CCNA ICND2
Official Exam Certification Guide
Second Edition

Wendell Odom, CCIE No. 1624

Cisco Press

800 East 96th Street
Indianapolis, IN 46240 USA

CCNA ICND2 Official Exam Certification Guide, Second Edition

Wendell Odom

Copyright © 2008 Cisco Systems, Inc.

Published by:
Cisco Press
800 East 96th Street
Indianapolis, IN 46240 USA

Printed in the United States of America

Seventh Printing September 2009

Library of Congress Cataloging-in-Publication Data:

Odom, Wendell.

 CCNA ICND2 official exam certification guide / Wendell Odom. -- 2nd ed.

   p. cm.

 ISBN 978-1-58720-181-3 (hbk : CD-ROM)

 1. Electronic data processing personnel--Certification. 2. Computer network protocols--Study guides. 3. Internetworking (Telecommunication)--Study guides. I. Title.

 QA76.3.O3618 2004

 004.6--dc22

2007029471

ISBN-13: 978-1-58720-181-3

ISBN-10: 1-58720-181-x

Warning and Disclaimer

Trademark Acknowledgments

Corporate and Government Sales

The publisher offers excellent discounts on this book when ordered in quantity for bulk purchases or special sales, which may include electronic versions and/or custom covers and content particular to your business, training goals, marketing focus, and branding interests. For more information, please contact:

U.S. Corporate and Government Sales
1-800-382-3419   corpsales@pearsontechgroup.com

For sales outside the United States please contact:
International Sales
international@pearsoned.com

Feedback Information

At Cisco Press, our goal is to create in-depth technical books of the highest quality and value. Each book is crafted with care and precision, undergoing rigorous development that involves the unique expertise of members from the professional technical community.

Readers' feedback is a natural continuation of this process. If you have any comments regarding how we could improve the quality of this book, or otherwise alter it to better suit your needs, you can contact us through email at feedback@ciscopress.com. Please make sure to include the book title and ISBN in your message.

We greatly appreciate your assistance.

Publisher: Paul Boger

Associate Publisher: David Dusthimer

Executive Editor: Brett Bartow

Managing Editor: Patrick Kanouse

Development Editor: Andrew Cupp

Senior Project Editor: Meg Shaw and Tonya Simpson

Editorial Assistant: Vanessa Evans

Designer: Louisa Adair

Composition: Mark Shirar

Indexer: Ken Johnson

Cisco Representative: Anthony Wolfenden

Cisco Press Program Manager: Jeff Brady

Copy Editors: Written Elegance and Gayle Johnson

Technical Editors: Teri Cook and Steve Kalman

Proofreader: Susan Eldridge

Americas Headquarters	Asia Pacific Headquarters	Europe Headquarters
Cisco Systems, Inc.	Cisco Systems, Inc.	Cisco Systems International BV
170 West Tasman Drive	168 Robinson Road	Haarlerbergpark
San Jose, CA 95134-1706	#28-01 Capital Tower	Haarlerbergweg 13-19
USA	Singapore 068912	1101 CH Amsterdam
www.cisco.com	www.cisco.com	The Netherlands
Tel: 408 526-4000	Tel: +65 6317 7777	www-europe.cisco.com
800 553-NETS (6387)	Fax: +65 6317 7799	Tel: +31 0 800 020 0791
Fax: 408 527-0883		Fax: +31 0 20 357 1100

Cisco has more than 200 offices worldwide. Addresses, phone numbers, and fax numbers are listed on the Cisco Website at **www.cisco.com/go/offices.**

©2007 Cisco Systems, Inc. All rights reserved. CCVP, the Cisco logo, and the Cisco Square Bridge logo are trademarks of Cisco Systems, Inc.; Changing the Way We Work, Live, Play, and Learn is a service mark of Cisco Systems, Inc.; and Access Registrar, Aironet, BPX, Catalyst, CCDA, CCDP, CCIE, CCIP, CCNA, CCNP, CCSP, Cisco, the Cisco Certified Internetwork Expert logo, Cisco IOS, Cisco Press, Cisco Systems, Cisco Systems Capital, the Cisco Systems logo, Cisco Unity, Enterprise/Solver, EtherChannel, EtherFast, EtherSwitch, Fast Step, Follow Me Browsing, FormShare, GigaDrive, GigaStack, HomeLink, Internet Quotient, IOS, IP/TV, iQ Expertise, the iQ logo, iQ Net Readiness Scorecard, iQuick Study, LightStream, Linksys, MeetingPlace, MGX, Networking Academy, Network Registrar, Packet, PIX, ProConnect, RateMUX, ScriptShare, SlideCast, SMARTnet, StackWise, The Fastest Way to Increase Your Internet Quotient, and TransPath are registered trademarks of Cisco Systems, Inc. and/or its affiliates in the United States and certain other countries.

All other trademarks mentioned in this document or Website are the property of their respective owners. The use of the word partner does not imply a partnership relationship between Cisco and any other company. (0609R)

About the Author

Wendell Odom, CCIE No. 1624, has been in the networking industry since 1981. He currently teaches QoS, MPLS, and CCNA courses for Skyline Advanced Technology Services (http://www.skyline-ats.com). Wendell also has worked as a network engineer, consultant, and systems engineer, and as an instructor and course developer. He is the author of all prior editions of *CCNA Exam Certification Guide*, as well as the *Cisco QoS Exam Certification Guide*, Second Edition, *Computer Networking First-Step*, *CCIE Routing and Switching Official Exam Certification Guide*, Second Edition, and *CCNA Video Mentor*, all from Cisco Press.

About the Technical Reviewers

Teri Cook (CCSI, CCDP, CCNP, CCDA, CCNA, MCT, and MCSE 2000/2003: Security) has more than 10 years of experience in the IT industry. She has worked with different types of organizations within the private business and DoD sectors, providing senior-level network and security technical skills in the design and implementation of complex computing environments. Since obtaining her certifications, Teri has been committed to bringing quality IT training to IT professionals as an instructor. She is an outstanding instructor that utilizes real-world experience to present complex networking technologies. As an IT instructor, Teri has been teaching Cisco classes for more than five years.

Stephen Kalman is a data security trainer and the author or tech editor of more than 20 books, courses, and CBT titles. His most recent book is *Web Security Field Guide*, published by Cisco Press. In addition to those responsibilities he runs a consulting company, Esquire Micro Consultants, which specializes in network security assessments and forensics.

Mr. Kalman holds SSCP, CISSP, ISSMP, CEH, CHFI, CCNA, CCSA (Checkpoint), A+, Network+, and Security+ certifications and is a member of the New York State Bar.

Dedications

For my wonderful, lovely, giving wife. Thanks so much for all your support, encouragement, love, and respect.

Acknowledgments

The team that helped produce this book has simply been awesome. Everyone who has touched the book has made it better, and the team has been particularly great at helping catch the errors that always creep into the manuscript.

Both Teri and Steve did great jobs as technical editors. Teri's ability to see each phrase in the context of an entire chapter, or whole book, was awesome, helping to catch things that no one would otherwise catch. Steve did his usual great job—something like 5–6 books of mine that he's done now—and as always, I get to learn a lot just by reading Steve's input. The depth of the reviews for this book was better than any of my other books because of Teri and Steve; thanks very much!

Drew Cupp got the "opportunity" to develop one of my books for the first time in a long time. Drew's insights and edits worked wonders, and a fresh set of eyes on the materials copied from the previous edition strengthened those parts a lot. All while juggling things in the middle of a whirlwind schedule—thanks, Drew, for doing a great job!

The wonderful and mostly hidden production folks did their usual great job. When I saw how they reworded something, and thought "Wow, why didn't I write that?" it made me appreciate the kind of team we have at Cisco Press. The final copy edit, figure review, and pages review process required a fair amount of juggling and effort as well—especially for the extra quality initiatives we've implemented. Thanks to you all!

Brett Bartow again was the executive editor on the book, as has been the case for almost all the books I've helped write. Brett did his usual great and patient job, being my advocate in so many ways. Brett, thanks for doing so many things on so many levels to help us be successful together.

Additionally, there are several folks who don't have any direct stake in the book who also helped it along. Thanks to Frank Knox for the discussions on the exams, why they're so difficult, and how to handle troubleshooting. Thanks to Rus Healy for the help with wireless. Thanks to the Mikes at Skyline for making my schedule work to get this book (and the ICND1 book) out the door. And thanks to the course and exam teams at Cisco for the great early communications and interactions about the changes to the courses and exams.

And as always, a special thanks to my Lord and Savior Jesus Christ—thanks for helping me rejoice in you even while doing the final reviews of 1400 pages of manuscript in just a few weeks!

This Book Is Safari Enabled

The Safari® Enabled icon on the cover of your favorite technology book means the book is available through Safari Bookshelf. When you buy this book, you get free access to the online edition for 45 days.

Safari Bookshelf is an electronic reference library that lets you easily search thousands of technical books, find code samples, download chapters, and access technical information whenever and wherever you need it.

To gain 45-day Safari Enabled access to this book:

- Go to http://www.ciscopress.com/safarienabled
- Complete the brief registration form
- Enter the coupon code 37R6-7E1Q-6HAX-5YQZ-G6KW

If you have difficulty registering on Safari Bookshelf or accessing the online edition, please e-mail customer-service@safaribooksonline.com.

Contents at a Glance

Contents

Icons Used in This Book

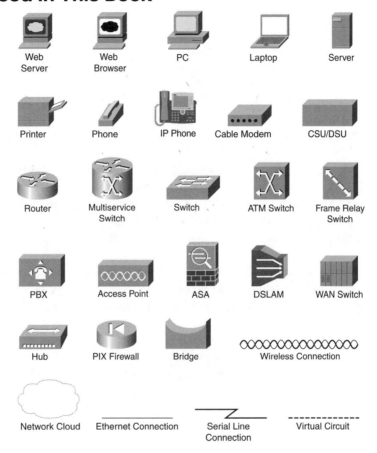

Command Syntax Conventions

The conventions used to present command syntax in this book are the same conventions used in the IOS Command Reference. The Command Reference describes these conventions as follows:

■ **Boldface** indicates commands and keywords that are entered literally as shown. In actual configuration examples and output (not general command syntax), boldface indicates commands that are manually input by the user (such as a **show** command).

■ *Italics* indicate arguments for which you supply actual values.

■ Vertical bars (|) separate alternative, mutually exclusive elements.

■ Square brackets [ ] indicate optional elements.

■ Braces { } indicate a required choice.

■ Braces within brackets [{ }] indicate a required choice within an optional element.

Foreword

CCNA ICND2 Official Exam Certification Guide, Second Edition, is an excellent self-study resource for the CCNA ICND2 exam. Passing the ICND2 exam validates the knowledge and skills required to successfully install, operate, and troubleshoot a small- to medium-size enterprise branch network. It is one of two exams required for CCNA certification.

Gaining certification in Cisco technology is key to the continuing educational development of today's networking professional. Through certification programs, Cisco validates the skills and expertise required to effectively manage the modern enterprise network.

Cisco Press exam certification guides and preparation materials offer exceptional—and flexible—access to the knowledge and information required to stay current in your field of expertise, or to gain new skills. Whether used as a supplement to more traditional training or as a primary source of learning, these materials offer users the information and knowledge validation required to gain new understanding and proficiencies.

Developed in conjunction with the Cisco certifications and training team, Cisco Press books are the only self-study books authorized by Cisco, and they offer students a series of exam practice tools and resource materials to help ensure that learners fully grasp the concepts and information presented.

Additional authorized Cisco instructor-led courses, e-learning, labs, and simulations are available exclusively from Cisco Learning Solutions Partners worldwide. To learn more, visit http://www.cisco.com/go/training.

I hope that you find these materials to be an enriching and useful part of your exam preparation.

Erik Ullanderson
Manager, Global Certifications
Learning@Cisco
August, 2007

Introduction

Congratulations! If you're reading far enough to look at the introduction to this book, you've probably already decided to go for your Cisco certification. If you want to succeed as a technical person in the networking industry, you need to know Cisco. Cisco has a ridiculously high market share in the router and switch marketplace, with more than 80 percent market share in some markets. In many geographies and markets around the world, networking equals Cisco. If you want to be taken seriously as a network engineer, Cisco certification makes perfect sense.

Historically speaking, the first entry-level Cisco certification has been the Cisco Certified Network Associate (CCNA) certification, first offered in 1998. The first three versions of the CCNA certification (1998, 2000, and 2002) required that you pass a single exam to become certified. However, over time, the exam kept growing, both in the amount of material covered and in the difficulty level of the questions. So, for the fourth major revision of the exams, announced in 2003, Cisco continued with a single certification (CCNA), but offered two options for the exams to get certified: a single-exam option and a two-exam option. The two-exam option allowed people to study roughly half of the material, and take and pass one exam, before moving on to the next.

Cisco announced changes to the CCNA certification and exams in June 2007. This announcement includes many changes, most notably:

- The exams collectively cover a broader range of topics.

- The exams increase the focus on proving the test taker's skills (as compared with just testing knowledge).

- Cisco created a new entry-level certification: the Cisco Certified Entry Network Technician (CCENT) certification.

For the current certifications, announced in June 2007, Cisco created the ICND1 (640-822) and ICND2 (640-816) exams, along with the CCNA (640-802) exam. To become CCNA certified, you can pass both the ICND1 and ICND2 exams, or just pass the CCNA exam. The CCNA exam simply covers all the topics on the ICND1 and ICND2 exams, giving you two options for gaining your CCNA certification. The two-exam path gives those people with less experience a chance to study for a smaller set of topics at a time, whereas the one-exam option provides a more cost-effective certification path for those who want to prepare for all the topics at once.

Although the two-exam option will be useful for some certification candidates, Cisco designed the ICND1 exam with a much more important goal in mind. The CCNA certification has grown to the point that it tested knowledge and skills beyond what an entry-level network technician would need to have. Cisco needed a certification that was more reflective of the skills required for entry-level networking jobs. So, Cisco designed its Interconnecting Cisco Networking Devices 1 (ICND1) course, and the corresponding ICND1 640-822 exam, to include the knowledge and skills most needed by an entry-level technician in a small enterprise network. And to show that you have the skills required for those entry-level jobs, Cisco created a new certification, CCENT, which is attained by passing the ICND1 exam.

Figure I-1 shows the basic organization of the certifications and the exams used for getting your CCENT and CCNA certifications. (Note that no separate certification exists for passing the ICND2 exam.)

Figure I-1 *Cisco Entry-Level Certifications and Exams*

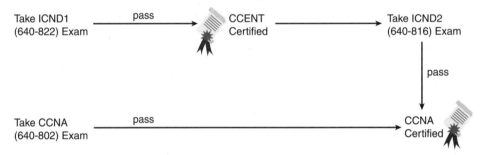

As you can see from the figure, while the CCENT certification is available by taking the ICND1 exam, you do not have to first be CCENT certified before getting your CCNA certification—you can choose to just take the CCNA exam and bypass the CCENT certification.

The ICND1 and ICND2 exams cover different sets of topics, with a minor amount of overlap. For example, ICND1 covers IP addressing and subnetting, while ICND2 covers a more complicated use of subnetting called variable-length subnet masking (VLSM), so ICND2 must then cover subnetting to some degree. The CCNA exam covers all the topics covered on both the ICND1 and ICND2 exams.

While the popularity of the CCENT certification cannot be seen until a few years have passed, certainly the Cisco CCNA certification enjoys a position as the most popular entry-level networking certification program. A CCNA certification proves that you have a firm foundation in the most important components of the Cisco product line—namely, routers and switches. It also proves that you have a broad knowledge of protocols and networking technologies.

Format of the CCNA Exams

The ICND1, ICND2, and CCNA exams all follow the same general format. When you get to the testing center and check in, the proctor will give you some general instructions and then take you into a quiet room with a PC. When you're at the PC, you have a few things to do before the timer starts on your exam. For example, you can take a sample quiz, just to get accustomed to the PC and to the testing engine. Anyone who has user-level skills in getting around a PC should have no problems with the testing environment. Additionally, Chapter 18, "Final Preparation," points to a Cisco website at which you can see a demo of the Cisco test engine.

When you start the exam, you are asked a series of questions. You answer a question and then move on to the next question. *The exam engine does not let you go back and change your answer.* Yes, that's true—when you move on to the next question, that's it for the earlier question.

The exam questions can be in one of the following formats:

- Multiple-choice (MC)

- Testlet

- Drag-and-drop (DND)

- Simulated lab (Sim)

- Simlet

The first three types of questions are relatively common in many testing environments. The multiple-choice format simply requires that you point and click a circle beside the correct answer(s). Cisco traditionally tells you how many answers you need to choose, and the testing software prevents you from choosing too many answers. Testlets are questions with one general scenario, with multiple MC questions about the overall scenario. Drag-and-drop questions require you to click and hold the mouse button, move a button or icon to another area, and release the mouse button to place the object somewhere else—typically into a list. So, for some questions, to get the question correct, you might need to put a list of five things into the proper order.

The last two types both use a network simulator to ask questions. Interestingly, the two types allow Cisco to assess two very different skills. First, Sim questions generally describe a problem, and your task is to configure one or more routers and switches to fix the problem. The exam then grades the question based on the configuration you changed or added. Interestingly, Sim questions are the only questions that Cisco (to date) has openly confirmed that partial credit is given.

The Simlet questions might well be the most difficult style of question on the exams. Simlet questions also use a network simulator, but instead of answering the question by changing the configuration, the question includes one or more MC questions. The questions require that you use the simulator to examine the current behavior of a network, interpreting the output of any **show** commands that you can remember to answer the question. While Sim questions require you to troubleshoot problems related to a configuration, Simlets require you to both analyze working networks and networks with problems, correlating **show** command output with your knowledge of networking theory and configuration commands.

What's on the CCNA Exam(s)?

Ever since I was in grade school, whenever the teacher announced that we were having a test soon, someone would always ask, "What's on the test?" Even in college, people would try to get more information about what would be on the exams. At heart, the goal is to know what to study hard, what to study a little, and what not to study.

Cisco does want the public to know both the variety of topics, and an idea about the kinds of knowledge and skills required for each topic, for every Cisco certification exam. To that end, Cisco publishes a set of exam objectives for each exam. The objectives list the specific topics, like IP addressing, RIP, and VLANs. The objectives also imply the kinds of skills required for that topic. For example, one objective might start with "Describe..." and another might begin with "Describe, configure, and troubleshoot...." The second objective clearly states that you need a thorough and deep understanding of that topic. By listing the topics and skill level, Cisco helps us all prepare for its exams.

While the exam objectives are helpful, keep in mind that Cisco adds a disclaimer that the posted exam topics for all its certification exams are *guidelines*. Cisco makes the effort to keep the exam questions within the confines of the stated exam objectives, and I know from talking to those involved that every question is analyzed for whether it fits within the stated exam topics.

ICND1 Exam Topics

Table I-1 lists the exam topics for the ICND1 exam, with the ICND2 exam topics following in Table I-2. Although the posted exam topics are not numbered at Cisco.com, Cisco Press does number the exam topics for easier reference. The table also notes the book parts in which each exam topic is covered. Because the exam topics might change over time, double-check the exam topics as listed on Cisco.com (specifically, http://www.cisco.com/go/ccna). If Cisco does happen to add exam topics at a later date, note that Appendix C of this book describes how to go to http://www.ciscopress.com and download additional information about those newly added topics.

> **NOTE** The table includes gray highlights that will be explained in the upcoming section "CCNA Exam Topics."

Table I-1 *ICND1 Exam Topics*

Reference Number	ICND1 Book Part(s) Where Topic Is Covered	Exam Topic
		Describe the operation of data networks
1	I	Describe the purpose and functions of various network devices
2	I	Select the components required to meet a given network specification
3	I, II, III	Use the OSI and TCP/IP models and their associated protocols to explain how data flows in a network
4	I	Describe common networking applications including web applications
5	I	Describe the purpose and basic operation of the protocols in the OSI and TCP models
6	I	Describe the impact of applications (Voice Over IP and Video Over IP) on a network
7	I–IV	Interpret network diagrams
8	I–IV	Determine the path between two hosts across a network
9	I, III, IV	Describe the components required for network and Internet communications
10	I–IV	Identify and correct common network problems at layers 1, 2, 3 and 7 using a layered model approach
11	II, III	Differentiate between LAN/WAN operation and features
		Implement a small switched network
12	II	Select the appropriate media, cables, ports, and connectors to connect switches to other network devices and hosts
13	II	Explain the technology and media access control method for Ethernet technologies
14	II	Explain network segmentation and basic traffic management concepts
15	II	Explain the operation of Cisco switches and basic switching concepts
16	II	Perform, save and verify initial switch configuration tasks including remote access management
17	II	Verify network status and switch operation using basic utilities (including: ping, traceroute, telnet, SSH, arp, ipconfig), SHOW & DEBUG commands

Table I-1 *ICND1 Exam Topics (Continued)*

Reference Number	ICND1 Book Part(s) Where Topic Is Covered	Exam Topic
18	II	Implement and verify basic security for a switch (port security, deactivate ports)
19	II	Identify, prescribe, and resolve common switched network media issues, configuration issues, autonegotiation, and switch hardware failures
		Implement an IP addressing scheme and IP services to meet network requirements for a small branch office
20	I, III	Describe the need and role of addressing in a network
21	I, III	Create and apply an addressing scheme to a network
22	III	Assign and verify valid IP addresses to hosts, servers, and networking devices in a LAN environment
23	IV	Explain the basic uses and operation of NAT in a small network connecting to one ISP
24	I, III	Describe and verify DNS operation
25	III, IV	Describe the operation and benefits of using private and public IP addressing
26	III, IV	Enable NAT for a small network with a single ISP and connection using SDM and verify operation using CLI and ping
27	III	Configure, verify and troubleshoot DHCP and DNS operation on a router. (including: CLI/SDM)
28	III	Implement static and dynamic addressing services for hosts in a LAN environment
29	III	Identify and correct IP addressing issues
		Implement a small routed network
30	I, III	Describe basic routing concepts (including: packet forwarding, router lookup process)
31	III	Describe the operation of Cisco routers (including: router bootup process, POST, router components)
32	I, III	Select the appropriate media, cables, ports, and connectors to connect routers to other network devices and hosts
33	III	Configure, verify, and troubleshoot RIPv2
34	III	Access and utilize the router CLI to set basic parameters
35	III	Connect, configure, and verify operation status of a device interface

Table I-1 *ICND1 Exam Topics (Continued)*

Reference Number	ICND1 Book Part(s) Where Topic Is Covered	Exam Topic
36	III	Verify device configuration and network connectivity using ping, traceroute, telnet, SSH or other utilities
37	III	Perform and verify routing configuration tasks for a static or default route given specific routing requirements
38	III	Manage IOS configuration files (including: save, edit, upgrade, restore)
39	III	Manage Cisco IOS
40	III	Implement password and physical security
41	III	Verify network status and router operation using basic utilities (including: ping, traceroute, telnet, SSH, arp, ipconfig), SHOW & DEBUG commands
		Explain and select the appropriate administrative tasks required for a WLAN
42	II	Describe standards associated with wireless media (including: IEEE, WI-FI Alliance, ITU/FCC)
43	II	Identify and describe the purpose of the components in a small wireless network. (including: SSID, BSS, ESS)
44	II	Identify the basic parameters to configure on a wireless network to ensure that devices connect to the correct access point
45	II	Compare and contrast wireless security features and capabilities of WPA security (including: open, WEP, WPA-1/2)
46	II	Identify common issues with implementing wireless networks
		Identify security threats to a network and describe general methods to mitigate those threats
47	I	Explain today's increasing network security threats and the need to implement a comprehensive security policy to mitigate the threats
48	I	Explain general methods to mitigate common security threats to network devices, hosts, and applications
49	I	Describe the functions of common security appliances and applications
50	I, II, III	Describe security recommended practices including initial steps to secure network devices
		Implement and verify WAN links
51	IV	Describe different methods for connecting to a WAN
52	IV	Configure and verify a basic WAN serial connection

ICND2 Exam Topics

Table I-2 lists the exam topics for the ICND2 (640-816) exam, along with the book parts in *CCNA ICND2 Official Exam Certification Guide* in which each topic is covered.

Table I-2 *ICND2 Exam Topics*

Reference Number	ICND2 Book Part(s) Where Topic Is Covered	Exam Topic
		Configure, verify and troubleshoot a switch with VLANs and interswitch communications
101	I	Describe enhanced switching technologies (including: VTP, RSTP, VLAN, PVSTP, 802.1q)
102	I	Describe how VLANs create logically separate networks and the need for routing between them
103	I	Configure, verify, and troubleshoot VLANs
104	I	Configure, verify, and troubleshoot trunking on Cisco switches
105	II	Configure, verify, and troubleshoot interVLAN routing
106	I	Configure, verify, and troubleshoot VTP
107	I	Configure, verify, and troubleshoot RSTP operation
108	I	Interpret the output of various show and debug commands to verify the operational status of a Cisco switched network
109	I	Implement basic switch security (including: port security, unassigned ports, trunk access, etc.)
		Implement an IP addressing scheme and IP Services to meet network requirements in a medium-size Enterprise branch office network
110	II	Calculate and apply a VLSM IP addressing design to a network
111	II	Determine the appropriate classless addressing scheme using VLSM and summarization to satisfy addressing requirements in a LAN/WAN environment
112	V	Describe the technological requirements for running IPv6 (including: protocols, dual stack, tunneling, etc)
113	V	Describe IPv6 addresses
114	II, III	Identify and correct common problems associated with IP addressing and host configurations
		Configure and troubleshoot basic operation and routing on Cisco devices
115	III	Compare and contrast methods of routing and routing protocols
116	III	Configure, verify and troubleshoot OSPF

Table I-2 *ICND2 Exam Topics (Continued)*

Reference Number	ICND2 Book Part(s) Where Topic Is Covered	Exam Topic
117	III	Configure, verify and troubleshoot EIGRP
118	II, III	Verify configuration and connectivity using ping, traceroute, and telnet or SSH
119	II, III	Troubleshoot routing implementation issues
120	II, III, IV	Verify router hardware and software operation using SHOW & DEBUG commands
121	II	Implement basic router security
		Implement, verify, and troubleshoot NAT and ACLs in a medium-size Enterprise branch office network.
122	II	Describe the purpose and types of access control lists
123	II	Configure and apply access control lists based on network filtering requirements
124	II	Configure and apply an access control list to limit telnet and SSH access to the router
125	II	Verify and monitor ACLs in a network environment
126	II	Troubleshoot ACL implementation issues
127	V	Explain the basic operation of NAT
128	V	Configure Network Address Translation for given network requirements using CLI
129	V	Troubleshoot NAT implementation issues
		Implement and verify WAN links
130	IV	Configure and verify Frame Relay on Cisco routers
131	IV	Troubleshoot WAN implementation issues
132	IV	Describe VPN technology (including: importance, benefits, role, impact, components)
133	IV	Configure and verify PPP connection between Cisco routers

CCNA Exam Topics

In the previous version of the exams, the CCNA exam covered a lot of what was in the ICND (640-811) exam, plus some coverage of topics in the INTRO (640-821) exam. The new CCNA exam (640-802) covers all the topics on both the ICND1 (640-822) and ICND2 (640-816) exams. One of the reasons for a more balanced coverage in the exams is that some of the topics that used to be in the second exam have been moved to the first exam.

The new CCNA (640-802) exam covers all topics in both the ICND1 and ICND2 exams. The official CCNA 640-802 exam topics, posted at http://www.cisco.com, include all the topics listed in Table I-2 for the ICND2 exam, plus most of the exam topics for the ICND1 exam listed in Table I-1. The only exam topics from these two tables that are not listed as CCNA exam topics are the topics highlighted in gray in Table I-1. However, note that the gray topics are still covered on the CCNA 640-802 exam. Those topics are just not listed in the CCNA exam topics because one of the ICND2 exam topics refers to the same concepts.

ICND1 and ICND2 Course Outlines

Another way to get some direction about the topics on the exams is to look at the course outlines for the related courses. Cisco offers two authorized CCNA-related courses: Interconnecting Cisco Network Devices 1 (ICND1) and Interconnecting Cisco Network Devices 2 (ICND2). Cisco authorizes Certified Learning Solutions Providers (CLSP) and Certified Learning Partners (CLP) to deliver these classes. These authorized companies can also create unique custom course books using this material, in some cases to teach classes geared toward passing the CCNA exam.

About the *CCENT/CCNA ICND1 Official Exam Certification Guide* and *CCNA ICND2 Official Exam Certification Guide*

As mentioned earlier, Cisco has separated the content covered by the CCNA exam into two parts: topics typically used by engineers who work in a small enterprise network (ICND1), with the additional topics commonly used by engineers in medium-sized enterprises being covered by the ICND2 exam. Likewise, the Cisco Press CCNA Exam Certification Guide series includes two books for CCNA—*CCENT/CCNA ICND1 Official Exam Certification Guide* and *CCNA ICND2 Official Exam Certification Guide*. These two books cover the breadth of topics on each exam, typically to a little more depth than is required for the exams, just to ensure that the books prepare you for the more difficult exam questions.

The following sections list the variety of features in both this book and *CCENT/CCNA ICND1 Official Exam Certification Guide*. Both books have the same basic features, so if you are reading both this book and the ICND1 book, you don't need to read the introduction to both books. Also, for those of you who are using both books to prepare for the CCNA 640-802 exam (rather than taking the two-exam option), the end of this introduction lists a suggested reading plan.

Objectives and Methods

The most important and somewhat obvious objective of this book is to help you pass the ICND2 exam or the CCNA exam. In fact, if the primary objective of this book were different, the book's title would be misleading! However, the methods used in this book to help you pass the exams are also designed to make you much more knowledgeable about how to do your job.

This book uses several key methodologies to help you discover the exam topics on which you need more review, to help you fully understand and remember those details, and to help you prove to yourself that you have retained your knowledge of those topics. So, this book does not try to help you pass the exams only by memorization, but by truly learning and understanding the topics. The CCNA certification is the foundation for many of the Cisco professional certifications, and it would be a disservice to you if this book did not help you truly learn the material. Therefore, this book helps you pass the CCNA exam by using the following methods:

- Helping you discover which exam topics you have not mastered

- Providing explanations and information to fill in your knowledge gaps

- Supplying exercises that enhance your ability to recall and deduce the answers to test questions

- Providing practice exercises on the topics and the testing process through test questions on the CD

Book Features

To help you customize your study time using these books, the core chapters have several features that help you make the best use of your time:

- **"Do I Know This Already?" Quizzes:** Each chapter begins with a quiz that helps you determine the amount of time you need to spend studying that chapter.

- **Foundation Topics:** These are the core sections of each chapter. They explain the protocols, concepts, and configuration for the topics in that chapter.

- **Exam Preparation Tasks:** At the end of the Foundation Topics section of each chapter, the Exam Preparation Tasks section lists a series of study activities that should be done at the end of the chapter. Each chapter includes the activities that make the most sense for studying the topics in that chapter. The activities include the following:

  — **Key Topics Review:** The Key Topics icon is shown next to the most important items in the Foundation Topics section of the chapter. The Key Topics Review activity lists the key topics from the chapter, and the page number. While the contents of the entire chapter could be on the exam, you should definitely know the information listed in each key topic, so these should be reviewed.

— **Complete Tables and Lists from Memory:** To help you exercise your memory and memorize some lists of facts, many of the more important lists and tables from the chapter are included in Appendix J on the CD. This document lists only partial information, allowing you to complete the table or list. Appendix K lists the same tables and lists, completed, for easy comparison.

— **Definition of Key Terms:** While the exams are unlikely to ask a question like "Define this term," the CCNA exams do require that you learn and know a lot of networking terminology. This section lists the most important terms from the chapter, asking you to write a short definition and compare your answer to the glossary at the end of the book.

— **Command Reference Tables:** Some book chapters cover a large amount of configuration and EXEC commands. These tables list the commands introduced in the chapter, along with an explanation. For exam preparation, use them for reference, but also read the tables once when performing the Exam Preparation Tasks to make sure that you remember what all the commands do.

■ **CD-based Practice Exam:** The companion CD contains an exam engine (from Boson software, http://www.boson.com) that includes a large number of exam-realistic practice questions. You can take simulated ICND2 exams, as well as simulated CCNA exams, with the CD in this book. (You can take simulated ICND1 and CCNA exams with the CD in *CCENT/CCNA ICND1 Official Exam Certification Guide*.)

■ **Subnetting Videos:** The companion DVD contains a series of videos that show how to calculate various facts about IP addressing and subnetting, in particular using the shortcuts described in this book.

■ **Subnetting Practice:** CD Appendix D contains a large set of subnetting practice problems, with the answers and with explanations of how the answers were found. This is a great resource to get ready to do subnetting well and fast.

■ **CD-based Practice Scenarios:** CD Appendix F contains several networking scenarios for additional study. These scenarios describe various networks and requirements, taking you through conceptual design, configuration, and verification. These scenarios are useful for building your hands-on skills, even if you do not have lab gear.

■ **Companion Website:** The website http://www.ciscopress.com/title/1587201828 posts up-to-the-minute materials that further clarify complex exam topics. Check this site regularly for new and updated postings written by the author that provide further insight into the more troublesome topics on the exam.

How This Book Is Organized

This book contains 18 core chapters—Chapters 1 through 18, with Chapter 18 including some summary materials and suggestions for how to approach the exams. Each core chapter covers a subset of the topics on the ICND2 exam. The core chapters are organized into sections and cover the following topics:

■ Part I: LAN Switching

— **Chapter 1, "Virtual LANs"**: This chapter explains the concepts and configuration surrounding virtual LANs, including VLAN trunking and VLAN Trunking Protocol.

— **Chapter 2, "Spanning Tree Protocol"**: This chapter dives deeply into the concepts behind the original Spanning Tree Protocol (STP), as well as the newer Rapid STP (RSTP), including concepts, configuration, and troubleshooting.

— **Chapter 3, "Troubleshooting LAN Switching"**: This chapter explains some general ideas about how to troubleshoot networking problems, with most of the chapter focusing on the forwarding process used by LAN switches.

■ Part II: IP Routing

— **Chapter 4, "IP Routing: Static and Connected Routes"**: This chapter examines how routers add both static routes and connected routes to the routing table, while also reviewing the concepts behind how routers route, or forward, packets.

— **Chapter 5, "VLSM and Route Summarization"**: This chapter explains how IP routing and routing protocols can support the use of different subnet masks in a single classful network (VLSM), as well as the math concepts behind how routers can summarize multiple routes into one routing table entry.

— **Chapter 6, "IP Access Control Lists"**: This chapter examines how ACLs can filter packets so that a router will not forward the packet. The chapter examines the concepts and configuration for standard and extended ACLs, including named and numbered ACLs.

— **Chapter 7, "Troubleshooting IP Routing"**: This chapter shows a structured plan for how to isolate problems related to two hosts that should be able to send packets to each other, but cannot. The chapter also includes a variety of tips and tools for helping attack routing problems.

■ Part III: Routing Protocols Configuration and Troubleshooting

— **Chapter 8, "Routing Protocol Theory"**: This chapter explains the theory behind distance vector and link-state protocols.

— **Chapter 9, "OSPF"**: This chapter examines OSPF, including more detail about link-state theory as implemented by OSPF, and OSPF configuration.

— **Chapter 10, "EIGRP"**: This chapter examines EIGRP, including a description of the theory behind EIGRP, as well as EIGRP configuration and verification.

— **Chapter 11, "Troubleshooting Routing Protocols"**: This chapter explains some of the typical reasons why routing protocols fail to exchange routing information, showing specific examples of common problems with both OSPF and EIGRP.

■ Part IV: Wide-Area Networks

— **Chapter 12, "Point-to-Point WANs"**: This short chapter reviews the basics of WANs and examines PPP, including CHAP, in more detail.

— **Chapter 13, "Frame Relay Concepts"**: This chapter focuses on the terminology and theory behind the Frame Relay protocol, including the IP addressing options when using Frame Relay.

— **Chapter 14, "Frame Relay Configuration and Troubleshooting"**: This chapter shows a variety of configuration options for Frame Relay, including both point-to-point and multipoint subinterfaces. It also explains how to best use **show** commands to isolate the root cause of common Frame Relay problems.

— **Chapter 15, "Virtual Private Networks"**: This chapter examines the concepts and protocols used to create secure VPNs over the Internet. This chapter includes the basics of IPsec.

- Part V: Scaling the IP Address Space

  — **Chapter 16, "Network Address Translation"**: This chapter closely examines the concepts behind the depletion of the IPv4 address space, and how NAT, in particular the Port Address Translation (PAT) option, helps solve the problem. The chapter also shows how to configure NAT on routers using the IOS CLI.

  — **Chapter 17, "IP Version 6"**: This chapter introduces the basics of IPv6, including the 128-bit address format, OSPF and EIGRP support for IPv6, and basic native IPv6 configuration. It also introduces the concept of IPv6 tunneling and migration strategies.

- Part VI: Final Preparation

  — **Chapter 18, "Final Preparation"**: This chapter suggests a plan for final preparation after you have finished the core parts of the book, in particular explaining the many study options available in the book.

- Part VII: Appendixes (in Print)

  — **Appendix A, "Answers to the 'Do I Know This Already?' Quizzes"**: Includes the answers to all the questions from Chapters 1 through 17.

  — **Appendix B, "Decimal-to-Binary Conversion Table"**: Lists decimal values 0 through 255, along with the binary equivalents.

  — **Appendix C, "ICND2 Exam Updates: Version 1.0"**: This appendix covers a variety of short topics that either clarify or expand upon topics covered earlier in the book. This appendix is updated from time to time and posted at http://www.ciscopress.com/ccna, with the most recent version available at the time of printing included here as Appendix C. (The first page of the appendix includes instructions on how to check whether a later version of Appendix C is available online.)

  — **Glossary**: The glossary contains definitions for all the terms listed in the "Definitions of Key Terms" section at the conclusion of Chapters 1–17.

■ Part VII: Appendixes (on CD)

The following appendixes are available in PDF format on the CD that accompanies this book:

— **Appendix D, "Subnetting Practice"**: Although not covered in any of the chapters printed in this book, subnetting is easily the most important prerequisite assumed skill for the ICND2 exam. This appendix, as well as Appendixes E, H, and I, include materials from *CCENT/CCNA ICND1 Official Exam Certification Guide* for those of you that bought this book, but not the ICND1 book. In particular, this appendix includes a large number of subnetting practice problems, with the answers listed. The answers use both binary and decimal-shortcut processes described in the ICND1 book's Chapter 12; Appendix H of this book is a duplicate of ICND1's Chapter 12.

— **Appendix E, "Subnetting Reference Pages"**: This appendix summarizes the process to find the answer to several key subnetting questions, with the details on a single page. The goal is to give you a handy reference page to refer to when practicing subnetting.

— **Appendix F, "Additional Scenarios"**: One method to improve your troubleshooting and network analysis skills is to examine as many unique network scenarios as is possible, think about them, and then get some feedback as to whether you came to the right conclusions. This appendix provides several such scenarios.

— **Appendix G, "Video Scenario Reference"**: The DVD includes several subnetting videos that show how to use the processes covered in Appendix H (copied from ICND1's Chapter 12). This appendix contains copies of the key elements from those videos, which can be useful when watching the videos (so that you do not have to keep moving back and forth in the video).

— **Appendix H, "ICND1 Chapter 12: IP Addressing and Subnetting"**: This appendix is a duplicate of Chapter 12 from *CCENT/CCNA ICND1 Official Exam Certification Guide*. This chapter explains IP addressing and subnetting, which is considered prerequisite knowledge for the ICND2 exam. Appendix H is included with this book for those of you who do not have a copy of *CCENT/CCNA ICND1 Official Exam Certification Guide*, but you need to review and learn more about subnetting.

— **Appendix I, "ICND1 Chapter 17: WAN Configuration"**: This appendix is a duplicate of Chapter 17 from *CCENT/CCNA ICND1 Official Exam Certification Guide*. Chapter 12 of this book (ICND2), "Point-to-Point WANs," makes a suggestion to review a few prerequisite points as listed in this chapter. This chapter is included in this book for those of you who do not have a copy of *CCENT/CCNA ICND1 Official Exam Certification Guide*.

— **Appendix J, "Memory Tables"**: This appendix holds the key tables and lists from each chapter, with some of the content removed. You can print this appendix and, as a memory exercise, complete the tables and lists. The goal is to help you memorize facts that can be useful on the exams.

— **Appendix K, "Memory Tables Answer Key"**: This appendix contains the answer key for the exercises in Appendix J.

— **Appendix L, "ICND2 Open-Ended Questions"**: This appendix is a holdover from previous editions of this book. The older edition had some open-ended questions for the purpose of helping you study for the exam, but the newer features make these questions unnecessary. For convenience, the old questions are included here, unedited since the last edition.

How to Use This Book to Prepare for the ICND2 (640-816) Exam

This book was designed with two primary goals in mind: to help you study for the ICND2 exam and to help you study for the CCNA exam by using both this book and the *CCENT/ CCNA ICND1 Official Exam Certification Guide*. Using this book to prepare for the ICND2 exam is straightforward—read each chapter in succession, and follow the study suggestions in Chapter 18, "Final Preparation."

For the core chapters of this book (Chapters 1–17), you do have some choices as to how much of the chapter you read. In some cases, you might already know most of or all the information covered in a given chapter. To help you decide how much time to spend on each chapter, the chapters begin with a "Do I Know This Already?" quiz. If you get all the quiz questions correct, or just miss one question, you might want to skip to the end of the chapter and the "Exam Preparation Tasks" section, and do those activities. Figure I-2 shows the overall plan.

Figure I-2 *How to Approach Each Chapter of This Book*

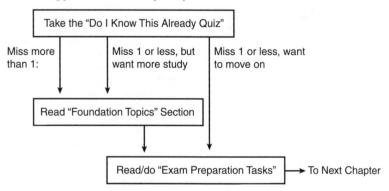

When you have completed Chapters 1–17, you can then use the guidance listed in Chapter 18 to detail the rest of the exam preparation tasks. That chapter includes the following suggestions:

■ Check http://www.ciscopress.com for the latest copy of Appendix C, which can include additional topics for study.

■ Practice subnetting using the tools available in the CD appendixes.

■ Repeat the tasks in all chapters' "Exam Preparation Tasks" chapter-ending sections.

■ Review the scenarios in CD Appendix F.

■ Review all the "Do I Know This Already?" questions.

■ Practice the exam using the exam engine.

How to Use These Books to Prepare for the CCNA 640-802 Exam

If you plan to get your CCNA certification using the one-exam option of taking the CCNA 640-802 exam, you can use this book along with *CCENT/CCNA ICND1 Official Exam Certification Guide*. If you've not yet bought either book, you can generally get the pair cheaper by buying both books as a two-book set, called the CCNA Certification Library.

These two books were designed to be used together when studying for the CCNA exam. You have two options for the order in which to read the two books. The first and most obvious option is to read the ICND1 book, and then move on to this (ICND2) book. The other option is to read all of ICND1's coverage of one topic area, then read ICND2's coverage of the same topics, and then go back to ICND1 again. Figure I-3 outlines my suggested option for reading the two books.

Figure I-3 *Reading Plan When Studying for CCNA Exam*

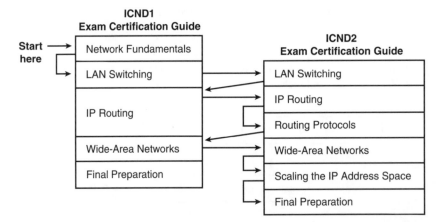

Both reading-plan options have some benefits. Moving back and forth between books can help you to focus on one general topic at a time. However, note that some overlap exists between the two exams, so you find some overlap between the two books as well. From reader comments about the previous edition of these books, those readers who were new to networking tended to do better by completing all of the first book and then moving on to the second, while readers that had more experience and knowledge before starting the books tended to prefer to follow a reading plan like the one shown in Figure I-3.

Note that for final preparation, you can use the final chapter (Chapter 18) of this book, rather than the final preparation chapter (Chapter 18) of the ICND1 book.

In addition to the flow shown in Figure I-3, when studying for the CCNA exam (rather than for the ICND1 and ICND2 exams), you must master IP subnetting before moving on to the IP routing and routing protocol parts (Parts II and III) of this book. This book does not review subnetting or the underlying math in the printed text, assuming that you know how to find the answers. Those ICND2 chapters, particularly Chapter 5 ("VLSM and Route Summarization"), will be much easier to understand if you can easily do the related subnetting math.

For More Information

If you have any comments about the book, you can submit those through Ciscopress.com. Just go to the website, click the Contact Us link, and type in your message.

Cisco might make changes that affect the CCNA certification from time to time. You should always check http://www.cisco.com/go/ccna for the latest details.

The CCNA certification is arguably the most important Cisco certification, with the new CCENT certification possibly surpassing CCNA in the future. CCNA certainly is the most popular Cisco certification, is required for several other certifications, and is the first step in distinguishing yourself as someone who has proven knowledge of Cisco.

CCNA ICND2 Official Exam Certification Guide is designed to help you attain CCNA certification. This is the CCNA ICND2 certification book from the only Cisco-authorized publisher. We at Cisco Press believe that this book certainly can help you achieve CCNA certification—but the real work is up to you! I trust that your time will be well spent.

Cisco Published ICND2 Exam Topics*
Covered in This Part

Configure, verify and troubleshoot a switch with VLANs and interswitch communications

- Describe enhanced switching technologies (including: VTP, RSTP, VLAN, PVSTP, 802.1q)

- Describe how VLANs create logically separate networks and the need for routing between them

- Configure, verify, and troubleshoot VLANs

- Configure, verify, and troubleshoot trunking on Cisco switches

- Configure, verify, and troubleshoot VTP

- Configure, verify, and troubleshoot RSTP operation

- Interpret the output of various show and debug commands to verify the operational status of a Cisco switched network

- Implement basic switch security (including: port security, unassigned ports, trunk access, etc.)

* Always recheck http://www.cisco.com for the latest posted exam topics.

Part I: LAN Switching

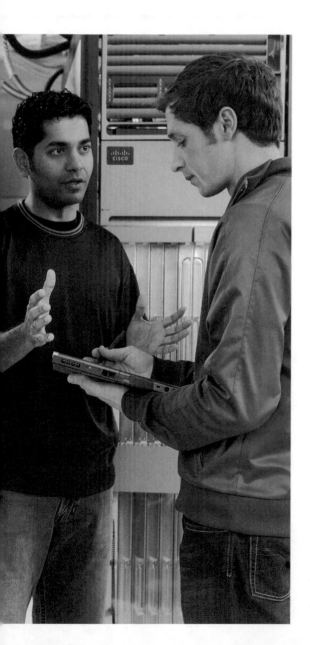

This chapter covers the following subjects:

Virtual LAN Concepts: This section explains the meaning and purpose for VLANs, VLAN trunking, and the VLAN Trunking Protocol (VTP).

VLAN and VLAN Trunking Configuration and Verification: This section shows how to configure VLANs and trunks on Cisco catalyst switches.

VTP Configuration and Verification: This final section explains how to configure and troubleshoot VTP installations.

CHAPTER 1

Virtual LANs

The first part of this book, which includes Chapters 1, 2, and 3, focuses on the world of LANs. Chapter 1 examines the concepts and configurations related to virtual LANs (VLANs), while Chapter 2, "Spanning Tree Protocol," covers how the Spanning Tree Protocol (STP) prevents loops in a switched network. Finally, Chapter 3, "Troubleshooting LAN Switching," pulls many LAN-related concepts together while exploring the process of troubleshooting common LAN problems.

As mentioned in the Introduction, this book assumes that you have a solid mastery of the most important topics covered on the ICND1 exam. If you are unclear about these prerequisites, you might want to glance over the list of prerequisite knowledge required by this book, under the heading "ICND1 Exam Topics" in the Introduction.

"Do I Know This Already?" Quiz

The "Do I Know This Already?" quiz allows you to assess whether you should read the entire chapter. If you miss no more than one of these ten self-assessment questions, you might want to move ahead to the "Exam Preparation Tasks" section. Table 1-1 lists the major headings in this chapter and the "Do I Know This Already?" quiz questions covering the material in those headings so that you can assess your knowledge of these specific areas. The answers to the "Do I Know This Already?" quiz appear in Appendix A.

Table 1-1 *"Do I Know This Already?" Foundation Topics Section-to-Question Mapping*

Foundation Topics Section	Questions
Virtual LAN Concepts	1–5
VLAN and VLAN Trunking Configuration and Verification	6–8
VTP Configuration and Verification	9–10

1. In a LAN, which of the following terms best equates to the term *VLAN*?

    a. Collision domain

    b. Broadcast domain

    c. Subnet domain

    d. Single switch

    e. Trunk

2. Imagine a switch with three configured VLANs. How many IP subnets are required, assuming that all hosts in all VLANs want to use TCP/IP?

    a. 0

    b. 1

    c. 2

    d. 3

    e. You can't tell from the information provided.

3. Which of the following fully encapsulates the original Ethernet frame in a trunking header rather than inserting another header inside the original Ethernet header?

    a. VTP

    b. ISL

    c. 802.1Q

    d. Both ISL and 802.1Q

    e. None of the other answers are correct.

4. Which of the following adds the trunking header for all VLANs except one?

    a. VTP

    b. ISL

    c. 802.1Q

    d. Both ISL and 802.1Q

    e. None of the other answers are correct.

5. Which of the following VTP modes allow VLANs to be configured on a switch?

    a. Client

    b. Server

    c. Transparent

    d. Dynamic

    e. None of the other answers are correct.

6. Imagine that you are told that switch 1 is configured with the **auto** parameter for trunking on its Fa0/5 interface, which is connected to switch 2. You have to configure switch 2. Which of the following settings for trunking could allow trunking to work?

   a. Trunking turned **on**

   b. **Auto**

   c. **Desirable**

   d. **Access**

   e. None of the other answers are correct.

7. A switch has just arrived from Cisco. The switch has never been configured with any VLANs, VTP configuration, or any other configuration. An engineer gets into configuration mode and issues the **vlan 22** command, followed by the **name Hannahs-VLAN** command. Which of the following are true?

   a. VLAN 22 is listed in the output of the **show vlan brief** command.

   b. VLAN 22 is listed in the output of the **show running-config** command.

   c. VLAN 22 is not created by this process.

   d. VLAN 22 does not exist in that switch until at least one interface is assigned to that VLAN.

8. Which of the following commands list the operational state of interface Gigabit 0/1 in regard to VLAN trunking?

   a. **show interfaces gi0/1**

   b. **show interfaces gi0/1 switchport**

   c. **show interfaces gi0/1 trunk**

   d. **show trunks**

9. An engineer has just installed four new 2960 switches and connected the switches to each other using crossover cables. All the interfaces are in an "up and up" state. The engineer configures each switch with the VTP domain name Fred and leaves all four switches in VTP server mode. The engineer adds VLAN 33 at 9:00 a.m., and then within 30 seconds, issues a **show vlan brief** command on the other three switches, but does not find VLAN 33 on the other three switches. Which answer gives the most likely reason for the problem in this case?

   a. VTP requires that all switches have the same VTP password.

   b. The engineer should have been more patient and waited for SW1 to send its next periodic VTP update.

   c. None of the links between the switches trunk because of the default 2960 trunking administrative mode of auto.

   d. None of the other answers are correct.

10. Switches SW1 and SW2 connect through an operational trunk. The engineer wants to use VTP to communicate VLAN configuration changes. The engineer configures a new VLAN on SW1, VLAN 44, but SW2 does not learn about the new VLAN. Which of the following configuration settings on SW1 and SW2 would *not* be a potential root cause why SW2 does not learn about VLAN 44?

   a.   VTP domain names of larry and LARRY, respectively

   b.   VTP passwords of bob and BOB, respectively

   c.   VTP pruning enabled and disabled, respectively

   d.   VTP modes of server and client, respectively

Foundation Topics

A Cisco Catalyst switch uses default settings that allow it to work with no additional configuration, right out of the box. However, most installations configure three major types of switch features: VLANs, as covered in this chapter; Spanning Tree, as covered in Chapter 2; and a variety of administrative settings that do not impact the forwarding behavior of the switch, which are explained in *CCENT/CCNA ICND1 Official Exam Certification Guide*.

All published objectives for the ICND1 exam are considered to be prerequisites for the ICND2 exam, although the ICND2 exam does not cover those topics as an end to themselves. For example, as described in the ICND1 book, switches learn MAC addresses by examining the source MAC address of incoming frames, and make forwarding/filtering decisions based on the destination MAC address of the frames. That book's LAN chapters (Chapter 3 plus Chapters 7 through 11) also explain the concepts of autonegotiation, collisions, collision domains, and broadcast domains. So, while the ICND2 exam might not have a specific question on these topics, these topics might be required to answer a question related to the exam objectives for the ICND2 exam. And, of course, the CCNA exam covers all the topics and objectives for both the ICND1 and ICND2 exams.

Besides the base concepts, the ICND1 book also describes a wide variety of small configuration tasks that either provide access to each switch or then help secure the switch when access has been granted. A switch should be configured with an IP address, subnet mask, and default gateway, allowing remote access to the switch. Along with that access, Cisco recommends several actions for better security beyond simply physically securing the router to prevent access from the switch console. In particular, passwords should be configured, and for remote access, Secure Shell (SSH) should be used instead of Telnet, if possible. The HTTP service should also be disabled, and banners should be configured to warn potential attackers away. Additionally, each switch's syslog messages should be monitored for any messages relating to various types of attacks.

The three chapters in this first part of the book pick up the LAN story, explaining the topics specifically related to ICND2 exam objectives. In particular, this chapter examines the concepts related to VLANs, and then covers the configuration and operation of VLANs. The first major section of this chapter explains the core concepts, including how to pass VLAN traffic between switches using VLAN trunks, and how the Cisco-proprietary VLAN Trunking Protocol (VTP) aids the process of configuring VLANs in a campus LAN. The second major section of this chapter shows how to configure VLANs and VLAN trunks, how to statically assign interfaces to a VLAN, and how to configure a switch so that a phone and PC on the same interface are in two different VLANs. The final major section covers VTP configuration and troubleshooting.

Virtual LAN Concepts

Before understanding VLANs, you must first have a specific understanding of the definition of a LAN. Although you can think about LANs from many perspectives, one perspective in particular can help you understand VLANs:

A LAN includes all devices in the same broadcast domain.

A broadcast domain includes the set of all LAN-connected devices that when any of the devices sends a broadcast frame, all the other devices get a copy of the frame. So, you can think of a LAN and a broadcast domain as being basically the same thing.

Without VLANs, a switch considers all its interfaces to be in the same broadcast domain; in others words, all connected devices are in the same LAN. With VLANs, a switch can put some interfaces into one broadcast domain and some into another, creating multiple broadcast domains. These individual broadcast domains created by the switch are called virtual LANs. Figure 1-1 shows an example, with two VLANs and two devices in each VLAN.

Figure 1-1   *Sample Network with Two VLANs Using One Switch*

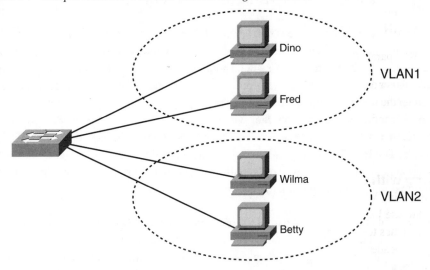

Putting hosts into different VLANs provides many benefits, although the reasons might not be obvious from Figure 1-1. The key to appreciating these benefits is to realize that a broadcast sent by one host in a VLAN will be received and processed by all the other hosts in the VLAN, but not by hosts in a different VLAN. The more hosts in a single VLAN, the larger the number of broadcasts, and the greater the processing time required by each host in the VLAN. Additionally, anyone can download several free software packages, generically called protocol analyzer software, which can capture all the frames received by a host. (Visit Wireshark, at http://www.wireshark.org, for a good free analyzer package.) As a result, larger VLANs expose larger numbers and types of broadcasts to other hosts, exposing more frames to hosts that could be used by an attacker that uses protocol analyzer software to try and perform a reconnaissance attack. These are just a few reasons for separating hosts into different VLANs. The following summarizes the most common reasons:

- To create more flexible designs that group users by department, or by groups that work together, instead of by physical location

- To segment devices into smaller LANs (broadcast domains) to reduce overhead caused to each host in the VLAN

- To reduce the workload for the Spanning Tree Protocol (STP) by limiting a VLAN to a single access switch

- To enforce better security by keeping hosts that work with sensitive data on a separate VLAN

- To separate traffic sent by an IP phone from traffic sent by PCs connected to the phones

This chapter does not examine the reasons for VLANs in any more depth, but it does closely examine the mechanics of how VLANs work across multiple Cisco switches, including the required configuration. To that end, the next section examines VLAN trunking, a feature required when installing a VLAN that exists on more than one LAN switch.

Trunking with ISL and 802.1Q

When using VLANs in networks that have multiple interconnected switches, the switches need to use *VLAN trunking* on the segments between the switches. VLAN trunking causes the switches to use a process called *VLAN tagging*, by which the sending switch adds another header to the frame before sending it over the trunk. This extra VLAN header includes a *VLAN identifier* (VLAN ID) field so that the sending switch can list the VLAN ID and the receiving switch can then know in what VLAN each frame belongs. Figure 1-2 outlines the basic idea.

Figure 1-2 *VLAN Trunking Between Two Switches*

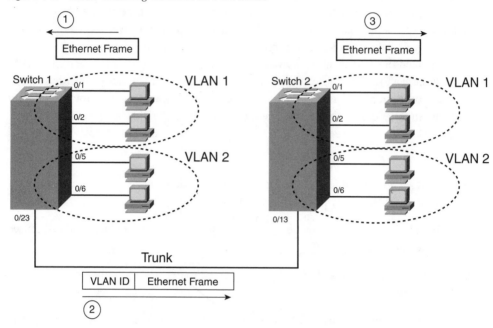

The use of trunking allows switches to pass frames from multiple VLANs over a single physical connection. For example, Figure 1-2 shows switch 1 receiving a broadcast frame on interface Fa0/1 at Step 1. To flood the frame, switch 1 needs to forward the broadcast frame to switch 2. However, switch 1 needs to let switch 2 know that the frame is part of VLAN 1. So, as shown at Step 2, before sending the frame, switch 1 adds a VLAN header to the original Ethernet frame, with the VLAN header listing a VLAN ID of 1 in this case. When switch 2 receives the frame, it sees that the frame was from a device in VLAN 1, so switch 2 knows that it should only forward the broadcast out its own interfaces in VLAN 1. Switch 2 removes the VLAN header, forwarding the original frame out its interfaces in VLAN 1 (Step 3).

For another example, consider the case when the device on switch 1's Fa0/5 interface sends a broadcast. Switch 1 sends the broadcast out port Fa0/6 (because that port is in VLAN 2) and out Fa0/23 (because it is a trunk, meaning that it supports multiple different VLANs). Switch 1 adds a trunking header to the frame, listing a VLAN ID of 2. Switch 2 strips off the trunking header after noticing that the frame is part of VLAN 2, so switch 2 knows to forward the frame out only ports Fa0/5 and Fa0/6, and not ports Fa0/1 and Fa0/2.

Cisco switches support two different trunking protocols: Inter-Switch Link (ISL) and IEEE 802.1Q. Trunking protocols provide several features, most importantly that they define headers which identify the VLAN ID, as shown in Figure 1-2. They do have some differences as well, as discussed next.

ISL

Cisco created ISL many years before the IEEE created the 802.1Q standard VLAN trunking protocol. Because ISL is Cisco proprietary, it can be used only between two Cisco switches that support ISL. (Some newer Cisco switches do not even support ISL, instead supporting only the standardized alternative, 802.1Q.) ISL fully encapsulates each original Ethernet frame in an ISL header and trailer. The original Ethernet frame inside the ISL header and trailer remains unchanged. Figure 1-3 shows the framing for ISL.

Figure 1-3 *ISL Header*

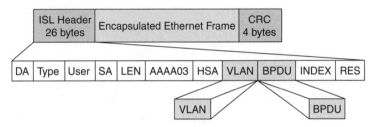

The ISL header includes several fields, but most importantly, the ISL header VLAN field provides a place to encode the VLAN number. By tagging a frame with the correct VLAN number inside the header, the sending switch can ensure that the receiving switch knows to which VLAN the encapsulated frame belongs. Also, the source and destination addresses in the ISL header use MAC addresses of the sending and receiving switch, as opposed to the devices that actually sent the original frame. Other than that, the details of the ISL header are not that important.

IEEE 802.1Q

The IEEE standardizes many of the protocols that relate to LANs today, and VLAN trunking is no exception. Years after Cisco created ISL, the IEEE completed work on the 802.1Q standard, which defines a different way to do trunking. Today, 802.1Q has become the more popular trunking protocol, with Cisco not even supporting ISL in some of its newer models of LAN switches, including the 2960 switches used in the examples in this book.

802.1Q uses a different style of header than does ISL to tag frames with a VLAN number. In fact, 802.1Q does not actually encapsulate the original frame in another Ethernet header and trailer. Instead, 802.1Q inserts an extra 4-byte VLAN header into the original frame's Ethernet header. As a result, unlike ISL, the frame still has the same original source and destination MAC addresses. Also, because the original header has been expanded, 802.1Q encapsulation forces a recalculation of the original frame check sequence (FCS) field in the

Ethernet trailer, because the FCS is based on the contents of the entire frame. Figure 1-4 shows the 802.1Q header and framing of the revised Ethernet header.

Figure 1-4   *802.1Q Trunking Header*

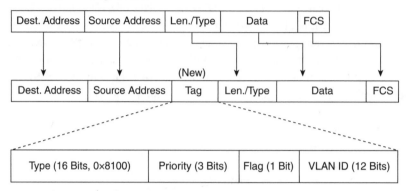

ISL and 802.1Q Compared

So far, the text has described one major similarity between ISL and 802.1Q, with a couple of differences. The similarity is that both ISL and 802.1Q define a VLAN header that has a VLAN ID field. However, each trunking protocol uses a different overall header, plus one is standardized (802.1Q) and one is proprietary (ISL). This section points out a few other key comparison points between the two.

Both trunking protocols support the same number of VLANs, specifically 4094 VLANs. Both protocols use 12 bits of the VLAN header to number VLANs, supporting 2^{12}, or 4096, VLAN IDs, minus two reserved values (0 and 4095). Of the supported VLANs, note that VLAN IDs 1–1005 are considered to be *normal range* VLANs, whereas values higher than 1005 are called *extended range* VLANs. This distinction matters in regard to the VLAN Trunking Protocol (VTP), which is covered in the next section.

ISL and 802.1Q both support a separate instance of Spanning Tree Protocol (STP) for each VLAN, but with different implementation details, as explained in Chapter 2. For campus LANs with redundant links, using only one instance of STP means that some links sit idle under normal operations, with those links only being used when another link fails. By supporting multiple instances of STP, engineers can tune the STP parameters so that under normal operations, some VLANs' traffic uses one set of links and other VLANs' traffic uses other links, taking advantage of all the links in the network.

NOTE   802.1Q has not always supported multiple instances of STP, so some older references might have accurately stated that, at that time, 802.1Q only supported a single instance of STP.

One final key difference between ISL and 802.1Q covered here relates to a feature called the *native VLAN*. 802.1Q defines one VLAN on each trunk as the native VLAN, whereas ISL does not use the concept. By default, the 802.1Q native VLAN is VLAN 1. By definition, 802.1Q simply does not add an 802.1Q header to frames in the native VLAN. When the switch on the other side of the trunk receives a frame that does not have an 802.1Q header, the receiving switch knows that the frame is part of the native VLAN. Note that because of this behavior, both switches must agree which VLAN is the native VLAN.

The 802.1Q native VLAN provides some interesting functions, mainly to support connections to devices that do not understand trunking. For example, a Cisco switch could be cabled to a switch that does not understand 802.1Q trunking. The Cisco switch could send frames in the native VLAN—meaning that the frame has no trunking header—so the other switch would understand the frame. The native VLAN concept gives switches the capability of at least passing traffic in one VLAN (the native VLAN), which can allow some basic functions, like reachability to telnet into a switch.

Table 1-2 summarizes the key features and points of comparison between ISL and 802.1Q.

Table 1-2   *ISL and 802.1Q Compared*

Function	ISL	802.1Q
Defined by	Cisco	IEEE
Inserts another 4-byte header instead of completely encapsulating the original frame	No	Yes
Supports normal-range (1–1005) and extended-range (1006–4094) VLANs	Yes	Yes
Allows multiple spanning trees	Yes	Yes
Uses a native VLAN	No	Yes

Key Topic

IP Subnets and VLANs

When including VLANs in a design, the devices in a VLAN need to be in the same subnet. Following the same design logic, devices in different VLANs need to be in different subnets.

Because of these design rules, many people think that a VLAN is a subnet and that a subnet is a VLAN. Although not completely true, because a VLAN is a Layer 2 concept and a subnet is a Layer 3 concept, the general idea is reasonable because the same devices in a single VLAN are the same devices in a single subnet.

As with all IP subnets, for a host in one subnet to forward packets to a host in another subnet, at least one router must be involved. For example, consider Figure 1-5, which shows a switch with three VLANs, shown inside the dashed lines, with some of the logic used when a host in VLAN 1 sends an IP packet to a host in VLAN 2.

Figure 1-5   *Routing Between VLANs*

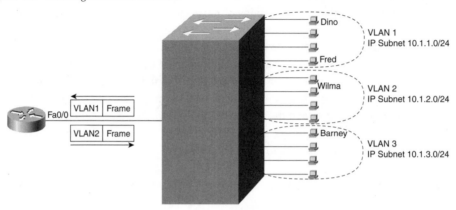

In this case, when Fred sends a packet to Wilma's IP address, Fred sends the packet to his default router, because Wilma's IP address is in a different subnet. The router receives the frame, with a VLAN header that implies the frame is part of VLAN 1. The router makes a forwarding decision, sending the frame back out the same physical link, but this time with a VLAN trunking header that lists VLAN 2. The switch forwards the frame in VLAN 2 to Wilma.

It might seem a bit inefficient to send the packet from the switch, to the router, and right back to the switch—and it is. A more likely option in real campus LANs today is to use a switch called either a multilayer switch or a Layer 3 switch. These switches can perform both Layer 2 switching and Layer 3 routing, combining the router function shown in Figure 1-5 into the switch.

VLAN Trunking Protocol (VTP)

The Cisco-proprietary VLAN Trunking Protocol (VTP) provides a means by which Cisco switches can exchange VLAN configuration information. In particular, VTP advertises about the existence of each VLAN based on its VLAN ID and the VLAN name. However, VTP does not advertise the details about which switch interfaces are assigned to each VLAN.

Because this book has not yet shown how to configure VLANs, to better appreciate VTP, consider this example of what VTP can do. Imagine that a network has ten switches connected somehow using VLAN trunks, and each switch has at least one port assigned to a VLAN with VLAN ID 3 and the name Accounting. Without VTP, an engineer would have to log in to all ten switches and enter the same two config commands to create the VLAN and define its name. With VTP, you would create VLAN 3 on one switch, and the other nine switches would learn about VLAN 3 and its name using VTP.

VTP defines a Layer 2 messaging protocol that the switches use to exchange VLAN configuration information. When a switch changes its VLAN configuration—in other words, when a VLAN is added or deleted, or an existing VLAN is changed—VTP causes all the switches to synchronize their VLAN configuration to include the same VLAN IDs and VLAN names. The process is somewhat like a routing protocol, with each switch sending periodic VTP messages. Switches also send VTP messages as soon as their VLAN configuration changes. For example, if you configured a new VLAN 3, with the name Accounting, the switch would immediately send VTP updates out all trunks, causing the distribution of the new VLAN information to the rest of the switches.

Each switch uses one of three VTP modes: server mode, client mode, or transparent mode. To use VTP, an engineer sets some switches to use server mode and the rest to use client mode. Then, VLAN configuration can be added on the servers, with all other servers and clients learning about the changes to the VLAN database. Clients cannot be used to configure VLAN information.

Oddly enough, Cisco switches cannot disable VTP. The closest option is to use transparent mode, which causes a switch to ignore VTP, other than to forward VTP messages so that any other clients or servers can receive a copy.

The next section explains the normal operations when the engineer uses server and client modes to take advantage of VTP's capabilities, followed by an explanation of the rather unusual way to essentially disable VTP by enabling VTP transparent mode.

Normal VTP Operation Using VTP Server and Client Modes

The VTP process begins with VLAN creation on a switch called a VTP server. The VTP server then distributes VLAN configuration changes through VTP messages, sent only over ISL and 802.1Q trunks, throughout the network. Both VTP servers and clients process the received VTP messages, update their VTP configuration database based on those messages, and then independently send VTP updates out their trunks. At the end of the process, all switches learn the new VLAN information.

VTP servers and clients choose whether to react to a received VTP update, and update their VLAN configurations based on whether the *VLAN database configuration revision number* increases. Each time a VTP server modifies its VLAN configuration, the VTP server increments the current configuration revision number by 1. The VTP update messages list the new configuration revision number. When another client or server switch receives a VTP message with a higher configuration revision number than its own, the switch updates its VLAN configuration. Figure 1-6 illustrates how VTP operates in a switched network.

Key Topic

Figure 1-6 *VTP Configuration Revision Numbers and the VTP Update Process*

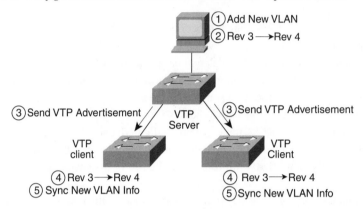

Figure 1-6 begins with all switches having the same VLAN configuration revision number, meaning that they have the same VLAN configuration database; this means that all switches know about the same VLAN numbers and VLAN names. The process begins with each switch knowing that the current configuration revision number is 3. The steps shown in Figure 1-6 are as follows:

1. Someone configures a new VLAN from the command-line interface (CLI) of a VTP server.

2. The VTP server updates its VLAN database revision number from 3 to 4.

3. The server sends VTP update messages out its trunk interfaces, stating revision number 4.

4. The two VTP client switches notice that the updates list a higher revision number (4) than their current revision numbers (3).

5. The two client switches update their VLAN databases based on the server's VTP updates.

While this example shows a very small LAN, the process works the same for larger networks. When a VTP server updates the VLAN configuration, the server immediately sends VTP messages out all trunks. The neighboring switches on the other end of the trunks process the received messages and update their VLAN databases, and then they send VTP messages to their neighbors. The process repeats on the neighboring switches, until eventually, all switches have heard of the new VLAN database.

> **NOTE**   The complete process by which a server changes the VLAN configuration, and all VTP switches learn the new configuration, resulting in all switches knowing the same VLAN IDs and name, is called *synchronization*.

VTP servers and clients also send periodic VTP messages every 5 minutes, in case any newly added switches need to know the VLAN configuration. Additionally, when a new trunk comes up, switches can immediately send a VTP message asking the neighboring switch to send its VLAN database.

So far, this chapter has referred to VTP messages as either VTP updates or VTP messages. In practice, VTP defines three different types of messages: summary advertisements, subset advertisements, and advertisement requests. The summary advertisements list the revision number, domain name, and other information, but no VLAN information. The periodic VTP messages that occur every five minutes are VTP summary advertisements. If something changes, as indicated by a new 1-larger revision number, the summary advertisement message is followed by one or more subset advertisements, each of which advertises some subset of the VLAN database. The third message, the advertisement request message, allows a switch to immediately request VTP messages from a neighboring switch as soon as a trunk comes up. However, the examples shown for the purposes of this book do not make distinctions about the use of the messages.

Three Requirements for VTP to Work Between Two Switches

When a VTP client or server connects to another VTP client or server switch, Cisco IOS requires that the following three facts be true before the two switches can exchange VTP messages:

- The link between the switches must be operating as a VLAN trunk (ISL or 802.1Q).

- The two switches' case-sensitive VTP domain name must match.

- If configured on at least one of the switches, the two switches' case-sensitive VTP password must match.

The VTP domain name provides a design tool by which engineers can create multiple groups of VTP switches, called domains, whose VLAN configurations are autonomous. To do so, the engineer can configure one set of switches in one VTP domain and another set in another VTP domain, and switches in the different domains will ignore each other's VTP messages. VTP domains allow engineers to break up the switched network into different administrative domains. For example, in a large building with a large IT staff, one division's

IT staff might use a VTP domain name of Accounting, while another part of the IT staff might use a domain name of Sales, maintaining control of their configurations but still being able to forward traffic between divisions through the LAN infrastructure.

The VTP password mechanism provides a means by which a switch can prevent malicious attackers from forcing a switch to change its VLAN configuration. The password itself is never transmitted in clear text.

Avoiding VTP by Using VTP Transparent Mode

Interestingly, to avoid using VTP to exchange VLAN information in Cisco switches, switches cannot simply disable VTP. Instead, switches must use the third VTP mode: VTP transparent mode. Transparent mode gives a switch autonomy from the other switches. Like VTP servers, VTP transparent mode switches can configure VLANs. However, unlike servers, transparent mode switches never update their VLAN databases based on incoming VTP messages, and transparent mode switches never try to create VTP messages to tell other switches about their own VLAN configuration.

VTP transparent mode switches essentially behave as if VTP does not exist, other than one small exception: Transparent mode switches forward VTP updates received from other switches, just to help out any neighboring VTP server or client switches.

From a design perspective, because of the dangers associated with VTP (as covered in the next section), some engineers just avoid VTP altogether by using VTP transparent mode on all switches. In other cases, engineers might make a few switches transparent mode switches to give autonomy to the engineers responsible for those switches, while using VTP server and client modes on other switches.

Storing VLAN Configuration

To forward traffic for a VLAN, a switch needs to know the VLAN's VLAN ID and its VLAN name. VTP's job is to advertise these details, with the full set of configuration for all VLANs being called the *VLAN configuration database*, or simply VLAN database.

Interestingly, Cisco IOS stores the information in the VLAN database differently than for most other Cisco IOS configuration commands. When VTP clients and servers store VLAN configuration—specifically, the VLAN ID, VLAN name, and other VTP configuration settings—the configuration is stored in a file called vlan.dat in flash memory. (The filename is short for "VLAN database.") Even more interesting is the fact that Cisco IOS does not put this VLAN configuration in the running-config file or the startup-config file. No command exists to view the VTP and VLAN configuration directly; instead, you need to use several **show** commands to list the information about VLANs and VTP output.

The process of storing the VLAN configuration in flash in the vlan.dat file allows both clients and servers to dynamically learn about VLANs, and have the configuration automatically stored, therefore making both client and server prepared for their next reload. If the dynamically learned VLAN configuration was only added to the running config file, the campus LAN could be exposed to cases in which all switches lost power around the same time (easily accomplished with a single power source into the building), resulting in loss of all VLAN configuration. By automatically storing the configuration in the vlan.dat file in flash memory, each switch has at least a recent VLAN configuration database, and can then rely on VTP updates from other switches if any VLAN configuration has changed recently.

An interesting side effect of this process is that when you use a VTP client or server switch in a lab, and you want to remove all the configuration to start with a clean switch, you must issue more than the **erase startup-config** command. If you only erase the startup-config and reload the switch, the switch remembers all VLAN config and VTP configuration that is instead stored in the vlan.dat file in flash. To remove those configuration details before reloading a switch, you would have to delete the vlan.dat file in flash with a command such as **delete flash:vlan.dat**.

Switches in transparent mode store VLAN configuration in both the running-config file as well as the vlan.dat file in flash. The running-config can be saved to the startup-config as well.

> **NOTE**   In some older switch Cisco IOS versions, VTP servers stored VLAN configuration in both vlan.dat and the running-config file.

VTP Versions

Cisco supports three VTP versions, aptly named versions 1, 2, and 3. Most of the differences between these versions are unimportant to the discussions in this book. However, VTP version 2 made one important improvement over version 1 relative to VTP transparent mode, an improvement that is briefly described in this section.

The section "Avoiding VTP by Using VTP Transparent Mode," earlier in this chapter, described how a switch using VTP version 2 would work. However, in VTP version 1, a VTP transparent mode switch would first check a received VTP update's domain name and password. If the transparent mode switch did not match both parameters, the transparent mode switch discarded the VTP update, rather than forwarding the update. The problem with VTP version 1 is that in cases where a transparent mode switch existed in a network with multiple VTP domains, the switch wouldn't forward all VTP updates. So, VTP version

2 changed transparent mode logic, ignoring the domain name and password, allowing a VTP version 2 transparent mode switch to forward all received VTP updates.

> **NOTE**   Version 3 is available only in higher-end Cisco switches today, and will be ignored for the purposes of this book.

VTP Pruning

By default, Cisco switches flood broadcasts (and unknown destination unicasts) in each active VLAN out all trunks, as long as the current STP topology does not block the trunk. (You find more on STP in Chapter 2.) However, in most campus networks, many VLANs exist on only a few switches, but not all switches. Therefore, it is wasteful to forward broadcasts over all trunks, causing the frames to arrive at switches that do not have any ports in that VLAN.

Switches support two methods by which an engineer can limit which VLAN's traffic flows over a trunk. One method requires the manual configuration of the *allowed VLAN list* on each trunk; this manual configuration is covered later in the chapter. The second method, VTP pruning, allows VTP to dynamically determine which switches do not need frames from certain VLANs, and then VTP prunes those VLANs from the appropriate trunks. Pruning simply means that the appropriate switch trunk interfaces do not flood frames in that VLAN. Figure 1-7 shows an example, with the dashed-line rectangles denoting the trunks from which VLAN 10 has been automatically pruned.

Figure 1-7   *VTP Pruning*

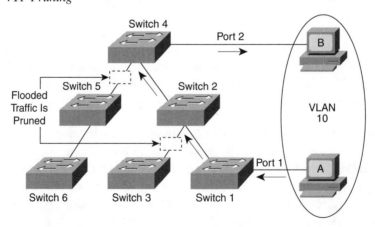

In Figure 1-7, switches 1 and 4 have ports in VLAN 10. With VTP pruning enabled network-wide, switch 2 and switch 4 automatically use VTP to learn that none of the switches in the lower-left part of the figure have any ports assigned to VLAN 10. As a result, switch 2 and switch 4 prune VLAN 10 from the trunks as shown. The pruning causes switch 2 and switch 4 to not send frames in VLAN 10 out these trunks. For example, when station A sends a broadcast, the switches flood the broadcast, as shown by the arrowed lines in Figure 1-7.

VTP pruning increases the available bandwidth by restricting flooded traffic. VTP pruning is one of the two most compelling reasons to use VTP, with the other reason being to make VLAN configuration easier and more consistent.

Summary of VTP Features

Table 1-3 offers a comparative overview of the three VTP modes.

Table 1-3 *VTP Features*

Key
Topic

Function	Server	Client	Transparent
Only sends VTP messages out ISL or 802.1Q trunks	Yes	Yes	Yes
Supports CLI configuration of VLANs	Yes	No	Yes
Can use normal-range VLANs (1–1005)	Yes	Yes	Yes
Can use extended-range VLANs (1006–4095)	No	No	Yes
Synchronizes (updates) its own config database when receiving VTP messages with a higher revision number	Yes	Yes	No
Creates and sends periodic VTP updates every 5 minutes	Yes	Yes	No
Does not process received VTP updates, but does forward received VTP updates out other trunks	No	No	Yes
Places the VLAN ID, VLAN name, and VTP configuration into the running-config file	No	No	Yes
Places the VLAN ID, VLAN name, and VTP configuration into the vlan.dat file in flash	Yes	Yes	Yes

VLAN and VLAN Trunking Configuration and Verification

Cisco switches do not require any configuration to work. You can purchase Cisco switches, install devices with the correct cabling, and turn on the switches, and they work. You would never need to configure the switch and it would work fine, even if you interconnected switches, until you needed more than one VLAN. Even the default STP settings would likely work just fine, but if you want to use VLANs—and most every enterprise network does—you need to add some configuration.

This chapter separates the VLAN configuration details into two major sections. The current section focuses on configuration and verification tasks when VTP is ignored, either by using the default VTP settings or if using VTP transparent mode. The final major section of this chapter, "VTP Configuration and Verification," examines VTP specifically.

Creating VLANs and Assigning Access VLANs to an Interface

This section shows how to create a VLAN, give the VLAN a name, and assign interfaces to a VLAN. To focus on these basic details, this section shows examples using a single switch, so VTP and trunking are not needed.

For a Cisco switch to forward frames in a particular VLAN, the switch must be configured to believe that the VLAN exists. Additionally, the switch must have nontrunking interfaces (called *access interfaces*) assigned to the VLAN and/or trunks that support the VLAN. The configuration steps for creating the VLAN, and assigning a VLAN to an access interface, are as follows. (Note that the trunk configuration is covered in the section "VLAN Trunking Configuration," later in this chapter.)

Step 1   To configure a new VLAN, follow these steps:

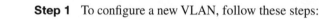

   a.   From configuration mode, use the **vlan** *vlan-id* global configuration command to create the VLAN and to move the user into VLAN configuration mode.

   b.   (Optional) Use the **name** *name* VLAN subcommand to list a name for the VLAN. If not configured, the VLAN name is VLANZZZZ, where *ZZZZ* is the 4-digit decimal VLAN ID.

Step 2   To configure a VLAN for each access interface, follow these steps:

   a.   Use the **interface** command to move into interface configuration mode for each desired interface.

   b.   Use the **switchport access vlan** *id-number* interface subcommand to specify the VLAN number associated with that interface.

c. (Optional) To disable trunking on that same interface, ensuring that
the interface is an access interface, use the **switchport mode access**
interface subcommand.

> **NOTE** VLANs can be created and named in configuration mode (as described in Step
> 1) or by using a configuration tool called VLAN database mode. The VLAN database
> mode is not covered in this book, and it is typically not covered for other Cisco exams,
> either.

> **NOTE** Cisco switches also support a dynamic method of assigning devices to VLANs,
> based on the device's MAC addresses, using a tool called the VLAN Management Policy
> Server (VMPS). This tool is seldom if ever used.

The previous process can be used on a switch either configured to be a transparent mode
switch or a switch with all default VTP settings. For reference, the following list outlines
the key Cisco switch defaults related to VLANs and VTP. For now, this chapter assumes
either default VTP settings or a setting of VTP transparent mode. Later in this chapter, the
section "Caveats When Moving Away from Default VTP Configuration" revisits Cisco
switch defaults and the implication of how to go from not using VTP, based on the default
settings, to how to use VTP.

- VTP server mode.

- No VTP domain name.

- VLAN 1 and VLANs 1002–1005 are automatically configured (and cannot be deleted).

- All access interfaces are assigned to VLAN 1 (an implied **switchport access vlan 1**
command).

VLAN Configuration Example 1: Full VLAN Configuration

Example 1-1 shows the configuration process of adding a new VLAN and assigning access
interfaces to that VLAN. Figure 1-8 shows the network used in the example, with one LAN
switch (SW1) and two hosts in each of three VLANs (1, 2, and 3). The example shows the
details of the two-step process for VLAN 2 and the interfaces in VLAN 2, with the
configuration of VLAN 3 deferred until the next example.

Figure 1-8 *Network with One Switch and Three VLANs*

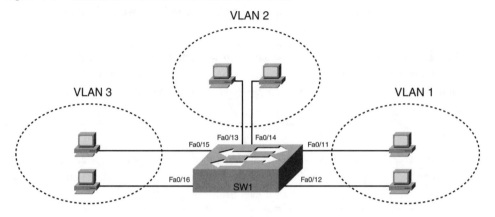

Example 1-1 *Configuring VLANs and Assigning VLANs to Interfaces*

```
sw1-2960#show vlan brief
VLAN Name                             Status    Ports
---- -------------------------------- --------- -------------------------------
1    default                          active    Fa0/1, Fa0/2, Fa0/3, Fa0/4
                                                Fa0/5, Fa0/6, Fa0/7, Fa0/8
                                                Fa0/9, Fa0/10, Fa0/11, Fa0/12
                                                Fa0/13, Fa0/14, Fa0/15, Fa0/16
                                                Fa0/17, Fa0/18, Fa0/19, Fa0/20
                                                Fa0/21, Fa0/22, Fa0/23, Fa0/24
                                                Gi0/1, Gi0/2
1002 fddi-default                     act/unsup
1003 token-ring-default               act/unsup
1004 fddinet-default                  act/unsup
1005 trnet-default                    act/unsup
! Above, VLAN 2 did not yet exist. Below, VLAN 2 is added, with name Freds-vlan,
! with two interfaces assigned to VLAN 2.
sw1-2960#configure terminal
Enter configuration commands, one per line.  End with CNTL/Z.
sw1-2960(config)#vlan 2
sw1-2960(config-vlan)#name Freds-vlan
sw1-2960(config-vlan)#exit
sw1-2960(config)#interface range fastethernet 0/13 - 14
sw1-2960(config-if)#switchport access vlan 2
sw1-2960(config-if)#exit
! Below, the show running-config command lists the interface subcommands on
! interfaces Fa0/13 and Fa0/14. The vlan 2 and name Freds-vlan commands do
! not show up in the running-config.
sw1-2960#show running-config
! lines omitted for brevity
interface FastEthernet0/13
```

Example 1-1   *Configuring VLANs and Assigning VLANs to Interfaces (Continued)*

```
 switchport access vlan 2
 switchport mode access
!
interface FastEthernet0/14
 switchport access vlan 2
 switchport mode access
!
SW1#show vlan brief

VLAN Name                             Status    Ports
---- -------------------------------- --------- -------------------------------
1    default                          active    Fa0/1, Fa0/2, Fa0/3, Fa0/4
                                                Fa0/5, Fa0/6, Fa0/7, Fa0/8
                                                Fa0/9, Fa0/10, Fa0/11, Fa0/12
                                                Fa0/15, Fa0/16, Fa0/17, Fa0/18
                                                Fa0/19, Fa0/20, Fa0/21, Fa0/22
                                                Fa0/23, Fa0/24, Gi0/1, Gi0/2
2    Freds-vlan                       active    Fa0/13, Fa0/14
1002 fddi-default                     act/unsup
1003 token-ring-default               act/unsup
1004 fddinet-default                  act/unsup
1005 trnet-default                    act/unsup
```

The example begins with the **show vlan brief** command, confirming the default settings of five nondeletable VLANs, with all interfaces assigned to VLAN 1. In particular, note that this 2960 switch has 24 Fast Ethernet ports (Fa0/1–Fa0/24) and two Gigabit Ethernet ports (Gi0/1 and Gi0/2), all of which are listed as being in VLAN 1.

Next, the example shows the process of creating VLAN 2 and assigning interfaces Fa0/13 and Fa0/14 to VLAN 2. Note in particular that the example uses the **interface range** command, which causes the **switchport access vlan 2** interface subcommand to be applied to both interfaces in the range, as confirmed in the **show running-config** command output at the end of the example.

After the configuration has been added, to list the new VLAN, the example repeats the **show vlan brief** command. Note that this command lists VLAN 2, name Freds-vlan, and the interfaces assigned to that VLAN (Fa0/13 and Fa0/14).

> **NOTE**   Example 1-1 uses default VTP configuration. However, if the switch had been configured for VTP transparent mode, the **vlan 2** and **name Freds-vlan** configuration commands would have also been seen in the output of the **show running-config** command. Because this switch is in VTP server mode (default), the switch stores these two commands only in the vlan.dat file.

A switch might not use the VLAN assigned by the **switchport access vlan** *vlan-id* command in some cases, depending on the operational mode of an interface. A Cisco switch's operational mode relates to whether the interface is currently using a trunking protocol. An interface that is currently using trunking is called a *trunk interface*, and all other interfaces are called *access interfaces*. So, engineers use phrases like "Fa0/12 is a trunk port" or "Fa0/13 is an access interface," referring to whether the design intends to use a particular interface to trunk (trunk mode) or to connect to just one VLAN (access mode).

The optional interface subcommand **switchport mode access** tells the switch to only allow the interface to be an access interface, which means that the interface will not use trunking and it will use the assigned access VLAN. If you omit the optional **switchport mode access** interface subcommand, the interface could negotiate to use trunking, becoming a trunk interface and ignoring the configured access VLAN.

VLAN Configuration Example 2: Shorter VLAN Configuration

Example 1-1 shows several of the optional configuration commands, with a side effect of being a bit longer than is required. Example 1-2 shows a much briefer alternative configuration, picking up the story where Example 1-1 ended, showing the addition of VLAN 3 (as seen in Figure 1-8). Note that SW1 does not know about VLAN 3 at the beginning of this example.

Example 1-2 *Shorter VLAN Configuration Example (VLAN 3)*

```
SW1#configure terminal
Enter configuration commands, one per line.  End with CNTL/Z.
SW1(config)#interface range Fastethernet 0/15 - 16
SW1(config-if-range)#switchport access vlan 3
% Access VLAN does not exist. Creating vlan 3
SW1(config-if-range)#^Z
SW1#show vlan brief

VLAN Name                             Status    Ports
---- -------------------------------- --------- -------------------------------
1    default                          active    Fa0/1, Fa0/2, Fa0/3, Fa0/4
                                                Fa0/5, Fa0/6, Fa0/7, Fa0/8
                                                Fa0/9, Fa0/10, Fa0/11, Fa0/12
                                                Fa0/17, Fa0/18, Fa0/19, Fa0/20
                                                Fa0/21, Fa0/22, Fa0/23, Fa0/24
                                                Gi0/1, Gi0/2
2    Freds-vlan                       active    Fa0/13, Fa0/14
3    VLAN0003                         active    Fa0/15, Fa0/16
1002 fddi-default                     act/unsup
1003 token-ring-default               act/unsup
1004 fddinet-default                  act/unsup
1005 trnet-default                    act/unsup
SW1#
```

Example 1-2 shows how a switch can dynamically create a VLAN—the equivalent of the **vlan** *vlan-id* global config command—when the **switchport access vlan** interface subcommand refers to a currently unconfigured VLAN. This example begins with SW1 not knowing about VLAN 3. When the **switchport access vlan 3** interface subcommand was used, the switch realized that VLAN 3 did not exist, and as noted in the shaded message in the example, the switch created VLAN 3, using a default name (VLAN0003). No other steps are required to create the VLAN. At the end of the process, VLAN 3 exists in the switch, and interfaces Fa0/15 and Fa0/16 are in VLAN 3, as noted in the shaded part of the **show vlan brief** command output.

As a reminder, note that some of the configuration shown in Examples 1-1 and 1-2 ends up only in the vlan.dat file in flash memory, and some ends up only in the running-config file. In particular, the interface subcommands are in the running-config file, so a **copy running-config startup-config** command would be needed to save the configuration. However, the definitions of new VLANs 2 and 3 have already been automatically saved in the vlan.dat file in flash. Table 1-7, later in this chapter, lists a reference of the various configuration commands, where they are stored, and how to confirm the configuration settings.

VLAN Trunking Configuration

Trunking configuration on Cisco switches involves two important configuration choices, as follows:

- The type of trunking: IEEE 802.1Q, ISL, or negotiate which one to use

- The *administrative mode*: Whether to trunk, not trunk, or negotiate

Cisco switches can either negotiate or configure the type of trunking to use (ISL or 802.1Q). By default, Cisco switches negotiate the type of trunking with the switch on the other end of the trunk, using the Dynamic Trunk Protocol (DTP). When negotiating, if both switches support both ISL and 802.1Q, they choose ISL. If one switch is willing to use either type, and the other switch is only willing to use one type of trunking, the two switches agree to use that one type of trunking supported by both switches. The type of trunking preferred on an interface, for switches that support both types, is configured using the **switchport trunk encapsulation** {**dot1q** | **isl** | **negotiate**} interface subcommand. (Many of the most recently developed Cisco switches, including 2960s, only support the IEEE-standard 802.1Q trunking today, so these switches simply default to a setting of **switchport trunk encapsulation dot1q**.)

The administrative mode refers to the configuration setting for whether trunking should be used on an interface. The term *administrative* refers to what is configured, whereas an interface's *operational* mode refers to what is currently happening on the interface. Cisco switches use an interface's *administrative mode*, as configured with the **switchport mode** interface subcommand, to determine whether to use trunking. Table 1-4 lists the options of the **switchport mode** command.

Table 1-4   *Trunking Administrative Mode Options with the **switchport mode** Command*

Command Option	Description
access	Prevents the use of trunking, making the port always act as an access (nontrunk) port
trunk	Always uses trunking
dynamic desirable	Initiates negotiation messages and responds to negotiation messages to dynamically choose whether to start using trunking, and defines the trunking encapsulation
dynamic auto	Passively waits to receive trunk negotiation messages, at which point the switch will respond and negotiate whether to use trunking, and if so, the type of trunking

For example, consider the two switches shown in Figure 1-9. This figure shows an expansion of the network of Figure 1-8, with a trunk to a new switch (SW2) and with parts of VLANs 1 and 3 on ports attached to SW2. The two switches use a Gigabit Ethernet link for the trunk. In this case, the trunk does not dynamically form by default, because both (2960) switches default to an administrative mode of *dynamic auto*, meaning that neither switch initiates the trunk negotiation process. By changing one switch to use *dynamic desirable* mode, which does initiate the negotiation, the switches negotiate to use trunking, specifically 802.1Q because the 2960s only support 802.1Q.

Figure 1-9   *Network with Two Switches and Three VLANs*

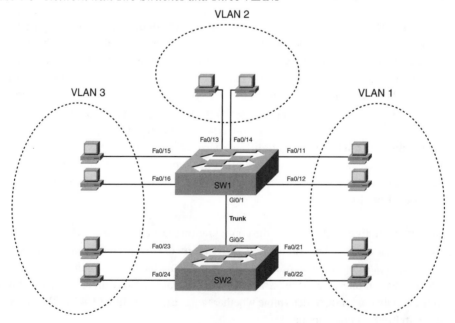

Example 1-3 begins by showing the two switches with the default configuration so that the two switches do not trunk. The example then shows the configuration of SW1 so that the two switches negotiate and use 802.1Q trunking.

Example 1-3 *Trunking Configuration and **show** Commands on 2960 Switches*

```
SW1#show interfaces gigabit 0/1 switchport
Name: Gi0/1
Switchport: Enabled
Administrative Mode: dynamic auto
Operational Mode: static access
Administrative Trunking Encapsulation: dot1q
Operational Trunking Encapsulation: native
Negotiation of Trunking: On
Access Mode VLAN: 1 (default)
Trunking Native Mode VLAN: 1 (default)
Administrative Native VLAN tagging: enabled
Voice VLAN: none
Access Mode VLAN: 1 (default)
Trunking Native Mode VLAN: 1 (default)
Administrative Native VLAN tagging: enabled
Voice VLAN: none
Administrative private-vlan host-association: none
Administrative private-vlan mapping: none
Administrative private-vlan trunk native VLAN: none
Administrative private-vlan trunk Native VLAN tagging: enabled
Administrative private-vlan trunk encapsulation: dot1q
Administrative private-vlan trunk normal VLANs: none
Administrative private-vlan trunk private VLANs: none
Operational private-vlan: none
Trunking VLANs Enabled: ALL
Pruning VLANs Enabled: 2-1001
Capture Mode Disabled
Capture VLANs Allowed: ALL

Protected: false
Unknown unicast blocked: disabled
Unknown multicast blocked: disabled
Appliance trust: none
! Note that the next command results in a single empty line of output.
SW1#show interfaces trunk

SW1#
! Next, the administrative mode is set to dynamic desirable.
SW1#configure terminal
Enter configuration commands, one per line.  End with CNTL/Z.
SW1(config)#interface gigabit 0/1
SW1(config-if)#switchport mode dynamic desirable
```

continues

Example 1-3 *Trunking Configuration and **show** Commands on 2960 Switches (Continued)*

```
SW1(config-if)#^Z
SW1#
01:43:46: %LINEPROTO-5-UPDOWN: Line protocol on Interface GigabitEthernet0/1, changed
state to down
SW1#
01:43:49: %LINEPROTO-5-UPDOWN: Line protocol on Interface GigabitEthernet0/1, changed
state to up
SW1#show interfaces gigabit 0/1 switchport
Name: Gi0/1
Switchport: Enabled
Administrative Mode: dynamic desirable
Operational Mode: trunk
Administrative Trunking Encapsulation: dot1q
Operational Trunking Encapsulation: dot1q
Negotiation of Trunking: On
Access Mode VLAN: 1 (default)
Trunking Native Mode VLAN: 1 (default)
! lines omitted for brevity
! The next command formerly listed a single empty line of output; now it lists
! information about the 1 operational trunk.
SW1#show interfaces trunk

Port        Mode        Encapsulation  Status      Native vlan
Gi0/1       desirable   802.1q         trunking    1

Port        Vlans allowed on trunk
Gi0/1       1-4094

Port        Vlans allowed and active in management domain
Gi0/1       1-3

Port        Vlans in spanning tree forwarding state and not pruned
Gi0/1       1-3
```

First, focus on important items from the output of the **show interfaces switchport** command at the beginning of Example 1-3. The output lists the default administrative mode setting of dynamic auto. Because SW2 also defaults to dynamic auto, the command lists SW1's operational status as access, meaning that it is not trunking. The third shaded line points out the only supported type of trunking (802.1Q) on this 2960 switch. (On a switch that supports both ISL and 802.1Q, this value would by default list "negotiate," to mean that the type or encapsulation is negotiated.) Finally, the operational trunking type is listed as "native," which is a subtle way to say that the switch does not add any trunking header to forwarded frames on this port, treating frames as if they are in an 802.1Q native VLAN.

To enable trunking, the two switches' administrative modes must be set to a combination of values that result in trunking. By changing SW1 to use dynamic desirable mode, as shown next in Example 1-3, SW1 will now initiate the negotiations, and the two switches will use trunking. Of particular interest is the fact that the switch brings the interface to a down state, and then back up again, as a result of the change to the administrative mode of the interface.

To verify that trunking is working now, the end of Example 1-3 lists the **show interfaces switchport** command. Note that the command still lists the administrative settings, which denote the configured values, along with the operational settings, which list what the switch is currently doing. In this case, SW1 now claims to be in an operational mode of trunk, with an operational trunking encapsulation of dot1Q.

For the ICND2 and CCNA exams, you should be ready to interpret the output of the **show interfaces switchport** command, realize the administrative mode implied by the output, and know whether the link should operationally trunk based on those settings. Table 1-5 lists the combinations of the trunking administrative modes and the expected operational mode (trunk or access) resulting from the configured settings. The table lists the administrative mode used on one end of the link on the left, and the administrative mode on the switch on the other end of the link across the top of the table.

Table 1-5 *Expected Trunking Operational Mode Based on the Configured Administrative Modes*

Key Topic

Administrative Mode	Access	Dynamic Auto	Trunk	Dynamic Desirable
access	Access	Access	Access	Access
dynamic auto	Access	Access	Trunk	Trunk
trunk	Access	Trunk	Trunk	Trunk
dynamic desirable	Access	Trunk	Trunk	Trunk

Controlling Which VLANs Can Be Supported on a Trunk

The *allowed VLAN list* feature provides a mechanism for engineers to administratively disable a VLAN from a trunk. By default, switches include all possible VLANs (1–4094) in each trunk's allowed VLAN list. However, the engineer can then limit the VLANs allowed on the trunk by using the following interface subcommand:

```
switchport trunk allowed vlan {add | all | except | remove} vlan-list
```

This command provides a way to easily add and remove VLANs from the list. For example, the **add** option permits the switch to add VLANs to the existing allowed VLAN list, and the **remove** option permits the switch to remove VLANs from the existing list. The **all** option means all VLANs, so you can use it to reset the switch to its original default setting (permitting VLANs 1–4094 on the trunk). The **except** option is rather tricky: It adds all

VLANs to the list that are not part of the command. For example, the **switchport trunk allowed vlan except 100-200** interface subcommand adds VLANs 1 through 99 and 201 through 4094 to the existing allowed VLAN list on that trunk.

In addition to the allowed VLAN list, a switch has three other reasons to prevent a particular VLAN's traffic from crossing a trunk. All four reasons are summarized in the following list:

- A VLAN has been removed from the trunk's *allowed VLAN* list.

- A VLAN does not exist, or is not active, in the switch's VLAN database (as seen with the **show vlan** command).

- A VLAN has been automatically pruned by VTP.

- A VLAN's STP instance has placed the trunk interface into a state other than a Forwarding State.

Of these additional three reasons, the second reason needs a little more explanation. (The third reason, VTP pruning, has already been covered in this chapter, and the fourth reason, STP, is covered thoroughly in Chapter 2.) If a switch does not know that a VLAN exists, as evidenced by the VLAN's absence from the output of the **show vlan** command, the switch will not forward frames in that VLAN over any interface. Additionally, a VLAN can be administratively shut down on any switch by using the **shutdown vlan** *vlan-id* global configuration command, which also causes the switch to no longer forward frames in that VLAN, even over trunks. So, switches do not forward frames in a nonexistent or shutdown VLAN over any of the switch's trunks.

The book lists the four reasons for limiting VLANs on a trunk in the same order in which IOS describes these reasons in the output of the **show interfaces trunk** command. This command includes a progression of three lists of the VLANs supported over a trunk. These three lists are as follows:

- VLANs in the allowed VLAN list on the trunk

- VLANs in the previous group that are also configured and active (not shut down) on the switch

- VLANs in the previous group that are also not pruned and are in an STP Forwarding State

To get an idea of these three lists inside the output of the **show interfaces trunk** command, Example 1-4 shows how VLANs might be disallowed on a trunk for various reasons. The command output is taken from SW1 in Figure 1-9, after the completion of the configuration as shown in Examples 1-1, 1-2, and 1-3. In other words, VLANS 1 through 3 exist, and trunking is operational. Then, during the example, the following items are configured on SW1:

Step 1   VLAN 4 is added.

Step 2   VLAN 2 is shut down.

Step 3   VLAN 3 is removed from the trunk's allowed VLAN list.

Example 1-4   *Allowed VLAN List and the List of Active VLANs*

```
! The three lists of VLANs in the next command list allowed VLANs (1-4094),
! Allowed and active VLANs (1-3), and allowed/active/not pruned/STP forwarding
! VLANs (1-3)
SW1#show interfaces trunk

Port        Mode        Encapsulation Status     Native vlan
Gi0/1       desirable   802.1q        trunking   1

Port        Vlans allowed on trunk
Gi0/1       1-4094

Port        Vlans allowed and active in management domain
Gi0/1       1-3

Port        Vlans in spanning tree forwarding state and not pruned
Gi0/1       1-3
! Next, the switch is configured with new VLAN 4; VLAN 2 is shutdown;
! and VLAN 3 is removed from the allowed VLAN list on the trunk.
SW1#configure terminal
Enter configuration commands, one per line.  End with CNTL/Z.
SW1(config)#vlan 4
SW1(config-vlan)#vlan 2
SW1(config-vlan)#shutdown
SW1(config-vlan)#interface gi0/1
SW1(config-if)#switchport trunk allowed vlan remove 3
SW1(config-if)#^Z
! The three lists of VLANs in the next command list allowed VLANs (1-2, 4-4094),
! allowed and active VLANs (1,4), and allowed/active/not pruned/STP forwarding
! VLANs (1,4)
SW1#show interfaces trunk

Port        Mode        Encapsulation Status     Native vlan
Gi0/1       desirable   802.1q        trunking   1


! VLAN 3 is omitted next, because it was removed from the allowed VLAN list.
Port        Vlans allowed on trunk
```

continues

Example 1-4 *Allowed VLAN List and the List of Active VLANs (Continued)*

```
Gi0/1      1-2,4-4094


! VLAN 2 is omitted below because it is shutdown. VLANs 5-4094 are omitted below
! because SW1 does not have them configured.
Port       Vlans allowed and active in management domain
Gi0/1      1,4


Port       Vlans in spanning tree forwarding state and not pruned
Gi0/1      1,4
```

Trunking to Cisco IP Phones

Cisco IP phones use Ethernet to connect to the IP network for the purpose of sending Voice over IP (VoIP) packets. Cisco IP phones can send VoIP packets to other IP phones to support voice calls, as well as send VoIP packets to voice gateways, which in turn connect to the existing traditional telephone network, supporting the ability to call most any phone in the world.

Cisco anticipated that each desk in an enterprise might have both a Cisco IP phone and a PC on it. To reduce cabling clutter, Cisco includes a small LAN switch in the bottom of each Cisco IP phone. The small switch allows one cable to run from the wiring closet to the desk and connect to the IP phone, and then the PC can connect to the switch by connecting a short Ethernet (straight-through) cable from the PC to the bottom of the IP phone. Figure 1-10 shows the cabling as well as a few more details.

Figure 1-10 *Typical Connection of a Cisco IP Phone and PC to a Cisco Switch*

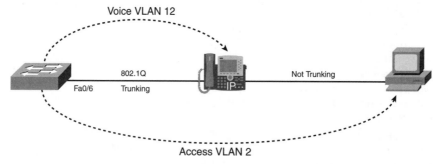

Cisco IP telephony design guidelines suggest that the link between the phone and switch should use 802.1Q trunking, and that the phone and PC should be in different VLANs (and therefore in different subnets). By placing the phones in one VLAN, and the PCs connected to the phones in a different VLAN, engineers can more easily manage the IP address space, more easily apply quality of service (QoS) mechanisms to the VoIP packets, and provide better security by separating the data and voice traffic.

Cisco calls the VLAN used for the phone's traffic the voice VLAN and the VLAN used for data the data or access VLAN. For the switch to forward traffic correctly, Cisco switches need to know the VLAN ID of both the voice VLAN and the data VLAN. The data (or access) VLAN is configured just as seen in the last few examples, using the **switchport access vlan** *vlan-id* command. The voice vlan is configured with the **switchport voice vlan** *vlan-id* interface subcommand. For example, to match Figure 1-10, interface Fa0/6 would need both the **switchport access vlan 2** interface subcommand and the **switchport voice vlan 12** subcommand.

Table 1-6 summarizes the key points about the voice VLAN.

Table 1-6 *Voice and Data VLAN Configuration*

Device	Name of the VLAN	Configured With This Command
Phone	Voice or auxiliary VLAN	**switchport voice vlan** *vlan-id*
PC	Data or access VLAN	**switchport access vlan** *vlan-id*

Securing VLANs and Trunking

Switches are exposed to several types of security vulnerabilities over both used ports and unused ports. For example, an attacker could connect a computer to a wall plug cabled to a switch port and cause problems on the VLAN assigned to that port. Additionally, the attacker could negotiate trunking and cause many other types of problems, some related to VTP.

Cisco makes some recommendations for how to protect unused switch ports. Instead of using default settings, Cisco recommends configuring these interfaces as follows:

■   Administratively disable the unused interface, using the **shutdown** interface subcommand.

■   Prevent trunking from being negotiated when the port is enabled by using the **switchport nonegotiate** interface subcommand to disable negotiation, or the **switchport mode access** interface subcommand to statically configure the interface as an access interface.

■   Assign the port to an unused VLAN, sometimes called a *parking lot VLAN*, using the **switchport access vlan** *number* interface subcommand.

Frankly, if you just shut down the interface, the security exposure goes away, but the other two tasks prevent any immediate problems if some other engineer enables the interface by configuring a **no shutdown** command.

Besides these recommendations on unused ports, Cisco recommends that the negotiation of trunking be disabled on all in-use access interfaces, with all trunks being manually configured to trunk. The exposure is that an attacker could disconnect a legitimate user's computer from the RJ-45 port, connect the attacker's PC, and try to negotiate trunking. By configuring all in-use interfaces that should not be trunking with the **switchport nonnegotiate** interface subcommand, these interfaces will not dynamically decide to trunk, reducing the exposure to trunking-related problems. For any interfaces that need to trunk, Cisco recommends manually configuring trunking.

VTP Configuration and Verification

VTP configuration requires only a few simple steps, but VTP has the power to cause significant problems, either by accidental poor configuration choices or by malicious attacks. The following sections first examine the overall configuration, followed by some comments about potential problems created by the VTP process. These sections then end with a discussion of how to troubleshoot problems related to VTP.

Using VTP: Configuring Servers and Clients

Before configuring VTP, several VTP settings must be chosen. In particular, assuming that the engineer wants to make use of VTP, the engineer needs to decide which switches will be in the same VTP domain, meaning that these switches will learn VLAN configuration information from each other. The VTP domain name must be chosen, along with an optional but recommended VTP password. (Both values are case sensitive.) The engineer must also choose which switches will be servers (usually at least two for redundancy), and which will be clients.

After the planning steps are completed, the following steps can be used to configure VTP:

Step 1   Configure the VTP mode using the **vtp mode** {**server** | **client**} global configuration command.

Step 2   Configure the VTP (case-sensitive) domain name using the **vtp domain** *domain-name* global configuration command.

Step 3   (Optional) On both clients and servers, configure the same case-sensitive password using the **vtp password** *password-value* global configuration command.

Step 4   (Optional) Configure VTP pruning on the VTP servers using the **vtp pruning** global configuration command.

Step 5   (Optional) Enable VTP version 2 with the **vtp version 2** global configuration command.

Step 6 Bring up trunks between the switches.

Example 1-5 shows a sample configuration, along with a **show vtp status** command, for the two switches in Figure 1-11. The figure points out the configuration settings on the two switches before Example 1-5 shows VTP configuration being added. In particular, note that both switches use default VTP configuration settings.

Figure 1-11 *Switch Configuration Before Example 1-5*

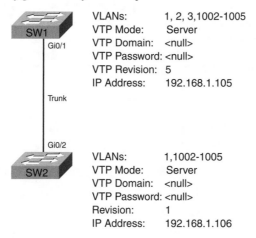

Example 1-5 shows the following configuration on both SW1 and SW2, and the results:

- **SW1:** Configured as a server, with VTP domain name Freds-domain, VTP password Freds-password, and VTP pruning enabled

- **SW2:** Configured as a client, with VTP domain name Freds-domain and VTP password Freds-password

Example 1-5 *Basic VTP Client and Server Configuration*

```
! IOS generates at least one informational message after each VTP command listed
! below. The comments added by the author begin with an exclamation point.
SW1#configure terminal
Enter configuration commands, one per line.  End with CNTL/Z.
SW1(config)#vtp mode server
Setting device to VTP SERVER mode
SW1(config)#vtp domain Freds-domain
Changing VTP domain name from NULL to Freds-domain
SW1(config)#vtp password Freds-password
Setting device VLAN database password to Freds-password
SW1(config)#vtp pruning
Pruning switched on
```

continues

Example 1-5 *Basic VTP Client and Server Configuration (Continued)*

```
SW1(config)#^Z
! Switching to SW2 now
SW2#configure terminal
Enter configuration commands, one per line.  End with CNTL/Z.
SW2(config)#vtp mode client
Setting device to VTP CLIENT mode.
SW2(config)#vtp domain Freds-domain
Domain name already set to Freds-domain.
SW2(config)#vtp password Freds-password
Setting device VLAN database password to Freds-password
SW2(config)#^Z
! The output below shows configuration revision number 5, with 7 existing VLANs
! (1 through 3, 1002 through 1005), as learned from SW1
SW2#show vtp status
VTP Version                     : 2
Configuration Revision          : 5
Maximum VLANs supported locally : 255
Number of existing VLANs        : 7
VTP Operating Mode              : Client
VTP Domain Name                 : Freds-domain
VTP Pruning Mode                : Enabled
VTP V2 Mode                     : Disabled
VTP Traps Generation            : Disabled
MD5 digest                      : 0x22 0x07 0xF2 0x3A 0xF1 0x28 0xA0 0x5D
Configuration last modified by 192.168.1.105 at 3-1-93 00:28:35
! The next command lists the known VLANs, including VLANs 2 and 3, learned
! from SW1
SW2#show vlan brief

VLAN Name                             Status    Ports
---- -------------------------------- --------- -------------------------------
1    default                          active    Fa0/1, Fa0/2, Fa0/3, Fa0/4
                                                Fa0/5, Fa0/6, Fa0/7, Fa0/8
                                                Fa0/9, Fa0/10, Fa0/11, Fa0/12
                                                Fa0/13, Fa0/14, Fa0/15, Fa0/16
                                                Fa0/17, Fa0/18, Fa0/19, Fa0/20
                                                Fa0/21, Fa0/22, Fa0/23, Fa0/24
                                                Gi0/1
2    Freds-vlan                       active
3    VLAN0003                         active
1002 fddi-default                     act/unsup
1003 token-ring-default               act/unsup
1004 fddinet-default                  act/unsup
1005 trnet-default                    act/unsup
! Switching to SW1 now
! Back on SW1, the output below confirms the same revision number as SW2, meaning
! that the two switches have synchronized their VLAN databases.
```

Example 1-5 *Basic VTP Client and Server Configuration (Continued)*

```
SW1#show vtp status
VTP Version                      : 2
Configuration Revision           : 5
Maximum VLANs supported locally  : 255
Number of existing VLANs         : 7
VTP Operating Mode               : Server
VTP Domain Name                  : Freds-domain
VTP Pruning Mode                 : Enabled
VTP V2 Mode                      : Disabled
VTP Traps Generation             : Disabled
MD5 digest                       : 0x22 0x07 0xF2 0x3A 0xF1 0x28 0xA0 0x5D
Configuration last modified by 192.168.1.105 at 3-1-93 00:28:35
Local updater ID is 192.168.1.105 on interface Vl1 (lowest numbered VLAN interface found)
SW1#show vtp password
VTP Password: Freds-password
```

The example is relatively long, but the configuration is straightforward. Both switches were configured with the VTP mode (server and client), the same domain name, and the same password, with trunking already having been configured. The configuration resulted in SW2 (client) synchronizing its VLAN database to match SW1 (server).

Cisco IOS switches in VTP server or client mode store the **vtp** configuration commands, and some other configuration commands, in the vlan.dat file in flash, and the switches do not store the configuration commands in the running-config file. Instead, to verify these configuration commands and their settings, the **show vtp status** and **show vlan** commands are used. For reference, Table 1-7 lists the VLAN-related configuration commands, the location in which a VTP server or client stores the commands, and how to view the settings for the commands.

Table 1-7 *Where VTP Clients and Servers Store VLAN-Related Configuration*

Key
Topic

Configuration Commands	Where Stored	How to View
vtp domain	vlan.dat	**show vtp status**
vtp mode	vlan.dat	**show vtp status**
vtp password	vlan.dat	**show vtp password**
vtp pruning	vlan.dat	**show vtp status**
vlan *vlan-id*	vlan.dat	**show vlan [brief]**
name *vlan-name*	vlan.dat	**show vlan [brief]**
switchport access vlan *vlan-id*	running-config	**show running-config, show interfaces switchport**
switchport voice vlan *vlan-id*	running-config	**show running-config, show interfaces switchport**

Any analysis of VTP and VLANs on Cisco switches depends on two important commands: the **show vtp status** and **show vlan** commands. First, note that when the domain is synchronized, the **show vtp status** command on all switches should have the same configuration revision number. Additionally, the **show vlan** command should list the same VLANs and VLAN names. For example, both SW1 and SW2 end Example 1-5 with a revision number of 5, and both know about seven VLANs: 1–3 and 1002–1005. Both instances of the **show vtp status** command in Example 1-5 list the IP address of the last switch to modify the VLAN database—namely SW1, 192.168.1.105—so it is easier to find which switch last changed the VLAN configuration. Only on VTP servers, the **show vtp status** command ends with a line that lists that switch's IP address that identifies itself when advertising VTP updates, making it easier to confirm which switch last changed the VLAN configuration.

Note that the VTP password can only be displayed with the **show vtp password** command. The **show vtp status** command displays an MD5 digest of the password.

> **NOTE**   Cisco switches send VTP messages and Cisco Discovery Protocol (CDP) messages on trunks using VLAN 1.

Caveats When Moving Away from Default VTP Configuration

The default behavior of VTP introduces the possibility of problems when first configuring VTP. To see why, consider the following five points about VTP:

- The default VTP configuration on Cisco switches is VTP server mode with a null domain name.

- With all default settings, a switch does not send VTP updates, even over trunks, but the switch can be configured with VLANs because it is in server mode.

- After configuring a domain name, that switch immediately starts sending VTP updates over all its trunks.

- If a switch that still has a (default) null domain name receives a VTP update—which by definition lists a domain name—and no password was used by the sending switch, the receiving switch starts using that VTP domain name.

- When the previous step occurs, the switch with the higher VLAN database revision number causes the switch with the lower revision number to overwrite its VLAN database.

Example 1-5 progresses through these same five facts. Example 1-5 begins with trunking enabled between the two switches, but with default VTP settings (items 1 and 2 from the list preceding this paragraph). As soon as SW1 configures its VTP domain name, SW1 sends VTP messages over the trunk to SW2 (item 3). SW2 reacts by starting to use the VTP domain name listed in the received VTP update (Freds-domain, in this case). By the time the **vtp domain Freds-domain** command was issued on SW2 in Example 1-5, SW2 was already using the dynamically learned domain name Freds-domain, so Cisco IOS on SW2 issued the response "Domain name already set to Freds-domain" (item 4). Finally, SW2, with a lower VTP revision number, synchronized its VLAN database to match SW1 (item 5).

The process worked exactly as intended in Example 1-5. However, this same process allows an engineer to innocently configure a switch's VTP domain name and completely crash a switched LAN. For example, imagine that SW2 had configured VLAN 4 and assigned several interfaces to VLAN 4, but SW1 does not have a definition for VLAN 4. Following this same process, when SW2 synchronizes its VLAN database to match SW1, SW2 overwrites the old database, losing the definition of VLAN 4. At that point, SW2 can no longer forward frames in VLAN 4, and all the users of VLAN 4 might start calling the help desk.

This same process could be used to perform a denial of service (DoS) attack using VTP. With only default VTP settings, any attacker that can manage to bring up a trunk between an attacking switch and the existing legitimate switch can cause the existing switches to synchronize to the attacking switch's VLAN database, which may well have no VLANs configured. So, for real networks, if you do not intend to use VTP when installing a switch, it is worth the effort to simply configure it to be a VTP transparent mode switch, as is covered in the next section. By doing so, the configuration of a VTP domain name on that new switch will not impact the existing switches, and the configuration of a domain name on another switch will not impact this new switch.

NOTE The section titled "Troubleshooting VTP" explains how to recognize when VTP might have caused problems like those mentioned in this section.

Avoiding VTP: Configuring Transparent Mode

To avoid using VTP, you need to configure VTP transparent mode. In transparent mode, a switch never updates its VLAN database based on a received VTP message, and never causes other switches to update their databases based on the transparent mode switch's VLAN database. The only VTP action performed by the switch is to forward VTP messages received on one trunk out all the other trunks, which allows other VTP clients and servers to work correctly.

Configuring VTP transparent mode is simple: Just issue the **vtp mode transparent** command in global configuration mode. You do not need a domain name or a password.

Troubleshooting VTP

VTP can have an enormous impact on a campus LAN built using Cisco switches, both a negative and positive impact. The following sections examine three aspects of VTP troubleshooting. First, the text suggests a process by which to troubleshoot VTP when VTP does not appear to be distributing VLAN configuration information (adds/deletions/ changes). Following that, the text examines a common class of problems that occur when a trunk comes up, possibly triggering the neighboring switches to send VTP updates and overwrite one of the switch's VLAN database. This topic ends with suggested best practices for preventing VTP problems.

Determining Why VTP Is Not Currently Working

The first step in troubleshooting VTP should be to determine whether a problem exists in the first place. For switches that should be using VTP, in the same domain, a problem can first be identified when any two neighboring switches have different VLAN databases. In other words, they know about different VLAN IDs, with different names, and with a different configuration revision number. After identifying two neighboring switches whose VLAN databases do not match, the next step is to check the configuration and the operational trunking mode (not the administrative mode), and to correct any problems. The following list details the specific steps:

Step 1   Confirm the switch names, topology (including which interfaces connect which switches), and switch VTP modes.

Step 2   Identify sets of two neighboring switches that should be either VTP clients or servers whose VLAN databases differ with the **show vlan** command.

Step 3   On each pair of two neighboring switches whose databases differ, verify the following:

   a.   At least one operational trunk should exist between the two switches (use the **show interfaces trunk**, **show interfaces switchport**, or **show cdp neighbors** command).

   b.   The switches must have the same (case-sensitive) VTP domain name (**show vtp status**).

   c.   If configured, the switches must have the same (case-sensitive) VTP password (**show vtp password**).

d. While VTP pruning should be enabled or disabled on all servers in the same domain, having two servers configured with opposite pruning settings does not prevent the synchronization process.

Step 4   For each pair of switches identified in Step 3, solve the problem by either troubleshooting the trunking problem or reconfiguring a switch to correctly match the domain name or password.

> **NOTE**   For real campus LANs, besides the items in this list, also consider the intended VTP design as well.

While the process does spell out several steps, it mainly shows how to attack the problem with knowledge covered earlier in this chapter. The process basically states that if the VLAN databases differ, and the switches should be either VTP clients or servers, that a VTP problem exists—and the root cause is usually some VTP configuration problem. However, on the exam, you might be forced to figure out the answer based on **show** command output. For example, consider a problem in which three switches (SW1, SW2, and SW3) all connect to each other. An exam question might require that you find any VTP problems in the network, based on the output of **show** commands like those in Example 1-6.

> **NOTE**   It would be a good exercise to read the example and apply the troubleshooting steps listed at the beginning of this section before reading any of the explanations that follow the example.

Example 1-6   *VTP Troubleshooting Example*

```
SW1#show cdp neighbors
Capability Codes: R - Router, T - Trans Bridge, B - Source Route Bridge
                  S - Switch, H - Host, I - IGMP, r - Repeater, P - Phone

Device ID          Local Intrfce      Holdtme   Capability   Platform   Port ID
SW2                Gig 0/1            163          S I        WS-C2960-2Gig 0/2
SW3                Gig 0/2            173          S I        WS-C3550-2Gig 0/1
SW1#show vlan brief

VLAN Name                            Status    Ports
---- -------------------------       --------- -------------------------------
1    default                         active    Fa0/1, Fa0/2, Fa0/3, Fa0/4
                                               Fa0/5, Fa0/6, Fa0/7, Fa0/8
                                               Fa0/9, Fa0/10, Fa0/13, Fa0/14
                                               Fa0/15, Fa0/16, Fa0/17, Fa0/18
                                               Fa0/19, Fa0/20, Fa0/21, Fa0/22
                                               Fa0/23, Fa0/24, Gi0/2
```

continues

Example 1-6 *VTP Troubleshooting Example (Continued)*

```
3    VLAN0003                     active     Fa0/11
4    VLAN0004                     active
5    VLAN0005                     active
49   VLAN0049                     active
50   VLAN0050                     active
1002 fddi-default                 act/unsup
1003 trcrf-default                act/unsup
1004 fddinet-default              act/unsup
1005 trbrf-default                act/unsup
SW1#show interfaces trunk


Port        Mode        Encapsulation  Status       Native vlan
Gi0/1       desirable   802.1q         trunking     1


Port        Vlans allowed on trunk
Gi0/1       1-4094


Port        Vlans allowed and active in management domain
Gi0/1       1,3-5,49-50


Port        Vlans in spanning tree forwarding state and not pruned
Gi0/1       3-5,49-50
SW1#show vtp status
VTP Version                  : 2
Configuration Revision       : 131
Maximum VLANs supported locally : 255
Number of existing VLANs     : 10
VTP Operating Mode           : Client
VTP Domain Name              : Larry
VTP Pruning Mode             : Disabled
VTP V2 Mode                  : Enabled
VTP Traps Generation         : Disabled
MD5 digest                   : 0x1D 0x27 0xA9 0xF9 0x46 0xDF 0x66 0xCF
Configuration last modified by 1.1.1.3 at 3-1-93 00:33:38
! SW2 next
SW2#show cdp neighbors
Capability Codes: R - Router, T - Trans Bridge, B - Source Route Bridge
                 S - Switch, H - Host, I - IGMP, r - Repeater, P - Phone


Device ID          Local Intrfce       Holdtme  Capability   Platform    Port ID
SW1                Gig 0/2             175          S I       WS-C2960-2Gig 0/1
SW3                Gig 0/1             155          S I       WS-C3550-2Gig 0/2
SW2#show vlan brief


VLAN Name                            Status    Ports
---- -------------------------------- --------- -------------------------------
1    default                         active    Fa0/1, Fa0/2, Fa0/3, Fa0/4
```

Example 1-6 *VTP Troubleshooting Example (Continued)*

```
                                        Fa0/5, Fa0/6, Fa0/7, Fa0/8
                                        Fa0/9, Fa0/10, Fa0/11, Fa0/12
                                        Fa0/13, Fa0/14, Fa0/15, Fa0/16
                                        Fa0/17, Fa0/18, Fa0/19, Fa0/20
                                        Fa0/21, Fa0/22, Fa0/23, Fa0/24
3    VLAN0003                  active
1002 fddi-default             act/unsup
1003 trcrf-default            act/unsup
1004 fddinet-default          act/unsup
1005 trbrf-default            act/unsup
SW2#show vtp status
VTP Version                   : 2
Configuration Revision        : 0
Maximum VLANs supported locally : 255
Number of existing VLANs      : 6
VTP Operating Mode            : Server
VTP Domain Name               : larry
VTP Pruning Mode              : Disabled
VTP V2 Mode                   : Enabled
VTP Traps Generation          : Disabled
MD5 digest                    : 0x8C 0x75 0xC5 0xDE 0xE9 0x7C 0x2D 0x8B
Configuration last modified by 1.1.1.2 at 0-0-00 00:00:00
Local updater ID is 1.1.1.2 on interface Vl1 (lowest numbered VLAN interface found)
! SW3 next
SW3#show vlan brief

VLAN Name                             Status    Ports
---- ------------------------------- --------- -------------------------------
1    default                         active    Fa0/1, Fa0/2, Fa0/3, Fa0/4
                                                Fa0/5, Fa0/6, Fa0/7, Fa0/8
                                                Fa0/9, Fa0/10, Fa0/11, Fa0/12
                                                Fa0/14, Fa0/15, Fa0/16, Fa0/17
                                                Fa0/18, Fa0/19, Fa0/20, Fa0/21
                                                Fa0/22, Fa0/23, Fa0/24, Gi0/1
3    VLAN0003                        active    Fa0/13
4    VLAN0004                        active
5    VLAN0005                        active
20   VLAN20                          active
1002 fddi-default                    act/unsup
1003 trcrf-default                   act/unsup
1004 fddinet-default                 act/unsup
1005 trbrf-default                   act/unsup
SW3#show interfaces trunk

Port        Mode        Encapsulation  Status        Native vlan
Gi0/2       desirable   n-802.1q       trunking      1
```

continues

Example 1-6   *VTP Troubleshooting Example (Continued)*

```
Port        Vlans allowed on trunk
Gi0/2        1-4094


Port        Vlans allowed and active in management domain
Gi0/2        1,3-5,20


Port        Vlans in spanning tree forwarding state and not pruned
Gi0/2        1,3-5,20
SW3#show vtp status
VTP Version                     : 2
Configuration Revision          : 134
Maximum VLANs supported locally : 1005
Number of existing VLANs        : 9
VTP Operating Mode              : Server
VTP Domain Name                 : Larry
VTP Pruning Mode                : Disabled
VTP V2 Mode                     : Enabled
VTP Traps Generation            : Disabled
MD5 digest                      : 0x76 0x1E 0x06 0x1E 0x1C 0x46 0x59 0x75
Configuration last modified by 1.1.1.3 at 3-1-93 01:07:29
Local updater ID is 1.1.1.3 on interface Vl1 (lowest numbered VLAN interface found)
```

For Step 1, the **show cdp neighbors** and **show interfaces trunk** commands provide
enough information to confirm the topology as well as show which links are operating as
trunks. The **show interfaces trunk** command lists only interfaces in an operationally
trunking state. Alternately, the **show interfaces switchport** command lists the operational
mode (trunk or access) as well. Figure 1-12 shows the network diagram. Note also that the
link between SW1 and SW3 does not currently use trunking.

Figure 1-12   *Switched Network Topology in Example 1-6*

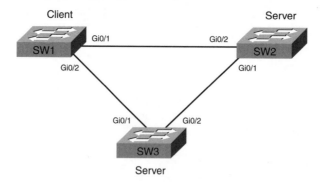

For Step 2, a quick review of the **show vlan brief** command output from each switch shows that all three switches have different VLAN databases. For example, all three switches know about VLAN 3, whereas SW1 is the only switch that knows about VLAN 50, and SW3 is the only switch that knows about VLAN 20.

Because all three pairs of neighboring switches have different VLAN databases, Step 3 of the troubleshooting process suggests that each pair be examined. Starting with SW1 and SW2, a quick look at the **show vtp status** command on both switches identifies the problem: SW1 uses the domain name Larry, whereas SW2 uses larry, and the names differ because of the different case of the first letter. Similarly, SW3 and SW2 have difficulties because of the mismatched VTP domain name. Because SW2 is the only switch with lowercase larry, a solution would be to reconfigure SW2 to use Larry as the domain name.

Continuing Step 3 for SW1 and SW3, the two switches have the same domain name (Step 3B), but a look at Step 3A shows that no trunk is connecting SW1 to SW3. CDP confirms that SW1's Gi0/2 interface connects to SW3, but the **show interfaces trunk** command on SW1 does not list the Gi0/2 interface. As a result, neither switch can send VTP messages to each other. The root cause of this problem is most likely an oversight in the configuration of the **switchport mode** interface subcommand.

While the example did not have any problems because of VTP password mismatches, it is important to know how to check the passwords. First, the password can be displayed on each switch with the **show vtp password** command. Additionally, the **show vtp status** command lists an MD5 hash derived from both the VTP domain name and VTP password. So, if two switches have the same case-sensitive domain name and password, the MD5 hash value listed in the **show vtp status** command output will be the same. However, if two switches list different MD5 hash values, you then need to examine the domain names. If the domain names are the same, the passwords must have been different because the MD5 hashes are different.

Before moving on to the next topic, here is a quick comment about VTP version and how it should not prevent switches from working. If you examine the **show vtp status** command output again in Example 1-6, note the headings VTP Version and V2 Mode Enabled. The first line lists the highest VTP version supported by that switch's software. The other line shows what the switch is currently using. If a switch has the VTP version 2 command configured, overriding the default of version 1, the switch will use **vtp version 2**—but only if the other switches in the domain also support version 2. So, a mismatch of the configured VTP version means that the switches work, but they would use VTP version 1, and the line reading "VTP V2 Mode" would list the word *disabled*, meaning that VTP version 1 is used.

Problems When Connecting New Switches and Bringing Up Trunks

VTP can be running just fine for months, and then one day, a rash of calls to the help desk describe cases in which large groups of users can no longer use the network. After further examination, it appears that most every VLAN in the campus has been deleted. The switches still have many interfaces with **switchport access vlan** commands that refer to the now-deleted VLANs. None of the devices on those now-deleted VLANs work, because Cisco switches do not forward frames for nonexistent VLANs.

This scenario can and does happen occasionally, mainly when a new switch is connected to an existing network. Whether this problem happens by accident or as a denial of service (DoS) attack, the root cause is that when a new VLAN trunk (ISL or 802.1Q) comes up between two switches, and the two switches are either VTP servers or clients, the switches send VTP updates to each other. If a switch receives a VTP advertisement that has the same domain name and was generated with the same VTP password, one or the other switch overwrites its VLAN database as part of the synchronization process. Specifically, the switch that had the lower revision number synchronizes its VLAN database to match the neighboring switch (which has the higher revision number). Summarizing the process more formally:

Step 1 Confirm that trunking will occur on the new link (refer to Table 1-5 for details).

Step 2 Confirm that the two switches use the same case-sensitive VTP domain name and password.

Step 3 If Steps 1 and 2 confirm that VTP will work, the switch with the lower revision number updates its VLAN database to match the other switch.

For example, Example 1-6 and Figure 1-12 show that the SW1-to-SW3 link is not trunking. If this link were to be configured to trunk, SW1 and SW3 would send VTP messages to each other, using the same VTP domain name and the same VTP password. So, one switch would update its VLAN database to match the other. Example 1-6 shows SW1 with revision number 131 and SW3 with revision number 134, so SW1 will overwrite its VLAN database to match SW3, thereby deleting VLANs 49 and 50. Example 1-7 picks up the story at the end of Example 1-6, showing the trunk between SW1 and SW3 coming up, allowing VTP synchronization, and resulting in changes to SW1's VLAN database.

Example 1-7 *VTP Troubleshooting Example*

```
SW1#configure terminal
Enter configuration commands, one per line.  End with CNTL/Z.
SW1(config)#interface gi0/2
SW1(config-if)#switchport mode dynamic desirable
SW1(config-if)#^Z
SW1#
01:43:46: %SYS-5-CONFIG_I: Configured from console by console
```

Example 1-7 *VTP Troubleshooting Example (Continued)*

```
01:43:46: %LINEPROTO-5-UPDOWN: Line protocol on Interface GigabitEthernet0/2, changed
state to down
SW1#01:43:49: %LINEPROTO-5-UPDOWN: Line protocol on Interface GigabitEthernet0/2,
changed state to up
SW1#show vlan brief

VLAN Name                             Status    Ports
---- -------------------------------- --------- -------------------------------
1    default                          active    Fa0/1, Fa0/2, Fa0/3, Fa0/4
                                                Fa0/5, Fa0/6, Fa0/7, Fa0/8
                                                Fa0/9, Fa0/10, Fa0/13, Fa0/14
                                                Fa0/15, Fa0/16, Fa0/17, Fa0/18
                                                Fa0/19, Fa0/20, Fa0/21, Fa0/22
                                                Fa0/23, Fa0/24, Gi0/1
3    VLAN0003                         active    Fa0/11
4    VLAN0004                         active
5    VLAN0005                         active
20   VLAN20                           active
1002 fddi-default                     act/unsup
1003 trcrf-default                    act/unsup
1004 fddinet-default                  act/unsup
1005 trbrf-default                    act/unsup
```

In real life, you have several ways to help reduce the chance of such problems when installing a new switch to an existing VTP domain. In particular, before connecting a new switch to an existing VTP domain, reset the new switch's VTP revision number to 0 by one of the following methods:

■ Configure the new switch for VTP transparent mode and then back to VTP client or server mode.

■ Erase the new switch's vlan.dat file in flash and reload the switch. This file contains the switch's VLAN database, including the revision number.

Avoiding VTP Problems Through Best Practices

Besides the suggestion of resetting the VLAN database revision number before installing a new switch, a couple of other good VTP conventions, called best practices, can help avoid some of the pitfalls of VTP. These are as follows:

■ If you do not intend to use VTP, configure each switch to use transparent mode.

■ If using VTP server or client mode, always use a VTP password.

Key
Topic

■   Disable trunking with the **switchport mode access** and **switchport nonegotiate** commands on all interfaces except known trunks, preventing VTP attacks by preventing the dynamic establishment of trunks.

By preventing the negotiation of trunking to most ports, the attacker can never see a VTP update from one of your switches. With a VTP password set, even if the attacker manages to get trunking working to an existing switch, the attacker would then have to know the password to do any harm. And by using transparent mode, you can avoid the types of problems described earlier, in the section "Caveats When Moving Away from Default VTP Configuration."

Exam Preparation Tasks

Review All the Key Topics

Review the most important topics from inside the chapter, noted with the Key Topics icon in the outer margin of the page. Table 1-8 lists these key topics and the page numbers on which each is found.

Key Topic

Table 1-8 *Key Topics for Chapter 1*

Key Topic Element	Description	Page Number
List	Reasons for using VLANs	11
Figure 1-2	Diagram of VLAN trunking	12
Figure 1-4	802.1Q header	14
Table 1-2	Comparisons of 802.1Q and ISL	15
Figure 1-6	VTP synchronization process concepts	18
List	Requirements for VTP to work between two switches	19
Table 1-3	VTP features summary	23
List	Configuration checklist for configuring VLANs and assigning to interfaces	24
List	Default VTP and VLAN configuration	25
Table 1-4	Options of the **switchport mode** command	30
Table 1-5	Expected trunking results based on the configuration of the **switchport mode** command	33
List	Four reasons why a trunk does not pass traffic for a VLAN	34
Table 1-6	Voice and data VLAN configuration and terms	37
List	Recommendations for how to protect unused switch ports	37
List	VTP configuration checklist	38
Table 1-7	VTP and VLAN configuration commands, and where they are stored	41
List	VTP troubleshooting process used when VTP is not performing as desired	44
List	Predicting what will happen with VTP when a new switch connects to a network	50
List	VTP best practices for preventing VTP problems	51

Complete the Tables and Lists from Memory

Print a copy of Appendix J, "Memory Tables," (found on the CD) or at least the section for this chapter, and complete the tables and lists from memory. Appendix K, "Memory Tables Answer Key," also on the CD, includes completed tables and lists to check your work.

Definitions of Key Terms

Define the following key terms from this chapter, and check your answers in the glossary:

802.1Q, ISL, trunk, trunking administrative mode, trunking operational mode, VLAN, VLAN configuration database, vlan.dat, VTP, VTP client mode, VTP pruning, VTP server mode, VTP transparent mode

Command Reference to Check Your Memory

While you should not necessarily memorize the information in the tables in this section, this section does include a reference for the configuration and EXEC commands covered in this chapter. Practically speaking, you should memorize the commands as a side effect of reading the chapter and doing all the activities in this exam preparation section. To check to see how well you have memorized the commands as a side effect of your other studies, cover the left side of the table with a piece of paper, read the descriptions in the right side, and see whether you remember the command.

Table 1-9 *Chapter 1 Configuration Command Reference*

Command	Description
vlan *vlan-id*	Global config command that both creates the VLAN and puts the CLI into VLAN configuration mode
name *vlan-name*	VLAN subcommand that names the VLAN
shutdown	VLAN subcommand that prevents that one switch from forwarding traffic in that VLAN
shutdown vlan *vlan-id*	Global config command that administratively disables a VLAN, preventing the switch from forwarding frames in that VLAN
vtp domain *domain-name*	Global config command that defines the VTP domain name
vtp password *password*	Global config command that defines the VTP password
**vtp {server	client	transparent}**	Global config command that defines the VTP mode

Table 1-9 *Chapter 1 Configuration Command Reference (Continued)*

Command	Description
vtp pruning	Global config command that tells the VTP server to tell all switches to use VTP pruning
switchport mode {access | dynamic {auto | desirable} | trunk}	Interface subcommand that configures the trunking administrative mode on the interface
switchport trunk allowed vlan {add | all | except | remove} *vlan-list*	Interface subcommand that defines the list of allowed VLANs
switchport access vlan *vlan-id*	Interface subcommand that statically configures the interface into that one VLAN
switchport trunk encapsulation {dot1q | isl | negotiate}	Interface subcommand that defines which type of trunking to use, assuming that trunking is configured or negotiated
switchport voice vlan *vlan-id*	Interface subcommand that defines the VLAN used for frames sent to and from a Cisco IP phone
switchport nonnegotiate	Interface subcommand that disables the negotiation of VLAN trunking

Table 1-10 *Chapter 1 EXEC Command Reference*

Command	Description
show interfaces *interface-id* switchport	Lists information about any interface regarding administrative settings and operational state
show interfaces *interface-id* trunk	Lists information about all operational trunks (but no other interfaces), including the list of VLANs that can be forwarded over the trunk
show vlan [brief | id *vlan-id* | name *vlan-name* | summary]	Lists information about the VLAN
show vlan [*vlan*]	Displays VLAN information
show vtp status	Lists VTP configuration and status information
show vtp password	Lists the VTP password

This chapter covers the following subjects:

Spanning Tree Protocol (IEEE 802.1d): This section explains the core concepts behind the operation of the original IEEE STP protocols.

Rapid STP (IEEE 802.1w): This section focuses on the differences between the earlier 802.1d STP standard and the new 802.1w RSTP standard.

STP Configuration and Verification: This section explains how to configure STP on Cisco IOS switches, and how to verify the current STP status on each switch and interface.

STP Troubleshooting: This section suggests an approach for how to predict the port role of each STP interface, thereby predicting the topology of the spanning tree.

CHAPTER 2

Spanning Tree Protocol

When LAN designs require multiple switches, most network engineers include redundant Ethernet segments between the switches. The goal is simple. The switches might fail, and cables might be cut or unplugged, but if redundant switches and cables are installed, the network service might still be available for most users.

LANs with redundant links introduce the possibility that frames might loop around the network forever. These looping frames would cause network performance problems. Therefore, LANs use Spanning Tree Protocol (STP), which allows the redundant LAN links to be used while preventing frames from looping around the LAN indefinitely through those redundant links. This chapter covers STP, along with a few configuration commands used to tune how STP behaves.

This chapter covers the details of STP, plus a newer variation called Rapid Spanning Tree Protocol (RSTP). The end of the chapter covers STP configuration on 2960 series switches, along with some suggestions on how to approach STP problems on the exams.

"Do I Know This Already?" Quiz

The "Do I Know This Already?" quiz allows you to assess whether you should read the entire chapter. If you miss no more than one of these ten self-assessment questions, you might want to move ahead to the "Exam Preparation Tasks" section. Table 2-1 lists the major headings in this chapter and the "Do I Know This Already?" quiz questions that cover the material in those headings so that you can assess your knowledge of these specific areas. The answers to the "Do I Know This Already?" quiz appear in Appendix A.

Table 2-1 *"Do I Know This Already?" Foundation Topics Section-to-Question Mapping*

Foundation Topics Section	Questions
Spanning Tree Protocol (IEEE 802.1d)	1–5
Rapid STP (IEEE 802.1w)	6–7
STP Configuration and Verification	8–9
STP Troubleshooting	10

1. Which of the following IEEE 802.1d port states are stable states used when STP has completed convergence?

   a. Blocking

   b. Forwarding

   c. Listening

   d. Learning

   e. Discarding

2. Which of the following are transitory IEEE 802.1d port states used only during the process of STP convergence?

   a. Blocking

   b. Forwarding

   c. Listening

   d. Learning

   e. Discarding

3. Which of the following bridge IDs would win election as root, assuming that the switches with these bridge IDs were in the same network?

   a. 32768:0200.1111.1111

   b. 32768:0200.2222.2222

   c. 200:0200.1111.1111

   d. 200:0200.2222.2222

   e. 40,000:0200.1111.1111

4. Which of the following facts determines how often a nonroot bridge or switch sends an 802.1d STP Hello BPDU message?

   a. The Hello timer as configured on that switch.

   b. The Hello timer as configured on the root switch.

   c. It is always every 2 seconds.

   d. The switch reacts to BPDUs received from the root switch by sending another BPDU 2 seconds after receiving the root BPDU.

5. What STP feature causes an interface to be placed in the Forwarding State as soon as the interface is physically active?

   a. STP

   b. RSTP

   c. Root Guard

   d. 802.1w

   e. PortFast

   f. EtherChannel

6. Which answer lists the name of the IEEE standard that improves the original STP standard and lowers convergence time?

   a. STP

   b. RSTP

   c. Root Guard

   d. 802.1w

   e. PortFast

   f. Trunking

7. Which of the following RSTP port states have the same name as a similar port state in traditional STP?

   a. Blocking

   b. Forwarding

   c. Listening

   d. Learning

   e. Discarding

   f. Disabled

8. On a 2960 switch, which of the following commands change the value of the bridge ID?

   a. **spanning-tree bridge-id** *value*

   b. **spanning-tree vlan** *vlan-number* **root** {**primary** I **secondary**}

   c. **spanning-tree vlan** *vlan-number* **priority** *value*

   d. **set spanning-tree priority** *value*

9. Examine the following extract from the **show spanning-tree** command on a Cisco switch:

    ```
    Bridge ID  Priority    32771  (priority 32768 sys-id-ext 3)
               Address     0019.e86a.6f80
    ```

    Which of the following answers is true regarding the switch on which this command output was gathered?

    a. The information is about the STP instance for VLAN 1.

    b. The information is about the STP instance for VLAN 3. ⌐

    c. The command output confirms that this switch cannot possibly be the root switch.

    d. The command output confirms that this switch is currently the root switch.

10. Switch SW3 is receiving only two Hello BPDUs, both from the same root switch, received on the two interfaces listed as follows:

    ```
    SW3#show interfaces status
    Port      Name      Status      Vlan  Duplex  Speed   Type
    Fa0/13              connected   1     a-half  a-100   10/100BaseTX
    Gi0/1               connected   1     a-full  a-1000  1000BaseTX
    ```

    SW3 has no STP-related configuration commands. The Hello received on Fa0/13 lists cost 10, and the Hello received on Gi0/1 lists cost 20. Which of the following is true about STP on SW3?

    a. SW3 will choose Fa0/13 as its root port.

    b. SW3 will choose Gi0/1 as its root port.

    c. SW3's Fa0/13 will become a designated port.

    d. SW3's Gi0/1 will become a designated port.

Foundation Topics

Without Spanning Tree Protocol (STP), a LAN with redundant links would cause Ethernet frames to loop for an indefinite period of time. With STP enabled, some switches block ports so that these ports do not forward frames. STP chooses which ports block so that only one active path exists between any pair of LAN segments (collision domains). As a result, frames can be delivered to each device, without causing the problems created when frames loop through the network.

This chapter begins by explaining the need for the original IEEE standard for STP and how the standard works. The second major section explains how the new and much faster Rapid STP (RSTP) works in comparison. The last two major sections examine the configuration and troubleshooting of STP, respectively.

Spanning Tree Protocol (IEEE 802.1d)

IEEE 802.1d, the first public standard for STP, defined a reasonable solution to the problem of frames looping around redundant links forever. The following sections begin with a more detailed description of the problem, followed by a description of the end result of how 802.1d STP solves the problem. The sections end with a lengthy description of how STP works, as a distributed process on all LAN switches, to prevent loops.

The Need for Spanning Tree

The most common problem that can be avoided by using STP is broadcast storms. Broadcast storms cause broadcasts (or multicasts or unknown-destination unicasts) to loop around a LAN indefinitely. As a result, some links can become saturated with useless copies of the same frame, crowding out good frames, as well as significantly impacting end-user PC performance by making the PCs process too many broadcast frames. To see how this occurs, Figure 2-1 shows a sample network in which Bob sends a broadcast frame. The dashed lines show how the switches forward the frame when STP does not exist.

Figure 2-1 *Broadcast Storm*

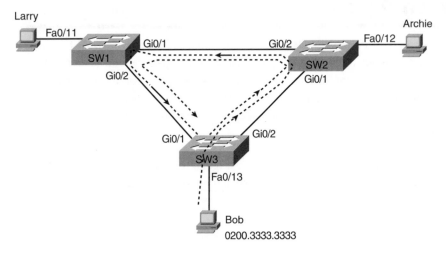

Switches flood broadcasts out all interfaces in the same VLAN, except the interface in which the frame arrived. In the figure, that means SW3 will forward Bob's frame to SW2; SW2 will forward the frame to SW1; SW1 will forward the frame back to SW3; and SW3 will forward it back to SW2 again. This frame will loop until something changes—someone shuts down an interface, reloads a switch, or does something else to break the loop. Also note that the same event happens in the opposite direction. When Bob sends the original frame, SW3 also forwards a copy to SW1, SW1 forwards it to SW2, and so on.

MAC table instability also occurs as a result of the looping frames. MAC table instability means that the switches' MAC address tables will keep changing the information listed for the source MAC address of the looping frame. For example, SW3 begins Figure 2-1 with a MAC table entry as follows:

> 0200.3333.3333   Fa0/13   VLAN 1

However, now think about the switch-learning process that occurs when the looping frame goes to SW2, then SW1, and then back into SW3's Gi0/1 interface. SW3 thinks, "Hmmm… the source MAC address is 0200.3333.3333, and it came in my Gi0/1 interface. Update my MAC table!" resulting in the following entry on SW3:

> 0200.3333.3333   Gi0/1   VLAN 1

At this point, if a frame arrives at SW3—a different frame than the looping frame that causes the problems—destined to Bob's MAC address of 0200.3333.3333, SW3 would incorrectly forward the frame out Gi0/1 to SW1. This new frame can also loop, or the frame might simply never be delivered to Bob.

The third class of problem caused by not using STP in a network with redundancy is that working hosts get multiple copies of the same frame. Consider a case in which Bob sends a frame to Larry, but none of the switches know Larry's MAC address. (Switches flood frames sent to unknown destination unicast MAC addresses.) When Bob sends the frame (destined to Larry's MAC address), SW3 sends a copy to SW1 and SW2. SW1 and SW2 also flood the frame, causing copies of the frame to loop. SW1 also sends a copy of each frame out Fa0/11 to Larry. As a result, Larry gets multiple copies of the frame, which may result in an application failure, if not more pervasive networking problems.

Table 2-2 summarizes the main three classes of problems that occur when STP is not used in a LAN with redundancy.

Table 2-2 *Three Classes of Problems Caused by Not Using STP in Redundant LANs*

Problem	Description
Broadcast storms	The forwarding of a frame repeatedly on the same links, consuming significant parts of the links' capacities
MAC table instability	The continual updating of a switch's MAC address table with incorrect entries, in reaction to looping frames, resulting in frames being sent to the wrong locations
Multiple frame transmission	A side effect of looping frames in which multiple copies of one frame are delivered to the intended host, confusing the host

What IEEE 802.1d Spanning Tree Does

STP prevents loops by placing each bridge/switch port in either a Forwarding State or a Blocking State. Interfaces in the Forwarding State act as normal, forwarding and receiving frames, but interfaces in a Blocking State do not process any frames except STP messages. All the ports in Forwarding State are considered to be in the current *spanning tree*. The collective set of forwarding ports creates a single path over which frames are sent between Ethernet segments.

Figure 2-2 shows a simple STP tree that solves the problem shown in Figure 2-1 by placing one port on SW3 in the Blocking State.

Figure 2-2   *Network with Redundant Links and STP*

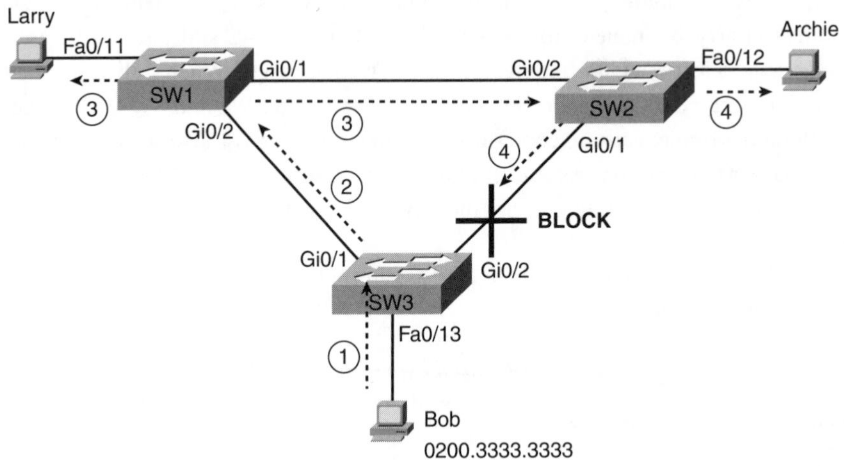

Now when Bob sends a broadcast frame, the frame does not loop. Bob sends the frame to SW3 (Step 1), which then forwards the frame only to SW1 (Step 2), because SW3's Gi0/2 interface is in a Blocking State. SW1 floods the frame out both Fa0/11 and Gi0/1 (Step 3). SW2 floods the frame out Fa0/12 and Gi0/1 (Step 4). However, SW3 ignores the frame received from SW2, again because that frame enters SW3's Gi0/2 interface, which is in a Blocking State.

With the STP topology in Figure 2-2, the switches simply do not use the link between SW2 and SW3 for traffic in this VLAN, which is the minor negative side effect of STP. However, if the link between SW1 and SW3 fails, STP converges so that SW3 forwards instead of blocks on its Gi0/2 interface.

NOTE   The term *STP convergence* refers to the process by which the switches collectively realize that something has changed in the LAN topology, so the switches might need to change which ports block and which ports forward.

How does STP manage to make switches block or forward on each interface? And how does it converge to change state from Blocking to Forwarding to take advantage of redundant links in response to network outages? The following sections answer these questions.

How Spanning Tree Works

The STP algorithm creates a spanning tree of interfaces that forward frames. The tree structure creates a single path to and from each Ethernet segment, just like you can trace a single path in a living, growing tree from the base of the tree to each leaf.

NOTE   Because Ethernet bridges are seldom used today, this chapter refers only to switches. However, both bridges and switches use STP.

The process used by STP, sometimes called the *Spanning Tree Algorithm (STA)*, chooses the interfaces that should be placed into a Forwarding State. For any interfaces not chosen to be in a Forwarding State, STA places the interfaces in Blocking State. In other words, STP simply picks which interfaces should forward.

STP uses three criteria to choose whether to put an interface in Forwarding State:

- STP elects a root switch. STP puts all working interfaces on the root switch in Forwarding State.

- Each nonroot switch considers one of its ports to have the least administrative cost between itself and the root switch. STP places this least-root-cost interface, called that switch's root port (RP), in Forwarding State.

- Many switches can attach to the same Ethernet segment. The switch with the lowest administrative cost from itself to the root bridge, as compared with the other switches attached to the same segment, is placed in Forwarding State. The lowest-cost switch on each segment is called the designated bridge, and that bridge's interface, attached to that segment, is called the *designated port (DP)*.

NOTE   The real reason the root places all working interfaces in a Forwarding State is that all its interfaces will become DPs, but it is easier to just remember that the all the root switches' working interfaces will forward frames.

All other interfaces are placed in Blocking State. Table 2-3 summarizes the reasons STP places a port in Forwarding or Blocking State.

Table 2-3   *STP: Reasons for Forwarding or Blocking*

Characterization of Port	STP State	Description
All the root switch's ports	Forwarding	The root switch is always the designated switch on all connected segments.
Each nonroot switch's root port	Forwarding	The port through which the switch has the least cost to reach the root switch.
Each LAN's designated port	Forwarding	The switch forwarding the lowest-cost BPDU onto the segment is the designated switch for that segment.
All other working ports	Blocking	The port is not used for forwarding frames, nor are any frames received on these interfaces considered for forwarding.

NOTE   STP only considers working interfaces. Failed interfaces (for example, interfaces with no cable installed) or administratively shut down interfaces are instead placed into an STP Disabled State. So, this section uses the term *working ports* to refer to interfaces that could forward frames if STP placed the interface into a Forwarding State.

The STP Bridge ID and Hello BPDU

The Spanning Tree Algorithm (STA) begins with an election of one switch to be the root switch. To better understand this election process, you need to understand the STP messages sent between switches as well as the concept and format of the identifier used to uniquely identify each switch.

The STP bridge ID (BID) is an 8-byte value unique to each switch. The bridge ID consists of a 2-byte priority field and a 6-byte system ID, with the system ID being based on a burned-in MAC address in each switch. Using a burned-in MAC address ensures that each switch's bridge ID will be unique.

STP defines messages called *bridge protocol data units* (BPDU), which bridges and switches use to exchange information with each other. The most common message, called a Hello BPDU, lists the sending switch's bridge ID. By listing its own unique bridge ID, switches can tell the difference between BPDUs sent by different switches. This message also lists the bridge ID of the current root switch.

STP defines several types of BPDU messages, with the Hello BPDU being the message that does most of the work. The Hello BPDU includes several fields, but most importantly, it contains the fields listed in Table 2-4.

Table 2-4   *Fields in the STP Hello BPDU*

Field	Description
Root bridge ID	The bridge ID of the bridge/switch that the sender of this Hello currently believes to be the root switch
Sender's bridge ID	The bridge ID of the bridge/switch sending this Hello BPDU
Cost to reach root	The STP cost between this switch and the current root
Timer values on the root switch	Includes the Hello timer, MaxAge timer, and Forward Delay timer

For the time being, just keep the first three items from Table 2-4 in mind as the following sections work through the three steps in how STP chooses the interfaces to place into a Forwarding State. Next, the text examines the three main steps in the STP process.

Electing the Root Switch

Switches elect a root switch based on the bridge IDs in the BPDUs. The root switch is the switch with the lowest numeric value for the bridge ID. Because the two-part bridge ID starts with the priority value, essentially the switch with the lowest priority becomes the root. For example, if one switch has priority 100, and another switch has priority 200, the switch with priority 100 wins, regardless of what MAC address was used to create the bridge ID for each bridge/switch.

If a tie occurs based on the priority portion of the bridge ID, the switch with the lowest MAC address portion of the bridge ID is the root. No other tiebreaker should be needed because switches use one of their own burned-in MAC addresses as the second part of their bridge IDs. So if the priorities tie, and one switch uses a MAC address of 0020.0000.0000 as part of the bridge ID, and the other uses 0FFF.FFFF.FFF, the first switch (MAC 0200.0000.0000) becomes the root.

STP elects a root switch in a manner not unlike a political election. The process begins with all switches claiming to be the root by sending Hello BPDUs listing their own bridge ID as the root bridge ID. If a switch hears a Hello that lists a better (lower) bridge ID—called a Superior Hello—that switch stops advertising itself as root and starts forwarding the superior Hello. The Hello sent by the better switch lists the better switch's bridge ID as the root. It works like a political race in which a less-popular candidate gives up and leaves the race, throwing her support behind another candidate. Eventually everyone agrees which switch has the best (lowest) bridge ID, and everyone supports the elected switch—which is where the political race analogy falls apart.

Figure 2-3 shows the beginning of the root election process. In this case, SW1 has advertised itself as root, as have SW2 and SW3. However, SW2 now believes that SW1 is a better root, so SW2 is now forwarding the Hello originating at SW1. This forwarded Hello lists SW1's BID as the root BID. However, at this point, SW1 and SW3 both still believe that they each are the best, so they still list their own BID as the root in their Hello BPDUs.

Figure 2-3   *Beginnings of the Root Election Process*

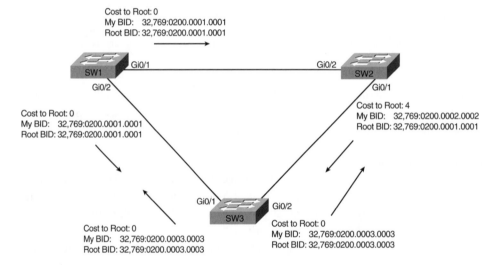

Two candidates still exist in Figure 2-3: SW1 and SW3. So who wins? Well, from the bridge ID, the lower-priority switch wins; if a tie occurs, the lower MAC address wins. As shown in the figure, SW1 has a lower bridge ID (32769:0200.0000.0001) than SW3 (32769:0200.0003.0003), so SW1 wins, and SW3 now also believes that SW1 is the better switch. Figure 2-4 shows the resulting Hello messages sent by the switches.

After the election is complete, only the root switch continues to originate STP Hello BPDU messages. The other switches receive the Hellos, update the sender's BID field (and cost-to-reach-the-root field), and forward the Hellos out other interfaces. The figure reflects this fact, with SW1 sending Hellos at Step 1, and SW2 and SW3 independently forwarding the Hello out their other interfaces at Step 2.

Figure 2-4 *SW1 Wins Election*

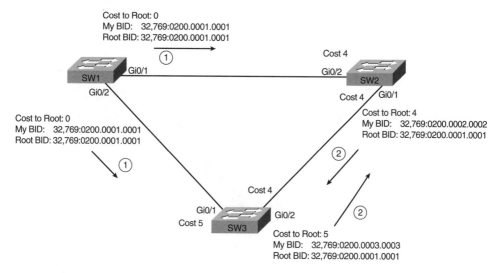

Choosing Each Switch's Root Port

The second part of the STP process occurs when each nonroot switch chooses its one and only *root port*. A switch's root port (RP) is its interface through which it has the least STP cost to reach the root switch.

To calculate the cost, a switch adds the cost listed in a received Hello to the STP port cost assigned to that same interface. The STP port cost is simply an integer value assigned to each interface for the purpose of providing an objective measurement that allows STP to choose which interfaces to add to the STP topology.

Figure 2-5 shows an example of how SW3 calculates its cost to reach the root over the two possible paths by adding the advertised cost (in Hello messages) to the interface costs listed in the figure.

Figure 2-5   *SW3 Calculating Cost to Reach the Root and Choosing Its RP*

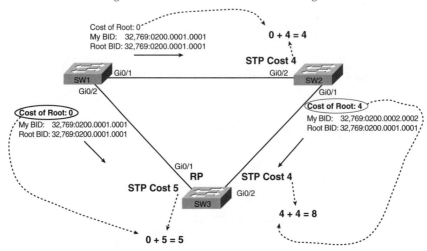

As a result of the process depicted in Figure 2-5, SW3 chooses Gi0/1 as its RP, because the cost to reach the root switch through that port (5) is lower than the other alternative (Gi0/2, cost 8). Similarly, SW2 will choose Gi0/2 as its RP, with a cost of 4 (SW1's advertised cost of 0 plus SW2's Gi0/2 interface cost of 4). Each switch places its root port into a Forwarding State.

In more complex topologies, the choice of root port will not be so obvious. The section "STP Troubleshooting," later in this chapter, shows an example in which the root port choice requires a little more thought.

Choosing the Designated Port on Each LAN Segment

STP's final step to choose the STP topology is to choose the designated port on each LAN segment. The designated port on each LAN segment is the switch port that advertises the lowest-cost Hello onto a LAN segment. When a nonroot switch forwards a Hello, the nonroot switch sets the cost field in the Hello to that switch's cost to reach the root. In effect, the switch with the lower cost to reach the root, among all switches connected to a segment, becomes the DP on that segment.

For example, in Figure 2-4, both SW2 and SW3 forward Hello messages onto the segment. Note that both SW2 and SW3 list their respective cost to reach the root switch (cost 4 on SW2 and cost 5 on SW3.) As a result, SW2's Gi0/1 port is the designated port on that LAN segment.

All DPs are placed into a forwarding state, so in this case, SW2's Gi0/1 interface will be in a forwarding state.

If the advertised costs tied, the switches break the tie by choosing the switch with the lower bridge ID. In this case, SW2 would have won, with a bridge ID of 32769:0200.0002.0002 versus SW3's 32769:0200.0003.0003.

> **NOTE** A switch can connect two or more interfaces to the same collision domain if hubs are used. In such cases, another tiebreaker is needed: The switch chooses the interface with the lower internal interface number.

The only interface that does not have a reason to be in a Forwarding State on the three switches in the examples shown in Figures 2-3, 2-4, and 2-5 is SW3's Gi0/2 port. So, the STP process is now complete. Table 2-5 outlines the state of each port and shows why it is in that state.

Table 2-5 *State of Each Interface*

Switch Interface	State	Reason Why the Interface Is in Forwarding State
SW1, Gi0/1	Forwarding	The interface is on the root switch.
SW1, Gi0/2	Forwarding	The interface is on the root switch.
SW2, Gi0/2	Forwarding	The root port.
SW2, Gi0/1	Forwarding	The designated port on the LAN segment to SW3.
SW3, Gi0/1	Forwarding	The root port.
SW3, Gi0/2	Blocking	Not the root port and not designated port.

Port costs can be configured, or you can use the default values. Table 2-6 lists the default port costs defined by IEEE; Cisco uses these same defaults. The IEEE revised the cost values because the original values, set in the early 1980s, did not anticipate the growth of Ethernet to support 10-Gigabit Ethernet.

Table 2-6 *Default Port Costs According to IEEE*

Key
Topic

Ethernet Speed	Original IEEE Cost	Revised IEEE Cost
10 Mbps	100	100
100 Mbps	10	19
1 Gbps	1	4
10 Gbps	1	2

With STP enabled, all working switch interfaces will settle into an STP Forwarding or Blocking State, even access ports. For switch interfaces connected to hosts or routers, which do not use STP, the switch will still forward Hellos onto those interfaces. By virtue of being the only device sending a Hello onto that LAN segment, the switch is sending the least-cost Hello onto that LAN segment, making the switch become the designated port on that LAN segment. So, STP puts working access interfaces into a Forwarding State as a result of the designated port part of the STP process.

Reacting to Changes in the Network

After the STP topology—the set of interfaces in a forwarding state—has been determined, this set of forwarding interfaces does not change unless the network topology changes. This section examines the ongoing operation of STP while the network is stable, and then it examines how STP converges to a new topology when something changes.

The root switch sends a new Hello BPDU every 2 seconds by default. Each switch forwards the Hello on all DPs, but only after changing two items. The cost is changed to reflect that switch's cost to reach the root, and the sender's bridge ID field is also changed. (The root's bridge ID field is not changed.) By forwarding the received (and changed) Hellos out all DPs, all switches continue to receive Hellos about every 2 seconds. The following list summarizes the steady-state operation when nothing is currently changing in the STP topology:

1. The root creates and sends a Hello BPDU, with a cost of 0, out all its working interfaces (those in a Forwarding State).

2. The nonroot switches receive the Hello on their root ports. After changing the Hello to list their own bridge ID as the sender's BID, and listing that switch's root cost, the switch forwards the Hello out all designated ports.

3. Steps 1 and 2 repeat until something changes.

Each switch relies on these periodic received Hellos from the root as a way to know that its path to the root is still working. When a switch ceases to receive the Hellos, something has failed, so the switch reacts and starts the process of changing the spanning-tree topology. For various reasons, the convergence process requires the use of three timers. Note that all switches use the timers as dictated by the root switch, which the root lists in its periodic Hello BPDU messages. The timer and their descriptions are listed in Table 2-7.

Table 2-7   *STP Timers*

Timer	Description	Default Value
Hello	The time period between Hellos created by the root.	2 sec.
Max Age	How long any switch should wait, after ceasing to hear Hellos, before trying to change the STP topology.	10 times Hello
Forward Delay	Delay that affects the process that occurs when an interface changes from Blocking State to Forwarding State. A port stays in an interim Listening State, and then an interim Learning State, for the number of seconds defined by the forward delay timer.	15 sec.

If a switch does not get an expected Hello BPDU within the Hello time, the switch continues as normal. However, if the Hellos do not show up again within MaxAge time, the switch reacts by taking steps to change the STP topology. At that point, the switch essentially reevaluates which switch should be the root switch, and if it is not the root, which port should be its RP, and which ports should be DPs, assuming that the Hellos it was formerly receiving have stopped arriving.

The best way to describe STP convergence is to show an example using the same familiar topology. Figure 2-6 shows the same familiar figure, with SW3's Gi0/2 in a Blocking State, but SW1's Gi0/2 interface has just failed.

Figure 2-6 *Reacting to Link Failure Between SW1 and SW3*

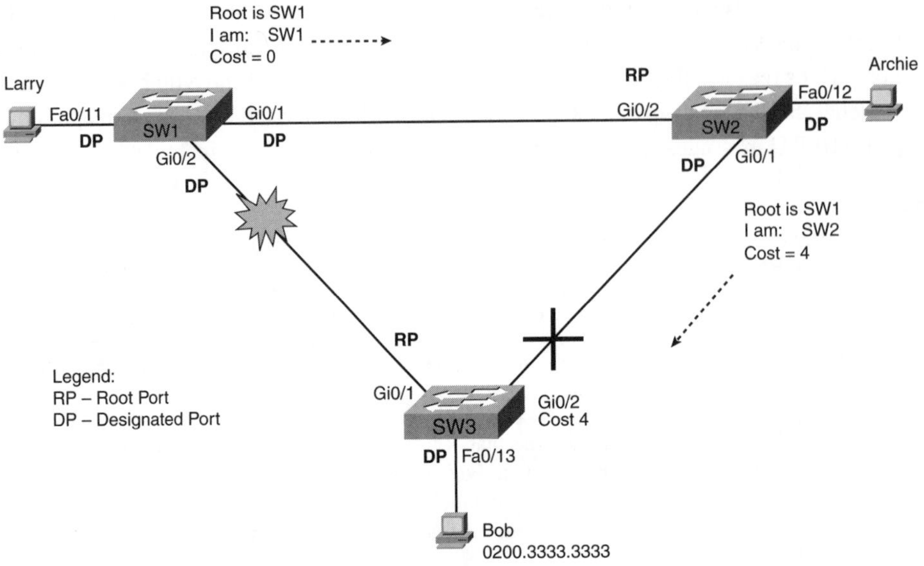

SW3 reacts to the change because SW3 fails to receive its expected Hellos on its Gi0/1 interface. However, SW2 does not need to react because SW2 continues to receive its periodic Hellos in its Gi0/2 interface. In this case, SW3 reacts either when MaxAge time passes without hearing the Hellos, or as soon as SW3 notices that interface Gi0/1 has failed. (If the interface fails, the switch can assume that the Hellos will not be arriving anymore.)

Now that SW3 can act, it begins by reevaluating the choice of root switch. SW3 still receives the Hello from SW1, forwarded by SW2, and SW1 has a lower bridge ID; otherwise, SW1 would not have already been the root. So, SW3 decides that SW1 is still the best switch and that SW3 is not the root.

Next, SW3 reevaluates its choice of RP. At this point, SW3 is only receiving Hellos on one interface, interface Gi0/2. Whatever the calculated cost, Gi0/2 will become SW3's new RP. (The cost would be 8: SW2's advertised cost of 4 plus Gi0/2's interface cost of 4.)

SW3 then reevaluates its role as DP on any other interfaces. In this example, no real work needs to be done. SW3 was already DP on interface Fa0/13, and it continues to be the DP, because no other switches connect to that port.

When STP converges, a switch chooses transition interfaces from one state to another. However, a transition from blocking to forwarding cannot be done immediately because an immediate change to forwarding could temporarily cause frames to loop. To prevent these temporary loops, STP transitions an interface through two intermediate interface states, as follows:

- **Listening**: Like the Blocking State, the interface does not forward frames. Old, now-incorrect MAC table entries are timed out during this state, because the old incorrect MAC table entries would be the root cause of the temporary loops.

- **Learning**: Interfaces in this state still do not forward frames, but the switch begins to learn the MAC addresses of frames received on the interface.

STP moves an interface from Blocking to Listening, then to Learning, and then to Forwarding State. STP leaves the interface in each interim state for a time equal to the forward delay timer. As a result, a convergence event that causes an interface to change from Blocking to Forwarding requires 30 seconds to transition from Blocking to Forwarding. Additionally, a switch might have to wait MaxAge seconds before even choosing to move an interface from Blocking to Forwarding state. Following the same example shown in the last several figures, SW3 might wait MaxAge seconds before deciding that it is no longer receiving the same root BPDU on its root port (20 seconds is the default), and then wait 15 seconds each in Listening and Learning States on interface Gi0/2, resulting in a 50-second convergence delay.

Table 2-8 summarizes Spanning Tree's various interface states for easier review.

Table 2-8   *IEEE 802.1d Spanning-Tree States*

State	Forwards Data Frames?	Learns MACs Based on Received Frames?	Transitory or Stable State?
Blocking	No	No	Stable
Listening	No	No	Transitory
Learning	No	Yes	Transitory
Forwarding	Yes	Yes	Stable
Disabled	No	No	Stable

Optional STP Features

STP has been around for over 20 years. Cisco switches implement the standard IEEE 802.1d STP, but over the intervening years, Cisco added proprietary features to make improvements to STP. In some cases, the IEEE added these improvements, or something like them, to later IEEE standards, whether as a revision of the 802.1d standard or as an additional standard. The following sections examine three of the proprietary additions to STP: EtherChannel, PortFast, and BPDU Guard.

> **NOTE**   If you plan to work on a production campus LAN network, you should probably learn more about STP features than is covered in this book. To do so, go to the Cisco software configuration guide for 2960 switches and look at the chapters on STP, RSTP, and optional STP features. The introduction to this book lists information about how to find Cisco documentation.

EtherChannel

One of the best ways to lower STP's convergence time is to avoid convergence altogether. EtherChannel provides a way to prevent STP convergence from being needed when only a single port or cable failure occurs.

EtherChannel combines multiple parallel segments of equal speed (up to eight) between the same pair of switches, bundled into an EtherChannel. The switches treat the EtherChannel as a single interface with regard to the frame-forwarding process as well as for STP. As a result, if one of the links fails, but at least one of the links is up, STP convergence does not have to occur. For example, Figure 2-7 shows the familiar three-switch network, but now with two Gigabit Ethernet connections between each pair of switches.

Figure 2-7   *Two-Segment EtherChannels Between Switches*

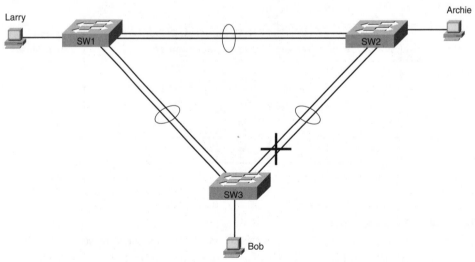

With each pair of Ethernet links configured as an EtherChannel, STP treats each EtherChannel as a single link. In other words, both links to the same switch must fail for a switch to need to cause STP convergence. Without EtherChannel, if you have multiple parallel links between two switches, STP blocks all the links except one. With EtherChannel, all the parallel links can be up and working at the same time, while reducing the number of times STP must converge, which in turn makes the network more available.

EtherChannel also provides more network bandwidth. All trunks in an EtherChannel are either forwarding or blocking, because STP treats all the trunks in the same EtherChannel as one trunk. When an EtherChannel is in Forwarding State, the switches load-balance traffic over all the trunks, providing more bandwidth.

PortFast

PortFast allows a switch to immediately place a port in Forwarding State when the port becomes physically active, bypassing any choices about the STP topology and bypassing the Listening and Learning States. However, the only ports on which you can safely enable PortFast are ports on which you know that no bridges, switches, or other STP-speaking devices are connected.

PortFast is most appropriate for connections to end-user devices. If you turn on PortFast on ports connected to end-user devices, when an end-user PC boots, as soon as the PC NIC is active, the switch port can move to an STP Forwarding State and forward traffic. Without PortFast, each port must wait while the switch confirms that the port is a DP, and then wait while the interface sits in the temporary Listening and Learning States before settling into the Forwarding State.

STP Security

Switch interfaces that connect to end-user locations in the LAN have some security exposures. An attacker could connect a switch to one of these ports, with a low STP priority value, and become the root switch. Also, by connecting the attacker's switch to multiple legitimate switches, the attacker's switch could end up forwarding a lot of traffic in the LAN, and the attacker could use a LAN analyzer to copy large numbers of data frames sent through the LAN. Also, users could innocently harm the LAN. For example, a user could buy and connect an inexpensive consumer LAN switch to an existing switch, possibly creating a loop, or possibly causing the new, relatively-low-powered switch to become the root.

The Cisco BPDU Guard feature helps defeat these kinds of problems by disabling a port if any BPDUs are received on the port. So, this feature is particularly useful on ports that should only be used as an access port and never connected to another switch. Additionally, the BPDU Guard feature is often used on the same interface that has PortFast enabled, because a PortFast-enabled port will already be in a Forwarding State, which increases the possibility for forwarding loops.

The Cisco Root Guard feature helps defeat the problem where the new rogue switch tries to become the root switch. The Root Guard feature allows another switch to be connected to the interface, and participate in STP by sending and receiving BPDUs. However, when the switch interface with Root Guard enabled receives a superior BPDU from the neighboring switch—a BPDU that has a lower/better bridge ID—the switch with Root Guard reacts. Not only does the switch ignore the superior BPDU, but the switch also disables the interface, not sending or receiving frames, as long as the superior BPDUs keep arriving. If the superior BPDUs stop arriving, the switch can start using the interface again.

Rapid STP (IEEE 802.1w)

As mentioned earlier in this chapter, the IEEE defines STP in the 802.1d IEEE standard. The IEEE has improved the 802.1d protocol with the definition of Rapid Spanning Tree Protocol (RSTP), as defined in standard 802.1w.

RSTP (802.1w) works just like STP (802.1d) in several ways:

Key Topic

■ It elects the root switch using the same parameters and tiebreakers.

■ It elects the root port on nonroot switches with the same rules.

■ It elects designated ports on each LAN segment with the same rules.

■ It places each port in either Forwarding or Blocking State, although RSTP calls the Blocking State the Discarding State.

RSTP can be deployed alongside traditional 802.1d STP switches, with RSTP features working in switches that support it, and traditional 802.1d STP features working in the switches that support only STP.

With all these similarities, you might be wondering why the IEEE bothered to create RSTP in the first place. The overriding reason is convergence. STP takes a relatively long time to converge (50 seconds with the default settings). RSTP improves network convergence when topology changes occur.

RSTP improves convergence by either eliminating or significantly reducing the waiting periods that 802.1d STP needs to avoid loops during convergence. 802.1d STP requires a waiting period of MaxAge (default 20 seconds) before reacting to some events, whereas RSTP only has to wait 3*Hello (default 6 seconds). Additionally, RSTP eliminates the forward delay (default 15 seconds) time in both Listening and Learning States. Traditional STP convergence has essentially three time periods, each of which RSTP improves upon. These three waiting periods of (by default) 20, 15, and 15 seconds create 802.1d STP's relatively slow convergence, and the reduction or elimination of these waiting periods makes RSTP convergence occur quickly.

RSTP convergence times are typically less than 10 seconds. In some cases, they can be as low as 1 to 2 seconds. The following sections explain the terminology and processes used by RSTP to overcome the shortcomings of 802.1d STP and improve convergence time.

> **NOTE**   Like most texts, when needing to distinguish between the older 802.1d and newer 802.1w standards, STP refers to 802.1d, and RSTP refers to 802.1w.

RSTP Link and Edge Types

RSTP characterizes the types of physical connectivity in a campus LAN into three different types:

- Link-type point-to-point

- Link-type shared

- Edge-type

Figure 2-8 shows each type.

Figure 2-8 *RSTP Link and Edge Types*

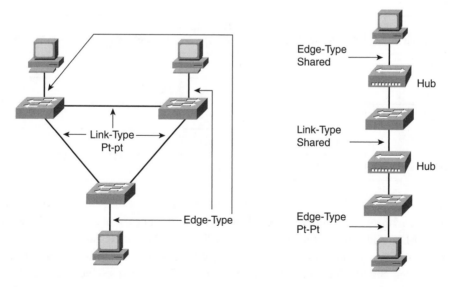

Figure 2-8 shows two sample networks. The network on the left is a typical campus design today, with no hubs. All the switches connect with Ethernet cables, and all the end-user devices also connect with Ethernet cables. The IEEE defined RSTP to improve convergence in these types of networks.

In the network on the right side of the figure, hubs are still in use for connections between the switches, as well as for connections to end-user devices. Most networks do not use hubs anymore. The IEEE did not attempt to make RSTP work in networks that use shared hubs, and RSTP would not improve convergence in the network on the right.

RSTP calls Ethernet connections between switches *links* and calls Ethernet connections to end-user devices *edges*. Two types of links exist: point-to-point, as shown on the left side of Figure 2-8, and shared, as shown on the right side. RSTP does not distinguish between point-to-point and shared types for edge connections.

RSTP reduces convergence time for link-type point-to-point and edge-type connections. It does not improve convergence over link-type shared connections. However, most modern networks do not use hubs between switches, so the lack of RSTP convergence improvements for link-type shared doesn't really matter.

RSTP Port States

You should also be familiar with RSTP's new terms to describe a port's state. Table 2-9 lists the states, with some explanation following the table.

Key
Topic

Table 2-9   *RSTP and STP Port States*

Operational State	STP State (802.1d)	RSTP State (802.1w)	Forwards Data Frames in This State?
Enabled	Blocking	Discarding	No
Enabled	Listening	Discarding	No
Enabled	Learning	Learning	No
Enabled	Forwarding	Forwarding	Yes
Disabled	Disabled	Discarding	No

Similar to STP, RSTP stabilizes with all ports either in Forwarding State or Discarding State. *Discarding* means that the port does not forward frames, process received frames, or learn MAC addresses, but it does listen for BPDUs. In short, it acts just like the STP Blocking State. RSTP uses an interim Learning State when moving an interface from a Discarding State to Forwarding State. However, RSTP needs to use Learning State for only a short time.

RSTP Port Roles

Both STP (802.1d) and RSTP (802.1w) use the concepts of port states and port roles. The STP process determines the role of each interface. For example, STP determines which interfaces are currently in the role of a root port or designated port. Then, STP determines the stable port state to use for interfaces in certain roles: the Forwarding State for ports in the RP or DP roles, and the Blocking State for ports in other roles.

RSTP adds three more port roles, two of which are shown in Figure 2-9. (The third new role, the disabled role, is not shown in the figure; it simply refers to shutdown interfaces.)

Figure 2-9 *RSTP Port Roles*

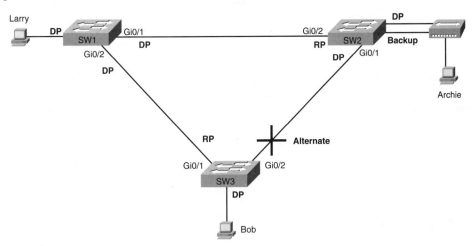

The RSTP *alternate* port role identifies a switch's best alternative to its current RP. In short, the alternate port role is an alternate RP. For example, SW3 lists Gi0/1 as its RP, but SW3 also knows that it is receiving Hello BPDUs on interface Gi0/2. Switch SW3 has a root port, just as it would with STP. (See Figure 2-4 for a reminder of the steady-state flow of BPDUs.) RSTP designates ports that receive suboptimal BPDUs (BPDUs that are not as "good" as the ones received on the root port) as alternate ports. If SW3 stops getting Hellos from the root bridge, RSTP on SW3 chooses the best alternate port as its new root port to begin the speedier convergence process.

The other new RSTP port type, *backup* port, applies only when a single switch has two links to the same segment (collision domain) . To have two links to the same collision domain, the switch must be attached to a hub, as shown in Figure 2-9 off SW2. In the figure, switch SW2 places one of the two ports into the designated port role (and eventually into a Forwarding State) and the other interface into the backup role (and eventually into the Discarding State). SW2 forwards BPDUs out the port in Forwarding State and gets the same BPDU back on the port that is in Discarding State. So SW2 knows it has an extra connection to that segment, called a *backup port*. If the DP port in Forwarding State fails, SW2 can quickly move that backup port from a Discarding State to a Learning State and then a Forwarding State.

Table 2-10 lists the port role terms for both STP and RSTP.

Table 2-10   *RSTP and STP Port Roles*

RSTP Role	STP Role	Definition
Root port	Root port	A single port on each nonroot switch in which the switch hears the best BPDU out of all the received BPDUs
Designated port	Designated port	Of all switch ports on all switches attached to the same segment/collision domain, the port that advertises the "best" BPDU
Alternate port	—	A port on a switch that receives a suboptimal BPDU
Backup port	—	A nondesignated port on a switch that is attached to the same segment/collision domain as another port on the same switch
Disabled	—	A port that is administratively disabled or is not capable of working for other reasons

RSTP Convergence

This section on RSTP started by telling you how similar RSTP is to STP: how they both choose a root using the same rules, choose designated ports using the same rules, and so forth. If RSTP did only the same things as STP, there would have been no need to update the original 802.1d STP standard with the new 802.1w RSTP standard. The main reason for the new standard is to improve convergence time.

The RSTP Spanning Tree Algorithm (STA) works somewhat differently than its older predecessor. For example, under stable conditions, every switch independently generates and sends Hello BPDUs, rather than only changing and forwarding the Hellos sent by the root switch. However, under stable conditions, the end results are the same: A switch that continues to hear the same Hellos, with the same cost and root switch BID listed, leaves the STP topology as is.

The main changes with RSTP's version of the STA occur when changes occur in the network. RSTP acts differently on some interfaces based on RSTP's characterization of the interface based on what is connected to the interface.

Edge-Type Behavior and PortFast

RSTP improves convergence for edge-type connections by immediately placing the port in Forwarding State when the link is physically active. In effect, RSTP treats these ports just like the Cisco-proprietary PortFast feature. In fact, on Cisco switches, to enable RSTP on edge interfaces, you simply configure PortFast.

Link-Type Shared

RSTP doesn't do anything differently from STP on link-type shared links. However, because most of the links between switches today are not shared, but are typically full-duplex point-to-point links, it doesn't matter.

Link-Type Point-to-Point

RSTP improves convergence over full-duplex links between switches—the links that RSTP calls "link-type point-to-point." The first improvement made by RSTP over these types of links relates to how STP uses MaxAge. STP requires that a switch that no longer receives root BPDUs in its root port must wait for MaxAge seconds before starting convergence. MaxAge defaults to 20 seconds. RSTP recognizes the loss of the path to the root bridge, through the root port, in 3 times the Hello timer, or 6 seconds with a default Hello timer value of 2 seconds. So RSTP recognizes a lost path to the root much more quickly.

RSTP removes the need for Listening State and reduces the time required for Learning State by actively discovering the network's new state. STP passively waits on new BPDUs and reacts to them during the Listening and Learning States. With RSTP, the switches negotiate with neighboring switches by sending RSTP messages. The messages enable the switches to quickly determine whether an interface can be immediately transitioned to a Forwarding State. In many cases, the process takes only a second or two for the entire RSTP domain.

An Example of Speedy RSTP Convergence

Rather than explain every nuance of RSTP convergence, one example can give you plenty of knowledge about the process. Figure 2-10 shows a network that explains RSTP convergence.

Figure 2-10 *RSTP Convergence Example: Steps 1 and 2*

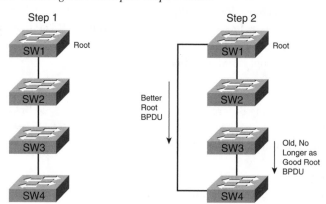

Figure 2-10 sets up the problem. On the left, in Step 1, the network has no redundancy. RSTP has placed all link-type point-to-point links in Forwarding State. To add redundancy, the network engineer adds another link-type point-to-point link between SW1 and SW4, as shown on the right as Step 2. So, RSTP convergence needs to occur..

The first step of convergence occurs when SW4 realizes that it is receiving a better BPDU than the one that entered from SW3. Because both the old and new root BPDUs advertise the same switch, SW1, the new, "better" BPDU coming over the direct link from SW1 must be better because of lower cost. Regardless of the reason, SW4 needs to transition to Forwarding State on the new link to SW1, because it is now SW4's root port.

At this point, RSTP behavior diverges from STP. RSTP on SW4 now temporarily blocks all other link-type ports. By doing so, SW4 prevents the possibility of introducing loops. Then SW4 negotiates with its neighbor on the new root port, SW1, using RSTP proposal and agreement messages. As a result, SW4 and SW1 agree that they can each place their respective ends of the new link into Forwarding State immediately. Figure 2-11 shows this third step.

Why can SW1 and SW4 place their ends of the new link in Forwarding State without causing a loop? Because SW4 blocks on all other link-type ports. In other words, it blocks on all other ports connected to other switches. That's the key to understanding RSTP convergence. A switch knows it needs to change to a new root port. It blocks on all other links and then negotiates to bring the new root port to Forwarding State. Essentially, SW4 tells SW1 to trust it and start forwarding, because SW4 promises to block all other ports until it is sure that it can move some of them back to Forwarding State.

Figure 2-11 *RSTP Convergence Example: Steps 3 and 4*

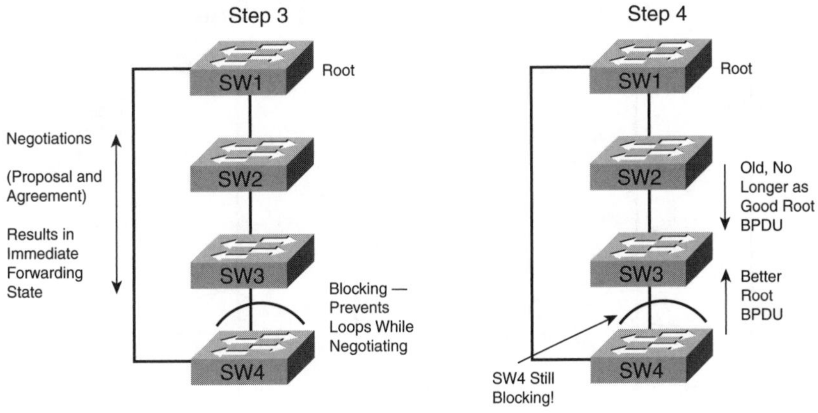

The process is not yet complete, however. The RSTP topology currently shows SW4 blocking, which in this example is not the final, best topology.

SW4 and SW3 repeat the same process that SW1 and SW4 just performed. In Step 4, SW4 still blocks, preventing loops. However, SW4 forwards the new root BPDU to SW3, so SW3 hears two BPDUs now. In this example, assume that SW3 thinks that the BPDU from SW4 is better than the one received from SW2; this makes SW3 repeat the same process that SW4 just performed. It follows this general flow from this point:

1. SW3 decides to change its root port based on this new BPDU from SW4.

2. SW3 blocks all other link-type ports. (RSTP calls this process *synchronization*.)

3. SW3 and SW4 negotiate.

4. As a result of the negotiation, SW4 and SW3 can transition to forwarding on their interfaces on either end of the link-type point-to-point link.

5. SW3 maintains Blocking State on all other link-type ports until the next step in the logic.

Figure 2-12 shows some of these steps in the Step 5 portion on the left and the resulting behavior in Step 6 on the right.

Figure 2-12   *RSTP Convergence Example: Steps 5 and 6*

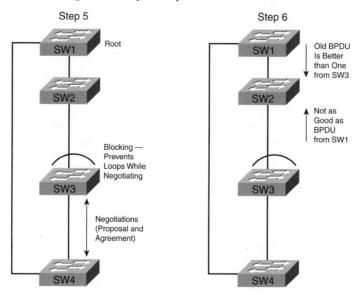

SW3 stills blocks on its upper interface at this point. Notice that SW2 is now receiving two BPDUs, but the same old BPDU it had been receiving all along is still the better BPDU. So SW2 takes no action. And RSTP is finished converging!

Although it took several pages to explain, the process in this example might take as little as 1 second to complete. For the CCNA exams, you should remember the terms relating to RSTP, as well as the concept that RSTP improves convergence time compared to STP.

STP Configuration and Verification

Cisco switches use STP (IEEE 802.1d) by default. You can buy some switches and connect them with Ethernet cables in a redundant topology, and STP will ensure that no loops exist. And you never even have to think about changing any settings!

Although STP works without any configuration, you should understand how STP works, understand how to interpret the STP-related **show** commands, and know how to tune STP by configuring various parameters. For example, by default, all switches use the same priority, so the switch with the lowest burned-in MAC address becomes the root. Instead, a switch can be configured with a lower priority, so the engineer always knows which switch is root, assuming that that switch is up and running.

The following sections begin by discussing several options for load-balancing traffic by using multiple instances of STP, followed by a short description of how to configure STP to take advantage of those multiple STP instances. The remainder of these sections show various configuration examples for both STP and RSTP.

Multiple Instances of STP

When IEEE standardized STP, VLANs did not yet exist. When VLANs were later standardized, the IEEE did not define any standards that allowed more than one instance of STP, even with multiple VLANs. At that time, if a switch only followed IEEE standards, the switch applied one instance of STP to all VLANs. In other words, if an interface was forwarding, it did so for all VLANs, and if it blocked, again it did so for all VLANs.

By default, Cisco switches use IEEE 802.1d, not RSTP (802.1w), with a Cisco-proprietary feature called Per-VLAN Spanning Tree Plus (PVST+). PVST+ (often abbreviated as simply PVST today) creates a different instance of STP for each VLAN. So, before looking at the tunable STP parameters, you need to have a basic understanding of PVST+, because the configuration settings can differ for each instance of STP.

PVST+ gives engineers a load-balancing tool. By changing some STP configuration parameters in different VLANs, the engineer could cause switches to pick different RPs and DPs in different VLANs. As a result, some traffic in some VLANs can be forwarded over one trunk, and traffic for other VLANs to be forwarded over a different trunk. Figure 2-13 shows the basic idea, with SW3 forwarding odd-numbered VLAN traffic over the left trunk (Gi0/1) and even-numbered VLANs over the right trunk (Gi0/2).

Figure 2-13 *Load Balancing with PVST+*

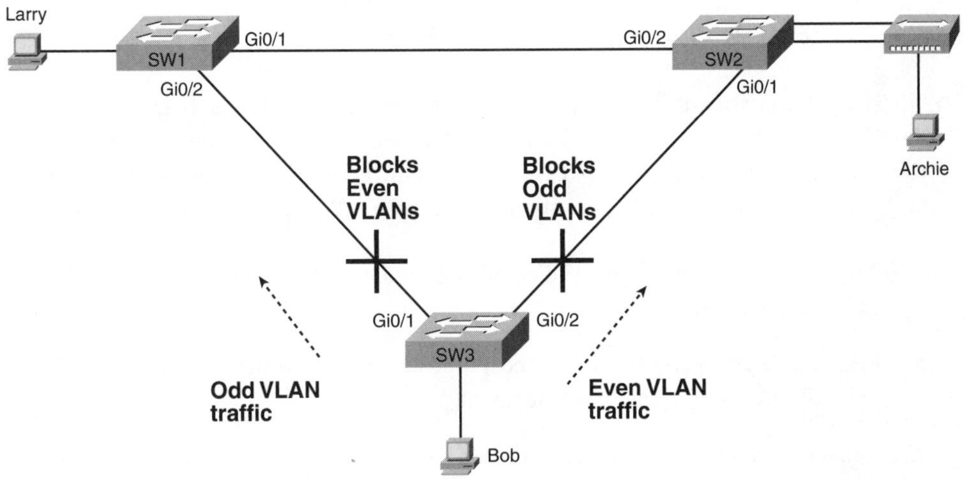

Later, when the IEEE introduced 802.1W RSTP, the IEEE still did not have a standard for using multiple instances of STP. So, Cisco implemented another proprietary solution to support one VLAN per RSTP spanning tree. Cisco has called this option both Rapid Per-VLAN Spanning Tree (RPVST) and Per-VLAN Rapid Spanning Tree (PVRST). Regardless of the acronyms, the idea is just like PVST+, but as applied to RSTP: one instance of RSTP to control each VLAN. So, not only do you get fast convergence, but you can also load-balance as shown in Figure 2-13.

Later, the IEEE created a standardized option for multiple spanning trees. The IEEE standard (802.1s) is often called either Multiple Spanning Trees (MST) or Multiple Instances of Spanning Trees (MIST). MIST allows the definition of multiple instances of RSTP, with each VLAN being associated with a particular instance. For example, to achieve the load-balancing effect in Figure 2-13, MIST would create two instances of RSTP: one for the even-numbered VLANs and one for the odd-numbered VLANs. If 100 VLANs existed, the switches still would only need two instances of RSTP, instead of the 100 instances used by PVRST. However, MIST requires more configuration on each switch, mainly to define the RSTP instances and associate each VLAN with an instance of STP.

Table 2-11 summarizes these three options for multiple spanning trees.

Table 2-11   *Comparing Three Options for Multiple Spanning Trees*

Option	Supports STP	Supports RSTP	Configuration Effort	Only One Instance Required for Each Redundant Path
PVST+	Yes	No	small	No
PVRST	No	Yes	small	No
MIST	No	Yes	medium	Yes

Configuration Options That Influence the Spanning Tree Topology

Regardless of whether PVST+, PVRST, or MIST is used, two main configuration options can be used to achieve the kind of load-balancing effects described around Figure 2-13: the bridge ID and the port cost. These options impact the per-VLAN STP topology as follows:

- The bridge IDs influence the choice of root switch, and for nonroot switches, their choice of root port.

- Each interface's (per-VLAN) STP cost to reach the root, which influences the choice of designated port on each LAN segment.

The following sections point out a few details particular to the implementation of STP on Cisco switches, beyond the generic concepts covered earlier in this chapter.

The Bridge ID and System ID Extension

As mentioned earlier in this chapter, a switch's bridge ID (BID) is formed by combining the switch's 2-byte priority and 6-byte MAC address. In practice, Cisco switches use a more detailed IEEE BID format that separates the priority into two parts. Figure 2-14 shows the more detailed format, with the former 16-bit priority field now including a 12-bit subfield called the *system ID extension*.

Figure 2-14 *STP System ID Extension*

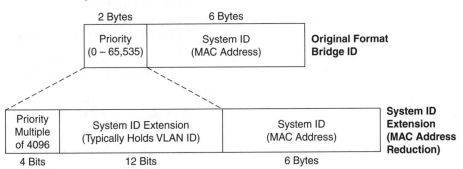

To build a switch's BID for a particular per-VLAN STP instance, the switch must use a base priority setting of a multiple of decimal 4096. (These multiples of 4096, when converted to binary, all end with 12 binary 0s.) To create the first 16 bits of the BID for a particular VLAN, the switch starts with a 16-bit version of the base priority value, which has all binary 0s in the last 12 digits. The switch then adds its base priority value to the VLAN ID. The result is that the low-order 12 bits in the original priority field then list the VLAN ID.

A nice side effect of using the system ID extension is that PVST+ then uses a different BID in each VLAN. For example, a switch configured with VLANs 1 through 4, with a default base priority of 32,768, has a default STP priority of 32,769 in VLAN 1, 32,770 in VLAN 2, 32,771 in VLAN 3, and so on.

Per-VLAN Port Costs

Each switch interface defaults its per-VLAN STP cost to the values shown earlier in Table 2-6 as the revised IEEE cost values. On Cisco switches, the STP cost is based on the actual speed of the interface, so if an interface negotiates to use a lower speed, the default STP cost reflects that lower speed per Table 2-6. If the interface negotiates to use a different speed, the switch dynamically changes the STP port cost as well.

Alternatively, a switch's port cost can be configured, either for all VLANs or for one VLAN at a time. After being configured, the switch ignores the negotiated speed on the interface, instead using the configured cost.

STP Configuration Option Summary

Table 2-12 summarizes the default settings for both the BID and the port costs, as well as lists the optional configuration commands covered in this chapter.

Table 2-12 *STP Defaults and Configuration Options*

Setting	Default	Command(s) to Change Default
Bridge ID	Priority: 32,768 + VLAN ID System: A burned-in MAC on the switch	**spanning-tree vlan** *vlan-id* **root** {**primary** | **secondary**} **spanning-tree vlan** *vlan-id* **priority** *priority*
Interface cost	Per Table 2-6: 100 for 10 Mbps, 19 for 100 Mbps, 4 for 1 Gbps, 2 for 10 Gbps	**spanning-tree vlan** *vlan-id* **cost** *cost*
PortFast	Not enabled	**spanning-tree portfast**
BPDU Guard	Not enabled	**spanning-tree bpduguard enable**

Next, the configuration section shows how to examine the operation of STP in a simple network, along with how to change these optional settings.

Verifying Default STP Operation

The following examples were taken from a small network with two switches, as shown in Figure 2-15. In this network, using default settings, all interfaces should forward except one interface on one switch on the links connecting the switches. Example 2-1 lists several **show** commands. The text following the example explains how the **show** command output identifies the details of the STP topology created in this small network.

Figure 2-15 *Two-Switch Network*

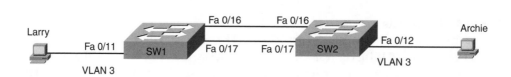

Example 2-1 *STP Status with Default STP Parameters*

```
SW1#show spanning-tree vlan 3


VLAN0003
  Spanning tree enabled protocol ieee
  Root ID    Priority    32771
             Address     0019.e859.5380
             Cost        19
             Port        16 (FastEthernet0/16)
             Hello Time   2 sec  Max Age 20 sec  Forward Delay 15 sec


  Bridge ID  Priority    32771  (priority 32768 sys-id-ext 3)
             Address     0019.e86a.6f80
             Hello Time   2 sec  Max Age 20 sec  Forward Delay 15 sec
             Aging Time 300


Interface        Role Sts Cost      Prio.Nbr Type
---------------- ---- --- --------- -------- --------------------------------
Fa0/11           Desg FWD 19        128.11   P2p
Fa0/16           Root FWD 19        128.16   P2p
Fa0/17           Altn BLK 19        128.17   P2p
SW1#show spanning-tree root

                                    Root   Hello Max Fwd
Vlan                  Root ID       Cost   Time  Age Dly Root Port
---------------- -------------------- --------- ----- --- --- ------------
VLAN0001         32769 0019.e859.5380    19     2    20  15  Fa0/16
VLAN0002         32770 0019.e859.5380    19     2    20  15  Fa0/16
VLAN0003         32771 0019.e859.5380    19     2    20  15  Fa0/16
VLAN0004         32772 0019.e859.5380    19     2    20  15  Fa0/16
! The next command supplies the same information as the show spanning-tree vlan 3
! command about the local switch, but in slightly briefer format
SW1#show span vlan 3 bridge

                                          Hello  Max  Fwd
Vlan                      Bridge ID       Time   Age  Dly Protocol
---------------- ------------------------------- ----- --- --- --------
VLAN0003         32771 (32768,   3) 0019.e86a.6f80   2   20  15  ieee
```

Example 2-1 begins with the output of the **show spanning-tree vlan 3** command on SW1. This command first lists three major groups of messages: one group of messages about the root switch, followed by another group about the local switch, and ending with interface role and status information. By comparing the shaded root ID and bridge ID in the first two groups of messages, you can quickly tell whether the local switch is root because the bridge ID and root ID would be the same. In this example, the local switch (SW1) is not the root.

The third group of messages in the **show spanning-tree vlan 3** command output identifies part of the STP topology in this example by listing all interfaces in that VLAN (both access interfaces and trunks that could possibly support the VLAN), their STP port roles, and their STP port states. For example, SW1 determines that Fa0/11 plays the role of a designated port because no other switches compete to become the DP on that port, as shown with the role of 'desg' in the command output. Therefore, SW1 must be advertising the lowest-cost Hello onto that segment. As a result, SW1 places Fa0/11 into a Forwarding State.

While the command output shows that SW1 chose interface Fa0/16 as its RP, SW1's logic in making this choice is not apparent from the command output. SW1 receives Hello BPDUs from SW2 on Fast Ethernet ports 0/16 and 0/17, both from SW2. Because both Fa0/16 and Fa0/17 default to the same port cost (19), SW1's path to the root is the same (19) over both paths. When a switch experiences a tie in regard to the cost to reach the root, the switch first uses the interfaces' *port priority* values as a tiebreaker. If the port priority values tie, the switch uses the lowest internal interface number. The interface priority and internal port number are listed under the heading "Prio.Nbr" in Example 2-1. In this case, SW1 is using the default port priority of 128 on each interface, so SW1 uses the lower port number, Fa0/16, as its root port, therefore placing Fa0/16 into a Forwarding State.

Note also that the command output shows Fa0/17 to be playing the role of an alternate (root) port, as shown with the "Altn" abbreviation in the command output. While the alternate port role is an RSTP concept, the Cisco 802.1d STP implementation also uses this concept, so the **show** command lists the alternate port role. However, because this port is neither an RP or DP, SW1 places this port into a Blocking State.

The next command in the example, **show spanning-tree root**, lists the bridge ID of the root switch in each VLAN. Note that both switches are using all default settings, so SW2 becomes root in all four existing VLANs. This command also lists the priority portion of the bridge ID separately, showing the differing priority values (32,769, 32,770, 32,771, and 32,772) based on the system ID extension explained earlier in this chapter. The last command in the example, **show spanning-tree vlan 3 bridge**, simply lists information about the local switch's bridge ID in VLAN 3.

Configuring STP Port Costs and Switch Priority

Example 2-2 shows how to impact the STP topology by configuring port cost and switch priority. First, on SW1, the port cost is lowered on FastEthernet 0/17, which makes SW1's path to the root through Fa0/17 better than the path out Fa0/16, therefore changing SW1's root port. Following that, the example shows SW1 becoming the root switch by changing SW1's bridge priority.

Example 2-2 *Manipulating STP Port Cost and Bridge Priority*

```
SW1#debug spanning-tree events
Spanning Tree event debugging is on
SW1#configure terminal
Enter configuration commands, one per line.  End with CNTL/Z.
SW1(config)#interface Fa0/17
SW1(config-if)#spanning-tree vlan 3 cost 2
00:45:39: STP: VLAN0003 new root port Fa0/17, cost 2
00:45:39: STP: VLAN0003 Fa0/17 -> listening
00:45:39: STP: VLAN0003 sent Topology Change Notice on Fa0/17
00:45:39: STP: VLAN0003 Fa0/16 -> blocking
00:45:54: STP: VLAN0003 Fa0/17 -> learning
00:46:09: STP: VLAN0003 sent Topology Change Notice on Fa0/17
00:46:09: STP: VLAN0003 Fa0/17 -> forwarding
SW1(config-if)#^Z
SW1#show spanning-tree vlan 3


VLAN0003
  Spanning tree enabled protocol ieee
  Root ID    Priority    32771
             Address     0019.e859.5380
             Cost        2
             Port        17 (FastEthernet0/17)
             Hello Time   2 sec  Max Age 20 sec  Forward Delay 15 sec

  Bridge ID  Priority    32771  (priority 32768 sys-id-ext 3)
             Address     0019.e86a.6f80
             Hello Time   2 sec  Max Age 20 sec  Forward Delay 15 sec
             Aging Time 15


Interface        Role Sts Cost      Prio.Nbr Type
---------------- ---- --- --------- -------- --------------------------------
Fa0/11           Desg FWD 19        128.11   P2p
Fa0/16           Altn BLK 19        128.16   P2p
Fa0/17           Root FWD 2         128.17   P2p
SW1#configure terminal
Enter configuration commands, one per line.  End with CNTL/Z.
SW1(config)#spanning-tree vlan 3 root primary
00:46:58: setting bridge id (which=1) prio 24579 prio cfg 24576 sysid 3
  (on) id 6003.0019.e86a.6f80
00:46:58: STP: VLAN0003 we are the spanning tree root
00:46:58: STP: VLAN0003 Fa0/16 -> listening
00:46:58: STP: VLAN0003 Topology Change rcvd on Fa0/16
00:47:13: STP: VLAN0003 Fa0/16 -> learning
00:47:28: STP: VLAN0003 Fa0/16 -> forwarding
```

This example starts with the **debug spanning-tree events** command on SW1. This command tells the switch to issue informational log messages whenever STP performs changes to an interface's role or state. These messages show up in the example as a result of the commands shown later in the example output.

Next, the port cost of the SW1 interface FastEthernet 0/17, in VLAN 3 only, is changed using the **spanning-tree vlan 3 cost 2** command, in interface Fa0/17 configuration mode. Immediately following this command, SW1 displays the first meaningful debug messages. These messages basically state that Fa0/17 is now SW1's root port, that Fa0/16 immediately transitions to a Blocking State, and that Fa0/17 slowly transitions to a Forwarding State by first going through the Listening and Learning States. You can see the timing of 15 seconds (per the default forward delay setting) in both the Learning and Listening States as shown in the shaded timestamps in the example.

> **NOTE**   Most of the configuration commands for setting STP parameters can omit the **vlan** parameter, thereby changing a setting for all VLANs. For example, the **spanning-tree cost 2** command would make an interface's STP cost be 2 for all VLANs.

Following the first set of debug messages, the output of the **show spanning-tree** command lists FastEthernet 0/16 as Blocking and FastEthernet 0/17 as Forwarding, with the cost to the root bridge now only 2, based on the changed cost of interface FastEthernet 0/17.

The next change occurs when the **spanning-tree vlan 3 root primary** command is issued on SW1. This command changes the base priority to 24,576, making SW1's VLAN 3 priority be 24,576 plus 3, or 24,579. As a result, SW1 becomes the root switch, as shown in the debug messages that follow.

The **spanning-tree vlan** *vlan-id* **root primary** command tells a switch to use a particular priority value in that VLAN only, with the switch choosing a value that will cause the switch to become the root switch in that VLAN. To do so, this command sets the base priority—the priority value that is then added to the VLAN ID to calculate the switch's priority—to a value lower than the current root switch's base priority. This command chooses the base priority as follows:

- 24,576, if the current root has a base priority higher than 24,576

- 4096 less than the current root's base priority if the current root's priority is 24,576 or lower

The **spanning-tree vlan** *vlan-id* **root secondary** command tells a switch to use a base priority value so that the local switch will become root if the primary root switch fails. This command sets the switch's base priority to 28,672 regardless of the current root's current priority value.

Note that the priority can also be explicitly set with the **spanning-tree vlan** *vlan-id* **priority** *value* global configuration command, which sets the base priority of the switch. However, because many LAN designs rely on one known root, with one backup to the root, the other commands are typically preferred.

Configuring PortFast and BPDU Guard

The PortFast and BPDU Guard features can be easily configured on any interface. To configure PortFast, just use the **spanning-tree portfast** interface subcommand. To also enable BPDU Guard, add the **spanning-tree bpduguard enable** interface subcommand.

Configuring EtherChannel

Finally, the two switches do have parallel Ethernet connections that could be configured for EtherChannel. By doing so, STP does not block on either interface, because STP treats both interfaces on each switch as one link. Example 2-3 shows the SW1 configuration and **show** commands for the new EtherChannel.

Example 2-3 *Configuring and Monitoring EtherChannel*

```
SW1#configure terminal
Enter configuration commands, one per line.  End with CNTL/Z.
SW1(config)#interface fa 0/16
SW1(config-if)#channel-group 1 mode on
SW1(config)#int fa 0/17
SW1(config-if)#channel-group 1 mode on
SW1(config-if)#^Z
00:32:27: STP: VLAN0001 Po1 -> learning
00:32:42: STP: VLAN0001 Po1 -> forwarding

SW1#show spanning-tree vlan 3


VLAN0003
  Spanning tree enabled protocol ieee
  Root ID    Priority    28675
             Address     0019.e859.5380
             Cost        12
             Port        72 (Port-channel1)
             Hello Time   2 sec  Max Age 20 sec  Forward Delay 15 sec

  Bridge ID  Priority    28675  (priority 28672 sys-id-ext 3)
             Address     0019.e86a.6f80
             Hello Time   2 sec  Max Age 20 sec  Forward Delay 15 sec
             Aging Time 300

Interface        Role Sts Cost      Prio.Nbr Type
---------------- ---- --- --------- -------- --------------------------------
```

continues

Example 2-3 *Configuring and Monitoring EtherChannel (Continued)*

```
Fa0/11           Desg FWD 19       128.11   P2p
Po1              Root FWD 12       128.72   P2p
SW1#show etherchannel 1 summary
Flags:  D - down          P - in port-channel
        I - stand-alone s - suspended
        H - Hot-standby (LACP only)
        R - Layer3      S - Layer2
        U - in use      f - failed to allocate aggregator
        u - unsuitable for bundling
        w - waiting to be aggregated
        d - default port


Number of channel-groups in use: 1
Number of aggregators:          1

Group  Port-channel  Protocol    Ports
------+-------------+-----------+---------------------------------------------
1      Po1(SU)          -         Fa0/16(P)    Fa0/17(P)
```

On 2960 switches, any port can be part of an EtherChannel, with up to eight on a single EtherChannel, so the EtherChannel commands are interface subcommands. The **channel-group 1 mode on** interface subcommands enable EtherChannel on interfaces FastEthernet 0/16 and 0/17. Both switches must agree on the number for the EtherChannel, 1 in this case, so SW2's portchannel configuration is identical to SW1's.

The **channel-group** command allows for configuring an interface to always be in a port channel (using the **on** keyword), or to be dynamically negotiated with the other switch using the **auto** or **desirable** keywords. With the **on** keyword used on SW1, if for some reason SW2 was not configured correctly for EtherChannel, the switches would not forward traffic over the interfaces. Alternatively, the EtherChannel **channel-group** configuration commands on each switch could use parameters of **auto** or **desirable** instead of **on**. With these other parameters, the switches negotiate whether to use EtherChannel. If negotiated, an EtherChannel is formed. If not, the ports can be used without forming an EtherChannel, with STP blocking some interfaces.

The use of the **auto** and **desirable** parameters can be deceiving. If you configure **auto** on both switches, the EtherChannel never comes up! The **auto** keyword tells the switch to wait for the other switch to start the negotiations. As long as one of the two switches is configured with as either **on** or **desirable**, the EtherChannel can be successfully negotiated.

In the rest of Example 2-3, you see several references to "port-channel" or "Po." Because STP treats the EtherChannel as one link, the switch needs some way to represent the entire

EtherChannel. The 2960 IOS uses the term "Po," short for "port channel," as a way to name the EtherChannel. (EtherChannel is sometimes called port channel.) For example, near the end of the example, the **show etherchannel 1 summary** command references Po1, for port channel/EtherChannel 1.

Configuring RSTP

RSTP configuration and verification are incredibly anticlimactic after fully understanding the STP configuration options covered in this chapter. Each switch requires a single global command, **spanning-tree mode rapid-pvst**. As you can tell from the command, it not only enables RSTP but also PVRST, running one RSTP instance for all defined VLANs.

The rest of the configuration commands covered in this section apply to RSTP and PVRST with no changes. The same commands impact the BID, the port cost, and EtherChannels. In fact, the **spanning-tree portfast** interface subcommand even works, technically making the interface an RSTP edge-type interface, instead of a link-type, and instantly moving the interface to a Forwarding State.

Example 2-4 shows an example of how to migrate from STP and PVST+ to RSTP and PVRST, and how to tell whether a switch is using RSTP or STP.

Example 2-4 *RSTP and PVRST Configuration and Verification*

```
SW1#configure terminal
Enter configuration commands, one per line.  End with CNTL/Z.
SW1(config)#spanning-tree mode ?
  mst         Multiple spanning tree mode
  pvst        Per-Vlan spanning tree mode
  rapid-pvst  Per-Vlan rapid spanning tree mode

! The next line configures this switch to use RSTP and PVRST.
!
SW1(config)#spanning-tree mode rapid-pvst
SW1(config)#^Z
! The "protocol RSTP" shaded text means that this switch uses RSTP, not IEEE STP.
SW1#show spanning-tree vlan 4


VLAN0004
  Spanning tree enabled protocol rstp
  Root ID    Priority    32772
             Address     0019.e859.5380
             Cost        19
             Port        16 (FastEthernet0/16)
             Hello Time   2 sec  Max Age 20 sec  Forward Delay 15 sec

  Bridge ID  Priority    32772  (priority 32768 sys-id-ext 4)
```

continues

Example 2-4 *RSTP and PVRST Configuration and Verification (Continued)*

```
          Address     0019.e86a.6f80
          Hello Time   2 sec  Max Age 20 sec  Forward Delay 15 sec
          Aging Time 300

Interface        Role Sts Cost     Prio.Nbr Type
---------------- ---- --- --------- -------- -------------------------------
Fa0/16           Root FWD 19        128.16   P2p Peer(STP)
Fa0/17           Altn BLK 19        128.17   P2p Peer(STP)
```

Of particular importance, take the time to compare the "protocol rstp" phrase shaded in the example with the earlier examples' output from the **show spanning-tree** command. The earlier examples all used the default setting of STP and PVST+, listing the text "protocol ieee," referring to the original IEEE 802.1d STP standard.

STP Troubleshooting

The final sections focus on how to apply the information covered in the earlier parts of this chapter to new scenarios. While this section helps you prepare to troubleshoot STP problems in real networks, the main goal for this section is to prepare you to answer STP questions on the CCNA exams. (Note that these sections do not introduce any new facts about STP.)

STP questions tend to intimidate many test takers. One reason STP causes exam takers more problems is that even those with on-the-job experience might not have ever needed to troubleshoot STP problems. STP runs by default and works well using default configuration settings in medium to small networks, so engineers seldom need to troubleshoot STP problems. Also, while the theory and commands covered in this chapter might be understandable, applying many of those concepts and commands to a unique problem on the exam takes time.

This section describes and summarizes a plan of attack for analyzing and answering different types of STP problems on the exam. Some exam questions might require you to determine which interfaces should forward or block. Other questions might want to know which switch is the root, which ports are root ports, and which ports are designated ports. Certainly, other variations of questions exist as well. Regardless of the type of question, the following three steps can be used to analyze STP in any LAN, and then, in turn, answer any STP questions on the exam:

Step 1   Determine the root switch.

Step 2   For each nonroot switch, determine its one root port (RP) and cost to reach the root switch through that RP.

Step 3   For each segment, determine the designated port (DP) and the cost advertised by the DP onto that segment.

The following sections review the key points about each of these steps, and then list some tips for helping you quickly find the answer for exam questions.

Determining the Root Switch

Determining the STP root switch is easy if you know all the switches' BIDs; just pick the lowest value. If the question lists the priority and MAC address separately, as is common in **show** command output, pick the switch with the lowest priority, or in the case of a tie, pick the lower MAC address value.

Much like with real networks, if a question requires you to issue **show** commands on various switches to find the root switch, an organized strategy can help you answer questions faster. First, remember that many variations of the **show spanning-tree** command list the root's BID, with priority on one line and the MAC address on the next, in the first part of the output; the local switch's BID is listed in the next section. (See Example 2-1 for a shaded example.) Also remember that Cisco switches default to use PVST+, so be careful to look at STP details for the correct VLAN. With these facts in mind, the following list outlines a good strategy:

Step 1   Pick a switch at which to begin, and find the root switch's BID and the local switch's BID in the VLAN in question using the **show spanning-tree vlan** *vlan-id* exec command.

Step 2   If the root BID and local BID are equal, the local switch is the root switch.

Step 3   If the root BID is not equal to the local switch's BID, follow these steps:

    a.   Find the RP interface on the local switch (also in the **show spanning-tree** command output).

    b.   Using Cisco Discovery Protocol (CDP) or other documentation, determine which switch is on the other end of the RP interface found in Step 3A.

    c.   Log in to the switch on the other end of the RP interface and repeat this process, starting at Step 1.

Example 2-5 shows the output of a **show spanning-tree vlan 1** command. Without even knowing the topology of the LAN, take the time now to try this troubleshooting strategy based on the output in the example, and compare your thoughts to the explanations following this example.

Example 2-5 *Finding the Root Switch*

```
SW2#show spanning-tree vlan 1
VLAN0001
  Spanning tree enabled protocol ieee
  Root ID    Priority    32769
             Address     000a.b7dc.b780
             Cost        19
             Port        1 (FastEthernet0/1)
             Hello Time   2 sec  Max Age 20 sec  Forward Delay 15 sec

  Bridge ID  Priority    32769  (priority 32768 sys-id-ext 1)
             Address     0011.92b0.f500
             Hello Time   2 sec  Max Age 20 sec  Forward Delay 15 sec
             Aging Time 300

Interface        Role Sts Cost      Prio.Nbr Type
---------------- ---- --- --------- -------- --------------------------------
Fa0/1            Root FWD 19          128.1    P2p
Fa0/19           Desg FWD 100         128.19   Shr
Fa0/20           Desg FWD 100         128.20   Shr
SW2#show spanning-tree vlan 1 bridge id
VLAN0001         8001.0011.92b0.f500
```

The shaded portions of the example point out the root's BID (priority and address) as well as SW2's differing BID. Because the root switch's BID is different, the next step should be to find the root port, which is listed in two different places in the command output (Fa0/1). The next step would be to repeat the process on the switch on the other end of SW2's Fa0/1 interface, but the example does not identify that switch.

Determining the Root Port on Nonroot Switches

Each nonroot switch has one, and only one, root port (RP). (Root switches do not have an RP.) To choose its RP, a switch listens for incoming Hello BPDUs. For each received Hello, the switch adds the cost listed in the Hello BPDU to that switch's port cost for the port on which the Hello was received. The least-calculated cost wins; in case of a tie, the switch picks the interface with the lower port priority, and if that ties, the switch picks the lower internal port number.

While the previous paragraph truly summarizes how a nonroot switch picks its RP, when an exam question supplies information about the root switch and interface port costs, a slightly different approach can possibly speed your way to an answer. For example, consider the following question, asked about the network shown in Figure 2-16:

> In the switched network shown in Figure 2-16, all switches and segments are up and working, with STP enabled in VLAN 1. SW1 has been elected root. SW2's Fa0/1 interface uses a cost setting of 20, with all other interfaces using the default STP cost. Determine the RP on SW4.

Figure 2-16 *STP Analysis Example 1*

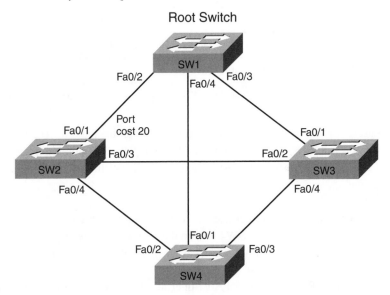

One way to go about solving this particular problem is to just apply the STP concepts as summarized in the first paragraph in this section. Alternately, you might find the solution a little more quickly with the following process, starting with a nonroot switch:

Step 1 Determine all possible paths over which a frame, sent by the nonroot switch, can reach the root switch.

Step 2 For each possible path in Step 1, add the costs of all outgoing interfaces in that path.

Step 3 The lowest cost found is the cost to reach the root, and the outgoing interface is that switch's RP.

Step 4 If the cost ties, use the port priority tiebreaker, and if that ties, use the lowest port number tiebreaker.

Table 2-13 shows the work done for Steps 1 and 2 of this process, listing the paths and the respective costs to reach the root over each path. In this network, SW4 has five possible paths to the root switch. The cost column lists the interface costs in the same order as in the first column, along with the total cost.

Table 2-13 *Finding SW4's RP: Calculating the Cost*

Physical Path (Outgoing Interfaces)	Cost
SW4 (Fa0/2) –> SW2 (Fa0/1) –> SW1	19 + 20 = 39
SW4 (Fa0/3) –> SW3 (Fa0/1) –> SW1	19 + 19 = 38
SW4 (Fa0/1) –> SW1	19 = 19
SW4 (Fa0/2) –> SW2 (Fa0/3) –> SW3 (Fa0/1) –> SW1	19 + 19 + 19 = 57
SW4 (Fa0/3) –> SW3 (Fa0/2) –> SW2 (Fa0/1) –> SW1	19 + 19 + 20 = 58

Just to ensure that the contents of the table are clear, examine the SW4 (Fa0/2) –> SW2 (Fa0/1) –> SW1 physical path for a moment. For this path, the outgoing interfaces are SW4's Fa0/2 interface, defaulting cost 19, and SW2's Fa0/1 interface, configured for cost 20, for a total of 39.

You should also realize which interfaces' costs are ignored with this process. Using the same example, the frame sent by SW4 toward the root would enter SW2's Fa0/4 interface and SW1's Fa0/2 interface. Neither interfaces' costs would be considered.

In this case, SW4's RP would be its FA0/1 interface, because the least-cost path (cost 19) begins with that interface.

Beware of making assumptions with questions that require you to find a switch's RP. For example, in this case, it might be intuitive to think that SW4's RP would be its Fa0/1 interface, because it is directly connected to the root. However, if SW4's Fa0/3 and SW3's Fa0/1 interfaces were changed to a port cost of 4 each, the SW4 (Fa0/3) –> SW3 (Fa0/1) –> SW1 path would total a cost of 8, and SW4's RP would be its Fa0/3 interface. So, just because the path looks better in the diagram, remember that the deciding point is the total cost.

Determining the Designated Port on Each LAN Segment

Each LAN segment has a single switch that acts as the designated port (DP) on that segment. On segments that connect a switch to a device that does not even use STP—for example, segments connecting a switch to a PC or a router—the switch port is elected as the DP because the only device sending a Hello onto the segment is the switch. However, segments that connect multiple switches require a little more work to discover which should be the DP. By definition, the DP for a segment is determined as follows:

> The switch interface that forwards the lowest-cost Hello BPDU onto the segment is the DP. In case of a tie, among the switches sending the Hellos whose cost tied, the switch with the lowest BID wins.

Again, the formal definition describes what STP does, and you can apply that concept to any STP question. However, for the exams, if you just finished finding the RP of each nonroot switch, and you noted the cost to reach the root on each switch (for example, as shown in Table 2-13), you can easily find the DP as follows:

Step 1   For switches connected to the same LAN segment, the switch with the lowest cost to reach the root is the DP on that segment.

Step 2   In case of a tie, among the switches that tied on cost, the switch with the lowest BID becomes the DP.

For example, consider Figure 2-17. This figure shows the same switched network as in Figure 2-16, but with the RPs and DPs noted, as well as each switch's least cost to reach the root over its respective RP.

Figure 2-17   *Picking the Designated Ports*

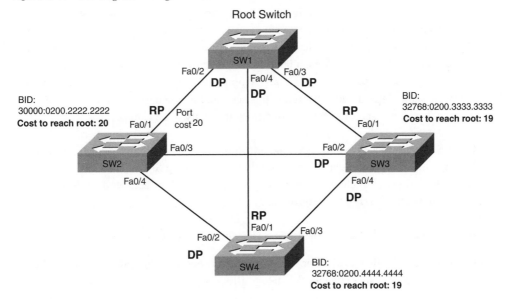

Focus on the segments that connect the nonroot switches for a moment. For the SW2–SW4 segment, SW4 wins by virtue of having a cost 19 path to the root, whereas SW2's best path is cost 20. For the same reason, SW3 becomes the DP on the SW2–SW3 segment. For the SW3–SW4 segment, both SW3 and SW4 tie on cost to reach the root. The figure lists the BIDs of the nonroot switches, so you can see that SW3's BID is lower. As a result, SW3 wins the tiebreaker, making SW3 the DP on that segment.

Note also that the root switch (SW1) becomes the DP on all its segments by virtue of the fact that the root switch always advertises Hellos of cost 0, and all other switches' calculated cost must be at least 1, because the lowest allowed port cost is 1.

For the exams, you should be able to find the root switch, then the RP on each switch, and then the DP on each segment, after you know the BIDs, port costs, and topology of the LAN. At that point, you also know which interfaces forward—those interfaces that are RPs or DPs—with the rest of the interfaces blocking.

STP Convergence

The STP topology—the set of interfaces in a Forwarding State—should remain stable as long as the network remains stable. When interfaces and switches go up or down, the resulting STP topology can change; in other words, STP convergence will occur. This section points out a few common-sense strategies for attacking these types of problems on the exams.

Some STP exam questions might ignore the transition details when convergence occurs, instead focusing on which interfaces change from Forwarding to Blocking, or Blocking to Forwarding, when a particular change happens. For example, a question might list details of a scenario and then ask, "Which interfaces change from a Blocking to a Forwarding State?" For these questions that compare the topologies both before and after a change, just apply the same steps already covered in this section, but twice: once for the conditions before the changes and once for the conditions that caused the change.

Other STP questions might focus on the transition process, including the Hello timer, MaxAge timer, forward delay timer, Listening and Learning States, and their usage, as described earlier in this chapter. For these types of questions, remember the following facts about what occurs during STP convergence:

■   For interfaces that stay in the same STP state, nothing needs to change.

■   For interfaces that need to move from a Forwarding State to a Blocking State, the switch immediately changes the state to Blocking.

■   For interfaces that need to move from a Blocking State to a Forwarding State, the switch first moves the interface to Listening State, then Learning State, each for the time specified by the forward delay timer (default 15 seconds). Only then will the interface be placed into Forwarding State.

Exam Preparation Tasks

Review All the Key Topics

Review the most important topics from this chapter, noted with the Key Topics icon in the outer margin of the page. Table 2-14 lists a reference of these key topics and the page numbers on which each is found.

Key
Topic

Table 2-14 *Key Topics for Chapter 2*

Key Topic Element	Description	Page Number
Table 2-2	Lists the three main problems that occur when not using STP in a LAN with redundant links	63
Table 2-3	Lists the reasons why a switch chooses to place an interface into Forwarding or Blocking State	66
Table 2-4	Lists the most important fields in Hello BPDU messages	67
Figure 2-5	Shows how switches calculate their root cost	70
Table 2-6	Lists the original and current default STP port costs for various interface speeds	71
List	A summary description of steady-state STP operations	72
Table 2-7	STP timers	73
List	Definitions of what occurs in the Listening and Learning States	75
Table 2-8	Summary of 802.1d states	75
List	Similarities between RSTP and STP	78
Table 2-9	Lists 802.1d and corresponding 802.1w interface states	80
Table 2-10	Lists STP and RSTP port roles and comparisons	82
Figure 2-13	Conceptual view of load-balancing benefits of PVST+	87
Table 2-11	Compares three options for multiple spanning trees	88
Figure 2-14	Shows the format of the system ID extension of the STP priority field	89
Table 2-12	Lists default settings for STP optional configuration settings and related configuration commands	90

continues

Table 2-14 *Key Topics for Chapter 2 (Continued)*

Key Topic Element	Description	Page Number
List	Two branches of logic in how the **spanning-tree root primary** command picks a new base STP priority	94
List	Strategy for solving STP problems on the exams	98

Complete the Tables and Lists from Memory

Print a copy of Appendix J, "Memory Tables," (found on the CD) or at least the section for this chapter, and complete the tables and lists from memory. Appendix K, "Memory Tables Answer Key," also on the CD, includes completed tables and lists to check your work.

Definitions of Key Terms

Define the following key terms from this chapter, and check your answers in the glossary.

Alternate port, backup port, Blocking State, BPDU Guard, bridge ID, bridge protocol data unit (BPDU), designated port, disabled port, Discarding State, EtherChannel, forward delay, Forwarding State, Hello BPDU, IEEE 802.1d, IEEE 802.1s, IEEE 802.1w, Inferior Hello, Learning State, Listening State, MaxAge, PortFast, Rapid Spanning Tree Protocol (RSTP), root port, root switch, Spanning Tree Protocol (STP)

Command Reference to Check Your Memory

While you should not necessarily memorize the information in the tables in this section, this section does include a reference for the configuration and EXEC commands covered in this chapter. Practically speaking, you should memorize the commands as a side effect of reading the chapter and doing all the activities in this exam preparation section. To check to see how well you have memorized the commands as a side effect of your other studies, cover the left side of the table with a piece of paper, read the descriptions in the right side, and see whether you remember the command.

Table 2-15 *Chapter 2 Configuration Command Reference*

Command	Description
spanning-tree vlan *vlan-number* **root primary**	Global configuration command that changes this switch to the root switch. The switch's priority is changed to the lower of either 24,576 or 4096 less than the priority of the current root bridge when the command was issued.

Table 2-15 *Chapter 2 Configuration Command Reference (Continued)*

Command	Description
spanning-tree vlan *vlan-number* **root secondary**	Global configuration command that sets this switch's STP base priority to 28,672.
spanning-tree [**vlan** *vlan-id*] {**priority** *priority*}	Global configuration command that changes the bridge priority of this switch for the specified VLAN.
spanning-tree [**vlan** *vlan-number*] **cost** *cost*	Interface subcommand that changes the STP cost to the configured value.
channel-group *channel-group-number* **mode** {**auto** | **desirable** | **on**}	Interface subcommand that enables EtherChannel on the interface.
spanning-tree portfast	Interface subcommand that enables PortFast on the interface.
spanning-tree bpduguard enable	Interface subcommand to enable BPDU Guard on an interface
spanning-tree mode {**mst** | **rapid-pvst** | **pvst**}	Global command to enable PVST+ and 802.1d (**pvst**), PVRST and 802.1w (**rapid-pvst**), or IEEE 802.1s (multiple spanning trees) and 802.1w (**mst**).

Table 2-16 *Chapter 2 EXEC Command Reference*

Command	Description
show spanning-tree	Lists details about the state of STP on the switch, including the state of each port
show spanning-tree *interface interface-id*	Lists STP information only for the specified port
show spanning-tree vlan *vlan-id*	Lists STP information for the specified VLAN
show spanning-tree [**vlan** *vlan-id*] **root**	Lists information about each VLAN's root or for just the specified VLAN
show spanning-tree [**vlan** *vlan-id*] **bridge**	Lists STP information about the local switch for each VLAN or for just the specified VLAN
debug spanning-tree events	Causes the switch to provide informational messages about changes in the STP topology
show etherchannel [*channel-group-number*] {**brief** | **detail** | **port** | **port-channel** | **summary**}	Lists information about the state of EtherChannels on this switch.

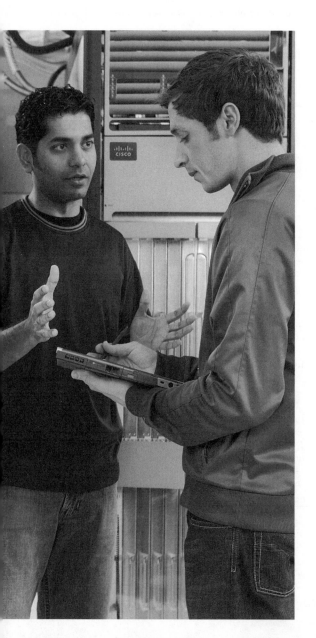

This chapter covers the following subjects:

Generalized Troubleshooting Methodologies: This section presents discussions and opinions about how to approach a networking problem when a general examination of the problem does not quickly identify the root cause.

Troubleshooting the LAN Switching Data Plane: This section suggests several organized steps for troubleshooting Ethernet LAN problems, with a detailed review of commands and methods.

Predicting Normal Operation of the LAN Switching Data Plane: This section suggests how to analyze switch **show** command output and figures to predict where a frame should be forwarded in an example switched LAN.

CHAPTER **3**

Troubleshooting LAN Switching

This chapter, along with Chapter 7, "Troubleshooting IP Routing," and Chapter 11, "Troubleshooting Routing Protocols," has an important job: to help you develop the troubleshooting skills required to quickly and confidently answer certain types of questions on the exams. At the same time, this chapter can hopefully make you better prepared to solve real networking problems.

> **NOTE** For some thoughts about why troubleshooting is so important for the exams, refer to the section "Format of the CCNA Exams" in the introduction to this book.

The troubleshooting chapters in this book do not have the same primary goal as the other chapters. Simply put, the nontroubleshooting chapters focus on individual features and facts about an area of technology, whereas the troubleshooting chapters pull a much broader set of concepts together. These troubleshooting chapters take a broader look at the networking world, focusing on how the parts work together, assuming that you already know about the individual components.

This chapter covers the same technology covered in the other chapters in this part of the book (Chapter 1, "Virtual LANs," and Chapter 2, "Spanning Tree Protocol") and the related prerequisite materials (as covered in *CCENT/CCNA ICND1 Official Exam Certification Guide*). Also, because this chapter is the first troubleshooting chapter in this book, it also explains some general concepts about troubleshooting methodology.

"Do I Know This Already?" Quiz

Because the troubleshooting chapters of this book pull in concepts from many other chapters, including some chapters in *CCENT/CCNA ICND1 Official Exam Certification Guide*, as well as show how to approach some of the more challenging questions on the CCNA exams, you should read these chapters regardless of your current knowledge level. For these reasons, the troubleshooting chapters do not include a "Do I Know This Already?" quiz. However, if you feel particularly confident about troubleshooting LAN switching features covered in this book and *CCENT/CCNA ICND1 Official Exam Certification Guide*, feel free to move to the "Exam Preparation Tasks" section, near the end of this chapter, to bypass the majority of the chapter.

Foundation Topics

This chapter has three major sections. The first section focuses on the troubleshooting process as an end to itself. The second section explains how to apply the general troubleshooting methods specifically to a LAN switching data plane. The last section then lists some hints and ideas about specific types of problems related to LAN switching.

Generalized Troubleshooting Methodologies

> **NOTE** The generic troubleshooting strategies and methods described here are a means to an end. You don't need to study these processes or memorize them for the purposes of the exam. Instead, these processes can help you think through problems on the exam so that you can answer the questions a little more quickly and with a little more confidence.

When faced with a need to solve a networking problem, everyone uses some troubleshooting methodology, whether informal or formal. Some people like to start by checking the physical cabling and interface status of all the physical links that could affect the problem. Some people like to start by pinging everything that could tell you more about the problem, and then drilling deeper into the details. Some people might even just try whatever comes to mind until they intuitively know the general problem. None of these methods is inherently bad or good; I've tried all these methods, and others, and had some success with each approach.

While most people develop troubleshooting habits and styles that work well based on their own experiences and strengths, a more systematic troubleshooting methodology can help anyone learn to troubleshoot problems with better success. The following sections describe one such systematic troubleshooting methodology for the purpose of helping you prepare to troubleshoot networking problems on the CCNA exams. This troubleshooting methodology has three major branches, which generally occur in the order shown here:

- **Analyzing/predicting normal operation**: The description and prediction of the details of what should happen if the network is working correctly, based on documentation, configuration, and **show** and **debug** command output.

- **Problem isolation**: When some problem might be occurring, find the component(s) that do not work correctly as compared to the predicted behavior, again based on documentation, configuration, and **show** and **debug** command output.

- **Root cause analysis**: Identify the underlying causes of the problems identified in the previous step, specifically the causes that have a specific action with which the problem can be fixed.

Following these three steps should result in the engineer knowing how to fix the problem, not just the problem symptoms. Next, the text explains some thoughts about how to approach each step of the troubleshooting process.

Analyzing and Predicting Normal Network Operation

Any network's job is to deliver data from one end-user device to another. To analyze a network, an engineer needs to understand the logic used by each successive device as it forwards the data to the next device. By thinking about what should happen at each device, the engineer can describe the entire flow of data.

The term *data plane* refers to any actions taken by networking devices for the forwarding of an individual frame or packet. To forward each frame or packet, a device applies its data plane logic and processes to the frame or packet. For example, when a LAN switch receives a frame in an interface in VLAN 3, the switch will make a forwarding decision based on the VLAN 3 entries in the MAC address table, and forward the packet. All this logic is part of a switch's data plane processing.

The term *control plane* refers to the overhead processes that do not need to be done for each packet or frame. Instead, some control plane processes support the forwarding process. For example, VLAN Trunking Protocol (VTP) and IP routing protocols are examples of control plane processes. Other control plane processes can only be indirectly related to the data plane. For example, Cisco Discovery Protocol (CDP) can be useful for confirming the accuracy of network documentation, but CDP can be disabled with no effect on the data plane forwarding processes.

To predict the expected operation of a network, or to explain the details of how a correctly functioning network is currently working, it can be helpful to begin by looking at either the control plane or data plane. This text shows the data plane first, but in real life, you can pick one or the other in part based on the known symptoms of the problem.

Data Plane Analysis

Data plane troubleshooting examines each device in the expected forwarding path for the data, in order. The analysis begins with the host creating the original data. That host sends the data to some other device, which then sends the data to another device, and so on, until the data reaches the endpoint host. The receiving host typically sends some sort of reply, so to fully understand how useful communications happen, you also need to analyze the reverse process as well. In particular, the outward problem symptoms typically identify two end-user devices that cannot communicate, but the underlying problem might only be related to frames or packets going in one direction.

Unless a particular problem's symptoms already suggest a specific problem, data plane troubleshooting should begin with an analysis of the Layer 3 data plane. If you start with Layer 3, you can see the major steps in sending and receiving data between two hosts. You can then examine each individual Layer 3 forwarding step more closely, looking at the underlying Layer 1 and 2 details. For example, Figure 3-1 shows the six major IP forwarding (data plane) steps in a small network.

Figure 3-1 *Major Steps in an IP Forwarding Example*

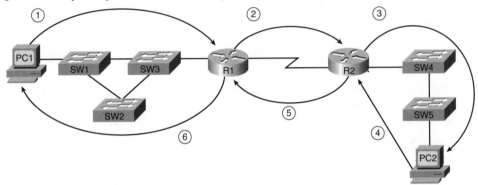

When understanding the expected behavior of Layer 3 in this case, you would need to consider how the packet flows from left to right, and then how the reply flows from right to left. Using the six steps in the figure, the following analysis could be done:

Step 1   Think about PC1's IP address and mask, the IP address and mask of PC2, and PC1's logic to realize that PC2 is in another subnet. This causes PC1 to choose to send the packet to its default gateway (R1).

Step 2   Consider R1's forwarding logic for matching the packet's destination IP address with R1's routing table, with the expectation that R1 chooses to send the packet to R2 next.

Step 3   On R2, consider the same routing table matching logic as used on R1 in the previous step, using R2's routing table. The matching entry should be a connected route on R2.

Step 4   This step relates to PC2's reply packet, which uses the same basic logic as Step 1. Compare PC2's IP address/mask with PC1's IP address, noting that they are in different subnets. As a result, PC2 should send the packet to its default gateway, R2.

Step 5   Consider R2's forwarding logic for packets destined to PC1's IP address, with the expectation that the matching route would cause R2 to send these packets to R1 next.

Step 6   The final routing step, on R1, should show that a packet destined to PC1's IP address matches a connected route on R1, which causes R1 to send the packet directly to PC1's MAC address.

After you have a good grasp of the expected behaviors of each step at Layer 3, you could then more closely examine Layer 2. Following the same ordering again, you could take a closer look at the first Layer 3 routing step in Figure 3-1 (PC1 sending a packet to R1), examining the Layer 1 and 2 details of how the frame is sent by PC1 to be delivered to R1, as shown in Figure 3-2.

Figure 3-2   *Major Steps in a LAN Switching Forwarding Example*

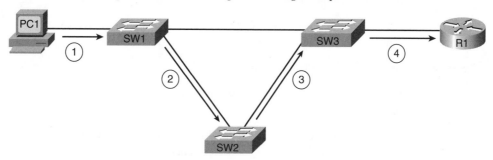

For this analysis, you would again begin with PC1, this time considering the Ethernet header and trailer, particularly the source and destination MAC addresses. Then, at Step 2, you would consider SW1's forwarding logic, which compares the frame's destination MAC address to SW1's MAC address table, telling SW1 to forward the frame to SW2. Steps 3 and 4 would repeat Step 2's logic from SW2 and SW3, respectively.

Control Plane Analysis

Many control plane processes directly affect the data plane process. For example, IP routing cannot work without appropriate IP routes, so routers typically use a dynamic routing protocol—a control plane protocol—to learn the routes. Routing protocols are considered to be control plane protocols in part because the work done by a routing protocol does not have to be repeated for each frame or packet.

While the data plane processes lend themselves to a somewhat generic troubleshooting process of examining the forwarding logic at each device, control plane processes differ too much to allow such a generalized troubleshooting process. However, it is helpful to consider a specific set of troubleshooting steps for each specific control plane protocol. For example, Chapter 1 explains how to approach troubleshooting various types of VTP problems.

Predicting Normal Operations: Summary of the Process

On the exams, some questions will simply require that you analyze and predict the normal operation of a working network. In other cases, predicting the normal behavior is just a precursor to isolating and fixing a problem. Regardless, if the question gives you no specific clues about the part of the network on which to focus, the following list summarizes a suggested approach for finding the answers:

Step 1 Examine the data plane as follows:

    a. Determine the major Layer 3 steps—including origin host to default router, each router to the next router, and last router to the destination host—in both directions.

    b. For each Layer 2 network between a host and router or between two routers, analyze the forwarding logic for each device.

Step 2 Examine the control plane as follows:

    a. Identify the control plane protocols that are used and vital to the forwarding process.

    b. Examine each vital control plane protocol for proper operation; the details of this analysis differ for each protocol.

    c. Defer any analysis of control plane protocols that do not affect the data plane's correct operation until you clearly see a need for the protocol to answer that question (for example, CDP).

Problem Isolation

The troubleshooting process is seldom a sequential process. For organizational purposes, this chapter lists problem isolation as the second of three troubleshooting steps. However, this step is more likely to happen as soon as the first step (predicting normal behavior) finds a problem. So, while the generic lists shown in this section help provide structure about how to troubleshoot a problem, the actual practice can be messy.

When you have no clues as to how to proceed, other than maybe that two hosts cannot communicate, it is again best to start with the Layer 3 data plane—in other words, IP forwarding logic. Then, when you find an IP forwarding step that doesn't work, examine that step more closely to further isolate where the problem is occurring. For example, consider Figure 3-1 again, which shows a packet being delivered from PC1 to PC2, and back, in six routing steps. In this case, however, you determine that R2 gets the packet, but the packet is never delivered to PC2. So, you take closer look at everything from R2 to PC2 to further isolate the problem.

After you isolate the problem to one IP forwarding step (as shown in Figure 3-1), you should continue to further isolate the problem to as small a number of components as possible. For example, if R2 gets the packet, but PC2 does not, the problem might be in R2, SW4, SW5, PC2, the cabling, or possibly devices left out of the network documentation.

The process to further isolate the problem typically requires thinking about functions at many layers of the OSI model, as well as both data plane and control plane functions. Continuing with the same example problem scenario, to be able to forward packets to PC2, R2 will need to know PC2's MAC address as learned using Address Resolution Protocol (ARP). If you discover that R2 does not have an ARP entry to PC2, you might be tempted to think that some sort of IP-related problem exists. However, this problem might be caused by the SW4–SW5 trunk being down, which means that R2's IP ARP request—a LAN broadcast—cannot be delivered by SW4 to SW5, and then to PC2. So, the problem with the packet-forwarding process from R2 to PC2 might be related to a control protocol (ARP), but the failed ARP request might be caused by yet other devices (SW4–SW5 trunk down), which might well be a Layer 2 or a Layer 1 problem.

If an exam question gives no hints as to where to start, the following process summarizes a good general systematic problem isolation strategy:

Step 1   Begin by examining the Layer 3 data plane (IP forwarding), comparing the results to the expected normal behavior, until you identify the first major routing step that fails.

Step 2   Further isolate the problem to as few components as possible:

    a.   Examine functions at all layers, but focusing on Layers 1, 2, and 3.

    b.   Examine both data plane and control plane functions.

On the exams, remember that you get no extra points for good troubleshooting methods, so just find the answer any way you can, even if that means you guessed a bit based on the context of the question. For example, the suggested process in Step 2A says to focus on Layers 1, 2, and 3; that suggestion is based on the fact that the CCNA exams focus mainly on these three layers. But you should look to shortcut this process as much as possible based on what the question says.

Root Cause Analysis

The final of the three steps, root cause analysis, strives to finish the troubleshooting process to identify the specific device and function that needs to be fixed. The root cause is the true reason the problem has occurred, and more importantly, it is the function that, when fixed, solves that particular problem.

Finding the root cause is vitally important because the root cause, unlike many of the problems identified by the problem isolation process, has a specific solution associated with it. For example, continuing the same problem with R2 not being able to forward packets to PC2, consider the list of problems identified through problem isolation:

■   R2 cannot forward packets to PC2.

■   R2 gets no ARP reply from PC2.

■   SW4's interface for the trunk to SW5 is in a down/down state.

■   The cable used between SW4 and SW5 uses the wrong cabling pinouts.

All these statements might be true about a particular problem scenario, but only the last item has an obvious actionable solution (replace with a correctly wired cable). While the other statements are valid and important facts found during problem isolation, they do not imply the specific action to take to solve the problem. As a result, the root cause analysis step reduces to two simple statements:

Step 1   Continue isolating the problem until you identify the true root cause, which in turn has an obvious solution.

Step 2   If you cannot reduce the problem to its true root cause, isolate the problem as much as is possible, and change something in the network, which will hopefully change the symptoms and help you identify the root cause.

Real World Versus the Exams

On the exam, you should look for clues as to the general topic for which you need to do some part of the troubleshooting process. For example, if the figure shows a network like the one in Figure 3-1, but all the multiple-choice answers refer to VLANs and VTP, start by looking at the LAN environment. Note that you might still want to consider Layers 1 through 3, and both the data and control plane details, to help you find the answers.

> **NOTE**   This section applies generally to troubleshooting, but it is included only in this chapter because this is the first chapter in the book dedicated to troubleshooting.

Troubleshooting the LAN Switching Data Plane

The generic troubleshooting strategies explained so far in this chapter suggest beginning with the IP routing process at Layer 3. If the engineer identifies a problem at a particular step in the IP forwarding process, the next step should be to examine that routing step more closely, including looking at the underlying Layer 1 and 2 status.

The following sections examine the tools and processes used to troubleshoot the LAN data plane processes at Layers 1 and 2. The rest of this chapter assumes that no Layer 3 problems exist; Chapters 7 and 11 examine Layer 3 troubleshooting. This chapter also makes some references to control plane protocols, specifically VTP and Spanning Tree Protocol (STP), but VTP and STP have already been well covered in the two previous chapters. So, these sections focus specifically on the LAN switching data plane.

These sections begin with a review of the LAN switch forwarding processes and an introduction to the four major steps in the LAN switching troubleshooting process as suggested in this chapter. Next, the text examines each of these four steps in succession. Finally, an example of how to apply the troubleshooting process is shown.

An Overview of the Normal LAN Switch Forwarding Process

The LAN switch forwarding process, described in detail in *CCENT/CCNA ICND1 Official Exam Certification Guide* Chapter 7, is relatively simple. However, before taking a closer look at how to use **show** command output to both predict normal operations and isolate the root cause of a forwarding problem, it is helpful to review how a switch thinks about the forwarding process when no problems exist. The following process steps outline that logic:

Step 1 Determine the VLAN in which the frame should be forwarded, as follows:

    a. If the frame arrives on an access interface, use the interface's access VLAN.

    b. If the frame arrives on a trunk interface, use the VLAN listed in the frame's trunking header.

Step 2 If the incoming interface is in an STP Learning or Forwarding State in that VLAN, add the source MAC address to the MAC address table, with incoming interface and VLAN ID (if not already in the table).

Step 3 If the incoming interface is not in an STP Forwarding State in that VLAN, discard the frame.

Step 4 Look for the destination MAC address of the frame in the MAC address table, but only for entries in the VLAN identified at Step 1. If the destination MAC is found or not found, follow these steps:

a. **Found:** Forward the frame out the only interface listed in the matched address table entry

b. **Not found:** Flood the frame out all other access ports in that same VLAN that are in an STP Forwarding State, and out all trunk ports that list this VLAN as fully supported (active, in the allowed list, not pruned, STP Forwarding)

To forward a frame, a switch must first determine in which VLAN the frame should be forwarded (Step 1), learn the source MAC addresses as needed (Step 2), and then choose where to forward the frame. Just to make sure that the process is clear, consider an example using Figure 3-3, in which PC1 sends a frame to its default gateway, R1, with the MAC addresses shown in the figure.

Figure 3-3 *Switched Network Used in Data Plane Analysis in Chapter 3*

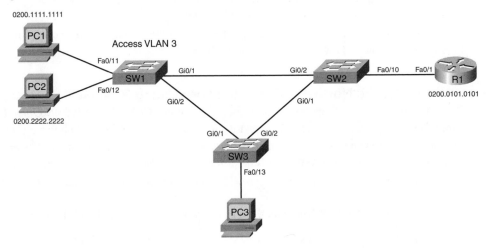

In this case, consider the frame as sent from PC1 (source MAC 0200.1111.1111) to R1 (destination MAC 0200.0101.0101). SW1, using Step 1 of the summarized forwarding logic, determines whether interface Fa0/11 is operating as an access interface or a trunk. In this case, it is an access interface assigned to VLAN 3. For Step 2, SW1 adds an entry to its MAC address table, listing MAC address 0200.1111.1111, interface Fa0/11, and VLAN 3. At Step 3, SW1 confirms that the incoming interface, Fa0/11, is in an STP Forwarding State. Finally, at Step 4, SW1 looks for an entry with MAC address 0200.0101.0101 in VLAN 3. If SW1 finds an entry that lists interface Gigabit 0/1, SW1 then forwards the frame only out Gi0/1. If the outgoing interface (Gi0/1) is a trunk interface, SW1 adds a VLAN trunking header that lists VLAN 3, the VLAN ID determined at Step 1.

For another slightly different example, consider a broadcast sent by PC1. Steps 1 through 3 occur as before, but at Step 4, SW1 floods the frame. However, SW3 only floods the frame out access ports in VLAN 3 and trunk ports that support VLAN 3, with the restriction that SW1 will not forward a copy of the frame out ports not in an STP Forwarding State.

Although this forwarding logic is relatively simple, the troubleshooting process requires the application of most every LAN-related concept in both the ICND1 and ICND2 books, plus other topics as well. For example, knowing that PC1 first sends frames to SW1, it makes sense to check the interface's status, ensure that the interface is "up and up," and fix the problem with the interface if it is not. Dozens of individual items might need to be checked to troubleshoot a problem. So, this chapter suggests a LAN data plane troubleshooting process that organizes the actions into four main steps:

Step 1   Confirm the network diagrams using CDP.

Step 2   Isolate interface problems.

Step 3   Isolate filtering and port security problems.

Step 4   Isolate VLANs and trunking problems.

The next four sections review and explain the concepts and tools to perform each of these four steps. While some facts and information are new, most of the specific underlying concepts have already been covered, either in *CCENT/CCNA ICND1 Official Exam Certification Guide* or in Chapters 1 and 2 of this book. The main goal is to help you pull all the concepts together so that analyzing unique scenarios—as will be required on the exams—takes a little less time, with a much better chance for success.

> **NOTE**   The next two sections, "Step 1: Confirm the Network Diagrams Using CDP," and "Step 2: Isolate Interface Problems," are also covered in the ICND1 book's Chapter 10. If you are reading both books to prepare for the CCNA exam, you don't need to read these sections of this chapter as well as the similarly named sections of ICND1's Chapter 10. If you are reading both books, feel free to skip to the section "Step 3: Isolate Filtering and Port Security Problems."

Step 1: Confirm the Network Diagrams Using CDP

The Cisco Discovery Protocol (CDP) can be useful to verify the information in the network diagram as well as to complete the rest of the necessary information about the devices and topology. In real life, the network diagrams can be old and outdated, and a problem might be caused because someone moved some cables and didn't update the diagrams. I doubt that Cisco would write a question with purposefully inaccurate information in the figure associated with the question, but the exam might easily include questions for which the network diagram does not list all the required information, and you need to use CDP to find the rest of the details. So, this section reviews CDP, and a good first LAN data plane troubleshooting step is as follows:

Step 1   Verify the accuracy of and complete the information listed in the network diagram using CDP.

> **NOTE**   This chapter shows a series of numbered troubleshooting steps for LAN switching, begun here with Step 1. The steps and their numbers are unimportant for the exam; the steps are just numbered in this chapter for easier reference.

Cisco routers, switches, and other devices use CDP for a variety of reasons, but routers and switches use it to announce basic information about themselves to their neighbors—information like the host name, device type, IOS version, and interface numbers. Three commands in particular list the CDP information learned from neighbors, as listed in Table 3-1. In fact, in cases for which no diagram exists, an engineer could create a diagram of routers and switches using **show cdp** command output.

Table 3-1   **show cdp** *Commands That List Information About Neighbors*

Command	Description
show cdp neighbors [*type number*]	Lists one summary line of information about each neighbor, or just the neighbor found on a specific interface if an interface was listed
show cdp neighbors detail	Lists one large set (approximately 15 lines) of information, one set for every neighbor
show cdp entry *name*	Lists the same information as the **show cdp neighbors detail** command, but only for the named neighbor

The only tricky part of the process of comparing CDP output to a diagram is that the output lists two interfaces or ports on many lines of output. Reading left to right, the output typically lists the host name of the neighboring device under the heading of "Device ID." However, the next heading of "Local Intrfce," meaning "local interface," is the local device's interface name/number. The neighboring device's interface name/number is on the right side of the command output under the heading "Port ID." Example 3-1 lists an example **show cdp neighbors** command from SW2 in Figure 3-3. Take the time to compare the shaded portions of the command output to the accurate details in Figure 3-3 to see which fields list interfaces for which devices.

Example 3-1 **show cdp** *Command Example*

```
SW2#show cdp neighbors
Capability Codes: R - Router, T - Trans Bridge, B - Source Route Bridge
                  S - Switch, H - Host, I - IGMP, r - Repeater, P - Phone

Device ID          Local Intrfce      Holdtme   Capability   Platform      Port ID
SW1                Gig 0/2            173          S I        WS-C2960-2    Gig 0/1
R1                 Fas 0/10           139          R S I      1841          Fas 0/1
```

CDP creates a security exposure when enabled. To avoid the exposure of allowing an attacker to learn details about each switch, CDP can be easily disabled. Cisco recommends that CDP be disabled on all interfaces that do not have a specific need for it. The most likely interfaces that need to use CDP are interfaces connected to other Cisco routers and switches and interfaces connected to Cisco IP phones. Otherwise, CDP can be disabled per interface using the **no cdp enable** interface subcommand. (The **cdp enable** interface subcommand reenables CDP.) Alternately, the **no cdp run** global command disables CDP for the entire switch, with the **cdp run** global command reenabling CDP globally.

Step 2: Isolate Interface Problems

A Cisco switch interface must be in a working state before the switch can process frames received on the interface or send frames out the interface. So, a somewhat obvious troubleshooting step should be to examine the state of each interface, specifically those expected to be used when forwarding frames, and verify that the interfaces are up and working.

This section examines the possible interface states on a Cisco IOS–based switch, lists root causes for the nonoperational states, and covers a popular problem that occurs even when the interface appears to be in a working state. The specific tasks for this step can be summarized with the following troubleshooting steps:

Step 2   Check for interface problems as follows:

  a. Determine interface status code(s) for each required interface, and if not in a connect or up/up state, resolve the problems until the interface reaches the connect or up/up state.

  b. For interfaces in a connect (up/up) state, also check for two other problems: duplex mismatches and some variations of port security purposefully dropping frames.

Interface Status Codes and Reasons for Nonworking States

Cisco switches use two different sets of status codes: one set of two codes (words) that uses the same conventions as do router interface status codes and another set with a single code (word). Both sets of status codes can determine whether an interface is working.

The switch **show interfaces** and **show interfaces description** commands list the two-code status just like routers. The two codes are named the *line status* and *protocol status*, with the codes generally referring to whether Layer 1 is working and whether Layer 2 is working, respectively. LAN switch interfaces typically show an interface with both codes as "up" or both codes as "down," because all switch interfaces use the same Ethernet data link layer protocols, so the data link layer protocol should never have a problem.

> **NOTE**   This book refers to these two status codes in shorthand by just listing the two codes with a slash between them, for example, "up/up."

The **show interfaces status** command lists a single interface status code. This single interface status code corresponds to different combinations of the traditional two-code interface status codes and can be easily correlated to those codes. For example, the **show interfaces status** command lists a "connect" state for working interfaces, which corresponds to the up/up state seen with the **show interfaces** and **show interfaces description** commands.

Any interface state other than connect or up/up means that the switch cannot forward or receive frames on the interface. Each nonworking interface state has a small set of root causes. Also, note that the exams could easily ask a question that only showed one or the other type of status code, so to be prepared for the exams, know the meanings of both sets of interface status codes. Table 3-2 lists the code combinations and some root causes that could have caused a particular interface status.

Table 3-2   *LAN Switch Interface Status Codes*

Line Status	Protocol Status	Interface Status	Typical Root Cause
admin. down	down	disabled	Interface is configured with the **shutdown** command.
down	down	notconnect	No cable; bad cable; wrong cable pinouts; speeds mismatched on the two connected devices; device on the other end of the cable is either powered off or the other interface is shut down.
up	down	notconnect	Not expected on LAN switch interfaces.

Table 3-2 *LAN Switch Interface Status Codes (Continued)*

Line Status	Protocol Status	Interface Status	Typical Root Cause
down	down (err-disabled)	err-disabled	Port security has disabled the interface.
up	up	connect	Interface is working.

The notconnect State and Cabling Pinouts

Table 3-2 lists several reasons why a switch interface can be in the notconnect state. Most of those reasons do not need much further explanation than the text in the table. For example, if an interface is connected to another switch, and the interface is in a notconnect state, check the other switch to find out whether the other switch's interface has been shut down. However, one of the reasons for a notconnect state—incorrect cable pinouts—deserves a little more attention because it is both a common mistake and is not otherwise covered in this book. (Ethernet cabling pinouts are covered in *CCENT/CCNA ICND1 Official Exam Certification Guide* Chapter 3.)

Ethernet unshielded twisted-pair (UTP) cabling standards specify the pins to which each of the wires should connect on the RJ-45 connectors on the ends of the cable. The devices transmit using pairs of wires, with 10BASE-T and 100BASE-Tx using two pairs: one to transmit and one to receive data. When connecting two devices that use the same pair of pins to transmit, the cable—a crossover cable—must connect or cross the wires connected to each device's transmit pair over to the other device's expected receive pair. Conversely, devices that already use opposite pairs for transmitting data need a straight-through cable that does not cross the pairs. Figure 3-4 shows an example in a typical switched LAN, with the types of cabling pinouts shown.

Figure 3-4 *Example Use of Crossover and Straight-Through Cables*

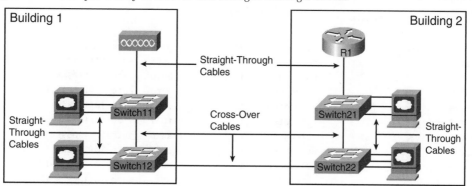

Effective troubleshooting requires knowledge of which devices transmit on which pairs. Table 3-3 lists the more common devices seen in the context of CCNA, along with the pairs used. Note that when connecting two types of devices from the same column, a crossover cable is required; when connecting two devices from different columns of the table, a straight-through cable is required.

Key Topic

Table 3-3 *10BASE-T and 100BASE-Tx Pin Pairs Used*

Devices That Transmit on 1,2 and Receive on 3,6	Devices That Transmit on 3,6 and Receive on 1,2
PC NICs	Hubs
Routers	Switches
Wireless access points (Ethernet interface)	—
Ethernet-connected network printers	—

Interface Speed and Duplex Issues

Switch interfaces can find their speed and duplex settings in several ways. By default, interfaces that use copper wiring and are capable of multiple speeds and duplex settings use the IEEE-standard (IEEE 802.3x) autonegotiation process. Alternately, switch interfaces, routers, and most network interface cards (NIC) can also be configured to use a specific speed or duplex setting. On switches and routers, the **speed {10 | 100 | 1000}** interface subcommand with the **duplex {half | full}** interface subcommand sets these values. Note that configuring both speed and duplex on a switch interface disables the IEEE-standard autonegotiation process on that interface.

The **show interfaces** and **show interfaces status** commands list both the speed and duplex settings on an interface, as shown in Example 3-2.

Example 3-2 *Displaying Speed and Duplex Settings on Switch Interfaces*

```
SW1#show interfaces status

Port      Name            Status       Vlan       Duplex  Speed Type
Fa0/1                     notconnect   1            auto   auto 10/100BaseTX
Fa0/2                     notconnect   1            auto   auto 10/100BaseTX
Fa0/3                     notconnect   1            auto   auto 10/100BaseTX
Fa0/4                     connected    1          a-full  a-100 10/100BaseTX
Fa0/5                     connected    1          a-full  a-100 10/100BaseTX
Fa0/6                     notconnect   1            auto   auto 10/100BaseTX
Fa0/7                     notconnect   1            auto   auto 10/100BaseTX
Fa0/8                     notconnect   1            auto   auto 10/100BaseTX
Fa0/9                     notconnect   1            auto   auto 10/100BaseTX
Fa0/10                    notconnect   1            auto   auto 10/100BaseTX
```

Example 3-2 *Displaying Speed and Duplex Settings on Switch Interfaces (Continued)*

```
Fa0/11                 connected     1       a-full    10 10/100BaseTX
Fa0/12                 connected     1         half   100 10/100BaseTX
Fa0/13                 connected     1       a-full a-100 10/100BaseTX
Fa0/14                 disabled      1         auto  auto 10/100BaseTX
Fa0/15                 notconnect    3         auto  auto 10/100BaseTX
Fa0/16                 notconnect    3         auto  auto 10/100BaseTX
Fa0/17                 connected     1       a-full a-100 10/100BaseTX
Fa0/18                 notconnect    1         auto  auto 10/100BaseTX
Fa0/19                 notconnect    1         auto  auto 10/100BaseTX
Fa0/20                 notconnect    1         auto  auto 10/100BaseTX
Fa0/21                 notconnect    1         auto  auto 10/100BaseTX
Fa0/22                 notconnect    1         auto  auto 10/100BaseTX
Fa0/23                 notconnect    1         auto  auto 10/100BaseTX
Fa0/24                 notconnect    1         auto  auto 10/100BaseTX
Gi0/1                  connected   trunk       full  1000 10/100/1000BaseTX
Gi0/2                  notconnect    1         auto  auto 10/100/1000BaseTX
SW1#show interfaces fa0/13
FastEthernet0/13 is up, line protocol is up (connected)
  Hardware is Fast Ethernet, address is 0019.e86a.6f8d (bia 0019.e86a.6f8d)
  MTU 1500 bytes, BW 100000 Kbit, DLY 100 usec,
     reliability 255/255, txload 1/255, rxload 1/255
  Encapsulation ARPA, loopback not set
  Keepalive set (10 sec)
  Full-duplex, 100Mb/s, media type is 10/100BaseTX
  input flow-control is off, output flow-control is unsupported
  ARP type: ARPA, ARP Timeout 04:00:00
  Last input 00:00:05, output 00:00:00, output hang never
  Last clearing of "show interface" counters never
  Input queue: 0/75/0/0 (size/max/drops/flushes); Total output drops: 0
  Queueing strategy: fifo
  Output queue: 0/40 (size/max)
  5 minute input rate 0 bits/sec, 0 packets/sec
  5 minute output rate 0 bits/sec, 0 packets/sec
     85022 packets input, 10008976 bytes, 0 no buffer
     Received 284 broadcasts (0 multicast)
     0 runts, 0 giants, 0 throttles
     0 input errors, 0 CRC, 0 frame, 0 overrun, 0 ignored
     0 watchdog, 281 multicast, 0 pause input
     0 input packets with dribble condition detected
     95226 packets output, 10849674 bytes, 0 underruns
     0 output errors, 0 collisions, 1 interface resets
     0 babbles, 0 late collision, 0 deferred
     0 lost carrier, 0 no carrier, 0 PAUSE output
     0 output buffer failures, 0 output buffers swapped out
```

While both commands can be useful, only the **show interfaces status** command implies how the switch determined the speed and duplex settings. The command output lists autonegotiated settings with an "a-". For example, "a-full" means full-duplex as autonegotiated, where as "full" means full-duplex but as manually configured. The example shades the command output that implies that the switch's Fa0/12 interfaces' speed and duplex were not found through autonegotiation, but Fa0/13 did use autonegotiation. Note that the **show interfaces Fa0/13** command (without the **status** option) simply lists the speed and duplex for interface Fa0/13, with nothing implying that the values were learned through autonegotiation.

Cisco switches have some interesting features related to interface speed that can help you determine some types of interface problems. If a Cisco switch interface has been configured to use a particular speed, and the speed does not match the device on the other end of the cable, the switch interface will be in a notconnect or down/down state. However, this kind of speed mismatch can only occur when the speed has been manually configured on the switch. Cisco switch interfaces that do not have the **speed** command configured can automatically detect the speed used by the other device—even if the other device turns off the IEEE autonegotiation process—and then use that speed.

For example, in Figure 3-3, imagine that SW2's Gi0/2 interface was configured with the **speed 100** and **duplex half** commands (not recommended settings on a Gigabit-capable interface, by the way). SW2 would use those settings and disable the IEEE-standard autonegotiation process because both the **speed** and **duplex** commands have been configured. If SW1's Gi0/1 interface did not have a **speed** command configured, SW1 would still recognize the speed (100 Mbps)—even though SW2 would not use IEEE-standard negotiation—and SW1 would also use a speed of 100 Mbps. Example 3-3 shows the results of this specific case on SW1.

Example 3-3 *Displaying Speed and Duplex Settings on Switch Interfaces*

```
SW1#show interfaces gi0/1 status

Port      Name            Status      Vlan     Duplex  Speed Type
Gi0/1                     connected   trunk    a-half  a-100 10/100/1000BaseTX
```

The speed and duplex still show up with a prefix of "a-" in the example, implying autonegotiation. The reason is that in this case, the speed was found automatically, and the duplex setting was chosen because of the default values used by the IEEE autonegotiation process. The IEEE standards state that for ports running at 100 Mbps, if autonegotiation fails, use a default half-duplex setting.

Finding a duplex mismatch can be much more difficult than finding a speed mismatch because *if the duplex settings do not match on the ends of an Ethernet segment, the switch interface will be in a connect (up/up) state.* In this case, the interface works, but it might work poorly, with poor performance and with symptoms of intermittent problems. The reason is that the device using half-duplex uses carrier sense multiple access collision detect (CSMA/CD) logic, waiting to send when receiving a frame, believing collisions occur when they physically do not, and stopping sending a frame because the switch thinks a collision occurred. With enough traffic load, the interface could be in a connect state, but essentially useless for passing traffic, even causing the loss of vital VTP and STP messages.

To identify duplex mismatch problems, try the following actions:

- Use commands like **show interfaces** on each end of the link to confirm the duplex setting on each end.

- Watch for increases to certain counters on half-duplex interfaces. The counters—runts, collisions, and late collisions—occur when the other device uses full duplex. (Note that these counters can also increment when legitimate collisions occur as well.)

Example 3-2 (earlier in this section) uses shading to indicate these counters in the output of the **show interfaces** command.

The root cause of duplex mismatches might be related to the defaults chosen by the IEEE autonegotiation process. When a device attempts autonegotiation, and the other device does not respond, the first device chooses the default duplex setting based on the current speed. The default duplex settings, per the IEEE, are chosen as follows:

- If the speed is 10 or 100 Mbps, default to use half-duplex.

- If the speed is 1000 Mbps, default to use full-duplex.

NOTE Ethernet interfaces using speeds faster than 1 Gbps always use full-duplex.

Step 3: Isolate Filtering and Port Security Problems

Generally speaking, any analysis of the forwarding process should consider any security features that might discard some frames or packets. For example, both routers and switches can be configured with access control lists (ACL) that examine the packets and frames being sent or received on an interface, with the router or switch discarding those packets/frames.

The CCNA exams do not include coverage of switch ACLs, but the exams do cover a similar switch feature called port security. As covered in *CCENT/CCNA ICND1 Official Exam Certification Guide*, Chapter 9, the port security feature can be used to cause the switch to discard some frames sent into and out of an interface. Port security has three basic features with which it determines which frames to filter:

- Limit which specific MAC addresses can send and receive frames on a switch interface, discarding frames to/from other MAC addresses.

- Limit the number of MAC addresses using the interface, discarding frames to/from MAC addresses learned after the maximum limit was reached.

- A combination of the previous two points.

The first port security troubleshooting step should be to find which interfaces have port security enabled, followed by a determination as to whether any violations are currently occurring. The trickiest part relates to the differences in what the IOS does in reaction to violations based on the **switchport port-security violation** *violation-mode* interface subcommand, which tells the switch what to do when a violation occurs. The general process is as follows:

Step 3   Check for port security problems as follows:

   a. Identify all interfaces on which port security is enabled (**show running-config** or **show port-security**).

   b. Determine whether a security violation is currently occurring based in part on the *violation mode* of the interface's port security configuration, as follows:

   — **shutdown**: The interface will be in an err-disabled state.

   — **restrict**: The interface will be in a connect state, but the **show port-security interface** command will show an incrementing violations counter.

   — **protect**: The interface will be in a connect state, and the **show port-security interface** command will not show an incrementing violations counter.

   c. In all cases, compare the port security configuration to the diagram as well as the "last source address" field in the output of the **show port-security interface** command.

One of the difficulties when troubleshooting port security relates to the fact that some port security configurations discard only the offending frames, but they do not disable the interface as a result, all based on the configured violation mode. All three violation modes discard the traffic as dictated by the configuration. For example, if only one predefined MAC address of 0200.1111.1111 is allowed, the switch discards all traffic on that interface, other than traffic to or from 0200.1111.1111. However, shutdown mode causes all future traffic to be discarded—even legitimate traffic from address 0200.1111.1111—after a violation has occurred. Table 3-4 summarizes some of these key points for easier study.

Table 3-4   *Port Security Behavior Based on Violation Mode*

Violation Mode	Discards Offending Traffic	Discards All Traffic After Violation Occurs	Violation Results in err-disabled Interface State	Counters Increment for Each New Violation
shutdown	Yes	Yes	Yes	Yes
restrict	Yes	No	No	Yes
protect	Yes	No	No	No

Troubleshooting Step 3B refers to the interface err-disabled (error disabled) state. This state verifies that the interface has been configured to use port security, that a violation has occurred, and that no traffic is allowed on the interface at the present time. This interface state implies that the shutdown violation mode is used, because it is the only one of the three port security modes that causes the interface to be disabled. To fix this problem, the interface must be shut down and then enabled with the **no shutdown** command. Example 3-4 lists an example in which the interface is in an err-disabled state.

Example 3-4   *Using Port Security to Define Correct MAC Addresses of Particular Interfaces*

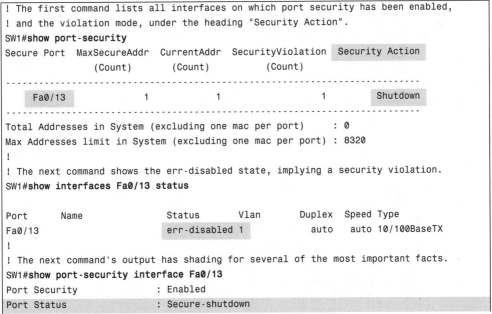

```
! The first command lists all interfaces on which port security has been enabled,
! and the violation mode, under the heading "Security Action".
SW1#show port-security
Secure Port  MaxSecureAddr  CurrentAddr  SecurityViolation  Security Action
             (Count)        (Count)      (Count)
---------------------------------------------------------------------------
    Fa0/13          1            1              1              Shutdown
---------------------------------------------------------------------------
Total Addresses in System (excluding one mac per port)     : 0
Max Addresses limit in System (excluding one mac per port) : 8320
!
! The next command shows the err-disabled state, implying a security violation.
SW1#show interfaces Fa0/13 status

Port       Name              Status         Vlan     Duplex  Speed Type
Fa0/13                       err-disabled 1          auto    auto  10/100BaseTX
!
! The next command's output has shading for several of the most important facts.
SW1#show port-security interface Fa0/13
Port Security              : Enabled
Port Status                : Secure-shutdown
```

continues

Example 3-4 *Using Port Security to Define Correct MAC Addresses of Particular Interfaces (Continued)*

```
Violation Mode            : Shutdown
Aging Time                : 0 mins
Aging Type                : Absolute
SecureStatic Address Aging : Disabled
Maximum MAC Addresses     : 1
Total MAC Addresses       : 1
Configured MAC Addresses  : 1
Sticky MAC Addresses      : 0
Last Source Address:Vlan  : 0200.3333.3333:2
Security Violation Count  : 1
```

The output of the **show port-security interface** command lists a couple of items helpful in the troubleshooting process. The port status of "secure-shutdown" means that the interface is disabled for all traffic as a result of a violation, and that the interface state should be "err-disabled." The end of the command output lists a violations counter, incremented by 1 for each new violation. Interestingly, with a violation mode of shutdown, the counter increments by 1, the interface is placed into err-disabled state, and the counter cannot increment anymore until the engineer uses the **shutdown** and **no shutdown** commands on the interface, in succession. Finally, note that the second-to-last line lists the source MAC address of the last frame received on the interface. This value can be useful in identifying the MAC address of the device that caused the violation.

The restrict and protect violation modes still cause frame discards, but with much different behavior. With these violation modes, the interface remains in a connect (up/up) state while still discarding the inappropriate frames because of port security. So, avoid the pitfall of assuming that an interface in a connect, or up/up, state cannot have any other reasons for not passing traffic.

Example 3-5 shows a sample configuration and **show** command when using protect mode. In this case, a PC with MAC address 0200.3333.3333 sent frames into port Fa0/13, with the port configured to restrict Fa0/13 to only receive frames sent by 0200.1111.1111.

Example 3-5 *Port Security Using Protect Mode*

```
SW1#show running-config
! Lines omitted for brevity
interface FastEthernet0/13
 switchport mode access
 switchport port-security
 switchport port-security mac-address 0200.1111.1111
 switchport port-security violation protect
! Lines omitted for brevity
```

Example 3-5 *Port Security Using Protect Mode (Continued)*

```
SW1#show port-security interface Fa0/13
Port Security              : Enabled
Port Status               : Secure-up
Violation Mode            : Protect
Aging Time                : 0 mins
Aging Type                : Absolute
SecureStatic Address Aging : Disabled
Maximum MAC Addresses     : 1
Total MAC Addresses       : 1
Configured MAC Addresses  : 1
Sticky MAC Addresses      : 0
Last Source Address:Vlan  : 0200.3333.3333:1
Security Violation Count  : 0
```

This **show** command output was gathered after many frames had been sent by a PC with MAC address 0200.3333.3333, with all the frames being discarded by the switch because of port security. The command output shows the disallowed PC's 0200.3333.3333 MAC address as the last source MAC address in a received frame. However, note that the port status is listed as secure-up and the violation count as 0—both indications that might make you think all is well. However, in protect mode, the **show port-security interface** command does not show any information confirming that an actual violation has occurred. The only indication is that end-user traffic does not make it to where it needs to go.

If this example had used violation mode restrict, the port status would have also stayed in a secure-up state, but the security violation counter would have incremented once for each violating frame.

For the exams, a port security violation might not be a problem; it might be the exact function intended. The question text might well explicitly state what port security should be doing. In these cases, it can be quicker to just immediately look at the port security configuration. Then, compare the configuration to the MAC addresses of the devices connected to the interface. The most likely problem on the exams is that the MAC addresses have been misconfigured or that the maximum number of MAC addresses has been set too low. (*CCENT/CCNA ICND1 Official Exam Certification Guide*, Chapter 9, explains the details of the configuration statements.)

One last security feature that needs a brief mention is IEEE 802.1x authentication. IEEE 802.1x (not to be confused with the IEEE 802.3x autonegotiation standard) defines a process to authenticate the user of the PC connected to a switch port. 802.1x can be used as part of an overall Network Admission Control (NAC) strategy, in which a user internal to an enterprise LAN cannot use the LAN until the user supplies some authentication credentials.

With 802.1x, each user communicates with a AAA server with a series of authentication messages. The access switch listens to the messages, discarding all frames on the link except for 802.1x messages to and from the PC. When the switch overhears the message from the AAA server that says that the user has been successfully authenticated, the switch then allows all traffic to flow on that port. If the user is not authenticated, the switch does not allow traffic on that interface. The details of how to configure 802.1x, and recognize an authentication failure as the root cause of a particular problem, is beyond the scope of this book.

Step 4: Isolate VLAN and Trunking Problems

A switch's forwarding process depends on both the definitions of access VLANs on access interfaces and on VLAN trunks that can pass traffic for many VLANs. Additionally, before a switch can forward frames in a particular VLAN, the switch must know about a VLAN, either through configuration or VTP, and the VLAN must be active. The following sections examine some of the tools regarding all these VLAN-related issues. This configuration step includes the following steps:

Step 4   Check VLANs and VLAN trunks as follows:

a.   Identify all access interfaces and their assigned access VLANs, and reassign into the correct VLANs as needed.

b.   Determine whether the VLANs both exist (configured or learned with VTP) and are active on each switch. If not, configure and activate the VLANs to resolve problems as needed.

c.   Identify the operationally trunking interfaces on each switch, and determine the VLANs that can be forwarded over each trunk.

The next three sections discuss Steps 4A, 4B, and 4C in succession.

Ensuring That the Right Access Interfaces Are in the Right VLANs

To ensure that each access interface has been assigned to the correct VLAN, engineers simply need to determine which switch interfaces are access interfaces instead of trunk interfaces, determine the assigned access VLANs on each interface, and compare the information to the documentation. The three **show** commands listed in Table 3-5 can be particularly helpful in this process.

Table 3-5   *Commands That Can Find Access Ports and VLANs*

EXEC Command	Description
show vlan brief show vlan	Lists each VLAN and all interfaces assigned to that VLAN, but does not include trunks

Table 3-5 *Commands That Can Find Access Ports and VLANs (Continued)*

EXEC Command	Description
show interfaces *type number* **switchport**	Identifies an interface's access VLAN, voice VLAN, and the administrative (configured) mode and operational mode (access or trunking)
show mac address-table dynamic	Lists MAC table entries: MAC addresses with associated interfaces and VLANs

If possible, start this step with the **show vlan** and **show vlan brief** commands, because they list all the known VLANs and the access interfaces assigned to each VLAN. Be aware, however, that the output of these commands includes all interfaces that are not currently operationally trunking. So, these commands list interfaces in a notconnect state, err-disabled state, and most importantly in this case, interfaces that might trunk after the interface comes up. For example, these commands might include interface Gi0/2 in the list of interfaces in VLAN 1, but as soon as Gi0/1 comes up, the interface might negotiate trunking—at which point the interface would no longer be an access interface and would no longer be listed in the output of the **show vlan brief** command.

If the **show vlan** and **show interface switchport** commands are not available in a particular test question, the **show mac address-table** command can also help identify the access VLAN. This command lists the MAC address table, with each entry including a MAC address, interface, and VLAN ID. If the test question implies that a switch interface connects to a single device PC, you should only see one MAC table entry that lists that particular access interface; the VLAN ID listed for that same entry identifies the access VLAN. (You cannot make such assumptions for trunking interfaces.)

After you determine the access interfaces and associated VLANs, if the interface is assigned to the wrong VLAN, use the **switchport access vlan** *vlan-id* interface subcommand to assign the correct VLAN ID.

Access VLANs Not Being Defined or Being Active

The next troubleshooting step, Step 4B, examines the fact that a switch does not forward frames in an undefined VLAN or in a defined VLAN that is not in the active state. This section summarizes the best ways to confirm that a switch knows that a particular VLAN exists, and if it exists, determines the state of the VLAN.

VTP servers and clients only display their current list of known VLANs with the **show vlan** command. Neither the running-config nor the startup-config file holds the **vlan** *vlan-id* global configuration commands that define the VLAN, or the associated **name** commands that name a VLAN. Transparent mode switches do put these configuration commands in both the vlan.dat and the running-config file, so you can see the configuration using the **show running-config** command.

After you determine that a VLAN does not exist, the problem might be that the VLAN simply needs to be defined. If so, follow the VLAN configuration process as covered in detail in Chapter 1, summarized as follows:

■ **On VTP servers and clients, assuming that VTP is working**: The VLAN must be configured on a VTP server, typically with the **vlan** *vlan-id* global configuration command, with the other VTP servers and clients learning about the VLAN. The VLAN can also be configured as a result of the **switchport access vlan** *vlan-id* interface subcommand, on the VTP server at which the VLAN does not yet exist, causing the server to automatically create the VLAN.

■ **On VTP servers and client, assuming that VTP is not working**: Troubleshoot VTP as covered in the section "VTP Troubleshooting" in Chapter 1.

■ **On a VTP transparent switch**: The configuration is the same as on a server, but it must be done on each switch, because VTP transparent mode switches do not advertise the new VLAN to other switches.

For any existing VLANs, also verify that the VLAN is active. The **show vlan** command should list one of two VLAN state values: active and act/lshut. The second of these states means that the VLAN is shut down. To solve this problem, use the **no shutdown vlan** *vlan-id* global configuration command. Note that this command must be issued on each switch, because this shutdown state is not advertised by VTP.

Identify Trunks and VLANs Forwarded on Those Trunks

At this step (4C), you can separate problems into two general categories as you begin to isolate the problem: problems with the details of how an operational trunk works and problems caused when an interface that should trunk does not trunk.

The first category in this step can be easily done using the **show interfaces trunk** command, which only lists information about currently operational trunks. The best place to begin with this command is the last section of output, which lists the VLANs whose traffic will be forwarded over the trunk. Any VLANs that make it to this final list of VLANs in the command output meet the following criteria:

■   The VLAN exists and is active on this switch (as covered in the previous section and seen in the **show vlan** command).

■   The VLAN has not been removed from the allowed VLAN list on the trunk (as configured with the **switchport trunk allowed vlan** interface subcommand).

■ The VLAN has not been VTP-pruned from the trunk (as done automatically by VTP, assuming that VTP pruning has been enabled with the **vtp pruning** global configuration command).

■ The trunk is in an STP Forwarding State in that VLAN (as also seen in the **show spanning-tree vlan** *vlan-id* command).

Example 3-6 shows a sample of the command output from the **show interfaces trunk** command, with the final section of the command output shaded. In this case, the trunk only forwards traffic in VLANs 1 and 4.

Example 3-6 *Allowed VLAN List and List of Active VLANs*

```
SW1#show interfaces trunk

Port        Mode        Encapsulation  Status       Native vlan
Gi0/1       desirable   802.1q         trunking     1

Port        Vlans allowed on trunk
Gi0/1       1-2,4-4094

Port        Vlans allowed and active in management domain
Gi0/1       1,4

Port        Vlans in spanning tree forwarding state and not pruned
Gi0/1       1,4
```

The absence of a VLAN in this last part of the command's output does not necessarily mean that a problem has occurred. In fact, a VLAN might be legitimately excluded from a trunk for any of the reasons in the list just before Example 3-6. However, for a given exam question, it can be useful to know why traffic for a VLAN will not be forwarded over a trunk. The output of the **show interfaces trunk** command's three lists of VLANs shows a progression of reasons why a VLAN is not forwarded over a trunk. To remember the details, review the details surrounding Chapter 1's Example 1-4 and the few paragraphs before the example.

A trunk's native VLAN configuration should also be checked at this step. The native VLAN ID can be manually set to different VLANs on either end of the trunk. If the native VLANs differ, the switches will accidentally cause frames to leave one VLAN and enter another. For example, if switch SW1 sends a frame using native VLAN 1 on an 802.1Q trunk, SW1 does not add a VLAN header, as is normal for the native VLAN. When switch SW2 receives the frame, noticing that no 802.1Q header exists, SW2 assumes that the frame is part of SW2's configured native VLAN. If SW2 has been configured to think VLAN 2 is the native VLAN on that trunk, SW2 will try to forward the received frame into VLAN 2.

The second general class of trunking problem is that an interface that should trunk does not. The most likely cause of this problem is a misconfiguration of trunking on the opposite ends of the link. The **switchport mode {access | trunk | dynamic {desirable | auto}}** interface subcommand tells the interface whether to trunk and the rules with which to negotiate trunking. You can display any interface's administrative (configured) trunking mode, as set by this configuration command, using the **show interface switchport** command. Make sure that you know the meaning of each of this configuration command's options as listed in Table 1-4 in Chapter 1, and the combinations on either end of the segment that result in trunking, as listed in Chapter 1's Table 1-5.

In some cases, an interface can fail to use trunking because of a misconfiguration of the type of trunking—in other words, whether to use ISL or 802.1Q. For example, if two switches on opposite ends of a segment configured the **switchport trunk encapsulation isl** and **switchport trunk encapsulation dot1Q** commands, respectively, the trunk would not form, because the types of trunks (the encapsulation) do not match.

Example: Troubleshooting the Data Plane

This section shows an example of how to apply the steps to a particular network and scenario. The scenario includes several problems based on Figure 3-5. At the beginning, PC1, PC2, and PC3 cannot ping their default gateway, R1, at IP address 2.2.2.9. This section shows how to apply the troubleshooting processes covered so far in this chapter to uncover the problems and fix them. For easier reference, the steps have been summarized here as follows:

Step 1   Verify the accuracy of and complete the information listed in the network diagram using CDP.

Step 2   Check for interface problems as follows:

   a. Determine the interface status code(s) for each required interface, and if not in a connect or up/up state, resolve the problems until the interface reaches the connect or up/up state.

   b. For interfaces in a connect (up/up) state, also check for two other problems: duplex mismatches and some variations of port security purposefully dropping frames.

Step 3   Check for port security problems as follows:

   a. Identify all interfaces on which port security is enabled (**show running-config** or **show port-security**).

b. Determine whether a security violation is currently occurring based in part on the *violation mode* of the interface's port security configuration, as follows:

— **shutdown**: The interface will be in an err-disabled state.

— **restrict**: The interface will be in a connect state, but the **show port-security interface** command will show an incrementing violations counter.

— **protect**: The interface will be in a connect state, and the **show port-security interface** command will not show an incrementing violations counter.

c. In all cases, compare the port security configuration to the diagram as well as the "last source address" field in the output of the **show port-security interface** command.

Step 4 Check VLANs and VLAN trunks as follows:

a. Identify all access interfaces and their assigned access VLANs, and reassign into the correct VLANs as needed.

b. Determine whether the VLANs both exist (configured or learned with VTP) and are active on each switch. If not, configure and activate the VLANs to resolve problems as needed.

c. Identify the operationally trunking interfaces on each switch, and determine the VLANs that can be forwarded over each trunk.

Figure 3-5 *Network Used in the Data Plane Troubleshooting Example*

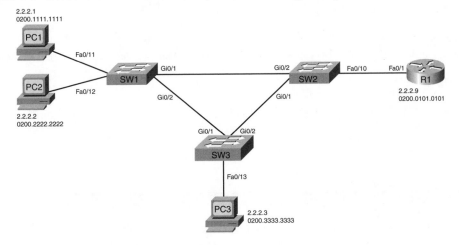

Step 1: Verify the Accuracy of the Diagram Using CDP

Example 3-7 shows a variety of example output from the **show cdp neighbors** and **show cdp entry** commands on the three switches in Figure 3-5. A simple comparison confirms the names and interfaces in the figure, with the exception that SW2's Fa0/9 interface connects to router R1, instead of SW2's Fa0/10 interface shown in Figure 3-5.

Example 3-7   *Verifying Figure 3-5 Using CDP*

```
SW1#show cdp neighbors
Capability Codes: R - Router, T - Trans Bridge, B - Source Route Bridge
                  S - Switch, H - Host, I - IGMP, r - Repeater, P - Phone


Device ID        Local Intrfce      Holdtme    Capability    Platform    Port ID
SW2              Gig 0/1            122          S I          WS-C2960-2  Gig 0/2
SW3              Gig 0/2            144          S I          WS-C3550-2  Gig 0/1
! SW2 commands next
SW2#show cdp neighbors
Capability Codes: R - Router, T - Trans Bridge, B - Source Route Bridge
                  S - Switch, H - Host, I - IGMP, r - Repeater, P - Phone


Device ID        Local Intrfce      Holdtme    Capability    Platform    Port ID
SW1              Gig 0/2            125          S I          WS-C2960-2  Gig 0/1
SW3              Gig 0/1            170          S I          WS-C3550-2  Gig 0/2
R1               Fas 0/9            157          R S I        1841        Fas 0/1
SW2#show cdp entry R1
-------------------------
Device ID: R1
Entry address(es):
  IP address: 2.2.2.10
Platform: Cisco 1841,  Capabilities: Router Switch IGMP
Interface: FastEthernet0/9,  Port ID (outgoing port): FastEthernet0/1
Holdtime : 150 sec


Version :
Cisco IOS Software, 1841 Software (C1841-ADVENTERPRISEK9-M), Version 12.4(9)T, RELEASE
SOFTWARE (fc1)
Technical Support: http://www.cisco.com/techsupport
Copyright  1986-2006 by Cisco Systems, Inc.
Compiled Fri 16-Jun-06 21:26 by prod_rel_team


advertisement version: 2
VTP Management Domain: ''
Duplex: full
Management address(es):
! SW3 command next
SW3#show cdp neighbors
Capability Codes: R - Router, T - Trans Bridge, B - Source Route Bridge
                  S - Switch, H - Host, I - IGMP, r - Repeater, P - Phone
```

Example 3-7 *Verifying Figure 3-5 Using CDP (Continued)*

```
Device ID          Local Intrfce      Holdtme   Capability   Platform    Port ID
SW1                Gig 0/1            154        S I          WS-C2960-2  Gig 0/2
SW2                Gig 0/2            178        S I          WS-C2960-2  Gig 0/1
```

This mistake in documentation in Figure 3-5 (listing SW2 interface Fa0/10 instead of Fa0/9) does not affect the current network's operation. However, had trunking been required between SW2 and R1, SW2 interface Fa0/9—not Fa0/10—would have to have been explicitly configured to enable trunking, because routers cannot automatically negotiate to use trunking. Chapter 4, "IP Routing: Static and Connected Routes," covers the details of router trunking configuration.

Note that CDP does not identify documentation problems with the interfaces that connect to the end-user PCs; for the purposes of this example, know that the rest of the interfaces shown in Figure 3-5 are the correct interfaces.

Step 2: Check for Interface Problems

The next step examines the interface status on each of the interfaces that should currently be used. Example 3-8 lists several **show interface status** commands on both SW1 and SW3. (For this chapter's purposes, assume that all interfaces on SW2 are working correctly.) Examine the output, identify any problems you see, and make a list of other interface-related problems you might want to investigate further based on this output.

Example 3-8 *Interface Problems on SW1*

```
SW1#show interfaces fa0/11 status

Port      Name              Status        Vlan      Duplex  Speed Type
Fa0/11                      connected     3         a-full  a-100 10/100BaseTX
SW1#show interfaces fa0/12 status

Port      Name              Status        Vlan      Duplex  Speed Type
Fa0/12                      notconnect    3          auto    auto 10/100BaseTX
SW1#show interfaces Gi0/1 status

Port      Name              Status        Vlan      Duplex  Speed Type
Gi0/1                       connected     trunk     a-full a-1000 10/100/1000BaseTX
SW1#show interfaces Gi0/2 status

Port      Name              Status        Vlan      Duplex  Speed Type
Gi0/2                       connected     1         a-full a-1000 10/100/1000BaseTX
! Switching to SW3 next
SW3#sh interfaces fa0/13 status
```

continues

Example 3-8 *Interface Problems on SW1 (Continued)*

```
Port        Name              Status      Vlan    Duplex  Speed Type
Fa0/13                        connected   3       a-half  a-100 10/100BaseTX
SW3#show interfaces Gi0/1 status

Port        Name              Status      Vlan    Duplex  Speed Type
Gi0/1                         connected   1       a-full a-1000 1000BaseTX
SW3#show interfaces Gi0/2 status

Port        Name              Status      Vlan    Duplex  Speed Type
Gi0/2                         connected   trunk   a-full a-1000 1000BaseTX
```

One obvious problem exists on SW1, with interface Fa0/12 in a notconnect state. Many reasons for this state exist, almost all relating to some cabling problem—anything from a cable that is not fully inserted into the switch port to difficult-to-find interference problems on the cable. (See Table 3-2 for suggested reasons.)

SW3's interfaces appear not to have any problems. However, all three interfaces have a duplex setting that is the same setting as what the switch would use if the autonegotiation process failed, with the use of half-duplex on Fa0/13 being notable. That raises the possibility of one of the two interface problems mentioned earlier in the chapter that could occur when the interface is in a connect state, namely, a duplex mismatch.

You can determine that SW3's Gigabit 0/1 and 0/2 interfaces do not have a mismatch by simply using the **show interfaces** status command on SW1 and SW2 on the other end of those links, respectively. However, ports connected to a PC pose a troubleshooting problem in that you probably will not be near the PC, so you might have to guide the end user through some steps to verify the speed and duplex settings. However, it is helpful to look for the telltale signs of runts, collisions, and early collisions, as listed in the output of the **show interfaces** command in Example 3-9.

Example 3-9 *Signs of a Duplex Mismatch*

```
SW3#show interfaces fa0/13
FastEthernet0/13 is up, line protocol is up (connected)
  Hardware is Fast Ethernet, address is 000a.b7dc.b78d (bia 000a.b7dc.b78d)
  MTU 1500 bytes, BW 100000 Kbit, DLY 100 usec,
     reliability 255/255, txload 1/255, rxload 1/255
  Encapsulation ARPA, loopback not set
  Keepalive set (10 sec)
  Half-duplex, 100Mb/s, media type is 10/100BaseTX
  input flow-control is off, output flow-control is unsupported
  ARP type: ARPA, ARP Timeout 04:00:00
  Last input never, output 00:00:01, output hang never
  Last clearing of "show interface" counters never
```

Example 3-9 *Signs of a Duplex Mismatch (Continued)*

```
Input queue: 0/75/0/0 (size/max/drops/flushes); Total output drops: 0
Queueing strategy: fifo
Output queue: 0/40 (size/max)
5 minute input rate 0 bits/sec, 0 packets/sec
5 minute output rate 0 bits/sec, 0 packets/sec
   108 packets input, 6946 bytes, 0 no buffer
   Received 3 broadcasts (0 multicast)
   54 runts, 0 giants, 0 throttles
   0 input errors, 0 CRC, 0 frame, 0 overrun, 0 ignored
   0 watchdog, 2 multicast, 0 pause input
   0 input packets with dribble condition detected
   722 packets output, 52690 bytes, 0 underruns
   0 output errors, 114 collisions, 5 interface resets
   0 babbles, 78 late collision, 19 deferred
   0 lost carrier, 0 no carrier, 0 PAUSE output
   0 output buffer failures, 0 output buffers swapped out
```

In this case, a duplex mismatch does indeed exist. However, note that these same counters do increment under normal half-duplex operations, so these counters do not definitively identify the problem as a duplex mismatch.

In this case, SW3's configuration was changed to use full-duplex on interface Fa0/13, matching the manual setting on PC3.

Step 3: Check for Port Security Problems

The next step examines the port security configuration and status on each switch. Starting with the **show port-security** command is particularly helpful because it lists the interfaces on which the feature has been enabled. Example 3-10 shows this command on SW1 and SW2, plus a few other commands. Note that both SW2 and SW3 do not have the port security feature enabled.

Examine the output in Example 3-10, and before reading beyond the end of the example, make a few notes about what next steps you would take to either rule out port security as a potential problem, or what command you would use to further isolate a potential problem.

Example 3-10 *Port Security on SW1 and SW2*

```
SW1#show port-security
Secure Port  MaxSecureAddr  CurrentAddr  SecurityViolation  Security Action
             (Count)        (Count)      (Count)
---------------------------------------------------------------------------
   Fa0/11          1             1            97             Restrict
---------------------------------------------------------------------------
Total Addresses in System (excluding one mac per port)   : 0
```

continues

Example 3-10 *Port Security on SW1 and SW2 (Continued)*

```
Max Addresses limit in System (excluding one mac per port) : 8320
! On SW2 below, no interfaces have port security enabled.
SW2#show port-security
Secure Port  MaxSecureAddr  CurrentAddr  SecurityViolation  Security Action
             (Count)        (Count)      (Count)
----------------------------------------------------------------------------
----------------------------------------------------------------------------
Total Addresses in System (excluding one mac per port)    : 0
Max Addresses limit in System (excluding one mac per port) : 8320
```

The **show port-security** commands in the example list the interfaces on which port security
has been enabled—specifically, SW1 interface Fa0/11 and no interfaces on SW2. On SW1,
the notable items for troubleshooting are that the security action heading, which matches
the violation mode setting, shows an action of restrict. With the restrict setting, SW1
interface Fa0/11 can be in the connect state (as seen in Example 3-8), but port security can
be discarding traffic that violates the port security configuration. So, a closer examination
of the port security configuration is in order, as shown in Example 3-11.

Example 3-11 *Port Security on SW1 and SW2*

```
SW1#show port-security interface fa0/11
Port Security              : Enabled
Port Status                : Secure-up
Violation Mode             : Restrict
Aging Time                 : 0 mins
Aging Type                 : Absolute
SecureStatic Address Aging : Disabled
Maximum MAC Addresses      : 1
Total MAC Addresses        : 1
Configured MAC Addresses   : 1
Sticky MAC Addresses       : 0
Last Source Address:Vlan   : 0200.1111.1111:3
Security Violation Count   : 97
!
! Next, the configuration shows that the configured MAC address does not
! match PC1's MAC address.
SW1#show running-config interface fa0/11

interface FastEthernet0/11
 switchport access vlan 3
 switchport mode access
 switchport port-security
 switchport port-security violation restrict
```

Example 3-11 *Port Security on SW1 and SW2 (Continued)*

```
 switchport port-security mac-address 0200.3333.3333
 !
 ! The following log message also points to a port security issue.
 01:46:58: %PORT_SECURITY-2-PSECURE_VIOLATION: Security violation occurred, caused by MAC
 address 0200.1111.1111 on port FastEthernet0/11.
```

The example begins by confirming the security mode and violation counter, as well as showing the last MAC address (0200.1111.1111) to send a frame into interface Fa0/11. PC1's MAC address (0200.1111.1111) does not match the port security configuration as seen in the second part of the example, a configuration that defaults to a maximum of one MAC address with an explicitly configured MAC address of 0200.3333.3333. A simple solution is to reconfigure port security to instead list PC1's MAC address. Note that the engineer would not need to use the **shutdown** and then the **no shutdown** commands on this interface to recover the interface, because the configuration uses violation mode restrict, which leaves the interface up while discarding the traffic to/from PC1.

Finally, the end of the example shows a log message generated by the switch for each violation when using restrict mode. This message would be seen from the console, or from a Telnet or Secure Shell (SSH) connection to the switch, if the remote user had issued the **terminal monitor** EXEC command.

Step 4: Check for VLAN and VLAN Trunk Problems

Step 4A begins by examining the access interfaces to ensure that the interfaces have been assigned to the correct VLANs. In this case, all interfaces connected to PCs and routers in Figure 3-5 should be assigned to VLAN 3. Example 3-12 provides some useful **show** command output. Take a few moments to read through the example, and look for any VLAN assignment problems.

Example 3-12 *Checking Access Interface VLAN Assignments*

```
SW1#show interfaces fa0/11 status

Port      Name            Status       Vlan     Duplex  Speed Type
Fa0/11                    connected    3        a-full  a-100 10/100BaseTX
SW1#show interfaces fa0/12 status

Port      Name            Status       Vlan     Duplex  Speed Type
Fa0/12                    notconnect   3         auto    auto 10/100BaseTX
! SW2 next
SW2#show interfaces status
! lines omitted for brevity
Fa0/9                     connected    1        a-full  a-100 10/100BaseTX
Fa0/10                    notconnect   3         auto    auto 10/100BaseTX
```

continues

Example 3-12 *Checking Access Interface VLAN Assignments (Continued)*

```
! SW3 next
SW3#show interfaces fa0/13 status

Port      Name            Status       Vlan     Duplex  Speed Type
Fa0/13                    connected    3        full  a-100 10/100BaseTX
```

The only problem in this case is the fact that while SW2's Fa0/10 interface was assigned to VLAN 3, per the drawing in Figure 3-5, SW2 connects to R1 using Fa0/9 (as seen with CDP in Example 3-7). Interface Fa0/9 defaults to be in VLAN 1. To solve this particular problem, on SW2, configure the **switchport access vlan 3** interface subcommand on interface Fa0/9.

The next part of Step 4 (Step 4B) suggests to check the VLANs to ensure that the VLANs are active on each switch. This ongoing example only uses VLAN 3, so Example 3-13 shows that VLAN 3 indeed is known on each switch. When reading the example, look for any problems with VLAN 3.

Example 3-13 *Finding a Half-Duplex Problem*

```
SW1#show vlan id 3

VLAN Name                          Status    Ports
---- ----------------------------- --------- ------------------------------
3    book-vlan3                    active    Fa0/11, Fa0/12, Gi0/1, Gi0/2
! lines omitted for brevity
! SW2 next
SW2#show vlan brief

VLAN Name                          Status    Ports
---- ----------------------------- --------- ------------------------------
1    default                       active    Fa0/1, Fa0/2, Fa0/3, Fa0/4
                                             Fa0/5, Fa0/6, Fa0/7, Fa0/8
                                             Fa0/11, Fa0/12, Fa0/13, Fa0/14
                                             Fa0/15, Fa0/16, Fa0/17, Fa0/18
                                             Fa0/19, Fa0/20, Fa0/21, Fa0/22
                                             Fa0/23, Fa0/24
3    VLAN0003                      active    Fa0/9, Fa0/10
! lines omitted for brevity
! SW3 next
SW3#show vlan brief

VLAN Name                          Status    Ports
---- ----------------------------- --------- ------------------------------
1    default                       active    Fa0/1, Fa0/2, Fa0/3, Fa0/4
                                             Fa0/5, Fa0/6, Fa0/7, Fa0/8
                                             Fa0/9, Fa0/10, Fa0/11, Fa0/12
```

Example 3-13 *Finding a Half-Duplex Problem (Continued)*

```
                                         Fa0/14, Fa0/15, Fa0/16, Fa0/17
                                         Fa0/18, Fa0/19, Fa0/20, Fa0/21
                                         Fa0/22, Fa0/23, Fa0/24
3    book-vlan3                 active   Fa0/13
! lines omitted for brevity
```

In this case, VLAN 3 exists and is active on all three switches. However, SW2 lists a different name than do the other two switches. The name is unimportant to the operation of the VLAN, so this difference does not matter. As it turns out, SW2 is using VTP transparent mode, with SW1 and SW3 as VTP client and server mode switches, respectively. So, the name of VLAN 3 (book-vlan3) matches on SW1 and SW3.

Finally, the last part of troubleshooting Step 4 (Step 4C) suggests that you confirm the trunking status of all expected trunk interfaces. It is also helpful to determine on which trunks the VLANs will be forwarded. Example 3-14 lists output that helps supply the answers. Examine the output in the example, and before reading past the end of the example, list any trunks that do not currently forward traffic in VLAN 3, and make a list of possible reasons why VLAN 3 is omitted from the trunk.

Example 3-14 *Verifying Trunking and VLAN 3*

```
SW1#show interfaces trunk

Port       Mode         Encapsulation  Status       Native vlan
Gi0/1      desirable    802.1q         trunking     1
Gi0/2      desirable    802.1q         trunking     1


Port       Vlans allowed on trunk
Gi0/1      1-4094
Gi0/2      1-4094


Port       Vlans allowed and active in management domain
Gi0/1      1,3
Gi0/2      1,3


Port       Vlans in spanning tree forwarding state and not pruned
Gi0/1      3
Gi0/2      1,3
! SW2 next
SW2#show interfaces trunk

Port       Mode         Encapsulation  Status       Native vlan
Gi0/1      auto         802.1q         trunking     1
Gi0/2      auto         802.1q         trunking     1
```

continues

Example 3-14   *Verifying Trunking and VLAN 3 (Continued)*

```
Port          Vlans allowed on trunk
Gi0/1         1-4094
Gi0/2         1-4094


Port          Vlans allowed and active in management domain
Gi0/1         1,3
Gi0/2         1,3


Port          Vlans in spanning tree forwarding state and not pruned
Gi0/1         1,3
Gi0/2         1
! SW3 next
SW3#show interfaces trunk

Port          Mode         Encapsulation  Status       Native vlan
Gi0/1         auto         n-802.1q       trunking     1
Gi0/2         desirable    n-802.1q       trunking     1


Port          Vlans allowed on trunk
Gi0/1         1-4094
Gi0/2         1-4094


Port          Vlans allowed and active in management domain
Gi0/1         1,3
Gi0/2         1,3


Port          Vlans in spanning tree forwarding state and not pruned
Gi0/1         1,3
Gi0/2         1,3
```

By examining the end of the **show interfaces trunk** command on each switch, you can see
that of both trunk interfaces on each switch, only SW2's Gi0/2 interface is not currently
forwarding traffic in VLAN 3. Earlier in this chapter, the section "Identify Trunks and
VLANs Forwarded on Those Trunks" listed four reasons a VLAN would be excluded from
a trunk. However, three of the four reasons can be ruled out based on the output in the
commands in Example 3-14 and in a few other examples in this chapter. First, if VLAN 3
were excluded because it was not in the allowed VLAN list, or because VLAN 3 was not
active, VLAN 3 would be omitted from the first two lists of VLANs in SW2's **show
interfaces trunk** command. Also, VTP pruning can be ruled out because earlier examples
showed that all three switches have at least one interface in VLAN 3 and in a connect state,

so even if all three switches used VTP correctly, with VTP pruning enabled, VLAN 3 would not be pruned. So, VLAN 3 is omitted in this case because of STP.

After finding all the problems in this ongoing example, and fixing the problems, PC1, PC3, and R1 can all ping each other. PC2, with an unspecified cabling problem, still does not work.

Predicting Normal Operation of the LAN Switching Data Plane

One of the steps in troubleshooting is to analyze what should be happening so that you can then compare that to what is happening—and hopefully isolate the root cause of any problems. These last sections of Chapter 3 complete this chapter's examination of how LANs should work by examining two examples of frames forwarded through a working version of the same sample network used in the just-completed troubleshooting example. The goal of these sections is to explain how to interpret the current **show** command output on switches to predict where the switches would each forward a particular frame. The first example shows a broadcast sent by PC1 in Figure 3-5, and the second example shows the forwarding process for a unicast frame sent by R1 to PC1's MAC address.

PC1 Broadcast in VLAN 3

The first working data plane example examines the path of a broadcast sent by PC1. PC1 might not have R1's MAC address in PC1's ARP cache, so in that case, PC1 sends an ARP broadcast, with an IP destination address of 255.255.255.255 and an Ethernet destination address of FFFF.FFFF.FFFF. This section examines what the various switches do to forward the broadcast to all parts of VLAN 3, as shown in Figure 3-6.

Figure 3-6 *Forwarding Path from PC1 to R1 per Example 3-14*

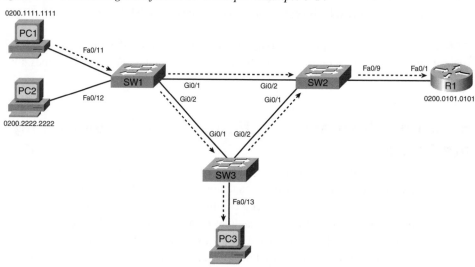

To analyze the flow of the broadcast, refer to the generic forwarding process, as summarized in the section "An Overview of the Normal LAN Switching Forwarding Process," earlier in this chapter. Earlier examples confirmed that SW1 port Fa0/11 is assigned to VLAN 3 and that SW1's Fa0/11 interface is an access interface. Because the frame is a broadcast, SW1 will flood the frame. Knowing these facts, Example 3-15 lists enough information to predict the interfaces out which SW1 will forward the broadcast frame sent by PC1 by listing the output of the **show spanning-tree vlan 3 active** command.

Example 3-15 *SW1's List of Active Interfaces*

```
SW1#show spanning-tree vlan 3 active

VLAN0003
  Spanning tree enabled protocol ieee
  Root ID    Priority    24579
             Address     000a.b7dc.b780
             Cost        1
             Port        26 (GigabitEthernet0/2)
             Hello Time   2 sec  Max Age 20 sec  Forward Delay 15 sec

  Bridge ID  Priority    32771  (priority 32768 sys-id-ext 3)
             Address     0019.e86a.6f80
             Hello Time   2 sec  Max Age 20 sec  Forward Delay 15 sec
             Aging Time 300

Interface        Role Sts Cost      Prio.Nbr Type
```

Example 3-15 *SW1's List of Active Interfaces (Continued)*

```
----------------  ---- ---  ---------  --------  -----------------------------
Fa0/11         Desg FWD 19        128.11   P2p
Gi0/1          Desg FWD 4         128.25   P2p
Gi0/2          Root FWD 1         128.26   P2p
```

Note that SW1 will not forward the frame back out Fa0/11, as the frame came in on Fa0/11. Also, SW1 will forward the frame out both trunk interfaces (Gi0/1 and Gi0/2). Also, earlier in this chapter, Example 3-14 shows evidence that both SW1's trunks use 802.1Q, with native VLAN 1, so SW1 will add an 802.1Q header, with VLAN ID 3, to each copy of the broadcast frame sent over those two trunks.

SW1's actions mean that both SW2 and SW3 should receive a copy of the broadcast frame sent by PC1. In SW2's case, SW2 happens to discard its copy of PC1's broadcast frame received on SW2's Gi0/2 interface. SW2 discards the frame because of Step 3 of the generic forwarding process from earlier in this chapter, because SW2's incoming interface (Gi0/2) is in a Blocking State in VLAN 3. (Example 3-14 and the text following that example showed SW2's Gi0/2 interface in a Blocking State for VLAN 3.) Note that SW2's Blocking State did not prevent SW1 from sending the frame to SW2; instead, SW2 silently discards the received frame.

For the copy of PC1's broadcast frame received by SW3 on its Gi0/1 interface, SW3 floods the frame. SW3 determines the frame's VLAN based on the incoming 802.1Q header and finds the incoming interface in an STP Forwarding State. Based on these facts, SW3 will forward the frame inside VLAN 3. Example 3-16 shows the information that's needed to know on which interfaces SW3 forwards the VLAN 3 broadcast.

Example 3-16 *SW3: Forwarding a Broadcast in VLAN 3*

```
SW3#show mac address-table dynamic vlan 3
          Mac Address Table
-------------------------------------------

Vlan    Mac Address       Type       Ports
----    -----------       --------   -----
   3    0200.0101.0101    DYNAMIC    Gi0/2
   3    0200.1111.1111    DYNAMIC    Gi0/1
   3    0200.3333.3333    DYNAMIC    Fa0/13
Total Mac Addresses for this criterion: 3

SW3#show spanning-tree vlan 3 active

VLAN0003
```

continues

Example 3-16 *SW3: Forwarding a Broadcast in VLAN 3 (Continued)*

```
 Spanning tree enabled protocol ieee
 Root ID    Priority    24579
            Address     000a.b7dc.b780
            This bridge is the root
            Hello Time   2 sec  Max Age 20 sec  Forward Delay 15 sec

 Bridge ID  Priority    24579  (priority 24576 sys-id-ext 3)
            Address     000a.b7dc.b780
            Hello Time   2 sec  Max Age 20 sec  Forward Delay 15 sec
            Aging Time 300

Interface        Role Sts Cost      Prio.Nbr Type
---------------- ---- --- --------- -------- --------------------------------
Fa0/13           Desg FWD 19        128.13   P2p
Gi0/1            Desg FWD 4         128.25   P2p
Gi0/2            Desg FWD 4         128.26   P2p
```

As with SW1, SW3 does not forward the broadcast out the same interface in which the frame arrived (Gi0/1 in this case), but SW3 does flood the frame out all other interfaces in that VLAN and in an STP Forwarding State, namely Fa0/13 and Gi0/2. Also, because SW3's Gi0/2 interface currently uses 802.1Q trunking, with native VLAN 1, SW3 adds an 802.1Q header with VLAN ID 3 listed.

Finally, when SW2 receives the copy of the broadcast in SW2's Gi0/1 interface from SW3, SW2 follows the same generic process as the other switches. SW2 identifies the VLAN based on the incoming 802.1Q header, confirms that the incoming interface is in a Forwarding State, and floods the broadcast out all its interfaces that are both in a Forwarding State and in VLAN 3. In this case, SW2 forwards the frame only out interface Fa0/9, connected to router R1. Example 3-17 shows the supporting command output.

Example 3-17 *SW2: Forwarding a Broadcast in VLAN 3 Received from SW3*

```
! First, note that the broadcast address FFFF.FFFF.FFFF is not
! in the VLAN 3 MAC table.
SW2#show mac address-table dynamic vlan 3
          Mac Address Table
-------------------------------------------

Vlan    Mac Address       Type        Ports
----    -----------       --------    -----
   3    000a.b7dc.b79a    DYNAMIC     Gi0/1
   3    0200.0101.0101    DYNAMIC     Fa0/9
   3    0200.1111.1111    DYNAMIC     Gi0/1
   3    0200.3333.3333    DYNAMIC     Gi0/1
```

Example 3-17 *SW2: Forwarding a Broadcast in VLAN 3 Received from SW3 (Continued)*

```
Total Mac Addresses for this criterion: 4
! Next, note that on Fa0/9 and Gi0/1 are in an STP forwarding state,
! and the broadcast came in Gi0/1 - so SW2 floods the frame only out Fa0/9.
SW2#show spanning-tree vlan 3 active
!lines omitted for brevity

Interface        Role Sts Cost      Prio.Nbr Type
---------------- ---- --- --------- -------- --------------------------------
Fa0/9            Desg FWD 19        128.9    P2p
Gi0/1            Root FWD 4         128.25   P2p
Gi0/2            Altn BLK 4         128.26   P2p
```

SW2 does not forward the frame out Gi0/1, because the frame entered SW2's Gi0/1
interface.

Forwarding Path: Unicast from R1 to PC1

The second data plane example examines how switches forward unicast frames. To analyze
the forwarding process for unicast frames, consider R1's ARP reply in response to PC1's
ARP request/broadcast. The destination addresses (both IP and MAC) of R1's ARP reply
are PC1's IP and MAC addresses, respectively. Figure 3-7 shows the forwarding path, with
the examples that follow spelling out how the generic frame-forwarding process applies to
this particular case.

Figure 3-7 *Forwarding Path from R1 to PC1 per Example 3-15*

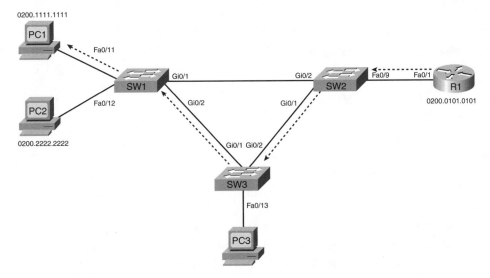

When SW2 receives the frame from R1, SW2 notes that the frame entered interface Fa0/9, an access interface in VLAN 3. The end of Example 3-17 previously showed Fa0/9 in an STP Forwarding State in VLAN 3, so SW2 will attempt to forward the frame instead of discarding the frame. As seen next in Example 3-18, SW2's MAC address table lists PC1's MAC address—0200.1111.1111—off interface Gi0/1 and in VLAN 3, so SW2 forwards the frame out Gi0/1 to SW3.

Example 3-18 *SW2's Logic When Forwarding a Known Unicast to PC1*

```
SW2#show mac address-table dynamic vlan 3
          Mac Address Table
-------------------------------------------

Vlan    Mac Address       Type        Ports
----    -----------       --------    -----
   3    000a.b7dc.b79a    DYNAMIC     Gi0/1
   3    0200.0101.0101    DYNAMIC     Fa0/9
   3    0200.1111.1111    DYNAMIC     Gi0/1
Total Mac Addresses for this criterion: 3
```

When SW3 receives the frame from SW2, SW3 notes that the frame entered interface Gi0/2, a trunking interface, and that the trunking header listed VLAN ID 3. The end of Example 3-16 previously showed Gi0/2 in an STP Forwarding State in VLAN 3 (forwarding Step 3), so SW3 will not discard the received frame because of STP. As seen next in Example 3-19, SW3's MAC address table lists PC1's MAC address— 0200.1111.1111—off interface Gi0/1 and in VLAN 3, so SW3 forwards the frame out Gi0/1 to SW1.

Example 3-19 *SW3's Logic When Forwarding a Known Unicast to PC1*

```
SW3#show mac address-table dynamic vlan 3
          Mac Address Table
-------------------------------------------

Vlan    Mac Address       Type        Ports
----    -----------       --------    -----
   3    0200.0101.0101    DYNAMIC     Gi0/2
   3    0200.1111.1111    DYNAMIC     Gi0/1
   3    0200.3333.3333    DYNAMIC     Fa0/13
Total Mac Addresses for this criterion: 3
```

When SW1 receives the frame from SW3, SW1 notes that the frame entered interface Gi0/2, a trunking interface, and that the trunking header listed VLAN ID 3. The end of Example 3-15 previously showed SW1's Gi0/2 in an STP Forwarding State in VLAN 3, so SW1 will not discard the frame because of the interface not being in an STP Forwarding

State. As seen next in Example 3-20, SW1's MAC address table lists PC1's MAC address—0200.1111.1111—off interface Fa0/11 and VLAN 3, so SW1 forwards the frame out Fa0/11 to PC1. In this case, SW1 strips off the 802.1Q VLAN header, because interface Fa0/11 is an access interface.

Example 3-20   *SW1's Logic When Forwarding a Known Unicast to PC1*

```
SW1#show mac address-table dynamic vlan 3
          Mac Address Table
-------------------------------------------

Vlan    Mac Address       Type        Ports
----    -----------       --------    -----
   3    000a.b7dc.b799    DYNAMIC     Gi0/2
   3    0200.0101.0101    DYNAMIC     Gi0/2
   3    0200.3333.3333    DYNAMIC     Gi0/2
Total Mac Addresses for this criterion: 3
SW1#show mac address-table vlan 3
          Mac Address Table
-------------------------------------------

Vlan    Mac Address       Type        Ports
----    -----------       --------    -----
 All    0100.0ccc.cccc    STATIC      CPU
 All    0100.0ccc.cccd    STATIC      CPU
 All    0180.c200.0000    STATIC      CPU
 All    0180.c200.0001    STATIC      CPU
 All    0180.c200.0002    STATIC      CPU
 All    0180.c200.0003    STATIC      CPU
 All    0180.c200.0004    STATIC      CPU
 All    0180.c200.0005    STATIC      CPU
 All    0180.c200.0006    STATIC      CPU
 All    0180.c200.0007    STATIC      CPU
 All    0180.c200.0008    STATIC      CPU
 All    0180.c200.0009    STATIC      CPU
 All    0180.c200.000a    STATIC      CPU
 All    0180.c200.000b    STATIC      CPU
 All    0180.c200.000c    STATIC      CPU
 All    0180.c200.000d    STATIC      CPU
 All    0180.c200.000e    STATIC      CPU
 All    0180.c200.000f    STATIC      CPU
 All    0180.c200.0010    STATIC      CPU
 All    ffff.ffff.ffff    STATIC      CPU
   3    000a.b7dc.b799    DYNAMIC     Gi0/2
   3    0200.0101.0101    DYNAMIC     Gi0/2
   3    0200.1111.1111    STATIC      Fa0/11
Total Mac Addresses for this criterion: 23
```

This last step points out an important fact about the MAC address table and port security. Note that the **show mac address-table dynamic** command on SW1 does not list PC1's MAC address of 0200.1111.1111, so you might have been tempted to think that SW1 will flood the frame because it is an unknown unicast frame. However, because SW1 has configured port security on Fa0/11, including the **switchport port-security mac-address 0200.1111.1111** interface subcommand, IOS considers this MAC address a static MAC address. So, by leaving off the **dynamic** keyword, the **show mac address-table vlan 3** command lists all MAC addresses known in the VLAN, including 0200.1111.1111. This command output confirms that SW1 will forward the unicast to 0200.1111.1111 only out interface Fa0/11.

Exam Preparation Tasks

Review All the Key Topics

Review the most important topics from this chapter, noted with the Key Topics icon in the outer margin of the page. Table 3-6 lists a reference of these key topics and the page numbers on which each is found.

Key Topic

Table 3-6   *Key Topics for Chapter 3*

Key Topic Element	Description	Page Number
Table 3-2	Lists both sets of interface status codes and typical root causes for each state	122-123
Figure 3-4	Typical uses of Ethernet straight-through and crossover cables	123
Table 3-3	Lists devices and the pins on which they transmit for 10BASE-T and 100BASE-Tx	124
List	Suggestions for noticing duplex mismatch problems	127
List	Default IEEE autonegotiation duplex choices based on current speed	127
List	Port security features	128
Table 3-4	Port security violation modes with differences in behavior and **show** commands	129
Table 3-5	Lists **show** commands useful for finding access interfaces and their assigned VLANs	132-133
List	The four reasons a switch does not pass a VLAN's traffic over a particular trunk	134-135
List	Lists the troubleshooting steps explained in this chapter (does not need to be memorized)	136

Complete the Tables and Lists from Memory

Print a copy of Appendix J, "Memory Tables," (found on the CD) or at least the section for this chapter, and complete the tables and lists from memory. Appendix K, "Memory Tables Answer Key," also on the CD, includes completed tables and lists to check your work.

Cisco Published ICND2 Exam Topics*
Covered in This Part

Configure, verify and troubleshoot a switch with VLANs and interswitch communications

- Configure, verify, and troubleshoot interVLAN routing

Implement an IP addressing scheme and IP Services to meet network requirements in a medium-size Enterprise branch office network

- Calculate and apply a VLSM IP addressing design to a network

- Determine the appropriate classless addressing scheme using VLSM and summarization to satisfy addressing requirements in a LAN/WAN environment

- Identify and correct common problems associated with IP addressing and host configurations

Configure and troubleshoot basic operation and routing on Cisco devices

- Verify configuration and connectivity using ping, traceroute, and telnet or SSH

- Troubleshoot routing implementation issues

- Verify router hardware and software operation using SHOW & DEBUG commands

- Implement basic router security

Implement, verify, and troubleshoot NAT and ACLs in a medium-size Enterprise branch office network.

- Describe the purpose and types of access control lists

- Configure and apply access control lists based on network filtering requirements

- Configure and apply an access control list to limit telnet and SSH access to the router

- Verify and monitor ACL's in a network environment

- Troubleshoot ACL implementation issues

* Always recheck http://www.cisco.com for the latest posted exam topics.

Part II: IP Routing

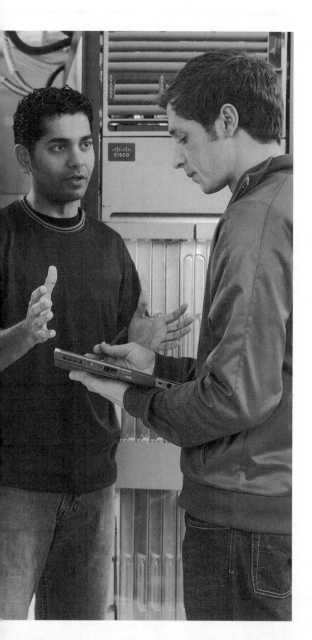

This chapter covers the following subjects:

IP Routing and Addressing: This section reviews the relationship between IP addressing and IP routing, and fills in more of the detail of how routing works with multiple overlapping routes.

Routes to Directly Connected Subnets: This section examines how routers add routes for subnets connected to a router's interfaces.

Static Routes: This section describes how to configure static routes, including static default routes.

CHAPTER **4**

IP Routing: Static and Connected Routes

This chapter begins Part II, "IP Routing." The four chapters in this part focus on features that impact the IP routing process—also called IP forwarding—by which hosts and routers deliver packets from the source host to the destination host. These four chapters also occasionally explain topics related to IP routing protocols, in part because IP routing, a data plane feature, relies heavily on the control plane work done by routing protocols.

This chapter covers several topics related to connected routes, which are routes to reach subnet attached to a router interface. This chapter also explains static routes, including default routes, as well as reviews the basic codependent topics of IP addressing and IP routing.

"Do I Know This Already?" Quiz

The "Do I Know This Already?" quiz allows you to assess whether you should read the entire chapter. If you miss no more than one of these eight self-assessment questions, you might want to move ahead to the section "Exam Preparation Tasks." Table 4-1 lists the major headings in this chapter and the "Do I Know This Already?" quiz questions covering the material in those headings so that you can assess your knowledge of these specific areas. The answers to the "Do I Know This Already?" quiz appear in Appendix A.

Table 4-1 *"Do I Know This Already?" Foundation Topics Section-to-Question Mapping*

Foundation Topics Section	Questions
IP Routing and Addressing	1–2
Routes to Directly Connected Subnets	3–4
Static Routes	5–8

1. A PC user turns on her computer, and as soon as the computer is up and working, she opens a web browser to browse http://www.ciscopress.com. Which protocol(s) would definitely not be used by the PC during this process?

    a. DHCP

    b. DNS

    c. ARP

    d. ICMP

2. A PC user turns on her computer, and as soon as the computer is up and working, she opens a command prompt. From there, she issues the **ping 2.2.2.2** command, and the ping shows 100 percent success. The PC's IP address is 1.1.1.1 with mask 255.255.255.0. Which of the following settings would be required on the PC to support the successful ping?

    a. The IP address of a DNS server

    b. The IP address of a default gateway

    c. The IP address of an ARP server

    d. The IP address of a DHCP server

3. Router 1 has a Fast Ethernet interface 0/0 with IP address 10.1.1.1. The interface is connected to a switch. This connection is then migrated to use 802.1Q trunking. Which of the following commands could be part of a valid configuration for Router 1's Fa0/0 interface?

    a. **interface fastethernet 0/0.4**

    b. **dot1q enable**

    c. **dot1q enable 4**

    d. **trunking enable**

    e. **trunking enable 4**

    f. **encapsulation dot1q**

4. A router is configured with the **no ip subnet-zero** global configuration command. Which of the following interface subcommands would not be accepted by this router?

    a. **ip address 10.1.1.1 255.255.255.0**

    b. **ip address 10.0.0.129 255.255.255.128**

    c. **ip address 10.1.2.2 255.254.0.0**

    d. **ip address 10.0.0.5 255.255.255.252**

5. Which of the following must be true before IOS lists a route as "S" in the output of a **show ip route** command?

    a. The IP address must be configured on an interface.

    b. The router must receive a routing update from a neighboring router.

    c. The **ip route** command must be added to the configuration.

    d. The **ip address** command must use the **special** keyword.

    e. The interface must be up and up.

6. Which of the following commands correctly configures a static route?

    a. **ip route 10.1.3.0 255.255.255.0 10.1.130.253**

    b. **ip route 10.1.3.0 serial 0**

    c. **ip route 10.1.3.0 /24 10.1.130.253**

    d. **ip route 10.1.3.0 /24 serial 0**

7. Which of the following is affected by whether a router is performing classful or classless routing?

    a. When to use a default route

    b. When to use masks in routing updates

    c. When to convert a packet's destination IP address to a network number

    d. When to perform queuing based on the classification of a packet into a particular queue

8. A router has been configured with the **ip classless** global configuration command. The router receives a packet destined to IP address 168.13.4.1. The following text lists the contents of the router's routing table. Which of the following is true about how this router forwards the packet?

    ```
    Gateway of last resort is 168.13.1.101 to network 0.0.0.0

         168.13.0.0/24 is subnetted, 2 subnets
    C       168.13.1.0 is directly connected,  FastEthernet0/0
    R       168.13.3.0 [120/1] via 168.13.100.3, 00:00:05, Serial0.1
    ```

    a. It is forwarded to 168.13.100.3.

    b. It is forwarded to 168.13.1.101.

    c. It is forwarded out interface Fa0/0, directly to the destination host.

    d. The router discards the packet.

Foundation Topics

This chapter introduces several straightforward concepts regarding how a router adds routes to its routing table without using a dynamic routing protocol. In particular, this chapter covers connected routes, including connected routes when a router uses LAN trunking. It also covers static routes, with some emphasis on how routers use special static routes called default routes. However, because this chapter is the first IP-centric chapter of this book, it begins with a brief review of two related topics: IP routing and IP addressing.

> **NOTE** The introduction to this book describes an alternate reading plan for readers pursuing the CCNA 640-802 exam, which you move back and forth between *CCENT/ CCNA ICND1 Official Exam Certification Guide* and this book. If you are using this plan, note that the first major section reviews topics from the ICND1 book. If you are following that reading plan, feel free to skip ahead to the section "IP Forwarding by Matching the Most Specific Route."

IP Routing and Addressing

IP routing depends on the rules of IP addressing, with one of the original core design goals for IP addressing being the creation of efficient IP routing. IP routing defines how an IP packet can be delivered from the host at which the packet is created to the destination host. IP addressing conventions group addresses into consecutively numbered sets of addresses called subnets, which then aids the IP forwarding or IP routing process.

> **NOTE** This book uses the terms *IP routing* and *IP forwarding* as synonymous terms. The term *IP routing protocols* refers to routing protocols that routers use to dynamically fill the routing tables with the currently best routes. Note that some texts and courses use the term *IP routing* when referring to both the packet-forwarding process and the protocols used to learn routes.

IP Routing

Both hosts and routers participate in the IP routing process. The next list summarizes a host's logic when forwarding a packet, assuming that the host is on an Ethernet LAN or wireless LAN:

1. When sending a packet, compare the destination IP address of the packet to the sending host's perception of the range of addresses in the connected subnet, based on the host's IP address and subnet mask.

    a. If the destination is in the same subnet as the host, send the packet directly to the destination host. Address Resolution Protocol (ARP) is needed to find the destination host's MAC address.

b. If the destination is not in the same subnet as the host, send the packet directly to the host's default gateway (default router). ARP is needed to find the default gateway's MAC address.

Routers use the following general steps, noting that with routers, the packet must first be received, whereas the sending host (as previously summarized) begins with the IP packet in memory:

1. For each received frame, use the data-link trailer frame check sequence (FCS) field to ensure that the frame had no errors; if errors occurred, discard the frame (and do not continue to the next step).

Key
Topic

2. Check the frame's destination data link layer address, and process only if addressed to this router or to a broadcast/multicast address.

3. Discard the incoming frame's old data-link header and trailer, leaving the IP packet.

4. Compare the packet's destination IP address to the routing table, and find the route that matches the destination address. This route identifies the outgoing interface of the router, and possibly the next-hop router.

5. Determine the destination data-link address used for forwarding packets to the next router or destination host (as directed in the routing table).

6. Encapsulate the IP packet inside a new data-link header and trailer, appropriate for the outgoing interface, and forward the frame out that interface.

For example, consider Figure 4-1, which shows a simple network with two routers and three hosts. In this case, PC1 creates a packet to be sent to PC3's IP address, namely 172.16.3.3. The figure shows three major routing steps, labeled A, B, and C: PC1's host routing logic that forwards the packet toward R1, R1's routing logic that forwards the packet toward R2, and R2's routing logic that forwards the packet toward PC3.

First, consider Step A from Figure 4-1. PC1 knows its own IP address of 172.16.1.1, mask 255.255.255.0. (All interfaces use an easy mask of 255.255.255.0 in this example.) PC1 can calculate its subnet number (172.16.1.0/24) and range of addresses (172.16.1.1– 172.16.1.254). Destination address 172.16.3.3 is not in PC1's subnet, so PC1 uses Step 1B in the summary of host routing logic—namely, PC1 sends the packet, inside an Ethernet frame, to its default gateway IP address of 172.16.1.251.

Figure 4-1 *Example of the IP Routing Process*

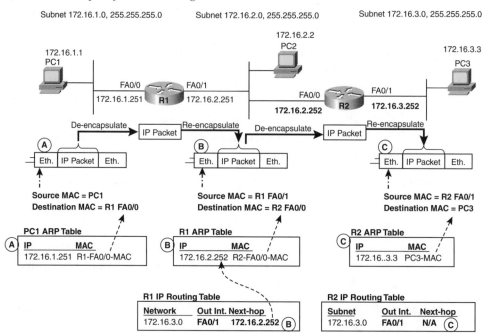

This first step (Step A) of PC1 sending the packet to its default gateway also reviews a couple of important concepts. As you can see from the lower part of the figure, PC1 uses its own MAC address as the source MAC address, but it uses R1's LAN MAC address as the destination MAC address. As a result, any LAN switches can deliver the frame correctly to R1's Fa0/0 interface. Also note that PC1 looked for and found 172.16.1.251's MAC address in PC1's ARP cache. If the MAC address had not been found, PC1 would have had to use ARP to dynamically discover the MAC address used by 172.16.1.251 (R1) before being able to send the frame shown in Figure 4-1.

Next focus on Step B from Figure 4-1, which is the work done by router R1 to forward the packet. Using the router's six summarized routing steps that preceded Figure 4-1, the following occurs at R1. Note that the figure denotes many of the details with letter *B*:

1. R1 checks the FCS, and the frame has no errors.

2. R1 finds its own Fa0/0 interface MAC address in the frame's destination MAC address field, so R1 should process the encapsulated packet.

3. R1 discards the old data-link header and trailer, leaving the IP packet (as shown directly under the R1 icon in Figure 4-1).

4. (In the bottom center of Figure 4-1) R1 compares the destination IP address (172.16.3.3) to R1's routing table, finding the matching route shown in the figure, with outgoing interface Fa0/1 and next-hop router 172.16.2.252.

5. R1 needs to find the next-hop device's MAC address (R2's MAC address), so R1 looks and finds that MAC address in its ARP table.

6. R1 encapsulates the IP packet in a new Ethernet frame, with R1's Fa0/1 MAC address as the source MAC address, and R2's Fa0/0 MAC address (per the ARP table) as the destination MAC address. R1 sends the frame.

While the steps might seem laborious, you can think of briefer versions of this logic in cases where a question does not require this level of depth. For example, when troubleshooting routing problems, focusing on Step 4—the matching of the packet's destination IP address to a router's routing table—is probably one of the most important steps. So, a briefer summary of the routing process might be: Router receives a packet, matches the packet's destination address with the routing table, and forwards the packet based on that matched route. While this abbreviated version ignores some details, it can make for quicker work when troubleshooting problems or discussing routing issues.

To complete the example, consider the same six-step router forwarding logic as applied on router R2, listed with letter C in Figure 4-1, as follows:

1. R2 checks the FCS, and the frame has no errors.

2. R2 finds its own Fa0/0 interface MAC address in the frame's destination MAC address field, so R2 should process the encapsulated packet.

3. R2 discards the old data-link header and trailer, leaving the IP packet (as shown directly under the R2 icon in Figure 4-1).

4. (In the bottom right of Figure 4-1) R2 compares the destination IP address (172.16.3.3) to R2's routing table, finding the matching route shown in the figure, with outgoing interface Fa0/1 and no next-hop router listed.

5. Because no next-hop router exists, R2 needs to find the true destination host's MAC address (PC3's MAC address), so R2 looks and finds that MAC address in its ARP table.

6. R2 encapsulates the IP packet in a new Ethernet frame, with R2's Fa0/1 MAC address as the source MAC address, and PC3's MAC address (per the ARP table) as the destination MAC address. R1 sends the frame.

Finally, when this frame arrives at PC3, PC3 sees its own MAC address listed as the destination MAC address, so PC3 begins to process the frame.

The same general process works with WAN links as well, with a few different details. On point-to-point links, as shown in Figure 4-2, an ARP table is not needed. Because a point-to-point link can have at most one other router connected to it, you can ignore the data-link addressing. However, with Frame Relay, the routing process does consider the data-link addresses, called data-link connection identifiers (DLCI). The routing details regarding Frame Relay DLCIs are covered later in this book in Chapter 13.

Figure 4-2   *Example of the IP Routing Process*

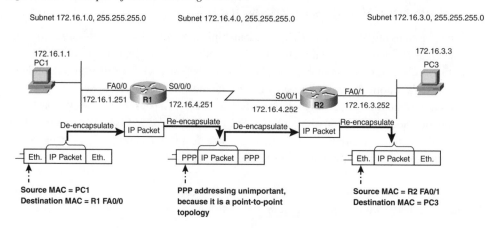

The IP routing process on both the hosts and the routers relies on these devices' abilities to understand IP addressing and predict which IP addresses are in each group or subnet. The next section provides a brief review of IP addresses and subnetting.

IP Addressing and Subnetting

IP addressing rules aid the IP routing processes by requiring that IP addresses be organized into groups of consecutively numbered IP addresses called subnets. To allow a concise way to refer to a subnet, IP addressing defines the concept of a subnet number and subnet mask, which together exactly identify the range of addresses in a subnet. For example, the routers in Figures 4-1 and 4-2 used routes that listed subnet number 172.16.3.0 when forwarding the packet destined for PC3 (172.16.3.3). The figures omitted the subnet mask to reduce clutter, but any device can look at subnet number 172.16.3.0, with mask 255.255.255.0, and know that these two numbers concisely represent the following subnet:

■   Subnet number 172.16.3.0

■   Range of usable addresses in the subnet: 172.16.3.1–172.16.3.254

■   Subnet broadcast address (not usable for individual hosts): 172.16.3.255

The following list provides a brief review of some of the major IP addressing concepts. Note that this chapter solely focuses on IP version 4 (IPv4) addresses, with Chapter 17, "IP Version 6," covering IPv6.

■ Unicast IP addresses are IP addresses that can be assigned to an individual interface for sending and receiving packets.

■ Each unicast IP address resides in a particular Class A, B, or C network, called a classful IP network.

■ If subnetting is used, which is almost always true in real life, each unicast IP address also resides in a specific subset of the classful network called a subnet.

■ The subnet mask, written in either dotted decimal form (for example, 255.255.255.0) or prefix notation form (for example, /24), identifies the structure of unicast IP addresses and allows devices and people to derive the subnet number, range of addresses, and broadcast address for a subnet.

■ Devices in the same subnet should all use the same subnet mask; otherwise, they have different opinions about the range of addresses in the subnet, which can break the IP routing process.

■ Devices in a single VLAN should be in the same single IP subnet.

■ Devices in different VLANs should be in different IP subnets.

■ To forward packets between subnets, a device that performs routing must be used. In this book, only routers are shown, but multilayer switches—switches that also perform routing functions—can also be used.

■ Point-to-point serial links use a different subnet than the LAN subnets, but these subnets only require two IP addresses, one for each router interface on either end of the link.

■ Hosts separated by a router must be in separate subnets.

Figure 4-3 shows an example internetwork that exhibits many of these features. Switch SW1 defaults to put all interfaces into VLAN 1, so all hosts on the left (PC1 included) are in a single subnet. Note that SW1's management IP address, also in VLAN 1, will be from that same subnet. Similarly, SW2 defaults to put all ports in VLAN 1, requiring a second subnet. The point-to-point link requires a third subnet. The figure shows the subnet numbers, masks, and range of addresses. Note that all addresses and subnets are part of the same single classful Class B network 172.16.0.0, and all subnets use a mask of 255.255.255.0.

Figure 4-3   *Example IP Addressing Design*

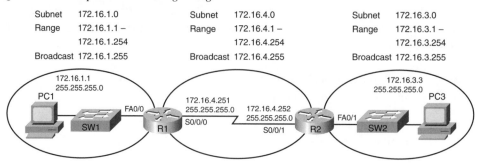

Subnet	172.16.1.0		Subnet	172.16.4.0		Subnet	172.16.3.0
Range	172.16.1.1 –		Range	172.16.4.1 –		Range	172.16.3.1 –
	172.16.1.254			172.16.4.254			172.16.3.254
Broadcast	172.16.1.255		Broadcast	172.16.4.255		Broadcast	172.16.3.255

Figure 4-3 lists the subnet numbers, ranges of addresses, and subnet broadcast addresses. However, each device in the figure can find the same information just based on its respective IP address and subnet mask configuration, deriving the subnet number, range of addresses, and broadcast address for each attached subnet.

The CCNA exams require mastery of these IP addressing and subnetting concepts, but more significantly, the exams require mastery of the math used to analyze existing IP networks and design new IP networks. If you have not already taken the time to master subnetting, it would be useful to study and practice before going further in your reading. While this section reviewed the basics of IP addressing, it does not cover subnetting math.

To learn about subnetting and the related math, you have a couple of options. For those of you who bought the two-book library that includes this book as well as *CCENT/CCNA ICND1 Official Exam Certification Guide*, dig into Chapter 12 of that book and do the practice problems listed. For those of you that bought this without the ICND1 book, all the resources for learning subnetting in the ICND1 book have been included on this book's CD. Refer to the following elements:

■   CD-only Appendix D, "Subnetting Practice"

■   CD-only Appendix E, "Subnetting Reference Pages"

■   CD-only Appendix H, "ICND1 Chapter 12: IP Addressing and Subnetting"

■   Subnetting videos

To be prepared to read the rest of this book without letting the subnetting math cause any difficulties, before reading any further in this book, you should be able to do the tasks in the following list, given plenty of time. You do not have to be able to find the answer quickly at this point in your preparation, but to be prepared for the exams, you need to be ready to do these tasks within the listed time limits:

■   Given a dotted decimal mask, convert it to prefix notation, or vice versa. (Suggested time for exam readiness: 5 seconds)

■ Given an IP address and mask, find the subnet number, range of addresses, and subnet broadcast address. (Suggested time: 15 seconds)

■ Given a subnet mask and class (A, B, or C) of a network, determine the number of subnets and hosts per subnet. (Suggested time: 15 seconds)

■ Given a class of network (A, B, or C) and design requirements for a number of subnets and number of hosts per subnet, find all masks that meet the requirements, and choose the mask that either maximizes the number of subnets or the number of hosts per subnet. (Suggested time: 30 seconds)

■ Given a classful network and a single subnet mask to use for all subnets, list the subnet numbers, and identify the zero subnet and broadcast subnet. (Suggested time: 30 seconds)

With these details of subnetting in mind, the next section examines how a router matches the routing table when the subnets listed in the routing table overlap so that one packet's destination matches more than one route.

IP Forwarding by Matching the Most Specific Route

Any router's IP routing process requires that the router compare the destination IP address of each packet with the existing contents of that router's IP routing table. Often, only one route matches a particular destination address. However, in some cases, a particular destination address matches more than one of the router's routes. Some legitimate and normal reasons for the overlapping routes in a routing table include the following:

■ The use of autosummary

■ Manual route summarization

■ The use of static routes

■ Incorrectly designed subnetting so that subnets overlap their address ranges

Chapter 5, "VLSM and Route Summarization," explains more detail about each of these reasons. While some cases of overlapping routes are problems, other cases are normal operation resulting from some other feature. This section focuses on how a router chooses which of the overlapping routes to use, with the features that cause the overlap being covered in Chapter 5.

The following statement summarizes a router's forwarding logic with overlapping routes:

When a particular destination IP address matches more than one route in a router's routing table, the router uses the most specific route—in other words, the route with the longest prefix length.

To see exactly what that means, the routing table listed in Example 4-1 shows a series of overlapping routes. First, before reading any text beneath the example, try to predict which route would be used for packets sent to the following IP addresses: 172.16.1.1, 172.16.1.2, 172.16.2.3, and 172.16.4.3.

Example 4-1   show ip route *Command with Overlapping Routes*

```
R1#show ip route rip


     172.16.0.0/16 is variably subnetted, 5 subnets, 4 masks
R       172.16.1.1/32 [120/1] via 172.16.25.2, 00:00:04, Serial0/1/1
R       172.16.1.0/24 [120/2] via 172.16.25.129, 00:00:09, Serial0/1/0
R       172.16.0.0/22 [120/1] via 172.16.25.2, 00:00:04, Serial0/1/1
R       172.16.0.0/16 [120/2] via 172.16.25.129, 00:00:09, Serial0/1/0
R       0.0.0.0/0 [120/3] via 172.16.25.129, 00:00:09, Serial0/1/0
R1#show ip route 172.16.4.3
Routing entry for 172.16.0.0/16
  Known via "rip", distance 120, metric 2
  Redistributing via rip
  Last update from 172.16.25.129 on Serial0/1/0, 00:00:19 ago
  Routing Descriptor Blocks:
  * 172.16.25.129, from 172.16.25.129, 00:00:19 ago, via Serial0/1/0
      Route metric is 2, traffic share count is 1
```

While a diagram of the internetwork might be supplied with the question, you really only need two pieces of information to determine which route will be matched: the destination IP address of the packet and the contents of the router's routing table. By examining each subnet and mask in the routing table, you can then determine the range of IP addresses in each subnet. In this case, the ranges defined by each route, respectively, are as follows:

- 172.16.1.1 (just this one address)

- 172.16.1.0–172.16.1.255

- 172.16.0.0–172.16.3.255

- 172.16.0.0–172.16.255.255

- 0.0.0.0–255.255.255.255 (all addresses)

NOTE   The route listed as 0.0.0.0/0 is the default route, which matches all IP addresses, and is explained later in this chapter.

As you can see from these ranges, several of the routes' address ranges overlap. When matching more than one route, the route with the longer prefix length is used. For example:

- **172.16.1.1:** Matches all five routes; longest prefix is /32, the route to 172.16.1.1/32.

- **172.16.1.2:** Matches last four routes; longest prefix is /24, the route to 172.16.1.0/24.

- **172.16.2.3:** Matches last three routes; longest prefix is /22, the route to 172.16.0.0/22.

- **172.16.4.3:** Matches the last two routes; longest prefix is /16, the route to 172.16.0.0/16.

Besides just doing the subnetting math on every route in the routing table, the **show ip route** *ip-address* command can also be particularly useful. This command lists detailed information about the route that the router matches for the IP address listed in the command. If multiple routes are matched for the IP address, this command lists the best route: the route with the longest prefix. For example, Example 4-1 lists the output of the **show ip route 172.16.4.3** command. The first line of (highlighted) output lists the matched route: the route to 172.16.0.0/16. The rest of the output lists the details of that particular route. This command can be handy command for both real life and for Sim questions on the exams.

DNS, DHCP, ARP, and ICMP

The IP routing process uses several related protocols, including the ARP protocol already mentioned in this chapter. Before moving on to the new topics for this chapter, this section reviews several related protocols.

Before a host can send any IP packets, the host needs to know several IP-related parameters. Hosts often use Dynamic Host Configuration Protocol (DHCP) to learn these key facts, including:

- The host's IP address

- The associated subnet mask

- The IP address of the default gateway (router)

- The IP address(s) of the DNS server(s)

Key
Topic

To learn this information, the host—a DHCP client—sends a broadcast that eventually reaches a DHCP server. The server can then lease an IP address to that host and supply the other information in the previous list. At that point, the host has an IP address with which to use as a source IP address, and enough information to make the simple host routing decision of whether to send packets directly to another host (same subnet) or to the default gateway (another subnet). (In Microsoft Windows XP, the **ipconfig /all** command lists the host's interfaces as the information listed before this paragraph.)

Typically the user either directly or indirectly refers to another host's host name, which in turn causes the host to need to send a packet to the other host. For example, opening a web browser and typing in **http://www.cisco.com** as the URL identifies the host name of a web server owned by Cisco. Opening an e-mail client like Microsoft Outlook indirectly references a host name. The e-mail client was likely configured to know the host name of both an incoming and outgoing e-mail server, so while the user does not look at the settings every day, the e-mail client software knows the name of the hosts with which to exchange mail.

Because hosts cannot send packets to a destination host name, most hosts use Domain Name System (DNS) protocols to resolve the name into its associated IP address. The host acts as a DNS client, sending messages to the unicast IP address of the DNS server. The DNS request lists the name (for example, www.cisco.com), with the server replying with the IP address that corresponds to that host name. After it is learned, the host can cache the name-to-address information, only needing to resolve that name again after the entry has timed out. (In Windows XP, the **ipconfig /displaydns** command lists the host's current list of names and addresses.)

Internet Control Message Protocol (ICMP) includes many different functions, all focused on the control and management of IP. ICMP defines a varied set of messages for different purposes, including the ICMP Echo Request and ICMP Echo Reply messages. The popular **ping** command tests the route to a remote host, and the reverse route back to the original host, by sending Echo Request messages to the destination IP address and with that destination host replying to each Echo Request message with an Echo Reply message. When the **ping** command receives the Echo Reply messages, the command knows that the route between the two hosts works.

All these protocols work together to help the IP routing process, but DHCP, DNS, ICMP, and ARP typically do not occur for every packet. For example, imagine a new host computer connects to a LAN, and the user types the **ping www.cisco.com** command. DHCP might well be used as the OS boots, when the PC uses DHCP to learn its IP address and other information, but then DHCP might not be used for days. The PC then uses DNS to resolve www.cisco.com into an IP address, but then the PC does not need to use DNS again until a new host name is referenced. If the host was pinging the remote host, the local host then creates an IP packet, with an ICMP Echo Request inside the packet, with a destination IP address of the addresses learned by the earlier DNS request. Finally, because the host just came up, it does not have an ARP entry for its default gateway, so the host must use ARP to find the default gateway's MAC address. Only then can the packet be sent to the true destination host, as described in the first part of this chapter. For subsequent packets sent to the same host name, these overhead protocols likely do not need to be used again, and the local host can just send the new packet.

The following list summarizes the steps used by a host, as needed, for the protocols mentioned in this section:

1. If not known yet, the host uses DHCP to learn its IP address, subnet mask, DNS IP addresses, and default gateway IP address. If already known, the host skips this step.

2. If the user references a host name not currently held in the host's name cache, the host makes a DNS request to resolve the name into its corresponding IP address. Otherwise, the host skips this step.

3. If the user issued the **ping** command, the IP packet contains an ICMP Echo Request; if the user instead used a typical TCP/IP application, it uses protocols appropriate to that application.

4. To build the Ethernet frame, the host uses the ARP cache's entry for the next-hop device—either the default gateway (when sending to a host on another subnet) or the true destination host (when sending to a host on the same subnet). If the ARP cache does not hold that entry, the host uses ARP to learn the information.

Fragmentation and MTU

TCP/IP defines a maximum length for an IP packet. The term used to describe that maximum length is *maximum transmission unit (MTU)*.

The MTU varies based on configuration and the interface's characteristics. By default, a computer calculates an interface's MTU based on the maximum size of the data portion of the data-link frame (where the packet is placed). For example, the default MTU value on Ethernet interfaces is 1500.

Routers, like any IP host, cannot forward a packet out an interface if the packet is longer than the MTU. If a router's interface MTU is smaller than a packet that must be forwarded, the router fragments the packet into smaller packets. Fragmentation is the process of breaking the packet into smaller packets, each of which is less than or equal to the MTU value. Figure 4-4 shows an example of fragmentation in a network where the MTU on the serial link has been lowered to 1000 bytes through configuration.

Figure 4-4   *IP Fragmentation*

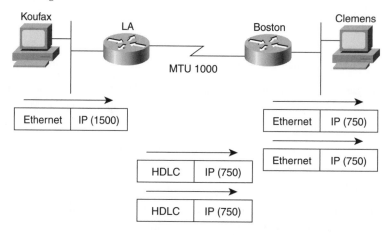

As Figure 4-4 illustrates, Koufax sends a 1500-byte packet toward Router LA. LA removes the Ethernet header but cannot forward the packet as is, because it is 1500 bytes and the High-Level Data Link Control (HDLC) link supports an MTU of only 1000. So LA fragments the original packet into two packets, each 750 bytes in length. The router does the math required to figure out the minimum number of fragments (two in this case) and breaks the original packet into equal-length packets. Because of this, any other routers the packets might go through are less likely to need to perform fragmentation. After forwarding the two packets, Boston receives the packets and forwards them *without reassembling them.* Reassembly is done by the endpoint host, which in this case is Clemens.

The IP header contains fields useful for reassembling the fragments into the original packet. The IP header includes an ID value that is the same in each fragmented packet, as well as an offset value that defines which part of the original packet is held in each fragment. Fragmented packets arriving out of order can be identified as a part of the same original packet and can be reassembled in the correct order using the offset field in each fragment.

Two configuration commands can be used to change the IP MTU size on an interface: the **mtu** interface subcommand and the **ip mtu** interface subcommand. The **mtu** command sets the MTU for all Layer 3 protocols; unless a need exists to vary the setting per Layer 3 protocol, this command is preferred. If a different setting is desired for IP, the **ip mtu** command sets the value used for IP. If both are configured on an interface, the IP MTU setting takes precedence on that interface. However, if the **mtu** command is configured after **ip mtu** is configured, the **ip mtu** value is reset to the same value as that of the **mtu** command. Use care when changing these values.

The review of IP routing and addressing is now complete. Next, this chapter examines connected routes, including connected routes related to VLAN trunking and secondary IP addresses.

Routes to Directly Connected Subnets

A router automatically adds a route to its routing table for the subnet connected to each interface, assuming that the following two facts are true:

■ The interface is in a working state—in other words, the interface status in the **show interfaces** command lists a line status of up and a protocol status of up.

■ The interface has an IP address assigned, either through the **ip address** interface subcommand or by using DHCP client services.

The concept of connected routes is relatively basic. The router of course needs to know the subnet number used on the physical network connected to each of its interfaces, but if the interface is not currently working, the router needs to remove the route from its routing table. The **show ip route** command lists these routes with a *c* as the route code, meaning connected, and the **show ip route connected** command lists only connected routes.

The following sections about connected routes focus on a couple of variations in configuration that affect connected routes, thereby affecting how routers forward packets. The first topic relates to a tool called secondary IP addressing, while the second relates to a router's configuration when using VLAN trunking.

Secondary IP Addressing

Imagine that you planned your IP addressing scheme for a network. Later, a particular subnet grows, and you have used all the valid IP addresses in the subnet. What should you do? Three main options exist:

■ Make the existing subnet larger

■ Migrate the hosts to use addresses in a different, larger subnet

■ Use secondary addressing

All three options are reasonable, but all have some problems.

To make the subnet larger, just change the mask used on that subnet. However, changing the mask could create overlapped subnets. For example, if subnet 10.1.4.0/24 is running out of addresses, and you make a change to mask 255.255.254.0 (9 host bits, 23 network/subnet bits), the new subnet includes addresses 10.1.4.0 to 10.1.5.255. If you have already assigned subnet 10.1.5.0/24, with assignable addresses 10.1.5.1 through 10.1.5.254, you would create an overlap, which is not allowed. However, if the 10.1.5.x addresses are unused, expanding the old subnet might be reasonable.

The second option is to simply pick a new, unused, but larger subnet. All the IP addresses would need to be changed. This is a relatively simple process if most or all hosts use DHCP, but a potentially laborious process if many hosts use statically configured IP addresses.

Note that both of the first two solutions imply a strategy of using different masks in different parts of the network. Use of these different masks is called variable-length subnet masking (VLSM), which introduces more complexity into the network, particularly for people who are monitoring and troubleshooting the network.

The third major option is to use a Cisco router features called *secondary IP addressing*. Secondary addressing uses multiple networks or subnets on the same data link. By using more than one subnet on the same medium, you increase the number of available IP addresses. To make it work, the router needs an IP address in each subnet so that the hosts in each subnet have a usable default gateway IP address in the same subnet. Additionally, packets that need to pass between these subnets must be sent to the router. For example, Figure 4-5 has subnet 10.1.2.0/24; assume that it has all IP addresses assigned. Assuming secondary addressing to be the chosen solution, subnet 10.1.7.0/24 also could be used on the same Ethernet. Example 4-2 shows the configuration for secondary IP addressing on Yosemite.

Figure 4-5 *TCP/IP Network with Secondary Addresses*

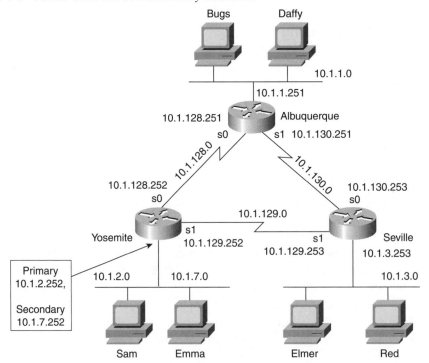

Example 4-2 *Secondary IP Addressing Configuration and the* **show ip route** *Command on Yosemite*

```
! Excerpt from show running-config follows...
Hostname Yosemite
ip domain-lookup
ip name-server 10.1.1.100 10.1.2.100
interface ethernet 0
 ip address 10.1.7.252  255.255.255.0 secondary
 ip address 10.1.2.252  255.255.255.0
interface serial 0
 ip address 10.1.128.252  255.255.255.0
interface serial 1
 ip address 10.1.129.252  255.255.255.0

Yosemite# show ip route connected
     10.0.0.0/24 is subnetted, 4 subnets
C       10.1.2.0 is directly connected, Ethernet0
C       10.1.7.0 is directly connected, Ethernet0
C       10.1.129.0 is directly connected, Serial1
C       10.1.128.0 is directly connected, Serial0
```

The router has connected routes to subnets 10.1.2.0/24 and 10.1.7.0/24, so it can forward packets to each subnet. The hosts in each subnet on the same LAN can use either 10.1.2.252 or 10.1.7.252 as their default gateway IP addresses, depending on the subnet in which they reside.

The biggest negative to secondary addressing is that packets sent between hosts on the LAN might be inefficiently routed. For example, when a host in subnet 10.1.2.0 sends a packet to a host in 10.1.7.0, the sending host's logic is to send the packet to its default gateway, because the destination is on a different subnet. So, the sending host sends the packet to the router, which then sends the packet back into the same LAN.

Supporting Connected Routes to Subnet Zero

IOS can restrict a router from configuring an **ip address** command with an address inside the zero subnet. The zero subnet (or subnet zero) is the one subnet in each classful network that has all binary 0s in the subnet part of the binary version of the subnet number. In decimal, the zero subnet happens to be the same number as the classful network number.

With the **ip subnet-zero** command configured, IOS allows the zero subnet to become a connected route as a result of an **ip address** command being configured on an interface. This command has been a default setting since at least IOS version 12.0, which was a relatively old IOS version by the time this book was published. So, for the exam, if you see the **ip subnet-zero** command configured, or if the question does not specify that the **no ip subnet-zero** command is configured, assume that the zero subnet can be configured.

> **NOTE**   Older editions of this book stated that you should assume that the zero subnet cannot be used, unless an exam question implied that the zero subnet was usable. The current CCNA exams, and therefore this book, allow the zero subnet to be used unless the exam question states or implies that it should not be used.

With the **no ip subnet-zero** command configured on a router, that router rejects any **ip address** command that uses an address/mask combination for the zero subnet. For example, the interface subcommand **ip address 10.0.0.1 255.255.255.0** implies zero subnet 10.0.0.0/ 24, so the router would reject the command if the **no ip subnet-zero** global configuration command was configured. Note that the error message simply says "bad mask," rather than stating that the problem was because of the zero subnet.

The **no ip subnet-zero** command on one router does not affect other routers, and it does not prevent a router from learning about a zero subnet through a routing protocol. It simply prevents the router from configuring an interface to be in a zero subnet.

Note that in today's CCNA exams, you can assume that the zero subnet is allowed to be used unless the question states that it should not be used. In particular, a question that uses a classful routing protocol (as discussed in Chapter 5), or uses the **no ip subnet-zero** command, implies that the zero and broadcast subnets should be avoided.

ISL and 802.1Q Configuration on Routers

As discussed in Chapter 1, "Virtual LANs," VLAN trunking can be used between two switches and between a switch and a router. By using trunking instead of using a physical router interface per VLAN, the number of required router interfaces can be reduced. Instead of a single physical interface on the router for each VLAN on the switch, one physical interface can be used, and the router can still route packets between the various VLANs.

Figure 4-6 shows a router with a single Fast Ethernet interface and a single connection to a switch. Either Inter-Switch Link (ISL) or 802.1Q trunking can be used, with only small differences in the configuration for each. For frames that contain packets that the router routes between the two VLANs, the incoming frame is tagged by the switch with one VLAN ID, and the outgoing frame is tagged by the router with the other VLAN ID. Example 4-3 shows the router configuration required to support ISL encapsulation and forwarding between these VLANs.

Figure 4-6 *Router Forwarding Between VLANs*

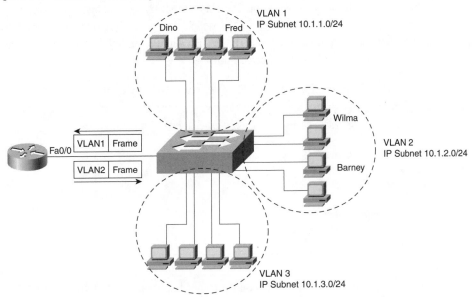

Example 4-3 *Router Configuration for the ISL Encapsulation Shown in Figure 4-6*

```
interface fastethernet 0/0.1
 ip address 10.1.1.1 255.255.255.0
 encapsulation isl 1
!
interface fastethernet 0/0.2
 ip address 10.1.2.1 255.255.255.0
 encapsulation isl 2
!
interface fastethernet 0/0.3
 ip address 10.1.3.1 255.255.255.0
 encapsulation isl 3
```

Example 4-3 shows the configuration for three *subinterfaces* of the Fast Ethernet interface on the router. A subinterface is a logical subdivision of a physical interface. The router assigns each subinterface an IP address and assigns the subinterface to a single VLAN. So, instead of three physical router interfaces, each attached to a different subnet/VLAN, the router uses one physical router interface with three logical subinterfaces, each attached to a different subnet/VLAN. The **encapsulation** command numbers the VLANs, which must match the configuration for VLAN IDs in the switch.

This example uses subinterface numbers that match the VLAN ID on each subinterface. There is no requirement that the numbers match, but most people choose to make them match, just to make the configuration more obvious and to make troubleshooting easier. In other words, the VLAN IDs can be 1, 2, and 3, but the subinterface numbers could have been 4, 5, and 6, because the subinterface numbers are just used internally by the router.

Example 4-4 shows the same network, but this time with 802.1Q used instead of ISL. IEEE 802.1Q has a concept called the native VLAN, which is a special VLAN on each trunk for which no 802.1Q headers are added to the frames. By default, VLAN 1 is the native VLAN. Example 4-4 shows the difference in configuration.

Example 4-4   *Router Configuration for the 802.1Q Encapsulation Shown in Figure 4-6*

```
interface fastethernet 0/0
 ip address 10.1.1.1 255.255.255.0
!
interface fastethernet 0/0.2
 ip address 10.1.2.1 255.255.255.0
 encapsulation dot1q 2
!
interface fastethernet 0/0.3
 ip address 10.1.3.1 255.255.255.0
 encapsulation dot1q 3
```

The configuration creates three VLANs on the router Fa0/0 interface. Two of the VLANs, VLANs 2 and 3, are configured just like Example 4-3, except that the **encapsulation** command lists 802.1Q as the type of encapsulation.

The native VLAN, VLAN 1 in this case, can be configured with two styles of configuration. Example 4-4 shows one style in which the native VLAN's IP address is configured on the physical interface. As a result, the router does not use VLAN trunking headers in this VLAN, as is intended for the native VLAN. The alternative is to configure the native VLAN's IP address on another subinterface and to use the **encapsulation dot1q 1 native** interface subcommand. This command tells the router that the subinterface is associated with VLAN 1, but the **native** keyword tells the router not to use any 802.1Q headers with that subinterface.

Routers do not perform dynamic negotiation of trunking. So, the switch connected to a router interface must manually configure trunking, as covered in Chapter 1. For example, a switch on the other end of the router's Fa0/0 interface would configure the **switchport mode trunk** interface subcommand (to enable trunking manually), and if the switch is capable of using either type of trunking, the **switchport trunk encapsulation dot1q** interface subcommand to statically configure the use of 802.1Q.

Static Routes

Routers use three main methods to add routes to their routing tables: connected routes, static routes, and dynamic routing protocols. Routers always add connected routes when interfaces have IP addresses configured and the interfaces are up and working. In most networks, engineers purposefully use dynamic routing protocols to cause each router to learn the rest of the routes in an internetwork. Using static routes—routes added to a routing table through direct configuration—is the least used of the three options.

Static routing consists of individual **ip route** global configuration commands that define a route to a router. The configuration command includes a reference to the subnet—the subnet number and mask—along with instructions about where to forward packets destined to that subnet. To see the need for static routes, and to see the configuration, look at Example 4-5, which shows two **ping** commands testing IP connectivity from Albuquerque to Yosemite (see Figure 4-7).

Figure 4-7 *Sample Network Used in Static Route Configuration Examples*

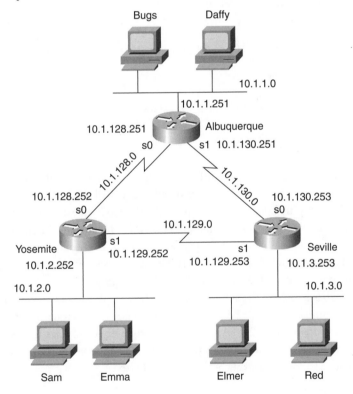

Example 4-5 *Albuquerque Router EXEC Commands with Only Connected Routers*

```
Albuquerque#show ip route
Codes: C - connected, S - static, I - IGRP, R - RIP, M - mobile, B - BGP
       D - EIGRP, EX - EIGRP external, O - OSPF, IA - OSPF inter area
       N1 - OSPF NSSA external type 1, N2 - OSPF NSSA external type 2
       E1 - OSPF external type 1, E2 - OSPF external type 2, E - EGP
```

continues

Example 4-5   *Albuquerque Router EXEC Commands with Only Connected Routers (Continued)*

```
        i - IS-IS, L1 - IS-IS level-1, L2 - IS-IS level-2, ia - IS-IS inter area
        * - candidate default, U - per-user static route, o - ODR
        P - periodic downloaded static route

Gateway of last resort is not set

     10.0.0.0/24 is subnetted, 3 subnets

C        10.1.1.0 is directly connected, Ethernet0
C        10.1.130.0 is directly connected, Serial1
C        10.1.128.0 is directly connected, Serial0
Albuquerque#ping 10.1.128.252
Type escape sequence to abort.
Sending 5, 100-byte ICMP Echos to 10.1.128.252, timeout is 2 seconds:
!!!!!
Success rate is 100 percent (5/5), round-trip min/avg/max = 4/4/8 ms

Albuquerque#ping 10.1.2.252
Type escape sequence to abort.
Sending 5, 100-byte ICMP Echos to 10.1.2.252, timeout is 2 seconds:
.....
Success rate is 0 percent (0/5)
```

The end of the example shows two different **ping** commands on router Albuquerque, one to 10.1.128.252 (Yosemite's S0 IP address) and one to 10.1.2.252 (Yosemite's LAN IP address). The IOS **ping** command sends five ICMP Echo Request packets by default, with the command output listing an exclamation point (!) to mean that an Echo Reply was received, and a period (.) to mean no reply was received. In the example, the first instance, **ping 10.1.128.252**, shows five responses (100%), and the second instance, **ping 10.1.2.252**, shows that no responses were received (0%). The first **ping** command works because Albuquerque has a route to the subnet in which 10.1.128.2 resides (subnet 10.1.128.0/24). However, the **ping** to 10.1.2.252 does not work because Albuquerque does not have a route that matches address 10.1.2.252. At this point, Albuquerque only has routes for its three connected subnets. So, Albuquerque's **ping 10.1.2.252** command creates the packets, but Albuquerque discards the packets because no routes exist.

Configuring Static Routes

One simple solution to the failure of the **ping 10.1.2.252** command is to enable an IP routing protocol on all three routers. In fact, in a real network, that is the most likely solution. As an alternative, you can configure static routes. Many networks have a few static routes, so you need to configure them occasionally. Example 4-6 shows the **ip route**

command on Albuquerque, which adds static routes and makes the failed ping from
Example 4-5 work.

Example 4-6 *Static Routes Added to Albuquerque*

```
ip route 10.1.2.0 255.255.255.0 10.1.128.252
ip route 10.1.3.0 255.255.255.0 10.1.130.253
```

The **ip route** command defines the static route by defining the subnet number and the next-
hop IP address. One **ip route** command defines a route to 10.1.2.0 (mask 255.255.255.0),
which is located off Yosemite, so the next-hop IP address as configured on Albuquerque is
10.1.128.252, which is Yosemite's Serial0 IP address. Similarly, a route to 10.1.3.0, the
subnet off Seville, points to Seville's Serial0 IP address, 10.1.130.253. Note that the next-
hop IP address is an IP address in a directly connected subnet; the goal is to define the next
router to send the packet to. Now Albuquerque can forward packets to these two subnets.

The **ip route** command has two basic formats. The command can refer to a next-hop IP
address, as shown in Example 4-6. Alternately, for static routes that use point-to-point serial
links, the command can list the outgoing interface instead of the next-hop IP address. For
example, Example 4-6 could instead use the **ip route 10.1.2.0 255.255.255.0 serial0** global
configuration command instead of the first **ip route** command.

Unfortunately, adding the two static routes in Example 4-6 to Albuquerque does not solve
all the network's routing problems. The static routes help Albuquerque deliver packets to
these two subnets, but the other two routers don't have enough routing information to
forward packets back toward Albuquerque. For example, PC Bugs cannot ping PC Sam in
this network, even after the addition of the commands in Example 4-6. The problem is that
although Albuquerque has a route to subnet 10.1.2.0, where Sam resides, Yosemite does not
have a route to 10.1.1.0, where Bugs resides. The **ping** request packet goes from Bugs to
Sam correctly, but Sam's ping response packet cannot be routed by the Yosemite router
back through Albuquerque to Bugs, so the ping fails.

The Extended ping Command

In real life, you might not be able to find a user, like Bugs, to ask to test your network by
pinging. Instead, you can use the extended **ping** command on a router to test routing in the
same way that a ping from Bugs to Sam tests routing. Example 4-7 shows Albuquerque with
the working **ping 10.1.2.252** command, but with an extended **ping 10.1.2.252** command

that works similarly to a **ping** from Bugs to Sam—a ping that fails in this case (only the two static routes from Example 4-6 have been added at this point).

Example 4-7   *Albuquerque: Working Ping After Adding Default Routes, Plus Failing Extended* **ping** *Command*

```
Albuquerque#show ip route
Codes: C - connected, S - static, I - IGRP, R - RIP, M - mobile, B - BGP
       D - EIGRP, EX - EIGRP external, O - OSPF, IA - OSPF inter area
       N1 - OSPF NSSA external type 1, N2 - OSPF NSSA external type 2
       E1 - OSPF external type 1, E2 - OSPF external type 2, E - EGP
       i - IS-IS, L1 - IS-IS level-1, L2 - IS-IS level-2, ia - IS-IS inter area
       * - candidate default, U - per-user static route, o - ODR
       P - periodic downloaded static route

Gateway of last resort is not set

     10.0.0.0/24 is subnetted, 5 subnets
S       10.1.3.0 [1/0] via 10.1.130.253
S       10.1.2.0 [1/0] via 10.1.128.252
C       10.1.1.0 is directly connected, Ethernet0
C       10.1.130.0 is directly connected, Serial1
C       10.1.128.0 is directly connected, Serial0
Albuquerque#ping 10.1.2.252

Type escape sequence to abort.
Sending 5, 100-byte ICMP Echos to 10.1.2.252, timeout is 2 seconds:
!!!!!
Success rate is 100 percent (5/5), round-trip min/avg/max = 4/4/8 ms

Albuquerque#ping
Protocol [ip]:
Target IP address: 10.1.2.252
Repeat count [5]:
Datagram size [100]:
Timeout in seconds [2]:
Extended commands [n]: y
Source address or interface: 10.1.1.251
Type of service [0]:
Set DF bit in IP header? [no]:
Validate reply data? [no]:
Data pattern [0xABCD]:
Loose, Strict, Record, Timestamp, Verbose[none]:
Sweep range of sizes [n]:
Type escape sequence to abort.
Sending 5, 100-byte ICMP Echos to 10.1.2.252, timeout is 2 seconds:
. . . . .
Success rate is 0 percent (0/5)
```

The simple **ping 10.1.2.252** command works for one obvious reason and one not-so-obvious reason. First, Albuquerque can forward a packet to subnet 10.1.2.0 because of the static route. The return packet, sent by Yosemite, is sent to address 10.1.128.251—Albuquerque's Serial0 IP address—and Yosemite has a connected route to reach subnet 10.2.128.0. But why does Yosemite send the Echo Reply to Albuquerque's S0 IP address of 10.1.128.251? Well, the following points are true about the **ping** command on a Cisco router:

■ The Cisco **ping** command uses, by default, the output interface's IP address as the packet's source address, unless otherwise specified in an extended ping. The first ping in Example 4-7 uses a source of 10.1.128.251, because the route used to send the packet to 10.1.2.252 sends packets out Albuquerque's Serial0 interface, whose IP address is 10.1.128.251.

■ Ping response packets (ICMP Echo Replies) reverse the IP addresses used in the received ping request to which they are responding. So, in this example, Yosemite's Echo Reply, in response to the first ping in Example 4-7, uses 10.1.128.251 as the destination address and 10.1.2.252 as the source IP address.

Because the **ping 10.1.2.252** command on Albuquerque uses 10.1.128.251 as the packet's source address, Yosemite can send back a response to 10.1.128.251, because Yosemite happens to have a (connected) route to 10.1.128.0.

The danger when troubleshooting with the standard **ping** command is that routing problems can still exist, but the **ping 10.1.2.252** command, which worked, gives you a false sense of security. A more thorough alternative is to use the extended **ping** command to act like you issued a ping from a computer on that subnet, without having to call a user and ask to enter a **ping** command for you on the PC. The extended version of the **ping** command can be used to refine the problem's underlying cause by changing several details of what the ping command sends in its request. In fact, when a ping from a router works, but a ping from a host does not, the extended ping could help you re-create the problem without needing to work with the end user on the phone.

For example, in Example 4-7, the extended **ping** command on Albuquerque sends a packet from source IP address 10.1.1.251 (Albuquerque's Ethernet) to 10.1.2.252 (Yosemite's Ethernet). According to the output, Albuquerque did not receive a response. Normally, the **ping** command would be sourced from the IP address of the outgoing interface. With the use of the extended ping source address option, the source IP address of the echo packet is set to Albuquerque's Ethernet IP address, 10.1.1.251. Because the ICMP echo generated by the extended ping is sourced from an address in subnet 10.1.1.0, the packet looks more like a packet from an end user in that subnet. Yosemite builds an Echo Reply, with destination

10.1.1.251, but it does not have a route to that subnet. So Yosemite cannot send the ping reply packet back to Albuquerque.

To solve this problem, all routers could be configured to use a routing protocol. Alternatively, you could simply define static routes on all the routers in the network.

Static Default Routes

A default route is a special route that matches all packet destinations. Default routes can be particularly useful when only one physical path exists from one part of the network to another, and in cases for which one enterprise router provides connectivity to the Internet for that enterprise. For example, in Figure 4-8, R1, R2, and R3 are connected to the rest of the network only through R1's LAN interface. All three routers can forward packets to the rest of the network as long as the packets get to R1, which in turn forwards packets to router Dist1.

Figure 4-8 *Sample Network Using a Default Route*

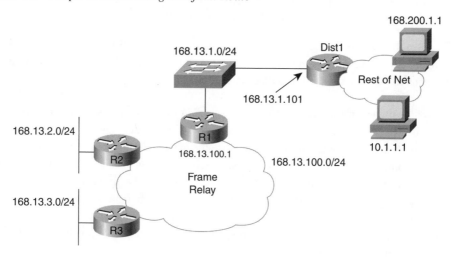

The following sections show two options for configuring static default routes: one using the **ip route** command and another using the **ip default-network** command.

Default Routes Using the ip route Command

By configuring a default route on R1, with next-hop router Dist1, and by having R1 advertise the default to R2 and R3, default routing can be accomplished. By using such a default route, R1, R2, and R3 should not need specific routes to the subnets to the right of router Dist1. Example 4-8 begins an examination of this design by showing the definition of a static default route on R1 and the resulting information in R1's IP routing table.

Example 4-8 *R1 Static Default Route Configuration and Routing Table*

```
R1(config)#ip route 0.0.0.0 0.0.0.0 168.13.1.101
R1#show ip route
Codes: C - connected, S - static, I - IGRP, R - RIP, M - mobile, B - BGP
       D - EIGRP, EX - EIGRP external, O - OSPF, IA - OSPF inter area
       N1 - OSPF NSSA external type 1, N2 - OSPF NSSA external type 2
       E1 - OSPF external type 1, E2 - OSPF external type 2, E - EGP
       i - IS-IS, L1 - IS-IS level-1, L2 - IS-IS level-2, ia - IS-IS inter area
       * - candidate default, U - per-user static route, o - ODR
       P - periodic downloaded static route

Gateway of last resort is 168.13.1.101 to network 0.0.0.0

     168.13.0.0/24 is subnetted, 4 subnets
C       168.13.1.0 is directly connected, FastEthernet0/0
R       168.13.3.0 [120/1] via 168.13.100.3, 00:00:05, Serial0.1
R       168.13.2.0 [120/1] via 168.13.100.2, 00:00:21, Serial0.1
C       168.13.100.0 is directly connected, Serial0.1
S*   0.0.0.0/0 [1/0] via 168.13.1.101
```

R1 defines the default route with a static **ip route** command, with destination 0.0.0.0, mask 0.0.0.0. As a result, R1's **show ip route** command lists a static route to 0.0.0.0, mask 0.0.0.0, with next hop 168.13.1.101—essentially, the same information in the **ip route 0.0.0.0 0.0.0.0 168.13.1.101** global configuration command. A destination of 0.0.0.0, with mask 0.0.0.0, represents all destinations by convention. With just that configuration, R1 has a static route that matches any and all IP packet destinations.

Note also in Example 4-8 that R1's **show ip route** command output lists a "Gateway of last resort" as 168.13.1.101. When a router knows about at least one default route, the router notes that route with an asterisk in the routing table. If a router learns about multiple default routes—either through static configuration or from routing protocols—the router notes each default route with an asterisk in the routing table. Then, the router chooses the best default route, noting that choice as the gateway of last resort. (The administrative distance of the source of the routing information, as defined by the administrative distance setting, has some impact on this choice. Administrative distance is covered in Chapter 8, "Routing Protocol Theory," in the section "Administrative Distance.")

While the Routing Information Protocol (RIP) configuration is not shown, R1 also advertises this default route to R2 and R3, as shown in the output of the **show ip route** command on R3 in Example 4-9.

Example 4-9 *R3: Nuances of the Successful Use of the Static Route on R1*

```
R3#show ip route
Codes: C - connected, S - static, I - IGRP, R - RIP, M - mobile, B - BGP
       D - EIGRP, EX - EIGRP external, O - OSPF, IA - OSPF inter area
       N1 - OSPF NSSA external type 1, N2 - OSPF NSSA external type 2
       E1 - OSPF external type 1, E2 - OSPF external type 2, E - EGP
       i - IS-IS, L1 - IS-IS level-1, L2 - IS-IS level-2, ia - IS-IS inter area
       * - candidate default, U - per-user static route, o - ODR
       P - periodic downloaded static route

Gateway of last resort is 168.13.100.1 to network 0.0.0.0

     168.13.0.0/24 is subnetted, 4 subnets
R       168.13.1.0 [120/1] via 168.13.100.1, 00:00:13, Serial0.1
C       168.13.3.0 is directly connected, Ethernet0
R       168.13.2.0 [120/1] via 168.13.100.2, 00:00:06, Serial0.1
C       168.13.100.0 is directly connected, Serial0.1
```

Different routing protocols advertise default routes in a couple of different ways. As an example, when R3 learns a default route from R1 using RIP, R3 lists the destination of the default route (0.0.0.0) and the next-hop router, which is R1 in this case (168.13.100.1), as highlighted in Example 4-9. So, when R3 needs to use its default route, it forwards packets to R1 (168.13.100.1)

Default Routes Using the ip default-network Command

Another style of configuration for the default route uses the **ip default-network** command. This command lists a classful IP network as its parameter, telling the router to use the routing details of the route for that classful network as the forwarding details for a default route.

This command is most useful when the engineer wants to use the default route to reach networks besides the networks used inside that enterprise. For example, in Figure 4-8, imagine that all subnets of the enterprise's 168.13.0.0 Class B network are known; they exist only near routers R1, R2, and R3; and these routes are all in the routing tables of R1, R2, and R3. Also, none of the subnets of 168.13.0.0 are to the right of Router Dist1. If the engineer wants to use a default route for forwarding packets to destinations to the right of Dist1, the **ip default-network** command works well.

To use the **ip default-network** command to configure a default route, the engineer relies on her knowledge that Dist1 is already advertising a route for classful network 10.0.0.0 to R1. R1's route to network 10.0.0.0 points to Dist1's 168.13.1.101 address as the next-hop address. Knowing that, the engineer can configure the **ip default-network 10.0.0.0** command on R1, which tells R1 to build its default route based on its learned route for network 10.0.0.0/8. Example 4-10 shows several details about this scenario on R1.

Example 4-10 *R1's Use of the* **ip default-network** *Command*

```
R1#configure terminal
R1(config)#ip default-network 10.0.0.0
R1(config)#exit
R1#show ip route
Codes: C - connected, S - static, I - IGRP, R - RIP, M - mobile, B - BGP
       D - EIGRP, EX - EIGRP external, O - OSPF, IA - OSPF inter area
       N1 - OSPF NSSA external type 1, N2 - OSPF NSSA external type 2
       E1 - OSPF external type 1, E2 - OSPF external type 2, E - EGP
       i - IS-IS, L1 - IS-IS level-1, L2 - IS-IS level-2, ia - IS-IS inter area
       * - candidate default, U - per-user static route, o - ODR
       P - periodic downloaded static route

Gateway of last resort is 168.13.1.101 to network 10.0.0.0

     168.13.0.0/24 is subnetted, 5 subnets
R       168.13.200.0 [120/1] via 168.13.1.101, 00:00:12, FastEthernet0/0
C       168.13.1.0 is directly connected, FastEthernet0/0
R       168.13.3.0 [120/1] via 168.13.100.3, 00:00:00, Serial0.1
R       168.13.2.0 [120/1] via 168.13.100.2, 00:00:00, Serial0.1
C       168.13.100.0 is directly connected, Serial0.1
R*   10.0.0.0/8 [120/1] via 168.13.1.101, 00:00:12, FastEthernet0/0
```

R1 shows both the result of having normally learned a route to network 10.0.0.0 through RIP, plus the additional results of the **ip default-network 10.0.0.0** global command. R1's RIP route for 10.0.0.0/8 lists a next-hop IP address of 168.13.1.101, Dist1's IP address on their common LAN, as normal. Because of the **ip default-network 10.0.0.0** command, R1 decides to use the details in the route to network 10.0.0.0 as its default route. The last part of the line about the gateway of last resort lists the default network, 10.0.0.0. Also, R1 lists an asterisk beside the route referenced in the **ip default-network** command.

Default Route Summary

Remembering the details of configuring default routes, and in particular the resulting details in the output of the **show ip route** command, can be a challenge. However, make it a point to remember these key points regarding default routes:

Key Topic

- Default static routes can be statically configured using the **ip route 0.0.0.0 0.0.0.0** *next-hop-address* or the **ip default-network** *net-number* command.

- When a router only matches a packet with the default route, that router uses the forwarding details listed in the gateway of last resort line.

Regardless of how the default route shows up—whether it's a gateway of last resort, a route to 0.0.0.0, or a route to some other network with an * beside it in the routing table—it is used according to the rules of classless or classful routing, as is explained in the next section.

Classful and Classless Routing

Cisco routers have two configurable options for how a router uses an existing default route: classless routing and classful routing. Classless routing causes a router to use its default routes for any packet that does not match some other route. Classful routing places one restriction on when a router can use its default route, resulting in cases in which a router has a default route but the router chooses to discard a packet rather than forwarding the packet based on the default route.

The terms *classless* and *classful* also characterize both IP addressing and IP routing protocols, so a fair amount of confusion exists as to the meaning of the terms. Before explaining the details of classful routing and classless routing, the next section summarizes the other use of these terms.

Summary of the Use of the Terms Classless and Classful

The terms *classless addressing* and *classful addressing* refer to two different ways to think about IP addresses. Both terms refer to a perspective on the structure of a subnetted IP address. Classless addressing uses a two-part view of IP addresses, and classful addressing has a three-part view. With classful addressing, the address always has an 8-, 16-, or 24-bit network field, based on the Class A, B, and C addressing rules. The end of the address has a host part that uniquely identifies each host inside a subnet. The bits in between the network and host part comprise the third part, namely the subnet part of the address. With classless addressing, the network and subnet parts from the classful view are combined into a single part, often called the subnet or prefix, with the address ending in the host part.

The terms *classless routing protocol* and *classful routing protocol* refer to features of different IP routing protocols. These features cannot be enabled or disabled; a routing protocol is, by its very nature, either classless or classful. In particular, classless routing protocols advertise mask information for each subnet, giving classless protocols the ability to support both VLSM and route summarization. Classful routing protocols do not advertise mask information, so they do not support VLSM or route summarization.

The third use of the terms *classless* and *classful*—the terms *classful routing* and *classless routing*—have to do with how the IP routing process makes use of the default route. Interestingly, this is the only one of the three uses of the terms that can be changed based on router configuration. Table 4-2 lists the three uses of the classless and classful terms, with a brief explanation. A more complete explanation of classless and classful routing follows the table. Chapter 5 explains more background information about the terms *classless routing protocol* and *classful routing protocol*.

Table 4-2   *Comparing the Use of the Terms Classless and Classful*

Key
Topic

As Applied To	Classful	Classless
Addresses	Addresses have three parts: network, subnet, and host.	Addresses have two parts: subnet or prefix, and host.
Routing protocols	Routing protocol does not advertise masks nor support VLSM; RIP-1 and IGRP.	Routing protocol does advertise masks and support VLSM; RIP-2, EIGRP, OSPF.
Routing (forwarding)	IP forwarding process is restricted in how it uses the default route.	IP forwarding process has no restrictions on using the default route.

Classless and Classful Routing Compared

Classless IP routing works just like most people think IP routing would work when a router knows a default route. Compared to classful routing, classless routing's core concepts are straightforward. Classful routing restricts the use of the default route. The following two statements give a general description of each, with an example following the definitions:

Key
Topic

- **Classless routing:** When a packet's destination only matches a router's default route, and does not match any other routes, forward the packet using that default route.

- **Classful routing:** When a packet's destination only matches a router's default route, and does not match any other routes, only use the default route if this router does not know any routes in the classful network in which the destination IP address resides.

The use of the term *classful* refers to the fact that the logic includes some consideration of classful IP addressing rules—namely, the classful (Class A, B, or C) network of the packet's destination address. To make sense of this concept, Example 4-11 shows a router with a default route, but classful routing allows the use of the default route in one case, but not another. The example uses the same default routes examples from earlier in this chapter, based on Figure 4-8. Both R3 and R1 have a default route that could forward packets to Router Dist1. However, as seen in Example 4-11, on R3, the **ping 10.1.1.1** works, but the **ping 168.13.200.1** fails.

> **NOTE**   This example uses the default route on R1 as defined with the **ip route** command and as explained in Examples 4-8 and 4-9, but it would have worked the same regardless of how the default route was learned.

Example 4-11   *Classful Routing Causes One Ping on R3 to Fail*

```
R3#show ip route
Codes: C - connected, S - static, I - IGRP, R - RIP, M - mobile, B - BGP
       D - EIGRP, EX - EIGRP external, O - OSPF, IA - OSPF inter area
       N1 - OSPF NSSA external type 1, N2 - OSPF NSSA external type 2
       E1 - OSPF external type 1, E2 - OSPF external type 2, E - EGP
       i - IS-IS, L1 - IS-IS level-1, L2 - IS-IS level-2, ia - IS-IS inter area
       * - candidate default, U - per-user static route, o - ODR
       P - periodic downloaded static route

Gateway of last resort is 168.13.100.1 to network 0.0.0.0

     168.13.0.0/24 is subnetted, 4 subnets
R       168.13.1.0 [120/1] via 168.13.100.1, 00:00:13, Serial0.1
C       168.13.3.0 is directly connected, Ethernet0
R       168.13.2.0 [120/1] via 168.13.100.2, 00:00:06, Serial0.1
C       168.13.100.0 is directly connected, Serial0.1
R3#ping 10.1.1.1

Type escape sequence to abort.
Sending 5, 100-byte ICMP Echos to 10.1.1.1, timeout is 2 seconds:
!!!!!
Success rate is 100 percent (5/5), round-trip min/avg/max = 84/89/114 ms
R3#
R3#ping 168.13.200.1

Type escape sequence to abort.
Sending 5, 100-byte ICMP Echos to 168.13.200.1, timeout is 2 seconds:
.....
Success rate is 0 percent (0/5)
```

First, consider R3's attempt to match both destinations (10.1.1.1 and 168.13.200.1) against the routes in the routing table. R3's routing table does not have any routes that match either destination IP address, other than the default route. So, R3's only option is to use its default route.

R3 is configured to use classful routing. With classful routing, the router first matches the Class A, B, or C network number in which a destination resides. If the Class A, B, or C network is found, Cisco IOS Software then looks for the specific subnet number. If it isn't found, the packet is discarded, as is the case with the ICMP echoes sent with the **ping 168.13.200.1** command. However, with classful routing, if the packet does not match a Class A, B, or C network in the routing table, and a default route exists, the default route is indeed used—which is why R3 can forward the ICMP echoes sent by the successful **ping 10.1.1.1** command.

In short, with classful routing, the only time the default route is used is when the router does not know about any subnets of the packet's destination Class A, B, or C network.

You can toggle between classless and classful routing with the **ip classless** and **no ip classless** global configuration commands, respectively. With classless routing, Cisco IOS Software looks for the best match, ignoring class rules. If a default route exists, with classless routing, the packet always at least matches the default route. If a more specific route matches the packet's destination, that route is used. Example 4-12 shows R3 changed to use classless routing, and the successful ping of 168.13.200.1.

Example 4-12   *Classless Routing Allows Ping 168.13.200.1 to Now Succeed*

```
R3#configure terminal
Enter configuration commands, one per line.  End with CNTL/Z.
R3(config)#ip classless
R3(config)#^Z
R3#ping 168.13.200.1

Type escape sequence to abort.
Sending 5, 100-byte ICMP Echos to 168.13.200.1, timeout is 2 seconds:
!!!!!
Success rate is 100 percent (5/5), round-trip min/avg/max = 80/88/112 ms
```

Exam Preparation Tasks

Review All the Key Topics

Key
Topic

Review the most important topics from this chapter, noted with the Key Topics icon in the outer margin of the page. Table 4-3 lists a reference of these key topics and the page numbers on which each is found.

Table 4-3 *Key Topics for Chapter 4*

Key Topic Element	Description	Page Number
List	Steps taken by a host when forwarding IP packets	162
List	Steps taken by a router when forwarding IP packets	163
List	Review of key points about IP addressing	167
Thought	Summary of the logic a router uses when a packet's destination matches more than one route	169
List	Items typically learned through DHCP	171
List	Steps and protocols used by a host when communicating with another host	173
List	Rules regarding when a router creates a connected route	175
List	Rules about the source address used for packets generated by the IOS **ping** command	185
List	Key facts regarding the definition of static default routes	190
Table 4-2	Summary of the three separate but related uses of the terms *classless* and *classful*	191
List	Definitions of classless routing and classful routing	191

Complete the Tables and Lists from Memory

Print a copy of Appendix J, "Memory Tables," (found on the CD) or at least the section for this chapter, and complete the tables and lists from memory. Appendix K, "Memory Tables Answer Key," also on the CD, includes completed tables and lists to check your work.

Definitions of Key Terms

Define the following key terms from this chapter, and check your answers in the glossary:

Classful addressing, classful routing, classful routing protocol, classless addressing, classless routing, classless routing protocol, extended ping, secondary IP address, zero subnet

Command Reference to Check Your Memory

While you should not necessarily memorize the information in the tables in this section, this section does include a reference for the configuration and EXEC commands covered in this chapter. Practically speaking, you should memorize the commands as a side effect of reading the chapter and doing all the activities in this exam preparation section. To check to see how well you have memorized the commands as a side effect of your other studies, cover the left side of the table with a piece of paper, read the descriptions on the right side, and see whether you remember the command.

Table 4-4 *Chapter 4 Configuration Command Reference*

Command	Description
encapsulation dot1q *vlan-id* [**native**]	A subinterface subcommand that tells the router to use 802.1Q trunking, for a particular VLAN, and with the **native** keyword, to not encapsulate in a trunking header
encapsulation isl *vlan-identifier*	A subinterface subcommand that tells the router to use ISL trunking, for a particular VLAN
[**no**] **ip classless**	Global command that enables (**ip classless**) or disables (**no ip classless**) classless routing
[**no**] **ip subnet-zero**	Global command that allows (**ip subnet-zero**) or disallows (**no ip subnet-zero**) the configuration of an interface IP address in a zero subnet
ip address *ip-address mask* [**secondary**]	Interface subcommand that assigns the interface's IP address, and optionally makes the address a secondary address
ip route *prefix mask* {*ip-address* | *interface-type interface-number*} [*distance*] [**permanent**]	Global configuration command that creates a static route
ip default-network *network-number*	Global command that creates a default route based on the router's route to reach the classful network listed in the command

Table 4-5   *Chapter 4 EXEC Command Reference*

Command	Description
show ip route	Lists the router's entire routing table
show ip route *ip-address*	Lists detailed information about the route that a router matches for the listed IP address
ping {*host-name* | *ip-address*}	Tests IP routes by sending an ICMP packet to the destination host
traceroute {*host-name* | *ip-address*}	Tests IP routes by discovering the IP addresses of the routes between a router and the listed destination

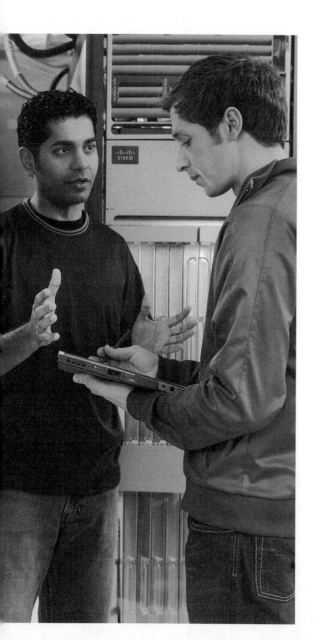

This chapter covers the following subjects:

VLSM: This section explains the issues and solutions when designing an internetwork that uses VLSM.

Manual Route Summarization: This section explains the concept of manual route summarization and describes how to design internetworks to allow easier summarization.

Autosummarization and Discontiguous Classful Networks: This section examines the autosummarization feature and explains how it must be considered in internetwork designs that use discontiguous networks.

CHAPTER 5

VLSM and Route Summarization

While Chapter 4, "IP Routing: Static and Connected Routes," focuses on topics related to IP routing, this chapter focuses on topics related to IP addressing: variable-length subnet masking (VLSM), manual route summarization, and automatic route summarization. These features relate to IP addressing in that they all require some thought about the range of IP addresses implied by a given address and mask, or by a subnet that is part of a summarized route. So, this chapter requires a full understanding of IP addressing for a full understanding of the examples in this chapter.

This chapter mainly focuses on concepts and **show** commands, with only a few configuration commands of interest.

"Do I Know This Already?" Quiz

The "Do I Know This Already?" quiz allows you to assess whether you should read the entire chapter. If you miss no more than one of these eight self-assessment questions, you might want to move ahead to the section "Exam Preparation Tasks." Table 5-1 lists the major headings in this chapter and the "Do I Know This Already?" quiz questions covering the material in those headings so that you can assess your knowledge of these specific areas. The answers to the "Do I Know This Already?" quiz appear in Appendix A.

Table 5-1 *"Do I Know This Already?" Foundation Topics Section-to-Question Mapping*

Foundation Topics Section	Questions
VLSM	1–3
Manual Route Summarization	4–6
Autosummarization and Discontiguous Classful Networks	7–8

1. Which of the following routing protocols support VLSM?

    a. RIP-1

    b. RIP-2

    c. EIGRP

    d. OSPF

2. What does the acronym VLSM stand for?

    a. Variable-length subnet mask

    b. Very long subnet mask

    c. Vociferous longitudinal subnet mask

    d. Vector-length subnet mask

    e. Vector loop subnet mask

3. R1 has configured interface Fa0/0 with the **ip address 10.5.48.1 255.255.240.0** command. Which of the following subnets, when configured on another interface on R1, would not be considered to be an overlapping VLSM subnet?

    a. 10.5.0.0 255.255.240.0

    b. 10.4.0.0 255.254.0.0

    c. 10.5.32.0 255.255.224.0

    d. 10.5.0.0 255.255.128.0

4. Which of the following summarized subnets is the smallest (smallest range of addresses) summary route that includes subnets 10.3.95.0, 10.3.96.0, and 10.3.97.0, mask 255.255.255.0?

    a. 10.0.0.0 255.0.0.0

    b. 10.3.0.0 255.255.0.0

    c. 10.3.64.0 255.255.192.0

    d. 10.3.64.0 255.255.224.0

5. Which of the following summarized subnets is not a valid summary that includes subnets 10.1.55.0, 10.1.56.0, and 10.1.57.0, mask 255.255.255.0?

    a. 10.0.0.0 255.0.0.0

    b. 10.1.0.0 255.255.0.0

    c. 10.1.55.0 255.255.255.0

    d. 10.1.48.0 255.255.248.0

    e. 10.1.32.0 255.255.224.0

6. Which of the following routing protocols support manual route summarization?

    a. RIP-1

    b. RIP-2

    c. EIGRP

    d. OSPF

7. Which routing protocol(s) perform(s) autosummarization by default?

    a. RIP-1

    b. RIP-2

    c. EIGRP

    d. OSPF

8. An internetwork has a discontiguous network 10.0.0.0, and it is having problems. All routers use RIP-1 with all default configurations. Which of the following answers lists an action that, by itself, would solve the problem and allow the discontiguous network?

    a. Migrate all routers to use OSPF, using as many defaults as is possible.

    b. Disable autosummarization with the **no auto-summary** RIP configuration command.

    c. Migrate to EIGRP, using as many defaults as is possible.

    d. The problem cannot be solved without first making network 10.0.0.0 contiguous.

Foundation Topics

This chapter discusses three related topics: VLSM, manual route summarization, and automatic route summarization. These topics mainly relate to each other because of the underlying math, which requires that the engineer be able to look at a subnet number and mask to quickly determine the implied range of addresses. This chapter begins with VLSM, moving on to manual route summarization, and finally autosummarization.

VLSM

VLSM occurs when an internetwork uses more than one mask in different subnets of a single Class A, B, or C network. VLSM allows engineers to reduce the number of wasted IP addresses in each subnet, allowing more subnets and avoiding having to obtain another registered IP network number from regional IP address assignment authorities. Also, even when using private IP networks (as defined in RFC 1918), large corporations might still need to conserve the address space, again creating a need to use VLSM.

Figure 5-1 shows an example of VLSM used in class A network 10.0.0.0.

Figure 5-1   *VLSM in Network 10.0.0.0: Masks 255.255.255.0 and 255.255.255.252*

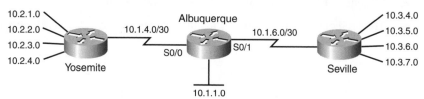

Mask: 255.255.255.0 Except Where Shown

Figure 5-1 shows a typical choice of using a /30 prefix (mask 255.255.255.252) on point-to-point serial links, with some other mask (255.255.255.0, in this example) on the LAN subnets. All subnets are of class A network 10.0.0.0, with two masks being used, therefore meeting the definition of VLSM.

Oddly enough, a common mistake occurs when people think that VLSM means "using more than one mask," rather than "using more than one mask in a single classful network." For example, if in one internetwork diagram, all subnets of network 10.0.0.0 use a 255.255.240.0 mask and all subnets of network 11.0.0.0 use a 255.255.255.0 mask, two different masks are used. However, only one mask is inside each respective classful network, so this particular design would not be using VLSM.

Example 5-1 lists the routing table on Albuquerque from Figure 5-1. Albuquerque uses two masks inside network 10.0.0.0, as noted in the highlighted line in the example.

Example 5-1   *Albuquerque Routing Table with VLSM*

```
Albuquerque#show ip route
Codes: C - connected, S - static, I - IGRP, R - RIP, M - mobile, B - BGP
       D - EIGRP, EX - EIGRP external, O - OSPF, IA - OSPF inter area
       N1 - OSPF NSSA external type 1, N2 - OSPF NSSA external type 2
       E1 - OSPF external type 1, E2 - OSPF external type 2, E - EGP
       i - IS-IS, L1 - IS-IS level-1, L2 - IS-IS level-2, ia - IS-IS inter area
       * - candidate default, U - per-user static route, o - ODR
       P - periodic downloaded static route

Gateway of last resort is not set

     10.0.0.0/8 is variably subnetted, 11 subnets, 2 masks
D        10.2.1.0/24 [90/2172416] via 10.1.4.2, 00:00:34, Serial0/0
D        10.2.2.0/24 [90/2172416] via 10.1.4.2, 00:00:34, Serial0/0
D        10.2.3.0/24 [90/2172416] via 10.1.4.2, 00:00:34, Serial0/0
D        10.2.4.0/24 [90/2172416] via 10.1.4.2, 00:00:34, Serial0/0
D        10.3.4.0/24 [90/2172416] via 10.1.6.2, 00:00:56, Serial0/1
D        10.3.5.0/24 [90/2172416] via 10.1.6.2, 00:00:56, Serial0/1
D        10.3.6.0/24 [90/2172416] via 10.1.6.2, 00:00:56, Serial0/1
D        10.3.7.0/24 [90/2172416] via 10.1.6.2, 00:00:56, Serial0/1
C        10.1.1.0/24 is directly connected, Ethernet0/0
C        10.1.6.0/30 is directly connected, Serial0/1
C        10.1.4.0/30 is directly connected, Serial0/0
```

Classless and Classful Routing Protocols

For a routing protocol to support VLSM, the routing protocol must advertise not only the subnet number but also the subnet mask when advertising routes. Additionally, a routing protocol must include subnet masks in its routing updates to support manual route summarization.

Each IP routing protocol is considered to be either classless or classful, based on whether the routing protocol does (classless) or does not (classful) send the mask in routing updates. Each routing protocol is either classless or classful by its very nature; no commands exist to enable or disable whether a particular routing protocol is a classless or classful routing protocol. Table 5-2 lists the routing protocols, shows whether each is classless or classful, and offers reminders of the two features (VLSM and route summarization) enabled by the inclusion of masks in the routing updates.

Table 5-2   *Classless and Classful Interior IP Routing Protocols*

Routing Protocol	Is It Classless?	Sends Mask in Updates	Supports VLSM	Supports Manual Route Summarization
RIP-1	No	No	No	No
IGRP	No	No	No	No
RIP-2	Yes	Yes	Yes	Yes
EIGRP	Yes	Yes	Yes	Yes
OSPF	Yes	Yes	Yes	Yes

Overlapping VLSM Subnets

The subnets chosen to be used in any IP internetwork design must not overlap their address ranges. With a single subnet mask in a network, the overlaps are somewhat obvious; however, with VLSM, the overlapping subnets might not be as obvious. When multiple subnets overlap, a router's routing table entries overlap. As a result, routing becomes unpredictable, and some hosts can be reached from only particular parts of the internetwork. In short, a design that uses overlapping subnets is considered to be an incorrect design, and should not be used.

Two general types of problems exist that relate to overlapping VLSM subnets, both in real jobs and for the exams: analyzing an existing design to find overlaps and choosing new VLSM subnets so that you do not create an overlapped subnet. To appreciate what the exam might cover for VLSM and overlapping subnets, consider Figure 5-2, which shows a single Class B network (172.16.0.0), using a VLSM design that includes three different masks, /23, /24, and /30.

Figure 5-2 *VLSM Design with Possible Overlap*

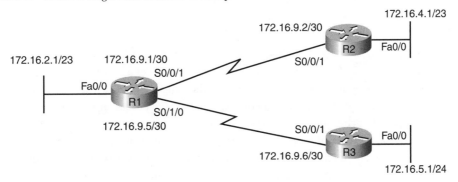

Now imagine that an exam question shows you the figure, and either directly or indirectly asks whether overlapping subnets exist. This type of question might simply tell you that some hosts cannot ping each other, or it might not even mention that the root cause could be that some of the subnets overlap. To answer such a question, you could follow this simple but possibly laborious task:

Step 1   Calculate the subnet number and subnet broadcast address of each subnet; this gives you the range of addresses in that subnet.

Step 2   Compare the ranges of addresses in each subnet and look for cases in which the address ranges overlap.

For example, in Figure 5-2, you would look at the five subnets, and using Step 1, calculate the subnet numbers, broadcast addresses, and range of addresses, with the answers listed in Table 5-3.

Table 5-3 *Subnets and Address Ranges in Figure 5-2*

Subnet Location	Subnet Number	First Address	Last Address	Broadcast Address
R1 LAN	172.16.2.0	172.16.2.1	172.16.3.254	172.16.3.255
R2 LAN	172.16.4.0	172.16.4.1	172.16.5.254	172.16.5.255
R3 LAN	172.16.5.0	172.16.5.1	172.16.5.254	172.16.5.255
R1-R2 serial	172.16.9.0	172.16.9.1	172.16.9.2	172.16.9.3
R1-R3 serial	172.16.9.4	172.16.9.5	172.16.9.6	172.16.9.7

Step 2 states the somewhat obvious step of comparing the address ranges to see whether any overlaps occur. Note that none of the subnet numbers are identical; however, a closer look at the R2 LAN and R3 LAN subnets shows that these two subnets overlap. In this case, the design is invalid because of the overlap, and one of the two subnets would need to be changed.

Designing a Subnetting Scheme Using VLSM

CCENT/CCNA ICND1 Official Exam Certification Guide explains how to design the IP addressing scheme for a new internetwork by choosing IP subnets when using a single subnet mask throughout a classful network. To do so, the process first analyzes the design requirements to determine the number of subnets and the number of hosts in the largest subnet. Then, a subnet mask is chosen. Finally, all possible subnets of the network, using that mask, are identified, and then the actual subnets used in the design are picked from that list. For example, in Class B network 172.16.0.0, a design might call for ten subnets, with a largest subnet of 200 hosts. Mask 255.255.255.0 meets the requirements, with 8 subnet bits and 8 host bits, supporting 256 subnets and 254 hosts per subnet. The subnet numbers would be 172.16.0.0, 172.16.1.0, 172.16.2.0, and so on.

When using VLSM in a design, the design process starts by deciding how many subnets of each size are required. For example, most installations use subnets with a /30 prefix for serial links because these subnets support exactly two IP addresses, which are all the addresses needed on a point-to-point link. The LAN-based subnets often have different requirements, with shorter prefix lengths (meaning more host bits) for larger numbers of hosts/subnet, and longer prefix lengths (meaning fewer host bits) for smaller numbers of hosts/subnet.

NOTE   To review subnetting design when using static-length subnet masks (SLSM), refer to *CCENT/CCNA ICND1 Official Exam Certification Guide*, Chapter 12, or the CD-only version of that chapter in this book's CD (Appendix H). (The CD-only Appendix D, "Subnetting Practice," of this book also includes some related practice problems.)

After the number of subnets with each mask has been determined, the next step is to find subnet numbers that match those requirements. This task is not particularly difficult if you already understand how to find subnet numbers when using static-length masks. However, a more formal process can help, which is outlined as follows:

Step 1   Determine the number of subnets needed for each mask/prefix based on the design requirements.

Step 2   Using the shortest prefix length (largest number of host bits), identify the subnets of the classful network when using that mask, until the required number of such subnets has been identified.

Step 3   Identify the next numeric subnet number using the same mask as in the previous step.

Step 4   Starting with the subnet number identified at the previous step, identify smaller subnets based on the next-longest prefix length required for the design, until the required number of subnets of that size have been identified.

Step 5   Repeat Steps 3 and 4 until all subnets of all sizes have been found.

Frankly, using the above process, as written, can be a little difficult, but an example can certainly help make sense of the process. So, imagine a network design for which the following design requirements were determined, per Step 1 of the previous process. The design calls for the use of Class B network 172.16.0.0:

■   Three subnets with mask /24 (255.255.255.0)

■   Three subnets with mask /26 (255.255.255.192)

■   Four subnets with mask /30 (255.255.255.252)

Step 2 in this case means that the first three subnets of network 172.16.0.0 should be identified, with mask /24, because /24 is the shortest prefix length of the three prefix lengths listed in the design requirements. Using the same math covered in detail in the ICND1 book, the first three subnets would be 172.16.0.0/24, 172.16.1.0/24, and 172.16.2.0/24:

■   172.16.0.0/24: Range 172.16.0.1–172.16.0.254

■   172.16.1.0/24: Range 172.16.1.1–172.16.1.254

■   172.16.2.0/24: Range 172.16.2.1–172.16.2.254

Step 3 in this case says to identify one more subnet using the /24 mask, so the next numeric subnet would be 172.16.3.0/24.

Before moving on to Step 4, take a few minutes to review Figure 5-3. The figure shows the results of Step 2 on the top part of the figure, listing the three subnets identified at this step as "allocated" because they will be used for subnets in this design. It also lists the next subnet, as found at Step 3, listing it as unallocated, because it has not yet been chosen to be used for a particular part of the design.

Figure 5-3 *Designing to Use VLSM Subnets*

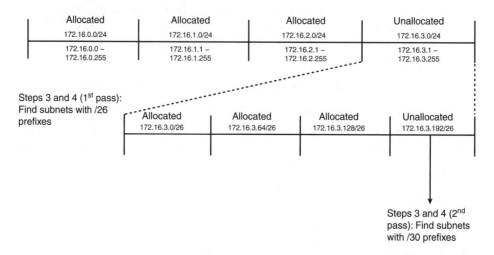

To find the subnets at Step 4, start with the unallocated subnet number found at Step 3 (172.16.3.0), but with Step 4 applying the next longer prefix length, or /26 in this example. The process always results in the first subnet number being the subnet number found at the previous step, or 172.16.3.0 in this case. The three subnets are as follows:

- 172.16.3.0/26: Range 172.16.3.1–172.16.3.62

- 172.16.3.64/26: Range 172.16.3.65–172.16.3.126

- 172.16.3.128/26: Range 172.16.3.129–172.16.3.190

Finally, Step 5 says to repeat Steps 3 and 4 until all subnets have been found. In this case, repeating Step 3, the next subnet is found, using the /26 prefix length—namely subnet 172.16.3.192/26. This subnet is considered unallocated for the time being. To repeat Step 4 for the next longest prefix length, Step 4 uses the /30 prefix, starting with subnet number 172.16.3.192. The first subnet will be 172.16.3.192, with mask /30, plus the next three subnets with that same mask, as follows:

- 172.16.3.192/30: Range 172.16.3.193–172.16.3.194

- 172.16.3.196/30: Range 172.16.3.197–172.16.3.198

- 172.16.3.200/30: Range 172.16.3.201–172.16.3.202

- 172.16.3.204/30: Range 172.16.3.205–172.16.3.206

The wording in the formalized process might seem to be a bit laborious, but it does result in a set of VLSM subnets that do not overlap. By using a structured approach of essentially allocating the larger subnets first, then the smaller subnets, you can generally choose subnets so that the address ranges do not overlap.

Adding a New Subnet to an Existing Design

Another task required when working with VLSM-based internetworks is to choose a new subnet number for an existing internetwork. In particular, extra care must be taken when choosing new subnet numbers to avoid causing an overlap between the new subnet and any existing subnets. For example, consider the internetwork in Figure 5-2, with classful network 172.16.0.0. An exam question might suggest that a new subnet, with a /23 prefix length, needs to be added to the design. The question might also say "Pick the smallest subnet number that can be used for the new subnet." So, the subnets must be identified, and a nonoverlapping subnet must be chosen.

To attack such a problem, you would essentially need to find all the subnet numbers that could be created in that classful network, using the stated or implied mask. Then, you would have to ensure that the new subnet did not overlap with any existing subnets. Specifically, you could use the following steps:

Step 1   If not already listed as part of the question, pick the subnet mask (prefix length) based on the design requirements, typically based on the number of hosts needed in the subnet.

Step 2   Calculate all possible subnet numbers of the classful network, using the mask determined at Step 1. (If the exam question asks for the numerically largest or smallest subnet number, you might choose to only do this math for the first few or last few subnets.)

Step 3   For the subnets found at Step 2, calculate the subnet broadcast address and range of addresses for each assumed subnet.

Step 4   Compare the lists of potential subnets and address ranges to the existing subnets and address ranges. Rule out any of the potential subnets that overlap with an existing subnet.

Step 5   Pick a subnet number from the list found at Step 2 that does not overlap with any existing subnets, noting whether the question asks for the smallest or largest subnet number.

Using this five-step process with the example started just before the step list with Figure 5-2, the question supplied the prefix length of /23 (Step 1). Table 5-4 lists the results for Steps

2 and 3, listing the subnet numbers, broadcast addresses, and range of addresses for the first five of the possible /23 subnets.

Table 5-4 *First Five Possible /23 Subnets*

Subnet	Subnet Number	First Address	Last Address	Broadcast Address
First (zero)	172.16.0.0	172.16.0.1	172.16.1.254	172.16.1.255
Second	172.16.2.0	172.16.2.1	172.16.3.254	172.16.3.255
Third	172.16.4.0	172.16.4.1	172.16.5.254	172.16.5.255
Fourth	172.16.6.0	172.16.6.1	172.16.7.254	172.16.7.255
Fifth	172.16.8.0	172.16.8.1	172.16.9.254	172.16.9.255

Step 4 compares the information in the table with the existing subnets. In this case, the second, third, and fourth subnets in Table 5-4 overlap with existing subnets in Figure 5-2.

Step 5 has more to do with the exam than with real networks. Multiple-choice questions sometimes need to force the question to have only a single answer, so asking for the numerically smallest or largest subnet solves the problem. This particular example problem asks for the smallest subnet number, and the zero subnet is still available (172.16.0.0/23, with broadcast address 172.16.1.255). If the question allowed the use of the zero subnet, the zero subnet (172.16.0.0/23) would be the correct answer. However, if the zero subnet was prohibited from use, the first three subnets listed in Table 5-4 would not be available, making the fourth subnet (172.16.8.0/23) the correct answer. Note that Scenario 5 in the CD-only Appendix F, "Additional Scenarios," gives you an opportunity to practice using this particular process.

> **NOTE**   For the exam, the zero subnet should be avoided if (a) the question implies the use of classful routing protocols or (b) the routers are configured with the **no ip subnet-zero** global configuration command. Otherwise, assume that the zero subnet can be used.

VLSM Configuration

Routers do not enable or disable VLSM as a configuration feature. From a configuration perspective, VLSM is simply a side effect of the **ip address** interface subcommand. Routers configure VLSM by virtue of having at least two router interfaces, on the same router or among all routers in the internetwork, with IP addresses in the same classful network but with different masks. Example 5-2 shows a simple example on Router R3 from Figure 5-2, with interface Fa0/0 being assigned IP address 172.16.5.1/24, and interface S0/0/1 being assigned IP address 172.16.9.6/30, thereby using at least two different masks in network 172.16.0.0.

Example 5-2 *Configuring VLSM*

```
R3#configure terminal
R3(config)#interface Fa0/0
R3(config-if)#ip address 172.16.5.1 255.255.255.0
R3(config-if)#interface S0/0/1
R3(config-if)#ip address 172.16.9.6 255.255.255.252
```

Classless routing protocols, which support VLSM, do not have to be configured to enable VLSM. Support for VLSM is simply a feature inherent to those routing protocols.

Next, the text moves on to the second major section of this chapter, the topic of manual route summarization.

Manual Route Summarization

Small networks might have only a few dozen routes in their routers' routing tables. The larger the network, the larger the number of routes. In fact, Internet routers have more than 100,000 routes in some cases.

The routing table might become too large in large IP networks. As routing tables grow, they consume more memory in a router. Also, each router can take more time to route a packet, because the router has to match a route in the routing table, and searching a larger table generally takes more time. And with a large routing table, it takes more time to troubleshoot problems, because the engineers working on the network need to sift through more information.

Route summarization reduces the size of routing tables while maintaining routes to all the destinations in the network. As a result, routing performance can be improved and memory can be saved inside each router. Summarization also improves convergence time, because the router that summarizes the route no longer has to announce any changes to the status of the individual subnets. By advertising only that the entire summary route is either up or down, the routers that have the summary route do not have to reconverge every time one of the component subnets goes up or down.

This chapter refers to route summarization as manual route summarization, in contrast to the last major topic in this chapter, autosummarization. The term *manual* refers to the fact that manual route summarization only occurs when an engineer configures one or more commands. Autosummarization occurs automatically without a specific configuration command.

The following sections first examine the concepts behind route summarization, followed by some suggestions of how to determine good summary routes. Note that while the concepts are covered, the configuration of manually summarized routes is not covered as an end to itself in this book.

Route Summarization Concepts

Engineers use route summarization to reduce the size of the routing tables in the network. Route summarization causes some number of more-specific routes to be replaced with a single route that includes all the IP addresses covered by the subnets in the original routes.

Summary routes, which replace multiple routes, must be configured by a network engineer. Although the configuration command does not look exactly like a **static ip route** command, the same basic information is configured. Now the routing protocol advertises just the summary route, as opposed to the original routes.

Route summarization works much better when the network was designed with route summarization in mind. For example, Figure 5-1, earlier in this chapter, shows the results of good planning for summarization. In this network, the engineer planned his choices of subnet numbers relative to his goal of using route summarization. All subnets off the main site (Albuquerque), including WAN links, start with 10.1. All LAN subnets off Yosemite start with 10.2, and likewise, all LAN subnets off Seville start with 10.3.

Earlier, Example 5-1 showed a copy of Albuquerque's routing table without summarization. That example shows Albuquerque's four routes to subnets that begin with 10.2, all pointing out its serial 0/0 interface to Yosemite. Similarly, Albuquerque shows four routes to subnets that begin with 10.3, all pointing out its serial 0/1 interface to Seville. This design allows the Yosemite and Seville routers to advertise a single summary route instead of the four routes they currently advertise to Albuquerque, respectively.

Example 5-3 shows the results of the configuration of manual route summarization on both Yosemite and Seville. In this case, Yosemite is advertising a summary route for 10.2.0.0/16, which represents address range 10.2.0.0–10.2.255.255 (all addresses that begin with 10.2). Seville advertises a summary route for 10.3.0.0/16, which represents the address range 10.3.0.0–10.3.255.255 (all addresses that begin 10.3).

Example 5-3 *Albuquerque Routing Table After Route Summarization*

```
Albuquerque#show ip route
Codes: C - connected, S - static, I - IGRP, R - RIP, M - mobile, B - BGP
       D - EIGRP, EX - EIGRP external, O - OSPF, IA - OSPF inter area
       N1 - OSPF NSSA external type 1, N2 - OSPF NSSA external type 2
       E1 - OSPF external type 1, E2 - OSPF external type 2, E - EGP
       i - IS-IS, L1 - IS-IS level-1, L2 - IS-IS level-2, ia - IS-IS inter area
```

Example 5-3 *Albuquerque Routing Table After Route Summarization (Continued)*

```
          * - candidate default, U - per-user static route, o - ODR
          P - periodic downloaded static route

Gateway of last resort is not set

     10.0.0.0/8 is variably subnetted, 5 subnets, 3 masks
D        10.2.0.0/16 [90/2172416] via 10.1.4.2, 00:05:59, Serial0/0
D        10.3.0.0/16 [90/2172416] via 10.1.6.3, 00:05:40, Serial0/1
C        10.1.1.0/24 is directly connected, Ethernet0/0
C        10.1.6.0/30 is directly connected, Serial0/1
C        10.1.4.0/30 is directly connected, Serial0/0
```

The resulting routing table on Albuquerque still routes packets correctly, but with more efficiency and less memory. Frankly, improving from 11 routes to 5 routes does not help much, but the same concept, applied to larger networks, does help.

The effects of route summarization can also be seen on the other two routers in the figure. Example 5-4 shows Yosemite, including both the route summarization configuration and Yosemite's routing table. Example 5-5 shows the same kind of information on Seville.

Example 5-4 *Yosemite Configuration and Routing Table After Route Summarization*

```
Yosemite#configure terminal
Enter configuration commands, one per line.  End with CNTL/Z.
Yosemite(config)#interface serial 0/0
Yosemite(config-if)#ip summary-address eigrp 1 10.2.0.0 255.255.0.0
Yosemite(config-if)#^Z

Yosemite#show ip route
Codes: C - connected, S - static, I - IGRP, R - RIP, M - mobile, B - BGP
       D - EIGRP, EX - EIGRP external, O - OSPF, IA - OSPF inter area
       N1 - OSPF NSSA external type 1, N2 - OSPF NSSA external type 2
       E1 - OSPF external type 1, E2 - OSPF external type 2, E - EGP
       i - IS-IS, L1 - IS-IS level-1, L2 - IS-IS level-2, ia - IS-IS inter area
       * - candidate default, U - per-user static route, o - ODR
       P - periodic downloaded static route

Gateway of last resort is not set

     10.0.0.0/8 is variably subnetted, 9 subnets, 3 masks
D        10.2.0.0/16 is a summary, 00:04:57, Null0
D        10.3.0.0/16 [90/2684416] via 10.1.4.1, 00:04:30, Serial0/0
C        10.2.1.0/24 is directly connected, FastEthernet0/0
D        10.1.1.0/24 [90/2195456] via 10.1.4.1, 00:04:52, Serial0/0
C        10.2.2.0/24 is directly connected, Loopback2
C        10.2.3.0/24 is directly connected, Loopback3
```

continues

Example 5-4 *Yosemite Configuration and Routing Table After Route Summarization (Continued)*

```
C       10.2.4.0/24 is directly connected, Loopback4
D       10.1.6.0/30 [90/2681856] via 10.1.4.1, 00:04:53, Serial0/0
C       10.1.4.0/30 is directly connected, Serial0/0
```

Example 5-5 *Seville Configuration and Routing Table After Route Summarization*

```
Seville#configure terminal
Enter configuration commands, one per line.  End with CNTL/Z.
Seville(config)#interface serial 0/0
Seville(config-if)#ip summary-address eigrp 1 10.3.0.0 255.255.0.0
Seville(config-if)#^Z
Seville#show ip route
Codes: C - connected, S - static, I - IGRP, R - RIP, M - mobile, B - BGP
       D - EIGRP, EX - EIGRP external, O - OSPF, IA - OSPF inter area
       N1 - OSPF NSSA external type 1, N2 - OSPF NSSA external type 2
       E1 - OSPF external type 1, E2 - OSPF external type 2, E - EGP
       i - IS-IS, L1 - IS-IS level-1, L2 - IS-IS level-2, ia - IS-IS inter area
       * - candidate default, U - per-user static route, o - ODR
       P - periodic downloaded static route

Gateway of last resort is not set

     10.0.0.0/8 is variably subnetted, 9 subnets, 3 masks
D       10.2.0.0/16 [90/2684416] via 10.1.6.1, 00:00:36, Serial0/0
D       10.3.0.0/16 is a summary, 00:00:38, Null0
D       10.1.1.0/24 [90/2195456] via 10.1.6.1, 00:00:36, Serial0/0
C       10.3.5.0/24 is directly connected, Loopback5
C       10.3.4.0/24 is directly connected, FastEthernet0/0
C       10.1.6.0/30 is directly connected, Serial0/0
C       10.3.7.0/24 is directly connected, Loopback7
D       10.1.4.0/30 [90/2681856] via 10.1.6.1, 00:00:36, Serial0/0
C       10.3.6.0/24 is directly connected, Loopback6
```

Route summarization configuration differs with different routing protocols; Enhanced IGRP (EIGRP) is used in this example. The summary routes for EIGRP are created by the **ip summary-address** interface subcommands on Yosemite and Seville in this case. Each command defines a new summarized route and tells EIGRP to only advertise the summary out this interface and not to advertise any routes contained in the larger summary. For example, Yosemite defines a summary route to 10.2.0.0, mask 255.255.0.0, which defines a route to all hosts whose IP addresses begin with 10.2. In effect, this command causes Yosemite and Seville to advertise routes 10.2.0.0 255.255.0.0 and 10.3.0.0 255.255.0.0, respectively, and not to advertise their original four LAN subnets.

Note that back in Example 5-3, Albuquerque's routing table now contains a route to 10.2.0.0 255.255.0.0 (the mask is listed in prefix notation as /16), but none of the original four subnets that begin with 10.2. The same thing occurs for route 10.3.0.0/16.

The routing tables on Yosemite and Seville look a little different from Albuquerque. Focusing on Yosemite (Example 5-4), notice that the four routes to subnets that begin with 10.2 show up because they are directly connected subnets. Yosemite does not see the four 10.3 routes. Instead, it sees a summary route, because Albuquerque now advertises the 10.3.0.0/16 summarized route only. The opposite is true on Seville (Example 5-5), which lists all four connected routes that begin with 10.3 and a summary route for 10.2.0.0/16.

The most interesting part of Yosemite's routing tables is the route to 10.2.0.0/16, with the outgoing interface set to **null0**. Routes referring to an outgoing interface of the null0 interface mean that packets matching this route are discarded. EIGRP added this route, with interface null0, as a result of the **ip summary-address** command. The logic works like this:

Yosemite needs this odd-looking route because now it might receive packets destined for other 10.2 addresses besides the four existing 10.2 subnets. If a packet destined for one of the four existing 10.2.x subnets arrives, Yosemite has a correct, more specific route to match the packet. If a packet whose destination starts with 10.2 arrives, but it is not in one of those four subnets, the null route matches the packet, causing Yosemite to discard the packet—as it should.

The routing table on Seville is similar to Yosemite's in terms of the table entries and why they are in the table.

Route Summarization Strategies

As mentioned earlier, manual route summarization works best when the network engineer plans his choice of subnet numbers anticipating route summarization. For example, the earlier examples assumed a well-thought-out plan, with the engineers only using subnets beginning with 10.2 for subnets off the Yosemite router. That convention allowed the creation of a summary route for all addresses beginning with 10.2 by having Yosemite advertise a route describing subnet 10.2.0.0, mask 255.255.0.0.

Some summarized routes combine many routes into one route, but that might not be the "best" summarization. The word *best*, when applied to choosing what summary route to configure, means that the summary should include all the subnets specified in the question but as few other addresses as is possible. For example, in the earlier summarization example, Yosemite summarized four subnets (10.2.1.0, 10.2.2.0, 10.2.3.0, and 10.2.4.0, all with mask 255.255.255.0) into the 10.2.0.0/16 summary route. However, this summary includes a lot of IP addresses that are not in those four subnets. Does the summary work given that network's design goals? Sure. However, instead of just defining a summary that encompasses lots of additional addresses that do not yet exist in a network, the engineer might instead want to configure the tightest, or most concise, or best summary: the summary that includes all the subnets but as few extra subnets (the ones that have not been assigned yet) as possible. This section describes a strategy for finding those concise best summary routes.

The following list describes a generalized binary process by which you can find a best summary route for a group of subnets:

Step 1   List all to-be-summarized subnet numbers in binary.

Step 2   Find the first N bits of the subnet numbers for which every subnet has the same value, moving from left to right. (For our purposes, consider this first part the "in-common" part.)

Step 3   To find the summary router's subnet number, write down the in-common bits from Step 2 and binary 0s for the remaining bits. Convert back to decimal, 8 bits at a time, when finished.

Step 4   To find the summary route's subnet mask, write down N binary 1s, with N being the number of in-common bits found at Step 2. Complete the subnet mask with all binary 0s. Convert back to decimal, 8 bits at a time, when finished.

Step 5   Check your work by calculating the range of valid IP addresses implied by the new summary route, comparing the range to the summarized subnets. The new summary should encompass all IP addresses in the summarized subnets.

By looking at the subnet numbers in binary, you can more easily discover the bits in common among all the subnet numbers. By using the longest number of bits in common, you can find the best summary. The next two sections show two examples using this process to find the best, most concise, tightest summary routes for the network shown in Figure 5-1.

Sample "Best" Summary on Seville

Seville has subnets 10.3.4.0, 10.3.5.0, 10.3.6.0, and 10.3.7.0, all with mask 255.255.255.0. You start the process by writing down all the subnet numbers in binary:

```
0000 1010 0000 0011 0000 01|00 0000 0000 - 10.3.4.0
0000 1010 0000 0011 0000 01|01 0000 0000 - 10.3.5.0
0000 1010 0000 0011 0000 01|10 0000 0000 - 10.3.6.0
0000 1010 0000 0011 0000 01|11 0000 0000 - 10.3.7.0
```

Step 2 requires that you find all in-common bits at the beginning of all the subnets. Even before looking at the numbers in binary, you can guess that the first two octets are identical in all four subnets. So, a quick look at the first 16 bits of all four subnet numbers confirms that all have the same value. This means that the in-common part (Step 2) is at least 16 bits long. Further examination shows that the first 6 bits of the third octet are also identical, but the seventh bit in the third octet has some different values among the different subnets. So the in-common part of these four subnets is the first 22 bits.

Step 3 says to create a subnet number for the summary by taking the same bits in the in-common part, and write down binary 0s for the rest. In this case:

   0000 1010 0000 0011 0000 01|00 0000 0000 - 10.3.4.0

Step 4 creates the mask by using binary 1s for the same bits as the in-common part, which is the first 22 bits in this case, and then binary 0s for the remaining bits, as follows:

   1111 1111 1111 1111 1111 11|00 0000 0000 - 255.255.252.0

So, the summary route uses subnet 10.3.4.0, mask 255.255.252.0.

Step 5 suggests a method to check your work. The summary route should include all the IP addresses in the summarized routes. In this case, the range of addresses for the summary route starts with 10.3.4.0. The first valid IP address is 10.3.4.1, the final valid IP address is 10.3.7.254, and the broadcast address is 10.3.7.255. In this case, the summary route includes all the IP addresses in the four routes it summarizes and no extraneous IP addresses.

Sample "Best" Summary on Yosemite

The four subnets on Yosemite cannot be summarized quite as efficiently as those on Seville. On Seville, the summary route itself covers the same set of IP addresses as the four subnets with no extra addresses. As you will see, the best summary route at Yosemite includes twice as many addresses in the summary as exist in the original four subnets.

Yosemite has subnets 10.2.1.0, 10.2.2.0, 10.2.3.0, and 10.2.4.0, all with mask 255.255.255.0. The process starts at Step 1 by writing down all the subnet numbers in binary:

   0000 1010 0000 0010 0000 0|001 0000 0000 - 10.2.1.0
   0000 1010 0000 0010 0000 0|010 0000 0000 - 10.2.2.0
   0000 1010 0000 0010 0000 0|011 0000 0000 - 10.2.3.0
   0000 1010 0000 0010 0000 0|100 0000 0000 - 10.2.4.0

At Step 2, it appears that the first two octets are identical in all four subnets, plus the first 5 bits of the third octet. So, the first 21 bits of the four subnet numbers are in common.

Step 3 says to create a subnet number for the summary route by taking the same value for the in-common part and binary 0s for the rest. In this case:

0000 1010 0000 0010 0000 0|000 0000 0000 - 10.2.0.0

Step 4 creates the mask used for the summary route by using binary 1s for the in-common part and binary 0s for the rest. The in-common part in this example is the first 21 bits:

1111 1111 1111 1111 1111 1|000 0000 0000 - 255.255.248.0

So, the best summary is 10.2.0.0, mask 255.255.248.0.

Step 5 suggests a method to check your work. The summary route should define a superset of the IP addresses in the summarized routes. In this case, the range of addresses starts with 10.2.0.0. The first valid IP address is 10.2.0.1, the final valid IP address is 10.2.7.254, and the broadcast address is 10.2.7.255. In this case, the summary route summarizes a larger set of addresses than just the four subnets, but it does include all addresses in all four subnets.

Autosummarization and Discontiguous Classful Networks

As covered in the previous sections, manual route summarization can improve routing efficiency, reduce memory consumption, and improve convergence by reducing the length of routing tables. The final sections of this chapter examine the automatic summarization of routes at the boundaries of classful networks, using a feature called autosummarization.

Because classful routing protocols do not advertise subnet mask information, the routing updates simply list subnet numbers but no accompanying mask. A router receiving a routing update with a classful routing protocol looks at the subnet number in the update, but the router must make some assumptions about what mask is associated with the subnet. For example, with Cisco routers, if R1 and R2 have connected networks of the same single Class A, B, or C network, and if R2 receives an update from R1, R2 assumes that the routes described in R1's update use the same mask that R2 uses. In other words, the classful routing protocols require a static-length subnet mask (SLSM) throughout each classful network so that each router can then reasonably assume that the mask configured for its own interfaces is the same mask used throughout that classful network.

When a router has interfaces in more than one Class A, B, or C network, it can advertise a single route for an entire Class A, B, or C network into the other classful network. This feature is called *autosummarization*. It can be characterized as follows:

> When advertised on an interface whose IP address is not in network X, routes related to subnets in network X are summarized and advertised as one route. That route is for the entire Class A, B, or C network X.

In other words, if R3 has interfaces in networks 10.0.0.0 and 11.0.0.0, when R3 advertises routing updates out interfaces with IP addresses that start with 11, the updates advertise a single route for network 10.0.0.0. Similarly, R3 advertises a single route to 11.0.0.0 out its interfaces whose IP addresses start with 10.

An Example of Autosummarization

As usual, an example makes the concept much clearer. Consider Figure 5-4, which shows two networks in use: 10.0.0.0 and 172.16.0.0. Seville has four (connected) routes to subnets of network 10.0.0.0. Example 5-6 shows the output of the **show ip route** command on Albuquerque, as well as RIP-1 **debug ip rip** output.

Figure 5-4   *Autosummarization*

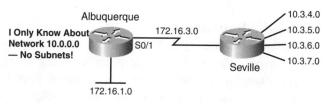

Example 5-6   *Albuquerque Routes and RIP Debugs*

```
Albuquerque#show ip route
Codes: C - connected, S - static, I - IGRP, R - RIP, M - mobile, B - BGP
       D - EIGRP, EX - EIGRP external, O - OSPF, IA - OSPF inter area
       N1 - OSPF NSSA external type 1, N2 - OSPF NSSA external type 2
       E1 - OSPF external type 1, E2 - OSPF external type 2, E - EGP
       i - IS-IS, L1 - IS-IS level-1, L2 - IS-IS level-2, ia - IS-IS inter area
       * - candidate default, U - per-user static route, o - ODR
       P - periodic downloaded static route

Gateway of last resort is not set

     172.16.0.0/24 is subnetted, 2 subnets
C       172.16.1.0 is directly connected, Ethernet0/0
```

continues

Example 5-6   *Albuquerque Routes and RIP Debugs (Continued)*

```
C     172.16.3.0 is directly connected, Serial0/1
R    10.0.0.0/8 [120/1] via 172.16.3.3, 00:00:28, Serial0/1


Albuquerque#debug ip rip
RIP protocol debugging is on

00:05:36: RIP: received v1 update from 172.16.3.3 on Serial0/1
00:05:36:      10.0.0.0 in 1 hops
```

As shown in Example 5-6, Albuquerque's received update on Serial0/1 from Seville advertises only the entire Class A network 10.0.0.0 because autosummarization is enabled on Seville (by default). As a result, the Albuquerque IP routing table lists just one route to network 10.0.0.0.

This example also points out another feature of how classful routing protocols make assumptions. Albuquerque does not have any interfaces in network 10.0.0.0. So, when Albuquerque receives the routing update, it assumes that the mask used with 10.0.0.0 is 255.0.0.0, the default mask for a Class A network. In other words, classful routing protocols expect autosummarization to occur.

Discontiguous Classful Networks

Autosummarization does not cause any problems as long as the summarized network is contiguous rather than discontiguous. U.S. residents can appreciate the concept of a discontiguous network based on the common term *contiguous 48*, referring to the 48 U.S. states besides Alaska and Hawaii. To drive to Alaska from the contiguous 48, for example, you must drive through another country (Canada, for the geographically impaired!), so Alaska is not contiguous with the 48 states. In other words, it is discontiguous.

To better understand what the terms *contiguous* and *discontiguous* mean in networking, refer to the following two formal definitions when reviewing the example of a discontiguous classful network that follows:

- **Contiguous network:** A classful network in which packets sent between every pair of subnets can pass only through subnets of that same classful network, without having to pass through subnets of any other classful network.

- **Discontiguous network:** A classful network in which packets sent between at least one pair of subnets must pass through subnets of a different classful network.

Figure 5-5 shows an example of a discontiguous network 10.0.0.0. In this case, packets sent from the subnets of network 10.0.0.0 on the left, near Yosemite, to the subnets of network 10.0.0.0 on the right, near Seville, have to pass through subnets of network 172.16.0.0.

Figure 5-5 *Discontiguous Network 10.0.0.0*

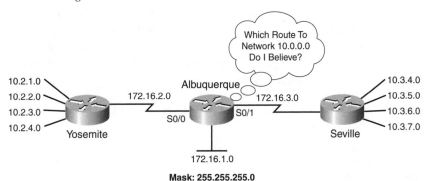

Autosummarization prevents an internetwork with a discontiguous network from working properly. Example 5-7 shows the results of using autosummarization in the internetwork shown in Figure 5-5, in this case using the classful RIP-1 routing protocol.

Example 5-7 *Albuquerque Routing Table: Autosummarization Causes Routing Problem with Discontiguous Network 10.0.0.0*

```
Albuquerque#show ip route
Codes: C - connected, S - static, I - IGRP, R - RIP, M - mobile, B - BGP
       D - EIGRP, EX - EIGRP external, O - OSPF, IA - OSPF inter area
       N1 - OSPF NSSA external type 1, N2 - OSPF NSSA external type 2
       E1 - OSPF external type 1, E2 - OSPF external type 2, E - EGP
       i - IS-IS, L1 - IS-IS level-1, L2 - IS-IS level-2, ia - IS-IS inter area
       * - candidate default, U - per-user static route, o - ODR
       P - periodic downloaded static route

Gateway of last resort is not set

     172.16.0.0/24 is subnetted, 3 subnets
C       172.16.1.0 is directly connected, Ethernet0/0
C       172.16.2.0 is directly connected, Serial0/0
C       172.16.3.0 is directly connected, Serial0/1
R    10.0.0.0/8 [120/1] via 172.16.3.3, 00:00:13, Serial0/1
                 [120/1] via 172.16.2.2, 00:00:04, Serial0/0
```

As shown in Example 5-7, Albuquerque now has two routes to network 10.0.0.0/8: one pointing left toward Yosemite and one pointing right toward Seville. Instead of sending packets destined for Yosemite's subnets out Serial 0/0, Albuquerque sends some packets out

S0/1 to Seville! Albuquerque simply balances the packets across the two routes, because as far as Albuquerque can tell, the two routes are simply equal-cost routes to the same destination: the entire network 10.0.0.0. So, applications would cease to function correctly in this network.

The solution to this problem is to disable the use of autosummarization. Because classful routing protocols must use autosummarization, the solution requires migration to a classless routing protocol and disabling the autosummarization feature. Example 5-8 shows the same internetwork from Figure 5-5 and Example 5-7, but this time with (classless) EIGRP, with autosummarization disabled.

Example 5-8 *Classless Routing Protocol with No Autosummarization Allows Discontiguous Network*

```
Albuquerque#show ip route
Codes: C - connected, S - static, I - IGRP, R - RIP, M - mobile, B - BGP
       D - EIGRP, EX - EIGRP external, O - OSPF, IA - OSPF inter area
       N1 - OSPF NSSA external type 1, N2 - OSPF NSSA external type 2
       E1 - OSPF external type 1, E2 - OSPF external type 2, E - EGP
       i - IS-IS, L1 - IS-IS level-1, L2 - IS-IS level-2, ia - IS-IS inter area
       * - candidate default, U - per-user static route, o - ODR
       P - periodic downloaded static route

Gateway of last resort is not set

     172.16.0.0/24 is subnetted, 3 subnets
C       172.16.1.0 is directly connected, Ethernet0/0
C       172.16.2.0 is directly connected, Serial0/0
C       172.16.3.0 is directly connected, Serial0/1
     10.0.0.0/24 is subnetted, 8 subnets
D       10.2.1.0/24 [90/2172416] via 172.16.2.2, 00:00:01, Serial0/0
D       10.2.2.0/24 [90/2297856] via 172.16.2.2, 00:00:01, Serial0/0
D       10.2.3.0/24 [90/2297856] via 172.16.2.2, 00:00:01, Serial0/0
D       10.2.4.0/24 [90/2297856] via 172.16.2.2, 00:00:01, Serial0/0
D       10.3.5.0/24 [90/2297856] via 172.16.3.3, 00:00:29, Serial0/1
D       10.3.4.0/24 [90/2172416] via 172.16.3.3, 00:00:29, Serial0/1
D       10.3.7.0/24 [90/2297856] via 172.16.3.3, 00:00:29, Serial0/1
D       10.3.6.0/24 [90/2297856] via 172.16.3.3, 00:00:29, Serial0/1
```

With autosummarization disabled on both Yosemite and Seville, neither router advertises an automatic summary of network 10.0.0.0/8 to Albuquerque. Instead, each router advertises the known subnets, so now Albuquerque knows the four LAN subnets off Yosemite as well as the four LAN subnets off Seville.

Autosummarization Support and Configuration

Classful routing protocols must use autosummarization. Some classless routing protocols support autosummarization, defaulting to use it, but with the ability to disable it with the **no auto-summary** router subcommand. Other classless routing protocols, notably Open Shortest Path First (OSPF), simply do not support autosummarization. Table 5-5 summarizes the facts about autosummarization on Cisco routers.

Table 5-5 *Autosummarization Support and Defaults*

Key
Topic

Routing Protocol	Classless?	Supports Autosummarization?	Defaults to Use Autosummarization?[1]	Can Disable Autosummarization?
RIP-1	No	Yes	Yes	No
RIP-2	Yes	Yes	Yes	Yes
EIGRP	Yes	Yes	Yes	Yes
OSPF	Yes	No	—	—

[1] As of IOS 12.4 mainline.

Also note that the autosummary feature impacts routers that directly connect to parts of more than one classful network, but it has no impact on routers whose interfaces all connect to the same single classful network. For example, in Figure 5-5, the solution (as shown in Example 5-8) required the **no auto-summary** EIGRP subcommand on both Yosemite and Seville. However, Albuquerque, whose interfaces all sit inside a single network (Class B network 172.16.0.0), would not change its behavior with either the **auto-summary** or **no auto-summary** command configured in this case.

Exam Preparation Tasks

Review All the Key Topics

Review the most important topics from this chapter, noted with the Key Topics icon in the outer margin of the page. Table 5-6 lists a reference of these key topics and the page numbers on which each is found.

Table 5-6 *Key Topics for Chapter 5*

Key Topic Element	Description	Page Number
Table 5-2	List of IP routing protocols, with facts about classless/classful, VLSM support, and summarization support	204
List	Two-step strategy for finding overlapping VLSM subnets	205
List	Five-step strategy for choosing a new nonoverlapping VLSM subnet	209
List	Five-step process for finding the best manual summary route	216
Definition	Generalized definition of autosummarization	219
Definitions	Definitions for contiguous network and discontiguous network	220
Table 5-5	List of routing protocols and facts related to autosummarization	223

Complete the Tables and Lists from Memory

Print a copy of Appendix J, "Memory Tables," (found on the CD) or at least the section for this chapter, and complete the tables and lists from memory. Appendix K, "Memory Tables Answer Key," also on the CD, includes completed tables and lists to check your work.

Definitions of Key Terms

Define the following key terms from this chapter, and check your answers in the glossary:

Autosummarization, classful network, classful routing protocol, classless routing protocol, contiguous network, discontiguous network, overlapping subnets, summary route, variable-length subnet masking

Read Appendix F Scenarios

Appendix F, "Additional Scenarios," contains five detailed scenarios that both give you a chance to analyze different designs, problems, and command output, and show you how concepts from several different chapters interrelate. Appendix F Scenario 1, Part A, and all of Scenario 5 provide an opportunity to practice and develop skills with VLSM.

Command Reference to Check Your Memory

This chapter introduces only one new command that has not already been introduced in this book, namely the [**no**] **auto-summary** router configuration mode command. This command enables autosummarization (omitting the **no** option) or disables autosummarization (using the **no** option).

This chapter includes this command reference section just as a reminder of the one command to remember from this chapter.

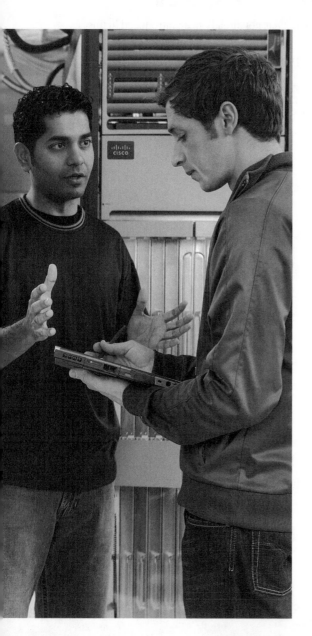

This chapter covers the following subjects:

Standard IP Access Control Lists: This section explains how standard IP ACLs work and how to configure them.

Extended IP Access Control Lists: This section examines the deeper complexity of extended IP ACLs, including how to configure them.

Advances in Managing ACL Configuration: This section examines the nuances of two major enhancements to ACL configuration over the years: named ACLs and sequence numbers.

Miscellaneous ACL Topics: This section explains a few additional ACL concepts.

IP Access Control Lists

Network security is one of the hottest topics in networking today. Although security has always been important, the explosion of the size and scope of the Internet has created more security exposures. In years past, most companies were not permanently connected to a global network—a network through which others could attempt to illegally access their networks. Today, because most companies connect to the Internet, many companies receive significant income through their network-based facilities—facts that increase the exposure and increase the impact when security is breached.

Cisco routers can be used as part of a good overall security strategy. One of the most important tools in Cisco IOS software used as part of that strategy are access control lists (ACL). ACLs define rules that can be used to prevent some packets from flowing through the network. Whether you simply want to restrict access to the payroll server to only people in the payroll department, or whether you are trying to stop Internet hackers from bringing your e-commerce web server to its knees, IOS ACLs can be a key security tool that is part of a larger security strategy.

This chapter is in Part II of this book, which is oriented toward IP routing topics. The reason that it is in Part II is that the most typical use of ACLs on the CCNA exams is to filter packets. So, whereas Chapters 4 and 5 discuss various features that impact the IP routing process to allow packets to flow, this chapter examines ACLs that then prevent selected packets from flowing.

"Do I Know This Already?" Quiz

The "Do I Know This Already?" quiz allows you to assess whether you should read the entire chapter. If you miss no more than one of these ten self-assessment questions, you might want to move ahead to the "Exam Preparation Tasks" section. Table 6-1 lists the major headings in this chapter and the "Do I Know This Already?" quiz questions covering the material in those sections. This helps you assess your knowledge of these specific areas. The answers to the "Do I Know This Already?" quiz appear in Appendix A.

Table 6-1   *"Do I Know This Already?" Foundation Topics Section-to-Question Mapping*

Foundation Topics Section	Questions
Standard IP Access Control Lists	1–3
Extended IP Access Control Lists	4–6
Advances in Managing ACL Configuration	7 and 8
Miscellaneous ACL Topics	9 and 10

1. Barney is a host with IP address 10.1.1.1 in subnet 10.1.1.0/24. Which of the following are things that a standard IP ACL could be configured to do?

   a. Match the exact source IP address

   b. Match IP addresses 10.1.1.1 through 10.1.1.4 with one **access-list** command without matching other IP addresses

   c. Match all IP addresses in Barney's subnet with one **access-list** command without matching other IP addresses

   d. Match only the packet's destination IP address

2. Which of the following wildcard masks is most useful for matching all IP packets in subnet 10.1.128.0, mask 255.255.255.0?

   a. 0.0.0.0

   b. 0.0.0.31

   c. 0.0.0.240

   d. 0.0.0.255

   e. 0.0.15.0

   f. 0.0.248.255

3. Which of the following wildcard masks is most useful for matching all IP packets in subnet 10.1.128.0, mask 255.255.240.0?

   a. 0.0.0.0

   b. 0.0.0.31

   c. 0.0.0.240

   d. 0.0.0.255

   e. 0.0.15.255

   f. 0.0.248.255

4. Which of the following fields cannot be compared based on an extended IP ACL?

   a. Protocol

   b. Source IP address

   c. Destination IP address

   d. TOS byte

   e. URL

   f. Filename for FTP transfers

5. Which of the following **access-list** commands permits traffic that matches packets going from host 10.1.1.1 to all web servers whose IP addresses begin with 172.16.5?

   a. **access-list 101 permit tcp host 10.1.1.1 172.16.5.0 0.0.0.255 eq www**

   b. **access-list 1951 permit ip host 10.1.1.1 172.16.5.0 0.0.0.255 eq www**

   c. **access-list 2523 permit ip host 10.1.1.1 eq www 172.16.5.0 0.0.0.255**

   d. **access-list 2523 permit tcp host 10.1.1.1 eq www 172.16.5.0 0.0.0.255**

   e. **access-list 2523 permit tcp host 10.1.1.1 172.16.5.0 0.0.0.255 eq www**

6. Which of the following **access-list** commands permits traffic that matches packets going to any web client from all web servers whose IP addresses begin with 172.16.5?

   a. **access-list 101 permit tcp host 10.1.1.1 172.16.5.0 0.0.0.255 eq www**

   b. **access-list 1951 permit ip host 10.1.1.1 172.16.5.0 0.0.0.255 eq www**

   c. **access-list 2523 permit tcp any eq www 172.16.5.0 0.0.0.255**

   d. **access-list 2523 permit tcp 172.16.5.0 0.0.0.255 eq www 172.16.5.0 0.0.0.255**

   e. **access-list 2523 permit tcp 172.16.5.0 0.0.0.255 eq www any**

7. Which of the following fields can be compared using a named extended IP ACL but not a numbered extended IP ACL?

   a. Protocol

   b. Source IP address

   c. Destination IP address

   d. TOS byte

   e. None of the other answers are correct.

8. In a router running IOS 12.3, an engineer needs to delete the second line in ACL 101, which currently has four commands configured. Which of the following options could be used?

    a. Delete the entire ACL and reconfigure the three ACL statements that should remain in the ACL.

    b. Delete one line from the ACL using the **no access-list...** command.

    c. Delete one line from the ACL by entering ACL configuration mode for the ACL and then deleting only the second line based on its sequence number.

    d. Delete the last three lines from the ACL from ACL configuration mode, and then add the last two statements back into the ACL.

9. What general guideline should you follow when placing extended IP ACLs?

    a. Perform all filtering on output if at all possible.

    b. Put more-general statements early in the ACL.

    c. Filter packets as close to the source as possible.

    d. Order the ACL commands based on the source IP addresses, lowest to highest, to improve performance.

10. Which of the following tools requires the end user to telnet to a router to gain access to hosts on the other side of the router?

    a. Named ACLs

    b. Reflexive ACLs

    c. Dynamic ACLs

    d. Time-based ACLs

Foundation Topics

Cisco IOS has supported IP ACLs almost since the original commercial Cisco routers were introduced in the late 1980s. IOS identified these ACLs with a number. Years later, as part of the introduction of IOS 11.2, Cisco added the ability to create named ACLs. These named ACLs provide some other minor benefits as compared to numbered ACLs, but both could be used to filter the exact same packets with the exact same rules. Finally, with the introduction of IOS 12.3, Cisco improved ACL support again, particularly with how IOS allows engineers to edit existing ACLs. This latest major step in the progression of ACLs over the years makes numbered and named ACLs support the exact same features, other than the one obvious difference of using either a number or a name to identify the ACL.

Because of the historical progression of Cisco's support for ACLs, the CCNA exams still cover a lot of the same information and configuration commands that have been used with Cisco routers for almost 20 years. To support all that history, this chapter spends most of its time explaining IP ACLs—numbered IP ACLs—using the same commands and syntax available in IOS for a long time. In particular, this chapter begins with a description of the simplest types of numbered IP ACLs—standard IP ACLs. The second major section then examines the more-complex extended IP ACLs, which can be used to examine many more fields inside an IP packet. Following that, the next section of the chapter describes the deepening support for ACLs in IOS—both the introduction of support for named ACLs with IOS version 11.2, and the later addition of support for ACL sequence numbers and enhanced ACL editing with IOS 12.3. The chapter concludes by covering miscellaneous ACL topics.

Standard IP Access Control Lists

IP ACLs cause a router to discard some packets based on criteria defined by the network engineer. The goal of these filters is to prevent unwanted traffic in the network—whether preventing hackers from penetrating the network or just preventing employees from using systems they shouldn't. Access lists should simply be part of an organization's security policy.

By the way, IP access lists can also be used to filter routing updates, to match packets for prioritization, to match packets for VPN tunneling, and to match packets for implementing quality-of-service features. You will also see ACLs used as part of configuring Network Address Translation (NAT) in Chapter 16, "Network Address Translation." So you will see ACLs in most of the other Cisco certification exams as you move on in your career.

This chapter covers two main categories of IOS IP ACLs—standard and extended. Standard ACLs use simpler logic, and extended ACLs use more-complex logic. The first section of this chapter covers standard IP ACLs, followed by a section on extended IP ACLs. Several sections related to both types of ACLs close the chapter.

Standard IP ACL Concepts

Engineers need to make two major choices for any ACL that will filter IP packets: which packets to filter, and where in the network to place the ACL. Figure 6-1 serves as an example. In this case, imagine that Bob is not allowed to access Server1, but Larry is.

Figure 6-1 *Locations Where Access List Logic Can Be Applied in the Network*

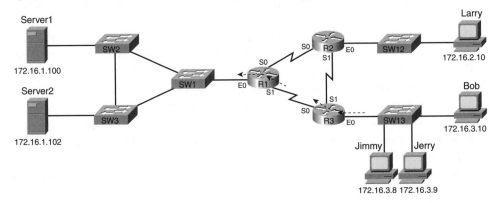

Filtering logic could be configured on any of the three routers and on any of their interfaces. The dotted arrowed lines in the figure show the most appropriate points at which to apply the filtering logic in an ACL. Because Bob's traffic is the only traffic that needs to be filtered, and the goal is to stop access to Server1, the access list could be applied at either R1 or R3. And because Bob's attempted traffic to Server1 would not need to go through R2, R2 would not be a good place to put the access list logic. For the sake of discussion, assume that R1 should have the access list applied.

Cisco IOS software applies the filtering logic of an ACL either as a packet enters an interface or as it exits the interface. In other words, IOS associates an ACL with an interface, and specifically for traffic either entering or exiting the interface. After you have chosen the router on which you want to place the access list, you must choose the interface on which to apply the access logic, as well as whether to apply the logic for inbound or outbound packets.

For instance, imagine that you want to filter Bob's packets sent to Server1. Figure 6-2 shows the options for filtering the packet.

Figure 6-2 *Internal Processing in R1 in Relation to Where R1 Can Filter Packets*

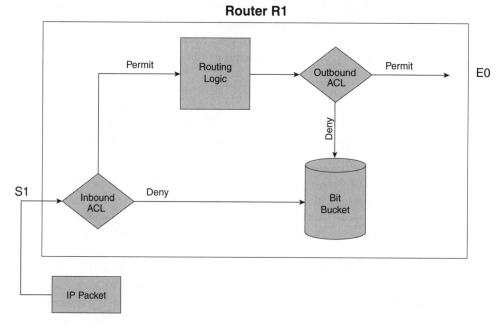

Filtering logic can be applied to packets entering S1 or to packets exiting E0 on R1 to match the packet sent by Bob to Server1. In general, you can filter packets by creating and enabling access lists for both incoming and outgoing packets on each interface. Here are some key features of Cisco access lists:

- Packets can be filtered as they enter an interface, before the routing decision.

- Packets can be filtered before they exit an interface, after the routing decision.

- *Deny* is the term used in Cisco IOS software to imply that the packet will be filtered.

- *Permit* is the term used in Cisco IOS software to imply that the packet will not be filtered.

- The filtering logic is configured in the access list.

- At the end of every access list is an implied "deny all traffic" statement. Therefore, if a packet does not match any of your access list statements, it is blocked.

For example, you might create an access list in R1 and enable it on R1's S1 interface. The access list would look for packets that came from Bob. Therefore, the access list would need to be enabled for inbound packets, because in this network, packets from Bob enter S1, and packets to Bob exit S1.

Access lists have two major steps in their logic: matching and action. Matching logic examines each packet and determines whether it matches the **access-list** statement. For instance, Bob's IP address would be used to match packets sent from Bob. IP ACLs tell the router to take one of two actions when a statement is matched: deny or permit. Deny means to discard the packet, and permit implies that the packet should continue on its way.

So the access list for preventing Bob's traffic to the server might go something like this:

> Look for packets with Bob's source IP address and Server1's destination IP address. When you see them, discard them. If you see any other packets, do not discard them.

Not surprisingly, IP ACLs can get a lot more difficult than those in real life. Even a short list of matching criteria can create complicated access lists on a variety of interfaces in a variety of routers. I've even heard of a couple of large networks with a few full-time people who do nothing but plan and implement access lists!

Cisco calls its packet-filtering features "access control lists" in part because the logic is created with multiple configuration commands that are considered to be in the same list. When an access list has multiple entries, IOS searches the list sequentially until the first statement is matched. The matched statement determines the action to be taken. The two diamond shapes in Figure 6-2 represent the application of access list logic.

The logic that IOS uses with a multiple-entry ACL can be summarized as follows:

1. The matching parameters of the **access-list** statement are compared to the packet.

2. If a match is made, the action defined in this **access-list** statement (permit or deny) is performed.

3. If a match is not made in Step 2, repeat Steps 1 and 2 using each successive statement in the ACL until a match is made.

4. If no match is made with an entry in the access list, the deny action is performed.

Wildcard Masks

IOS IP ACLs match packets by looking at the IP, TCP, and UDP headers in the packet. Extended access lists can check source and destination IP addresses, as well as source and destination port numbers, along with several other fields. However, standard IP access lists can examine only the source IP address.

Regardless of whether you use standard or extended IP ACLs, you can tell the router to match based on the entire IP address or just a part of the IP address. For instance, if you wanted to stop Bob from sending packets to Server1, you would look at the entire IP address of Bob and Server1 in the access list. But what if the criteria were to stop all hosts in Bob's subnet from getting to Server1? Because all hosts in Bob's subnet have the same numbers in their first 3 octets, the access list could just check the first 3 octets of the address to match all packets with a single **access-list** command.

Cisco *wildcard masks* define the portion of the IP address that should be examined. When defining the ACL statements, as you'll see in the next section of this chapter, you can define a wildcard mask along with the IP address. The wildcard mask tells the router which part of the IP address in the configuration statement must be compared with the packet header.

For example, suppose that one mask implies that the whole packet should be checked and another implies that only the first 3 octets of the address need to be examined. (You might choose to do that to match all IP hosts in the same subnet when using a subnet mask of 255.255.255.0.) To perform this matching, Cisco access lists use wildcard masks.

Wildcard masks look similar to subnet masks, but they are not the same. Wildcard masks represent a 32-bit number, as do subnet masks. However, the wildcard mask's 0 bits tell the router that those corresponding bits in the address must be compared when performing the matching logic. The binary 1s in the wildcard mask tell the router that those bits do not need to be compared. In fact, many people call these bits the "don't care" bits.

To get a sense of the idea behind a wildcard mask, Table 6-2 lists some of the more popular wildcard masks, along with their meanings.

Table 6-2   *Sample Access List Wildcard Masks*

Key
Topic

Wildcard Mask	Binary Version of the Mask	Description
0.0.0.0	00000000.00000000.00000000.00000000	The entire IP address must match.
0.0.0.255	00000000.00000000.00000000.11111111	Just the first 24 bits must match.
0.0.255.255	00000000.00000000.11111111.11111111	Just the first 16 bits must match.
0.255.255.255	00000000.11111111.11111111.11111111	Just the first 8 bits must match.

continues

Table 6-2   *Sample Access List Wildcard Masks (Continued)*

Wildcard Mask	Binary Version of the Mask	Description
255.255.255.255	11111111.11111111.11111111.11111111	Automatically considered to match any and all addresses.
0.0.15.255	00000000.00000000.00001111.11111111	Just the first 20 bits must match.
0.0.3.255	00000000.00000000.00000011.11111111	Just the first 22 bits must match.

The first several examples show typical uses of the wildcard mask. As you can see, it is not a subnet mask. A wildcard of 0.0.0.0 means that the entire IP address must be examined, and be equal, to be considered a match. 0.0.0.255 means that the last octet automatically matches, but the first 3 must be examined, and so on. More generally, the wildcard mask means the following:

> Bit positions of binary 0 mean that the access list compares the corresponding bit position in the IP address and makes sure it is equal to the same bit position in the address configured in the **access-list** statement. Bit positions of binary 1 are "don't care" bits. Those bit positions are immediately considered to be a match.

The last two rows of Table 6-2 show two reasonable, but not obvious, wildcard masks. 0.0.15.255 in binary is 20 binary 0s followed by 12 binary 1s. This means that the first 20 bits must match. Similarly, 0.0.3.255 means that the first 22 bits must be examined to find out if they match. Why are these useful? If the subnet mask is 255.255.240.0, and you want to match all hosts in the same subnet, the 0.0.15.255 wildcard means that all network and subnet bits must be matched, and all host bits are automatically considered to match. Likewise, if you want to filter all hosts in a subnet that uses subnet mask 255.255.252.0, the wildcard mask 0.0.3.255 matches the network and subnet bits. In general, if you want a wildcard mask that helps you match all hosts in a subnet, invert the subnet mask, and you have the correct wildcard mask.

A Quicker Alternative for Interpreting Wildcard Masks

Both IP standard ACLs (source IP address only) and extended ACLs (both source and destination addresses) can be configured to examine all or part of an IP address based on the wildcard mask. However, particularly for the exams, working with the masks in binary may be slow and laborious unless you master binary-to-decimal and decimal-to-binary conversions. This section suggests an easier method of working with ACL wildcard masks that works well if you have already mastered subnetting math.

In many cases, an ACL needs to match all hosts in a particular subnet. To match a subnet with an ACL, you can use the following shortcut:

■ Use the subnet number as the address value in the **access-list** command.

■ Use a wildcard mask found by subtracting the subnet mask from 255.255.255.255.

For example, for subnet 172.16.8.0 255.255.252.0, use the subnet number (172.16.8.0) as the *address* parameter, and then do the following math to find the wildcard mask:

$$
\begin{array}{r}
255.255.255.255 \\
-\ 255.255.252.0 \\
\hline
0.\ \ 0.\ \ 3.255
\end{array}
$$

Some exam questions may not ask that you pick the ACL statement that needs to be configured, instead asking that you interpret some existing **access-list** commands. Typically, these questions list preconfigured ACL statements, or you need to display the contents of an ACL from a router simulator, and you need to decide which statement a particular packet matches. To do that, you need to determine the range of IP addresses matched by a particular address/wildcard mask combination in each ACL statement.

If you have mastered subnetting math using any of the decimal shortcuts, avoiding binary math, another shortcut can be used to analyze each existing address/wildcard pair in each ACL command. To do so:

Step 1   Use the address in the **access-list** command as if it were a subnet number.

Step 2   Use the number found by subtracting the wildcard mask from 255.255.255.255 as a subnet mask.

Step 3   Treat the values from the first two steps as a subnet number and subnet mask, and find the broadcast address for the subnet. The ACL matches the range of addresses between the subnet number and broadcast address, inclusively.

The range of addresses identified by this process is the same range of addresses matched by the ACL. So, if you can already find a subnet's range of addresses quickly and easily, using this process to change an ACL's math may help you find the answer more quickly on the exams. For example, with the command **access-list 1 permit 172.16.200.0 0.0.7.255**, you would first think of 172.16.200.0 as a subnet number. Then you could calculate the assumed subnet mask of 255.255.248.0, as follows:

```
  255.255.255.255
– 0.  0.  7.255
  255.255.248.0
```

From there, using any process you like, use subnetting math to determine that the broadcast address of this subnet would be 172.16.207.255. So, the range of addresses matched by this ACL statement would be 172.16.200.0 through 172.16.207.255.

> **NOTE**   CD-only Appendix F, Scenario 3, provides an opportunity to practice choosing a wildcard mask to match hosts in a particular subnet.

Standard IP Access List Configuration

ACL configuration tends to be simpler than the task of interpreting the meaning and actions taken by an ACL. To that end, this section presents a plan of attack for configuring ACLs. Then it shows a couple of examples that review both the configuration and the concepts implemented by those ACLs.

The generic syntax of the standard ACL configuration command is

access-list *access-list-number* {**deny** | **permit**} *source* [*source-wildcard*]

A standard access list uses a series of **access-list** commands that have the same number. The **access-list** commands with the same number are considered to be in the same list, with the commands being listed in the same order in which they were added to the configuration. Each **access-list** command can match a range of source IP addresses. If a match occurs, the ACL either allows the packet to keep going (**permit** action) or discards the packet (**deny** action). Each standard ACL can match all, or only part, of the packet's source IP address. Note that for standard IP ACLs, the number range for ACLs is 1 to 99 and 1300 to 1999.

The following list outlines a suggested configuration process. You do not need to memorize the process itself for the exam; it is simply listed here as a convenient study review aid.

Step 1 Plan the location (router and interface) and direction (in or out) on that interface:

  a. Standard ACLs should be placed near to the destination of the packets so that it does not unintentionally discard packets that should not be discarded.

  b. Because standard ACLs can only match a packet's source IP address, identify the source IP addresses of packets as they go in the direction that the ACL is examining.

Step 2 Configure one or more **access-list** global configuration commands to create the ACL, keeping the following in mind:

  a. The list is searched sequentially, using first-match logic. In other words, when a packet matches one of the **access-list** statements, the search is over, even if the packet would match subsequent statements.

  b. The default action, if a packet does not match any of the **access-list** commands, is to **deny** (discard) the packet.

Step 3 Enable the ACL on the chosen router interface, in the correct direction, using the **ip access-group** *number* {**in** | **out**} interface subcommand.

Next, two examples of standard ACLs are shown.

Standard IP ACL: Example 1

Example 6-1 attempts to stop Bob's traffic to Server1. As shown in Figure 6-1, Bob is not allowed to access Server1. In Example 6-1, the configuration enables an ACL for all packets going out R1's Ethernet0 interface. The ACL matches the source address in the packet—Bob's IP address. Note that the **access-list** commands are at the bottom of the example because the **show running-config** command also lists them near the bottom, after the interface configuration commands.

Example 6-1 *Standard Access List on R1 Stopping Bob from Reaching Server1*

```
interface Ethernet0
 ip address 172.16.1.1 255.255.255.0
 ip access-group 1 out
!
access-list 1 remark stop all traffic whose source IP is Bob
access-list 1 deny 172.16.3.10 0.0.0.0
access-list 1 permit 0.0.0.0 255.255.255.255
```

First, focus on the basic syntax of the commands. Standard IP access lists use a number in the range of 1 to 99 or 1300 to 1999. This example uses ACL number 1 versus the other available numbers for no particular reason. (There is absolutely no difference in using one number or another, as long as it is in the correct range. In other words, list 1 is no better or worse than list 99.) The **access-list** commands, under which the matching and action logic are defined, are global configuration commands. To enable the ACL on an interface and define the direction of packets to which the ACL is applied, the **ip access-group** command is used. In this case, it enables the logic for ACL 1 on Ethernet0 for packets going out the interface.

ACL 1 keeps packets sent by Bob from exiting R1's Ethernet interface, based on the matching logic of the **access-list 1 deny 172.16.3.10 0.0.0.0** command. The wildcard mask of 0.0.0.0 means "match all 32 bits," so only packets whose IP address exactly matches 172.16.3.10 match this statement and are discarded. The **access-list 1 permit 0.0.0.0 255.255.255.255** command, the last statement in the list, matches all packets, because the wildcard mask of 255.255.255.255 means "don't care" about all 32 bits. In other words, the statement matches all IP source addresses. These packets are permitted.

Finally, note that the engineer also added an **access-list 1 remark** command to the ACL. This command allows the addition of a text comment, or remark, so that you can track the purpose of the ACL. The remark only shows up in the configuration; it is not listed in **show** command output.

Although it's a seemingly simple example, in this case access list 1 also prevents Bob's packets sent to Server2 from being delivered. With the topology shown in Figure 6-1, an outbound standard ACL on R1's E0 interface cannot somehow deny Bob access to Server1 while permitting access to Server2. To do that, an extended ACL is needed that can check both the source and destination IP addresses.

Interestingly, if the commands in Example 6-1 are entered in configuration mode, IOS changes the configuration syntax of a couple of commands. The output of the **show running-config** command in Example 6-2 shows what IOS actually places in the configuration file.

Example 6-2 *Revised Standard Access List Stopping Bob from Reaching Server1*

```
interface Ethernet0
 ip address 172.16.1.1 255.255.255.0
 ip access-group 1 out

access-list 1 remark stop all traffic whose source IP is Bob
access-list 1 deny host 172.16.3.10
access-list 1 permit any
```

The commands in Example 6-1 are changed based on three factors. Cisco IOS allows both an older style and newer style of configuration for some parameters. Example 6-1 shows the older style, and the router changes to the equivalent newer-style configuration in Example 6-2. First, the use of a wildcard mask of 0.0.0.0 does indeed mean that the router should match that specific host IP address. The newer-style configuration uses the **host** keyword in *front* of the specific IP address. The other change to the newer-style configuration involves the use of wildcard mask 255.255.255.255 to mean "match anything." The newer-style configuration uses the keyword **any** to replace both the IP address and 255.255.255.255 wildcard mask. **any** simply means that any IP address is matched.

Standard IP ACL: Example 2

The second standard IP ACL example exposes more ACL issues. Figure 6-3 and Examples 6-3 and 6-4 show a basic use of standard IP access lists, with two typical oversights in the first attempt at a complete solution. The criteria for the access lists are as follows:

- Sam is not allowed access to Bugs or Daffy.

- Hosts on the Seville Ethernet are not allowed access to hosts on the Yosemite Ethernet.

- All other combinations are allowed.

Figure 6-3 *Network Diagram for Standard Access List Example*

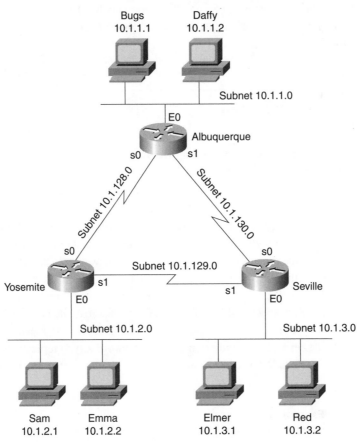

Example 6-3 *Yosemite Configuration for Standard Access List Example*

```
interface serial 0
 ip access-group 3 out
!
access-list 3 deny host 10.1.2.1
access-list 3 permit any
```

Example 6-4 *Seville Configuration for Standard Access List Example*

```
interface serial 1
 ip access-group 4 out
!
access-list 4 deny 10.1.3.0    0.0.0.255
access-list 4 permit any
```

At first glance, these two access lists seem to perform the desired function. ACL 3, enabled for packets exiting Yosemite's S0 interface, takes care of criterion 1, because ACL 3 matches Sam's IP address exactly. ACL 4 in Seville, enabled for packets exiting its S1 interface, takes care of criterion 2, because ACL 4 matches all packets coming from subnet 10.1.3.0/24. Both routers meet criterion 3: A wildcard **permit any** is used at the end of each access list to override the default, which is to discard all other packets. So all the criteria appear to be met.

However, when one of the WAN links fails, some holes can appear in the ACLs. For example, if the link from Albuquerque to Yosemite fails, Yosemite learns a route to 10.1.1.0/24 through Seville. Packets from Sam, forwarded by Yosemite and destined for hosts in Albuquerque, leave Yosemite's serial 1 interface without being filtered. So criterion 1 is no longer met. Similarly, if the link from Seville to Yosemite fails, Seville routes packets through Albuquerque, routing around the access list enabled on Seville, so criterion 2 is no longer met.

Example 6-5 illustrates an alternative solution, with all the configuration on Yosemite—one that works even when some of the links fail.

Example 6-5 *Yosemite Configuration for Standard Access List Example: Alternative Solution to Examples 6-3 and 6-4*

```
interface serial 0
 ip access-group 3 out
!
interface serial 1
 ip access-group 3 out
!
interface ethernet 0
 ip access-group 4 out
!
access-list 3 remark meets criteria 1
access-list 3 deny host 10.1.2.1
access-list 3 permit any
!
access-list 4 remark meets criteria 2
access-list 4 deny 10.1.3.0 0.0.0.255
access-list 4 permit any
```

The configuration shown in Example 6-5 solves the problem from Examples 6-3 and 6-4. ACL 3 checks for Sam's source IP address, and it is enabled on both serial links for outbound traffic. So, of the traffic that is rerouted because of a WAN link failure, the packets from Sam are still filtered. To meet criterion 2, Yosemite filters packets as they exit its

Ethernet interface. Therefore, regardless of which of the two WAN links the packets enter, packets from Seville's subnet are not forwarded to Yosemite's Ethernet.

Extended IP Access Control Lists

Extended IP access lists have both similarities and differences compared to standard IP ACLs. Just like standard lists, you enable extended access lists on interfaces for packets either entering or exiting the interface. IOS searches the list sequentially. The first statement matched stops the search through the list and defines the action to be taken. All these features are true of standard access lists as well.

The one key difference between the two is the variety of fields in the packet that can be compared for matching by extended access lists. A single extended ACL statement can examine multiple parts of the packet headers, requiring that all the parameters be matched correctly to match that one ACL statement. That matching logic is what makes extended access lists both much more useful and much more complex than standard IP ACLs.

This section starts with coverage of the extended IP ACL concepts that differ from standard ACLs—namely, the matching logic. Following that, the configuration details are covered.

Extended IP ACL Concepts

Extended access lists create powerful matching logic by examining many parts of a packet. Figure 6-4 shows several of the fields in the packet headers that can be matched.

Figure 6-4 *Extended Access List Matching Options*

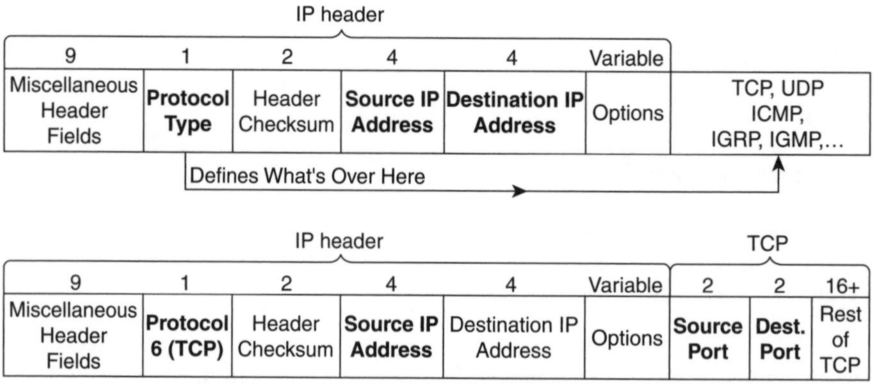

The top set of headers shows the IP protocol type, which identifies what header follows the IP header. You can specify all IP packets, or those with TCP headers, UDP headers, ICMP, and so on, by checking the Protocol field. You can also check both the source and destination IP addresses, as shown. The lower part of the figure shows an example with a TCP header following the IP header, pointing out the location of the TCP source and destination port numbers. These port numbers identify the application. For instance, the web uses port 80 by default. If you specify a protocol of TCP or UDP, you can also check the port numbers.

Table 6-3 summarizes the most commonly used fields that can be matched with an extended IP ACL, as compared with standard IP ACLs.

Table 6-3 *Standard and Extended IP Access Lists: Matching*

Type of Access List	What Can Be Matched
Both standard and extended ACLs	Source IP address
	Portions of the source IP address using a wildcard mask
Only extended ACLs	Destination IP address
	Portions of the destination IP address using a wildcard mask
	Protocol type (TCP, UDP, ICMP, IGRP, IGMP, and others)
	Source port
	Destination port
	All TCP flows except the first
	IP TOS
	IP precedence

Knowing what to look for is just half the battle. IOS checks all the matching information configured in a single **access-list** command. Everything must match for that single command to be considered a match and for the defined action to be taken. The options start with the protocol type (IP, TCP, UDP, ICMP, and others), followed by the source IP address, source port, destination IP address, and destination port number. Table 6-4 lists several sample **access-list** commands, with several options configured and some explanations. Only the matching options are shaded.

Table 6-4   *Extended access-list Commands and Logic Explanations*

access-list Statement	What It Matches
access-list 101 deny ip any host 10.1.1.1	Any IP packet, any source IP address, with a destination IP address of 10.1.1.1.
access-list 101 deny tcp any gt 1023 host 10.1.1.1 eq 23	Packets with a TCP header, any source IP address, with a source port greater than (**gt**) 1023, a destination IP address of exactly 10.1.1.1, and a destination port equal to (**eq**) 23.
access-list 101 deny tcp any host 10.1.1.1 eq 23	The same as the preceding example, but any source port matches, because that parameter is omitted in this case.
access-list 101 deny tcp any host 10.1.1.1 eq telnet	The same as the preceding example. The **telnet** keyword is used instead of port 23.
access-list 101 deny udp 1.0.0.0 0.255.255.255 lt 1023 any	A packet with a source in network 1.0.0.0, using UDP with a source port less than (**lt**) 1023, with any destination IP address.

Matching TCP and UDP Port Numbers

Extended IP ACLs allow for the matching of the IP header protocol field, as well as matching the source and destination TCP or UDP port numbers. However, many people have difficultly when first configuring ACLs that match port numbers, particularly when matching the source port number.

When considering any exam question that involves TCP or UDP ports, keep the following key points in mind:

Key
Topic

- The **access-list** command must use protocol keyword **tcp** to be able to match TCP ports and the **udp** keyword to be able to match UDP ports. The **ip** keyword does not allow for matching the port numbers.

- The source port and destination port parameters on the **access-list** command are positional. In other words, their location in the command determines if the parameter examines the source or destination port.

- Remember that ACLs can match packets sent to a server by comparing the destination port to the well-known port number. However, ACLs need to match the source port for packets sent by the server.

- It is useful to memorize the most popular TCP and UDP applications, and their well-known ports, as listed in Table 6-5, as shown later in this chapter.

For example, consider the simple network shown in Figure 6-5. The FTP server sits on the right, with the client on the left. The figure shows the syntax of an ACL that matches

- Packets that include a TCP header

- Packets sent from the client subnet

- Packets sent to the server subnet

- Packets with TCP destination port 21

Figure 6-5 *Filtering Packets Based on Destination Port*

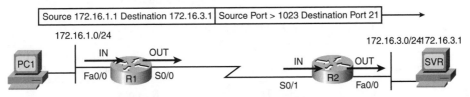

access-list 101 permit tcp 172.16.1.0 0.0.0.255 172.16.3.0 0.0.0.255 eq 21

To fully appreciate the matching of the destination port with the **eq 21** parameter, consider packets moving left to right, from PC1 to the server. If the server is using well-known port 21 (FTP control port), the packet sent by PC1, in the TCP header, has a destination port value of 21. The ACL syntax includes the **eq 21** parameter *after* the destination IP address, with this position in the command implying that this parameter matches the destination port. As a result, the ACL statement shown in the figure would match this packet, and the destination port of 21, if used in any of the four locations implied by the four thick arrowed lines in the figure.

Conversely, Figure 6-6 shows the reverse flow, with a packet sent by the server back toward PC1. In this case, the packet's TCP header has a source port of 21, so the ACL must check the source port value of 21, and the ACL must be located on different interfaces.

Figure 6-6 *Filtering Packets Based on Source Port*

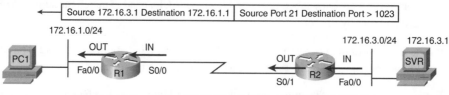

access-list 101 permit tcp 172.16.3.0 0.0.0.255 eq 21 172.16.1.0 0.0.0.255

For exam questions that require ACLs and matching of port numbers, first consider whether the question requires that the ACL be placed in a certain location and direction. If so, you can then determine if that ACL would process packets either sent to the server or sent by the server. At that point, you can decide whether you need to check the source or destination port in the packet.

For reference, Table 6-5 lists many of the popular port numbers and their transport layer protocols and applications. Note that the syntax of the **access-list** commands accepts both the port numbers and a shorthand version of the application name.

Table 6-5 *Popular Applications and Their Well-Known Port Numbers*

Port Number(s)	Protocol	Application	Application Name Keyword in access-list Command Syntax
20	TCP	FTP data	**ftp-data**
21	TCP	FTP control	**ftp**
22	TCP	SSH	—
23	TCP	Telnet	**telnet**
25	TCP	SMTP	**smtp**
53	UDP, TCP	DNS	**domain**
67, 68	UDP	DHCP	**bootps(67)** **bootpc(68)**
69	UDP	TFTP	**tftp**
80	TCP	HTTP (WWW)	**www**
110	TCP	POP3	**pop3**
161	UDP	SNMP	**snmp**
443	TCP	SSL	—
16,384–32,767	UDP	RTP-based voice (VoIP) and video	—

Extended IP ACL Configuration

Because extended ACLs can match so many different fields in the various headers in an IP packet, the command syntax cannot be easily summarized in a single generic command. For reference, Table 6-6 lists the syntax of the two most common generic commands.

Table 6-6 *Extended IP Access List Configuration Commands*

Command	Configuration Mode and Description
access-list *access-list-number* {**deny** | **permit**} *protocol source source-wildcard destination destination-wildcard* [**log** | **log-input**]	Global command for extended numbered access lists. Use a number between 100 and 199 or 2000 and 2699, inclusive.
access-list *access-list-number* {**deny** | **permit**} {**tcp** | **udp**} *source source-wildcard* [*operator* [*port*]] *destination destination-wildcard* [*operator* [*port*]] [**established**] [**log**]	A version of the **access-list** command with TCP-specific parameters.

The configuration process for extended ACLs mostly matches the same process used for standard ACLs. The location and direction should be chosen first so that the ACL's parameters can be planned based on the information in the packets flowing in that direction. The ACL should be configured with **access-list** commands. Then the ACL should be enabled with the same **ip access-group** command used with standard ACLs. All these steps remain the same as with standard ACLs. However, the differences in configuration are summarized as follows:

- Extended ACLs should be placed as close as possible to the source of the packets to be filtered, because extended ACLs can be configured so that they do not discard packets that should not be discarded. So filtering close to the source of the packets saves some bandwidth.

- All fields in one **access-list** command must match a packet for the packet to be considered to match that **access-list** statement.

- The extended **access-list** command uses numbers between 100–199 and 2000–2699, with no number being inherently better than another.

The extended version of the **access-list** command allows for matching of port numbers using several basic operations, such as equal-to and less-than. However, the commands use abbreviations, so Table 6-7 lists the abbreviations and a fuller explanation.

Table 6-7 *Operators Used When Matching Port Numbers*

Operator in the access-list Command	Meaning
eq	Equal to
neq	Not equal to
lt	Less than
gt	Greater than
range	Range of port numbers

Extended IP Access Lists: Example 1

This example focuses on understanding the basic syntax. In this case, Bob is denied access to all FTP servers on R1's Ethernet, and Larry is denied access to Server1's web server. Figure 6-7 is a reminder of the network topology. Example 6-6 shows the configuration on R1.

Figure 6-7 *Network Diagram for Extended Access List Example 1*

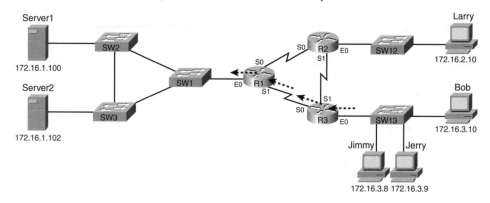

Example 6-6 *R1's Extended Access List: Example 1*

```
interface Serial0
 ip address 172.16.12.1 255.255.255.0
 ip access-group 101 in
!
interface Serial1
 ip address 172.16.13.1 255.255.255.0
 ip access-group 101 in
!
access-list 101 remark Stop Bob to FTP servers, and Larry to Server1 web
access-list 101 deny tcp host 172.16.3.10 172.16.1.0 0.0.0.255 eq ftp
access-list 101 deny tcp host 172.16.2.10 host 172.16.1.100 eq www
access-list 101 permit ip any any
```

In Example 6-6, the first ACL statement prevents Bob's access to FTP servers in subnet 172.16.1.0. The second statement prevents Larry's access to web services on Server1. The final statement permits all other traffic.

Focusing on the syntax for a moment, there are several new items to review. First, the access list number for extended access lists falls in the range of 100 to 199 or 2000 to 2699. Following the **permit** or **deny** action, the *protocol* parameter defines whether you want to check for all IP packets or just those with TCP or UDP headers. When you check for TCP or UDP port numbers, you must specify the TCP or UDP protocol.

This example uses the **eq** parameter, meaning "equals," to check the destination port numbers for FTP control (keyword **ftp**) and HTTP traffic (keyword **www**). You can use the numeric values—or, for the more popular options, a more obvious text version is valid. (If you were to enter **eq 80**, the config would show **eq www**.)

In this first extended ACL example, the access lists could have been placed on R2 and R3 instead of on R1. As you will read near the end of this chapter, Cisco makes some specific recommendations about where to locate IP ACLs. With extended IP ACLs, Cisco suggests that you locate them as close as possible to the source of the packet. Therefore, Example 6-7 achieves the same goal as Example 6-6 of stopping Bob's access to FTP servers at the main site, and it does so with an ACL on R3.

Example 6-7 *R3's Extended Access List Stopping Bob from Reaching FTP Servers Near R1*

```
interface Ethernet0
 ip address 172.16.3.1 255.255.255.0
 ip access-group 101 in

access-list 101 remark deny Bob to FTP servers in subnet 172.16.1.0/24
access-list 101 deny tcp host 172.16.3.10 172.16.1.0 0.0.0.255 eq ftp
access-list 101 permit ip any any
```

ACL 101 looks a lot like ACL 101 from Example 6-6, but this time, the ACL does not bother to check for the criteria to match Larry's traffic, because Larry's traffic will never enter R3's Ethernet 0 interface. Because the ACL has been placed on R3, near Bob, it watches for packets Bob sends that enter its Ethernet0 interface. Because of the ACL, Bob's FTP traffic to 172.16.1.0/24 is denied, with all other traffic entering R3's E0 interface making it into the network. Example 6-7 does not show any logic for stopping Larry's traffic.

Extended IP Access Lists: Example 2

Example 6-8, based on the network shown in Figure 6-8, shows another example of how to use extended IP access lists. This example uses the same criteria and network topology as the second standard IP ACL example, as repeated here:

- Sam is not allowed access to Bugs or Daffy.

- Hosts on the Seville Ethernet are not allowed access to hosts on the Yosemite Ethernet.

- All other combinations are allowed.

Figure 6-8 *Network Diagram for Extended Access List Example 2*

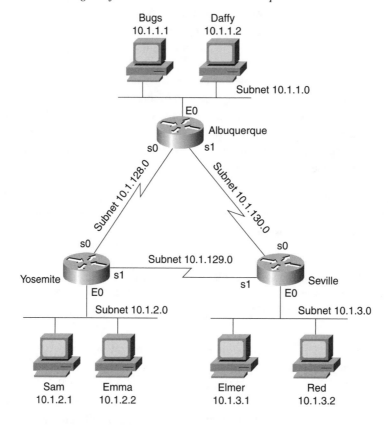

Example 6-8 *Yosemite Configuration for Extended Access List Example 2*

```
interface ethernet 0
 ip access-group 110 in
!
access-list 110 deny ip host 10.1.2.1 10.1.1.0 0.0.0.255
access-list 110 deny ip 10.1.2.0 0.0.0.255 10.1.3.0 0.0.0.255
access-list 110 permit ip any any
```

This configuration solves the problem with few statements while keeping to Cisco's design guideline of placing extended ACLs as close as possible to the source of the traffic. The ACL filters packets that enter Yosemite's E0 interface, which is the first router interface that packets sent by Sam enter. The issue of having packets "routed around" access lists on serial interfaces is taken care of with the placement on Yosemite's only Ethernet interface. Also, the filtering mandated by the second requirement (to disallow Seville's LAN hosts from accessing Yosemite's) is met by the second **access-list** statement. Stopping packet flow from Yosemite's LAN subnet to Seville's LAN subnet stops effective communication between the two subnets. Alternatively, the opposite logic could have been configured at Seville.

Advances in Managing ACL Configuration

Now that you have a good understanding of the core concepts in IOS IP ACLs, this next section examines a couple of enhancements to IOS support for ACLs: named ACLs and ACL sequence numbers. Although both features are useful and important, neither adds any function as to what a router can and cannot filter, as compared to the numbered ACLs already covered in this chapter. Instead, named ACLs and ACL sequence numbers provide the engineer with configuration options that make it easier to remember ACL names and easier to edit existing ACLs when an ACL needs to change.

Named IP Access Lists

Named ACLs, introduced with IOS version 11.2, can be used to match the same packets, with the same parameters, that can be matched with standard and extended IP ACLs. Named IP ACLs do have some differences, however, some of which make them easier to work with. The most obvious difference is that IOS identifies named ACLs using names you make up, as opposed to numbers—and you have a better chance of remembering names.

In addition to using more memorable names, the other major advantage of named ACLs over numbered ACLs, at the time they were introduced into IOS, was that you could delete individual lines in a named IP access list. Throughout the history of numbered IP ACLs and the **ip access-list** global command, until the introduction of IOS 12.3, a single line in a numbered ACL could not be deleted. For example, if you had earlier configured the **ip access-list 101 permit tcp any any eq 80** command, and then you entered the **no ip access-list 101 permit tcp any any eq 80** command, the whole ACL 101 would be deleted! The advantage of the introduction of named ACLs is that you can enter a command that removes individual lines in an ACL.

> **NOTE**   With IOS 12.3, Cisco expanded IOS to be able to delete individual lines in numbered ACLs, making IOS support for editing both named and numbered ACLs equivalent. These details are explained in the next section.

The configuration syntax is very similar between named and numbered IP access lists. The items that can be matched with a numbered standard IP access list are identical to the items that can be matched with a named standard IP access list. Likewise, the items are identical with both numbered and named extended IP access lists.

Two important configuration differences exist between old-style numbered ACLs and the newer named access lists. One key difference is that named access lists use a global command that places the user in a named IP access list submode, under which the matching and permit/deny logic is configured. The other key difference is that when a named matching statement is deleted, only that one statement is deleted.

Example 6-9 shows an example that uses named IP ACLs. It shows the changing command prompt in configuration mode, showing that the user has been placed in ACL configuration mode. It also lists the pertinent parts of the output of a **show running-config** command. It ends with an example of how you can delete individual lines in a named ACL.

Example 6-9   *Named Access List Configuration*

```
conf t
Enter configuration commands, one per line.  End with Ctrl-Z.
Router(config)#ip access-list extended barney
Router(config-ext-nacl)#permit tcp host 10.1.1.2 eq www any
Router(config-ext-nacl)#deny udp host 10.1.1.1 10.1.2.0 0.0.0.255
Router(config-ext-nacl)#deny ip 10.1.3.0 0.0.0.255 10.1.2.0 0.0.0.255
! The next statement is purposefully wrong so that the process of changing
! the list can be seen.
Router(config-ext-nacl)#deny ip 10.1.2.0 0.0.0.255 10.2.3.0 0.0.0.255

Router(config-ext-nacl)#deny ip host 10.1.1.130 host 10.1.3.2
Router(config-ext-nacl)#deny ip host 10.1.1.28 host 10.1.3.2
Router(config-ext-nacl)#permit ip any any
Router(config-ext-nacl)#interface serial1
Router(config-if)#ip access-group barney out
Router(config-if)#^Z
Router#show running-config
Building configuration...
```

Example 6-9 *Named Access List Configuration (Continued)*

```
Current configuration:

.
. (unimportant statements omitted)
.
interface serial 1
 ip access-group barney out
!
ip access-list extended barney
 permit tcp host 10.1.1.2 eq www any
 deny    udp host 10.1.1.1 10.1.2.0 0.0.0.255
 deny    ip 10.1.3.0 0.0.0.255 10.1.2.0 0.0.0.255
 deny    ip 10.1.2.0 0.0.0.255 10.2.3.0 0.0.0.255
 deny    ip host 10.1.1.130 host 10.1.3.2
 deny    ip host 10.1.1.28 host 10.1.3.2
 permit ip any any
Router#conf t
Enter configuration commands, one per line.  End with Ctrl-Z.
Router(config)#ip access-list extended barney
Router(config-ext-nacl)#no deny ip 10.1.2.0 0.0.0.255 10.2.3.0 0.0.0.255
Router(config-ext-nacl)#^Z
Router#show access-list

Extended IP access list barney
    10 permit tcp host 10.1.1.2 eq www any
    20 deny    udp host 10.1.1.1 10.1.2.0 0.0.0.255
    30 deny    ip 10.1.3.0 0.0.0.255 10.1.2.0 0.0.0.255
    50 deny    ip host 10.1.1.130 host 10.1.3.2
    60 deny    ip host 10.1.1.28 host 10.1.3.2
    70 permit ip any any
```

Example 6-9 begins with the creation of an ACL named barney. The **ip access-list extended barney** command creates the ACL, naming it barney and placing the user in ACL configuration mode. This command also tells the IOS that barney is an extended ACL. Next, seven different **permit** and **deny** statements define the matching logic and action to be taken upon a match. The **permit** and **deny** commands use the exact same syntax that the numbered **access-list** commands use, starting with the **deny** and **permit** keywords. In this example, a comment is added just before the command that is deleted later in the example.

The **show running-config** command output lists the named ACL configuration before the single entry is deleted. Next, the **no deny ip...** command deletes a single entry from the ACL. Notice that the output of the **show access-list** command still lists the ACL, with six **permit** and **deny** commands instead of seven.

Editing ACLs Using Sequence Numbers

Numbered ACLs have existed in IOS since the early days of Cisco routers. From their creation, up through IOS version 12.2, the only way to edit an existing numbered ACL—for example, to simply delete a line from the ACL—was to delete the whole ACL and then reconfigure the entire ACL. Besides being an inconvenience to the engineer, this process also caused some unfortunate side effects. When deleting the ACL, it is important to disable the ACL from all interfaces, and then delete it, reconfigure it, and enable it on the interface. Otherwise, during the reconfiguration process, before all the statements have been reconfigured, the ACL will not perform all the checks it should, sometimes causing problems, or exposing the network to various attacks.

As mentioned in the preceding section, the original IOS support for named ACLs, introduced in IOS 11.2, solved some of the editing problem. The original commands for named ACLs allowed the engineer to delete a line from an ACL, as shown in the preceding section in Example 6-9. However, the configuration commands did not allow the user to insert a new **permit** or **deny** command into the list. All new commands were added to the end of the ACL.

With IOS 12.3, Cisco introduced several more configuration options for ACLs—options that apply to both named and numbered IP ACLs. These options take advantage of an ACL sequence number that is added to each ACL **permit** or **deny** statement, with the numbers representing the sequence of statements in the ACL. ACL sequence numbers provide the following features for both numbered and named ACLs:

- An individual ACL **permit** or **deny** statement can be deleted just by referencing the sequence number, without deleting the rest of the ACL.

- Newly added **permit** and **deny** commands can be configured with a sequence number, dictating the location of the statement within the ACL.

- Newly added **permit** and **deny** commands can be configured *without* a sequence number, with IOS creating a sequence number and placing the command at the end of the ACL.

To take advantage of the ability to delete and insert lines in an ACL, both numbered and named ACLs must use the same overall configuration style and commands used for named ACLs. The only difference in syntax is whether a name or number is used. Example 6-10 shows the configuration of a standard numbered IP ACL, using this alternative configuration style. The example shows the power of the ACL sequence number for editing. In this example, the following occurs:

Step 1   Numbered ACL 24 is configured, using this new-style configuration, with three **permit** commands.

Step 2   The **show ip access-list** command shows the three permit commands, with sequence numbers 10, 20, and 30.

Step 3 The engineer deletes only the second **permit** command, using the **no 20** ACL subcommand, which simply refers to sequence number 20.

Step 4 The **show ip access-list** command confirms that the ACL now has only two lines (sequence numbers 10 and 30).

Step 5 The engineer adds a new **permit** command to the beginning of the ACL, using the **5 deny 10.1.1.1** ACL subcommand.

Step 6 The **show ip access-list** command again confirms the changes, this time listing three **permit** commands, sequence numbers 5, 10, and 30.

NOTE For this example, note that the user does not leave configuration mode, instead using the **do** command to tell IOS to issue the **show ip access-list** EXEC command from configuration mode.

Example 6-10 *Editing ACLs Using Sequence Numbers*

```
! Step 1: The 3-line Standard Numbered IP ACL is configured.
R1#configure terminal
Enter configuration commands, one per line.  End with Ctrl-Z.
R1(config)#ip access-list standard 24
R1(config-std-nacl)#permit 10.1.1.0 0.0.0.255
R1(config-std-nacl)#permit 10.1.2.0 0.0.0.255
R1(config-std-nacl)#permit 10.1.3.0 0.0.0.255
! Step 2: Displaying the ACL's contents, without leaving configuration mode.
R1(config-std-nacl)#do show ip access-list 24
Standard IP access list 24
    10 permit 10.1.1.0, wildcard bits 0.0.0.255
    20 permit 10.1.2.0, wildcard bits 0.0.0.255
    30 permit 10.1.3.0, wildcard bits 0.0.0.255
! Step 3: Still in ACL 24 configuration mode, the line with sequence number 20 is deleted.
R1(config-std-nacl)#no 20
! Step 4: Displaying the ACL's contents again, without leaving configuration mode.
! Note that line number 20 is no longer listed.
R1(config-std-nacl)#do show ip access-list 24
Standard IP access list 24
    10 permit 10.1.1.0, wildcard bits 0.0.0.255
    30 permit 10.1.3.0, wildcard bits 0.0.0.255
! Step 5: Inserting a new first line in the ACL.
R1(config-std-nacl)#5 deny 10.1.1.1
! Step 6: Displaying the ACL's contents one last time, with the new statement (sequence
! number 5) listed first.
R1(config-std-nacl)#do show ip access-list 24
Standard IP access list 24
    5 deny   10.1.1.1
    10 permit 10.1.1.0, wildcard bits 0.0.0.255
    30 permit 10.1.3.0, wildcard bits 0.0.0.255
```

Interestingly, numbered ACLs can be configured with the new-style configuration, as shown in Example 6-10, or with the old-style configuration, using **access-list** global configuration commands, as shown in the first several examples in this chapter. In fact, you can use both styles of configuration on a single ACL. However, no matter which style of configuration is used, the **show running-config** command output still shows the old-style configuration commands. Example 6-11 demonstrates these facts, picking up where Example 6-10 ended, with the following additional steps:

Step 7 The engineer lists the configuration (**show running-config**), which lists the old-style configuration commands—even though the ACL was created with the new-style commands.

Step 8 The engineer adds a new statement to the end of the ACL, using the old-style **access-list 24 permit 10.1.4.0 0.0.0.255** global configuration command.

Step 9 The **show ip access-list** command confirms that the old-style **access-list** command from the previous step followed the rule of being added only to the end of the ACL.

Step 10 The engineer displays the configuration to confirm that the parts of ACL 24 configured with both new-style commands and old-style commands are all listed in the same old-style ACL (**show running-config**).

Example 6-11 *Adding to and Displaying a Numbered ACL Configuration*

```
! Step 7: A configuration snippet for ACL 24.
R1#show running-config
! The only lines shown are the lines from ACL 24
access-list 24 deny    10.1.1.1
access-list 24 permit 10.1.1.0 0.0.0.255
access-list 24 permit 10.1.3.0 0.0.0.255


! Step 8: Adding a new access-list 24 command
R1#configure terminal
Enter configuration commands, one per line.  End with CNTL/Z.
R1(config)#access-list 24 permit 10.1.4.0 0.0.0.255
R1(config)#^Z
! Step 9: Displaying the ACL's contents again, with sequence numbers. Note that even
! the new statement has been automatically assigned a sequence number.
R1#show ip access-list 24
Standard IP access list 24
    5 deny    10.1.1.1
    10 permit 10.1.1.0, wildcard bits 0.0.0.255
    30 permit 10.1.3.0, wildcard bits 0.0.0.255
    40 permit 10.1.4.0, wildcard bits 0.0.0.255
!
```

Example 6-11 *Adding to and Displaying a Numbered ACL Configuration (Continued)*

```
! Step 10: The numbered ACL configuration remains in old-style configuration commands.
R1#show running-config
! The only lines shown are the lines from ACL 24
access-list 24 deny    10.1.1.1
access-list 24 permit 10.1.1.0 0.0.0.255
access-list 24 permit 10.1.3.0 0.0.0.255
access-list 24 permit 10.1.4.0 0.0.0.255
```

Miscellaneous ACL Topics

This short section covers a couple of small topics: how to filter Telnet and SSH traffic using ACLs, and some general implementation guidelines.

Controlling Telnet and SSH Access with ACLs

An engineer can control remote access to a router by using ACLs that look for the well-known ports used by both Telnet (23) and SSH (22). However, to do the job by enabling ACLs on interfaces using the **ip access-group** interface subcommand, the ACL would need to check for all the router's IP addresses, and both the Telnet and SSH port. As new interfaces are configured, the ACL would need to be updated.

IOS provides a much easier option for protecting access into and out of the virtual terminal line (vty) ports. Telnet and SSH users connect to vty lines on a router, so to protect that access, an IP ACL can be applied to the vty lines. You can use ACLs to limit the IP hosts that can telnet into the router, and you can also limit the hosts to which a user of the router can telnet.

For instance, imagine that only hosts in subnet 10.1.1.0/24 are supposed to be able to telnet into any of the Cisco routers in a network. In such a case, the configuration shown in Example 6-12 could be used on each router to deny access from IP addresses not in that subnet.

Example 6-12 *vty Access Control Using the **access-class** Command*

```
line vty 0 4
 login
 password cisco
 access-class 3 in
!
! Next command is a global command
 access-list 3 permit 10.1.1.0 0.0.0.255
```

The **access-class** command refers to the matching logic in **access-list 3**. The keyword **in** refers to Telnet connections into this router—in other words, people telnetting into this router. As configured, ACL 3 checks the source IP address of packets for incoming Telnet connections.

If the command **access-class 3 out** had been used, it would have checked for not only outgoing Telnets, but also the packets' destination IP address. When filtering outbound Telnet and SSH connections, checking the source IP address, which by definition must be one of the interface IP addresses in that router, would not really make any sense. For filtering outgoing Telnet sessions, it makes the most sense to filter based on the destination IP address. So, the use of the **access-class 3 out** command, particularly the **out** keyword, is one of those rare cases in which a standard IP ACL actually looks at the destination IP address and not the source.

ACL Implementation Considerations

In production IP networks, IP ACL creation, troubleshooting, and updates can consume a large amount of time and effort. The ICND2 exam does not have many questions about things to watch for when you implement IP ACLs in live networks, but it does cover a few small items, which are discussed in this section.

Cisco makes the following general recommendations in the courses on which the CCNA exams are based:

- Create your ACLs using a text editor outside the router, and copy and paste the configurations into the router. (Even with the ability to delete and insert lines into an ACL, creating the commands in an editor will still likely be an easier process.)

- Place extended ACLs as close as possible to the source of the packet to discard the packets quickly.

- Place standard ACLs as close as possible to the packet's destination, because standard ACLs often discard packets that you do not want discarded when they are placed close to the source.

- Place more-specific statements early in the ACL.

- Disable an ACL from its interface (using the **no ip access-group** command) before making changes to the ACL.

The first suggestion states that you should create the ACLs outside the router using an editor. That way, if you make mistakes when typing, you can fix them in the editor. This suggestion is not as important as it was before IOS version 12.3, because IOS 12.3 supports

ACL line numbers and the deletion and insertion of single lines in an ACL, as described earlier, in the section "Editing ACLs Using Sequence Numbers."

> **NOTE**   If you create all your ACLs in a text editor, it may be useful to begin each file with the **no access-list** *number* command, followed by the configuration commands in the ACL. Then, each time you edit the text file to change the ACL, all you have to do is copy/paste the entire file's contents, with the first line deleting the entire existing ACL, and the rest of the statements re-creating the new ACL.

The second and third points deal with the concept of where to locate your ACLs. If you intend to filter a packet, filtering closer to the packet's source means that the packet takes up less bandwidth in the network, which seems to be more efficient—and it is. Therefore, Cisco suggests locating extended ACLs as close to the source as possible.

However, Cisco also suggests, at least in the CCNA-related courses, to locate standard ACLs close to the destination. Why not close to the source of the packets? Well, because standard ACLs look only at the source IP address, they tend to filter more than you want filtered when placed close to the source. For instance, imagine that Fred and Barney are separated by four routers. If you filter Barney's traffic sent to Fred on the first router, Barney can't reach any hosts near the other three routers. So the Cisco ICND2 course makes a blanket recommendation to locate standard ACLs closer to the destination to avoid filtering traffic you don't mean to filter.

By placing more-specific matching parameters early in each list, you are less likely to make mistakes in the ACL. For instance, imagine that you have a statement that permits all traffic from 10.1.1.1 to 10.2.2.2, destined for port 80 (the web), and another statement that denies all other packets sourced in subnet 10.1.1.0/24. Both statements would match packets sent by host 10.1.1.1 to a web server at 10.2.2.2, but you probably meant to match the more-specific statement (permit) first. In general, placing the more-specific statements first tends to ensure that you don't miss anything.

Finally, Cisco recommends that you disable the ACLs on the interfaces before you change the statements in the list. Thankfully, if you have an IP ACL enabled on an interface with the **ip access-group** command, and you delete the entire ACL, IOS does not filter any packets. (That was not always the case in earlier IOS versions!) Even so, as soon as you add a command to the ACL, the IOS starts filtering packets. Suppose you have ACL 101 enabled on S0 for output packets. You delete list 101 so that all packets are allowed through. Then you enter a single **access-list 101** command. As soon as you press Enter, the list exists, and the router filters all packets exiting S0 based on the one-line list. If you want to enter a long ACL, you might temporarily filter packets you don't want to filter! Therefore, the better way is to disable the list from the interface, make the changes to the list, and then reenable it on the interface.

Reflexive Access Lists

Reflexive ACLs, also called IP session filtering, provide a way to prevent a class of security attacks by permitting each allowed TCP or UDP session on an individual basis. To do so, the router reacts when seeing the first packet in a new session between two hosts. It reacts to the packet to add a permit statement to the ACL, allowing that session's traffic based on the source and destination IP address and TCP/UDP port.

Figure 6-9 shows a classic case in which traditional ACLs create a security hole, but reflexive ACLs could plug the hole. Most Enterprises want to allow users to use a web browser to connect to Internet-based web servers. A traditional extended ACL could permit the traffic by allowing traffic to and from any two IP addresses, but with the additional check on the TCP port used by HTTP (port 80). In this case, the figure shows an ACL that checks source port 80 for packets coming into the Enterprise, meaning that the packets came from a web server.

Figure 6-9 *The Need for Reflexive ACLs*

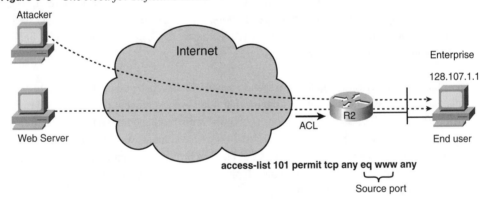

The ACL used on R2 filters all incoming traffic except traffic from web servers. This allows the Internet-based web server on the left to send packets to the user in the Enterprise on the right. However, it also allows the attacker to send packets, with source port 80, with the router allowing the packets through. Although these packets may not be part of an existing TCP connection, several known attacks can be made using these packets—from a simple DoS attack by flooding packets into the Enterprise, to the leveraging of known bugs in the operating system.

Reflexive ACLs still allow legitimate users to send and receive packets through the router, while discarding the packets from other hosts, like packets from the attacker shown in Figure 6-9. With reflexive ACLs, when the Enterprise user first creates a new session, the router notices the new session and records the source and destination IP addresses and ports used for that session. The reflexive ACL on R2 would not allow all port 80 traffic in. Instead, it would allow only packets whose addresses and ports matched the original packet. For example, if the PC on the right started a session with the legitimate web server, source port 1030, R2 would allow packets in from the Internet if they had the following characteristics: source IP address 64.100.2.2, destination IP address 128.107.1.1, source port 80, destination port 1030. As a result, only the packets from that legitimate session are allowed through the router, and the packets sent by the attacker are discarded.

Reflexive ACLs require some additional configuration, as well as the use of named extended ACL configuration.

Dynamic ACLs

Dynamic ACLs solve a different problem that also cannot be easily solved using traditional ACLs. Imagine a set of servers that need to be accessed by a small set of users. With ACLs, you can match the IP addresses of the hosts used by the users. However, if the user borrows another PC, or leases a new address using DHCP, or takes her laptop home, and so on, the legitimate user now has a different IP address. So a traditional ACL would have to be edited to support each new IP address. Over time, maintaining an ACL that checked for all these IP addresses would be painful. Additionally, it would introduce the possibility of security holes when other users' hosts start using one of the old IP addresses.

Dynamic ACLs, also called Lock-and-Key Security, solve this problem by tying the ACL to a user authentication process. Instead of starting by trying to connect to the server, the users must be told to first telnet to a router. The router asks for a username/password combination. If it is authentic, the router dynamically changes its ACL, permitting traffic from the IP address of the host that just sent the authentication packets. After a period of inactivity, the router removes the dynamic entry in the ACL, closing the potential security hole. Figure 6-10 shows the idea.

Figure 6-10 *Dynamic ACLs*

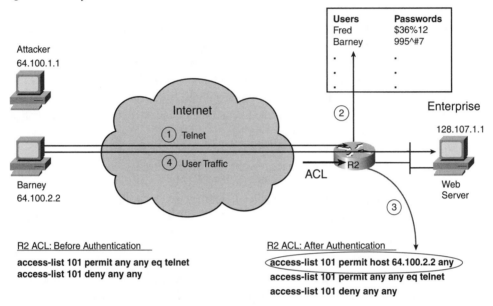

R2 ACL: Before Authentication

access-list 101 permit any any eq telnet
access-list 101 deny any any

R2 ACL: After Authentication

access-list 101 permit host 64.100.2.2 any
access-list 101 permit any any eq telnet
access-list 101 deny any any

The process shown in the figure begins with the router denying all traffic except Telnet. (Although the figure shows an ACL that allows telnetting to any IP address, in practice, the Telnet traffic only needs to be allowed into a router IP address.) To trigger the process, the following steps occur:

Step 1   The user connects to the router using Telnet.

Step 2   The user supplies a username/password, which the router compares to a list, authenticating the user.

Step 3   After authentication, the router dynamically adds an entry to the beginning of the ACL, permitting traffic sourced by the authenticated host.

Step 4   Packets sent by the permitted host go through the router to the server.

Time-Based ACLs

The term time-based ACL refers to a feature of normal IP ACLs (both numbered and named) in which a time constraint can be added to the configuration commands. In some cases, it may be useful to match packets in an ACL, but only at certain times in the day, or even on particular days of the week. Time-based ACLs allow the addition of time constraints, with IOS keeping or removing the statements from the ACL during the appropriate times of day.

Exam Preparation Tasks

Review All the Key Topics

Review the most important topics from this chapter, noted with the key topics icon.
Table 6-8 lists these key topics and where each is discussed.

Table 6-8   Key Topics for Chapter 6

Key Topic Element	Description	Page Number
Figure 6-2	Logic diagram showing when a router examines packets with inbound and outbound ACLs	233
List	Four steps that describe how a router processes a multiline ACL	234
Table 6-2	Explains sample wildcard masks and their meanings	235-236
List	Shortcut to find values in the **access-list** command to match a subnet number, given the subnet number and subnet mask	237
List	Shortcut to interpret the address and wildcard mask in an **access-list** command as a subnet number and mask	237
List	ACL planning and configuration checklist	239
Table 6-3	List of IP packet fields matchable with standard and extended ACLs	245
List	Hints and tips on matching TCP and UDP ports using IP ACLs	246
Figure 6-6	Shows a packet with source and destination port, with the corresponding location of the source port parameter in the **access-list** command	248
List	Three items that differ between standard and extended IP ACLs	249
Table 6-7	List of operators that can be used when comparing port numbers in extended **access-list** commands	250
List	Features for both numbered and named ACLs provided by ACL sequence numbers	256
List	List of suggested best practices for ACLs according to the authorized Cisco CCNA courses	260

Complete the Tables and Lists from Memory

Print a copy of Appendix J, "Memory Tables" (found on the CD), or at least the section for this chapter, and complete the tables and lists from memory. Appendix K, "Memory Tables Answer Key," also on the CD, includes completed tables and lists for you to check your work.

Read the Appendix F Scenarios

Appendix F, "Additional Scenarios," contains five detailed scenarios that give you a chance to analyze different designs, problems, and command output. They also demonstrate how concepts from several different chapters interrelate. Scenario 3 focuses on IP ACLs, including practice with how to choose ACL wildcard masks to match all hosts in a single subnet.

Definitions of Key Terms

Define the following key terms from this chapter, and check your answers in the glossary:

Extended access list, named access list, standard access list, wildcard mask, dynamic ACL, reflexive ACL

Command Reference to Check Your Memory

Although you should not necessarily memorize the information in the tables in this section, this section does include a reference for the configuration and EXEC commands covered in this chapter. Practically speaking, you should memorize the commands as a side effect of reading the chapter and doing all the activities in this exam preparation section. To see how well you have memorized the commands as a side effect of your other studies, cover the left side of the table, read the descriptions on the right side, and see if you remember the command.

Table 6-9 *Chapter 6 Configuration Command Reference*

Command	Description
access-list *access-list-number* {**deny** | **permit**} *source* [*source-wildcard*] [**log**]	Global command for standard numbered access lists. Use a number between 1 and 99 or 1300 and 1999, inclusive.
access-list *access-list-number* {**deny** | **permit**} *protocol source source-wildcard destination destination-wildcard* [**log**]	Global command for extended numbered access lists. Use a number between 100 and 199 or 2000 and 2699, inclusive.

Table 6-9   *Chapter 6 Configuration Command Reference (Continued)*

Command	Description
access-list *access-list-number* {**deny** I **permit**} **tcp** *source source-wildcard* [*operator* [*port*]] *destination destination-wildcard* [*operator* [*port*]] [**log**]	A version of the **access-list** command with TCP-specific parameters.
access-list *access-list-number* **remark** *text*	Defines a remark that helps you remember what the ACL is supposed to do.
ip access-group {*number* I *name* [**in** I **out**]}	Interface subcommand to enable access lists.
access-class *number* I *name* [**in** I **out**]	Line subcommand to enable either standard or extended access lists.
ip access-list {**standard** I **extended**} *name*	Global command to configure a named standard or extended ACL and enter ACL configuration mode.
{**deny** I **permit**} *source* [*source-wildcard*] [**log**]	ACL mode subcommand to configure the matching details and action for a standard named ACL.
{**deny** I **permit**} *protocol source source-wildcard destination destination-wildcard* [**log**]	ACL mode subcommand to configure the matching details and action for an extended named ACL.
{**deny** I **permit**} **tcp** *source source-wildcard* [*operator* [*port*]] *destination destination-wildcard* [*operator* [*port*]] [**log**]	ACL mode subcommand to configure the matching details and action for a named ACL that matches TCP segments.
remark *text*	ACL mode subcommand to configure a description of a named ACL.

Table 6-10   *Chapter 6 EXEC Command Reference*

Command	Description
show ip interface [*type number*]	Includes a reference to the access lists enabled on the interface.
show access-lists [*access-list-number* I *access-list-name*]	Shows details of configured access lists for all protocols.
show ip access-list [*access-list-number* I *access-list-name*]	Shows IP access lists.

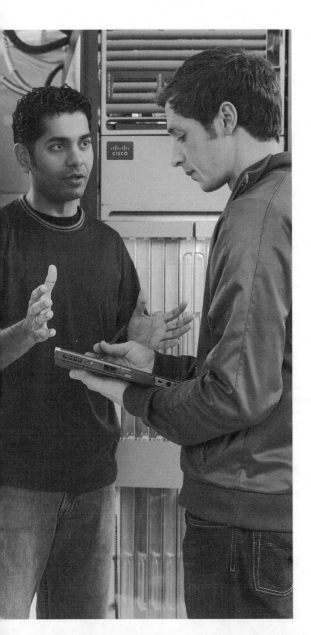

This chapter covers the following subjects:

The ping and traceroute Commands: This section explains how the **ping** and **traceroute** commands work, along with the nuances of how they can be used to better troubleshoot routing problems.

Troubleshooting the Packet Forwarding Process: This section examines the packet forwarding process, focusing on host routing and how routers route packets. It also covers issues related to forwarding packets in both directions between two hosts.

Troubleshooting Tools and Tips: This section covers a wide variety of topics that have some effect on the packet forwarding process. It includes many tips about various commands and concepts that can aid the troubleshooting process.

CHAPTER 7

Troubleshooting IP Routing

This troubleshooting chapter has several goals. First, it explains several tools and functions not covered in Chapters 4 through 6—specifically, tools that can be very helpful when you're analyzing problems. This chapter also reviews concepts from all three of the other chapters in Part II, "IP Routing." It pulls together the concepts by showing a suggested process for troubleshooting routing problems, as well as examples of how to use the process. The second half of the chapter focuses on a series of troubleshooting tips for many of the specific topics covered in Chapters 4 through 6.

"Do I Know This Already?" Quiz

The troubleshooting chapters of this book pull in concepts from many other chapters, including some chapters in *CCENT/CCNA ICND1 Official Exam Certification Guide*. They also show you how to approach some of the more challenging questions on the CCNA exams. Therefore, it is useful to read these chapters regardless of your current knowledge level. For these reasons, the troubleshooting chapters do not include a "Do I Know This Already?" quiz. However, if you feel particularly confident about troubleshooting IP routing features covered in this book and *CCENT/CCNA ICND1 Official Exam Certification Guide*, feel free to move to the "Exam Preparation Tasks" section near the end of this chapter to bypass the majority of the chapter.

Foundation Topics

This chapter focuses on troubleshooting the IP routing process. To that end, it begins with a section about two important troubleshooting tools: ping and traceroute. Following that, the chapter examines the IP routing process from a troubleshooting perspective, particularly focusing on how to isolate routing problems to identify the root cause of the problem. The final section covers a wide variety of small topics, all of which can be useful when you're troubleshooting IP routing problems.

> **NOTE**   This chapter, and Chapter 15 in *CCENT/CCNA ICND1 Official Exam Certification Guide*, both explain details of how to troubleshoot the IP routing process. IP routing is vitally important on both the ICND1 and ICND2 exams, as well as on the CCNA exam, so there is overlap between the exams, requiring some overlap in the books. However, this chapter covers many topics that go beyond the details required for the ICND1 exam. To be fully prepared, read this entire chapter, but feel free to skim portions if the chapter seems repetitive with the ICND1 book.

The ping and traceroute Commands

This section examines a suggested process of troubleshooting IP routing—in other words, the data plane process of how hosts and routers forward IP packets. To that end, this section first examines a set of useful tools and protocols—in particular, ICMP, **ping**, and **traceroute**. Following that, the text suggests a good general troubleshooting process for IP problems, with a few examples to show how to use the processes.

Internet Control Message Protocol (ICMP)

TCP/IP includes ICMP, a protocol designed to help manage and control the operation of a TCP/IP network. The ICMP protocol provides a wide variety of information about a network's health and operational status. *Control Message* is the most descriptive part of the name. ICMP helps control and manage IP's work by defining a set of messages and procedures about the operation of IP. Therefore, ICMP is considered part of TCP/IP's network layer. Because ICMP helps control IP, it can provide useful troubleshooting information. In fact, the ICMP messages sit inside an IP packet, with no transport layer header, so ICMP is truly an extension of the TCP/IP network layer.

RFC 792 defines ICMP. The following excerpt from RFC 792 describes the protocol well:

> Occasionally a gateway (router) or destination host will communicate with a source host, for example, to report an error in datagram processing. For such

purposes, this protocol, the Internet Control Message Protocol (ICMP), is used. ICMP uses the basic support of IP as if it were a higher level protocol; however, ICMP is actually an integral part of IP and must be implemented by every IP module.

ICMP defines several different types of messages to accomplish its varied tasks, as summarized in Table 7-1.

Table 7-1   *ICMP Message Types*

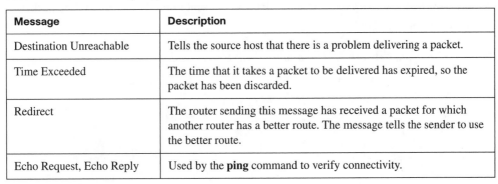

Key
Topic

Message	Description
Destination Unreachable	Tells the source host that there is a problem delivering a packet.
Time Exceeded	The time that it takes a packet to be delivered has expired, so the packet has been discarded.
Redirect	The router sending this message has received a packet for which another router has a better route. The message tells the sender to use the better route.
Echo Request, Echo Reply	Used by the **ping** command to verify connectivity.

The ping Command and the ICMP Echo Request and Echo Reply

The **ping** command uses the ICMP Echo Request and Echo Reply messages. In fact, when people say they sent a ping packet, they really mean that they sent an ICMP Echo Request. These two messages are somewhat self-explanatory. The Echo Request simply means that the host to which it is addressed should reply to the packet. The Echo Reply is the ICMP message type that should be used in the reply. The Echo Request includes some data that can be specified by the **ping** command; whatever data is sent in the Echo Request is sent back in the Echo Reply.

The **ping** command itself supplies many creative ways to use Echo Requests and Replies. For instance, the **ping** command lets you specify the length as well as the source and destination addresses, and it also lets you set other fields in the IP header. Chapter 4, "IP Routing: Static and Connected Routes," shows an example of the extended **ping** command that lists the various options.

The Destination Unreachable ICMP Message

This book focuses on IP. But if you take a broader view, the role of the entire set of TCP/IP protocols is to deliver data from the sending application to the receiving application. Hosts and routers send ICMP Destination Unreachable messages back to the sending host when that host or router cannot deliver the data completely to the application at the destination host.

To aid in troubleshooting, the ICMP Unreachable message includes five separate unreachable functions (codes) that further identify the reason why the packet cannot be delivered. All five code types pertain directly to an IP, TCP, or UDP feature.

For example, the internetwork shown in Figure 7-1 can be used to better understand some of the Unreachable codes. Assume that Fred is trying to connect to the web server, called Web. (Web uses HTTP, which in turn uses TCP as the transport layer protocol.) Three of the ICMP unreachable codes can possibly be used by Routers A and B. The other two codes are used by the web server. These ICMP codes are sent to Fred as a result of the packet originally sent by Fred.

Figure 7-1   *Sample Network for Discussing ICMP Unreachable Codes*

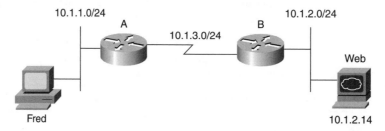

Table 7-2 summarizes the more common ICMP unreachable codes. After the table, the text explains how each ICMP code might be needed for the network shown in Figure 7-1.

Table 7-2   *ICMP Unreachable Codes*

Unreachable Code	When It Is Used	What Typically Sends It
Network unreachable	There is no match in a routing table for the packet's destination.	Router
Host unreachable	The packet can be routed to a router connected to the destination subnet, but the host is not responding.	Router
Can't fragment	The packet has the Don't Fragment bit set, and a router must fragment to forward the packet.	Router
Protocol unreachable	The packet is delivered to the destination host, but the transport layer protocol is not available on that host.	Host
Port unreachable	The packet is delivered to the destination host, but the destination port has not been opened by an application.	Host

The following list explains each code in Table 7-2 in greater detail using the network in Figure 7-1 as an example:

- **Network unreachable:** Router A uses this code if it does not have a route telling it where to forward the packet. In this case, Router A needs to route the packet to subnet 10.1.2.0/24. If it cannot, Router A sends Fred the ICMP Destination Unreachable message with the code "network unreachable" in response to Fred's packet destined for 10.1.2.14.

- **Host unreachable:** This code implies that the single destination host is unavailable. If Router A has a route to 10.1.2.0/24, the packet is delivered to Router B. If Router B's LAN interface is working, B also has a connected route to 10.1.2.0/24, so B tries to ARP and learn the web server's MAC address. However, if the web server is down, Router B does not get an ARP reply from the web server. Router B sends Fred the ICMP Destination Unreachable message with the code "host unreachable," meaning that B has a route but cannot forward the packet directly to 10.1.2.14.

- **Can't fragment:** This code is the last of the three ICMP unreachable codes that a router might send. Fragmentation defines the process in which a router needs to forward a packet, but the outgoing interface allows only packets that are smaller than the packet. The router is allowed to fragment the packet into pieces, but the packet header can be set with the "Do Not Fragment" bit in the IP header. In this case, if Router A or B needs to fragment the packet, but the Do Not Fragment bit is set in the IP header, the router discards the packet and sends Fred an ICMP Destination Unreachable message with the code "can't fragment."

- **Protocol unreachable:** If the packet successfully arrives at the web server, two other unreachable codes are possible. One implies that the protocol above IP, typically TCP or UDP, is not running on that host. This is highly unlikely, because most operating systems that use TCP/IP use a single software package that provides IP, TCP, and UDP functions. But if the host receives the IP packet and TCP or UDP is unavailable, the web server host sends Fred the ICMP Destination Unreachable message with the code "protocol unreachable" in response to Fred's packet destined for 10.1.2.14.

- **Port unreachable:** This final code field value is more likely today. If the server—the computer—is up and running, but the web server software is not running, the packet can get to the server but cannot be delivered to the web server software. In effect, the server is not listening on that application protocol's well-known port. So, host 10.1.2.14 sends Fred the ICMP Destination Unreachable message with the code "port unreachable" in response to Fred's packet destined for 10.1.2.14.

NOTE   Most security policies today filter these various unreachable messages to help bolster the network's security profile.

The **ping** command lists various responses that in some cases imply that an unreachable message was received. Table 7-3 lists the various unreachable codes that may be displayed by the Cisco IOS Software **ping** command.

Table 7-3   *Codes That the* **ping** *Command Receives in Response to Its ICMP Echo Request*

ping Command Code	Description
!	ICMP Echo Reply received
.	Nothing was received before the **ping** command timed out
U	ICMP unreachable (destination) received
N	ICMP unreachable (network/subnet) received
M	ICMP Can't Fragment message received
?	Unknown packet received

The Redirect ICMP Message

The ICMP Redirect message provides a means by which routers can tell hosts to use another router as default gateway for certain destination addresses. Most hosts use the concept of a default router IP address, sending packets destined for subnets to their default router. However, if multiple routers connect to the same subnet, a host's default gateway may not be the best router on that subnet to which to forward packets sent to some destinations. The default gateway can recognize that a different router is a better option. Then it can send ICMP redirect messages to the host to tell it to send the packets for that destination address to this different router.

For example, in Figure 7-2, the PC uses Router B as its default router. However, Router A's route to subnet 10.1.4.0 is a better route. (Assume the use of mask 255.255.255.0 in each subnet in Figure 7-2.) The PC sends a packet to Router B (Step 1 in Figure 7-2). Router B then forwards the packet based on its own routing table (Step 2); that route points through Router A, which has a better route. Finally, Router B sends the ICMP redirect message to the PC (Step 3), telling it to forward future packets destined for 10.1.4.0 to Router A instead. Ironically, the host can ignore the redirect and keep sending the packets to Router B, but in this example, the PC believes the redirect message, sending its next packet (Step 4) directly to Router A.

The ICMP Time Exceeded Message

The ICMP Time Exceeded message notifies a host when a packet it sent has been discarded because it was "out of time." Packets are not actually timed, but to prevent them from being forwarded forever when there is a routing loop, each IP header uses a Time to Live (TTL) field. Routers decrement the TTL by 1 every time they forward a packet; if a router decrements the TTL to 0, it throws away the packet. This prevents packets from rotating forever. Figure 7-3 shows the basic process.

Figure 7-2 *ICMP Redirect*

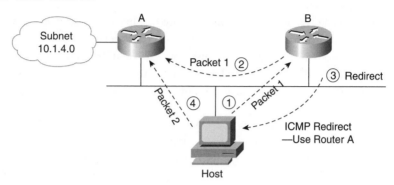

Figure 7-3 *TTL Decremented to 0*

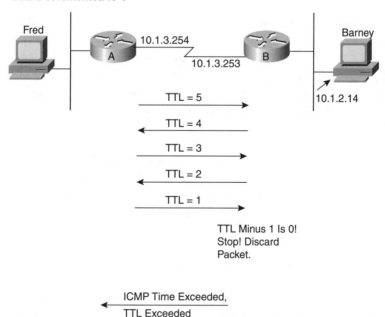

As you can see in the figure, the router that discards the packet also sends an ICMP Time Exceeded message, with a Code field of "time exceeded" to the host that sent the packet. That way, the sender knows that the packet was not delivered. Getting a Time Exceeded message can also help you when you troubleshoot a network. Hopefully, you do not get too many of these; otherwise, you have routing problems.

The traceroute Command

The **ping** command is a powerful troubleshooting tool that can be used to answer the question "Does the route from here to there work?" The **traceroute** command provides an arguably better troubleshooting tool because not only can it determine if the route works, but it can supply the IP address of each router in the route. If the route is not working, **traceroute** can identify the best places to start troubleshooting the problem.

The IOS **traceroute** command uses the Time Exceeded message and the IP TTL field to identify each successive router in a route. The **traceroute** command sends a set of messages with increasing TTL values, starting with 1. The **traceroute** command expects these messages to be discarded when routers decrement the TTL to 0, returning Time Exceeded messages to the **traceroute** command. The source IP addresses of the Time Exceeded messages identify the routers that discarded the messages, which can then be displayed by the **traceroute** command.

To see how this command works, consider the first set of packets (three packets by default) sent by the **traceroute** command. The packets are IP packets, with a UDP transport layer, and with the TTL set to 1. When the packets arrive at the next router, the router decrements the TTL to 0 in each packet, discards the packet, and sends a Time Exceeded message back to the host that sent the discarded packet. The **traceroute** command looks at the first router's source IP address in the received Time Exceeded packet.

Next, the **traceroute** command sends another set of three IP packets, this time with TTL = 2. The first router decrements TTL to 1 and forwards the packets, and the second router decrements the TTL to 0 and discards the packets. This second router sends Time Exceeded messages back to the router where the **traceroute** command was used, and the **traceroute** command now knows the second router in the route.

The **traceroute** command knows when the test packets arrive at the destination host because the host sends back an ICMP Port Unreachable message. The original packets sent by the IOS **traceroute** command use a destination UDP port number that is very unlikely to be used on the destination host, so as soon as the TTL is large enough to allow the packet to arrive at the destination host, the host notices that it does not have an application listening at that particular UDP port. So, the destination host returns a Port Unreachable message, which tells the **traceroute** command that the complete route has been found, and the command can stop.

Figure 7-4 shows an example, but with only one of the three messages at each TTL setting (to reduce clutter). Router A uses the **traceroute** command to try to find the route to Barney. Example 7-1 shows this **traceroute** command on Router A, with debug messages from Router B, showing the three resulting Time Exceeded messages.

Figure 7-4   *Cisco IOS Software* **traceroute** *Command: Messages Generated*

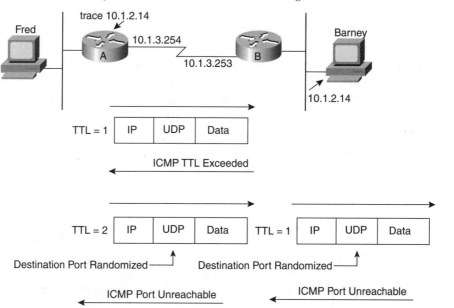

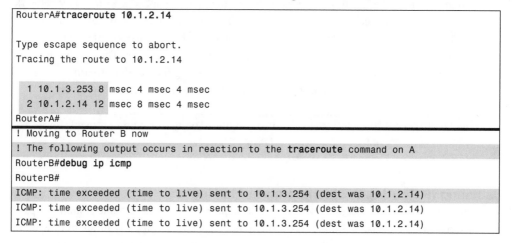

Example 7-1   *ICMP* **debug** *on Router B When Running the* **traceroute** *Command on Router A*

```
RouterA#traceroute 10.1.2.14

Type escape sequence to abort.
Tracing the route to 10.1.2.14

  1 10.1.3.253 8 msec 4 msec 4 msec
  2 10.1.2.14 12 msec 8 msec 4 msec
RouterA#
! Moving to Router B now
! The following output occurs in reaction to the traceroute command on A
RouterB#debug ip icmp
RouterB#
ICMP: time exceeded (time to live) sent to 10.1.3.254 (dest was 10.1.2.14)
ICMP: time exceeded (time to live) sent to 10.1.3.254 (dest was 10.1.2.14)
ICMP: time exceeded (time to live) sent to 10.1.3.254 (dest was 10.1.2.14)
```

The **traceroute** command lists the IP address of Router B in the first line and the IP address of the destination host in the second line. Note that it lists Router B's left-side IP address. B replies with the Time Exceeded message, using B's outgoing interface IP address as the source address in that packet. As a result, the **traceroute** command lists that IP address. If the address is known to a DNS server, or if it's in Router A's hostname table, the command can list the hostname instead of the IP address.

Similar to the extended **ping** command as described in the section titled, "The Extended **ping** Command" in Chapter 4, the extended version of the **traceroute** command does a much better job of simulating packets sent by end-user hosts, especially for testing reverse routes. For example, in Example 7-1, A's **traceroute** command uses A's 10.1.3.254 IP address as the source address of sent packets, because A uses the interface with address 10.1.3.254 to send the packets generated by the **traceroute** command. So, the **traceroute** command in Example 7-1 tests the forward route toward 10.1.2.14 and the reverse route to 10.1.3.254. By using the extended **traceroute** command, the command can be used to test a more appropriate reverse route, such as the route to the LAN subnet on the left side of Router A. Example 7-2, later in this chapter, shows an example of the extended **traceroute** command.

> **NOTE** The **tracert** command on Microsoft operating systems works much like the IOS **traceroute** command. However, it is important to note that the Microsoft **tracert** command sends ICMP Echo Requests and does not use UDP. So, IP ACLs could cause the IOS **traceroute** to fail while the Microsoft **tracert** worked, and vice versa.

Troubleshooting the Packet Forwarding Process

Troubleshooting the IP routing process is one of the more complex tasks faced by network engineers. As usual, using a structured approach can help. Chapter 4 in particular, as well as Chapters 5 and 6, have already explained a lot about the first major part of the troubleshooting process—namely, what should happen in a network. This section focuses on the second major step: problem isolation. (For a more general reference on troubleshooting techniques, refer to Chapter 3, "Troubleshooting LAN Switching.")

> **NOTE** This chapter defers any detailed troubleshooting of routing protocols until Chapter 11, "Troubleshooting Routing Protocols."

Isolating IP Routing Problems Related to Hosts

The troubleshooting process outlined in this chapter separates the troubleshooting steps—one part for the hosts, and one part for the routers. Essentially, for any problem in which two hosts cannot communicate, the first part of this troubleshooting process examines the issues that might impact each host's ability to send packets to and from its respective default gateway. The second part isolates problems related to how routers forward packets.

The following list outlines the troubleshooting steps focused on testing the host's connectivity to the first router:

Step 1 Check the host's ability to send packets inside its own subnet. Either ping the host's default gateway IP address from the host, or ping the host's IP address from the default gateway. If the ping fails, do the following:

  a. Ensure that the router's interface used at the default gateway is in an "up and up" state.

  b. Check the source host's IP address and mask setting as compared to the router's interface used as the default gateway. Ensure that both agree as to the subnet number and mask, and therefore agree to the range of valid addresses in the subnet.

  c. If the router uses VLAN trunking, solve any trunk configuration issues, ensuring that the router is configured to support the same VLAN in which the host resides.

  d. If the other steps do not lead to a solution, investigate Layer 1/2 problems with the LAN, as covered in Chapter 3. For example, look for an undefined VLAN.

Step 2 Verify the default gateway setting on the host by pinging one of the default router's other interface IP addresses. Or, from the default router, use an extended ping of the host's IP address with a source address from another of the router's interfaces.

For example, in Figure 7-5, the problem symptoms may be that PC1 cannot browse the web server at PC4. To test PC1's ability to send packets over its local subnet, PC1 could use the **ping 10.1.1.1** command to test connectivity to the default router in its same subnet. Or the engineer could simply **ping 10.1.1.10** from R1 (Step 1). Either location for the **ping** works fine, because both ping locations require that a packet be sent in each direction. If the **ping** fails, further problem isolation should uncover the two specific problem areas listed in Steps 1A, 1B, and 1C. If not, the problem is likely to be some Layer 1 or 2 problem, as discussed in Chapter 3.

Figure 7-5   *Sample Network for Troubleshooting Scenarios*

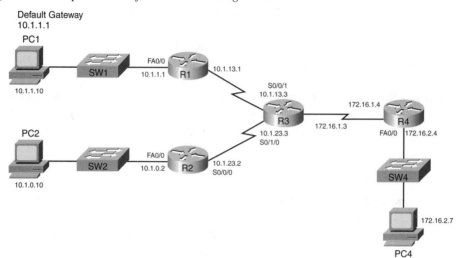

Step 2 stresses an often-overlooked troubleshooting concept to verify that the default gateway setting is working. Neither **ping** option listed in Step 1 requires the host to use its default gateway setting, because the source and destination address in each packet are in the same subnet. Step 2 forces the host to send a packet to an IP address in another subnet, thereby testing the host's default gateway setting. Also, by pinging an IP address on the default gateway (router), instead of some faraway host IP address, this step removes much of the IP routing complexity from the test. Instead, the focus is on whether the host's default gateway setting works. For example, in Figure 7-5, a **ping 10.1.13.1** command on PC1 forces PC1 to use its default gateway setting because 10.1.13.1 is not in PC1's subnet (10.1.1.0/24). But the IP address is on router R1, which removes most of the rest of the network as being a possible cause if the ping fails.

Isolating IP Routing Problems Related to Routers

When the host problem isolation process is complete, and the pings all work, on both the sending and receiving hosts, any remaining IP routing issues should be between the first and last router in both the forward and reverse route between the two hosts. The following list picks up the troubleshooting process with the source host's default gateway/router, relying on the **traceroute** command on the router. (Note that the host's equivalent command, such as **tracert** on Microsoft operating systems, can also be used.)

> **NOTE**   Although the following list may be useful for reference, it is rather long. Do not get bogged down in the details, but do read the examples of its use that follow this list; that should clarify many of the steps. As usual, you do not need to memorize any troubleshooting processes listed here. They are meant as learning tools to help you build your skills.

Step 3   Test connectivity to the destination host by using the extended **traceroute** command on the host's default gateway, using the router's interface attached to the source host for the source IP address of the packets. If the command successfully completes:

    a. No routing problems exist in the forward route or reverse route directions.

    b. If the end-user traffic still does not work (even though the **traceroute** worked), troubleshoot any ACLs on each interface on each router in the route, in both directions.

Step 4   If the **traceroute** command in Step 3 does not complete, test the *forward route* as follows:

    a. **telnet** to the last traced router (the last router listed in the **traceroute** command).

    b. Find that router's route that matches the destination IP address that was used in the original **traceroute** command (**show ip route**, **show ip route** *ip-address*).

    c. If no matching route is found, investigate why the expected route is missing. Typically it's either a routing protocol issue or a static route misconfiguration. It could also be related to a missing connected route.

    d. If a matching route is found, and the route is a default route, confirm that it will be used based on the setting for the **ip classless/no ip classless** commands.

    e. If a matching route is found, **ping** the next-hop IP address listed in the route. Or, if the route is a connected route, **ping** the true destination IP address.

       • If the **ping** fails, investigate Layer 2 problems between this router and the IP address that was pinged, and investigate possible ACL problems.

       • If the **ping** works, investigate ACL issues.

   f. If a matching route is found, and no other problems are found,
         confirm that the route is not errantly pointing in the wrong direction.

Step 5 If Step 4 does not identify a problem in the forward route, test the *reverse
         route*:

   a. If the forward route on the last traced router refers to another router
         as the next-hop router, repeat the substeps of Step 3 from that next-
         hop router. Analyze the reverse route—the route to reach the source
         IP address used by the failed **traceroute** command.

   b. If the forward route on the last traced router refers to a connected
         subnet, check the destination host's IP settings. In particular, confirm
         the settings for the IP address, mask, and default gateway.

For example, if PC1 cannot communicate with PC4 in Figure 7-5, and the hosts can both
communicate through their respective default gateways, Step 3 of the router-oriented
problem isolation process could start with a **traceroute 172.16.2.7**, using R1's Fa0/0 IP
address (10.1.1.1) as the source IP address. If that **traceroute** command lists 10.1.13.3 as
the last IP address in the command output, rather than completing, you would then start
Step 4, which examines R3's forward route toward 172.16.2.7. If the analysis at Step 4 does
not uncover the problem, Step 5 would then move on to the next-hop router, R4 in this case,
and examine R4's reverse route—its route back to the original source address of 10.1.1.1.

Next, two separate scenarios show how to use these troubleshooting steps to isolate some
sample problems.

Troubleshooting Scenario 1: Forward Route Problem

This first example of the router troubleshooting process uses the same internetwork shown
in Figure 7-5. In this case, PC1 cannot use a web browser to connect to the web service
running on PC4. After further investigation, PC1 cannot ping 172.16.2.7 (PC4). Example
7-2 shows the commands used on R1 and R4 for the host-oriented Steps 1 and 2, as well as
a beginning of the router-oriented Step 3.

Example 7-2 *Troubleshooting Scenario 1: Steps 1 and 2 and Part of Step 3*

```
R1#ping 10.1.1.10

Type escape sequence to abort.
Sending 5, 100-byte ICMP Echos to 10.1.1.10, timeout is 2 seconds:
!!!!!
Success rate is 100 percent (5/5), round-trip min/avg/max = 1/2/4 ms
R1#ping
Protocol [ip]:
Target IP address: 10.1.1.10
Repeat count [5]:
```

Example 7-2 *Troubleshooting Scenario 1: Steps 1 and 2 and Part of Step 3 (Continued)*

```
Datagram size [100]:
Timeout in seconds [2]:
Extended commands [n]: y
Source address or interface: 10.1.13.1
Type of service [0]:
Set DF bit in IP header? [no]:
Validate reply data? [no]:
Data pattern [0xABCD]:
Loose, Strict, Record, Timestamp, Verbose[none]:
Sweep range of sizes [n]:
Type escape sequence to abort.
Sending 5, 100-byte ICMP Echos to 10.1.1.10, timeout is 2 seconds:
Packet sent with a source address of 10.1.13.1
!!!!!
Success rate is 100 percent (5/5), round-trip min/avg/max = 1/2/4 ms
R1#
```

```
! Now moving to R4 to repeat the test
R4#ping 172.16.2.7

Type escape sequence to abort.
Sending 5, 100-byte ICMP Echos to 172.16.2.7, timeout is 2 seconds:
.....
Success rate is 0 percent (0/5)
R4#show ip interface brief
Interface              IP-Address      OK? Method Status                 Protocol
FastEthernet0/0        172.16.2.4      YES manual administratively down  down
FastEthernet0/1        172.16.1.4      YES manual up                     up
Serial0/0/0            unassigned      YES unset  administratively down  down
Serial0/0/1            unassigned      YES unset  administratively down  down
Serial0/1/0            unassigned      YES unset  administratively down  down
```

The standard and extended pings on R1 at the beginning of the example essentially perform Steps 1 and 2, the host-oriented steps, to confirm that PC1 seems to be working well. However, the example next shows that R4 cannot reach PC4 because R4's LAN interface has been shut down, as shown at the end of the example. Although this scenario may seem a bit simple, it provides a good starting point for troubleshooting a problem.

To get a fuller view of the troubleshooting process, next consider this same scenario, with the same root problem, but now you do not have access to router R4. So, you can only perform Steps 1 and 2 for PC1, which work, but you cannot do those same steps for PC4 from R4. So, Example 7-3 moves on to Steps 3 and 4. The beginning of the example shows Step 3, where R1 uses **traceroute 172.16.2.7**, with a source IP address of 10.1.1.1. This command does not complete, referencing 10.1.13.3 (R3) as the last router. Step 4 proceeds by looking at how R3 then routes packets destined for 172.16.2.7.

Example 7-3 *Troubleshooting Scenario 1: Step 4*

```
R1#traceroute
Protocol [ip]:
Target IP address: 172.16.2.7
Source address: 10.1.1.1
Numeric display [n]:
Timeout in seconds [3]:
Probe count [3]:
Minimum Time to Live [1]:
Maximum Time to Live [30]:
Port Number [33434]:
Loose, Strict, Record, Timestamp, Verbose[none]:
Type escape sequence to abort.
Tracing the route to 172.16.2.7


  1 10.1.13.3 0 msec 4 msec 0 msec
  2 10.1.13.3 !H  *  !H
! Note above that the command did stop by itself, but it does not list the
! destination host 172.16.2.7
R3#show ip route 172.16.2.7
% Subnet not in table
R3#show ip route
Codes: C - connected, S - static, R - RIP, M - mobile, B - BGP
       D - EIGRP, EX - EIGRP external, O - OSPF, IA - OSPF inter area
       N1 - OSPF NSSA external type 1, N2 - OSPF NSSA external type 2
       E1 - OSPF external type 1, E2 - OSPF external type 2
       i - IS-IS, su - IS-IS summary, L1 - IS-IS level-1, L2 - IS-IS level-2
       ia - IS-IS inter area, * - candidate default, U - per-user static route
       o - ODR, P - periodic downloaded static route

Gateway of last resort is not set

     172.16.0.0/24 is subnetted, 1 subnets
C       172.16.1.0 is directly connected, FastEthernet0/0
     10.0.0.0/24 is subnetted, 4 subnets
C       10.1.13.0 is directly connected, Serial0/0/1
R       10.1.1.0 [120/1] via 10.1.13.1, 00:00:04, Serial0/0/1
R       10.1.0.0 [120/1] via 10.1.23.2, 00:00:01, Serial0/1/0
C       10.1.23.0 is directly connected, Serial0/1/0
```

The extended **traceroute** command at the beginning of the example shows output identifying R3 (10.1.13.3) as the last listed device in the command output (Step 3). Step 4 then proceeds with an examination of the forward route on R3 toward IP address 172.16.2.7. The **show ip route 172.16.2.7** command gets right to the point. The message "subnet not in table" means that R3 does not have a route matching destination address 172.16.2.7. If the question does not supply access to a simulator, only the output of the **show ip route** command, you would need to examine the routes to determine that none of them refer to a range of addresses that includes 172.16.2.7.

Any time the problem isolation process points to a missing route, the next step is to determine how the router should have learned about the route. In this case, R3 should have used RIP-2 to learn the route. So, the next steps would be to troubleshoot any problems with the dynamic routing protocol.

The root cause of this problem has not changed—R4 has shut down its Fa0/0 interface— but the symptoms are somewhat interesting. Because the interface is shut down, R4 does not advertise a route for subnet 172.16.2.0/24 to R3. However, R3 advertises an autosummarized route to network 172.16.0.0/16 to both R1 and R2, so both R1 and R2, because of RIP-2's default autosummary setting, can forward packets destined for 172.16.2.7 to R3. As a result, the **traceroute** command on R1 can forward packets to R3.

Troubleshooting Scenario 2: Reverse Route Problem

This next example uses the same network diagram as shown in Figure 7-5, with all the information shown in the figure still being true. However, the details mentioned in the previous section may have changed—particularly the problem that exists to make the example more interesting. So, approach this second problem only relying on the figure as being true.

In this scenario, PC1 again cannot ping 172.16.2.7 (PC4). The host default gateway checks suggested in Steps 1 and 2 again work for PC1, but the tests cannot be performed for the reverse direction, because the engineer cannot access PC4 or router R4. So, Example 7-4 picks up the suggested troubleshooting process at Step 3, showing the result of the extended **traceroute** command on R1. Note that the command does not even list R3's 10.1.13.3 IP address in this case. So, the rest of Example 7-4 shows the investigations into the specific substeps of Step 4.

Example 7-4   *Troubleshooting Scenario 2: Steps 3 and 4*

```
R1#traceroute ip 172.16.2.7 source fa0/0

Type escape sequence to abort.
Tracing the route to 172.16.2.7

  1  *   *   *
  2  *   *   *
  3  *
```

continues

Example 7-4 *Troubleshooting Scenario 2: Steps 3 and 4 (Continued)*

```
R1#show ip route 172.16.2.7
Routing entry for 172.16.0.0/16
  Known via "rip", distance 120, metric 1
  Redistributing via rip
  Last update from 10.1.13.3 on Serial0/1/0, 00:00:05 ago
  Routing Descriptor Blocks:
  * 10.1.13.3, from 10.1.13.3, 00:00:05 ago, via Serial0/1/0
      Route metric is 1, traffic share count is 1

R1#ping 10.1.13.3

Type escape sequence to abort.
Sending 5, 100-byte ICMP Echos to 10.1.13.3, timeout is 2 seconds:
!!!!!
Success rate is 100 percent (5/5), round-trip min/avg/max = 1/2/4 ms
R1#show ip access-lists

! Switching to router R3 next
R3#show ip access-lists

R3#
```

The example starts by showing the Step 3 part of the process, with the **traceroute** command only listing lines of asterisks. This means that the command did not successfully identify even the very next router in the route.

Next, moving on to Step 4, the following list outlines the substeps of Step 4 as applied to this example:

Step 4a   The example had already begun with a Telnet into R1, so no extra work is required.

Step 4b   The next command, **show ip route 172.16.2.7**, shows that R1 has a nondefault route for network 172.16.0.0, pointing to R3 (10.1.13.3) as the next hop.

Step 4c   This step does not apply in this case, because a matching route was found in Step 4B.

Step 4d   This step does not apply in this case, because the matching route is not a route to 0.0.0.0/0 (the default route).

Step 4e   The next listed command, **ping 10.1.13.3**, tests R1's ability to send packets over the link to the next-hop router identified in Step 4B. The ping works.

Step 4f   On both R1 and the next-hop router (R3), the **show ip access-lists**
command confirms that neither router has any IP ACLs configured.

Because all the steps to examine the forward route passed, the process then moves on to
Step 5. The original **traceroute** command in Example 7-4 used R1's Fa0/0 interface IP
address, 10.1.1.1, as the source IP address. For Step 5, the process begins at R3 with an
analysis of R3's reverse route to reach 10.1.1.1. Examine the output in Example 7-5, and
look for any problems before reading the explanations following the example.

Example 7-5   *Troubleshooting Scenario 2: Step 5*

```
! The next command shows the matched route, for subnet 10.1.1.0/26,
! with next-hop 10.1.23.2.
R3#show ip route 10.1.1.1
Routing entry for 10.1.1.0/26
  Known via "static", distance 1, metric 0
  Routing Descriptor Blocks:
  * 10.1.23.2
      Route metric is 0, traffic share count is 1

! The next command shows the overlapping subnets - 10.1.1.0/26 and 10.1.1.0/24.
R3#show ip route
Codes: C - connected, S - static, R - RIP, M - mobile, B - BGP
       D - EIGRP, EX - EIGRP external, O - OSPF, IA - OSPF inter area
       N1 - OSPF NSSA external type 1, N2 - OSPF NSSA external type 2
       E1 - OSPF external type 1, E2 - OSPF external type 2
       i - IS-IS, su - IS-IS summary, L1 - IS-IS level-1, L2 - IS-IS level-2
       ia - IS-IS inter area, * - candidate default, U - per-user static route
       o - ODR, P - periodic downloaded static route

Gateway of last resort is not set

     172.16.0.0/24 is subnetted, 2 subnets
C       172.16.1.0 is directly connected, FastEthernet0/0
R       172.16.2.0 [120/1] via 172.16.1.4, 00:00:18, FastEthernet0/0
     10.0.0.0/8 is variably subnetted, 5 subnets, 2 masks
C       10.1.13.0/24 is directly connected, Serial0/0/1
S       10.1.1.0/26 [1/0] via 10.1.23.2
R       10.1.1.0/24 [120/1] via 10.1.13.1, 00:00:10, Serial0/0/1
R       10.1.0.0/24 [120/1] via 10.1.23.2, 00:00:11, Serial0/1/0
C       10.1.23.0/24 is directly connected, Serial0/1/0
```

R3 has an incorrectly configured static route for subnet 10.1.1.0/26. This subnet includes
the address range 10.1.1.0–10.1.1.63, which includes IP address 10.1.1.1. When R3
attempts to send a packet back to 10.1.1.1, R3 has two routes that match the destination
address. But R3 picks the more specific (longer prefix) route for subnet 10.1.1.0/26. This
route causes R3 to forward packets intended for 10.1.1.1 out R3's link to R2, instead of to
R1.

Although you cannot necessarily determine the true intent of this static route, this process has identified the root cause—the static route to 10.1.1.0/26 on R3. If the LAN off R1 should include all addresses between 10.1.1.0 and 10.1.1.255, the static route should just be deleted.

An Alternative Problem Isolation Process for Steps 3, 4, and 5

The router-oriented steps of the IP routing problem isolation process depend on the **traceroute** command, relying on this command's ability to identify on which router the router-oriented troubleshooting should begin. As an alternative, the **ping** and **telnet** commands can be used. However, because these commands cannot quickly identify the most likely routers on which the problem exists, using **ping** and **telnet** requires that you perform a set of tasks on the first router (the host's default gateway/router) in a route, and then the next router, and the next, and so on, until the problem is identified.

So, just to be complete, note that you can do the same specific subtasks as already explained in Steps 4 and 5, but when using **ping**, just repeat the steps at each successive router. For example, to apply this revised process to the first of the two just-completed scenarios, the process would begin with router R1, PC1's default router. In the first scenario, R1 did not have any forward route issues for forwarding packets to 172.16.2.7 (PC4), and R1 had no reverse route issues and no ACLs. This new alternative process would then suggest moving on to the next router (R3). In this example, R3's forward route problem—not having a route that matches destination address 172.16.2.7—would be found.

Troubleshooting Tools and Tips

The second half of this chapter covers a wide variety of troubleshooting tools and tips that can be helpful when you're troubleshooting real networks. Some of the information in this section may apply directly to the CCNA exams. Other parts of this section will be indirectly useful for the exams. The information may help you learn as you work with networks in your job, making you better prepared for the unique scenarios on the exams.

Host Routing Tools and Perspectives

This section covers two short topics related to how hosts process IP packets. The first topic lists several tips for troubleshooting hosts. The second topic reviews information covered in *CCENT/CCNA ICND1 Official Exam Certification Guide* on how a LAN switch's IP configuration works like a host.

Host Troubleshooting Tips

When you're trying to isolate the cause of networking problems, the tips in Table 7-4 may help you more quickly find problems related to hosts. The tips are organized by typical symptoms, along with common root causes. Note that the table does not list all possible causes, just the more common ones.

Table 7-4 *Common Host Problem Symptoms and Typical Reasons*

Symptom	Common Root Cause
The host can send packets to hosts in the same subnet, but not to other subnets.	The host does not have a default gateway configured, or the default gateway IP address is incorrect.
The host can send packets to hosts in the same subnet, but not to other subnets.	The host's default gateway is in a different subnet than the host's IP address (according to the host's perception of the subnet).
Some hosts in a subnet can communicate with hosts in other subnets, but others cannot.	This may be caused by the default gateway (router) using a different mask than the hosts. This may result in the router's connected route not including some of the hosts on the LAN.
Some hosts on the same VLAN can send packets to each other, but others cannot.	The hosts may not be using the same mask.

When troubleshooting networking problems in real life, it's helpful to get used to thinking about the symptoms, because that's where the problem isolation process typically begins. However, for the exams, most host communication problems are caused by just a handful of issues:

Step 1 Check all hosts and routers that should be in the same subnet to ensure that they all use the same mask and that their addresses are indeed all in the same subnet.

Key
Topic

Step 2 Compare each host's default gateway setting with the router's configuration to ensure that it is the right IP address.

Step 3 If the first two items are correct, next look at Layer 1/2 issues, as covered in Chapters 1 through 3.

LAN Switch IP Support

Ethernet switches do not need to know anything about Layer 3 to perform their basic Layer 2 function of forwarding Ethernet frames. However, to support several important features, such as the ability to telnet and SSH to the switch to troubleshoot problems, LAN switches need an IP address.

Switches act like hosts when it comes to IP configuration. As compared to a PC, a Cisco switch does not use a NIC. Instead, it uses an internal virtual interface associated with VLAN 1 that essentially gives the switch itself an interface in VLAN 1. Then, the same kinds of items that can be configured on a host for IP can be configured on this VLAN interface: IP address, mask, and default gateway. DNS server IP addresses can also be configured.

The following list repeats the LAN switch IP configuration checklist from *CCENT/CCNA ICND1 Official Exam Certification Guide*. Following the list, Example 7-6 shows the IP address configuration for switch SW1 in Figure 7-5 from earlier in the chapter.

Step 1 Enter VLAN 1 configuration mode using the **interface vlan 1** global configuration command (from any config mode).

Step 2 Assign an IP address and mask using the **ip address** *ip-address mask* interface subcommand.

Step 3 Enable the VLAN 1 interface using the **no shutdown** interface subcommand.

Step 4 Add the **ip default-gateway** *ip-address* global command to configure the default gateway.

Example 7-6 *Switch Static IP Address Configuration*

```
SW1#configure terminal
SW1(config)#interface vlan 1
SW1(config-if)#ip address 10.1.1.200 255.255.255.0
SW1(config-if)#no shutdown
00:25:07: %LINK-3-UPDOWN: Interface Vlan1, changed state to up
00:25:08: %LINEPROTO-5-UPDOWN: Line protocol on Interface Vlan1, changed
  state to up
SW1(config-if)#exit
SW1(config)#ip default-gateway 10.1.1.1
```

NOTE The VLAN interface on a switch stays in an administratively down state until the user issues the **no shutdown** command; the switch cannot send IP packets until the VLAN 1 interface is up.

A common oversight when configuring or troubleshooting IP connectivity problems to LAN switches relates to VLAN trunking. Cisco generally suggests that you avoid putting end-user devices into VLAN 1, but the switch IP address may well be configured in VLAN 1. To support the ability for the switch to send and receive packets to hosts in different subnets, thereby supporting Telnet into the switch from those end-user subnets, the router's trunking configuration must include configuration for VLAN 1 as well as the end-user VLANs.

show ip route Reference

The **show ip route** command plays a huge role in troubleshooting IP routing and IP routing protocol problems. Many chapters in this book and in the ICND1 book mention various facts about this command. This section pulls the concepts together in one place for easier reference and study.

Figure 7-6 shows the output of the **show ip route** command from back in Example 7-3. The figure numbers various parts of the command output for easier reference, with Table 7-5 describing the output noted by each number.

Figure 7-6   **show ip route** *Command Output Reference*

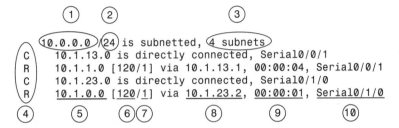

Table 7-5   *Descriptions of the* **show ip route** *Command Output*

Item Number	Item	Value in the Figure	Description
1	Classful network	10.0.0.0	The routing table is organized by classful network. This line is the heading line for classful network 10.0.0.0.
2	Prefix length	/24	When this router knows only one subnet mask for all subnets of the network, this location lists that one mask, by default in prefix notation.
3	Number of subnets	4 subnets	Lists the number of routes for subnets of the classful network known to this router.
4	Legend code	R, C	A short code that identifies the source of the routing information. R is for RIP, and C is for connected. The figure omits the legend text at the top of the **show ip route** command output, but it can be seen in Example 7-3.
5	Subnet number	10.1.0.0	The subnet number of this particular route.
6	Administrative distance	120	If a router learns routes for the listed subnet from more than one source of routing information, the router uses the source with the lowest AD.
7	Metric	1	The metric for this route.
8	Next-hop router	10.1.23.2	For packets matching this route, the IP address of the next router to which the packet should be forwarded.
9	Timer	00:00:01	Time since this route was learned in a routing update.
10	Outgoing interface	Serial0/1/0	For packets matching this route, the interface out which the packet should be forwarded.

The output of the command differs slightly when VLSM is used. The figure shows an example in which VLSM is not used in network 10.0.0.0, with mask /24 used for all subnets of that network. So, IOS lists the mask once, in the heading line (/24 in this case). If VLSM were in use, the heading line would simply note that the network is variably subnetted, and each route would list the mask. For an example, see Example 5-1 in Chapter 5, "VLSM and Route Summarization."

Interface Status

One of the steps in the IP routing troubleshooting process described earlier, in the "Troubleshooting the Packet Forwarding Process" section, says to check the interface status, ensuring that the required interface is working. For a router interface to be working, the two interface status codes must both be listed as "up," with engineers usually saying the interface is "up and up."

This chapter does not explain the troubleshooting steps for router interfaces, simply assuming that each interface is indeed in an up/up state. Chapter 12's section titled "Troubleshooting Serial Links" covers many of the details for troubleshooting router interfaces. For router LAN interfaces connected to a LAN switch, the main items to check on routers are that the router and switch match each other's duplex and speed settings, and that if trunking is configured, both the router and switch have been manually configured for trunking, because routers do not dynamically negotiate LAN trunking.

VLSM Issues

This section examines several issues when using VLSM:

- Recognizing whether VLSM is used and, if so, which routing protocols can be used
- Understanding the conditions in which routers can allow the misconfiguration of overlapping VLSM subnets
- Understanding the outward symptoms that can occur when overlapping VLSM subnets exist

Recognizing When VLSM Is Used

One common oversight when troubleshooting a problem in an unfamiliar internetwork is failing to recognize whether VLSM is used. As defined in Chapter 5, an internetwork uses VLSM when multiple subnet masks are used for different subnets of *a single classful network*. For example, if in one internetwork all subnets of network 10.0.0.0 use a 255.255.240.0 mask, and all subnets of network 172.16.0.0 use a 255.255.255.0 mask, the design does not use VLSM. If multiple masks were used for subnets of network 10.0.0.0, VLSM would be in use.

The follow-on concept is that only classless routing protocols (RIP-2, EIGRP, OSPF) can support VLSM; classful routing protocols (RIP-1, IGRP) cannot. So, a quick determination of whether VLSM is actually used can then tell you whether a classless routing protocol is required. Note that the routing protocol does not require any special configuration to support VLSM. It is just a feature of the routing protocol.

Configuring Overlapping VLSM Subnets

IP subnetting rules require that the address ranges in the subnets used in an internetwork should not overlap. IOS can recognize when a new **ip address** command creates an overlapping subnet, but only in some cases. This section examines the conditions under which overlapping subnets can be configured, beginning with the following general statements about when the overlaps cannot and can be configured:

- **Preventing the overlap:** IOS detects the overlap when the **ip address** command implies an overlap with another **ip address** command *on the same router*. If the interface being configured is up/up, IOS rejects the **ip address** command. If not, IOS accepts the **ip address** command, but IOS will never bring up the interface.

- **Allowing the overlap:** IOS cannot detect an overlap when an **ip address** command overlaps with an **ip address** command on another router.

The router shown in Example 7-7 prevents the configuration of an overlapping VLSM subnet. The example shows router R3 configuring Fa0/0 with IP address 172.16.5.1/24, and Fa0/1 with 172.16.5.193/26. The ranges of addresses in each subnet are:

Subnet 172.16.5.0/24:   172.16.5.1–   172.16.5.254
Subnet 172.16.5.192/26: 172.16.5.193–172.16.5.254

Example 7-7   *Single Router Rejects Overlapped Subnets*

```
R3#configure terminal
R3(config)#interface Fa0/0
R3(config-if)#ip address 172.16.5.1 255.255.255.0
R3(config-if)#interface Fa0/1
R3(config-if)#ip address 172.16.5.193 255.255.255.192
% 172.16.5.192 overlaps with FastEthernet0/0
R3(config-if)#
```

IOS knows that it is illegal to overlap the ranges of addresses implied by a subnet. In this case, because both subnets would be connected subnets, this single router knows that these two subnets should not coexist, because that would break subnetting rules, so IOS rejects the second command.

However, it is possible to configure overlapping subnets if they are connected to different routers. Figure 7-7 shows a figure very similar to Figure 5-2 in Chapter 5—used in that chapter to explain the problem of overlapping subnets. Example 7-8 shows the configuration of the two overlapping subnets on R2 and R3.

Figure 7-7   *Internetwork That Allows the Configuration of Overlapped Subnets*

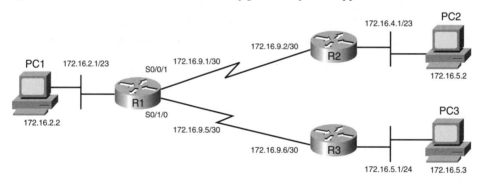

Example 7-8   *Two Routers Accept Overlapped Subnets*

```
R2#configure terminal
R2(config)#interface Fa0/0
R2(config-if)#ip address 172.16.4.1 255.255.254.0
R3#configure terminal
R3(config)#interface Fa0/0
R3(config-if)# ip address 172.16.5.1 255.255.255.0
```

For the exams, keep in mind that overlapped subnets can be configured if the subnets do not connect to the same router. So, if a question asks you to pick a new subnet number and configure an interface to be in that subnet, the router's acceptance of your **ip address** command does not necessarily tell you that you did the math correctly.

The next topic explains some of the problem symptoms you might see if such an overlap exists.

Symptoms with Overlapping Subnets

> **NOTE**   Although this section is included for the sake of completeness, the types of problems described here may well be beyond the scope of the CCNA exams.

The outward problem symptoms differ depending on whether the address in question is in the overlapped portion of the subnets and if multiple hosts are attempting to use the exact same IP address. The addresses in the nonoverlapped parts of the subnet typically work fine, whereas those in the overlapped area may or may not work at all. For example, continuing with the overlapped subnets shown in Figure 7-7, subnets 172.16.4.0/23 and 172.16.5.0/24 overlap—specifically, addresses 172.16.5.0–172.16.5.255. Hosts in the nonoverlapped range of 172.16.4.0–172.16.4.255 probably work fine.

For the addresses in the overlapped address range, in many cases, hosts in the smaller of the two overlapped subnets work fine, but hosts in the larger of the two subnets do not. To see why, consider the case in which PC1 in Figure 7-7 tries to ping both 172.16.5.2 (PC2, off R2) and 172.16.5.3 (PC3, off R3). (For the sake of this example, assume that PC2's and PC3's IP addresses are not duplicated in the opposite overlapped subnet.) As you can see from the routing tables on R1 and R3 and the **traceroute 172.16.5.2** command in Example 7-9, the packet sent by PC1 to PC2 would actually be delivered from R1 to R3, and then onto R3's LAN.

Example 7-9   *Two Routers Accept Overlapped Subnets*

```
! R1's route to reach 172.16.5.2, off R2, points to R3
R1#show ip route 172.16.5.2
Routing entry for 172.16.5.0/24
  Known via "rip", distance 120, metric 1
  Redistributing via rip
  Last update from 172.16.9.6 on Serial0/1/0, 00:00:25 ago
  Routing Descriptor Blocks:
  * 172.16.9.6, from 172.16.9.6, 00:00:25 ago, via Serial0/1/0
      Route metric is 1, traffic share count is 1
! R1's route to reach 172.16.5.3, off R3, points to R3
R1#show ip route 172.16.5.3
Routing entry for 172.16.5.0/24
  Known via "rip", distance 120, metric 1
```

continues

Example 7-9   *Two Routers Accept Overlapped Subnets (Continued)*

```
 Redistributing via rip
 Last update from 172.16.9.6 on Serial0/1/0, 00:00:01 ago
 Routing Descriptor Blocks:
 * 172.16.9.6, from 172.16.9.6, 00:00:01 ago, via Serial0/1/0
     Route metric is 1, traffic share count is 1

! The traceroute to PC2 shows R3, not R2, as the first router, so the packet never
! reaches PC2, and the command never completes until stopped by the user.
R1#traceroute 172.16.5.2

Type escape sequence to abort.
Tracing the route to 172.16.5.2

  1 172.16.9.6 4 msec 0 msec 4 msec
  2  *   *   *
  3  *   *   *
  4
R1#traceroute 172.16.5.3

Type escape sequence to abort.
Tracing the route to 172.16.5.3

  1 172.16.9.6 0 msec 4 msec 0 msec
  2 172.16.5.3 4 msec *  0 msec
```

The example shows that R1 forwards packets to hosts 172.16.5.2 (PC2) and 172.16.5.3 (PC3) by sending them to R3 next. R3 then tries to send them onto R3's LAN subnet, which works well for PC3 but not so well for PC2. So, PC3, in the smaller of the two overlapped subnets, works fine, whereas PC2, in the larger of the two overlapped subnets, does not.

The symptoms can get even worse when addresses are duplicated. For example, imagine that PC22 has been added to R2's LAN subnet, with IP address 172.16.5.3 duplicating PC3's IP address. Now when the PC22 user calls to say that his PC cannot communicate with other devices, the network support person uses a **ping 172.16.5.3** to test the problem—and the ping works! The ping works to the wrong instance of 172.16.5.3, but it works. So, the symptoms may be particularly difficult to track down.

Another difficultly with overlapped VLSM subnets is that the problem may not show up for a while. In this same example, imagine that all addresses in both subnets were to be assigned by a DHCP server, beginning with the smallest IP addresses. For the first six months, the server assigned only IP addresses that began with 172.16.4.*x* on the R2 LAN subnet. Finally, enough hosts were installed on the R2 LAN to require the use of addresses that begin with 172.16.5, like PC2's address of 172.16.5.2 used in the preceding example.

Unfortunately, no one can send packets to those hosts. At first glance, the fact that the problem showed up long after the installation and configuration were complete may actually cloud the issue.

VLSM Troubleshooting Summary

The following list summarizes the key troubleshooting points to consider when you're troubleshooting potential VLSM problems on the exams:

■ Pay close attention to whether the design really uses VLSM. If it does, note whether a classless routing protocol is used.

■ Be aware that overlapping subnets can indeed be configured.

■ The outward problem symptoms may be that some hosts in a subnet work well, but others cannot send packets outside the local subnet.

■ Use the **traceroute** command to look for routes that direct packets to the wrong part of the network. This could be a result of the overlapped subnets.

■ On the exams, you might see a question you think is related to VLSM and IP addresses. In that case, the best plan of attack may well be to analyze the math for each subnet and ensure that no overlaps exist, rather than troubleshooting using **ping** and **traceroute**.

Discontiguous Networks and Autosummary

Chapter 5 explained the concept of discontiguous networks, along with the solution: using a classless routing protocol with autosummarization disabled. This section examines one particular case in which a discontiguous network exists only part of the time. Figure 7-8 shows an internetwork with two classful networks: 10.0.0.0 and 172.16.0.0. The design shows two contiguous networks because a route consisting of only subnets of each network exists between all subnets of that network.

Figure 7-8   *Internetwork with (Currently) Contiguous Networks*

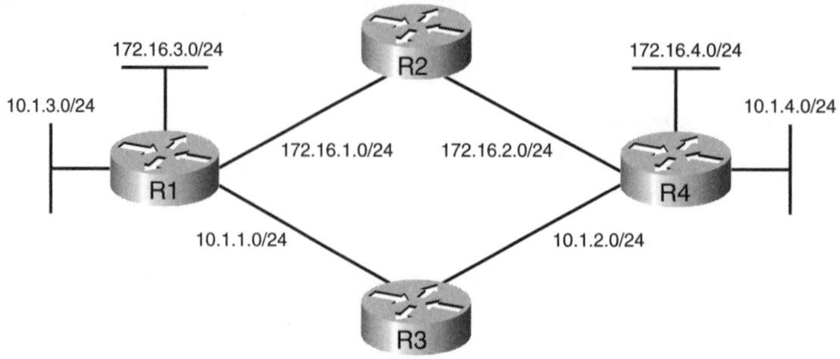

In this figure, with all links up and working, using a routing protocol with autosummary enabled by default, all hosts can ping all other hosts. In this design, packets for network 172.16.0.0 flow over the high route, and packets for network 10.0.0.0 flow over the low route.

Unfortunately, a problem can occur later when one of the four links between routers fails. If any link between the routers fails, one of the two classful networks becomes discontiguous. For example, if the link between R3 and R4 fails, the route from R1 to R4 passes through subnets of network 172.16.0.0, so network 10.0.0.0 is discontiguous. Even with a classless routing protocol, but with autosummarization enabled, both R1 and R4 advertise a route for 10.0.0.0/8 to R2, and R2 sees two routes to all of network 10.0.0.0— one through R1, and another through R4. The solution, as always, is to use a classless routing protocol with autosummary disabled.

Although the design in Figure 7-8 may seem a bit contrived, it happens more often than you might think—particularly as companies are bought and sold. Both for real life and the exams, keep the concept of discontiguous networks in mind for normal working cases and for cases in which redundant links fail.

Access List Troubleshooting Tips

Troubleshooting problems that are impacted by ACLs may well be one of the most difficult tasks for real networking jobs. One of the major difficulties is that the traditional troubleshooting tools such as **ping** and **traceroute** do not send packets that look like the packets matched by the variety of fields in extended ACLs. So, although a **ping** may work, the end-user host may not be able to get to the right application, or vice versa.

This section summarizes some tips for attacking ACL-related problems in real life and on the exams:

Step 1   Determine on which interfaces ACLs are enabled, and in which direction (**show running-config, show ip interfaces**).

Step 2 Determine which ACL statements are matched by test packets (**show access-lists, show ip access-lists**).

Step 3 Analyze the ACLs to predict which packets should match the ACL, focusing on the following points:

a. Remember that the ACL uses first-match logic.

b. Consider using the (possibly) faster math described in Chapter 6, "IP Access Control Lists," which converts ACL address/wildcard mask pairs into address/subnet mask pairs that allow the use of the same math as subnetting.

c. Note the direction of the packet in relation to the server (going to the server, coming from the server). Make sure that the packets have particular values as either the source IP address and port, or as the destination IP address and port, when processed by the ACL enabled for a particular direction (in or out).

d. Remember that the **tcp** and **udp** keywords must be used if the command needs to check the port numbers. (See Table 6-5 in Chapter 6 for a list of popular TCP and UDP port numbers.)

e. Note that ICMP packets do not use UDP or TCP. ICMP is considered to be another protocol matchable with the **icmp** keyword (instead of **ip**, **tcp**, and **udp**).

f. Instead of using the implicit deny any at the end of each ACL, use an explicit configuration command to deny all traffic at the end of the ACL so that the **show** command counters increment when that action is taken.

Chapter 6 covered the background information behind the tips listed in Step 3. The remainder of this section focuses on commands available for you to investigate problems in the first two steps.

If a problem in forwarding IP packets is occurring, and existing ACLs may be impacting the problem, the first problem isolation step is to find the location and direction of the ACLs. The fastest way to do this is to look at the output of the **show running-config** command and to look for **ip access-group** commands under each interface. However, in some cases, enable mode access may not be allowed, and **show** commands are required. The only way to find the interfaces and direction for any IP ACLs is the **show ip interfaces** command, as shown in Example 7-10.

Example 7-10 *Sample* **show ip interface** *Command*

```
R1>show ip interface s0/0/1
Serial0/0/1 is up, line protocol is up
  Internet address is 10.1.2.1/24
  Broadcast address is 255.255.255.255
  Address determined by setup command
  MTU is 1500 bytes
  Helper address is not set
  Directed broadcast forwarding is disabled
  Multicast reserved groups joined: 224.0.0.9
  Outgoing access list is not set
  Inbound  access list is 102
! roughly 26 more lines omitted for brevity
```

Note that the command output lists whether an ACL is enabled, in both directions, and which ACL it is. The example shows an abbreviated version of the **show ip interface S0/0/1** command, which lists messages for just this one interface. The **show ip interface** command would list the same messages for every interface in the router.

Step 2 then says that the contents of the ACL must be found. Again, the most expedient way to look at the ACL is to use the **show running-config** command. If enable mode is not allowed, the **show access-lists** and **show ip access-lists** commands give the same output. The only difference is that if other non-IP ACLs have been configured, the **show access-lists** command lists the non-IP ACLs as well. The output provides the same details shown in the configuration commands, as well as a counter for the number of packets matching each line in the ACL. Example 7-11 shows an example.

Example 7-11 *Sample* **show ip access-lists** *Command*

```
R1#show ip access-lists
Extended IP access list 102
    10 permit ip 10.1.2.0 0.0.0.255 10.1.1.0 0.0.0.255 (15 matches)
```

After the locations, directions, and configuration details of the various ACLs have been discovered in Steps 1 and 2, the hard part begins—interpreting what the ACL really does. Of particular interest is the last item in the troubleshooting tips list, item 3E. In the ACL shown in Example 7-11, some packets (15 so far) have matched the single configured **access-list** statement in ACL 102. However, some packets have probably been denied because of the implied deny all packets logic at the end of an ACL. By configuring the **access-list 102 deny ip any any** command at the end of the ACL, which explicitly matches all packets and discards them, the **show ip access-lists** command would then show the number of packets being denied at the end of the ACL. Cisco sometimes recommends adding the explicit deny all statement at the end of the ACL for easier troubleshooting.

Exam Preparation Tasks

Review All the Key Topics

Review the most important topics from this chapter, noted with the key topics icon. Table 7-6 lists these key topics and where each is discussed.

Key
Topic

Table 7-6 *Key Topics for Chapter 7*

Key Topic Element	Description	Page Number
Table 7-1	Popular ICMP messages and their purpose	271
Figure 7-3	Diagram of how the TTL IP header field and the ICMP Time Exceeded message work	275
Figure 7-4	Demonstration of how the **traceroute** command uses the TTL field and Time Exceeded message	277
List	Two major steps and several substeps in a suggested host routing problem isolation process	279
List	Three major steps for problem isolation with IP routing in routers, with the list numbered as a continuation of the host routing problem isolation list	281
List	Three tips for general items to check when troubleshooting host connectivity problems	289
List	Configuration step list for LAN switch IP details	290
List	Conditions under which overlapping subnets can be configured, and when IOS can prevent this error	293
List	Summary of troubleshooting tips for questions in which VLSM may be causing a problem	297
List	Three steps for troubleshooting ACL problems, particularly when the configuration cannot be displayed	298-299

Complete the Tables and Lists from Memory

Print a copy of Appendix J, "Memory Tables" (found on the CD), or at least the section for this chapter, and complete the tables and lists from memory. Appendix K, "Memory Tables Answer Key," also on the CD, includes completed tables and lists for you to check your work.

Definitions of Key Terms

Define the following key terms from this chapter, and check your answers in the glossary:

Forward route, reverse route

Cisco Published ICND2 Exam Topics*
Covered in This Part

Implement an IP addressing scheme and IP Services to meet network requirements in a medium-size Enterprise branch office network

- Identify and correct common problems associated with IP addressing and host configurations

Configure and troubleshoot basic operation and routing on Cisco devices

- Compare and contrast methods of routing and routing protocols

- Configure, verify and troubleshoot OSPF

- Configure, verify and troubleshoot EIGRP

- Verify configuration and connectivity using ping, traceroute, and telnet or SSH

- Troubleshoot routing implementation issues

- Verify router hardware and software operation using SHOW & DEBUG commands

* Always recheck http://www.cisco.com for the latest posted exam topics.

Part III: Routing Protocols Configuration and Troubleshooting

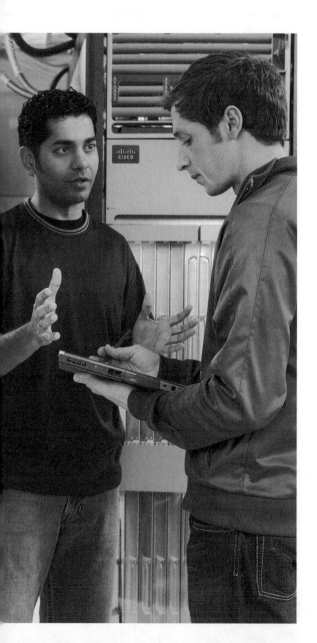

This chapter covers the following subjects:

Dynamic Routing Protocol Overview: This section introduces the core concepts behind how routing protocols work and many terms related to routing protocols.

Distance Vector Routing Protocol Features: This section explains how distance vector routing protocols work, focusing on the loop-avoidance features.

Link-State Routing Protocol Features: This section explains how link-state routing protocols work, using OSPF as a specific example.

CHAPTER **8**

Routing Protocol Theory

Part II, "IP Routing," focused on the IP routing (packet forwarding) process, with some coverage of how routers fill their routing tables. Part III, "Routing Protocols Configuration and Troubleshooting," which begins with this chapter, changes the focus to how routers fill their routing tables by using dynamic routing protocols.

IP routing protocols work on a set of routers, sending messages to nearby routers to help those routers learn all the best routes to reach each subnet. Although this core goal is simple, the processes used by routing protocols tend to be some of the more complex and detailed topics on the CCNA exams. This chapter begins this book's examination of IP routing protocols by explaining the fundamental concepts and theory behind how routing protocols work. Chapters 9 and 10 go on to provide much more detail about how OSPF and EIGRP work, respectively. Chapter 11 ends this part of the book by examining some troubleshooting processes and tips for OSPF and EIGRP.

"Do I Know This Already?" Quiz

The "Do I Know This Already?" quiz allows you to assess whether you should read the entire chapter. If you miss no more than one of these ten self-assessment questions, you might want to move ahead to the "Exam Preparation Tasks" section. Table 8-1 lists the major headings in this chapter and the "Do I Know This Already?" quiz questions covering the material in those sections. This helps you assess your knowledge of these specific areas. The answers to the "Do I Know This Already?" quiz appear in Appendix A.

Table 8-1 *"Do I Know This Already?" Foundation Topics Section-to-Question Mapping*

Foundation Topics Section	Questions
Dynamic Routing Protocol Overview	1–5
Distance Vector Routing Protocol Features	6–8
Link-State Routing Protocol Features	9 and 10

1. Which of the following routing protocols are considered to use distance vector logic?

    a. RIP-1

    b. RIP-2

    c. EIGRP

    d. OSPF

    e. BGP

    f. Integrated IS-IS

2. Which of the following routing protocols are considered to use link-state logic?

    a. RIP-1

    b. RIP-2

    c. EIGRP

    d. OSPF

    e. BGP

    f. Integrated IS-IS

3. Which of the following routing protocols use a metric that is, by default, at least partially affected by link bandwidth?

    a. RIP-1

    b. RIP-2

    c. EIGRP

    d. OSPF

    e. BGP

4. Which of the following interior routing protocols support VLSM?

    a. RIP-1

    b. RIP-2

    c. EIGRP

    d. OSPF

    e. Integrated IS-IS

5. Which of the following situations would cause a router using RIP-2 to remove all the routes learned from a particular neighboring router?

    a. RIP keepalive failure

    b. No longer receiving updates from that neighbor

    c. Updates received 5 or more seconds after the last update was sent to that neighbor

    d. Updates from that neighbor have the global "route bad" flag

6. Which of the following distance vector features prevents routing loops by causing the routing protocol to advertise only a subset of known routes, as opposed to the full routing table, under normal stable conditions?

    a. Counting to infinity

    b. Poison reverse

    c. Holddown

    d. Split horizon

    e. Route poisoning

7. Which of the following distance vector features prevents routing loops by advertising an infinite metric route when a route fails?

    a. Holddown

    b. Full updates

    c. Split horizon

    d. Route poisoning

8. A router that is using a distance vector protocol just received a routing update that lists a route as having an infinite metric. The previous routing update from that neighbor listed a valid metric. Which of the following is not a normal reaction to this scenario?

    a. Immediately send a partial update that includes a poison route for the failed route

    b. Put the route into holddown state

    c. Suspend split horizon for that route and send a poison reverse route

    d. Send a full update listing a poison route for the failed route

9. An internetwork is using a link-state routing protocol. The routers have flooded all LSAs, and the network is stable. Which of the following describes what the routers will do to reflood the LSAs?

    a. Each router refloods each LSA using a periodic timer that has a time similar to distance vector update timers.

    b. Each router refloods each LSA using a periodic timer that is much longer than distance vector update timers.

    c. The routers never reflood the LSAs as long as the LSAs do not change.

    d. The routers reflood all LSAs whenever one LSA changes.

10. Which of the following is true about how a router using a link-state routing protocol chooses the best route to reach a subnet?

    a. The router finds the best route in the link-state database.

    b. The router calculates the best route by running the SPF algorithm against the information in the link-state database.

    c. The router compares the metrics listed for that subnet in the updates received from each neighbor and picks the best (lowest) metric route.

Foundation Topics

Routing protocols define various ways that routers chat among themselves to determine the best routes to each destination. As networks grew more complex over time, routers gained both processing power and RAM. As a result, engineers designed newer routing protocols, taking advantage of faster links and faster routers, transforming routing protocols. This chapter follows that progression to some degree, starting with an introduction to routing protocols. Following that, the theory behind distance vector routing protocols, used with the earliest IP routing protocols, is explained. The final section of this chapter examines the theory behind link-state routing protocols, which is used by some of the more recently defined routing protocols.

Dynamic Routing Protocol Overview

> **NOTE**   If you are using the reading plan suggested in the Introduction, you should have already read about routing protocols in *CCENT/CCNA ICND1 Official Exam Certification Guide*. If so, you may want to skim the text from here to the heading "IGP Comparisons: Summary," because the next several pages cover topics already covered in Chapter 14 of the ICND1 book.

Routers add IP routes to their routing tables using three methods: connected routes, static routes, and routes learned by using dynamic routing protocols. Before we get too far into the discussion, however, it is important to define a few related terms and clear up any misconceptions about the terms *routing protocol*, *routed protocol*, and *routable protocol*. The concepts behind these terms are not that difficult, but because the terms are so similar, and because many documents pay poor attention to when each of these terms is used, they can be a bit confusing. These terms are generally defined as follows:

- **Routing protocol:** A set of messages, rules, and algorithms used by routers for the overall purpose of learning routes. This process includes the exchange and analysis of routing information. Each router chooses the best route to each subnet (path selection) and finally places those best routes in its IP routing table. Examples include RIP, EIGRP, OSPF, and BGP.

- **Routed protocol** and **routable protocol:** Both terms refer to a protocol that defines a packet structure and logical addressing, allowing routers to forward or route the packets. Routers forward, or route, packets defined by routed and routable protocols. Examples include IP and IPX (a part of the Novell NetWare protocol model).

> **NOTE**   The term *path selection* sometimes refers to part of the job of a routing protocol, in which the routing protocol chooses the best route.

Even though routing protocols (such as RIP) are different from routed protocols (such as IP), they do work together very closely. The routing process forwards IP packets, but if a router does not have any routes in its IP routing table that match a packet's destination address, the router discards the packet. Routers need routing protocols so that the routers can learn all the possible routes and add them to the routing table so that the routing process can forward (route) routable protocols such as IP.

Routing Protocol Functions

Cisco IOS software supports several IP routing protocols, performing the same general functions:

1. Learn routing information about IP subnets from other neighboring routers.

2. Advertise routing information about IP subnets to other neighboring routers.

3. If more than one possible route exists to reach one subnet, pick the best route based on a metric.

4. If the network topology changes—for example, a link fails—react by advertising that some routes have failed, and pick a new currently best route. (This process is called convergence.)

> **NOTE**   A neighboring router connects to the same link (for example, the same WAN link or the same Ethernet LAN) as another router, with the two routers being neighbors.

Figure 8-1 shows an example of three of the four functions in the list. Both R1 and R3 learn about a route to subnet 172.16.3.0/24 from R2 (function 1). After R3 learns about the route to 172.16.3.0/24 from R2, R3 advertises that route to R1 (function 2). Then R1 must make a decision about the two routes it learned about for reaching subnet 172.16.3.0/24: one with metric 1 from R2, and one with metric 2 from R3. R1 chooses the lower metric route through R2 (function 3).

Convergence is the fourth routing protocol function listed here. The term *convergence* refers to a process that occurs when the topology changes—that is, when either a router or link fails or comes back up again. When something changes, the best routes available in the network may change. Convergence simply refers to the process by which all the routers collectively realize something has changed, advertise the information about the changes to all the other routers, and all the routers then choose the currently best routes for each subnet. The ability to converge quickly, without causing loops, is one of the most important considerations when choosing which IP routing protocol to use.

Figure 8-1   *Three of the Four Basic Functions of Routing Protocols*

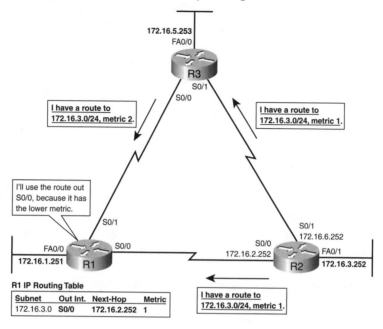

In Figure 8-1, convergence might occur if the link between R1 and R2 failed. In that case, R1 should stop using its old route for subnet 172.16.3.0/24 (directly through R2), instead sending packets to R3.

Interior and Exterior Routing Protocols

IP routing protocols fall into one of two major categories: *Interior Gateway Protocols (IGP)* or *Exterior Gateway Protocols (EGP)*. The definitions of each are as follows:

■ **IGP:** A routing protocol that was designed and intended for use inside a single autonomous system (AS)

■ **EGP:** A routing protocol that was designed and intended for use between different autonomous systems

> **NOTE**   The terms IGP and EGP include the word gateway because routers used to be called gateways.

These definitions use another new term: autonomous system (AS). An AS is an internetwork under the administrative control of a single organization. For instance, an internetwork created and paid for by a single company is probably a single AS, and an internetwork created by a single school system is probably a single AS. Other examples include large divisions of a state or national government, where different government agencies may be able to build their own internetworks. Each ISP is also typically a single different AS.

Some routing protocols work best inside a single AS by design, so these routing protocols are called IGPs. Conversely, routing protocols designed to exchange routes between routers in different autonomous systems are called EGPs. (Currently, only one legitimate EGP exists: the Border Gateway Protocol [BGP]).

Each AS can be assigned a number called (unsurprisingly) an *AS number (ASN)*. Like public IP addresses, the Internet Corporation for Assigned Network Numbers (ICANN, http://www.icann.org) controls the worldwide rights to assigning ASNs. It delegates that authority to other organizations around the world, typically to the same organizations that assign public IP addresses. For example, in North America, the American Registry for Internet Numbers (ARIN, http://www.arin.net/) assigns public IP address ranges and ASNs.

Figure 8-2 shows a small view of the worldwide Internet. The figure shows two Enterprises and three ISPs using IGPs (OSPF and EIGRP) inside their own networks, and with BGP being used between the ASNs.

Figure 8-2 *Comparing Locations for Using IGPs and EGPs*

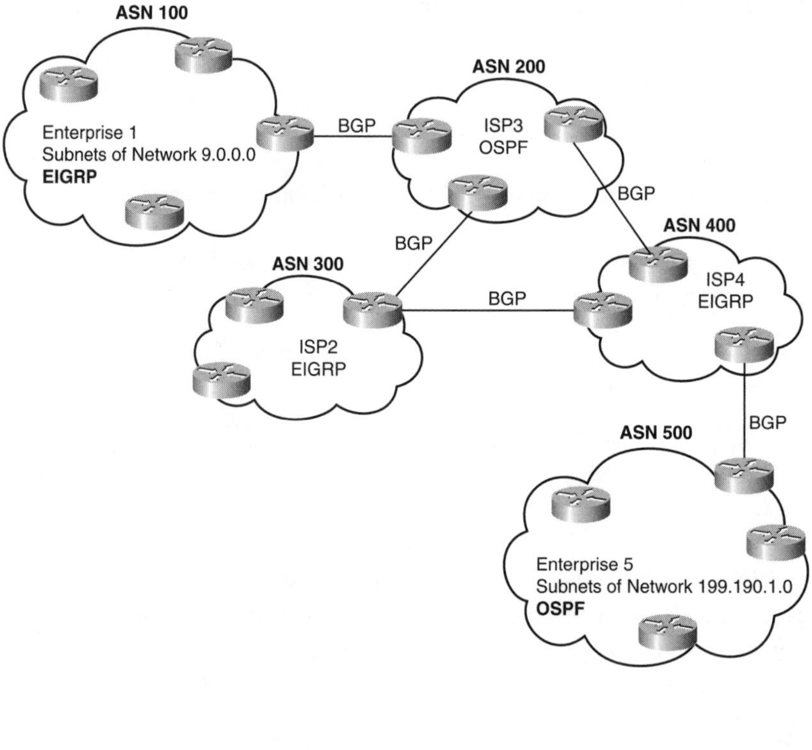

Comparing IGPs

Today, there is no real choice of what EGP to use: you simply use BGP. However, when choosing an IGP to use inside a single organization, you have several choices. The most reasonable choices today are RIP-2, EIGRP, and OSPF. Of these three IGPs, RIP-2 has already been covered to some depth in *CCENT/CCNA ICND1 Official Exam Certification Guide*, and this book covers OSPF and EIGRP in more depth in Chapters 9 and 10, respectively. This section introduces a few key comparison points between the various IP IGPs.

IGP Routing Protocol Algorithms

A routing protocol's underlying algorithm determines how the routing protocol does its job. The term *routing protocol algorithm* simply refers to the logic and processes used by different routing protocols to solve the problem of learning all routes, choosing the best route to each subnet, and converging in reaction to changes in the internetwork. Three main branches of routing protocol algorithms exist for IGP routing protocols:

- Distance vector (sometimes called Bellman-Ford after its creators)

- Link-state

- Balanced hybrid (sometimes called enhanced distance vector)

Historically speaking, distance vector protocols were invented first, mainly in the early 1980s. RIP was the first popularly used IP distance vector protocol, with the Cisco-proprietary Interior Gateway Routing Protocol (IGRP) being introduced a little later. By the early 1990s, distance vector protocols' somewhat slow convergence and potential for routing loops drove the development of new alternative routing protocols that used new algorithms. Link-state protocols—in particular, OSPF and Integrated IS-IS—solved the main issues with distance vector protocols, but they required a fair amount more planning in medium- to larger-sized networks.

Around the same time as the introduction of OSPF, Cisco created a proprietary routing protocol called Enhanced Interior Gateway Routing Protocol (EIGRP), which used some features of the earlier IGRP protocol. EIGRP solved the same problems as did link-state routing protocols, but less planning was required when implementing the network. As time went on, EIGRP was classified as a unique type of routing protocol—neither distance vector nor link state—so EIGRP is called either a balanced hybrid protocol or an advanced distance vector protocol.

The second and third major sections of this chapter examine distance vector and link-state algorithms in more detail. Chapter 10 explains balanced hybrid concepts in the context of the discussion of EIGRP.

Metrics

Routing protocols choose the best route to reach a subnet by choosing the route with the lowest metric. For example, RIP uses a counter of the number of routers (hops) between a router and the destination subnet. Table 8-2 lists the most important IP routing protocols for the CCNA exams and some details about the metric in each case.

Table 8-2 *IP IGP Metrics*

IGP	Metric	Description
RIP-1, RIP-2	Hop count	The number of routers (hops) between a router and the destination subnet.
OSPF	Cost	The sum of all interface cost settings for all links in a route, with the cost defaulting to be based on interface bandwidth.
EIGRP	Composite of bandwidth and delay	Calculated based on the route's slowest link and the cumulative delay associated with each interface in the route.

Unlike RIP-1 and RIP-2, both the OSPF and EIGRP metrics are impacted by the various interface bandwidth settings. Figure 8-3 compares the impact of the metrics used by RIP and EIGRP.

Figure 8-3 *RIP and EIGRP Metrics Compared*

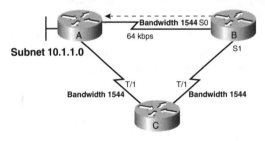

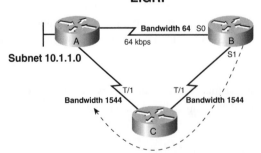

As shown at the top of the figure, Router B's RIP route to 10.1.1.0 points through Router A because that route has a lower hop count (1) than the route through Router C (2). However, in the lower half of the figure, Router B chooses the two-hop route through Router C when using EIGRP because the bandwidths of the two links in the route are much faster (better) than that of the single-hop route. Note that so that EIGRP would make the right choice, the engineer correctly configured the interface bandwidth to match the actual link speeds, thereby allowing EIGRP to choose the faster route. (The **bandwidth** interface subcommand does not change the actual physical speed of the interface. It just tells the IOS what speed to assume the interface is using.)

IGP Comparisons: Summary

For convenient comparison and study, Table 8-3 summarizes many of the features supported by various IGPs. The table includes items specifically mentioned in this chapter or in earlier chapters in this book.

Table 8-3 *Interior IP Routing Protocols Compared*

Feature	RIP-1	RIP-2	EIGRP	OSPF	IS-IS
Classless	No	Yes	Yes	Yes	Yes
Supports VLSM	No	Yes	Yes	Yes	Yes
Sends mask in update	No	Yes	Yes	Yes	Yes
Distance vector	Yes	Yes	No[1]	No	No
Link-state	No	No	No[1]	Yes	Yes
Supports autosummarization	Yes	Yes	Yes	No	No
Supports manual summarization	No	Yes	Yes	Yes	Yes
Proprietary	No	No	Yes	No	No
Routing updates are sent to a multicast IP address	No	Yes	Yes	Yes	—
Supports authentication	No	Yes	Yes	Yes	Yes
Convergence	Slow	Slow	Very fast	Fast	Fast

[1]EIGRP is often described as a balanced hybrid routing protocol, instead of link-state or distance vector. Some documents refer to EIGRP as an advanced distance vector protocol.

In addition to Table 8-3, Table 8-4 lists several other items about RIP-2, OSPF, and EIGRP. The items in Table 8-4 are explained more fully in Chapters 9 and 10, but they are included here for your reference when studying.

Table 8-4 *Comparing Features of IGPs: RIP-2, EIGRP, and OSPF*

Features	RIP-2	OSPF	EIGRP
Metric	Hop count	Link cost	Function of bandwidth, delay
Sends periodic updates	Yes (30 seconds)	No	No
Full or partial routing updates	Full	Partial	Partial
Where updates are sent	(224.0.0.9)[1]	(224.0.0.5, 224.0.0.6)	(224.0.0.10)
Metric considered to be "infinite"	16	$(2^{24} - 1)$	$(2^{32} - 1)$
Supports unequal-cost load balancing	No	No	Yes

[1]This table specifically refers to features of RIP-2, but the only difference with RIP-1 in this table is that RIP-1 broadcasts updates to IP address 255.255.255.255.

Administrative Distance

Many companies and organizations use a single routing protocol. However, in some cases, a company needs to use multiple routing protocols. For instance, if two companies connect their networks so that they can exchange information, they need to exchange some routing information. If one company uses RIP, and the other uses EIGRP, on at least one router, both RIP and EIGRP must be used. Then, that router can take routes learned by RIP and advertise them into EIGRP, and vice versa, through a process called route redistribution.

Depending on the network topology, the two routing protocols might learn routes to the same subnets. When a single routing protocol learns multiple routes to the same subnet, the metric tells it which route is best. However, when two different routing protocols learn routes to the same subnet, because each routing protocol's metric is based on different information, IOS cannot compare the metrics. For instance, RIP might learn a route to subnet 10.1.1.0 with metric 1, and EIGRP might learn a route to 10.1.1.0 with metric 2,195,416, but the EIGRP may be the better route—or it may not. There is simply no basis for comparison between the two metrics.

When IOS must choose between routes learned using different routing protocols, IOS uses a concept called *administrative distance*. Administrative distance is a number that denotes how believable an entire routing protocol is on a single router. The lower the number, the better, or more believable, the routing protocol. For instance, RIP has a default administrative distance of 120, and EIGRP defaults to 90, making EIGRP more believable than RIP. So, when both routing protocols learn routes to the same subnet, the router adds only the EIGRP route to the routing table.

The administrative distance values are configured on a single router and are not exchanged with other routers. Table 8-5 lists the various sources of routing information, along with the default administrative distances.

Table 8-5 *Default Administrative Distances*

Route Type	Administrative Distance
Connected	0
Static	1
BGP (external routes)	20
EIGRP (internal routes)	90
IGRP	100
OSPF	110
IS-IS	115
RIP	120
EIGRP (external routes)	170
BGP (internal routes)	200
Unusable	255

NOTE   The **show ip route** command lists each route's administrative distance as the first of the two numbers inside the brackets. The second number in brackets is the metric.

The table shows the default administrative distance values, but IOS can be configured to change the administrative distance of a particular routing protocol, a particular route, or even a static route. For instance, the command **ip route 10.1.3.0 255.255.255.0 10.1.130.253** defines a static route with a default administrative distance of 1, but the command **ip route 10.1.3.0 255.255.255.0 10.1.130.253 210** defines the same static route with an administrative distance of 210.

Distance Vector Routing Protocol Features

This section explains the basics of distance vector routing protocols, using RIP as an example. This section begins by examining the basic normal operations of distance vector protocols, followed by a thorough explanation of the many distance vector loop-avoidance features.

The Concept of a Distance and a Vector

The term *distance vector* describes what a router knows about each route. At the end of the process, when a router learns about a route to a subnet, all the router knows is some measurement of distance (the metric) and the next-hop router and outgoing interface to use for that route (a vector, or direction). To show you more exactly what a distance vector protocol does, Figure 8-4 shows a view of what a router learns with a distance vector routing protocol. The figure shows an internetwork in which R1 learns about three routes to reach subnet X:

■   The four-hop route through R2

■   The three-hop route through R5

■   The two-hop route through R7

Figure 8-4   *Information Learned Using Distance Vector Protocols*

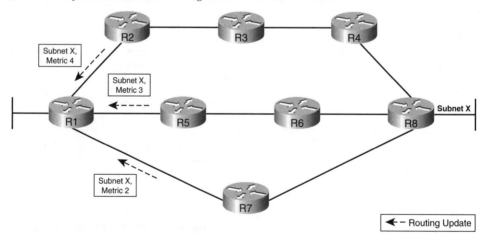

R1 learns about the subnet, and a metric associated with that subnet, and nothing more. R1 must then pick the best route to reach subnet X. In this case, it picks the two-hop route through R7, because that route has the lowest metric. To further appreciate the meaning of the term distance vector, consider Figure 8-5, which shows what R1 really knows about subnet X in Figure 8-4.

Figure 8-5 *Graphical Representation of the Distance Vector Concept*

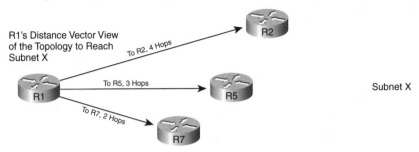

Effectively, all R1 knows about subnet X is three vectors. The length of the vectors represents the metric, which describes how good (or bad) each route is. The direction of the vector represents the next-hop router. So, with distance vector logic, routing protocols do not learn much about the network when they receive routing updates. All the routing protocols know is some concept of a vector: a vector's length is the distance (metric) to reach a subnet, and a vector's direction is through the neighbor that advertised the route.

Distance Vector Operation in a Stable Network

Distance vector routing protocols send periodic full routing updates. Figure 8-6 illustrates this concept in a simple internetwork with two routers, three LAN subnets, and one WAN subnet. The figure shows both routers' full routing tables, listing all four routes, and the periodic full updates sent by each router.

Figure 8-6 *Normal Steady-State RIP Operations*

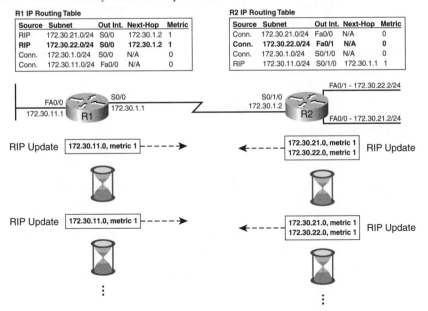

To more fully understand distance vector operations in this figure, focus on some of the more important facts about what router R1 learns for subnet 172.30.22.0/24, which is the subnet connected to R2's Fa0/1 interface:

1. R2 considers itself to have a 0 hop route for subnet 172.30.22.0/24, so in the routing update sent by R2 (shown below the R2 router icon), R2 advertises a metric 1 (hop count 1) route.

2. R1 receives the RIP update from R2, and because R1 has learned of no other possible routes to 172.30.22.0/24, this route must be R1's best route to the subnet.

3. R1 adds the subnet to its routing table, listing it as a RIP learned route.

4. For the learned route, R1 uses an outgoing interface of S0/0, because R1 received R2's routing update on R1's S0/0 interface.

5. For the learned route, R1 uses a next-hop router of 172.30.1.2, because R1 learned the route from a RIP update whose source IP address was 172.30.1.2.

At the end of this process, R1 has learned a new route. The rest of the RIP learned routes in this example follow the same process.

Besides the process of advertising and learning routes, Figure 8-6 also highlights a few other particularly important facts about distance vector protocols:

- **Periodic:** The hourglass icons represent the fact that the updates repeat on a regular cycle. RIP uses a 30-second update interval by default.

- **Full updates:** The routers send full updates every time instead of just sending new or changed routing information.

- **Full updates limited by split-horizon rules:** The routing protocol omits some routes from the periodic full updates because of split-horizon rules. Split horizon is a loop-avoidance feature that is covered in the next few pages.

Distance Vector Loop Prevention

As you can see, the actual distance vector process is pretty simple. Unfortunately, the simplicity of distance vector protocols introduced the possibility of routing loops. Routing loops occur when the routers forward packets such that the same single packet ends up back at the same routers repeatedly, wasting bandwidth and never delivering the packet. In production networks, the number of looping packets could congest the network to the point that the network becomes unusable, so routing loops must be avoided as much as possible. The rest of this chapter's coverage of distance vector protocols is devoted to describing a variety of distance vector features that help prevent loops.

Route Poisoning

When a route fails, distance vector routing protocols risk causing routing loops until every router in the internetwork believes and knows that the original route has failed. As a result, distance vector protocols need a way to specifically identify which routes have failed.

Distance vector protocols spread the bad news about a route failure by poisoning the route. *Route poisoning* refers to the practice of advertising a route, but with a special metric value called *infinity*. Simply put, routers consider routes advertised with an infinite metric to have failed. Note that each distance vector routing protocol uses the concept of an actual metric value that represents infinity. RIP defines infinity as 16.

Figure 8-7 shows an example of route poisoning with RIP, with R2's Fa0/1 interface failing, meaning that R2's route for 172.30.22.0/24 has failed.

> **NOTE** Even though routes poisoned by RIP have a metric of 16, the **show ip route** command does not list the metric's value. Instead, it lists the phrase "possibly down."

Figure 8-7 *Route Poisoning*

Key Topic

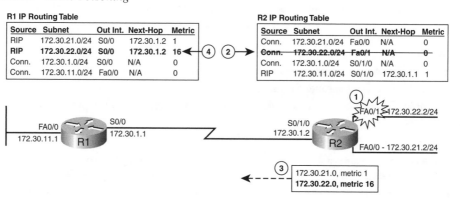

Figure 8-7 shows the following process:

1. R2's Fa0/1 interface fails.

2. R2 removes its connected route for 172.30.22.0/24 from its routing table.

3. R2 advertises 172.30.22.0 with an infinite metric, which for RIP is metric 16.

4. R1 keeps the route in its routing table, with an infinite metric, until it removes the route from the routing table.

Any metric value below infinity can be used as a valid metric for a valid route. With RIP, that means that a 15-hop route would be a valid route. Some of the largest enterprise networks in the world have at most four or five routers in the longest route between any two subnets, so a valid maximum metric of 15 hops is enough.

Problem: Counting to Infinity over a Single Link

Distance vector routing protocols risk causing routing loops during the time between when the first router realizes a route has failed until all the routers know that the route has failed. Without the loop-prevention mechanisms explained in this chapter, distance vector protocols can experience a problem called counting to infinity. Certainly, routers could never literally count to infinity, but they can count to their version of infinity—for example, to 16 with RIP.

Counting to infinity causes two related problems. Several of the distance vector loop-prevention features focus on preventing these problems:

■   Packets may loop around the internetwork while the routers count to infinity, with the bandwidth consumed by the looping packets crippling an internetwork.

■   The counting-to-infinity process may take several minutes, meaning that the looping could cause users to believe that the network has failed.

When routers count to infinity, they collectively keep changing their minds about the metric of a failed route. The metric grows slowly until it reaches infinity, at which point the routers finally believe that the route has failed. The best way to understand this concept is to see an example; Figure 8-8 shows the beginnings of the counting-to-infinity problem.

Figure 8-8   *R2 Incorrectly Believes That R1 Has a Route to 172.30.22.0/24*

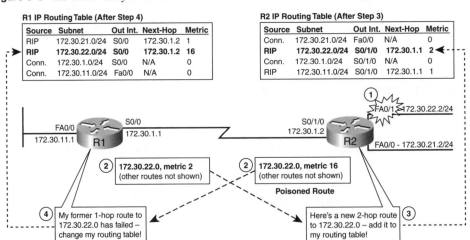

The key to this example is to know that R1's periodic update to R2 (left-to-right in Figure 8-8) occurs at almost the same instant as R2's poison route advertisement to R1. Figure 8-8 shows the following process:

1. R2's Fa0/1 interface fails, so R2 removes its connected route for 172.30.22.0/24 from its routing table.

2. R2 sends a poisoned route advertisement (metric 16 for RIP) to R1, but *at about the same time*, R1's periodic update timer expires, so R1 sends its regular update, including an advertisement about 172.30.22.0, metric 2.

3. R2 hears about the metric 2 route to reach 172.30.22.0 from R1. Because R2 no longer has a route for subnet 172.30.22.0, it adds the two-hop route to its routing table, next-hop router R1.

4. At about the same time as Step 3, R1 receives the update from R2, telling R1 that its former route to 172.30.22.0, through R2, has failed. As a result, R1 changes its routing table to list a metric of 16 for the route to 172.30.22.0.

At this point, R1 and R2 forward packets destined for 172.30.22.0/24 back and forth to each other. R2 has a route for 172.30.22.0/24, pointing to R1, and R1 has the reverse. The looping occurs until R1 and R2 both count to infinity. Figure 8-9 shows the next step in their cooperative march toward infinity.

Figure 8-9 *R1 and R2 Count to Infinity*

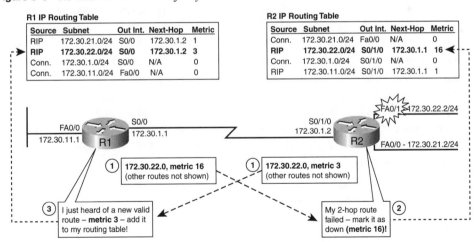

Figure 8-9 shows both routers' next periodic updates, as follows:

1. Both R1's and R2's update timers expire at about the same time. R1 advertises a poison (metric 16) route, and R2 advertises a metric 3 route. (Remember, RIP routers add 1 to the metric before advertising the route.)

2. R2 receives R1's update, so R2 changes its route for 172.30.22.0 to use a metric of 16.

3. At about the same time as Step 2, R1 receives R2's update, so R1 changes its route for 172.30.22.0 to use a metric of 3.

The process continues through each periodic update cycle, with both routers eventually reaching metric 16. At that point, the routers could time out the routes and remove them from their routing tables.

Split Horizon

In the simple internetwork used in Figures 8-8 and 8-9, router R2 has a connected route to 172.30.22.0, and R1 learns the route because of a routing update sent by R2. However, there is little need for R1 to advertise that same route back to R2, because R1 learned that route from R2 in the first place. So, one way to prevent the counting-to-infinity problem shown in these figures is to have R1 simply not advertise subnet 172.30.22.0, using a feature called split horizon. Split horizon is defined as follows:

In routing updates sent out interface X, do not include routing information about routes that refer to interface X as the outgoing interface.

Distance vector protocols work a lot like how people in a neighborhood spread rumors. People tell their neighbors, who tell other neighbors, until eventually everyone in the neighborhood learns the latest gossip. Following that analogy, if you heard a rumor from your neighbor Fred, you wouldn't turn around and tell him the same rumor. Likewise, split horizon means that when router R1 learns a route from router R2, R1 has no need to advertise that same route back to router R2.

Figure 8-10 shows the effect of split horizon on routers R1 and R2 in the same familiar internetwork. R1's routing table (at the top of the figure) lists four routes, three of which have R1's S0/0 interface as the outgoing interface. So, split horizon prevents R1 from including those three routes in the update sent by R1 out its S0/0 interface.

Figure 8-10 *Effects of Split Horizon Without Poison Reverse*

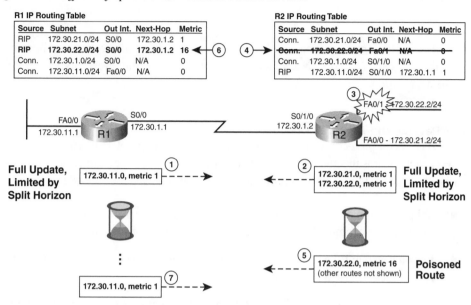

Figure 8-10 shows the following process:

1. R1 sends its normal periodic full update, which, because of split-horizon rules, includes only one route.

2. R2 sends its normal periodic full update, which, because of split-horizon rules, includes only two routes.

3. R2's Fa0/1 interface fails.

4. R2 removes its connected route for 172.30.22.0/24 from its routing table.

5. R2 advertises 172.30.22.0 with an infinite metric, which for RIP is metric 16.

6. R1 temporarily keeps the route for 172.30.22.0 in its routing table, later removing the route from the routing table.

7. In its next regular update, R1, because of split horizon, still does not advertise the route for 172.30.22.0.

Split horizon prevents the counting-to-infinity problem shown in Figures 8-8 and 8-9 because R1 does not advertise 172.30.22.0 to R2 at all. As a result, R2 never hears about an (incorrect) alternative route to 172.30.22.0. Cisco IOS defaults to use split horizon on most interfaces.

> **NOTE**   RIP implementation with Cisco IOS does not act exactly as described in Step 7 of this particular example. Instead, it uses a feature called poison reverse, as described in the next section.

Poison Reverse and Triggered Updates

Distance vector protocols can attack the counting-to-infinity problem by ensuring that every router learns that the route has failed, through every means possible, as quickly as possible. The next two loop-prevention features do just that and are defined as follows:

- **Triggered update:** When a route fails, do not wait for the next periodic update. Instead, send an immediate triggered update listing the poisoned route.

- **Poison reverse:** When learning of a failed route, suspend split-horizon rules for that route, and advertise a poisoned route.

Figure 8-11 shows an example of each of these features, with R2's interface Fa0/1 failing yet again. Note that the figure begins with all interfaces working, and all routes known.

Figure 8-11   *R2 Sending a Triggered Update, with R1 Advertising a Poison Reverse Route*

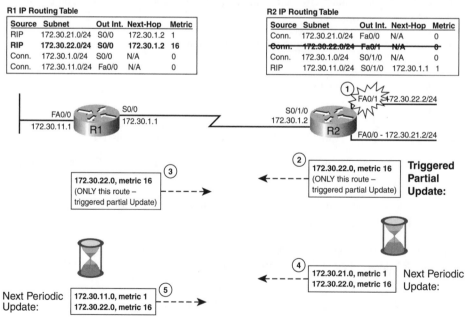

The process shown in Figure 8-11 runs as follows:

1. R2's Fa0/1 interface fails.

2. R2 immediately sends a triggered partial update with only the changed information— in this case, a poison route for 172.30.22.0.

3. R1 responds by changing its routing table and sending back an immediate (triggered) partial update, listing only 172.30.22.0 with an infinite metric (metric 16). This is a poison reverse route.

4. On R2's next regular periodic update, R2 advertises all the typical routes, including the poison route for 172.30.22.0, for a time.

5. On R1's next regular periodic update, R1 advertises all the typical routes, plus the poison reverse route for 172.30.22.0, for a time.

In this example, R2 reacts immediately by sending the triggered update. R1 also reacts immediately, suspending split-horizon rules for the failed route to send a poison reverse route. In fact, R2's poison route is not considered to be a poison reverse route, because R2 was already advertising a route for 172.30.22.0. However, R1's poison route is a poison reverse route because it was advertised back to the router from which R1 learned about the failed route. In fact, some books also refer to poison reverse as *split horizon with poison reverse*, because the router suspends the split-horizon rule for the failed route.

Problem: Counting to Infinity in a Redundant Network

Split horizon prevents the counting-to-infinity problem from occurring between two routers. However, with redundant paths in an internetwork, which is true of most internetworks today, split horizon alone does not prevent the counting-to-infinity problem. To see the problem, Figure 8-12 shows the new working network in its normal, stable, everything-working state. Figures 8-13 and 8-14 show in a moment how the counting-to-infinity problem occurs, even when split horizon is enabled.

Figure 8-12 *Periodic Updates in a Stable Triangle Internetwork*

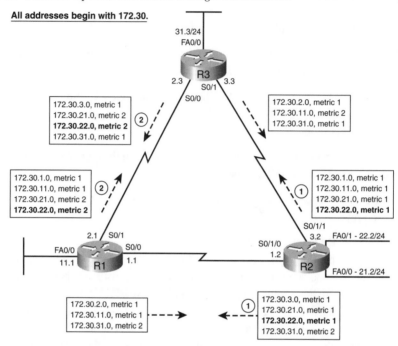

NOTE   Figure 8-12 omits the RIP updates that would be sent out the LAN interfaces to make the figure less cluttered.

Besides showing the normal operation of another network, Figure 8-12 provides a good example of how split horizon works. Again using subnet 172.30.22.0 as an example, the following process occurs in this internetwork:

1. R2 advertises a metric 1 route in its updates to both R1 and R3.

2. R1 then advertises a metric 2 route for 172.30.22.0 to R3, and R3 advertises a metric 2 route for 172.30.22.0 to R1.

3. Both R1 and R3 add the metric 1 route, learned directly from R2, to their routing tables, and ignore the two-hop routes they learn from each other. For example, R1 places route 172.30.22.0, using outgoing interface S0/0, next-hop router 172.30.1.2 (R2), in its routing table.

Split horizon prevents R1 and R3 from advertising subnet 172.30.22.0 back to R2. Note that Figure 8-12 shows all the route advertisements for 172.30.22.0 in bold text. R1 and R3 do not list 172.30.22.0 in their updates sent back to R2. In fact, all the routing updates shown in Figure 8-12 show the effects of split horizon.

Now that you have a good understanding of the internetwork shown in Figure 8-12, Figure 8-13 shows the same internetwork, but with the beginning of the counting-to-infinity problem, even though split horizon is enabled. Again, R2's fa0/1 begins the example by failing.

Figure 8-13 *Counting to Infinity in a Redundant Internetwork*

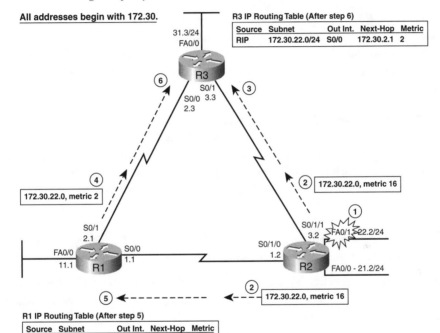

The process shown in Figure 8-13 is as follows. As usual, this example relies on some unfortunate timing of periodic routing updates around the time that the route fails.

1. R2's Fa0/1 interface fails.

2. R2 immediately sends a triggered partial update, poisoning the route for 172.30.22.0. R2 sends the updates out all still-working interfaces.

3. R3 receives R2's triggered update that poisons the route for 172.30.22.0, so R3 updates its routing table to list metric 16 for this route.

4. Before the update described in Step 2 arrives at R1, R1 sends its normal periodic update to R3, listing 172.30.22.0, metric 2, as normal. (Note that Figure 8-13 omits some of what would be in R1's periodic update to reduce clutter.)

5. R1 receives R2's triggered update (described in Step 2) that poisons the route for 172.30.22.0, so R1 updates its routing table to list metric 16 for this route.

6. R3 receives the periodic update sent by R1 (described in Step 4), listing a metric 2 route for 172.30.22.0. As a result, R3 updates its routing table to list a metric 2 route, through R1 as the next-hop router, with outgoing interface S0/0.

At this point, R3 has an incorrect metric 2 route for 172.30.22.0, pointing back to R1. Depending on the timing of when the entries enter and leave the routing table, the routers may end up forwarding the packets sent to subnet 172.30.22.0/24 through the network, possibly looping some packets around the network several times, while the counting-to-infinity process continues.

The Holddown Process and Holddown Timer

The last loop-prevention feature covered in this chapter, a process called *holddown*, prevents the looping and counting-to-infinity problem shown in Figure 8-13. Distance vector protocols use holddown to specifically prevent the loops created by the counting-to-infinity problems that occur in redundant internetworks. The term holddown gives a hint as to its meaning:

> As soon as the route is considered to be down, *hold it down for a while* to give the routers time to make sure every router knows that the route has failed.

The holddown process tells a router to ignore new information about the failed route, for a time period called the holddown time, as counted using the *holddown timer*. The holddown process can be summarized as follows:

> After hearing a poisoned route, start a holddown timer for that one route. Until the timer expires, do not believe any other routing information about the failed route, because believing that information may cause a routing loop. However, information learned from the neighbor that originally advertised the working route can be believed before the holddown timer expires.

The holddown concept may be better understood with an example. Figure 8-14 repeats the example of Figure 8-13, but with R3's holddown process preventing the counting-to-infinity problem. The figure shows how R3 ignores any new information about subnet 172.30.22.0 because of holddown. As usual, the figure begins with all interfaces up and working, and all routes known, and with Step 1 being the failure of the same interface off router R2.

Figure 8-14 *Using Holddown to Prevent Counting to Infinity*

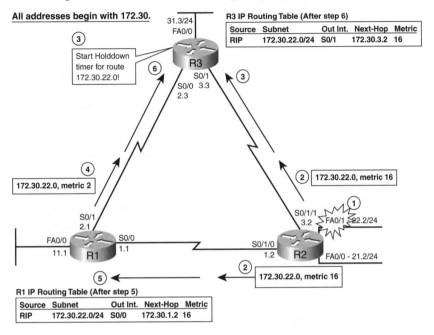

The process shown in Figure 8-14 is as follows, with Steps 3 and 6 differing from Figure 8-13's steps:

1. R2's Fa0/1 interface fails.

2. R2 immediately sends a triggered partial update, poisoning the route for 172.30.22.0. R2 sends the updates out all still-working interfaces.

3. R3 receives R2's triggered update that poisons the route for 172.30.22.0, so R3 updates its routing table to list metric 16 for this route. R3 also puts the route for 172.30.22.0 in holddown and starts the holddown timer for the route (the default is 180 seconds with RIP).

4. Before the update described in Step 2 arrives at R1, R1 sends its normal periodic update to R3, listing 172.30.22.0, metric 2, as normal. (Note that Figure 8-14 omits some details in R1's periodic update to reduce clutter.)

5. R1 receives R2's triggered update (described in Step 2) that poisons the route for 172.30.22.0, so R1 updates its routing table to list metric 16 for this route.

6. R3 receives the update from R1 (described in Step 4), listing a metric 2 route for 172.30.22.0. Because R3 has placed this route in a holddown state, and this new metric 2 route was learned from a different router (R1) than the original route (R2), R3 ignores the new routing information.

As a result of R3's holddown logic described in Step 6, all three routers have a metric 16 route for 172.30.22.0. At this point, any future routing updates will list only metric 16 routes for this subnet—at least until a real route to the subnet becomes available again.

The definition of holddown allows the routers to believe the same router that originally advertised the route, even before the holddown timer expires. For example, the entire process of Figure 8-14 may occur within just a few seconds because of all the triggered updates. If R2's Fa0/1 interface comes up again, R2 then advertises a metric 1 route for 172.30.22.0 again. If R1 and R3 would believe R2's advertisement, they could avoid waiting almost 3 more minutes for their holddown timers to expire for subnet 172.30.22.0. As it turns out, believing the routing update from the same router that originally advertised the route does not risk causing a loop. Therefore, holddown allows the routers (in this case R1 and R3) to believe R2's advertisement.

Distance Vector Summary

Before closing the coverage of distance vector loop avoidance, it is useful to review the concepts covered here. This section covered a lot of theory, some of which can be a little tricky, but the main features can be summarized easily:

- During periods of stability, routers send periodic full routing updates based on a short update timer (the RIP default is 30 seconds). The updates list all known routes except the routes omitted because of split-horizon rules.

- When changes occur that cause a route to fail, the router that notices the failure reacts by immediately sending triggered partial updates, listing only the newly poisoned (failed) routes, with an infinite metric.

- Other routers that hear the poisoned route also send triggered partial updates, poisoning the failed route.

- Routers suspend split-horizon rules for the failed route by sending a poison reverse route back toward the router from which the poisoned route was learned.

- All routers place the route in holddown state and start a holddown timer for that route after learning that the route has failed. Each router ignores all new information about this route until the holddown timer expires, unless that information comes from the same router that originally advertised the good route to that subnet.

Link-State Routing Protocol Features

Like distance vector protocols, link-state protocols send routing updates to neighboring routers, which in turn send updates to their neighboring routers, and so on. At the end of the process, like distance vector protocols, routers that use link-state protocols add the best routes to their routing tables, based on metrics. However, beyond this level of explanation, these two types of routing protocol algorithms have little in common.

This section covers the most basic mechanics of how link-state protocols work, with the examples using Open Shortest Path First (OSPF), the first link-state IP routing protocol, in the examples. The section begins by showing how link-state routing protocols flood routing information throughout the internetwork. Then it describes how link-state protocols process the routing information to choose the best routes.

Building the Same LSDB on Every Router

Routers using link-state routing protocols need to collectively advertise practically every detail about the internetwork to all the other routers. At the end of the process, called flooding, every router in the internetwork has the exact same information about the internetwork. Routers use this information, stored in RAM inside a data structure called the link-state database (LSDB), to perform the other major link-state process to calculate the currently best routes to each subnet. Flooding a lot of detailed information to every router sounds like a lot of work, and relative to distance vector routing protocols, it is.

Open Shortest Path First (OSPF), the most popular link-state IP routing protocol, advertises information in routing update messages of various types, with the updates containing information called link-state advertisements (LSA). LSAs come in many forms, including the following two main types:

- **Router LSA:** Includes a number to identify the router (router ID), the router's interface IP addresses and masks, the state (up or down) of each interface, and the cost (metric) associated with the interface.

- **Link LSA:** Identifies each link (subnet) and the routers that are attached to that link. It also identifies the link's state (up or down).

Some routers must first create the router and link LSAs, and then flood the LSAs to all other routers. Each router creates a router LSA for itself and then floods that LSA to other routers in routing update messages. To flood an LSA, a router sends the LSA to its neighbors. Those neighbors in turn forward the LSA to their neighbors, and so on, until all the routers have learned about the LSA. For the link LSAs, one router attached to a subnet also creates and floods a link LSA for each subnet. (Note that in some cases, a link LSA is not required, typically when only one router connects to the subnet.) At the end of the process, every router has every other router's router LSA and a copy of all the link LSAs as well.

Figure 8-15 shows the general idea of the flooding process, with R8 creating and flooding its router LSA. Note that Figure 8-15 actually shows only a subset of the information in R8's router LSA.

Figure 8-15   *Flooding LSAs Using a Link-State Routing Protocol*

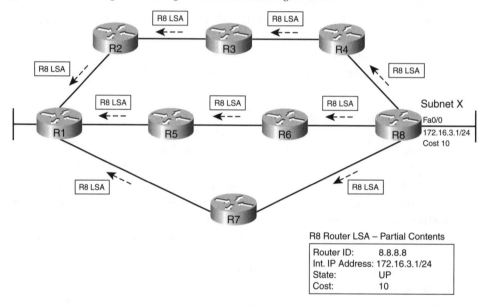

Figure 8-15 shows the rather basic flooding process, with R8 sending the original LSA for itself, and the other routers flooding the LSA by forwarding it until every router has a copy. To prevent looping LSA advertisements, a router that knows about the LSA first asks its neighbor if that neighbor already knows about this LSA. For example, R8 would begin by separately asking R4, R6, and R7 if they know about the router LSA for R8. Those three routers would reply, stating that they do not know about the R8 router LSA. Only at that point does R8 send the LSA to each of those neighboring routers. The process repeats with every neighbor. If a router has already learned the LSA—no matter over what path—it could politely say that it already has the LSA, thereby preventing the LSA from being advertised in loops around the network.

The origins of the term *link state* can be explained by considering the (partial) contents of the router LSA shown in Figure 8-15. The figure shows one of the four interface IP addresses that would be listed in R8's router LSA, along with the interface's state. Link-state protocols get their name from the fact that the LSAs advertise each interface (link) and whether the interface is up or down (state). So, the LSDB contains information about not only the up and working routers and interfaces and links (subnets), but all routers and interfaces and links (subnets), even if the interfaces are down.

After the LSA has been flooded, even if the LSAs do not change, link-state protocols do require periodic reflooding of the LSAs, similar to the periodic updates sent by distance vector protocols. However, distance vector protocols typically use a short timer; for example, RIP sends periodic updates every 30 seconds and RIP sends a full update listing all normally advertised routes. OSPF refloods each LSA based on each LSA's separate aging timer (default 30 minutes). As a result, in a stable internetwork, link-state protocols actually use less network bandwidth to send routing information than do distance vector protocols. If an LSA changes, the router immediately floods the changed LSA. For example, if Figure 8-15's Router R8's LAN interface failed, R8 would need to reflood the R8 LSA, stating that the interface is now down.

Applying Dijkstra SPF Math to Find the Best Routes

The link-state flooding process results in every router having an identical copy of the LSDB in memory, but the flooding process alone does not cause a router to learn what routes to add to the IP routing table. Although incredibly detailed and useful, the information in the LSDB does not explicitly state each router's best route to reach a destination. Link-state protocols must use another major part of the link-state algorithm to find and add routes to the IP routing table—routes that list a subnet number and mask, an outgoing interface, and a next-hop router IP address. This process uses something called the Dijkstra Shortest Path First (SPF) algorithm.

The SPF algorithm can be compared to how humans think when taking a trip using a road map. Anyone can buy the same road map, so anyone can know all the information about the roads. However, when you look at the map, you first find your starting and ending locations, and then you analyze the map to find the possible routes. If several routes look similar in length, you may decide to take a longer route if the roads are highways rather than country roads. Someone else may own the same map, but they might be starting from a different location, and going to a different location, so they may choose a totally different route.

In the analogy, the LSDB works like the map, and the SPF algorithm works like the person reading the map. The LSDB holds all the information about all the possible routers and links. The SPF algorithm defines how a router should process the LSDB, with each router considering itself to be the starting point for the route. Each router uses itself as the starting point because each router needs to put routes in its own routing table. The SPF algorithm calculates all the possible routes to reach a subnet, and the cumulative metric for each entire route, for each possible destination subnet. In short, each router must view itself as the starting point, and each subnet as the destination, and use the SPF algorithm to look at the LSDB road map to find and pick the best route to each subnet.

Figure 8-16 shows a graphical view of the results of the SPF algorithm run by router R1 when trying to find the best route to reach subnet 172.16.3.0/24 (based on Figure 8-15). Figure 8-16 shows R1 at the top of the figure rather than on the left because SPF creates a mathematical tree. These trees are typically drawn with the base or root of the tree at the top of the figure, and the leaves (subnets) at the bottom.

Figure 8-16 *SPF Tree to Find R1's Route to 172.16.3.0/24*

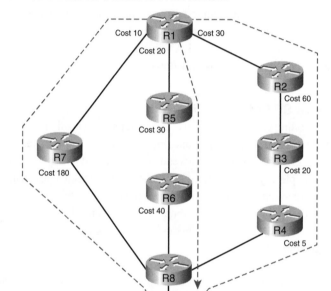

Figure 8-16 does not show the SPF algorithm's math (frankly, almost no one bothers looking at the math), but it does show a drawing of the kind of analysis done by the SPF algorithm on R1. Generally, each router runs the SPF process to find all routes to each subnet, and then the SPF algorithm can pick the best route. To pick the best route, a router's SPF algorithm adds the cost associated with each link between itself and the destination subnet, over each possible route. Figure 8-16 shows the costs associated with each route beside the links, with the dashed lines showing the three routes R1 finds between itself and subnet X (172.16.3.0/24).

Table 8-6 lists the three routes shown in Figure 8-16, with their cumulative costs, showing that R1's best route to 172.16.3.0/24 starts by going through R5.

Table 8-6   *Comparing R1's Three Alternatives for the Route to 172.16.3.0/24*

Route	Location in Figure 8-16	Cumulative Cost
R1–R7–R8	Left	10 + 180 + 10 = 200
R1–R5–R6–R8	Middle	20 + 30 + 40 + 10 = 100
R1–R2–R3–R4–R8	Right	30 + 60 + 20 + 5 + 10 = 125

As a result of the SPF algorithm's analysis of the LSDB, R1 adds a route to subnet 172.16.3.0/24 to its routing table, with the next-hop router of R5.

Convergence with Link-State Protocols

As soon as the internetwork is stable, link-state protocols reflood each LSA on a regular basis. (OSPF defaults to 30 minutes.) However, when an LSA changes, link-state protocols react swiftly, converging the network and using the currently best routes as quickly as possible. For example, imagine that the link between R5 and R6 fails in the internetwork of Figures 8-15 and 8-16. The following list explains the process R1 uses to switch to a different route. (Similar steps would occur for changes to other routers and routes.)

1. R5 and R6 flood LSAs that state that their interfaces are now in a "down" state. (In a network of this size, the flooding typically takes maybe a second or two.)

2. All routers run the SPF algorithm again to see if any routes have changed. (This process may take another second in a network this size.)

3. All routers replace routes, as needed, based on the results of SPF. (This takes practically no additional time after SPF has completed.) For example, R1 changes its route for subnet X (172.16.3.0/24) to use R2 as the next-hop router.

These steps allow the link-state routing protocol to converge quickly—much more quickly than distance vector routing protocols.

Summary and Comparisons to Distance Vector Protocols

Link-state routing protocols provide fast convergence, which is probably the most important feature of a routing protocol, with built-in loop avoidance. Link-state routing protocols do not need to use the large variety of loop-avoidance features used by distance vector protocols, which in itself greatly reduces the convergence time. The main features of a link-state routing protocol are as follows:

- All routers learn the same detailed information about all routers and subnets in the internetwork.

- The individual pieces of topology information are called LSAs. All LSAs are stored in RAM in a data structure called the link-state database (LSDB).

- Routers flood LSAs when 1) they are created, 2) on a regular (but long) time interval if the LSAs do not change over time, and 3) immediately when an LSA changes.

- The LSDB does not contain routes, but it does contain information that can be processed by the Dijkstra SPF algorithm to find a router's best route to reach each subnet.

- Each router runs the SPF algorithm, with the LSDB as input, resulting in the best (lowest-cost/lowest-metric) routes being added to the IP routing table.

- Link-state protocols converge quickly by immediately reflooding changed LSAs and rerunning the SPF algorithm on each router.

One of the most important comparison points between different routing protocols is how fast the routing protocol converges. Certainly, link-state protocols converge much more quickly than distance vector protocols. The following list summarizes some of the key comparison points for different routing protocols, comparing the strengths of the underlying algorithms:

- **Convergence:** Link-state protocols converge much more quickly.

- **CPU and RAM:** Link-state protocols consume much more CPU and memory than distance vector protocols, although with proper design, this disadvantage can be reduced.

- **Avoiding routing loops:** Link-state protocols inherently avoid loops, whereas distance vector protocols require many additional features (for example, split horizon).

- **Design effort:** Distance vector protocols do not require much planning, whereas link-state protocols require much more planning and design effort, particularly in larger networks.

- **Configuration:** Distance vector protocols typically require less configuration, particularly when the link-state protocol requires the use of more-advanced features.

Exam Preparation Tasks

Review All the Key Topics

Review the most important topics from this chapter, noted with the key topics icon. Table 8-7 lists these key topics and where each is discussed.

Table 8-7 *Key Topics for Chapter 8*

Key Topic Element	Description	Page Number
List	Definitions and comparison of the terms routing protocol, routed protocol, and routable protocol	309
List	List of the main functions of a routing protocol	310
List	Definitions of IGP and EGP	311
List	Three types of IGP routing protocol algorithms	313
Table 8-3	Comparison points for IGP protocols	315
Table 8-4	More comparisons between RIP-2, OSPF, and EIGRP	316
Table 8-5	List of routing information sources and their respective administrative distance	317
Figure 8-5	Graphical view of the meaning of distance vector	319
List	Description of distance vector periodic updates, full updates, and full updates limited by split horizon	320
Figure 8-7	Example of route poisoning	321
Definition	Split horizon	324
Definitions	Triggered updates, poison reverse	326
Definition	Holddown	330
Figure 8-16	Graphical representation of a link-state SPF calculation	336
List	Summary of link-state operations	338

Complete the Tables and Lists from Memory

Print a copy of Appendix J, "Memory Tables" (found on the CD), or at least the section for this chapter, and complete the tables and lists from memory. Appendix K, "Memory Tables Answer Key," also on the CD, includes completed tables and lists for you to check your work.

Definitions of Key Terms

Define the following key terms from this chapter, and check your answers in the glossary:

> Balanced hybrid, convergence, counting to infinity, Dijkstra Shortest Path First (SPF) algorithm, distance vector, exterior gateway protocol (EGP), full update, holddown (holddown timer), infinity, interior gateway protocol (IGP), link state, link-state advertisement (LSA), link-state database (LSDB), metric, partial update, periodic update, poison reverse, poisoned route, routable protocol, routed protocol, routing protocol, split horizon, triggered update

Command Reference to Check Your Memory

This chapter does not refer to any commands that are not otherwise covered more fully in another chapter. Therefore, this chapter, unlike most others in this book, does not have any command reference tables.

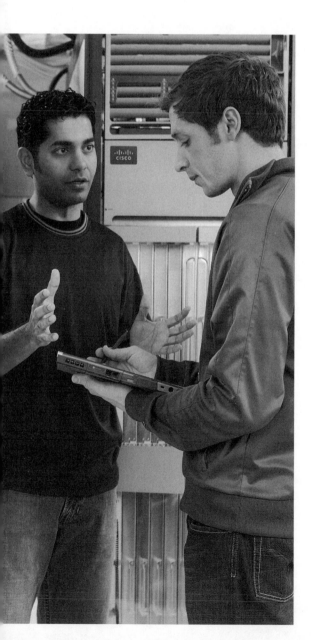

This chapter covers the following subjects:

OSPF Protocols and Operation: This section completes the discussion of link-state protocols begun in Chapter 8, "Routing Protocol Theory," by describing the specifics of OSPF operation.

OSPF Configuration: This section examines how to configure OSPF in a single area and in multiple areas, OSPF authentication, and a few other small features.

CHAPTER **9**

OSPF

Link-state routing protocols were originally developed mainly in the early to mid-1990s. The protocol designers assumed that link speeds, router CPUs, and router memory would continue to improve over time, so the protocols were designed to provide much more powerful features by taking advantage of these improvements. By sending more information, and requiring the routers to perform more processing, link-state protocols gain some important advantages over distance vector protocols—in particular, much faster convergence. The goal remains the same—adding the currently best routes to the routing table—but these protocols use different methods to find and add those routes.

This chapter explains the most commonly used IP link-state routing protocol—Open Shortest Path First (OSPF). The other link-state protocol for IP, Integrated IS-IS, is mainly ignored on the CCNA exams.

"Do I Know This Already?" Quiz

The "Do I Know This Already?" quiz allows you to assess whether you should read the entire chapter. If you miss no more than one of these ten self-assessment questions, you might want to move ahead to the "Exam Preparation Tasks" section. Table 9-1 lists the major headings in this chapter and the "Do I Know This Already?" quiz questions covering the material in those sections. This helps you assess your knowledge of these specific areas. The answers to the "Do I Know This Already?" quiz appear in Appendix A.

Table 9-1 *"Do I Know This Already?" Foundation Topics Section-to-Question Mapping*

Foundation Topics Section	Questions
OSPF Protocols and Operation	1–5
OSPF Configuration	6–10

1. Which of the following affects the calculation of OSPF routes when all possible default values are used?

   a. Bandwidth

   b. Delay

    c.   Load

    d.   Reliability

    e.   MTU

    f.   Hop count

2. OSPF runs an algorithm to calculate the currently best route. Which of the following terms refer to that algorithm?

    a.   SPF

    b.   DUAL

    c.   Feasible successor

    d.   Dijkstra

    e.   Good old common sense

3. Two OSPF routers connect to the same VLAN using their Fa0/0 interfaces. Which of the following settings on the interfaces of these two potentially neighboring routers would prevent the two routers from becoming OSPF neighbors?

    a.   IP addresses of 10.1.1.1/24 and 10.1.1.254/25, respectively

    b.   The addition of a secondary IP address on one router's interface, but not the other

    c.   Both router interfaces assigned to area 3

    d.   One router is configured to use MD5 authentication, and the other is not configured to use authentication

4. Which of the following OSPF neighbor states is expected when the exchange of topology information is complete so that neighboring routers have the same LSDB?

    a.   Two-way

    b.   Full

    c.   Exchange

    d.   Loading

5. Which of the following is true about an existing OSPF designated router?

    a.   A newly connected router in the same subnet, with a higher OSPF priority, preempts the existing DR to become the new DR.

    b.   A newly connected router in the same subnet, with a lower OSPF priority, preempts the existing DR to become the new DR.

    c.   The DR may be elected based on the lowest OSPF Router ID.

    d.   The DR may be elected based on the highest OSPF Router ID.

    e.   The DR attempts to become fully adjacent with every other neighbor on the subnet.

6. Which of the following **network** commands, following the command **router ospf 1**, tells this router to start using OSPF on interfaces whose IP addresses are 10.1.1.1, 10.1.100.1, and 10.1.120.1?

    a.   **network 10.0.0.0 255.0.0.0 area 0**

    b.   **network 10.0.0.0 0.255.255.255 area 0**

    c.   **network 10.0.0.1 255.0.0.255 area 0**

    d.   **network 10.0.0.1 0.255.255.0 area 0**

7. Which of the following **network** commands, following the command **router ospf 1**, tells this router to start using OSPF on interfaces whose IP addresses are 10.1.1.1, 10.1.100.1, and 10.1.120.1?

    a.   **network 0.0.0.0 255.255.255.255 area 0**

    b.   **network 10.0.0.0 0.255.255.0 area 0**

    c.   **network 10.1.1.0 0.x.1x.0 area 0**

    d.   **network 10.1.1.0 255.0.0.0 area 0**

    e.   **network 10.0.0.0 255.0.0.0 area 0**

8. Which of the following commands list the OSPF neighbors off interface serial 0/0?

    a.   **show ip ospf neighbor**

    b.   **show ip ospf interface**

    c.   **show ip neighbor**

    d.   **show ip interface**

    e.   **show ip ospf neighbor serial 0/0**

9. OSPF routers R1, R2, and R3 attach to the same VLAN. R2 has been configured with the **ip ospf authentication message-digest** interface subcommand on the LAN interface connected to the common VLAN. The **show ip ospf neighbor** command lists R1 and R3 as neighbors, in an Init and Full state, respectively. Which of the following are true?

    a.   R3 must have an **ip ospf message-digest** interface subcommand configured.

    b.   R3 must have an **ip ospf message-digest-key** interface subcommand configured.

    c.   R1's failure must be because of having configured an incorrect OSPF authentication type.

    d.   R1's failure may or may not be related to authentication.

10. An OSPF router learns about six possible routes to reach subnet 10.1.1.0/24. All six routes have a cost of 55, and all six are interarea routes. By default, how many of these routes are placed in the routing table?

    a.   1

    b.   2

    c.   3

    d.   4

    e.   5

    f.   6

Foundation Topics

This chapter examines Open Shortest Path First (OSPF) concepts and configuration, picking up where the link-state coverage in Chapter 8 ended. In particular, the first half of this chapter explains a variety of the basics related to how OSPF works. The second half examines how to configure OSPF on Cisco routers.

OSPF Protocols and Operation

The OSPF protocol has a wide variety of sometimes-complex features. To aid the learning process, OSPF features can be broken into three major categories: neighbors, database exchange, and route calculation. OSPF routers first form a neighbor relationship that provides a foundation for all continuing OSPF communications. After routers become neighbors, they exchange the contents of their respective LSDBs, through a process called database exchange. Finally, as soon as a router has topology information in its link-state database (LSDB), it uses the Dijkstra Shortest Path First (SPF) algorithm to calculate the now-best routes and add those to the IP routing table.

Interestingly, the IOS **show** commands also support this same structure. IOS has an OSPF neighbor table (**show ip ospf neighbor**), an OSPF LSDB (**show ip ospf database**), and of course an IP routing table (**show ip route**). The processes explained in the first half of this chapter can then be seen in action on routers by displaying the contents of these three tables.

OSPF Neighbors

Although some variations exist, a general definition of an OSPF neighbor is, from one router's perspective, another router that connects to the same data link with which the first router can and should exchange routing information using OSPF. Although this definition is correct, you can better understand the true meaning of the OSPF neighbor concept by thinking about the purpose of OSPF neighbor relationships. First, neighbors check and verify basic OSPF settings before exchanging routing information—settings that must match for OSPF to work correctly. Second, the ongoing process of one router knowing when the neighbor is healthy, and when the connection to a neighbor has been lost, tells the router when it must recalculate the entries in the routing table to reconverge to a new set of routes. Additionally, the OSPF Hello process defines how neighbors can be dynamically discovered, which means that new routers can be added to a network without requiring every router to be reconfigured.

The OSPF Hello process by which new neighbor relationships are formed works somewhat like when you move to a new house and meet your various neighbors. When you see each other outside, you might walk over, say hello, and learn each others' names. After talking a bit, you form a first impression, particularly as to whether you think you'll enjoy chatting with this neighbor occasionally, or whether you may just wave and not take the time to talk the next time you see him outside. Similarly, with OSPF, the process starts with messages called OSPF Hello messages. The Hellos in turn list each router's Router ID (RID), which serves as each router's unique name or identifier for OSPF. Finally, OSPF does several checks of the information in the Hello messages to ensure that the two routers should become neighbors.

Identifying OSPF Routers with a Router ID

OSPF needs to uniquely identify each router for many reasons. First, neighbors need a way to know which router sent a particular OSPF message. Additionally, the OSPF LSDB lists a set of Link State Advertisements (LSA), some of which describe each router in the internetwork, so the LSDB needs a unique identifier for each router. To that end, OSPF uses a concept called the *OSPF router ID* (RID).

OSPF RIDs are 32-bit numbers written in dotted decimal, so using an IP address is a convenient way to find a default RID. Alternatively, the OSPF RID can be directly configured, as covered in the later section "Configuring the OSPF Router ID."

Meeting Neighbors by Saying Hello

As soon as a router has chosen its OSPF RID, and some interfaces come up, the router is ready to meet its OSPF neighbors. OSPF routers can become neighbors if they are connected to the same subnet (and in some other special cases not covered on the CCNA exams). To discover other OSPF-speaking routers, a router sends multicast OSPF Hello packets to each interface and hopes to receive OSPF Hello packets from other routers connected to those interfaces. Figure 9-1 outlines the basic concept.

Figure 9-1 *Link-State Hello Packets*

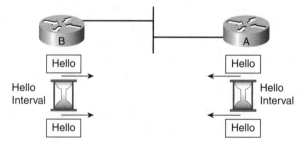

Routers A and B both send Hello messages onto the LAN. They continue to send Hellos based on their Hello Timer settings. Soon afterward, the two routers can begin exchanging topology information with each other. Then they run the Dijkstra algorithm to fill the routing table with the best routes. The Hello messages themselves have the following features:

- The Hello message follows the IP packet header, with IP packet protocol type 89.

- Hello packets are sent to multicast IP address 224.0.0.5, a multicast IP address intended for all OSPF-speaking routers.

- OSPF routers listen for packets sent to IP multicast address 224.0.0.5, in part hoping to receive Hello packets and learn about new neighbors.

Routers learn several important pieces of information from looking at the received Hello packets. The Hello message includes the sending router's RID, Area ID, Hello interval, dead interval, router priority, the RID of the designated router, the RID of the backup designated router, and a list of neighbors that the sending router already knows about on the subnet. (There's more to come on most of these items.)

The list of neighbors is particularly important to the Hello process. For example, when Router A receives a Hello from Router B, Router A needs to somehow tell Router B that Router A got the Hello. To do so, Router A adds Router B's RID to the list of OSPF neighbors inside the next (and future) Hello that Router A multicasts onto the network. Likewise, when Router B receives Router A's Hello, Router B's next (and ongoing) Hellos include Router A's RID in the list of neighbors.

As soon as a router sees its own RID in a received Hello, the router believes that *two-way* communication has been established with that neighbor. The two-way state for a neighbor is important, because at that point, more detailed information, such as LSAs, can be exchanged. Also, in some cases on LANs, neighbors might reach the two-way state and stop there. You'll read more about that in the section "Choosing a Designated Router."

Potential Problems in Becoming a Neighbor

Interestingly, receiving a Hello from a router on the same subnet does not always result in two routers becoming neighbors. It's like meeting a new neighbor in real life. If you disagree about a lot of things, and you don't get along, you might not talk all that much. Similarly, with OSPF, routers on the same subnet must agree about several of the parameters exchanged in the Hello; otherwise, the routers simply do not become neighbors. Specifically, the following must match before a pair of routers become neighbors:

- Subnet mask used on the subnet

- Subnet number (as derived using the subnet mask and each router's interface IP address)

- Hello interval

Key
Topic

- Dead interval

- OSPF area ID

- Must pass authentication checks (if used)

- Value of the stub area flag

If any one of these parameters differs, the routers do not become neighbors. In short, if you're troubleshooting OSPF when routers should be neighbors, and they are not, check this list!

> **NOTE**   The stub area flag relates to concepts outside the scope of the CCNA exams, but it is listed as a requirement for two routers to become neighbors just so the list will be complete.

A couple of the items in the list need further explanation. First, a potential neighbor confirms that it is in the same subnet by comparing the neighboring router's IP address and subnet mask, as listed in the Hello message, with its own address and mask. If they are in the exact same subnet, with the same range of addresses, this check passes.

Next, two timer settings, the Hello Interval and Dead Interval, must match. OSPF routers send Hello messages every Hello Interval. When a router no longer hears a Hello from a neighbor for the time defined by the Dead Interval, the router believes the neighbor is no longer reachable, and the router reacts and reconverges the network. For instance, on Ethernet interfaces, Cisco routers default to a Hello interval of 10 seconds and a dead interval of 4 times the Hello interval, or 40 seconds. If a router does not hear any Hello messages from that neighbor for 40 seconds, it marks the now-silent router as "down" in its neighbor table. At that point, the routers can react and converge to use the now-currently best routes.

Neighbor States

OSPF defines a large set of potential actions that two neighbors use to communicate with each other. To keep track of the process, OSPF routers set each neighbor to one of many OSPF neighbor states. An OSPF neighbor state is the router's perception of how much work has been completed in the normal processes done by two neighboring routers. For example, if Routers R1 and R2 connect to the same LAN and become neighbors, R1 lists a neighbor state for R2, which is R1's perception of what has happened between the two routers so far. Likewise, R2 lists a neighbor state for R1, representing R2's view of what has happened between R2 and R1 so far. (The most common command to list the neighbors and states is **show ip ospf neighbor**.)

Because the neighbor states reflect various points in the normal OSPF processes used between two routers, it is useful to discuss neighbor states along with these processes and OSPF messages. Also, by understanding the OSPF neighbor states and their meanings, an engineer can more easily determine if an OSPF neighbor is working normally, or if a problem exists.

Figure 9-2 shows several of the neighbor states used by the early formation of a neighbor relationship. The figure shows the Hello messages and the resulting neighbor states.

Figure 9-2 *Early Neighbor States*

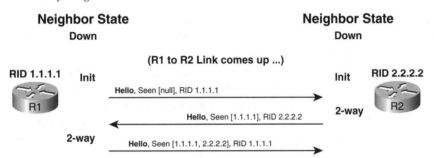

The first two states, the Down state and the Init state, are relatively simple. In cases when a router previously knew about a neighbor, but the interface failed, the neighbor is listed as a Down state. As soon as the interface comes up, the two routers can send Hellos, transitioning that neighbor to an Init state. Init means that the neighbor relationship is being initialized.

A router changes from Init to a two-way state when two major facts are true: a received Hello lists that router's RID as having been seen, and that router has checked all parameters for the neighbor and they look good. These two facts mean that the router is willing to communicate with this neighbor. To make the process work, when each router receives a Hello from a new neighbor, the router checks the neighbor's configuration details, as described earlier. If all looks good, the router's next Hello lists the neighbor's RID in the list of "seen" routers. After both routers have checked the parameters and sent a Hello listing the other router's RID as "seen," both routers should have reached the two-way state.

For example, in Figure 9-2, R2 receives the first Hello, which lists "Seen [null]." This notation means that R1 has not yet seen any approved potential neighbors. When R2 sends its Hello, R2 lists R1's RID, implying that R2 has seen R1's Hello and has verified that all parameters look good. R1 returns the favor in the third Hello, sent one Hello-interval later than R1's first Hello.

After they are in a two-way state, the two routers are ready to exchange topology information, as covered in the next section.

OSPF Topology Database Exchange

OSPF routers exchange the contents of their LSDBs so that both neighbors have an exact copy of the same LSDB at the end of the database exchange process—a fundamental principle of how link-state routing protocols work. The process has many steps, with much more detail than is described here. This section begins by explaining an overview of the entire process, followed by a deeper look at each of the steps.

Overview of the OSPF Database Exchange Process

Interestingly, after two OSPF routers become neighbors and reach a two-way state, the next step may not be to exchange topology information. First, based on several factors, the routers must first decide if they should directly exchange topology information, or if the two neighbors should learn each other's topology information, in the form of LSAs, indirectly. As soon as a pair of OSPF neighbors knows that they should share topology information directly, they exchange the topology data (LSAs). After this is completed, the process moves to a relatively quiet maintenance state in which the routers occasionally reflood the LSAs and watch for changes to the network.

The overall process flows as follows, with each step explained in the following pages:

Step 1   Based on the OSPF interface type, the routers may or may not collectively elect a Designated Router (DR) and Backup Designated Router (BDR).

Step 2   For each pair of routers that need to become fully adjacent, mutually exchange the contents of their respective LSDBs.

Step 3   When completed, the neighbors monitor for changes and periodically reflood LSAs while in the Full (fully adjacent) neighbor state.

Choosing a Designated Router

OSPF dictates that a subnet either should or should not use a Designated Router (DR) and Backup Designated Router (BDR) based on the OSPF interface type (also sometimes called the OSPF network type). Several OSPF interface types exist, but for the CCNA exams you should be aware of two main types: point-to-point and broadcast. (These types can be configured with the **ip ospf network** *type* command.) These OSPF interface types make a general reference to the type of data-link protocol used. As you might guess from the names, the point-to-point type is intended for use on point-to-point links, and the broadcast type is for use on data links that support broadcast frames, such as LANs.

Figure 9-3 shows a classic example of two sets of neighbors—one using the default OSPF interface type of point-to-point on a serial link, and the other using the default OSPF interface type of broadcast on a LAN. The end result of the DR election is that topology information is exchanged only between neighbors shown with arrowed lines in the figure. Focus on the lower-right part of the figure.

Figure 9-3 *No DR on a Point-to-Point Link, with a DR on the LAN*

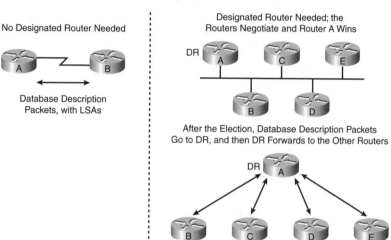

When a DR is not required, neighboring routers can go ahead and start the topology exchange process, as shown on the left side of the figure. In OSPF terminology, the two routers on the left should continue working to exchange topology information and become fully adjacent. On the right side of the figure, the top part shows a LAN topology where a DR election has been held, with Router A winning the election. With a DR, the topology exchange process happens between the DR and every other router, but not between every pair of routers. As a result, all routing updates flow to and from Router A, with Router A essentially distributing the topology information to the other routers. All routers learn all topology information from all other routers, but the process only causes a direct exchange of routing information between the DR and each of the non-DR routers.

The DR concept prevents overloading a subnet with too much OSPF traffic when many routers are on a subnet. Of course, lots of routers could be attached to one LAN, which is why a DR is required for routers attached to a LAN. For instance, if ten routers were attached to the same LAN subnet, and they were allowed to forward OSPF updates to each of the other nine routers, topology updates would flow between 45 different pairs of neighbors—with almost all the information being redundant. With the DR concept, as shown on the right side of Figure 9-3, that same LAN would require routing updates only between the DR and the nine other routers, significantly reducing the flooding of OSPF information across the LAN.

Because the DR is so important to the exchange of routing information, the loss of the elected DR could cause delays in convergence. OSPF includes the concept of a *Backup DR* (BDR) on each subnet, so when the DR fails or loses connectivity to the subnet, the BDR can take over as the DR. (All routers except the DR and BDR are typically called "DROther" in IOS **show** command output.)

> **NOTE**   All non-DR and non-BDR routers attempt to become fully adjacent with both the DR and BDR, but Figure 9-3 shows only the relationships with the DR to reduce clutter.

When a DR is required, the neighboring routers hold an election. To elect a DR, the neighboring routers look at two fields inside the Hello packets they receive and choose the DR based on the following criteria:

- The router sending the Hello with the *highest OSPF priority* setting becomes the DR.

- If two or more routers tie with the highest priority setting, the router sending the Hello with the *highest RID* wins.

- It's not always the case, but typically the router with the second-highest priority becomes the BDR.

- A priority setting of 0 means that the router does not participate in the election and can never become the DR or BDR.

- The range of priority values that allow a router to be a candidate are 1 through 255.

- If a new, better candidate comes along after the DR and BDR have been elected, the new candidate does not preempt the existing DR and BDR.

Database Exchange

The database exchange process can be quite involved with several OSPF messages. The details of the process can be ignored for the purposes of this book, but a brief overview can help give some perspective on the overall process.

After two routers decide to exchange databases, they do not simply send the contents of the entire database. First, they tell each other a list of LSAs in their respective databases—not all the details of the LSAs, just a list. Each router then compares the other router's list to its own LSDB. For any LSAs that a router does not have a copy of, the router asks the neighbor for a copy of the LSA, and the neighbor sends the full LSA.

When two neighbors complete this process, they are considered to have *fully completed* the database exchange process. So OSPF uses the *Full* neighbor state to mean that the database exchange process has been completed.

Maintaining the LSDB While Being Fully Adjacent

Neighbors in a Full state still do some maintenance work. They keep sending Hellos every Hello interval. The absence of Hellos for a time equal to the Dead Interval means that the connection to the neighbor has failed. Also, if any topology changes occur, the neighbors send new copies of the changed LSAs to each neighbor so that the neighbor can change its LSDBs. For example, if a subnet fails, a router updates the LSA for that subnet to reflect its state as being down. That router then sends the LSA to its neighbors, and they in turn send it to their neighbors, until all routers again have an identical copy of the LSDB. Each router can then also use SPF to recalculate any routes affected by the failed subnet.

The router that creates each LSA also has the responsibility to reflood the LSA every 30 minutes (the default), even if no changes occur. This process is quite different than the distance vector concept of periodic updates. Distance vector protocols send full updates over a short time interval, listing all routes (except those omitted due to loop-avoidance tools such as split horizon). OSPF does not send all routes every 30 minutes. Instead, each LSA has a separate timer, based on when the LSA was created. So, there is no single moment when OSPF sends a lot of messages to reflood all LSAs. Instead, each LSA is reflooded by the router that created the LSA, every 30 minutes.

As a reminder, some routers do not attempt to become fully adjacent. In particular, on interfaces on which a DR is elected, routers that are neither DR nor BDR become neighbors, but they do not become fully adjacent. These non-fully adjacent routers do not directly exchange LSAs. Also, the **show ip ospf neighbor** command on such a router lists these neighbors in a two-way state as the normal stable neighbor state, and Full as the normal stable state for the DR and BDR.

Summary of Neighbor States

For easier reference and study, Table 9-2 lists and briefly describes the neighbor states mentioned in this chapter.

Table 9-2 *OSPF Neighbor States and Their Meanings*

Key Topic

Neighbor State	Meaning
Down	A known neighbor is no longer reachable, often because of an underlying interface failure.
Init	An interim state in which a Hello has been heard from the neighbor, but that Hello does not list the router's RID as having been seen yet.
Two-way	The neighbor has sent a Hello that lists the local router's RID in the list of seen routers, also implying that neighbor verification checks all passed.
Full	Both routers know the exact same LSDB details and are fully adjacent.

Building the IP Routing Table

OSPF routers send messages to learn about neighbors, listing those neighbors in the OSPF neighbor table. OSPF routers then send messages to exchange topology data with these same neighbors, storing the information in the OSPF topology table, more commonly called the LSDB or the OSPF database. To fill the third major table used by OSPF, the IP routing table, OSPF does not send any messages. Each router runs the Dijkstra SPF algorithm against the OSPF topology database, choosing the best routes based on that process.

The OSPF topology database consists of lists of subnet numbers (called *links*, hence the name *link-state database*). It also contains lists of routers, along with the links (subnets) to which each router is connected. Armed with the knowledge of links and routers, a router can run the SPF algorithm to compute the best routes to all the subnets. The concept is very much like putting together a jigsaw puzzle. The color and shape of each piece help you identify what pieces might fit next to it. Similarly, the detailed information in each LSA—things such as a *link LSA* listing the routers attached to the subnet, and a *router LSA* listing its IP addresses and masks—gives the SPF algorithm enough information to figure out which routers connect to each subnet and create the mathematical equivalent of a network diagram.

Each router independently uses the Dijkstra SPF algorithm, as applied to the OSPF LSDB, to find the best route from that router to each subnet. The algorithm finds the shortest path from that router to each subnet in the LSDB. Then the router places the best route to each subnet in the IP routing table. It sounds simple, and it is with a drawing of an internetwork that lists all the information. Fortunately, although the underlying math of the SPF algorithm can be a bit daunting, you do not need to know SPF math for the exams or for real networking jobs. However, you do need to be able to predict the routes SPF will choose using network diagrams and documentation.

OSPF chooses the least-cost route between the router and a subnet by adding up the outgoing interfaces' OSPF costs. Each interface has an OSPF cost associated with it. The router looks at each possible route, adds up the costs on the interfaces out which packets would be forwarded on that route, and then picks the least-cost route. For example, Figure 9-4 shows a simple internetwork with the OSPF cost values listed beside each interface. In this figure, router R4 has two possible paths with which to reach subnet 10.5.1.0/24. The two routes are as follows, listing each router and its outgoing interface:

R4 Fa0/0—R1 S0/1—R5 Fa0/0
R4 Fa0/0—R2 S0/1—R5 Fa0/0

Figure 9-4   *Sample OSPF Network with Costs Shown*

Route R4 – R1 – R5 : cost 1 + 100 + 10 = 111
Route R4 – R2 – R5 : cost 1 + 64 + 10 = 75

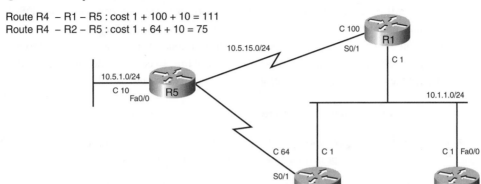

If you add up the cost associated with each interface, the first of the two routes totals a cost of 111, and the second totals 75. So, R4 adds the route through R2 as the best route and lists R2's IP address as the next-hop IP address.

Now that you have seen how OSPF routers perform the most fundamental functions of OSPF, the next section takes a broader look at OSPF, particularly some important design points.

Scaling OSPF Through Hierarchical Design

OSPF can be used in some networks with very little thought about design issues. You just turn on OSPF in all the routers, and it works! However, in large networks, engineers need to think about and plan how to use several OSPF features that allow it to scale well in larger networks. To appreciate the issues behind OSPF scalability, and the need for good design to allow scalability, examine Figure 9-5.

Figure 9-5   *Single-Area OSPF*

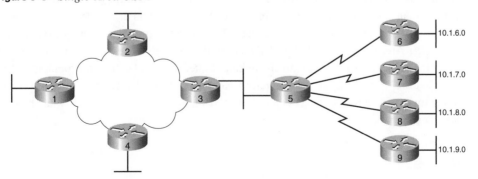

In the network shown in Figure 9-5, the topology database on all nine routers is the same full topology that matches the figure. With a network that size, you can just enable OSPF, and it works fine. But imagine a network with 900 routers instead of only nine, and several thousand subnets. In that size of network, the sheer amount of processing required to run the complex SPF algorithm might cause convergence time to be slow, and the routers might experience memory shortages. The problems can be summarized as follows:

- A larger topology database requires more memory on each router.

- Processing the larger-topology database with the SPF algorithm requires processing power that grows exponentially with the size of the topology database.

- A single interface status change (up to down or down to up) forces every router to run SPF again!

Although there is no exact definition of "large" in this context, in networks with at least 50 routers and at least a few hundred subnets, engineers should use OSPF scalability features to reduce the problems just described. These numbers are gross generalizations. They depend largely on the network design, the power of the router CPU, the amount of RAM, and so on.

OSPF Areas

Using OSPF areas solves many, but not all, of the most common problems with running OSPF in larger networks. OSPF areas break up the network so that routers in one area know less topology information about the subnets in the other area—and they do not know about the routers in the other area at all. With smaller-topology databases, routers consume less memory and take less processing time to run SPF. Figure 9-6 shows the same network as Figure 9-5, but with two OSPF areas, labeled Area 1 and Area 0.

The same topology is shown in the upper part of the figure, but the lower part of the figure shows the topology database on Routers 1, 2, and 4. By placing part of the network in another area, the routers inside Area 1 are shielded from some of the details. Router 3 is known as an OSPF Area Border Router (ABR), because it is on the border between two different areas. Router 3 does not advertise full topology information about the part of the network in Area 0 to Routers 1, 2, and 4. Instead, Router 3 advertises summary information about the subnets in Area 0, effectively making Routers 1, 2, and 4 think the topology looks like the lower part of Figure 9-6. Therefore, Routers 1, 2, and 4 view the world as if it has fewer routers. As a result, the SPF algorithm takes less time, and the topology database takes less memory.

Figure 9-6 *Two-Area OSPF*

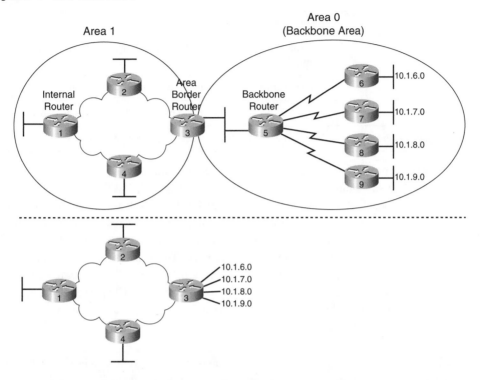

OSPF design introduces a few important terms you should know for the exams; they are defined in Table 9-3.

Table 9-3 *OSPF Design Terminology*

Term	Description
Area Border Router (ABR)	An OSPF router with interfaces connected to the backbone area and to at least one other area.
Autonomous System Border Router (ASBR)	An OSPF router that connects to routers that do not use OSPF for the purpose of exchanging external routes into and out of the OSPF domain.
Backbone router	A router in one area, the backbone area.
Internal router	A router in a single nonbackbone area.
Area	A set of routers and links that share the same detailed LSDB information, but not with routers in other areas, for better efficiency.
Backbone area	A special OSPF area to which all other areas must connect. Area 0.

continues

Key Topic

Table 9-3 *OSPF Design Terminology (Continued)*

Term	Description
External route	A route learned from outside the OSPF domain and then advertised into the OSPF domain.
Intra-area route	A route to a subnet inside the same area as the router.
Interarea route	A route to a subnet in an area of which the router is not a part.
Autonomous system	In OSPF, a reference to a set of routers that use OSPF.

It is very important to note the difference between the summarized information shown in Figure 9-6 versus summarized routes as covered in Chapter 5, "VLSM and Route Summarization." In this case, the term "summary" just means that a router inside one area receives briefer information in the LSA for a subnet, thereby decreasing the amount of memory needed to store the information. For example, in Figure 9-6, router R1 (in Area 1) learns only a very brief LSA about subnets in Area 0. This process reduces the size and complexity of the SPF algorithm. In addition, the term "summary" can refer to a summary route configured in OSPF, with the general concepts covered in Chapter 5. OSPF manual route summarization reduces the number of subnets, which in turn also reduces the size and effort of the SPF calculation.

> **NOTE** Although the perspectives of the routers in Area 1 are shown in Figure 9-6, the same thing happens in reverse—routers in Area 0 do not know the details of Area 1's topology.

Notice that the dividing line between areas is not a link, but a router. In Figure 9-6, Router 3 is in both Area 1 and Area 0. OSPF uses the term Area Border Router (ABR) to describe a router that sits in both areas. An ABR has the topology database for both areas and runs SPF when links change status in either area. So, although using areas helps scale OSPF by reducing the size of the LSDB and the time to compute a routing table, the amount of RAM and CPU consumed on ABRs can actually increase. As a result, the routers acting as ABRs should be faster routers with relatively more memory.

OSPF Area Design Advantages

Using areas improves OSPF operations in many ways, particularly in larger internetworks:

■ The smaller per-area LSDB requires less memory.

■ The router requires fewer CPU cycles to process the smaller per-area LSDB with the SPF algorithm, reducing CPU overhead and improving convergence time.

- The SPF algorithm has to be run on internal routers only when an LSA inside the area changes, so routers have to run SPF less often.

- Less information must be advertised between areas, reducing the bandwidth required to send LSAs.

- Manual summarization can only be configured on ABRs and ASBRs, so areas allow for smaller IP routing tables by allowing for the configuration of manual route summarization.

OSPF Configuration

OSPF configuration includes only a few required steps, but it has many optional steps. After an OSPF design has been chosen—a task that may be complex in larger IP internetworks—the configuration may be as simple as enabling OSPF on each router interface and placing that interface in the correct OSPF area.

This section shows several configuration examples, starting with a single-area OSPF internetwork and then a multiarea OSPF internetwork. Following those examples, the text goes on to cover several of the additional optional configuration settings. For reference, the following list outlines the configuration steps covered in this chapter, as well as a brief reference to the required commands:

Step 1   Enter OSPF configuration mode for a particular OSPF process using the **router ospf** *process-id* global command.

Step 2   (Optional) Configure the OSPF router ID by:

    a. Configuring the **router-id** *id-value* router subcommand.

    b. Configuring an IP address on a loopback interface.

Step 3   Configure one or more **network** *ip-address wildcard-mask* **area** *area-id* router subcommands, with any matched interfaces being added to the listed area.

Step 4   (Optional) Change the interface Hello and Dead intervals using the **ip ospf hello-interval** *time* and **ip ospf dead-interval** *time* interface subcommands.

Step 5   (Optional) Impact routing choices by tuning interface costs as follows:

    a. Configure costs directly using the **ip ospf cost** *value* interface subcommand.

    b. Change interface bandwidths using the **bandwidth** *value* interface subcommand.

c. Change the numerator in the formula to calculate the cost based on the interface bandwidth, using the **auto-cost reference-bandwidth** *value* router subcommand.

Step 6 (Optional) Configure OSPF authentication:

a. On a per-interface basis using the **ip ospf authentication** interface subcommand.

b. For all interfaces in an area using the **area authentication** router subcommand.

Step 7 (Optional) Configure support for multiple equal-cost routes using the **maximum-paths** *number* router subcommand.

OSPF Single-Area Configuration

OSPF configuration differs only slightly from RIP configuration when a single OSPF area is used. The best way to describe the configuration, and the differences with the configuration of the other routing protocols, is to use an example. Figure 9-7 shows a sample network, and Example 9-1 shows the configuration on Albuquerque.

Figure 9-7 *Sample Network for OSPF Single-Area Configuration*

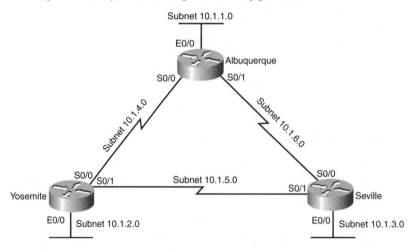

Example 9-1 *OSPF Single-Area Configuration on Albuquerque*

```
interface ethernet 0/0
 ip address 10.1.1.1 255.255.255.0
interface serial 0/0
 ip address 10.1.4.1 255.255.255.0
interface serial 0/1
 ip address 10.1.6.1 255.255.255.0
```

Example 9-1   *OSPF Single-Area Configuration on Albuquerque (Continued)*

```
!
router ospf 1
 network 10.0.0.0 0.255.255.255 area 0
```

The configuration correctly enables OSPF on all three interfaces on Albuquerque. First, the **router ospf 1** global command puts the user in OSPF configuration mode. The **router ospf** command has a parameter called the OSPF *process-id*. In some instances, you might want to run multiple OSPF processes in a single router, so the **router** command uses the *process-id* to distinguish between the processes. The *process-id* does not have to match on each router, and it can be any integer between 1 and 65,535.

The **network** command tells a router to enable OSPF on each matched interface, discover neighbors on that interface, assign the interface to that area, and advertise the subnet connected to each interface. In this case, the **network 10.0.0.0 0.255.255.255 area 0** command matches all three of Albuquerque's interfaces because the OSPF **network** command matches interfaces using an address and a wildcard-style mask like those used with IP ACLs. The wildcard mask shown in Example 9-1 is 0.255.255.255, with address 10.0.0.0. From the details included in Chapter 6, "IP Access Control Lists," this combination matches all addresses that begin with 10 in the first octet. So, this one **network** command matches all three of Albuquerque's interfaces, puts them in Area 0, and causes Albuquerque to try to discover neighbors on those interfaces. It also causes Albuquerque to advertise the three connected subnets.

The wildcard mask in the OSPF **network** command works like an ACL wildcard mask, but there is one restriction on the values used. The OSPF wildcard mask must have only one string of consecutive binary 1s and one string of consecutive binary 0s. For example, a mask of 0.0.255.255 represents 16 binary 0s and 16 binary 1s and would be allowed. Likewise, a mask of 255.255.255.0 would be allowed, because it has a string of 24 binary 1s followed by eight binary 0s. However, a value of 0.255.255.0 would not be allowed, because it has two sets of eight binary 0s, separated by a string of 16 binary 1s.

Example 9-2 shows an alternative configuration for Albuquerque that also enables OSPF on every interface. In this case, the IP address for each interface is matched with a different **network** command. The wildcard mask of 0.0.0.0 means that all 32 bits must be compared, and they must match—so the **network** commands include the specific IP address of each interface, respectively. Many people prefer this style of configuration in production networks, because it removes any ambiguity about the interfaces on which OSPF is running.

Example 9-2 *OSPF Single-Area Configuration on Albuquerque Using Three* **network**
            Commands

```
interface ethernet 0/0
 ip address 10.1.1.1 255.255.255.0
interface serial 0/0
 ip address 10.1.4.1 255.255.255.0
interface serial 0/1
 ip address 10.1.6.1 255.255.255.0
!
router ospf 1
 network 10.1.1.1 0.0.0.0 area 0
 network 10.1.4.1 0.0.0.0 area 0
 network 10.1.6.1 0.0.0.0 area 0
```

OSPF Configuration with Multiple Areas

Configuring OSPF with multiple areas is simple when you understand OSPF configuration
in a single area. Designing the OSPF network by making good choices about which subnets
should be placed in which areas is the hard part! After the area design is complete, the
configuration is easy. For instance, consider Figure 9-8, which shows some subnets in Area
0 and some in Area 1.

Figure 9-8 *Multiarea OSPF Network*

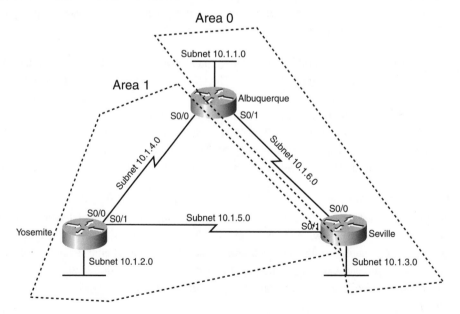

Multiple areas are not needed in such a small network, but two areas are used in this example to show the configuration. Note that Albuquerque and Seville are both ABRs, but Yosemite is totally inside Area 1, so it is not an ABR. Examples 9-3 and 9-4 show the configuration on Albuquerque and Yosemite, along with several **show** commands.

Example 9-3 *OSPF Multiarea Configuration and* **show** *Commands on Albuquerque*

```
! Only the OSPF configuration is shown to conserve space
!
router ospf 1
 network 10.1.1.1 0.0.0.0 area 0
 network 10.1.4.1 0.0.0.0 area 1
 network 10.1.6.1 0.0.0.0 area 0
Albuquerque#show ip route
Codes: C - connected, S - static, I - IGRP, R - RIP, M - mobile, B - BGP
       D - EIGRP, EX - EIGRP external, O - OSPF, IA - OSPF inter area
       N1 - OSPF NSSA external type 1, N2 - OSPF NSSA external type 2
       E1 - OSPF external type 1, E2 - OSPF external type 2, E - EGP
       i - IS-IS, L1 - IS-IS level-1, L2 - IS-IS level-2, ia - IS-IS inter area
       * - candidate default, U - per-user static route, o - ODR
       P - periodic downloaded static route

Gateway of last resort is not set

     10.0.0.0/24 is subnetted, 6 subnets
O       10.1.3.0 [110/65] via 10.1.6.3, 00:01:04, Serial0/1
O       10.1.2.0 [110/65] via 10.1.4.2, 00:00:39, Serial0/0
C       10.1.1.0 is directly connected, Ethernet0/0
C       10.1.6.0 is directly connected, Serial0/1
O       10.1.5.0 [110/128] via 10.1.4.2, 00:00:39, Serial0/0
C       10.1.4.0 is directly connected, Serial0/0

Albuquerque#show ip route ospf
     10.0.0.0/24 is subnetted, 6 subnets
O       10.1.3.0 [110/65] via 10.1.6.3, 00:01:08, Serial0/1
O       10.1.2.0 [110/65] via 10.1.4.2, 00:00:43, Serial0/0
O       10.1.5.0 [110/128] via 10.1.4.2, 00:00:43, Serial0/0
```

Example 9-4 *OSPF Multiarea Configuration and* **show** *Commands on Yosemite*

```
! Only the OSPF configuration is shown to conserve space
router ospf 1
 network 10.0.0.0 0.255.255.255 area 1
Yosemite#show ip route
Codes: C - connected, S - static, I - IGRP, R - RIP, M - mobile, B - BGP
       D - EIGRP, EX - EIGRP external, O - OSPF, IA - OSPF inter area
       N1 - OSPF NSSA external type 1, N2 - OSPF NSSA external type 2
       E1 - OSPF external type 1, E2 - OSPF external type 2, E - EGP
```

continues

Example 9-4   *OSPF Multiarea Configuration and* **show** *Commands on Yosemite (Continued)*

```
        i - IS-IS, L1 - IS-IS level-1, L2 - IS-IS level-2, ia - IS-IS inter area
        * - candidate default, U - per-user static route, o - ODR
        P - periodic downloaded static route

Gateway of last resort is not set

     10.0.0.0/24 is subnetted, 6 subnets
IA      10.1.3.0 [110/65] via 10.1.5.1, 00:00:54, Serial0/1
IA      10.1.1.0 [110/65] via 10.1.4.1, 00:00:49, Serial0/0
C       10.1.2.0 is directly connected, Ethernet0/0
C       10.1.5.0 is directly connected, Serial0/1
IA      10.1.6.0 [110/128] via 10.1.4.1, 00:00:38, Serial0/0
C       10.1.4.0 is directly connected, Serial0/0
```

The configuration needs to set the correct area number on the appropriate interfaces. For instance, the **network 10.1.4.1 0.0.0.0 area 1** command at the beginning of Example 9-3 matches Albuquerque's Serial 0/0 interface IP address, placing that interface in Area 1. The **network 10.1.6.1 0.0.0.0 area 0** and **network 10.1.1.1 0.0.0.0 area 0** commands place Serial 0/1 and Ethernet 0/0, respectively, in Area 0. Unlike Example 9-1, Albuquerque cannot be configured to match all three interfaces with a single **network** command, because one interface (Serial 0/0) is in a different area than the other two interfaces.

Continuing with Example 9-3, the **show ip route ospf** command just lists OSPF-learned routes, as opposed to the entire IP routing table. The **show ip route** command lists all three connected routes, as well as the three OSPF learned routes. Note that Albuquerque's route to 10.1.2.0 has the **O** designation beside it, meaning *intra-area,* because that subnet resides in Area 1, and Albuquerque is part of Area 1 and Area 0.

In Example 9-4, notice that the OSPF configuration in Yosemite requires only a single **network** command because all interfaces in Yosemite are in Area 1. Also note that the routes learned by Yosemite from the other two routers show up as *interarea (IA) routes,* because those subnets are in Area 0, and Yosemite is in Area 1.

Configuring the OSPF Router ID

OSPF-speaking routers must have a Router ID (RID) for proper operation. To find its RID, a Cisco router uses the following process when the router reloads and brings up the OSPF process. Note that when one of these steps identifies the RID, the process stops.

1. If the **router-id** *rid* OSPF subcommand is configured, this value is used as the RID.

2. If any loopback interfaces have an IP address configured and the interface has a line and protocol status of up/up, the router picks the highest numeric IP address among the up/up loopback interfaces.

3. The router picks the highest numeric IP address from all other working (up/up) interfaces.

The first and third criteria should make some sense right away: the RID is either configured or is taken from a working interface's IP address. However, this book has not yet explained the concept of a *loopback interface*, as mentioned in Step 2. A loopback interface is a virtual interface that can be configured with the **interface loopback** *interface-number* command, where *interface-number* is an integer. Loopback interfaces are always in an "up and up" state unless administratively placed in a shutdown state. For instance, a simple configuration of the command **interface loopback 0**, followed by **ip address 192.168.200.1 255.255.255.0**, would create a loopback interface and assign it an IP address. Because loopback interfaces do not rely on any hardware, these interfaces can be up/up whenever IOS is running, making them good interfaces on which to base an OSPF RID.

Each router chooses its OSPF RID when OSPF is initialized. Initialization happens during the initial load of IOS. So, if OSPF comes up, and later other interfaces come up that happen to have higher IP addresses, the OSPF RID does not change until the OSPF process is restarted. OSPF can be restarted with the **clear ip ospf process** command as well, but depending on circumstances, IOS still may not change its OSPF RID until the next IOS reload.

Many commands list the OSPF RID of various routers. For instance, in Example 9-5, the first neighbor in the output of the **show ip ospf neighbor** command lists Router ID 10.1.5.2, which is Yosemite's RID. Following that, **show ip ospf** lists Albuquerque's own RID.

Example 9-5 *Displaying OSPF-Related Information in Albuquerque*

```
Albuquerque#show ip ospf neighbor

Neighbor ID     Pri   State         Dead Time   Address      Interface
10.1.6.3          1   FULL/   -     00:00:35    10.1.6.3     Serial0/1
10.1.5.2          1   FULL/   -     00:00:37    10.1.4.2     Serial0/0
Albuquerque#show ip ospf
Routing Process "ospf 1" with ID 10.1.6.1
! lines omitted for brevity
```

OSPF Hello and Dead Timers

The default settings for the OSPF Hello and dead timers typically work just fine. However, it is important to note that a mismatch on either setting causes two potential neighbors to never become neighbors, never reaching the two-way state. Example 9-6 lists the most common way to see the current settings using the **show ip ospf interface** command, as taken from Albuquerque, when configured as shown in the multiarea OSPF example (Examples 9-3 and 9-4).

Example 9-6 *Displaying the Hello and Dead Timers on Albuquerque*

```
Albuquerque#show ip ospf interface
Serial0/1 is up, line protocol is up
  Internet Address 10.1.6.1/24, Area 0
  Process ID 1, Router ID 10.1.6.1, Network Type POINT_TO_POINT, Cost: 64
  Transmit Delay is 1 sec, State POINT_TO_POINT,
  Timer intervals configured, Hello 10, Dead 40, Wait 40, Retransmit 5
    Hello due in 00:00:07
  Index 2/3, flood queue length 0
  Next 0x0(0)/0x0(0)
  Last flood scan length is 2, maximum is 2
  Last flood scan time is 0 msec, maximum is 0 msec
  Neighbor Count is 1, Adjacent neighbor count is 1
    Adjacent with neighbor 10.1.6.3
  Suppress hello for 0 neighbor(s)
Ethernet0/0 is up, line protocol is up
  Internet Address 10.1.1.1/24, Area 0
  Process ID 1, Router ID 10.1.6.1, Network Type BROADCAST, Cost: 10
  Transmit Delay is 1 sec, State DR, Priority 1
  Designated Router (ID) 10.1.6.1, Interface address 10.1.1.1
  No backup designated router on this network
  Timer intervals configured, Hello 10, Dead 40, Wait 40, Retransmit 5
    Hello due in 00:00:08
  Index 1/1, flood queue length 0
  Next 0x0(0)/0x0(0)
  Last flood scan length is 0, maximum is 0
  Last flood scan time is 0 msec, maximum is 0 msec
  Neighbor Count is 0, Adjacent neighbor count is 0
  Suppress hello for 0 neighbor(s)
Serial0/0 is up, line protocol is up
  Internet Address 10.1.4.1/24, Area 1
  Process ID 1, Router ID 10.1.6.1, Network Type POINT_TO_POINT, Cost: 64
  Transmit Delay is 1 sec, State POINT_TO_POINT,
  Timer intervals configured, Hello 10, Dead 40, Wait 40, Retransmit 5
    Hello due in 00:00:01
  Index 1/2, flood queue length 0
  Next 0x0(0)/0x0(0)
  Last flood scan length is 1, maximum is 1
  Last flood scan time is 0 msec, maximum is 0 msec
  Neighbor Count is 1, Adjacent neighbor count is 1
    Adjacent with neighbor 10.1.5.2
  Suppress hello for 0 neighbor(s)
```

Note also that the **show ip ospf interface** command lists more detailed information about OSPF operation on each interface. For instance, this command lists the area number, OSPF cost, and any neighbors known on each interface. The timers used on the interface, including the Hello and dead timer, are also listed.

To configure the Hello and Dead intervals, you can use the **ip ospf hello-interval** *value* and **ip ospf dead-interval** *value* interface subcommands. Interestingly, if the Hello interval is configured, IOS automatically reconfigures the interface's dead interval to be 4 times the Hello interval.

OSPF Metrics (Cost)

OSPF calculates the metric for each possible route by adding up the outgoing interfaces' OSPF costs. The OSPF cost for an interface can be configured, or a router can calculate the cost based on the interface's bandwidth setting.

As a reminder, the bandwidth setting on an interface can be configured using the **bandwidth** interface subcommand. This command sets the router's perception of interface speed, with a unit of Kbps. Note that the interface's bandwidth setting does not have to match the physical interface speed, but it usually makes sense to set the bandwidth to match the physical interface speed. On Ethernet interfaces, the bandwidth reflects the current negotiated speed—10,000 (meaning 10,000 Kbps or 10 Mbps) for 10 Mbps Ethernet, and 100,000 (meaning 100,000 Kbps or 100 Mbps) for 100 Mbps. For serial interfaces, the bandwidth defaults to 1544 (meaning 1544 Kbps, or T1 speed), but IOS cannot adjust this setting dynamically.

IOS chooses an interface's cost based on the following rules:

1. The cost can be explicitly set using the **ip ospf cost** *x* interface subcommand, to a value between 1 and 65,535, inclusive.

2. IOS can calculate a value based on the generic formula *Ref-BW / Int-BW*, where *Ref-BW* is a reference bandwidth that defaults to 100 Mbps, and *Int-BW* is the interface's bandwidth setting.

3. The reference bandwidth can be configured from its default setting of 100 (100 Mbps) using the router OSPF subcommand **auto-cost reference-bandwidth** *ref-bw*, which in turn affects the calculation of the default interface cost.

The simple formula to calculate the default OSPF cost has one potentially confusing part. The calculation requires that the numerator and denominator use the same units, whereas the **bandwidth** and **auto-cost reference-bandwidth** commands use different units. For instance, Cisco IOS software defaults Ethernet interfaces to use a bandwidth of 10,000, meaning 10,000 Kbps, or 10 Mbps. The reference bandwidth defaults to a value of 100, meaning 100 Mbps. So, the default OSPF cost on an Ethernet interface would be 100 Mbps / 10 Mbps, after making both values use a unit of Mbps. Higher-speed serial interfaces default to a bandwidth of 1544, giving a default cost of 10^8 bps / 1,544,000 bps, which is rounded down to a value of 64, as shown for interface S0/1 in Example 9-6. If the reference bandwidth had been changed to 1000, using the router OSPF subcommand **auto-cost reference-bandwidth 1000**, the calculated metric would be 647.

The main motivation for changing the reference bandwidth is so that routers can have different cost values for interfaces running at speeds of 100 Mbps and higher. With the default setting, an interface with a 100 Mbps bandwidth setting (for example, an FE interface) and an interface with a 1000 Mbps bandwidth (for example, a GE interface) would both have a default cost of 1. By changing the reference bandwidth to 1000, meaning 1000 Mbps, the default cost on a 100-Mbps bandwidth interface would be 10, versus a default cost of 1 on an interface with a bandwidth of 1000 Mbps.

> **NOTE**   Cisco recommends making the OSPF reference bandwidth setting the same on all OSPF routers in a network.

OSPF Authentication

Authentication is arguably the most important of the optional configuration features for OSPF. The lack of authentication opens the network to attacks in which an attacker connects a router to the network, with the legitimate routers believing the OSPF data from the rogue router. As a result, the attacker can easily cause a denial-of-service (DoS) attack by making all routers remove the legitimate routes to all subnets, instead installing routes that forward packets to the attacking router. The attacker can also perform a reconnaissance attack, learning information about the network by listening for and interpreting the OSPF messages.

OSPF supports three types of authentication—one called null authentication (meaning no authentication), one that uses a simple text password and therefore is easy to break, and one that uses MD5. Frankly, if you bother to configure an option in real life, the MD5 option is the only reasonable option. As soon as a router has configured OSPF authentication on an interface, that router must pass the authentication process for every OSPF message, with every neighboring router on that interface. This means that each neighboring router on that interface must also have the same authentication type and the same authentication password configured.

The configuration can use two interface subcommands on each interface—one to enable the particular type of authentication, and one to set the password used for the authentication.

Example 9-7 shows a sample configuration in which simple password authentication is configured on interface Fa0/0, and MD5 authentication is configured on Fa0/1.

Example 9-7 *OSPF Authentication Using Only Interface Subcommands*

```
! The following commands enable OSPF simple password authentication and
! set the password to a value of "key-t1".
R1#show running-config
! lines omitted for brevity
interface FastEthernet0/0
 ip ospf authentication
 ip ospf authentication-key key-t1
! Below, the neighbor relationship formed, proving that authentication worked.
R1# show ip ospf neighbor fa 0/0
Neighbor ID     Pri   State         Dead Time   Address      Interface
2.2.2.2           1   FULL/BDR      00:00:37    10.1.1.2     FastEthernet0/0
! Next, each interface's OSPF authentication type can be seen in the last line
! or two in the output of the show ip ospf interface command.
R1# show ip ospf interface fa 0/0
! Lines omitted for brevity
 Simple password authentication enabled


! Below, R1's Fa0/1 interface is configured to use type 2 authentication.
! Note that the key must be defined with
! the ip ospf message-digest-key interface subcommand.
R1#show running-config
! lines omitted for brevity
interface FastEthernet0/1
 ip ospf authentication message-digest
 ip ospf message-digest-key 1 md5 key-t2
! Below, the command confirms type 2 (MD5) authentication, key number 1.
R1# show ip ospf interface fa 0/1
! Lines omitted for brevity
Message digest authentication enabled
Youngest key id is 1
```

The trickiest part of the configuration is to remember the command syntax used on two interface subcommands. Note the interface subcommands used to configure the authentication keys, with the syntax differing depending on the type of authentication. For reference, Table 9-4 lists the three OSPF authentication types and the corresponding commands.

Key
Topic

Table 9-4 *OSPF Authentication Types*

Type	Meaning	Command to Enable Authentication	What the Password Is Configured With
0	None	**ip ospf authentication null**	—
1	Clear text	**ip ospf authentication**	**ip ospf authentication-key** *key-value*
2	MD5	**ip ospf authentication message-digest**	**ip ospf message-digest-key** *key-number* **md5** *key-value*

Note that the passwords, or authentication keys, are kept in clear text in the configuration, unless you add the **service password-encryption** global command to the configuration. (If you have a copy of *CCENT/CCNA ICND1 Official Exam Certification Guide*, you might want to refer to Chapter 9 of that book for more information on the **service password-encryption** command.)

The default setting to use type 0 authentication—which really means no authentication—can be overridden on an area-by-area basis by using the **area authentication** router command. For example, Router R1 in Example 9-7 could be configured with the **area 1 authentication message-digest** router subcommand, which makes that router default to use MD5 authentication on all its interfaces in Area 1. Similarly, the **area 1 authentication** router subcommand enables simple password authentication for all interfaces in Area 1, making the **ip ospf authentication** interface subcommand unnecessary. Note that the authentication keys (passwords) must still be configured with the interface subcommands listed in Table 9-4.

OSPF Load Balancing

When OSPF uses SPF to calculate the metric for each of several routes to reach one subnet, one route may have the lowest metric, so OSPF puts that route in the routing table. However, when the metric is a tie, the router can put up to 16 different equal-cost routes in the routing table (the default is four different routes) based on the setting of the **maximum-paths** *number* router subcommand. For example, if an internetwork had six possible paths between some parts of the network, and the engineer wanted all routes to be used, the routers could be configured with the **maximum-paths 6** subcommand under **router ospf**.

The more challenging concept relates to how the routers use those multiple routes. A router could load-balance the packets on a per-packet basis. For example, if the router had three equal-cost OSPF routes for the same subnet in the routing table, the router could send the next packet over the first route, the next packet over the second route, the next packet over the third route, and then start over with the first route for the next packet. Alternatively, the load balancing could be on a per-destination IP address basis.

Exam Preparation Tasks

Review All the Key Topics

Review the most important topics from this chapter, noted with the key topics icon. Table 9-5 lists these key topics and where each is discussed.

Table 9-5 *Key Topics for Chapter 9*

Key Topic Element	Description	Page Number
List	Items that must match on OSPF neighbors before they will become neighbors and reach the two-way state (at least)	349
Figure 9-2	Neighbor states and messages during OSPF neighbor formation	351
List	Three-step summary of the OSPF topology database exchange process	352
Figure 9-3	Drawing comparing full adjacencies formed with and without a DR	353
List	Rules for electing a designated router	354
Table 9-2	OSPF neighbor states and their meanings	355
List	List of reasons why OSPF needs areas to scale well	358
Table 9-3	OSPF design terms and definitions	359-360
List	Configuration checklist for OSPF	361-362
List	Details of how IOS determines an interface's OSPF cost	366
Table 9-4	OSPF authentication types and configuration commands	372

Definitions of Key Terms

Define the following key terms from this chapter, and check your answers in the glossary:

Two-way state, Area Border Router (ABR), Autonomous System Border Router (ASBR), Backup Designated Router, database description, dead interval, designated router, Full state, fully adjacent, Hello interval, link-state advertisement, link-state request, link-state update, neighbor, neighbor table, router ID (RID), topology database

Command Reference to Check Your Memory

Although you should not necessarily memorize the information in the tables in this section, this section does include a reference for the configuration and EXEC commands covered in this chapter. Practically speaking, you should memorize the commands as a side effect of reading the chapter and doing all the activities in this exam preparation section. To see how well you have memorized the commands as a side effect of your other studies, cover the left side of the table, read the descriptions on the right side, and see if you remember the command.

Table 9-6 *Chapter 9 Configuration Command Reference*

Command	Description
router ospf *process-id*	Enters OSPF configuration mode for the listed process.
network *ip-address wildcard-mask* **area** *area-id*	Router subcommand that enables OSPF on interfaces matching the address/wildcard combination and sets the OSPF area.
ip ospf cost *interface-cost*	Interface subcommand that sets the OSPF cost associated with the interface.
bandwidth *bandwidth*	Interface subcommand that directly sets the interface bandwidth (Kbps).
auto-cost reference-bandwidth *number*	Router subcommand that tells OSPF the numerator in the *Ref-BW/Int-BW* formula used to calculate the OSPF cost based on the interface bandwidth.
ip ospf hello *number*	Interface subcommand that sets the OSPF Hello interval, and also resets the Dead interval to 4 times this number.
ip ospf dead-interval *number*	Interface subcommand that sets the OSPF dead timer.
ip ospf network *type*	Interface subcommand that defines the OSPF network type.

Table 9-6   *Chapter 9 Configuration Command Reference (Continued)*

Command	Description
router-id *id*	OSPF command that statically sets the router ID.
ip ospf hello-interval *seconds*	Interface subcommand that sets the interval for periodic Hellos.
ip ospf priority *number-value*	Interface subcommand that sets the OSPF priority on an interface.
maximum-paths *number-of-paths*	Router subcommand that defines the maximum number of equal-cost routes that can be added to the routing table.
ip ospf authentication [null | message-digest]	Interface subcommand that enables type 0 (null), type 1 (no optional parameter listed), or type 2 (message-digest) authentication.
ip ospf message-digest-key *key-number* **md5** *key-value*	Interface subcommand that sets the OSPF authentication key if MD5 authentication is used.
ip ospf authentication-key *key-value*	Interface subcommand that sets the OSPF authentication key if simple password authentication is used.
area *area* **authentication [message-digest | null]**	Router subcommand that configures the default authentication service for interfaces in the listed area.

Table 9-7   *Chapter 9 EXEC Command Reference*

Command	Description
show ip route ospf	Lists routes in the routing table learned by OSPF.
show ip protocols	Shows routing protocol parameters and current timer values.
show ip ospf interface	Lists the area in which the interface resides, neighbors adjacent on this interface, and Hello and dead timers.
show ip ospf neighbor [*neighbor-RID*]	Lists neighbors and current status with neighbors, per interface, and optionally lists details for the router ID listed in the command.
debug ip ospf events	Issues log messages for each OSPF packet.
debug ip ospf packet	Issues log messages describing the contents of all OSPF packets.
debug ip ospf hello	Issues log messages describing Hellos and Hello failures.

This chapter covers the following subjects:

EIGRP Concepts and Operation: This section explains the concepts behind EIGRP neighbors, exchanging topology information, and calculating routes.

EIGRP Configuration and Verification: This section shows how to configure EIGRP, including authentication and tuning the metric, as well as how to determine the successor and feasible successor routes in the output of **show** commands.

CHAPTER **10**

EIGRP

Enhanced Interior Gateway Routing Protocol (EIGRP) provides an impressive set of features and attributes for its main purpose of learning IP routes. EIGRP converges very quickly, on par with or even faster than OSPF, but without some of the negatives of OSPF. In particular, EIGRP requires much less processing time, much less memory, and much less design effort than OSPF. The only significant negative is that EIGRP is Cisco-proprietary, so if an internetwork uses some non-Cisco routers, EIGRP cannot be used on those routers.

EIGRP does not fit neatly into the general categories of distance vector and link-state routing protocols. Sometimes Cisco refers to EIGRP as simply an advanced distance vector protocol, but in other cases, Cisco refers to EIGRP as a new type: a balanced hybrid routing protocol. Regardless of the category, the underlying concepts and processes used by EIGRP may have some similarities with other routing protocols, but EIGRP has far more differences, making EIGRP a unique routing protocol unto itself.

This chapter begins by examining some of the key concepts behind how EIGRP does its work. The second half of this chapter explains EIGRP configuration and verification.

"Do I Know This Already?" Quiz

The "Do I Know This Already?" quiz allows you to assess whether you should read the entire chapter. If you miss no more than one of these nine self-assessment questions, you might want to move ahead to the "Exam Preparation Tasks" section. Table 10-1 lists the major headings in this chapter and the "Do I Know This Already?" quiz questions covering the material in those sections. This helps you assess your knowledge of these specific areas. The answers to the "Do I Know This Already?" quiz appear in Appendix A.

Table 10-1 *"Do I Know This Already?" Foundation Topics Section-to-Question Mapping*

Foundation Topics Section	Questions
EIGRP Concepts and Operation	1–4
EIGRP Configuration and Verification	5–9

1. Which of the following affect the calculation of EIGRP metrics when all possible default values are used?

    a. Bandwidth

    b. Delay

    c. Load

    d. Reliability

    e. MTU

    f. Hop count

2. How does EIGRP notice when a neighboring router fails?

    a. The failing neighbor sends a message before failing.

    b. The failing neighbor sends a "dying gasp" message.

    c. The router notices a lack of routing updates for a period of time.

    d. The router notices a lack of Hello messages for a period of time.

3. Which of the following is true about the concept of EIGRP feasible distance?

    a. A route's feasible distance is the calculated metric of a feasible successor route.

    b. A route's feasible distance is the calculated metric of the successor route.

    c. The feasible distance is the metric of a route from a neighboring router's perspective.

    d. The feasible distance is the EIGRP metric associated with each possible route to reach a subnet.

4. Which of the following is true about the concept of EIGRP reported distance?

    a. A route's reported distance is the calculated metric of a feasible successor route.

    b. A route's reported distance is the calculated metric of the successor route.

    c. A route's reported distance is the metric of a route from a neighboring router's perspective.

    d. The reported distance is the EIGRP metric associated with each possible route to reach a subnet.

5. Which of the following **network** commands, following the command **router eigrp 1**, tells this router to start using EIGRP on interfaces whose IP addresses are 10.1.1.1, 10.1.100.1, and 10.1.120.1?

    a. **network 10.0.0.0**

    b. **network 10.1.1x.0**

    c. **network 10.0.0.0 0.255.255.255**

    d. **network 10.0.0.0 255.255.255.0**

6. Routers R1 and R2 attach to the same VLAN with IP addresses 10.0.0.1 and 10.0.0.2, respectively. R1 is configured with the commands **router eigrp 99** and **network 10.0.0.0.** Which of the following commands might be part of a working EIGRP configuration on R2 that ensures that the two routers become neighbors and exchange routes?

   a. **network 10**

   b. **router eigrp 98**

   c. **network 10.0.0.2 0.0.0.0**

   d. **network 10.0.0.0**

7. Examine the following excerpt from a router's CLI:

```
P 10.1.1.0/24, 1 successors, FD is 2172416
        via 10.1.6.3 (2172416/28160), Serial0/1
        via 10.1.4.2 (2684416/2284156), Serial0/0
        via 10.1.5.4 (2684416/2165432), Serial1/0
```

   Which of the following identifies a next-hop IP address on a feasible successor route?

   a. 10.1.6.3

   b. 10.1.4.2

   c. 10.1.5.4

   d. It cannot be determined from this command output.

8. Which of the following must occur to configure MD5 authentication for EIGRP?

   a. Setting the MD5 authentication key via some interface subcommand

   b. Configuring at least one key chain

   c. Defining a valid lifetime for the key

   d. Enabling EIGRP MD5 authentication on an interface

9. In the **show ip route** command, what code designation implies that a route was learned with EIGRP?

   a. E

   b. I

   c. G

   d. R

   e. P

   f. D

Foundation Topics

EIGRP Concepts and Operation

Like OSPF, EIGRP follows three general steps to be able to add routes to the IP routing table:

1. **Neighbor discovery**: EIGRP routers send Hello messages to discover potential neighboring EIGRP routers and perform basic parameter checks to determine which routers should become neighbors.

2. **Topology exchange**: Neighbors exchange full topology updates when the neighbor relationship comes up, and then only partial updates as needed based on changes to the network topology.

3. **Choosing routes**: Each router analyzes its respective EIGRP topology tables, choosing the lowest-metric route to reach each subnet.

As a result of these three steps, IOS maintains three important EIGRP tables. The EIGRP neighbor table lists the neighboring routers and is viewed with the **show ip eigrp neighbor** command. The EIGRP topology table holds all the topology information learned from EIGRP neighbors and is displayed with the **show ip eigrp topology** command. Finally, the IP routing table holds all the best routes and is displayed with the **show ip route** command.

The next few sections describe some details about how EIGRP forms neighbor relationships, exchanges routes, and adds entries to the IP routing table. In addition to these three steps, this section explains some unique logic EIGRP uses when converging and reacting to changes in an internetwork—logic that is not seen with the other types of routing protocols.

EIGRP Neighbors

An EIGRP neighbor is another EIGRP-speaking router, connected to a common subnet, with which the router is willing to exchange EIGRP topology information. EIGRP uses EIGRP Hello messages, sent to multicast IP address 224.0.0.10, to dynamically discover potential neighbors. A router learns of potential neighbors by receiving a Hello.

Routers perform some basic checking of each potential neighbor before that router becomes an EIGRP neighbor. A potential neighbor is a router from which an EIGRP Hello has been received. Then the router checks the following settings to determine if the router should be allowed to be a neighbor:

- It must pass the authentication process.

- It must use the same configured AS number.

- The source IP address used by the neighbor's Hello must be in the same subnet.

> **NOTE**   The router's EIGRP K values must also match, but this topic is outside the scope of this book.

The verification checks are relatively straightforward. If authentication is configured, the two routers must be using the same type of authentication and the same authentication key. EIGRP configuration includes a parameter called an autonomous system number (ASN), which must be the same on two neighboring routers. Finally, the IP addresses used to send the EIGRP Hello messages—the routers' respective interface IP addresses—must be in the range of addresses on the other routers' respective connected subnet.

The EIGRP neighbor relationship is much simpler than OSPF. EIGRP does not have an additional concept of being fully adjacent like OSPF, and there are no neighbor states like OSPF. As soon as an EIGRP neighbor is discovered and passes the basic verification checks, the router becomes a neighbor. At that point, the two routers can begin exchanging topology information. The neighbors send Hellos every EIGRP Hello interval. A router considers its EIGRP neighbor to no longer be reachable after the neighbor's Hellos cease to occur for the number of seconds defined by the EIGRP Hold Timer—the rough equivalent of the OSPF Dead Interval.

Exchanging EIGRP Topology Information

EIGRP uses EIGRP *Update messages* to send topology information to neighbors. These Update messages can be sent to multicast IP address 224.0.0.10 if the sending router needs to update multiple routers on the same subnet; otherwise, the updates are sent to the unicast IP address of the particular neighbor. (Hello messages are always sent to the 224.0.0.10 multicast address.) Unlike OSPF, there is no concept of a Designated Router (DR) or Backup Designated Router (BDR), but the use of multicast packets on LANs allows EIGRP to exchange routing information with all neighbors on the LAN efficiently.

The update messages are sent using *Reliable Transport Protocol (RTP)*. The significance of RTP is that, like OSPF, EIGRP resends routing updates that are lost in transit. By using RTP, EIGRP can better avoid loops.

> **NOTE** The acronym RTP also refers to a different protocol, Real-time Transport Protocol (RTP), which is used to transmit voice and video IP packets.

Neighbors use both full routing updates and partial updates, as shown in Figure 10-1. A full update means that a router sends information about all known routes, whereas a partial update includes only information about recently changed routes. Full updates occur when neighbors first come up. After that, the neighbors send only partial updates in reaction to changes to a route. From top to bottom, Figure 10-1 shows neighbor discovery with Hellos, the sending of full updates, the maintenance of the neighbor relationship with ongoing Hellos, and partial updates.

Figure 10-1 *Full and Partial EIGRP Updates*

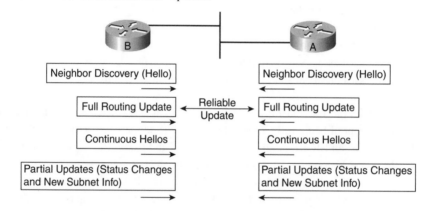

Calculating the Best Routes for the Routing Table

Metric calculation is one of the more interesting features of EIGRP. EIGRP uses a composite metric, calculated as a function of bandwidth and delay by default. The calculation can also include interface load and interface reliability, although Cisco recommends against using either. EIGRP calculates the metric for each possible route by inserting the values of the composite metric into a formula.

> **NOTE** Past documents and books often stated that EIGRP, and its predecessor, IGRP, also could use MTU as a part of the metric, but MTU cannot be used and was never considered as part of the calculation.

EIGRP's metric calculation formula actually helps describe some of the key points about the metric. The formula, assuming that the default settings use just bandwidth and delay, is as follows:

$$\text{Metric} = \left(\left(\frac{10^7}{\text{least-bandwidth}} \right) + \text{cumulative-delay} \right) * 256$$

In this formula, the term *least-bandwidth* represents the lowest-bandwidth link in the route, using a unit of kilobits per second. For instance, if the slowest link in a route is a 10-Mbps Ethernet link, the first part of the formula is $10^7 / 10^4$, which equals 1000. You use 10^4 in the formula because 10 Mbps is equal to 10,000 kbps (10^4 kbps). The cumulative-delay value used in the formula is the sum of all the delay values for all links in the route, with a unit of "tens of microseconds." You can set both bandwidth and delay for each link, using the cleverly named **bandwidth** and **delay** interface subcommands.

> **NOTE**   Most **show** commands, including **show ip eigrp topology** and **show interfaces**, list delay settings as the number of microseconds of delay. The metric formula uses a unit of tens of microseconds.

EIGRP updates list the subnet number and mask, along with the cumulative delay, minimum bandwidth, along with the other typically unused portions of the composite metric. The router then considers the bandwidth and delay settings on the interface on which the update was received and calculates a new metric. For example, Figure 10-2 shows Albuquerque learning about subnet 10.1.3.0/24 from Seville. The update lists a minimum bandwidth of 100,000 kbps, and a cumulative delay of 100 microseconds. R1 has an interface bandwidth set to 1544 kbps—the default bandwidth on a serial link—and a delay of 20,000 microseconds.

Figure 10-2   *How Albuquerque Calculates Its EIGRP Metric for 10.1.3.0/24*

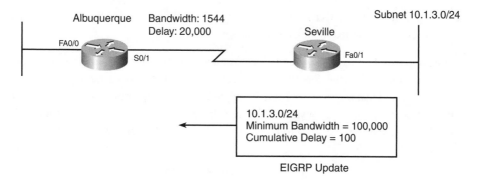

In this case, Albuquerque discovers that its S0/1 interface bandwidth (1544) is less than the advertised minimum bandwidth of 100,000, so Albuquerque uses this new, slower bandwidth in the metric calculation. (If Albuquerque's S0/1 interface had a bandwidth of 100,000 or more in this case, Albuquerque would instead use the minimum bandwidth listed in the EIGRP Update from Seville.) Albuquerque also adds the interface S0/1 delay (20,000 microseconds, converted to 2000 tens-of-microseconds for the formula) to the cumulative delay received from Seville in the update (100 microseconds, converted to 10 tens-of-microseconds). This results in the following metric calculation:

$$\text{Metric} = \left(\left(\frac{10^7}{1544}\right) + (10 + 2000)\right) * 256 = 2{,}172{,}416$$

NOTE   IOS rounds down the division in this formula to the nearest integer before performing the rest of the formula. In this case, $10^7 / 1544$ is rounded down to 6476.

If multiple possible routes to subnet 10.1.3.0/24 existed, Albuquerque would also calculate the metric for those routes and would choose the route with the best (lowest) metric to be added to the routing table. If the metric is a tie, by default a router would place up to four equal-metric routes into the routing table, sending some traffic over each route. The later section "EIGRP Maximum Paths and Variance" explains a few more details about how EIGRP can add multiple equal-metric routes, and multiple unequal-metric routes, to the routing table.

Feasible Distance and Reported Distance

The example described for Figure 10-2 provides a convenient backdrop to define a couple of EIGRP terms:

- **Feasible Distance (FD)**: The metric of the best route to reach a subnet, as calculated on a router

- **Reported Distance (RD)**: The metric as calculated on a neighboring router and then reported and learned in an EIGRP Update

For example, in Figure 10-2, Albuquerque calculates an FD of 2,172,416 to reach subnet 10.1.3.0/24 through Seville. Seville also calculates its own metric to reach subnet 10.1.3.0/24. Seville also lists that metric in its EIGRP update sent to Albuquerque. In fact, based on the information in Figure 10-2, Seville's FD to reach subnet 10.1.3.0/24, which is then known by Albuquerque as Seville's RD to reach 10.1.3.0/24, could be easily calculated:

$$\left(\left(\frac{10^7}{100{,}000}\right) + (10)\right) * 256 = 28{,}160$$

FD and RD are mentioned in an upcoming discussion of how EIGRP reacts and converges when a change occurs in an internetwork.

Caveats with Bandwidth on Serial Links

EIGRP's robust metric gives it the ability to choose routes that include more router hops but with faster links. However, to ensure that the right routes are chosen, engineers must take care to configure meaningful bandwidth and delay settings. In particular, serial links default to a bandwidth of 1544 and a delay of 20,000 microseconds, as used in the example shown in Figure 10-2. However, IOS cannot automatically change the bandwidth and delay settings based on the Layer 1 speed of a serial link. So, using default bandwidth settings on serial links can lead to problems.

Figure 10-3 shows the problem with using default bandwidth settings and how EIGRP uses the better (faster) route when the bandwidth is set correctly. The figure focuses on router B's route to subnet 10.1.1.0/24 in each case. In the top part of the figure, all serial interfaces use defaults, even though the top serial link is a slow 64 kbps. The bottom figure shows the results when the slow serial link's **bandwidth** command is changed to reflect the correct (slow) speed.

Figure 10-3   *Impact of the Bandwidth on EIGRP's Metric Calculation*

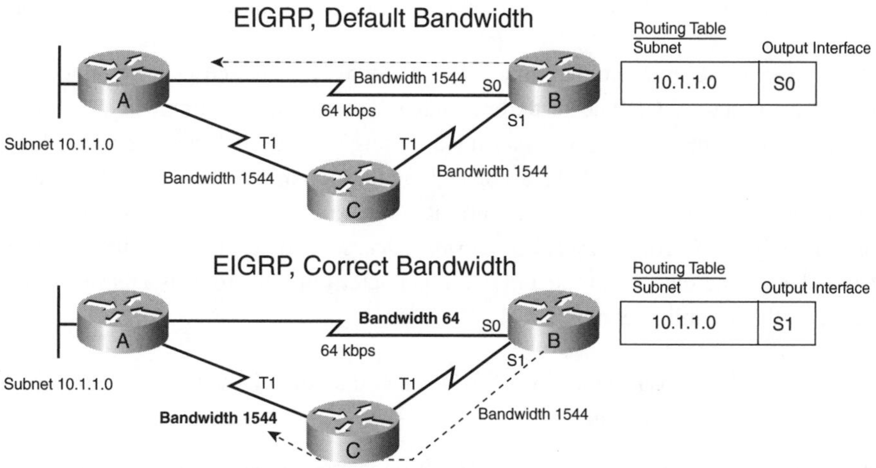

EIGRP Convergence

Loop avoidance poses one of the most difficult problems with any dynamic routing protocol. Distance vector protocols overcome this problem with a variety of tools, some of which create a large portion of the minutes-long convergence time after a link failure. Link-state protocols overcome this problem by having each router keep a full topology of the network, so by running a rather involved mathematical model, a router can avoid any loops.

EIGRP avoids loops by keeping some basic topological information, but it avoids spending too much CPU and memory by keeping the information brief. When a router learns multiple routes to the same subnet, it puts the best route in the IP routing table. EIGRP keeps some topological information for the same reason as OSPF—so that it can very quickly converge and use a new route without causing a loop. Essentially, EIGRP keeps a record of each possible next-hop router, and some details related to those routes, but no information about the topology beyond the next-hop routers. This sparser topology information does not require the sophisticated SPF algorithm, resulting in quick convergence and less overhead, with no loops.

The EIGRP convergence process uses one of two branches in its logic, based on whether the failed route does or does not have a *feasible successor* route. If a feasible successor route exists, the router can immediately use that route. If not, the router must use a *query and response* process to find a loop-free alternative route. Both processes result in fast convergence, typically quicker than 10 seconds, but the query and response process takes slightly longer.

EIGRP Successors and Feasible Successors

EIGRP calculates the metric for each route to reach each subnet. For a particular subnet, the route with the best metric is called the successor, with the router filling the IP routing table with this route. (This route's metric is called the feasible distance, as introduced earlier.)

Of the other routes to reach that same subnet—routes whose metrics were larger than the FD for the route—EIGRP needs to determine which can be used immediately if the currently best route fails, without causing a routing loop. EIGRP runs a simple algorithm to identify which routes could be used, keeping these loop-free backup routes in its topology table and using them if the currently best route fails. These alternative, immediately usable routes are called *feasible successor* routes, because they can feasibly be used when the successor route fails. A router determines if a route is a feasible successor based on the feasibility condition:

> If a nonsuccessor route's RD is less than the FD, the route is a feasible successor route.

Although it is technically correct, this definition is much more understandable with the example shown in Figure 10-4. The figure illustrates how EIGRP figures out which routes are feasible successors for subnet 1. In the figure, Router E learns three routes to Subnet 1, from Routers B, C, and D. After calculating each route's metric, based on bandwidth and delay information received in the routing update and on E's corresponding outgoing interfaces, Router E finds that the route through Router D has the lowest metric, so Router E adds that route to its routing table, as shown. The FD is the metric calculated for this route, a value of 14,000 in this case.

Figure 10-4 *Successors and Feasible Successors with EIGRP*

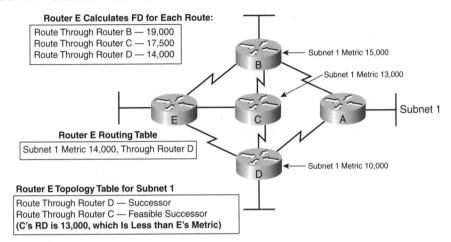

EIGRP decides if a route can be a feasible successor if the reported distance for that route (the metric as calculated on that neighbor) is less than its own best computed metric (the FD). When that neighbor has a lower metric for its route to the subnet in question, that route is said to have met the *feasibility condition*. For example, Router E computes a metric (FD) of 14,000 on its best route (through Router D). Router C's computed metric—its reported distance for this route—is lower than 14,000 (it's 13,000). As a result, E knows that C's best route for this subnet could not possibly point toward router E, so Router E believes that it could start using the route through Router C and not cause a loop. As a result, Router E adds a route through Router C to the topology table as a feasible successor route. Conversely, Router B's reported distance is 15,000, which is larger than Router E's FD of 14,000, so Router E does not consider the route through Router B a feasible successor.

If the route to Subnet 1 through Router D fails, Router E can immediately put the route through Router C into the routing table without fear of creating a loop. Convergence occurs almost instantly in this case.

The Query and Reply Process

When a route fails and has no feasible successor, EIGRP uses a distributed algorithm called *Diffusing Update Algorithm (DUAL)*. DUAL sends queries looking for a loop-free route to the subnet in question. When the new route is found, DUAL adds it to the routing table.

The EIGRP DUAL process simply uses messages to confirm that a route exists, and would not create a loop, before deciding to replace a failed route with an alternative route. For instance, in Figure 10-4, imagine that both Routers C and D fail. Router E does not have a feasible successor route for subnet 1, but there is an obvious physically available path through Router B. To use the route, Router E sends EIGRP *query* messages to its working neighbors (in this case, Router B). Router B's route to subnet 1 is still working fine, so Router B replies to Router E with an EIGRP *reply* message, simply stating the details of the working route to subnet 1 and confirming that it is still viable. Router E can then add a new route to subnet 1 to its routing table, without fear of a loop.

Replacing a failed route with a feasible successor takes a very short amount of time, typically less than a second or two. When queries and replies are required, convergence can take slightly longer, but in most networks, convergence can still occur in less than 10 seconds.

EIGRP Summary and Comparisons with OSPF

EIGRP is a popular IGP for many reasons. It works well, converging quickly while avoiding loops as a side effect of its underlying balanced hybrid/advanced distance vector algorithms. It does not require a lot of configuration or a lot of planning, even when scaling to support larger internetworks.

EIGRP also has another advantage that is not as important today as in years past: the support of Novell's IPX and Apple's AppleTalk Layer 3 protocols. Routers can run EIGRP to learn IP routes, IPX routes, and AppleTalk routes, with the same wonderful performance features. However, like many other Layer 3 protocols, IP has mostly usurped IPX and AppleTalk, making support for these Layer 3 protocols a minor advantage.

Table 10-2 summarizes several important features of EIGRP as compared to OSPF.

Table 10-2   *EIGRP Features Compared to OSPF*

Feature	EIGRP	OSPF
Converges quickly	Yes	Yes
Built-in loop prevention	Yes	Yes
Sends partial routing updates, advertising only new or changed information	Yes	Yes
Classless; therefore, supports manual summarization and VLSM	Yes	Yes
Allows manual summarization at any router	Yes	No
Sends routing information using IP multicast on LANs	Yes	Yes

Table 10-2 *EIGRP Features Compared to OSPF (Continued)*

Feature	EIGRP	OSPF
Uses the concept of a designated router on a LAN	No	Yes
Flexible network design with no need to create areas	Yes	No
Supports both equal-metric and unequal-metric load balancing	Yes	No
Robust metric based on bandwidth and delay	Yes	No
Can advertise IP, IPX, and AppleTalk routes	Yes	No
Public standard	No	Yes

EIGRP Configuration and Verification

Basic EIGRP configuration closely resembles RIP and OSPF configuration. The **router eigrp** command enables EIGRP and puts the user in EIGRP configuration mode, in which one or more **network** commands are configured. For each interface matched by a **network** command, EIGRP tries to discover neighbors on that interface, and EIGRP advertises the subnet connected to the interface.

This section examines EIGRP configuration, including several optional features. It also explains the meaning of the output of many **show** commands to help connect the theory covered in the first part of this chapter with the reality of the EIGRP implementation in IOS. The following configuration checklist outlines the main configuration tasks covered in this chapter:

Step 1 Enter EIGRP configuration mode, and define the EIGRP ASN by using the **router eigrp** *as-number* global command.

Step 2 Configure one or more **network** *ip-address* [*wildcard-mask*] router subcommands. This enables EIGRP on any matched interface and causes EIGRP to advertise the connected subnet.

Step 3 (Optional) Change the interface Hello and hold timers using the **ip hello-interval eigrp** *asn time* and **ip hold-time eigrp** *asn time* interface subcommands.

Step 4 (Optional) Impact metric calculations by tuning bandwidth and delay using the **bandwidth** *value* and **delay** *value* interface subcommands.

Step 5 (Optional) Configure EIGRP authentication.

Step 6   (Optional) Configure support for multiple equal-cost routes using the
maximum-paths *number* and **variance** *multiplier* router subcommands.

Basic EIGRP Configuration

Example 10-1 shows a sample EIGRP configuration, along with **show** commands, on
Albuquerque in Figure 10-5. The EIGRP configuration required on Yosemite and Seville
matches exactly the two lines of EIGRP configuration on Albuquerque.

Figure 10-5   *Sample Internetwork Used in Most of the EIGRP Examples*

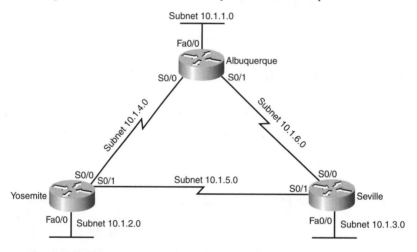

Example 10-1   *Sample Router Configuration with EIGRP Enabled*

```
router eigrp 1
 network 10.0.0.0
Albuquerque#show ip route
Codes: C - connected, S - static, I - IGRP, R - RIP, M - mobile, B - BGP
       D - EIGRP, EX - EIGRP external, O - OSPF, IA - OSPF inter area
       N1 - OSPF NSSA external type 1, N2 - OSPF NSSA external type 2
       E1 - OSPF external type 1, E2 - OSPF external type 2, E - EGP
       i - IS-IS, L1 - IS-IS level-1, L2 - IS-IS level-2, ia - IS-IS inter area
       * - candidate default, U - per-user static route, o - ODR
       P - periodic downloaded static route

Gateway of last resort is not set

     10.0.0.0/24 is subnetted, 6 subnets
D       10.1.3.0 [90/2172416] via 10.1.6.3, 00:00:43, Serial0/1
D       10.1.2.0 [90/2172416] via 10.1.4.2, 00:00:43, Serial0/0
C       10.1.1.0 is directly connected, FastEthernet0/0
C       10.1.6.0 is directly connected, Serial0/1
```

Example 10-1   *Sample Router Configuration with EIGRP Enabled (Continued)*

```
D        10.1.5.0 [90/2681856] via 10.1.6.3, 00:00:45, Serial0/1
                  [90/2681856] via 10.1.4.2, 00:00:45, Serial0/0
C        10.1.4.0 is directly connected, Serial0/0

Albuquerque#show ip route eigrp
     10.0.0.0/24 is subnetted, 6 subnets
D        10.1.3.0 [90/2172416] via 10.1.6.3, 00:00:47, Serial0/1
D        10.1.2.0 [90/2172416] via 10.1.4.2, 00:00:47, Serial0/0
D        10.1.5.0 [90/2681856] via 10.1.6.3, 00:00:49, Serial0/1
                  [90/2681856] via 10.1.4.2, 00:00:49, Serial0/0

Albuquerque#show ip eigrp neighbors
IP-EIGRP neighbors for process 1
H    Address                  Interface    Hold Uptime   SRTT   RTO  Q  Seq Type
                                           (sec)         (ms)        Cnt Num
0    10.1.4.2                 Se0/0         11 00:00:54    32   200  0  4
1    10.1.6.3                 Se0/1         12 00:10:36    20   200  0  24

Albuquerque#show ip eigrp interfaces
IP-EIGRP interfaces for process 1

                  Xmit Queue    Mean   Pacing Time   Multicast    Pending
Interface   Peers Un/Reliable   SRTT   Un/Reliable   Flow Timer   Routes
Fa0/0       0      0/0           0       0/10          0            0
Se0/0       1      0/0           32      0/15          50           0
Se0/1       1      0/0           20      0/15          95           0
Albuquerque#show ip eigrp topology summary
IP-EIGRP Topology Table for AS(1)/ID(10.1.6.1)
Head serial 1, next serial 9
6 routes, 0 pending replies, 0 dummies
IP-EIGRP(0) enabled on 3 interfaces, 2 neighbors present on 2 interfaces
Quiescent interfaces:  Se0/1/0 Se0/0/1
```

For EIGRP configuration, all three routers must use the same AS number in the **router eigrp** command. For instance, they all use **router eigrp 1** in this example. The actual number used doesn't really matter, as long as it is the same on all three routers. (The range of valid AS numbers is 1 through 65,535, as is the range of valid Process IDs with the **router ospf** command.) The **network 10.0.0.0** command enables EIGRP on all interfaces whose IP addresses are in network 10.0.0.0, which includes all three interfaces on Albuquerque. With the identical two EIGRP configuration statements on the other two routers, EIGRP is enabled on all three interfaces on those routers as well, because those interfaces are also in network 10.0.0.0.

The **show ip route** and **show ip route eigrp** commands both list the EIGRP-learned routes with a "D" beside them. "D" signifies EIGRP. The letter E was already being used for Exterior Gateway Protocol (EGP) when Cisco created EIGRP, so Cisco chose the next-closest unused letter, D, to denote EIGRP-learned routes.

You can see information about EIGRP neighbors with the **show ip eigrp neighbors** command and information about the number of active neighbors (called peers in the command output) with the **show ip eigrp interfaces** command, as shown in the last part of the example. These commands also provide some insight into EIGRP's underlying processes, such as the use of RTP for reliable transmission. For instance, the **show ip eigrp neighbors** command shows a "Q Cnt" (Queue Count) column, listing either the number of packets waiting to be sent to a neighbor or packets that have been sent but for which no acknowledgment has been received. The **show ip eigrp interfaces** command lists similar information in the "Xmit Queue Un/Reliable" column, which separates statistics for EIGRP messages that are sent with RTP (reliable) or without it (unreliable).

Finally, the end of the example displays Albuquerque's RID. EIGRP allocates its RID just like OSPF—based on the configured value, or the highest IP address of an up/up loopback interface, or the highest IP address of a nonloopback interface, in that order of precedence. The only difference compared to OSPF is that the EIGRP RID is configured with the **eigrp router-id** *value* router subcommand.

The EIGRP **network** command can be configured without a wildcard mask, as shown in Example 10-1. Without a wildcard mask, the **network** command must use a classful network as the lone parameter, and all interfaces in the classful network are matched. Example 10-2 shows an alternative configuration that uses a **network** command with an address and wildcard mask. In this case, the command matches an interface IP address that would be matched if the address and mask in the **network** command were part of an ACL. The example shows three **network** commands on Albuquerque, one matching each of the three interfaces.

Example 10-2 *Using Wildcard Masks with EIGRP Configuration*

```
Albuquerque#router eigrp 1
Albuquerque(config-router)#network 10.1.1.0 0.0.0.255
Albuquerque(config-router)#network 10.1.4.0 0.0.0.255
Albuquerque(config-router)#network 10.1.6.0 0.0.0.255
```

EIGRP Metrics, Successors, and Feasible Successors

As defined earlier in this chapter, an EIGRP successor route is a route that has the best metric for reaching a subnet, and a Feasible Successor (FS) route is a route that could be used if the successor route failed. This section examines how to see successor and FS routes with EIGRP, along with the calculated metrics. To that end, Example 10-3 shows Albuquerque's single best route to reach subnet 10.1.3.0/24, both in the routing table and as the successor route in the EIGRP topology table. It also lists the two equal-metric successor routes for subnet 10.1.5.0/24, with both of these successor routes being highlighted in the EIGRP topology table. Some of the explanations are listed in the example, and the longer explanations follow the example.

Example 10-3 *Using Wildcard Masks with EIGRP Configuration, and Feasible Successor Examination*

```
! Below, note the single route to subnet 10.1.3.0, and the two
! equal-metric routes to 10.1.5.0.
Albuquerque#show ip route
Codes: C - connected, S - static, R - RIP, M - mobile, B - BGP
       D - EIGRP, EX - EIGRP external, O - OSPF, IA - OSPF inter area
       N1 - OSPF NSSA external type 1, N2 - OSPF NSSA external type 2
       E1 - OSPF external type 1, E2 - OSPF external type 2
       i - IS-IS, L1 - IS-IS level-1, L2 - IS-IS level-2, ia - IS-IS inter area
       * - candidate default, U - per-user static route, o - ODR
       P - periodic downloaded static route


Gateway of last resort is not set


     10.0.0.0/24 is subnetted, 6 subnets
D       10.1.3.0 [90/2172416] via 10.1.6.3, 00:00:57, Serial0/1
D       10.1.2.0 [90/2172416] via 10.1.4.2, 00:00:57, Serial0/0
C       10.1.1.0 is directly connected, Ethernet0/0
C       10.1.6.0 is directly connected, Serial0/1
D       10.1.5.0 [90/2681856] via 10.1.4.2, 00:00:57, Serial0/0
                 [90/2681856] via 10.1.6.3, 00:00:57, Serial0/1
C       10.1.4.0 is directly connected, Serial0/0
! Next, the EIGRP topology table shows one successor for the route to 10.1.3.0,
! and two successors for 10.1.5.0, reconfirming that EIGRP installs successor
! routes (not feasible successor routes) into the IP routing table.
Albuquerque#show ip eigrp topology
IP-EIGRP Topology Table for AS(1)/ID(10.1.6.1)


Codes: P - Passive, A - Active, U - Update, Q - Query, R - Reply,
       r - reply Status, s - sia Status


P 10.1.3.0/24, 1 successors, FD is 2172416
         via 10.1.6.3 (2172416/28160), Serial0/1
P 10.1.2.0/24, 1 successors, FD is 2172416
         via 10.1.4.2 (2172416/28160), Serial0/0
P 10.1.1.0/24, 1 successors, FD is 281600
         via Connected, Ethernet0/0
P 10.1.6.0/24, 1 successors, FD is 2169856
         via Connected, Serial0/1
```

continues

Example 10-3 *Using Wildcard Masks with EIGRP Configuration, and Feasible Successor Examination (Continued)*

```
P 10.1.5.0/24, 2 successors, FD is 2681856
        via 10.1.4.2 (2681856/2169856), Serial0/0
        via 10.1.6.3 (2681856/2169856), Serial0/1
P 10.1.4.0/24, 1 successors, FD is 2169856
        via Connected, Serial0/0
```

The comments in the example explain the main key points, most of which are relatively straightforward. However, a closer look at the **show ip eigrp topology** command can provide a few insights. First, focus on the EIGRP topology table's listing of the number of successor routes. The entry for 10.1.3.0/24 states that there is one successor, so the IP routing table lists one EIGRP-learned route for subnet 10.1.3.0/24. In comparison, the EIGRP topology table entry for subnet 10.1.5.0/24 states that two successors exist, so the IP routing table shows two EIGRP-learned routes for that subnet.

Next, focus on the numbers in brackets for the EIGRP topology table entry for 10.1.3.0/24. The first number is the metric calculated by Albuquerque for each route. The second number is the RD—the metric as calculated on neighboring router 10.1.6.3 (Seville) and as reported to Albuquerque. Because these routers have defaulted all bandwidth and delay settings, the metric values match the sample metric calculations shown in the earlier section "Calculating the Best Routes for the Routing Table."

Creating and Viewing a Feasible Successor Route

With all default settings in this internetwork, none of Albuquerque's routes meet the feasibility condition, in which an alternative route's RD is less than the FD (the metric of the best route). Example 10-4 changes the bandwidth on one of Yosemite's interfaces, lowering Yosemite's FD to reach subnet 10.1.3.0/24. In turn, Yosemite's RD for this same route, as reported to Albuquerque, will now be lower, meeting the feasibility condition, so Albuquerque will now have an FS route.

Example 10-4 *Creating a Feasible Successor Route on Albuquerque*

```
! Below, the bandwidth of Yosemite's link to Seville (Yosemite's S0/1 interface)
! is changed from 1544 to 2000, which lowers Yosemite's metric for
! subnet 10.1.3.0.
Yosemite(config)#interface S0/1
Yosemite(config-if)#bandwidth 2000
! Moving back to Albuquerque
! Below, the EIGRP topology table shows a single successor route for 10.1.3.0,
! but two entries listed - the new entry is a feasible successor route. The new
! entry shows a route to 10.1.3.0 through 10.1.4.2 (which is Yosemite).
Albuquerque#show ip eigrp topology
IP-EIGRP Topology Table for AS(1)/ID(10.1.6.1)
```

Example 10-4 *Creating a Feasible Successor Route on Albuquerque (Continued)*

```
Codes: P - Passive, A - Active, U - Update, Q - Query, R - Reply,
       r - reply Status, s - sia Status

P 10.1.3.0/24, 1 successors, FD is 2172416
         via 10.1.6.3 (2172416/28160), Serial0/1
         via 10.1.4.2 (2684416/1794560), Serial0/0
! the rest of the lines omitted for brevity
! Moving back to Yosemite here
Yosemite#show ip route eigrp
     10.0.0.0/24 is subnetted, 5 subnets
D       10.1.3.0 [90/1794560] via 10.1.5.3, 00:40:14, Serial0/1
D       10.1.1.0 [90/2195456] via 10.1.4.1, 00:42:19, Serial0/0
```

To see the feasible successor route, and why it is a feasible successor, look at the two numbers in parentheses in the second highlighted line from the **show ip eigrp topology** command on Albuquerque. The first of these is Albuquerque's router's calculated metric for the route, and the second number is the neighbor's RD. Of the two possible routes—one through 10.1.6.3 (Seville) and one through 10.1.4.2 (Yosemite)—the route through Seville has the lowest metric (2,172,416), making it the successor route, and making the FD also be 2,172,416. Albuquerque puts this route into the IP routing table. However, note the RD on the second of the two routes (the route through Yosemite), with an RD value of 1,794,560. The feasibility condition is that the route's RD must be smaller than that router's best calculated metric—its FD—for that same destination subnet. So, the route through Yosemite meets this condition, making it a feasible successor route. The following points summarize the key information about the successor and feasible successor routes in this example:

■   The route to 10.1.3.0 through 10.1.6.3 (Seville) is the successor route, because the calculated metric (2,172,416), shown as the first of the two numbers in parentheses, is the best calculated metric.

■   The route to 10.1.3.0 through 10.1.4.2 (Yosemite) is a feasible successor route, because the neighbor's Reported Distance (1,794,560, shown as the second number in parentheses) is lower than Albuquerque's FD.

■   Although both the successor and feasible successor routes are in the EIGRP topology table, only the successor route is added to the IP routing table.

NOTE   The **show ip eigrp topology** command lists only successor and feasible successor routes. To see other routes, use the **show ip eigrp topology all-links** command.

Convergence Using the Feasible Successor Route

One of the advantages of EIGRP is that it converges very quickly. Example 10-5 shows one such example, using **debug** messages to show the process. Some of the **debug** messages may not make a lot of sense, but the example does highlight a few interesting and understandable **debug** messages.

For this example, the link between Albuquerque and Seville is shut down, but this is not shown in the example. The **debug** messages on Albuquerque show commentary about EIGRP's logic in changing from the original route for 10.1.3.0/24 to the new route through Yosemite. Pay particular attention to the time stamps, which show that the convergence process takes less than 1 second.

Example 10-5 *Debug Messages During Convergence to the Feasible Successor Route for Subnet 10.1.3.0/24*

```
!!!!!!!!!!!!!!!!!!!!!!!!!!!!!!!!!!!!!!!!!!!!!!!!!!!!!!!!!!!!!!!!!!!!!!!!!!!!!!!!
! Below, debug eigrp fsm is enabled, and then Seville's link to Albuquerque
! (Seville's S0/0 interface) will be disabled, but not shown in the example text.
! SOME DEBUG MESSAGES are omitted to improve readability.
Albuquerque#debug eigrp fsm
EIGRP FSM Events/Actions debugging is on
Albuquerque#
*Mar  1 02:35:31.836: %LINK-3-UPDOWN: Interface Serial0/1, changed state to down
*Mar  1 02:35:31.848: DUAL: rcvupdate: 10.1.6.0/24 via Connected metric 42949672
95/4294967295
*Mar  1 02:35:31.848: DUAL: Find FS for dest 10.1.6.0/24. FD is 2169856, RD is 2
169856
*Mar  1 02:35:31.848: DUAL: 0.0.0.0 metric 4294967295/4294967295 not found D
min is 4294967295
*Mar  1 02:35:31.848: DUAL: Peer total/stub 2/0 template/full-stub 2/0
*Mar  1 02:35:31.848: DUAL: Dest 10.1.6.0/24 entering active state.
*Mar  1 02:35:31.852: DUAL: Set reply-status table. Count is 2.
*Mar  1 02:35:31.852: DUAL: Not doing split horizon
!
! Next, Albuquerque realizes that neighbor 10.1.6.3 (Seville) is down, so
! Albuquerque can react.
!
*Mar  1 02:35:31.852: %DUAL-5-NBRCHANGE: IP-EIGRP(0) 1: Neighbor 10.1.6.3
  (Serial0/1) is down: interface down
!
! The next two highlighted messages imply that the old route to 10.1.3.0 is
! removed, and the new successor route (previously the feasible successor route)
! is added to the "RT" (routing table).
!
*Mar  1 02:35:31.852: DUAL: Destination 10.1.3.0/24
*Mar  1 02:35:31.852: DUAL: Find FS for dest 10.1.3.0/24. FD is 2172416,
  RD is 2172416
```

Example 10-5 *Debug Messages During Convergence to the Feasible Successor Route for Subnet 10.1.3.0/24 (Continued)*

```
*Mar  1 02:35:31.856: DUAL: 10.1.6.3 metric 4294967295/4294967295
*Mar  1 02:35:31.856: DUAL: 10.1.4.2 metric 2684416/1794560 found Dmin is 2684416
!
! The next two highlighted messages state that the old route is removed, and the
! new route through Yosemite is added to the "RT" (routing table).
!
*Mar  1 02:35:31.856: DUAL: Removing dest 10.1.3.0/24, nexthop 10.1.6.3
*Mar  1 02:35:31.856: DUAL: RT installed 10.1.3.0/24 via 10.1.4.2
*Mar  1 02:35:31.856: DUAL: Send update about 10.1.3.0/24.  Reason: metric chg
*Mar  1 02:35:31.860: DUAL: Send update about 10.1.3.0/24.  Reason: new if
```

EIGRP Authentication

EIGRP supports one type of authentication: MD5. Configuring MD5 authentication requires several steps:

Step 1 Create an (authentication) key chain:

    a. Create the chain and give it a name with the **key chain** *name* global command (this also puts the user into key chain config mode).

    b. Create one or more key numbers using the **key** *number* command in key chain configuration mode.

    c. Define the authentication key's value using the **key-string** *value* command in key configuration mode.

    d. (Optional) Define the lifetime (time period) for both sending and accepting this particular key.

Step 2 Enable EIGRP MD5 authentication on an interface, for a particular EIGRP ASN, using the **ip authentication mode eigrp** *asn* **md5** interface subcommand.

Step 3 Refer to the correct key chain to be used on an interface using the **ip authentication key-chain eigrp** *asn name-of-chain* interface subcommand.

The configuration in Step 1 is fairly detailed, but Steps 2 and 3 are relatively simple. Essentially, IOS configures the key values separately, then requires an interface subcommand to refer to the key values. To support the ability to have multiple keys, and even multiple sets of keys, the configuration includes the concept of a key chain and multiple keys on each key chain.

The IOS key chain concept resembles key chains and keys used in everyday life. Most people have at least one key chain, with the keys they typically use every day. If you have a lot of keys for work and home, you might have two key chains to make it a little easier to find the right key. You might even have a key chain with seldom-used keys that you keep on a shelf somewhere. Similarly, IOS allows lets you configure multiple key chains so that different key chains can be used on different interfaces. Each key chain can include multiple keys. Having multiple keys in one key chain allows neighbors to still be up and working while the keys are being changed. (As with all passwords and authentication keys, changing the keys occasionally enhances security.) To configure these main details, follow Steps 1A, 1B, and 1C to create the key chain, create one or more keys, and assign the text key (password).

The last and optional item that can be configured for EIGRP authentication is the useful lifetime of each key. If this isn't configured, the key is valid forever. However, if it is configured, the router uses the key only during the listed times. This feature allows the key chain to include several keys, each with different successive lifetimes. For example, 12 keys could be defined, one for each month of the year. The routers then automatically use the lowest-numbered key whose time range is valid, changing keys automatically every month in this example. This feature allows an engineer to configure the keys once and have the routers use new keys occasionally, improving security.

To support the useful lifetime concept, a router must know the time and date. Routers can set the time and date with the **clock set** EXEC command. Routers can also use Network Time Protocol (NTP), a protocol that allows routers to synchronize their time-of-day clocks.

The best way to appreciate the configuration is to see an example. Example 10-6 shows a sample configuration that uses two key chains. Key chain "carkeys" has two keys, each with different lifetimes, so that the router will use new keys automatically over time. It also shows the two key chains being referenced on two different interfaces.

Example 10-6 *EIGRP Authentication*

```
! Chain "carkeys" will be used on R1's Fa0/0 interface. R1 will use key "fred"
! for about a month and then start using "wilma."
!
key chain carkeys
  key 1
  key-string fred
  accept-lifetime 08:00:00 Jan 11 2005 08:00:00 Feb 11 2005
  send-lifetime 08:00:00 Jan 11 2005 08:00:00 Feb 11 2005
 key 2
  key-string wilma
  accept-lifetime 08:00:00 Feb 10 2005 08:00:00 Mar 11 2005
  send-lifetime 08:00:00 Feb 10 2005 08:00:00 Mar 11 2005
```

Example 10-6 *EIGRP Authentication (Continued)*

```
! Next, key chain "anothersetofkeys" defines the key to be used on
! interface Fa0/1.
key chain anothersetofkeys
 key 1
 key-string barney
!
! Next, R1's interface subcommands are shown. First, the key chain is referenced
! using the ip authentication key-chain command, and the ip authentication mode eigrp
! command causes the router to use an MD5 digest of the key string.
interface FastEthernet0/0
 ip address 172.31.11.1 255.255.255.0
 ip authentication mode eigrp 1 md5
 ip authentication key-chain eigrp 1 carkeys
!
! Below, R1 enables EIGRP authentication on interface Fa0/1,
! using the other key chain.
interface FastEthernet0/1
 ip address 172.31.12.1 255.255.255.0
 ip authentication mode eigrp 1 md5
 ip authentication key-chain eigrp 1 anothersetofkeys
```

For authentication to work, neighboring routers must both have EIGRP MD5 authentication enabled, and the key strings they currently use must match. Note that the key chain name does not need to match. The most common problems relate to when the useful lifetime settings do not match, or one of the router's clocks has the wrong time. For real-life implementations, NTP should be enabled and used before restricting keys to a particular time frame.

To verify that the authentication worked, use the **show ip eigrp neighbors** command. If the authentication fails, the neighbor relationship will not form. Also, if you see routes learned from a neighbor on that interface, it also proves that authentication worked. You can see more details about the authentication process using the **debug eigrp packets** command, particularly if the authentication fails.

EIGRP Maximum Paths and Variance

Like OSPF, EIGRP supports the ability to put multiple equal-metric routes in the routing table. Like OSPF, EIGRP defaults to support four such routes for each subnet, and it can be configured to support up to 16 using the **maximum-paths** *number* EIGRP subcommand. However, EIGRP's metric calculation often prevents competing routes from having the exact same metric. The formula may result in similar metrics, but given that the metric values can easily be in the millions, calculating the exact same metric is statistically unlikely.

IOS includes the concept of EIGRP variance to overcome this problem. Variance allows routes whose metrics are relatively close in value to be considered equal, allowing multiple unequal-metric routes to the same subnet to be added to the routing table.

The **variance** *multiplier* EIGRP router subcommand defines an integer between 1 and 128. The router then multiplies the variance times a route's FD—the best metric with which to reach that subnet. Any FS routes whose metric is less than the product of the variance times the FD are considered to be equal routes and may be placed in the routing table, depending on the setting of the **maximum-paths** command.

An example of variance can make this concept clear. To keep the numbers more obvious, Table 10-3 lists an example with small metric values. The table lists the metric for three routes to the same subnet, as calculated on router R4. The table also lists the neighboring routers' RD, and the decision to add routes to the routing table based on various variance settings.

Table 10-3 *Example of Routes Chosen as Equal Because of Variance*

Next Hop	Metric	RD	Added to RT at Variance 1?	Added to RT at Variance 2?	Added to RT at Variance 3?
R1	50	30	Yes	Yes	Yes
R2	90	40	No	Yes	Yes
R3	120	60	No	No	No

Before considering the variance, note that in this case, the route through R1 is the successor route because it has the lowest metric. This also means that the metric for the route through R1, 50, is the FD. The route through R2 is an FS route because its RD of 40 is less than the FD of 50. The route through R3 is not an FS route, because R3's RD of 60 is more than the FD of 50.

At a default variance setting of 1, the metrics must be exactly equal to be considered equal, so only the successor route is added to the routing table. With variance 2, the FD (50) is multiplied by the variance (2) for a product of 100. The route through R2, with FD 90, is less than 100, so R4 adds the route through R2 to the routing table as well. The router can then load-balance traffic across these two routes.

In the third case, with variance 3, the product of the FD (50) times 3 results in a product of 150, and all three routes' calculated metrics are less than 150. However, the route through R3 is not an FS route, so it cannot be added to the routing table for fear of causing a routing loop.

The following list summarizes the key points about variance:

- The variance is multiplied by the current FD (the metric of the best route to reach the subnet).

- Any FS routes whose calculated metric is less than or equal to the product of variance times the FD are added to the IP routing table, assuming that the **maximum-paths** setting allows more routes.

- Routes that are neither successor nor feasible successor can never be added to the IP routing table, regardless of the variance setting.

As soon as the routes have been added to the routing table, the router supports a variety of options for how to load-balance traffic across the routes. The router can balance the traffic proportionally with the metrics, meaning that lower metric routes send more packets. The router can send all traffic over the lowest-metric route, with the other routes just being in the routing table for faster convergence in case the best route fails. However, the details of the load-balancing process require a much deeper discussion of the internals of the forwarding process in IOS, and this topic is outside the scope of this book.

Tuning the EIGRP Metric Calculation

By default, EIGRP calculates an integer metric based on the composite metric of bandwidth and delay. Both settings can be changed on any interface using the **bandwidth** *value* and the **delay** *value* interface subcommands.

Cisco recommends setting each interface's bandwidth to an accurate value, rather than setting the bandwidth to change EIGRP's metric calculation. Although LAN interfaces default to accurate bandwidth settings, router serial links should be configured with the **bandwidth** *speed* command, with a speed value in kbps, matching the interface's actual speed.

Because fewer features rely on the interface delay setting, Cisco recommends that if you want to tune EIGRP metric, change the interface delay settings. To change an interface's delay setting, use the **delay** *value* command, where the value is the delay setting with an unusual unit: tens-of-microseconds. Interestingly, the EIGRP metric formula also uses the unit of tens-of-microseconds; however, **show** commands list the delay with a unit of microseconds. Example 10-7 shows an example, with the following details:

1. The router's Fa0/0 has a default delay setting of 100 microseconds (usec).

2. The **delay 123** command is configured on the interface, meaning 123 tens-of-microseconds.

3. The **show interfaces fa0/0** command now lists a delay of 1230 microseconds.

Example 10-7 *Configuring Interface Delay*

```
Yosemite#show interfaces fa0/0
FastEthernet0/0 is up, line protocol is up
  Hardware is Gt96k FE, address is 0013.197b.5026 (bia 0013.197b.5026)
  Internet address is 10.1.2.252/24
  MTU 1500 bytes, BW 100000 Kbit, DLY 100 usec,
! lines omitted for brevity


Yosemite#configure terminal
Enter configuration commands, one per line.  End with CNTL/Z.
Yosemite(config)#interface fa0/0
Yosemite(config-if)#delay 123
Yosemite(config-if)#^Z


Yosemite#show interfaces fa0/0
FastEthernet0/0 is up, line protocol is up
  Hardware is Gt96k FE, address is 0013.197b.5026 (bia 0013.197b.5026)
  Internet address is 10.1.2.252/24
  MTU 1500 bytes, BW 100000 Kbit, DLY 1230 usec,
! lines omitted for brevity
```

Exam Preparation Tasks

Review All the Key Topics

Review the most important topics from this chapter, noted with the key topics icon. Table 10-4 lists these key topics and where each is discussed.

Key
Topic

Table 10-4 *Key Topics for Chapter 10*

Key Topic Element	Description	Page Number
List	Reasons why EIGRP routers are prevented from becoming neighbors	381
Figure 10-1	Depicts the normal progression through neighbor discovery, full routing updates, ongoing Hellos, and partial updates	382
List	Definitions of Feasible Distance and Reported Distance	384
Figure 10-4	Example of how routers determine which routes are feasible successors	387
Table 10-2	Comparisons of EIGRP and OSPF features	388
List	EIGRP configuration checklist	389
List	Key points about how to determine a feasible successor route from **show** command output	395
List	EIGRP MD5 authentication configuration checklist	397
List	Key points about EIGRP variance	401

Complete the Tables and Lists from Memory

Print a copy of Appendix J, "Memory Tables" (found on the CD), or at least the section for this chapter, and complete the tables and lists from memory. Appendix K, "Memory Tables Answer Key," also on the CD, includes completed tables and lists for you to check your work.

Definitions of Key Terms

Define the following key terms from this chapter, and check your answers in the glossary:

> feasibility condition, feasible distance, feasible successor, full update, partial update, reported distance, successor

Command Reference to Check Your Memory

Although you should not necessarily memorize the information in the tables in this section, this section does include a reference for the configuration and EXEC commands covered in this chapter. Practically speaking, you should memorize the commands as a side effect of reading the chapter and doing all the activities in this exam preparation section. To see how well you have memorized the commands as a side effect of your other studies, cover the left side of the table, read the descriptions on the right side, and see if you remember the command.

Table 10-5 *Chapter 10 Configuration Command Reference*

Command	Description
router eigrp *autonomous-system*	Global command to move the user into EIGRP configuration mode for the listed ASN.
network *network-number* [*wildcard-mask*]	EIGRP router subcommand that matches either all interfaces in a classful network, or a subset of interfaces based on the ACL-style wildcard mask, enabling EIGRP on those interfaces.
maximum-paths *number-paths*	Router subcommand that defines the maximum number of equal-cost routes that can be added to the routing table.
variance *multiplier*	Router subcommand that defines an EIGRP multiplier used to determine if a feasible successor route's metric is close enough to the successor's metric to be considered equal.
bandwidth *bandwidth*	Interface subcommand directly sets the interface bandwidth (kbps).
delay *delay-value*	Interface subcommand to set the interface delay value, with a unit of tens-of-microseconds.
ip hello-interval eigrp *as-number timer-value*	Interface subcommand that sets the EIGRP Hello interval for that EIGRP process.
ip hold-time eigrp *as-number timer-value*	Interface subcommand that sets the EIGRP hold time for the interface.
maximum-paths *number-of-paths*	Router subcommand that defines the maximum number of equal-cost routes that can be added to the routing table.

Table 10-5 *Chapter 10 Configuration Command Reference (Continued)*

Command	Description
ip authentication key-chain eigrp *asn chain-name*	Interface subcommand that references the key chain used for MD5 authentication with EIGRP.
ip authentication mode eigrp *asn* **md5**	Interface subcommand that enables EIGRP MD5 authentication for all neighbors reached on the interface.
key chain *name*	Global command to create and name an authentication key chain.
key *integer-number*	Key chain mode command to create a new key number.
key-string *text*	Key chain mode command to create the authentication key's value.
accept-lifetime *start-time* {**infinite** | *end-time* | **duration** *seconds*}	Key chain mode command to set the time frame during which a router will accept the use of a particular key.
send-lifetime *start-time* {**infinite** | *end-time* | **duration** *seconds*}	Key chain mode command to set the time frame during which a router will send EIGRP messages using a particular key.

Table 10-6 *Chapter 10 EXEC Command Reference*

Command	Description
show ip route eigrp	Lists routes in the routing table learned by EIGRP.
show ip route *ip-address* [*mask*]	Shows the entire routing table, or a subset if parameters are entered.
show ip protocols	Shows routing protocol parameters and current timer values.
show ip eigrp neighbors	Lists EIGRP neighbors and status.
show ip eigrp topology	Lists the contents of the EIGRP topology table, including successors and feasible successors.
show ip eigrp traffic	Lists statistics on the number of EIGRP messages sent and received by a router.
debug eigrp packets	Displays the contents of EIGRP packets.
debug eigrp fsm	Displays changes to the EIGRP successor and feasible successor routes.
debug ip eigrp	Displays similar output to the **debug eigrp packets** command, but specifically for IP.

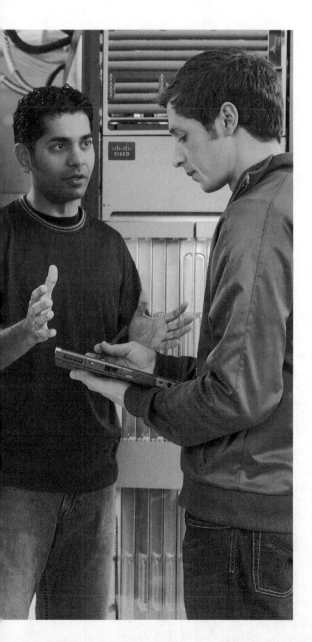

This chapter covers the following subjects:

Perspectives on Troubleshooting Routing Protocol Problems: This short introductory section explains the troubleshooting process this book suggests for routing protocol problems.

Interfaces Enabled with a Routing Protocol: This section shows how to determine the interfaces on which a router attempts to form neighbor relationships and whose connected subnets to advertise.

Neighbor Relationships: This section examines why routers may fail to become neighbors with routers they should become neighbors with.

CHAPTER 11

Troubleshooting Routing Protocols

Chapters 3 and 7, the other two chapters of this book that are dedicated to troubleshooting, focus on the process of forwarding data. In particular, Chapter 7, "Troubleshooting IP Routing," mostly ignores how routes are added to the routing table, focusing entirely on the data plane process of IP packet forwarding and how to troubleshoot that process. Chapter 7 assumes that the control plane processes related to filling the routing table will be covered elsewhere—mainly in Part III of this book.

This chapter wraps up the coverage of the IPv4 control plane—the process of filling routers' routing tables with good routes—by examining how to troubleshoot problems with OSPF and EIGRP. The troubleshooting process itself is relatively straightforward, at least to the depth required for the CCNA exams. However, as usual, you need to think about many different details while troubleshooting, so the process can help ensure that you verify each component before moving on to the next function.

This chapter concludes Part III of this book. If you are preparing specifically for the CCNA exam by using the reading plan mentioned in the Introduction, note that after this chapter, you should go back to *CCENT/CCNA ICND1 Official Exam Certification Guide*, Part IV.

"Do I Know This Already?" Quiz

The troubleshooting chapters of this book pull in concepts from many other chapters, including some chapters in *CCENT/CCNA ICND1 Official Exam Certification Guide*. They also show you how to approach some of the more challenging questions on the CCNA exams. Therefore, it is useful to read these chapters regardless of your current knowledge level. For these reasons, the troubleshooting chapters do not include a "Do I Know This Already?" quiz. However, if you feel particularly confident about troubleshooting OSPF and EIGRP, feel free to move to the "Exam Preparation Tasks" section near the end of this chapter to bypass the majority of the chapter.

Foundation Topics

The best first step when troubleshooting a routing protocol is to examine the configuration on the various routers. Comparing the routing protocol configuration, particularly the **network** subcommands, to the interface IP addresses can quickly confirm whether the routing protocol has been enabled on all the intended interfaces. If it is enabled on all the correct interfaces on all the routers, further examination of interface configuration and authentication configuration can verify whether some configuration settings might prevent two routers on the same subnet from becoming neighbors. A failure to pass all the requirements to become neighbors will prevent two routers from exchanging routing information.

Chapter 9, "OSPF," and Chapter 10, "EIGRP," cover routing protocol configuration in depth, so this chapter makes no attempt to explain how to troubleshoot a problem by looking for configuration mistakes. However, the configuration may not always be available for the exams or in real life. This chapter focuses on how to troubleshoot routing protocol problems using only **show** and **debug** commands. First, this chapter discusses some options for troubleshooting routing protocol problems, including a suggested process that has two major steps. The other two major sections of this chapter examine how to perform each of the major troubleshooting steps, for both EIGRP and OSPF.

Perspectives on Troubleshooting Routing Protocol Problems

Because a routing protocol's job is to fill a router's routing table with the currently best routes, it makes sense that troubleshooting potential problems with routing protocols could begin with the IP routing table. Given basic information about an internetwork, including the routers, their IP addresses and masks, and the routing protocol, you could calculate the subnet numbers that should be in the router's routing table and list the likely next-hop router(s) for each route. For example, Figure 11-1 shows an internetwork with six subnets. Router R1's routing table should list all six subnets, with three connected routes, two routes learned from R2 (172.16.4.0/24 and 172.16.5.0/24), and one route learned from R3 (172.16.6.0/24).

So, one possible troubleshooting process would be to analyze the internetwork, look at the routing table, and look for missing routes. If one or more expected routes are missing, the next step would be to determine if that router has learned any routes from the expected next-hop (neighbor) router. The next steps to isolate the problem differ greatly if a router is having problems forming a neighbor relationship with another router, versus having a working neighbor relationship but not being able to learn all routes.

Figure 11-1 *Internetwork with Six Subnets*

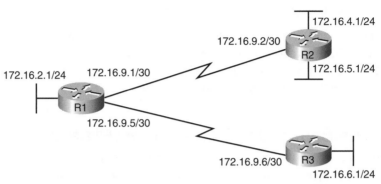

For example, imagine that R1 in Figure 11-1 has learned a route for subnet 172.16.4.0/24 in Figure 11-1 but not for subnet 172.16.5.0/24. In this case, it is clear that R1 has a working neighbor relationship with R2. In these cases, the root cause of this problem may still be related to the routing protocol, or it might be unrelated to the routing protocol. For example, the problem may be that R2's lower LAN interface is down. However, if R1 did not have a route for either 172.16.4.0/24 or 172.16.5.0/24, R1's neighbor relationship with R2 could be the problem.

Troubleshooting routing protocol problems in real internetworks can be very complex—much more complex than even the more difficult CCNA exam questions. Defining a generic troubleshooting process with which to attack both simple and complex routing protocol problems would require a lot of space, and be counter-productive for preparing for the CCNA exams. This chapter offers a straightforward process for attacking routing protocol problems—specifically, problems similar to the depth and complexity of the CCNA exams.

If an exam question appears to be related to a problem with a routing protocol, you can quickly identify some common configuration errors with the following process—even without the configuration or the ability to use the **show running-config** command. The process has three main branches:

Step 1 Examine the internetwork design to determine on which interfaces the routing protocol should be enabled and which routers are expected to become neighbors.

Step 2 Verify whether the routing protocol is enabled on each interface (as per Step 1). If it isn't, determine the root cause and fix the problem.

Step 3   Verify that each router has formed all expected neighbor relationships. If it hasn't, find the root cause and fix the problem.

At this point, having completed chapters 9 and 10, Step 1 should not require any further explanation. The two remaining major sections of this chapter examine Steps 2 and 3. By completing these steps and fixing any problems found throughout this process, you should have fixed the CCNA-level routing protocol problems.

Interfaces Enabled with a Routing Protocol

This section examines the second major troubleshooting step outlined in the previous section of the chapter: how to verify the interfaces on which the routing protocol has been enabled. Both EIGRP and OSPF configuration enables the routing protocol on an interface by using the **network** router subcommand. For any interfaces matched by the **network** commands, the routing protocol tries the following two actions:

- Attempt to find potential neighbors on the subnet connected to the interface

- Advertise the subnet connected to that interface

At the same time, the **passive-interface** router subcommand can be configured so that the router does not attempt to find neighbors on the interface (the first action just listed) but still advertises the connected subnet (the second action).

Three **show** commands are all that is needed to know exactly which interfaces have been enabled with EIGRP and OSPF and which interfaces are passive. In particular, the **show ip eigrp interfaces** command lists all EIGRP-enabled interfaces that are not passive interfaces. The **show ip protocols** command essentially lists the contents of the configured **network** commands for each routing protocol, as well as a separate list of the passive interfaces. Comparing these two commands identifies all EIGRP-enabled interfaces and those that are passive. For OSPF, the command works slightly differently, with the **show ip ospf interface brief** command listing all OSPF-enabled interfaces (including passive interfaces). Table 11-1 summarizes these commands for easier reference.

Table 11-1   *Key Commands to Find Routing Protocol Enabled Interfaces*

Command	Key Information
show ip eigrp interfaces	Lists the interfaces on which the routing protocol is enabled (based on the **network** commands), except passive interfaces.
show ip ospf interface brief	Lists the interfaces on which the OSPF is enabled (based on the **network** commands), including passive interfaces.
show ip protocols	Lists the contents of the **network** configuration commands for each routing process, and lists enabled but passive interfaces.

> **NOTE**   All the commands in Table 11-1 list the interfaces regardless of interface status, in effect telling you the results of the **network** and **passive-interface** configuration commands.

So, for the major troubleshooting step covered in this section, the task is to use the commands in Table 11-1 and analyze the output. First an EIGRP example will be shown, followed by an OSPF example.

EIGRP Interface Troubleshooting Example

This section shows a few examples of the commands in the context of Figure 11-2, which is used in all the examples in this chapter.

Figure 11-2   *Sample Internetwork for EIGRP/OSPF Troubleshooting Examples*

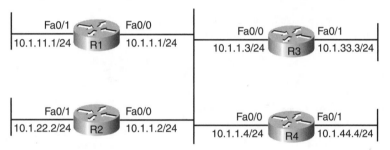

This example includes four routers, with the following scenario in this case:

- R1 and R2 are configured correctly on both LAN interfaces.

- R3 is mistakenly not enabled with EIGRP on its Fa0/1 interface.

- R4 meant to use a **passive-interface fa0/1** command, because no other routers are off R4's Fa0/1 LAN, but instead R4 has configured a **passive-interface fa0/0** command.

Example 11-1 begins by showing the pertinent commands, with an example on either R1 or on R2. It also shows the configuration on R1 for the sake of comparison.

Example 11-1   *EIGRP Problems with Interfaces*

```
R1#show running-config
! only pertinent lines shown
router eigrp 99
 network 10.0.0.0
!
R1>show ip eigrp interfaces
```

continues

Example 11-1   *EIGRP Problems with Interfaces (Continued)*

```
IP-EIGRP interfaces for process 99

                         Xmit Queue   Mean   Pacing Time   Multicast    Pending
Interface      Peers   Un/Reliable   SRTT   Un/Reliable   Flow Timer   Routes
Fa0/0            2        0/0        620       0/10          50           0
Fa0/1            0        0/0          0       0/10           0           0
R1>show ip protocols
Routing Protocol is "eigrp 99"
  Outgoing update filter list for all interfaces is not set
  Incoming update filter list for all interfaces is not set
  Default networks flagged in outgoing updates
  Default networks accepted from incoming updates
  EIGRP metric weight K1=1, K2=0, K3=1, K4=0, K5=0
  EIGRP maximum hopcount 100
  EIGRP maximum metric variance 1
  Redistributing: eigrp 99
  EIGRP NSF-aware route hold timer is 240s
  Automatic network summarization is in effect
  Maximum path: 4
  Routing for Networks:
    10.0.0.0
  Routing Information Sources:
    Gateway         Distance      Last Update
    10.1.1.2            90        00:13:11
    10.1.1.3            90        00:13:09
  Distance: internal 90 external 170
! The next commands are on router R2
!
R2>show ip eigrp interfaces
IP-EIGRP interfaces for process 99

                         Xmit Queue   Mean   Pacing Time   Multicast    Pending
Interface      Peers   Un/Reliable   SRTT   Un/Reliable   Flow Timer   Routes
Fa0/0            2        0/0        736       0/1         3684           0
Fa0/1            0        0/0          0       0/1            0           0
R2>show ip protocols
Routing Protocol is "eigrp 99"
  Outgoing update filter list for all interfaces is not set
  Incoming update filter list for all interfaces is not set
  Default networks flagged in outgoing updates
  Default networks accepted from incoming updates
  EIGRP metric weight K1=1, K2=0, K3=1, K4=0, K5=0
  EIGRP maximum hopcount 100
  EIGRP maximum metric variance 1
  Redistributing: eigrp 99
  EIGRP NSF-aware route hold timer is 240s
  Automatic network summarization is in effect
```

Example 11-1 *EIGRP Problems with Interfaces (Continued)*

```
 Maximum path: 4
 Routing for Networks:
   10.0.0.0
 Routing Information Sources:
   Gateway         Distance      Last Update
   10.1.1.3              90      00:13:25
   10.1.1.1              90      00:13:25
 Distance: internal 90 external 170

R2>show ip route eigrp
     10.0.0.0/24 is subnetted, 3 subnets
D       10.1.11.0 [90/30720] via 10.1.1.1, 00:13:38, FastEthernet0/0
```

The **show ip eigrp interfaces** command output on both R1 and R2 shows how both R1 and R2 have configured EIGRP using process ID 99, and that EIGRP has been enabled on both Fa0/0 and Fa0/1 on R1 and R2. This command lists only interfaces on which EIGRP has been enabled, excluding passive interfaces.

The highlighted parts of the **show ip protocols** command output on each router are particularly interesting. These sections show the parameters of the configured **network** commands. For each **network** command, the **show ip protocols** command lists a separate line under the header "Routing for Networks," with each line listing the contents of the various **network** router subcommands. For example, R1 uses the **network 10.0.0.0** configuration command (shown at the beginning of the example), which matches the "10.0.0.0" line in the output of the **show ip protocols** command.

The end of the example gives brief insight into the current problem on R3 from R2's perspective. The end of the **show ip protocols** command on R2 lists two routing information sources: 10.1.1.1 (R1) and 10.1.1.3 (R3). However, R2 has learned only one EIGRP route (10.1.11.0/24), as shown in the **show ip route eigrp** command output. When working properly, R2 should learn three EIGRP routes—one for each of the outer LAN subnets shown in Figure 11-2.

Next, Example 11-2 shows the problems on R3 and R4 that prevent R1 and R2 from learning about subnets 10.1.33.0/24 and 10.1.44.0/24. The example shows the pertinent configuration on each router for perspective, as well as **show** commands that point out the problems.

Example 11-2 *EIGRP Problems on R3 and R4*

```
R3#show running-config
! lines omitted for brevity
router eigrp 99
```

continues

Example 11-2 *EIGRP Problems on R3 and R4 (Continued)*

```
 network 10.1.1.3 0.0.0.0
 network 10.1.13.3 0.0.0.0
 auto-summary
R3#show ip eigrp interfaces
IP-EIGRP interfaces for process 99

                          Xmit Queue   Mean   Pacing Time   Multicast    Pending
Interface        Peers   Un/Reliable   SRTT   Un/Reliable   Flow Timer   Routes
Fa0/0              2        0/0          1        0/10          50          0
R3#show ip protocols
Routing Protocol is "eigrp 99"
  Outgoing update filter list for all interfaces is not set
  Incoming update filter list for all interfaces is not set
  Default networks flagged in outgoing updates
  Default networks accepted from incoming updates
  EIGRP metric weight K1=1, K2=0, K3=1, K4=0, K5=0
  EIGRP maximum hopcount 100
  EIGRP maximum metric variance 1
  Redistributing: eigrp 99
  EIGRP NSF-aware route hold timer is 240s
  Automatic network summarization is in effect
  Maximum path: 4
  Routing for Networks:
    10.1.1.3/32
    10.1.13.3/32
  Routing Information Sources:
    Gateway         Distance      Last Update
    10.1.1.2             90       00:28:16
    10.1.1.1             90       00:28:14
  Distance: internal 90 external 170
! R4 output starts here

R4#show running-config
! lines omitted for brevity
router eigrp 99
 passive-interface FastEthernet0/0
 network 10.0.0.0
 auto-summary

R4#show ip eigrp interfaces
IP-EIGRP interfaces for process 99

                          Xmit Queue   Mean   Pacing Time   Multicast    Pending
Interface        Peers   Un/Reliable   SRTT   Un/Reliable   Flow Timer   Routes
Fa0/1              0        0/0          0        0/1           0           0
R4#show ip protocols
Routing Protocol is "eigrp 99"
```

Example 11-2 *EIGRP Problems on R3 and R4 (Continued)*

```
Outgoing update filter list for all interfaces is not set
Incoming update filter list for all interfaces is not set
Default networks flagged in outgoing updates
Default networks accepted from incoming updates
EIGRP metric weight K1=1, K2=0, K3=1, K4=0, K5=0
EIGRP maximum hopcount 100
EIGRP maximum metric variance 1
Redistributing: eigrp 99
EIGRP NSF-aware route hold timer is 240s
Automatic network summarization is in effect
Maximum path: 4
Routing for Networks:
  10.0.0.0
Passive Interface(s):
  FastEthernet0/0
Routing Information Sources:
  Gateway         Distance      Last Update
Distance: internal 90 external 170
```

The root cause of R3's problem is that R3 has a **network 10.1.13.3 0.0.0.0** configuration command, which does not match R3's 10.1.33.3 Fa0/1 IP address. If the configuration was not available in the exam question, the **show ip protocols** command could be used to essentially see the same configuration details. In this case, the **show ip protocols** command on R3 lists the text "10.1.13.3/32" as a reference to the contents of the incorrect **network** command's parameters. As a result, R3 does not try to find neighbors on its Fa0/1 interface, which is not a big deal in this case, but R3 also does not advertise subnet 10.1.33.0/24, the connected subnet off its Fa0/1 interface. Also note that R3's **show ip eigrp interfaces** command omits interface Fa0/1, which does not by itself determine the root cause, but it can help you isolate the problem.

On R4, the engineer could have correctly used a **passive-interface fastethernet0/1** router subcommand, because no other routers should exist off R4's Fa0/1 interface. However, the engineer mistakenly referred to R4's Fa0/0 interface instead of Fa0/1. R4's **show ip eigrp interfaces** command purposefully omits the (Fa0/0) passive interface, and the highlighted part of R4's **show ip protocols** command output lists Fa0/0 as a passive interface. Because R4's Fa0/0 is passive, R4 does not even attempt to become neighbors with other routers on the same LAN.

OSPF Interface Troubleshooting Example

OSPF has the same basic requirements as EIGRP for interfaces, with a few exceptions. First, EIGRP routers need to use the same ASN or process ID as their neighboring routers, as configured in the **router** global configuration command. OSPF routers can use any process ID, with no need to match their neighbors. Second, OSPF requires that the interfaces connected to the same subnet be assigned to the same OSPF area, whereas EIGRP has no concept of areas.

Example 11-3 shows a mostly working OSPF internetwork, again based on Figure 11-2. The following problems exist:

> R2 has been configured to put both interfaces in area 1. R1, R3, and R4 have been configured to put their common LAN interfaces (Fa0/0 in each case) in area 0, breaking OSPF design rules.

Example 11-3 shows how to isolate the root cause of the problem. It also shows the normal working output, with the **show ip ospf interface brief** and **show ip protocols** commands.

Example 11-3   *OSPF Problems on R2*

```
R1>show ip ospf interface brief
Interface    PID   Area        IP Address/Mask    Cost  State Nbrs F/C
Fa0/1        11    0           10.1.11.1/24       1     DR    0/0
Fa0/0        11    0           10.1.1.1/24        1     DROTH 2/2
R1>show ip protocols
Routing Protocol is "ospf 11"
  Outgoing update filter list for all interfaces is not set
  Incoming update filter list for all interfaces is not set
  Router ID 1.1.1.1
  Number of areas in this router is 1. 1 normal 0 stub 0 nssa
  Maximum path: 4
  Routing for Networks:
    10.0.0.0 0.255.255.255 area 0
  Routing Information Sources:
    Gateway         Distance      Last Update
    3.3.3.3              110      00:01:12
    4.4.4.4              110      00:01:12
    1.1.1.1              110      00:01:12
  Distance: (default is 110)
R1>show ip route ospf
      10.0.0.0/24 is subnetted, 5 subnets
O        10.1.44.0 [110/2] via 10.1.1.4, 00:01:19, FastEthernet0/0
O        10.1.33.0 [110/2] via 10.1.1.3, 00:01:19, FastEthernet0/0
! Now moving to router R2
R2>show ip ospf interface brief
Interface    PID   Area        IP Address/Mask    Cost  State Nbrs F/C
Fa0/1        22    1           10.1.22.2/24       1     DR    0/0
Fa0/0        22    1           10.1.1.2/24        1     DR    0/0
R2>show ip protocols
Routing Protocol is "ospf 22"
```

Example 11-3   *OSPF Problems on R2 (Continued)*

```
 Outgoing update filter list for all interfaces is not set
 Incoming update filter list for all interfaces is not set
 --More--  _____         _____  Router ID 2.2.2.2
 Number of areas in this router is 1. 1 normal 0 stub 0 nssa
 Maximum path: 4
 Routing for Networks:
   10.0.0.0 0.255.255.255 area 1
Reference bandwidth unit is 100 mbps
 Routing Information Sources:
   Gateway         Distance      Last Update
Distance: (default is 110)
R2>
!!!!!!!!!!!!!!!!!!!!!!!!!!!!!!!!!!!!!!!!!!!!!!!!!!!!!!!!!!!!!!!!!!!!!!!!!!!!!!!!!!!!!
May 28 18:30:26.659: %OSPF-4-ERRRCV: Received invalid packet: mismatch area ID,
from backbone area must be virtual-link but not found from 10.1.1.4,
FastEthernet0/0
```

For OSPF, the **show ip ospf interface brief** command lists output similar to the **show ip eigrp interface** command, with one line for each enabled interface. (The **show ip ospf interface** command, not shown in the example, lists detailed OSPF information for each interface.) In this example, both R1 and R2 have OSPF enabled on both LAN interfaces, but this command also lists the area number for each interface, with R2 having both LAN interfaces in area 1. As a result, R2's Fa0/0 interface is in a different area than the other three routers' interfaces on the same LAN.

A closer look at R2's **show ip protocols** command output, particularly the highlighted portion, points out the configuration error. The highlighted phrase "10.0.0.0 0.255.255.255 area 1" is actually the exact syntax of the one **network** command on router R2, minus the word "network." Reconfiguring R2 so that its Fa0/0 interface matches the other three routers would solve this particular problem.

The end of the example shows an unsolicited log message generated by router R2, notifying the console user that this router has received a Hello from a router in a different area.

As you check the interfaces, you could also check several other details mentioned in Chapter 7's IP troubleshooting coverage. It makes sense to go ahead and check the interface IP addresses, masks, and interface status, using the **show interfaces** and **show ip interface brief** commands. In particular, it is helpful to note which interfaces are up/up, because a routing protocol will not attempt to find neighbors or advertise connected subnets for an interface that is not in an up/up state. These verification checks were discussed in detail in Chapter 7, so they are not repeated here.

Neighbor Relationships

As mentioned near the beginning of this chapter, when a routing protocol has been enabled on an interface, and the interface is not configured as a passive interface, the routing protocol attempts to discover neighbors and form a neighbor relationship with each neighbor that shares the common subnet. This section examines the large number of facts that each router must check with each potential neighbor before the two routers become neighbors.

OSPF and EIGRP both use Hello messages to learn about new neighbors and to exchange information used to perform some basic verification checks. For example, as just shown in Example 11-3, an OSPF router should not become neighbors with another router in another area, because all routers on a common subnet should be in the same area by design. (The border between areas is a router, not a link.)

After an EIGRP or OSPF router hears a Hello from a new neighbor, the routing protocol examines the information in the Hello, along with some local settings, to decide if the two neighbors should even attempt to become neighbors. Because there is no formal term for all these items that a routing protocol considers, this book just calls them *neighbor requirements*. Table 11-2 lists the neighbor requirements for both EIGRP and OSPF. Following the table, the next few pages examine some of these settings for both EIGRP and OSPF, again using examples based on Figure 11-2.

Table 11-2 *Neighbor Requirements for EIGRP and OSPF*

Requirement	EIGRP	OSPF
Interfaces must be in an up/up state	Yes	Yes
Interfaces must be in the same subnet	Yes	Yes
Must pass neighbor authentication (if configured)	Yes	Yes
Must use the same ASN/process-ID on the **router** configuration command	Yes	No
Hello and hold/dead timers must match	No	Yes
IP MTU must match	No	Yes
Router IDs must be unique	No[1]	Yes
K-values must match	Yes	N/A
Must be in the same area	N/A	Yes

[1]Having duplicate EIGRP RIDs does not prevent routers from becoming neighbors, but it can cause problems when external EIGRP routes are added to the routing table.

> **NOTE**   Even though it is important to study and remember the items in this table, it may be best not to study this table right now. Instead, read the rest of the chapter first, because the items in the table will be mentioned and reviewed throughout the rest of this chapter.

Unlike the rest of the neighbor requirements listed in Table 11-2, the first requirement has very little to do with the routing protocols themselves. The two routers must be able to send packets to each other over the physical network to which they are both connected. To do that, the router interfaces must be up/up. In practice, before examining the rest of the details of why two routers do not become neighbors, confirm that the two routers can ping each other on the local subnet. If the ping fails, investigate all the Layer 1, 2, and 3 issues that could prevent the ping from working (such as an interface not being up/up), as covered in various chapters of this book and in *CCENT/CCNA ICND1 Official Exam Certification Guide*.

Because the details differ slightly between the two routing protocols, this section first examines EIGRP, followed by OSPF.

> **NOTE**   This section assumes that the routing protocol has actually been enabled on each required interface, as covered earlier in this chapter in the section titled "Interfaces Enabled with a Routing Protocol."

EIGRP Neighbor Requirements

Any two EIGRP routers that connect to the same data link, and whose interfaces have been enabled for EIGRP and are not passive, will at least consider becoming neighbors. To quickly and definitively know which potential neighbors have passed all the neighbor requirements for EIGRP, just look at the output of the **show ip eigrp neighbors** command. This command lists only neighbors that have passed all the neighbor verification checks. Example 11-4 shows an example, with the four routers from Figure 11-2 again, but with all earlier EIGRP configuration problems having been fixed.

Example 11-4   *R1* **show ip eigrp neighbors** *Command with All Problems Fixed*

```
R1#show ip eigrp neighbors
IP-EIGRP neighbors for process 99
H   Address                 Interface       Hold Uptime    SRTT   RTO  Q   Seq
                                            (sec)          (ms)        Cnt Num
2   10.1.1.3                Fa0/0             13 00:00:04   616   3696  0   8
1   10.1.1.4                Fa0/0             12 00:00:54    1     200  0   45
0   10.1.1.2                Fa0/0             14 00:01:19   123    738  0   43
```

If the **show ip eigrp neighbors** command does not list one or more expected neighbors, and the two routers can ping each other's IP address on their common subnet, the problem is probably related to one of the neighbor requirements listed in Tables 11-2 and 11-3. Table 11-3 summarizes the EIGRP neighbor requirements and notes the best commands with which to determine which requirement is the root cause of the problem.

Key
Topic

Table 11-3   *EIGRP Neighbor Requirements and the Best* **show/debug** *Commands*

Requirement	Best Command(s) to Isolate the Problem
Must be in the same subnet	**show interfaces**
Must pass any neighbor authentication	**debug eigrp packets**
Must use the same ASN on the **router** configuration command	**show ip eigrp interfaces**, **show protocols**
K-values must match	**show protocols**

All the requirements listed in Table 11-3, except the last one, were explained in Chapter 10. EIGRP K-values refer to the parameters that can be configured to change what EIGRP uses in its metric calculation. Cisco recommends leaving these values at their default settings, using only bandwidth and delay in the metric calculation. Because Cisco recommends that you not change these values, this particular problem is not very common. However, you can check the K-values on both routers with the **show ip protocols** command.

Example 11-5 shows three problems that can cause two routers that should become EIGRP neighbors to fail to do so. For this example, the following problems have been introduced:

■   R2 has been configured with IP address 10.1.2.2/24, in a different subnet than R1, R3, and R4.

■   R3 has been configured to use ASN 199 with the **router eigrp 199** command, instead of ASN 99, as used on the other three routers.

■   R4 has been configured to use MD5 authentication, like the other routers, but R4 has a key value of "FRED" instead of the value "fred," used by the other three routers.

R1 can actually detect two of the problems without having to use commands on the other routers. R1 generates an unsolicited log message for the mismatched subnet problem, and a **debug** command on R1 can reveal the authentication failure. A quick examination of a few **show** commands on R3 can identify that the wrong ASN has been used in the **router** configuration command. Example 11-5 shows the details.

Example 11-5 *Common Problems Preventing the Formation of EIGRP Neighbors*

```
! First, R1 has no neighbor relationships yet. R1 uses ASN (process) 99.
R1#show ip eigrp neighbors
IP-EIGRP neighbors for process 99


R1#
! Next, R1 generates a log message, which shows up at the console, stating
! that the router with IP address 10.1.2.2 is not on the same subnet as R1.
!
*May 28 20:02:22.355: IP-EIGRP(Default-IP-Routing-Table:99): Neighbor
   10.1.2.2 not on common subnet for FastEthernet0/0


! Next, R1 enables a debug that shows messages for each packet received from R4,
! which uses the wrong password (authentication key string)
!
R1#debug eigrp packets
EIGRP Packets debugging is on
    (UPDATE, REQUEST, QUERY, REPLY, HELLO, IPXSAP, PROBE, ACK, STUB, SIAQUERY,
     SIAREPLY)
*May 28 20:04:00.931: EIGRP: pkt key id = 1, authentication mismatch
*May 28 20:04:00.931: EIGRP: FastEthernet0/0: ignored packet from 10.1.1.4,
   opcode = 5 (invalid authentication)
! The rest of the output is from R3
! The first line of output from the show ip protocols command lists ASN 199
!
R3#show ip protocols
Routing Protocol is "eigrp 199"
!
! The first line of output from show ip eigrp interfaces lists ASN 199
!
R3#show ip eigrp interfaces
IP-EIGRP interfaces for process 199

                       Xmit Queue    Mean   Pacing Time   Multicast    Pending
Interface      Peers   Un/Reliable   SRTT   Un/Reliable   Flow Timer   Routes
Fa0/0            0        0/0          0        0/10           0          0
Fa0/1            0        0/0          0        0/10           0          0
```

OSPF Neighbor Requirements

Similar to EIGRP, a router's **show ip ospf neighbor** command lists all the neighboring routers that have met all the requirements to become an OSPF neighbor as listed in Table 11-2—with one minor exception (mismatched MTU). (If the MTU is mismatched, the two routers are listed in the **show ip ospf neighbor** command. This particular problem is discussed later, in the section "The MTU Matching Requirement.") So, the first step in troubleshooting OSPF neighbors is to look at the list of neighbors.

Example 11-6 lists the output of a **show ip ospf neighbor** command on router R2, from Figure 11-2, with the configuration correct on each of the four routers in the figure.

Example 11-6 *Normal Working* **show ip ospf neighbors** *Command on Router R2*

```
R2#show ip ospf neighbor

Neighbor ID     Pri    State           Dead Time    Address       Interface
1.1.1.1           1    FULL/BDR        00:00:37     10.1.1.1      FastEthernet0/0
3.3.3.3           1    2WAY/DROTHER    00:00:37     10.1.1.3      FastEthernet0/0
4.4.4.4           1    FULL/DR         00:00:31     10.1.1.4      FastEthernet0/0
```

A brief review of OSPF neighbor states (as explained in Chapter 9) can help you understand a few of the subtleties of the output in the example. A router's listed status for each of its OSPF neighbors—the neighbor's state—should settle into either a *two-way* or *Full* state under normal operation. For neighbors that do not need to directly exchange their databases, typically two non-DR routers on a LAN, the routers should settle into a *two-way* neighbor state. In most cases, two neighboring routers need to directly exchange their complete full LSDBs with each other. As soon as that process has been completed, the two routers settle into a Full neighbor state. In Example 11-6, router R4 is the DR, and R1 is the BDR, so R2 and R3 (as non-DRs) do not need to directly exchange routes. Therefore, R2's neighbor state for R3 (RID 3.3.3.3) in Example 11-6 is listed as two-way.

> **NOTE**   Notably, OSPF neighbors do not have to use the same process ID on the **router ospf** *process-id* command to become neighbors. In Example 11-6, all four routers use different process IDs.

If the **show ip ospf neighbor** command does not list one or more expected neighbors, before moving on to look at OSPF neighbor requirements, you should confirm that the two routers can ping each other on the local subnet. As soon as the two neighboring routers can ping each other, if the two routers still do not become OSPF neighbors, the next step is to examine each of the OSPF neighbor requirements. Table 11-4 summarizes the requirements, listing the most useful commands with which to find the answers.

Key Topic

Table 11-4 *OSPF Neighbor Requirements and the Best* **show/debug** *Commands*

Requirement	Best Command(s) to Isolate the Problem
Must be in the same subnet	**show interfaces**, **debug ip ospf hello**
Must pass any neighbor authentication	**debug ip ospf adj**
Hello and hold/dead timers must match	**show ip ospf interface**, **debug ip ospf hello**

Table 11-4 *OSPF Neighbor Requirements and the Best* **show/debug** *Commands (Continued)*

Requirement	Best Command(s) to Isolate the Problem
Must be in the same area	**debug ip ospf adj**, **show ip ospf interface brief**
Router IDs must be unique	**show ip ospf**

The rest of this section looks at a couple of examples in which two OSPF routers could become neighbors but do not because of some of the reasons in the table. This is followed by information on the MTU matching requirement.

OSPF Neighbor Example 1

In this first example of OSPF neighbor problems, the usual four-router network from Figure 11-2 is used. This internetwork is designed to use a single area, area 0. In this case, the following problems have been introduced into the design:

- R2 has been configured with both LAN interfaces in area 1, whereas the other three routers' Fa0/0 interfaces are assigned to area 0.

- R3 is using the same RID (1.1.1.1) as R1.

- R4 is using MD5 authentication like the other three routers, but R4 has misconfigured its authentication key value (FRED instead of fred).

Example 11-7 shows the evidence of the problems, with comments following the example.

Example 11-7 *Finding Mismatch Area, Same RID, and Authentication Problems*

```
R1#debug ip ospf adj
OSPF adjacency events debugging is on
R1#
*May 28 23:59:21.031: OSPF: Send with youngest Key 1
*May 28 23:59:24.463: OSPF: Rcv pkt from 10.1.1.2, FastEthernet0/0, area 0.0.0.0
     mismatch area 0.0.0.1 in the header
*May 28 23:59:24.907: OSPF: Rcv pkt from 10.1.1.4, FastEthernet0/0 :
  Mismatch Authentication Key - Message Digest Key 1

R1#undebug all
All possible debugging has been turned off
R1#show ip ospf interface brief
Interface   PID   Area      IP Address/Mask    Cost  State Nbrs F/C
Fa0/1       11    0         10.1.11.1/24       1     DR    0/0
Fa0/0       11    0         10.1.1.1/24        1     DR    0/0
! Now to R2
! R2 shows that Fa0/0 is in area 1
!
R2#show ip ospf interface brief
```

continues

Example 11-7   *Finding Mismatch Area, Same RID, and Authentication Problems (Continued)*

```
Interface     PID  Area           IP Address/Mask    Cost  State Nbrs F/C
Fa0/1         22   1              10.1.22.2/24       1     DR    0/0
Fa0/0         22   1              10.1.1.2/24        1     DR    0/0
! Next, on R3
! R3 lists the RID of 1.1.1.1
!
R3#show ip ospf
 Routing Process "ospf 33" with ID 1.1.1.1
 Supports only single TOS(TOS0) routes
! lines omitted for brevity
! Back to R1 again
! Next command confirms that R1 is also trying to use RID 1.1.1.1
!
R1#show ip ospf
 Routing Process "ospf 11" with ID 1.1.1.1
 Supports only single TOS(TOS0) routes
 ! lines omitted for brevity
*May 29 00:01:25.679: %OSPF-4-DUP_RTRID_NBR: OSPF detected duplicate router-id
1.1.1.1 from 10.1.1.3 on interface FastEthernet0/0
```

As noted in Table 11-4, the **debug ip ospf adj** command helps troubleshoot mismatched OSPF area problems as well as authentication problems. The highlighted messages in the first few lines of the example point out that the router with address 10.1.1.2 (R2) has a mismatched area ID 0.0.0.1, meaning area 1. Indeed, R2 was misconfigured to put its Fa0/0 interface in area 1. Immediately following is a reference to a "mismatched authentication key," meaning that the correct authentication type was used, but the configured keys have different values, specifically for router 10.1.1.4 (R4).

> **NOTE**   Routers treat debug messages as log messages, which IOS sends to the console by default. To see these messages from a Telnet or SSH connection, use the **terminal monitor** command. To disable the display of these messages, use the **terminal no monitor** command.

The next part of the example shows the **show ip ospf interface brief** command on both R1 and R2, pointing out how each router's Fa0/0 interface is in a different OSPF area.

The end of the example lists the information that shows R1 and R3 both trying to use RID 1.1.1.1. Interestingly, both routers automatically generate a log message for the duplicate OSPF RID problem between R1 and R3. A duplicate RID causes significant problems with OSPF, far beyond just whether two routers can become neighbors. The end of Example 11-7 shows the (highlighted) log message. The **show ip ospf** commands on both R3 and R1 also show how you can easily list the RID on each router, noting that they both use the same value.

OSPF Neighbor Example 2

In this next example, the same network from Figure 11-2 is used again. The problems on R2, R3, and R4 from the previous example have been fixed, but new problems have been introduced on R2 and R4 to show the symptoms. In this case, the following problems have been introduced into the design:

- R2 has been configured with a Hello/Dead timer of 5/20 on its Fa0/0 interface, instead of the 10/40 used (by default) on R1, R3, and R4.

- R3's problems have been solved; no problems related to OSPF neighbors exist.

- R4 is now using the correct key string (fred), but with clear-text authentication instead of the MD5 authentication used by the other three routers.

Example 11-8 shows the evidence of the problems, with comments following the example. As usual, the **debug ip ospf adj** command helps discover authentication problems. Also, the **debug ip ospf hello** command helps uncover mismatches discovered in the Hello message, including mismatched IP addresses/masks and timers.

Example 11-8 *Finding Mismatched Hello/Dead Timers and Wrong Authentication Types*

```
R1#debug ip ospf adj
OSPF adjacency events debugging is on
R1#
*May 29 10:41:30.639: OSPF: Rcv pkt from 10.1.1.4, FastEthernet0/0 :
  Mismatch Authentication type. Input packet specified type 1, we use type 2
R1#
R1#undebug all
All possible debugging has been turned off
R1#debug ip ospf hello
OSPF hello events debugging is on
R1#
*May 29 10:41:42.603: OSPF: Rcv hello from 2.2.2.2 area 0 from
  FastEthernet0/0 10.1.1.2
*May 29 10:41:42.603: OSPF: Mismatched hello parameters from 10.1.1.2
*May 29 10:41:42.603: OSPF: Dead R 20 C 40, Hello R 5 C 10
  Mask R 255.255.255.0 C 255.255.255.0
R1#undebug all
All possible debugging has been turned off
R1#show ip ospf interface fa0/0
FastEthernet0/0 is up, line protocol is up
  Internet Address 10.1.1.1/24, Area 0
  Process ID 11, Router ID 1.1.1.1, Network Type BROADCAST, Cost: 1
```

continues

Example 11-8   *Finding Mismatched Hello/Dead Timers and Wrong Authentication Types (Continued)*

```
   Transmit Delay is 1 sec, State DR, Priority 1
   Designated Router (ID) 1.1.1.1, Interface address 10.1.1.1
   Backup Designated router (ID) 3.3.3.3, Interface address 10.1.1.3
   Timer intervals configured, Hello 10, Dead 40, Wait 40, Retransmit 5
! lines omitted for brevity
! Moving on to R2 next
!
R2#show ip ospf interface fa0/0
FastEthernet0/0 is up, line protocol is up
   Internet Address 10.1.1.2/24, Area 0
   Process ID 22, Router ID 2.2.2.2, Network Type BROADCAST, Cost: 1
   Transmit Delay is 1 sec, State DR, Priority 1
   Designated Router (ID) 2.2.2.2, Interface address 10.1.1.2
   No backup designated router on this network
   Timer intervals configured, Hello 5, Dead 20, Wait 20, Retransmit 5
! lines omitted for brevity
```

The example begins with the debug messages related to the authentication problem between R1, which uses MD5 authentication, and R4, which now uses clear-text authentication. As listed in Chapter 9's Table 9-4, IOS considers OSPF clear-text authentication to be type 1 authentication and MD5 to be type 2. The highlighted debug message confirms that thinking, stating that R1 received a packet from 10.1.1.4 (R4), with type 1 authentication, but with R1 expecting type 2 authentication.

Next, the example shows the messages generated by the **debug ip ospf hello** command— specifically, those related to the Hello/Dead timer mismatch. The highlighted message uses a "C" to mean "configured value"—in other words, the value on the local router, or R1 in this case. The "R" in the message means "Received value," or the value listed in the received Hello. In this case, the phrase "Dead R 20 C 40" means that the router that generated this message, R1, received a Hello with a Dead timer set to 20, but R1's configured value on the interface is 40, so the values don't match. Similarly, the message shows the mismatch in the Hello timers as well. Note that any IP subnet mismatch problems could also be found with this same debug, based on the received and configured subnet masks.

The majority of the space in the example shows the output of the **show ip ospf interface** command on both R1 and R2, which lists the Hello and Dead timers on each interface, confirming the details listed in the debug messages.

The MTU Matching Requirement

Of all the potential problems between two potential OSPF neighbors listed in Table 11-2, only one problem, the mismatched MTU problem, allows the neighbor to be listed in the other router's **show ip ospf neighbor** command output. When two routers connect to the same subnet, with different interface IP MTU settings, the two routers can become neighbors and reach the two-way state. However, when the two routers attempt to exchange LSDBs, the database exchange process fails because of the MTU mismatch.

When the MTU mismatch occurs, the routers typically move between a few neighbor states while trying to overcome the problem. The most common state is the Exchange state, as shown in Example 11-9. In this case, R1 and R3 have no other problems that prevent them from becoming OSPF neighbors, except that R3 has been configured with an IP MTU of 1200 bytes on its Fa0/0 interface, instead of the default 1500 used by R1.

Example 11-9 *Results of Mismatched MTUs on OSPF Neighbors*

```
R1#show ip ospf neighbor

Neighbor ID     Pri   State         Dead Time   Address     Interface
3.3.3.3           1   EXCHANGE/DR   00:00:36    10.1.1.3    FastEthernet0/0
```

The state typically cycles from Exchange state, back to Init state, and then back to Exchange state.

Exam Preparation Tasks

Review All the Key Topics

Review the most important topics from this chapter, noted with the key topics icon. Table 11-5 lists these key topics and where each is discussed.

Table 11-5 *Key Topics for Chapter 11*

Key Topic Element	Description	Page Number
List	Two things that happen when EIGRP or OSPF is enabled on a router's interface	410
Table 11-1	List of three commands that are useful when determining on which interfaces EIGRP or OSPF has been enabled	410
Table 11-2	List of neighbor requirements for both EIGRP and OSPF	418
Table 11-3	List of EIGRP neighbor requirements and useful commands to isolate that requirement as the root cause of a neighbor problem	420
Table 11-4	The same information as Table 11-3, but for OSPF	422-423

Complete the Tables and Lists from Memory

Print a copy of Appendix J, "Memory Tables" (found on the CD), or at least the section for this chapter, and complete the tables and lists from memory. Appendix K, "Memory Tables Answer Key," also on the CD, includes completed tables and lists for you to check your work.

Command Reference to Check Your Memory

Although you should not necessarily memorize the information in the tables in this section, this section does include a reference for the configuration and EXEC commands covered in this chapter. Practically speaking, you should memorize the commands as a side effect of reading the chapter and doing all the activities in this exam preparation section. To see how well you have memorized the commands as a side effect of your other studies, cover the left side of the table, read the descriptions on the right side, and see if you remember the command.

Table 11-6 *Chapter 11 Configuration Command Reference*

Command	Description
ip hello-interval eigrp *as-number timer-value*	Interface subcommand that sets the EIGRP Hello interval for that EIGRP process.
ip hold-time eigrp *as-number timer-value*	Interface subcommand that sets the EIGRP hold time for the interface.
ip ospf hello-interval *seconds*	Interface subcommand that sets the interval for periodic Hellos.
ip ospf dead-interval *number*	Interface subcommand that sets the OSPF Dead Timer.

Table 11-7 *Chapter 11 EXEC Command Reference*

Command	Description
show ip protocols	Shows routing protocol parameters and current timer values, including an effective copy of the routing protocols' **network** commands, and a list of passive interfaces.
show ip eigrp interfaces	Lists the interfaces on which EIGRP has been enabled for each EIGRP process, except passive interfaces.
show ip route eigrp	Lists only EIGRP-learned routes from the routing table.
debug eigrp packets	Displays the contents of EIGRP packets, including many useful notices about reasons why neighbor relationships fail to form.
show ip eigrp neighbors	Lists EIGRP neighbors and status.
show ip ospf interface brief	Lists the interfaces which the OSPF protocol is enabled (based on the **network** commands), including passive interfaces.
show ip ospf interface [*type number*]	Lists detailed OSPF settings for all interfaces, or the listed interface, including Hello and Dead timers and OSPF area.
show ip route ospf	Lists routes in the routing table learned by OSPF.
show ip ospf neighbor	Lists neighbors and current status with neighbors, per interface.
debug ip ospf events	Issues log messages for each action taken by OSPF, including the receipt of messages.
debug ip ospf packet	Issues log messages describing the contents of all OSPF packets.
debug ip ospf hello	Issues log messages describing Hellos and Hello failures.

Cisco Published ICND2 Exam Topics*
Covered in This Part

Configure and troubleshoot basic operation and routing on Cisco devices

- Verify router hardware and software operation using SHOW & DEBUG commands

Implement and verify WAN links

- Configure and verify Frame Relay on Cisco routers

- Troubleshoot WAN implementation issues

- Describe VPN technology (including: importance, benefits, role, impact, components)

- Configure and verify PPP connection between Cisco routers

* Always recheck http://www.cisco.com for the latest posted exam topics.

Part IV: Wide-Area Networks

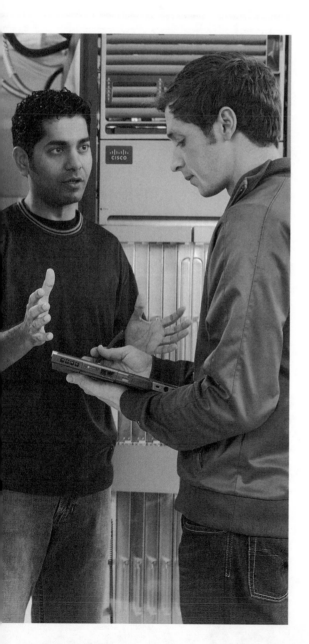

This chapter covers the following subjects:

PPP Concepts: This section examines PPP concepts, including control protocols and PAP/CHAP.

PPP Configuration: This section looks at how to configure a simple PPP serial link, as well as how to configure CHAP.

Troubleshooting Serial Links: This section examines the overall serial link troubleshooting process, including typical reasons why an interface has a particular status code.

CHAPTER 12

Point-to-Point WANs

This chapter is the first of four chapters in Part IV of this book. This part focuses on WAN technologies. This chapter completes the examination of point-to-point links by examining more details about how PPP works, along with a wide variety of troubleshooting topics related to point-to-point leased lines. Chapter 13, "Frame Relay Concepts," and Chapter 14, "Frame Relay Configuration and Troubleshooting," explore Frame Relay technologies. Chapter 15, "Virtual Private Networks," looks at the concepts behind virtual private networks (VPN). VPNs let you create secure communication paths that work like WAN links, while using other, less-secure networks, such as the Internet.

"Do I Know This Already?" Quiz

The "Do I Know This Already?" quiz allows you to assess whether you should read the entire chapter. If you miss no more than one of these seven self-assessment questions, you might want to move ahead to the "Exam Preparation Tasks" section. Table 12-1 lists the major headings in this chapter and the "Do I Know This Already?" quiz questions covering the material in those sections. This helps you assess your knowledge of these specific areas. The answers to the "Do I Know This Already?" quiz appear in Appendix A.

Table 12-1 *"Do I Know This Already?" Foundation Topics Section-to-Question Mapping*

Foundation Topics Section	Questions
PPP Concepts	1 and 2
PPP Configuration	3–5
Troubleshooting Serial Links	6 and 7

1. Which of the following PPP authentication protocols authenticates a device on the other end of a link without sending any password information in clear text?

   a. MD5

   b. PAP

   c. CHAP

   d. DES

2. Which of the following PPP protocols controls the operation of CHAP?

    a. CDPCP

    b. IPCP

    c. LCP

    d. IPXCP

3. Two routers have no initial configuration whatsoever. They are connected in a lab using a DTE cable connected to R1 and a DCE cable connected to R2, with the DTE and DCE cables then connected to each other. The engineer wants to create a working PPP link. Which of the following commands are required on R1 for the link to reach a state in which R1 can ping R2's serial IP address, assuming that the physical back-to-back link physically works?

    a. **encapsulation ppp**

    b. **no encapsulation hdlc**

    c. **clock rate**

    d. **ip address**

4. Imagine that two routers, R1 and R2, have a leased line between them. Each router had its configuration erased and was then reloaded. R1 was then configured with the following commands:

    ```
    hostname R1
    interface s0/0
     encapsulation ppp
     ppp authentication chap
    ```

    Which of the following configuration commands can complete the configuration on R1 so that CHAP can work correctly? Assume that R2 has been configured correctly and that the password is fred.

    a. No other configuration is needed.

    b. **ppp chap** (global command)

    c. **username R1 password fred**

    d. **username R2 password fred**

    e. **ppp chap password fred**

5. Consider the following excerpt from the output of a **show** command:

    ```
    Serial0/0/1 is up, line protocol is up
      Hardware is GT96K Serial
      Internet address is 192.168.2.1/24
      MTU 1500 bytes, BW 1544 Kbit, DLY 20000 usec,
        reliability 255/255, txload 1/255, rxload 1/255
      Encapsulation PPP, LCP Open
      Open: CDPCP, IPCP, loopback not set
    ```

Which of the following are true about this router's S0/0/1 interface?

a. The interface is using HDLC.

b. The interface is using PPP.

c. The interface currently cannot pass IPv4 traffic.

d. The link should be able to pass PPP frames at the present time.

6. Consider the following excerpt from the output of a **show interfaces** command on an interface configured to use PPP:

```
Serial0/0/1 is up, line protocol is down
  Hardware is GT96K Serial
  Internet address is 192.168.2.1/24
```

A ping of the IP address on the other end of the link fails. Which of the following are reasons for the failure, assuming that the problem listed in that answer is the only problem with the link?

a. The CSU/DSU connected to the other router is not powered on.

b. The IP address on the router at the other end of the link is not in subnet 192.168.2.0/24.

c. CHAP authentication failed.

d. The router on the other end of the link has been configured to use HDLC.

e. None of the other answers is correct.

7. Two routers have a serial link between them, with the link configured to use PPP, and with EIGRP configured correctly for all interfaces. The engineer can ping the IP address on the other end of the link, but not the IP address of the other router's LAN interface. Which of the following answers is a likely cause of the problem?

a. The CSU/DSU connected to the other router is not powered on.

b. The serial IP address on the router at the other end of the link is not in the same subnet as the local router.

c. CHAP authentication failed.

d. The router on the other end of the link has been configured to use HDLC.

Foundation Topics

Point-to-Point Protocol (PPP) defines a data-link protocol with many features besides just helping two devices send data over the link. This chapter starts by explaining the many PPP features available on routers, followed by PPP configuration, including the configuration of PPP authentication. The chapter ends with a section on troubleshooting serial links, covering a wide variety of topics, including PPP.

> **NOTE**   WAN options such as leased lines, packet switching, and CSUs/DSUs, as well as basic knowledge of HDLC and PPP, are all considered prerequisite knowledge for the ICND2 exam and for this book. However, if you do not have a copy of *CCENT/CCNA ICND1 Official Exam Certification Guide*, this book's CD includes a copy of that book's Chapter 17 as an appendix; it covers this prerequisite information. The appendix on the CD is Appendix I, "ICND1 Chapter 17: WAN Configuration and Troubleshooting." If you have not yet read Chapter 17 in the ICND1 book, or if you do not have that book, now may be a good time to review Appendix I before continuing with this chapter.

PPP Concepts

PPP provides several basic but important functions that are useful on a leased line that connects two devices, as reviewed in the following list:

- Definition of a header and trailer that allows delivery of a data frame over the link

- Support for both synchronous and asynchronous links

- A protocol type field in the header, allowing multiple Layer 3 protocols to pass over the same link

- Built-in authentication tools: Password Authentication Protocol (PAP) and Challenge Handshake Authentication Protocol (CHAP)

- Control protocols for each higher-layer protocol that rides over PPP, allowing easier integration and support of those protocols

The next several pages take a closer look at the protocol field, authentication, and the control protocols.

The PPP Protocol Field

One of the more important features included in the PPP standard, but not in the HDLC standard, is the protocol field. The protocol field identifies the type of packet inside the frame. When PPP was created, this field allowed packets from the many different Layer 3 protocols to pass over a single link. Today, the protocol type field still provides the same function, even for the support of two different versions of IP (IPv4 and IPv6). Figure 12-1 compares the framing details of HDLC and PPP, showing the proprietary HDLC Protocol field and the standardized PPP Protocol field.

Figure 12-1 *PPP and HDLC Framing*

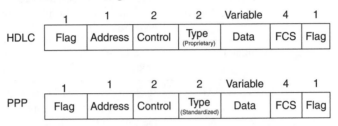

PPP defines a set of Layer 2 control messages that perform various link control functions. These control functions fall into two main categories:

■ Those needed regardless of the Layer 3 protocol sent across the link

■ Those specific to each Layer 3 protocol

The PPP *Link Control Protocol* (LCP) implements the control functions that work the same regardless of the Layer 3 protocol. For features related to any higher-layer protocols, typically Layer 3 protocols, PPP uses a series of PPP *control protocols* (CP), such as IP Control Protocol (IPCP). PPP uses one instance of LCP per link, and one CP for each Layer 3 protocol defined on the link. For example, on a PPP link using IPv4, IPv6, and Cisco Discovery Protocol (CDP), the link uses one instance of LCP, plus IPCP (for IPv4), IPv6CP (for IPv6), and CDPCP (for CDP).

The next section first summarizes the functions of LCP and then explains one of those functions, authentication, in more detail.

PPP Link Control Protocol (LCP)

LCP provides four notable features, which are covered in this chapter. Table 12-2 summarizes the functions, gives the LCP feature names, and describes the features briefly. Following the table, the text explains each feature in more detail. Note that the features listed in the table are optional and are disabled by default.

Key Topic

Table 12-2 *PPP LCP Features*

Function	LCP Feature	Description
Looped link detection	Magic number	Detects if the link is looped, and disables the interface, allowing rerouting over a working route.
Error detection	Link Quality Monitoring (LQM)	Disables an interface that exceeds an error percentage threshold, allowing rerouting over better routes.
Multilink support	Multilink PPP	Load-balances traffic over multiple parallel links.
Authentication	PAP and CHAP	Exchanges names and passwords so that each device can verify the identity of the device on the other end of the link.

Looped Link Detection

Error detection and looped link detection are two key features of PPP. Looped link detection allows for faster convergence when a link fails because it is looped. What does "looped" mean? Well, to test a circuit, the phone company might loop the circuit. The telco technician can sit at his desk and, using commands, cause the phone company's switch to loop the circuit. This means that the phone company takes the electrical signal sent by the CPE device and sends the same electrical current right back to the same device.

The routers cannot send bits to each other while the link is looped, of course. However, the router might not notice that the link is looped, because the router is still receiving something over the link! PPP helps the router recognize a looped link quickly so that it can bring down the interface and possibly use an alternative route.

In some cases, routing protocol convergence can be sped up by LCP's recognition of the loop. If the router can immediately notice that the link is looped, it can put the interface in a "down and down" status, and the routing protocols can change their routing updates based on the fact that the link is down. If a router does not notice that the link has been looped, the routing protocol must wait for timeouts—things such as not hearing from the router on the other end of the link for some period of time.

LCP notices looped links quickly using a feature called *magic numbers*. When using PPP, the router sends PPP LCP messages instead of Cisco-proprietary keepalives across the link; these messages include a magic number, which is different on each router. If a line is looped, the router receives an LCP message with its own magic number instead of getting a message with the other router's magic number. When a router receives its own magic number, that router knows that the frame it sent has been looped back, so the router can take down the interface, which speeds convergence.

Enhanced Error Detection

Similar to many other data-link protocols, PPP uses an FCS field in the PPP trailer to determine if an individual frame has an error. If a frame is received in error, it is discarded. However, PPP can monitor the frequency with which frames are received in error so that it can take down an interface if too many errors occur.

PPP LCP analyzes the error rates on a link using a PPP feature called Link Quality Monitoring (LQM). LCP at each end of the link sends messages describing the number of correctly received packets and bytes. The router that sent the packets compares this number of correctly-received frames to the number of frames and bytes it sent, and it calculates percentage loss. The router can take down the link after a configured error rate has been exceeded.

The only time LQM helps is when you have redundant routes in the network. By taking down a link that has many errors, you can cause packets to use an alternative path that might not have as many errors.

PPP Multilink

When multiple PPP links exist between the same two routers—referred to as parallel links—the routers must then determine how to use those links. With HDLC links, and with PPP links using the simplest configuration, the routers must use Layer 3 load balancing. This means that the routers have multiple routes for the same destination subnets. For example, the upper part of Figure 12-2 shows the load-balancing effect on R1 when forwarding packets to subnet 192.168.3.0/24.

Figure 12-2 *Load Balancing Without Multilink PPP*

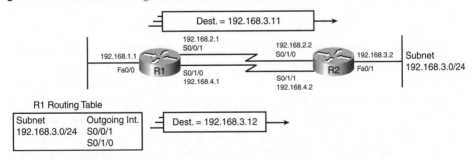

The figure shows two packets, one large and one small. Using Layer 3 logic, the router may choose to send one packet over one link, and the next packet over another. However, because the packets might be of different sizes, the router may not balance the traffic equally over each link. In some cases, particularly when most packets are sent to just a few destination hosts, the numbers of packets sent over each link might not even be balanced, which may overload one of the links and leave another link idle.

Multilink PPP load-balances the traffic equally over the links while allowing the Layer 3 logic in each router to treat the parallel links as a single link. When encapsulating a packet, PPP fragments the packet into smaller frames, sending one fragment over each link. For example, for the network shown in Figure 12-2, with two links, R1 would create two frames for each Layer 3 packet, with each frame holding roughly half the original packet. Then, PPP sends one fragment of each original packet over each of the two links. By sending about half of each packet over each link, multilink PPP can more evenly load-balance the traffic. As an added benefit, multilink PPP allows the Layer 3 routing tables to use a single route that refers to the combined links, keeping the routing table smaller. For example, in Figure 12-2, R1 would instead use one route for subnet 192.168.3.0/24, referring to the group of interfaces as a concept called a *multilink group*.

PPP Authentication

The term *authentication* refers to a set of security functions that help one device confirm that the other device should be allowed to communicate and is not some imposter. For instance, if R1 and R2 are supposed to be communicating over a serial link, R1 might want R2 to somehow prove that it really is R2. Authentication provides a way to prove one's identity.

WAN authentication is most often needed when dial lines are used. However, the configuration of the authentication features remains the same whether a leased line or dial line is used.

PAP and CHAP authenticate the endpoints on either end of a point-to-point serial link. CHAP is the preferred method today because the identification process uses values hidden with a Message Digest 5 (MD5) one-way hash, which is more secure than the clear-text passwords sent by PAP.

Both PAP and CHAP require the exchange of messages between devices. When a dialed line is used, the dialed-to router expects to receive a username and password from the dialing router with both PAP and CHAP. With a leased line, typically both routers mutually authenticate the other router. Whether leased line or dial, with PAP, the username and password are sent in the first message. With CHAP, the protocol begins with a message called a *challenge*, which asks the other router to send its username and password. Figure 12-3 outlines the different processes in the case where the links are dialed. The process works the same when the link uses a leased line.

Figure 12-3 *PAP and CHAP Authentication Process*

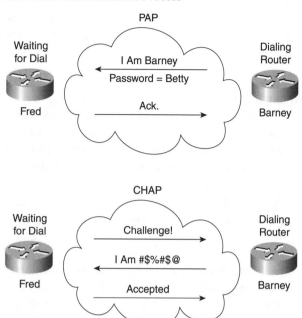

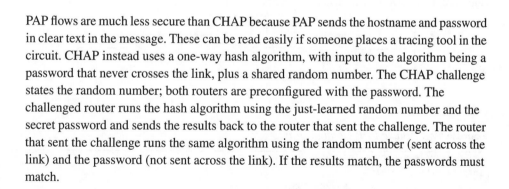

PAP flows are much less secure than CHAP because PAP sends the hostname and password in clear text in the message. These can be read easily if someone places a tracing tool in the circuit. CHAP instead uses a one-way hash algorithm, with input to the algorithm being a password that never crosses the link, plus a shared random number. The CHAP challenge states the random number; both routers are preconfigured with the password. The challenged router runs the hash algorithm using the just-learned random number and the secret password and sends the results back to the router that sent the challenge. The router that sent the challenge runs the same algorithm using the random number (sent across the link) and the password (not sent across the link). If the results match, the passwords must match.

The most interesting part of the CHAP process is that at no time does the password itself ever cross the link. With the random number, the hash value is different every time. So even if someone sees the calculated hash value using a trace tool, the value is meaningless as a way to break in next time. CHAP authentication is difficult to break, even with a tracing tool on the WAN link.

PPP Configuration

This section examines how to configure PPP and then how to add CHAP configuration. At the same time, this section also examines a couple of commands that help verify if PPP is up and working.

Basic PPP Configuration

Configuring PPP requires only the **encapsulation ppp** command on both ends of the link. To change back to use the default of HDLC, the engineer just needs to use the **encapsulation hdlc** command on both ends of the link as well. However, besides this basic configuration, the physical serial link needs to be ordered and installed. This section assumes that the physical link has been installed and is working. If you want to read more details about the physical link, refer to Chapter 17 of *CCENT/CCNA ICND1 Official Exam Certification Guide*, or to the copy of that chapter included as this book's CD-only Appendix I.

Example 12-1 shows a simple configuration using the two routers shown in Figure 12-4. The example includes the IP address configuration, but the IP addresses do not have to be configured for PPP to work. Because most installations will use IP, the configuration is added for some perspectives in the **show** commands in the second part of the example.

Figure 12-4 *Two-Router Internetwork Used in PPP Examples*

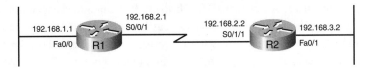

Example 12-1 *Basic PPP Configuration*

```
! The example starts with router R1
interface Serial0/0/1
 ip address 192.168.2.1 255.255.255.0
 encapsulation ppp
 clockrate 1536000
! Next, the configuration on router R2
interface Serial0/1/1
 ip address 192.168.2.2 255.255.255.0
 encapsulation ppp
! Back to router R1 again
R1#show interfaces serial 0/0/1
Serial0/0/1 is up, line protocol is up
  Hardware is GT96K Serial
```

Example 12-1 *Basic PPP Configuration (Continued)*

```
 Internet address is 192.168.2.1/24
 MTU 1500 bytes, BW 1544 Kbit, DLY 20000 usec,
    reliability 255/255, txload 1/255, rxload 1/255
 Encapsulation PPP, LCP Open
 Open: CDPCP, IPCP, loopback not set
! lines omitted for brevity
```

This example shows the simple configuration, with both routers needing to use PPP encapsulation. If either router defaulted to use HDLC, and the other configured PPP as shown, the link would not come up, staying in an "up and down" interface state.

The **show interfaces** command at the bottom of the example shows the normal output when the link is up and working. The second interface status code typically refers to the data-link status, with the "up" value meaning that the data link is working. Additionally, a few lines into the output, the highlighted phrases show that PPP is indeed configured, and that LCP has completed its work successfully, as noted with the "LCP Open" phrase. Additionally, the output lists the fact that two CPs, CDPCP and IPCP, have also successfully been enabled—all good indications that PPP is working properly.

CHAP Configuration and Verification

The simplest version of CHAP configuration requires only a few commands. The configuration uses a password configured on each router. As an alternative, the password could be configured on an external Authentication, Authorization, and Accounting (AAA) server outside the router. The configuration steps are as follows:

Step 1   Configure the routers' hostnames using the **hostname** *name* global configuration command.

Step 2   Configure the name of the other router, and the shared secret password, using the **username** *name* **password** *password* global configuration command.

Step 3   Enable CHAP on the interface on each router using the **ppp authentication chap** interface subcommand.

Example 12-2 shows a sample configuration, using the same two routers as the previous example (see Figure 12-4).

Example 12-2 *CHAP Configuration Example*

```
hostname R1                              hostname R2

username R2 password mypass              username R1 password mypass
!                                        !
interface serial 0/0/1                   interface serial 0/1/1
 encapsulation ppp                        encapsulation ppp
 ppp authentication chap                  ppp authentication chap
```

The commands themselves are not complicated, but it is easy to misconfigure the hostnames and passwords. Notice that each router refers to the other router's hostname in the **username** command, but both routers must configure the same password value. Also, not only are the passwords (mypass in this case) case-sensitive, but the hostnames, as referenced in the **username** command, also are also case-sensitive.

Because CHAP is a function of LCP, if the authentication process fails, LCP does not complete, and the interface falls to an "up and down" interface state.

PAP Configuration

PAP uses the exact same configuration commands as CHAP, except that the **ppp authentication pap** command is used instead of **ppp authentication chap**. The rest of the verification commands work the same, regardless of which of the two types of authentication are used. For example, if PAP authentication fails, LCP fails, and the link settles into an "up and down" state.

Cisco IOS Software also supports the capability to configure the router to first try one authentication method and, if the other side does not respond, try the other option. For example, the **ppp authentication chap pap** interface subcommand tells the router to send CHAP messages, and if no reply is received, to try PAP. Note that the second option is not tried if the CHAP messages flow between the two devices, and the result is that authentication failed. It uses the other option only if the other device does not send back any messages.

The next section discusses a wide range of WAN troubleshooting topics, including a few more details about troubleshooting CHAP issues.

Troubleshooting Serial Links

This section discusses how to isolate and find the root cause of problems related to topics covered earlier in this chapter, as well as some point-to-point WAN topics covered in *CCENT/CCNA ICND1 Official Exam Certification Guide*. Also, this section does not attempt to repeat the IP troubleshooting coverage in Parts II and III of this book, but it does point out some of the possible symptoms on a serial link when a Layer 3 subnet mismatch occurs on opposite ends of a serial link, which prevents the routers from routing packets over the serial link.

A simple **ping** command can determine whether a serial link can or cannot forward IP packets. A **ping** of the other router's serial IP address—for example, a working **ping 192.168.2.2** command on R1 in Figure 12-4—proves that the link either works or does not.

If the **ping** does not work, the problem could be related to functions at OSI Layer 1, 2, or 3. The best way to isolate which layer is the most likely cause is to examine the interface status codes described in Table 12-3. (As a reminder, router interfaces have two status codes—line status and protocol status.)

Table 12-3 *Interface Status Codes and Typical Meanings When a Ping Does Not Work*

Line Status	Protocol Status	Likely Reason/Layer
Administratively down	Down	Interface is shut down
Down	Down	Layer 1
Up	Down	Layer 2
Up	Up	Layer 3

The serial link verification and troubleshooting process should begin with a simple three-step process:

Step 1   From one router, ping the other router's serial IP address.

Step 2   If the ping fails, examine the interface status on both routers, and investigate problems related to the likely problem areas listed in Table 12-4 (shown later in this chapter).

Step 3   If the ping works, also verify that any routing protocols are exchanging routes over the link.

NOTE   The interface status codes can be found using the **show interfaces**, **show ip interface brief**, and **show interfaces description** commands.

The rest of this chapter explores the specific items to be examined when the ping fails, based on the combinations of interface status codes listed in Table 12-3.

Troubleshooting Layer 1 Problems

The interface status codes, or interface state, play a key role in isolating the root cause of problems on serial links. In fact, the status on both ends of the link may differ, so it is important to examine the status on both ends of the link to help determine the problem.

One simple and easy-to-find Layer 1 problem occurs when either one of the two routers has administratively disabled its serial interface with the **shutdown** interface subcommand. If a router's serial interface is in an administratively down line status, the solution is simple— just configure a **no shutdown** interface configuration command on the interface. Also, if one router's interface has a line status of down, the other router may be shut down, so check both sides of the link.

The combination of a *down* line status on both ends of the serial link typically points to a Layer 1 problem. The following list describes the most likely reasons:

- The leased line is down (a telco problem).

- The line from the telco is not plugged in to either or both CSU/DSUs.

- A CSU/DSU has failed or is misconfigured.

- A serial cable from a router to its CSU/DSU is disconnected or faulty.

The details of how to further isolate these four problems is beyond the scope of this book.

Interestingly, one other common physical layer problem can occur that results in both routers' interfaces being in an up/down state. On a back-to-back serial link, if the required **clock rate** command is missing on the router with a DCE cable installed, both routers' serial interfaces will fail and end up with a line status of up but a line protocol status of down. Example 12-3 shows just such an example, pointing out a couple of ways to check to see if a missing **clock rate** command is the problem. The two best ways to find this problem are to notice the absence of the **clock rate** command on the router with the DCE cable, and to note the "no clock" phrase in the output of the **show controllers serial** command. (This example shows R1 from Figure 12-4, with the **clock rate** command removed.)

Example 12-3   *Problem: No **clock rate** Command on the DCE End*

```
R1#show controller s0/0/1
Interface Serial0/0/1
Hardware is PowerQUICC MPC860
  Internet address is 192.168.2.1/24
DCE V.35, no clock
! lines omitted for brevity
R1#show running-config interface S0/0/1
```

Example 12-3 *Problem: No* **clock rate** *Command on the DCE End (Continued)*

```
Building configuration...

Current configuration : 42 bytes
!
interface Serial0/0/1
 ip address 192.168.2.1 255.255.255.0
end
```

> **NOTE** Some recent IOS releases actually prevent the user from removing the **clock rate** command on the interface if a DCE cable or no cable is installed, in an effort to prevent the unintentional omission of the **clock rate** command. Also, IOS sometimes spells the **clock rate** command as the **clockrate** command; both are acceptable.

Troubleshooting Layer 2 Problems

When both routers' serial line status is up, but at least one of the routers' line protocol status (the second interface status code) either is down or continually switches between up and down, the interface probably has one of two types of data link layer problems. This section explains both problems, which are summarized in Table 12-4.

Table 12-4 *Likely Reasons for Data-Link Problems on Serial Links*

Key
Topic

Line Status	Protocol Status	Likely Reason
Up	Down (stable) on both ends or Down (stable) on one end, flapping between up and down on the other	Mismatched **encapsulation** commands
Up	Down on one end, up on the other	Keepalive is disabled on the end in an up state
Up	Down (stable) on both ends	PAP/CHAP authentication failure

> **NOTE** As with the other troubleshooting topics in this book, Table 12-4 lists some of the more common types of failures but not all.

The first of these two problems—a mismatch between the configured data-link protocols—is easy to identify and fix. The **show interfaces** command lists the encapsulation type in the seventh line of the output, so using this command on both routers can quickly identify the problem. Alternatively, a quick look at the configuration, plus remembering that HDLC is the default serial encapsulation, can confirm whether the encapsulations are mismatched. The solution is simple—reconfigure one of the two routers to match the other router's **encapsulation** command.

The other two root causes require a little more discussion to understand the issue and determine if they are the real root cause. The next two headings take a closer look at each.

Keepalive Failure

The second item relates to a feature called *keepalive*. The *keepalive* feature helps a router recognize when a link is no longer functioning so that the router can bring down the interface, hoping to then use an alternative IP route.

The keepalive function (by default) causes routers to send keepalive messages to each other every 10 seconds (the default setting). (Cisco defines a proprietary HDLC keepalive message, with PPP defining a keepalive message as part of LCP.) This 10-second timer is the keepalive interval. If a router does not receive any keepalive messages from the other router for a number of keepalive intervals (three or five intervals by default, depending on the IOS version), the router brings down the interface, thinking that the interface is no longer working.

For real networks, it is useful to just leave keepalives enabled. However, you can make a mistake and turn off keepalives on one end of a serial link, leave them enabled on the other, and cause the link to fail. For example, if R1 were configured with the **no keepalive** interface subcommand, disabling keepalives, R1 would no longer send the keepalive messages. If R2 continued to default to use keepalives, R2 would keep sending keepalive messages, plus R2 would expect to receive keepalive messages from R1. After several keepalive intervals pass, R2, having not received any keepalive messages from R1, would change the interface to an "up and down" state. Then, R2 would continually bring the link back up, still not get any keepalives from R1, and then fall back to an "up and down" state again, and flapping up and down repeatedly. R1, not caring about keepalives, would leave the interface in an "up and up" state the whole time. Example 12-4 shows this exact example, again with the routers in Figure 12-4.

Example 12-4 *Line Problems Because of Keepalive Only on R2*

```
! R1 disables keepalives, and remains in an up/up state.
R1#configure terminal
Enter configuration commands, one per line.  End with CNTL/Z.
R1(config)#interface s 0/0/1
R1(config-if)#no keepalive
R1(config-if)#^Z
R1#show interfaces s0/0/1
Serial0/0/1 is up, line protocol is up
  Hardware is PowerQUICC Serial
```

Example 12-4 *Line Problems Because of Keepalive Only on R2 (Continued)*

```
  Internet address is 192.168.2.1/24  MTU 1500 bytes, BW 1544 Kbit, DLY 20000 usec,
     reliability 255/255, txload 1/255, rxload 1/255
  Encapsulation HDLC, loopback not set
  Keepalive not set
! lines omitted for brevity
! Below, R2 still has keepalives enabled (default)
R2#show interfaces S0/1/1
Serial0/1/1 is up, line protocol is down
  Hardware is PowerQUICC Serial
  Internet address is 192.168.2.2/24
  MTU 1500 bytes, BW 1544 Kbit, DLY 20000 usec,
     reliability 255/255, txload 1/255, rxload 1/255
  Encapsulation HDLC, loopback not set
  Keepalive set (10 sec)
! lines omitted for brevity
```

> **NOTE** It is a configuration mistake to enable keepalives on only one end of a point-to-point serial link. It appears that some very recent IOS versions notice when the keepalives are mistakenly disabled on one end of a link and prevent the problem described here from happening. For the CCNA exams, just be aware that keepalives should be enabled on both ends of the link, or disabled on both ends.

PAP and CHAP Authentication Failure

As mentioned earlier, a failure in the PAP/CHAP authentication process results in both routers falling to an "up and down" state. To discover whether a PAP/CHAP failure is really the root cause, you can use the **debug ppp authentication** command. For perspective, Example 12-5 shows the output of this command when CHAP has been configured as in earlier Example 12-2, with CHAP working correctly in this case.

Example 12-5 *Debug Messages Confirming the Correct Operation of CHAP*

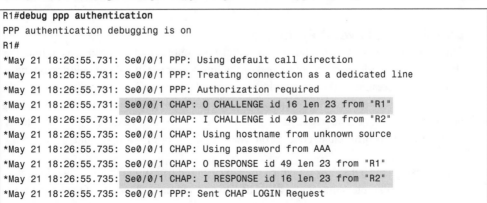

```
R1#debug ppp authentication
PPP authentication debugging is on
R1#
*May 21 18:26:55.731: Se0/0/1 PPP: Using default call direction
*May 21 18:26:55.731: Se0/0/1 PPP: Treating connection as a dedicated line
*May 21 18:26:55.731: Se0/0/1 PPP: Authorization required
*May 21 18:26:55.731: Se0/0/1 CHAP: O CHALLENGE id 16 len 23 from "R1"
*May 21 18:26:55.731: Se0/0/1 CHAP: I CHALLENGE id 49 len 23 from "R2"
*May 21 18:26:55.735: Se0/0/1 CHAP: Using hostname from unknown source
*May 21 18:26:55.735: Se0/0/1 CHAP: Using password from AAA
*May 21 18:26:55.735: Se0/0/1 CHAP: O RESPONSE id 49 len 23 from "R1"
*May 21 18:26:55.735: Se0/0/1 CHAP: I RESPONSE id 16 len 23 from "R2"
*May 21 18:26:55.735: Se0/0/1 PPP: Sent CHAP LOGIN Request
```

continues

Example 12-5 *Debug Messages Confirming the Correct Operation of CHAP (Continued)*

```
*May 21 18:26:55.735: Se0/0/1 PPP: Received LOGIN Response PASS
*May 21 18:26:55.735: Se0/0/1 PPP: Sent LCP AUTHOR Request
*May 21 18:26:55.735: Se0/0/1 PPP: Sent IPCP AUTHOR Request
*May 21 18:26:55.735: Se0/0/1 LCP: Received AAA AUTHOR Response PASS
*May 21 18:26:55.739: Se0/0/1 IPCP: Received AAA AUTHOR Response PASS
*May 21 18:26:55.739: Se0/0/1 CHAP: O SUCCESS id 16 len 4
*May 21 18:26:55.739: Se0/0/1 CHAP: I SUCCESS id 49 len 4
```

CHAP uses a three-message exchange, as shown back in Figure 12-3, with a set of messages flowing for authentication in each direction by default. The three highlighted lines show the authentication process by which R1 authenticates R2; it begins with R1 sending a challenge message. The first highlighted message in Example 12-5 lists an "O," meaning "output." This indicates that the message is a challenge message and that it was sent from R1. The next highlighted message is the received response message (noted with an "I" for input), from R2. The last highlighted line is the third message, sent by R1, stating that the authentication was successful. You can see the same three messages for R2's authentication of R1 in the output as well, but those messages are not highlighted in the example.

When CHAP authentication fails, the **debug** output shows a couple of fairly obvious messages. Example 12-6 shows the results using the same two-router internetwork shown in Figure 12-4, this time with the passwords misconfigured, so CHAP fails.

Example 12-6 *Debug Messages Confirming the Failure of CHAP*

```
R1#debug ppp authentication
PPP authentication debugging is on
! Lines omitted for brevity
*May 21 18:24:03.171: Se0/0/1 PPP: Sent CHAP LOGIN Request
*May 21 18:24:03.171: Se0/0/1 PPP: Received LOGIN Response FAIL
*May 21 18:24:03.171: Se0/0/1 CHAP: O FAILURE id 15 len 25 msg is "Authentication failed"
```

Troubleshooting Layer 3 Problems

This chapter suggests that the best starting place to troubleshoot serial links is to ping the IP address of the router on the other end of the link—specifically, the IP address on the serial link. Interestingly, the serial link can be in an "up and up" state but the ping can still fail because of Layer 3 misconfiguration. In some cases, the ping may work, but the routing protocols may not be able to exchange routes. This short section examines the symptoms, which are slightly different depending on whether HDLC or PPP is used, and the root cause.

First, consider an HDLC link on which the physical and data-link details are working fine. In this case, both routers' interfaces are in an "up and up" state. However, if the IP addresses configured on the serial interfaces on the two routers are in different subnets, a ping to the IP address on the other end of the link will fail, because the routers do not have a matching route. For example, in Figure 12-4, if R1's serial IP address remained 192.168.2.1, and R2's was changed to 192.168.3.2 (instead of 192.168.2.2), still with a mask of /24, the two routers would have connected routes to different subnets. They would not have a route matching the opposite router's serial IP address.

Finding and fixing a mismatched subnet problem with HDLC links is relatively simple. You can find the problem by doing the usual first step of pinging the IP address on the other end of the link, and failing. If both interface status codes on both routers' interfaces are up, the problem is likely this mismatched IP subnet.

For PPP links, with the same IP address/mask misconfiguration, both routers' interfaces also are in an "up and up" state, but the ping to the other router's IP address actually works. As it turns out, a router using PPP advertises its serial interface IP address to the other router, with a /32 prefix, which is a route to reach just that one host. So, both routers have a route with which to route packets to the other end of the link, even though two routers on opposite ends of a serial link have mismatched their IP addresses. For example, in Figure 12-4 again, if R2's IP address were 192.168.4.2/24, while R1's remained 192.168.2.1/24, the two addresses would be in different subnets, but the pings would work because of PPP's advertisement of the host routes. Example 12-7 shows this exact scenario.

NOTE   A route with a /32 prefix, representing a single host, is called a *host route*.

Example 12-7 *PPP Allowing a Ping over a Serial Link, Even with Mismatched Subnets*

```
R1#show ip route
Codes: C - connected, S - static, R - RIP, M - mobile, B - BGP
       D - EIGRP, EX - EIGRP external, O - OSPF, IA - OSPF inter area
       N1 - OSPF NSSA external type 1, N2 - OSPF NSSA external type 2
       E1 - OSPF external type 1, E2 - OSPF external type 2
       i - IS-IS, su - IS-IS summary, L1 - IS-IS level-1, L2 - IS-IS level-2
       ia - IS-IS inter area, * - candidate default, U - per-user static route
       o - ODR, P - periodic downloaded static route

C    192.168.1.0/24 is directly connected, FastEthernet0/0
C    192.168.2.0/24 is directly connected, Serial0/0/1
     192.168.4.0/32 is subnetted, 1 subnets
C       192.168.4.2 is directly connected, Serial0/0/1
R1#ping 192.168.4.2

Type escape sequence to abort.
Sending 5, 100-byte ICMP Echos to 192.168.4.2, timeout is 2 seconds:
!!!!!
Success rate is 100 percent (5/5), round-trip min/avg/max = 1/2/4 ms
```

The first highlighted line in the example shows the normal connected route on the serial link, for network 192.168.2.0/24. R1 thinks this subnet is the subnet connected to S0/0/1 because of R1's configured IP address (192.168.2.1/24). The second highlighted line shows the host route created by PPP, specifically for R2's new serial IP address (192.168.4.2). (R2 will have a similar route for 192.168.2.1/32, R1's serial IP address.) So, both routers have a route to allow them to forward packets to the IP address on the other end of the link, which allows the **ping** to the other side of the serial link to work in spite of the addresses on each end being in different subnets.

Although the **ping** to the other end of the link works, the routing protocols still do not advertise routes because of the IP subnet mismatch on the opposite ends of the link. So, when troubleshooting a network problem, do not assume that a serial interface in an up/up state is fully working, or even that a serial interface over which a ping works is fully working. Also make sure the routing protocol is exchanging routes and that the IP addresses are in the same subnet. Table 12-5 summarizes the behavior on HDLC and PPP links when the IP addresses on each end do not reside in the same subnet but no other problems exist.

Table 12-5 *Summary of Symptoms for Mismatched Subnets on Serial Links*

Symptoms When IP Addresses on a Serial Link Are in Different Subnets	HDLC	PPP
Does a ping of the other router's serial IP address work?	No	Yes
Can routing protocols exchange routes over the link?	No	No

Exam Preparation Tasks

Review All the Key Topics

Review the most important topics from this chapter, noted with the key topics icon. Table 12-6 lists these key topics and where each is discussed.

Table 12-6 *Key Topics for Chapter 12*

Key Topic Element	Description	Page Number
List	PPP features	436
Table 12-2	PPP LCP features	438
Figure 12-3	Comparison of messages sent by PAP and CHAP	441
List	Configuration checklist for CHAP	443
Table 12-3	List of typical combinations of serial interface status codes, and the typical general reason for each combination	445
List	Common reasons for Layer 1 serial link problems	446
Table 12-4	Common symptoms and reasons for common Layer 2 problems on serial links	447
Example 12-5	Sample **debug** messages showing a successful CHAP authentication process	449

Complete the Tables and Lists from Memory

Print a copy of Appendix J, "Memory Tables" (found on the CD), or at least the section for this chapter, and complete the tables and lists from memory. Appendix K, "Memory Tables Answer Key," also on the CD, includes completed tables and lists for you to check your work.

Definitions of Key Terms

Define the following key terms from this chapter, and check your answers in the glossary:

CHAP, IP control protocol, keepalive, Link Control Protocol, PAP

Command Reference to Check Your Memory

Although you should not necessarily memorize the information in the tables in this section, this section does include a reference for the configuration and EXEC commands covered in this chapter. Practically speaking, you should memorize the commands as a side effect of reading the chapter and doing all the activities in this exam preparation section. To see how well you have memorized the commands as a side effect of your other studies, cover the left side of the table, read the descriptions on the right side, and see if you remember the command.

Table 12-7   *Chapter 12 Configuration Command Reference*

Command	Description
encapsulation {**hdlc** l **ppp**}	Interface subcommand that defines the serial data-link protocol.
ppp authentication {**pap** l **chap** l **pap chap** l **chap pap**}	Interface subcommand that enables only PAP, only CHAP, or both (order-dependent).
username *name* **password** *secret*	Global command that sets the password that this router expects to use when authenticating the router with the listed hostname.

Table 12-8   *Chapter 12 EXEC Command Reference*

Command	Description
show interfaces [*type number*]	Lists statistics and details of interface configuration, including the encapsulation type.
debug ppp authentication	Generates messages for each step in the PAP or CHAP authentication process.
debug ppp negotiation	Generates **debug** messages for the LCP and NCP negotiation messages sent between the devices.

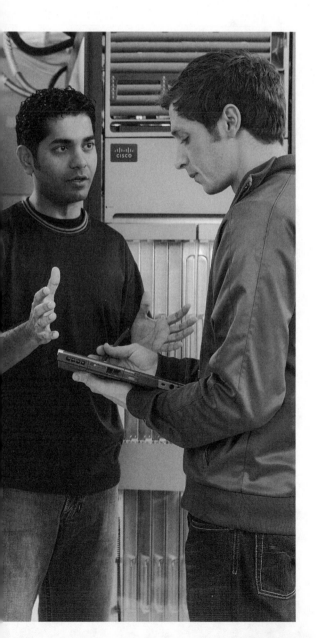

This chapter covers the following subjects:

Frame Relay Overview: This section introduces the terminology, functions, and purpose of Frame Relay protocols.

Frame Relay Addressing: This section examines the DLCI, the Frame Relay data-link address, and how it is used to transfer frames over the Frame Relay cloud.

Network Layer Concerns with Frame Relay: This section mainly examines the various options for the use of Layer 3 subnets over a Frame Relay network.

Controlling Speed and Discards in the Frame Relay Cloud: This short section explains a few features related to controlling the flow of data over the Frame Relay network.

CHAPTER 13

Frame Relay Concepts

Frame Relay remains the most popular WAN technology used today. However, its popularity is waning. It is being replaced mainly by virtual private network (VPN) technology of two main types: Internet VPNs, which use the Internet to transport packets, and Multiprotocol Label Switching (MPLS) VPNs, which follow the same basic service model as Frame Relay, typically offered by the same Frame Relay providers, but with significant technical advantages. However, Frame Relay is still used by many companies today, and it can also be used to connect to MPLS and Internet VPNs, so Frame Relay will be an important networking topic for some time.

Frame Relay most closely compares to the OSI data link layer (Layer 2). If you remember that the word "frame" describes the data link layer protocol data unit (PDU), it will be easy to remember that Frame Relay relates to OSI Layer 2. Like other data-link protocols, Frame Relay can be used to deliver packets (Layer 3 PDUs) between routers. Frame Relay protocol headers and trailers are simply used to let a packet traverse the Frame Relay network, just like Ethernet headers and trailers are used to help a packet traverse an Ethernet segment.

This chapter describes Frame Relay protocol details. Chapter 14, "Frame Relay Configuration and Troubleshooting," examines the configuration, verification, and troubleshooting of Frame Relay networks.

"Do I Know This Already?" Quiz

The "Do I Know This Already?" quiz allows you to assess whether you should read the entire chapter. If you miss no more than one of these eight self-assessment questions, you might want to move ahead to the "Exam Preparation Tasks" section. Table 13-1 lists the major headings in this chapter and the "Do I Know This Already?" quiz questions covering the material in those sections. This helps you assess your knowledge of these specific areas. The answers to the "Do I Know This Already?" quiz appear in Appendix A.

Table 13-1   *"Do I Know This Already?" Foundation Topics Section-to-Question Mapping*

Foundation Topics Section	Questions
Frame Relay Overview	1–3
Frame Relay Addressing	4 and 5
Network Layer Concerns with Frame Relay	6 and 7
Controlling Speed and Discards in the Frame Relay Cloud	8

1. Which of the following is a protocol used between the Frame Relay DTE and the Frame Relay switch?

   a. VC

   b. CIR

   c. LMI

   d. Q.921

   e. DLCI

   f. FRF.5

   g. Encapsulation

2. Which of the following statements about Frame Relay are true?

   a. The DTE typically sits at the customer site.

   b. Routers send LMI messages to each other to signal the status of a VC.

   c. A frame's source DLCI must remain unchanged, but the frame's destination DLCI is allowed to change, as the frame traverses the Frame Relay cloud.

   d. The Frame Relay encapsulation type on the sending router should match the encapsulation type on the receiving router for the receiving router to be able to understand the frame's contents.

3. What does DLCI stand for?

   a. Data-link connection identifier

   b. Data-link connection indicator

   c. Data-link circuit identifier

   d. Data-link circuit indicator

4. Router R1 receives a frame from router R2 with DLCI value 222 in it. Which of the following statements about this network is the most accurate?

   a. 222 represents Router R1.

   b. 222 represents Router R2.

   c. 222 is the local DLCI on R1 that represents the VC between R1 and R2.

   d. 222 is the local DLCI on R2 that represents the VC between R1 and R2.

5. A Frame Relay planning diagram shows the number 101 beside R1, 102 by R2, 103 by R3, and 104 by R4. No other DLCIs are listed. The lead network engineer tells you that the planning diagram uses global DLCI addressing and that a full mesh of VCs exists. Which of the following are true?

   a. Frames sent by R1 to R2, as they cross R2's access link, have DLCI 102.

   b. Frames sent by R1 to R2, as they cross R2's access link, have DLCI 101.

   c. Frames sent by R3 to R2, as they cross R3's access link, have DLCI 102.

   d. Frames sent by R3 to R1, as they cross R3's access link, have DLCI 102.

6. FredsCo has five sites, with routers connected to the same Frame Relay network. Virtual circuits (VC) have been defined between each pair of routers. What is the fewest subnets that FredsCo could use on the Frame Relay network?

   a. 1

   b. 2

   c. 3

   d. 4

   e. 5

   f. 10

7. BarneyCo has five sites, with routers connected to the same Frame Relay network. VCs have been defined between each pair of routers. Barney, the company president, will fire anyone who configures Frame Relay without using point-to-point subinterfaces. What is the fewest subnets that BarneyCo could use on the Frame Relay network?

   a. 1

   b. 4

   c. 8

   d. 10

   e. 12

   f. 15

8. R1 sends a Frame Relay frame over a VC to router R2. About the same time, a Frame Relay switch notices that too many packets are trying to exit the Frame Relay network over the access link connected to R2. Which of the following is the most likely result that could be caused by this scenario?

a. R1 eventually receives a frame with BECN set.

b. R1 eventually receives a frame with FECN set.

c. R1 eventually receives a frame with DE set.

d. None of the other answers is correct.

Foundation Topics

With point-to-point serial links, a company orders a leased line, or circuit, between two points. The telco creates the circuit, installing a two-pair (four-wire) cable into the buildings on either end of the circuit. The telco creates the circuit so that it will run at the preset speed requested by the customer, typically some multiple of 64 kbps. As soon as the Telcos' cable has been connected to a CSU/DSU, and a router, on each end of the circuit, the routers have a dedicated physical link, with the ability to send data in both directions simultaneously.

Frame Relay is a set of WAN standards that create a more efficient WAN service as compared to point-to-point links, while still allowing pairs of routers to send data directly to each other. With leased lines, each leased line requires a serial interface on each router and a separate (and expensive) physical circuit built by the telco. Frame Relay supports the ability to send data to multiple remote routers over a single physical WAN circuit. For example, a company with one central site and ten remote sites would require ten leased lines to communicate with the main site and ten serial interfaces on the central site router. With Frame Relay, the main site could have a single leased line connecting it to the Frame Relay service, and a single serial interface on the router at the central site, and still be able to communicate with each of the ten remote-site routers.

The first section of this chapter focuses on the basics of Frame Relay, including a lot of new terminology. The second section examines Frame Relay data-link addressing. This topic requires some attention because Frame Relay addresses are needed for both router configuration and troubleshooting. The last two major sections of this chapter examine some network layer concerns when using Frame Relay, along with a few features that impact the speed and frame discard rates inside the Frame Relay cloud.

Frame Relay Overview

Frame Relay networks provide more features and benefits than simple point-to-point WAN links, but to do that, Frame Relay protocols are more detailed. For example, Frame Relay networks are multiaccess networks, which means that more than two devices can attach to the network, similar to LANs. Unlike with LANs, you cannot send a data link layer broadcast over Frame Relay. Therefore, Frame Relay networks are called *nonbroadcast multiaccess* (*NBMA*) networks. Also, because Frame Relay is multiaccess, it requires the use of an address that identifies to which remote router each frame is addressed.

Figure 13-1 outlines the basic physical topology and related terminology in a Frame Relay network.

Key
Topic

Figure 13-1 *Frame Relay Components*

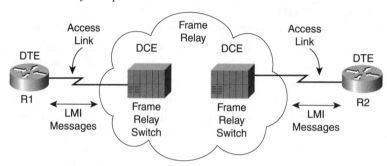

Figure 13-1 shows the most basic components of a Frame Relay network. A leased line is installed between the router and a nearby Frame Relay switch; this link is called the *access link*. To ensure that the link is working, the device outside the Frame Relay network, called the *data terminal equipment (DTE)*, exchanges regular messages with the Frame Relay switch. These keepalive messages, along with other messages, are defined by the Frame Relay *Local Management Interface (LMI)* protocol. The routers are considered DTE, and the Frame Relay switches are *data communications equipment (DCE)*.

Whereas Figure 13-1 shows the physical connectivity at each connection to the Frame Relay network, Figure 13-2 shows the logical, or virtual, end-to-end connectivity associated with a virtual circuit (VC).

Figure 13-2 *Frame Relay PVC Concepts*

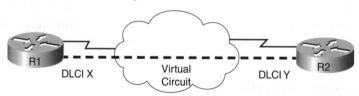

The logical communications path between each pair of DTEs is a VC. The dashed line in the figure represents a single VC; this book uses a thick dashed line style to make sure you notice the line easily. Typically, the service provider preconfigures all the required details of a VC; predefined VCs are called permanent virtual circuits (PVC).

Routers use the data-link connection identifier (DLCI) as the Frame Relay address; it identifies the VC over which the frame should travel. So, in Figure 13-2, when R1 needs to forward a packet to R2, R1 encapsulates the Layer 3 packet into a Frame Relay header and trailer and then sends the frame. The Frame Relay header includes the correct DLCI so that the provider's Frame Relay switches correctly forward the frame to R2.

Table 13-2 lists the components shown in Figures 13-1 and 13-2 and some associated terms. After the table, the most important features of Frame Relay are described in further detail.

Table 13-2 *Frame Relay Terms and Concepts*

Key
Topic

Term	Description
Virtual circuit (VC)	A logical concept that represents the path that frames travel between DTEs. VCs are particularly useful when you compare Frame Relay to leased physical circuits.
Permanent virtual circuit (PVC)	A predefined VC. A PVC can be equated to a leased line in concept.
Switched virtual circuit (SVC)	A VC that is set up dynamically when needed. An SVC can be equated to a dial connection in concept.
Data terminal equipment (DTE)	DTEs are connected to a Frame Relay service from a telecommunications company. They typically reside at sites used by the company buying the Frame Relay service.
Data communications equipment (DCE)	Frame Relay switches are DCE devices. DCEs are also known as data circuit-terminating equipment. DCEs are typically in the service provider's network.
Access link	The leased line between the DTE and DCE.
Access rate (AR)	The speed at which the access link is clocked. This choice affects the connection's price.
Committed Information Rate (CIR)	The speed at which bits can be sent over a VC, according to the business contract between the customer and provider.
Data-link connection identifier (DLCI)	A Frame Relay address used in Frame Relay headers to identify the VC.
Nonbroadcast multiaccess (NBMA)	A network in which broadcasts are not supported, but more than two devices can be connected.
Local Management Interface (LMI)	The protocol used between a DCE and DTE to manage the connection. Signaling messages for SVCs, PVC status messages, and keepalives are all LMI messages.

Frame Relay Standards

The definitions for Frame Relay are contained in documents from the International Telecommunications Union (ITU) and the American National Standards Institute (ANSI). The Frame Relay Forum (http://www.frforum.com), a vendor consortium, also defines several Frame Relay specifications, many of which predate the original ITU and ANSI specifications, with the ITU and ANSI picking up many of the forum's standards. Table 13-3 lists the most important of these specifications.

Table 13-3 *Frame Relay Protocol Specifications*

What the Specification Defines	ITU Document	ANSI Document
Data-link specifications, including LAPF header/trailer	Q.922 Annex A (Q.922-A)	T1.618
PVC management, LMI	Q.933 Annex A (Q.933-A)	T1.617 Annex D (T1.617-D)
SVC signaling	Q.933	T1.617
Multiprotocol encapsulation (originated in RFC 1490/2427)	Q.933 Annex E (Q.933-E)	T1.617 Annex F (T1.617-F)

Virtual Circuits

Frame Relay provides significant advantages over simply using point-to-point leased lines. The primary advantage has to do with virtual circuits. Consider Figure 13-3, which shows a typical Frame Relay network with three sites.

Figure 13-3 *Typical Frame Relay Network with Three Sites*

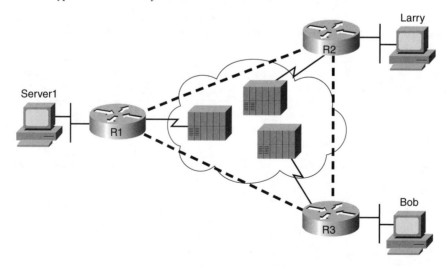

A virtual circuit defines a logical path between two Frame Relay DTEs. The term *virtual circuit* describes the concept well. It acts like a point-to-point circuit, providing the ability to send data between two endpoints over a WAN. There is no physical circuit directly between the two endpoints, so it's virtual. For example, R1 terminates two VCs—one whose other endpoint is R2, and one whose other endpoint is R3. R1 can send traffic directly to either of the other two routers by sending it over the appropriate VC.

VCs share the access link and the Frame Relay network. For example, both VCs terminating at R1 use the same access link. In fact, many customers share the same Frame Relay network. Originally, people with leased-line networks were reluctant to migrate to Frame Relay, because they would be competing with other customers for the provider's capacity inside the cloud. To address these fears, Frame Relay is designed with the concept of a committed information rate (CIR). Each VC has a CIR, which is a guarantee by the provider that a particular VC gets at least that much bandwidth. So you can migrate from a leased line to Frame Relay, getting a CIR of at least as much bandwidth as you previously had with your leased line.

Interestingly, even with a three-site network, it's probably less expensive to use Frame Relay than to use point-to-point links. Imagine an organization with 100 sites that needs any-to-any connectivity. How many leased lines are required? 4950! And besides that, the organization would need 99 serial interfaces per router if it used point-to-point leased lines. With Frame Relay, an organization could have 100 access links to local Frame Relay switches, one per router, and have 4950 VCs running over them. That requires a lot fewer actual physical links, and you would need only one serial interface on each router!

Service providers can build their Frame Relay networks more cost-effectively than for leased lines. As you would expect, that makes it less expensive for the Frame Relay customer as well. For connecting many WAN sites, Frame Relay is simply more cost-effective than leased lines.

Two types of VCs are allowed—permanent (PVC) and switched (SVC). PVCs are predefined by the provider; SVCs are created dynamically. PVCs are by far the more popular of the two. Frame Relay providers seldom offer SVCs as a service. (The rest of this chapter and Chapter 14 ignore SVCs.)

When the Frame Relay network is engineered, the design might not include a VC between each pair of sites. Figure 13-3 includes PVCs between each pair of sites; this is called a full-mesh Frame Relay network. When not all pairs have a direct PVC, it is called a partial-mesh network. Figure 13-4 shows the same network as Figure 13-3, but this time with a partial mesh and only two PVCs. This is typical when R1 is at the main site and R2 and R3 are at remote offices that rarely need to communicate directly.

Figure 13-4 *Typical Partial-Mesh Frame Relay Network*

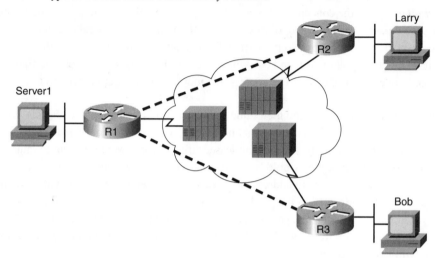

The partial mesh has some advantages and disadvantages compared to a full mesh. The primary advantage is that partial mesh is cheaper, because the provider charges per VC. The downside is that traffic from R2's site to R3's site must go to R1 first and then be forwarded. If that's a small amount of traffic, it's a small price to pay. If it's a lot of traffic, a full mesh is probably worth the extra money, because traffic going between two remote sites would have to cross R1's access link twice.

One conceptual hurdle with PVCs is that there is typically a single access link across which multiple PVCs flow. For example, consider Figure 13-4 from R1's perspective. Server1 sends a packet to Larry. It comes across the Ethernet. R1 gets it and matches Larry's routing table, which tells him to send the packet out Serial0, which is R1's access link. He encapsulates the packet in a Frame Relay header and trailer and then sends it. Which PVC does it use? The Frame Relay switch should forward it to R2, but why does it?

To solve this problem, Frame Relay uses an address to differentiate one PVC from another. This address is called a data-link connection identifier (DLCI). The name is descriptive: The address is for an OSI Layer 2 (data-link) protocol, and it identifies a VC, which is sometimes called a *virtual connection*. So, in this example, R1 uses the DLCI that identifies the PVC to R2, so the provider forwards the frame correctly over the PVC to R2. To send frames to R3, R1 uses the DLCI that identifies the VC for R3. DLCIs and how they work are covered in more detail later in this chapter.

LMI and Encapsulation Types

When you're first learning about Frame Relay, it's often easy to confuse the LMI and the encapsulation used with Frame Relay. The LMI is a definition of the messages used between the DTE (for example, a router) and the DCE (for example, the Frame Relay switch owned by the service provider). The encapsulation defines the headers used by a DTE to communicate some information to the DTE on the other end of a VC. The switch and its connected router care about using the same LMI; the switch does not care about the encapsulation. The endpoint routers (DTE) do care about the encapsulation.

The most important LMI message relating to topics on the exam is the LMI status inquiry message. Status messages perform two key functions:

- They perform a keepalive function between the DTE and DCE. If the access link has a problem, the absence of keepalive messages implies that the link is down.

- They signal whether a PVC is active or inactive. Even though each PVC is predefined, its status can change. An access link might be up, but one or more VCs could be down. The router needs to know which VCs are up and which are down. It learns that information from the switch using LMI status messages.

Three LMI protocol options are available in Cisco IOS software: Cisco, ITU, and ANSI. Each LMI option is slightly different and therefore is incompatible with the other two. As long as both the DTE and DCE on each end of an access link use the same LMI standard, LMI works fine.

The differences between LMI types are subtle. For example, the Cisco LMI calls for the use of DLCI 1023, whereas ANSI T1.617-D and ITU Q.933-A specify DLCI 0. Some of the messages have different fields in their headers. The DTE simply needs to know which of the three LMIs to use so that it can use the same one as the local switch.

Configuring the LMI type is easy. Today's most popular option is to use the default LMI setting. This setting uses the LMI autosense feature, in which the router simply figures out which LMI type the switch is using. So you can simply let the router autosense the LMI and never bother coding the LMI type. If you choose to configure the LMI type, the router disables the autosense feature.

Table 13-4 outlines the three LMI types, their origin, and the keyword used in the Cisco IOS software **frame-relay lmi-type** interface subcommand.

Table 13-4   *Frame Relay LMI Types*

Name	Document	IOS LMI-Type Parameter
Cisco	Proprietary	**cisco**
ANSI	T1.617 Annex D	**ansi**
ITU	Q.933 Annex A	**q933a**

A Frame Relay-connected router encapsulates each Layer 3 packet inside a Frame Relay header and trailer before it is sent out an access link. The header and trailer are defined by the Link Access Procedure Frame Bearer Services (LAPF) specification, ITU Q.922-A. The sparse LAPF framing provides error detection with an FCS in the trailer, as well as the DLCI, DE, FECN, and BECN fields in the header (which are discussed later). Figure 13-5 diagrams the frame.

Figure 13-5   *LAPF Header*

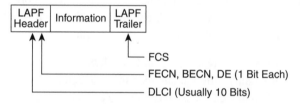

However, the LAPF header and trailer do not provide all the fields typically needed by routers. In particular, Figure 13-5 does not show a Protocol Type field. Each data-link header needs a field to define the type of packet that follows the data-link header. If Frame Relay is using only the LAPF header, DTEs (including routers) cannot support multiprotocol traffic, because there is no way to identify the type of protocol in the Information field.

Two solutions were created to compensate for the lack of a Protocol Type field in the standard Frame Relay header:

- Cisco and three other companies created an additional header, which comes between the LAPF header and the Layer 3 packet shown in Figure 13-5. It includes a 2-byte Protocol Type field, with values matching the same field Cisco uses for HDLC.

- RFC 1490 (which was later superceded by RFC 2427; you should know both numbers), *Multiprotocol Interconnect over Frame Relay*, defined the second solution. RFC 1490 was written to ensure multivendor interoperability between Frame Relay DTEs. This RFC defines a similar header, also placed between the LAPF header and

Layer 3 packet, and includes a Protocol Type field as well as many other options. ITU and ANSI later incorporated RFC 1490 headers into their Q.933 Annex E and T1.617 Annex F specifications, respectively.

Figure 13-6 outlines these two alternatives.

Figure 13-6   *Cisco and RFC 1490/2427 Encapsulation*

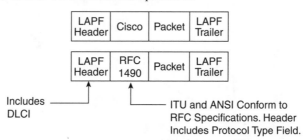

DTEs use and react to the fields specified by these two types of encapsulation, but Frame Relay switches ignore these fields. *Because the frames flow from DTE to DTE, both DTEs should agree on the encapsulation used. The switches don't care.* However, each VC can use a different encapsulation. In the configuration, the encapsulation created by Cisco is called **cisco**, and the other one is called **ietf**.

Now that you have a broad understanding of Frame Relay concepts and terminology, the next section takes a much closer look at Frame Relay DLCIs.

Frame Relay Addressing

Frame Relay defines the rules by which devices deliver Frame Relay frames across a Frame Relay network. Because a router uses a single access link that has many VCs connecting it to many routers, there must be something to identify each of the remote routers—in other words, an address. The DLCI is the Frame Relay address.

DLCIs work slightly differently from the other data-link addresses covered on the CCNA exams. This difference is mainly because of the use of the DLCI and the fact that *the header has a single DLCI field, not both Source and Destination DLCI fields.*

Frame Relay Local Addressing

You should understand a few characteristics of DLCIs before we get into their use. Frame Relay DLCIs are locally significant; this means that the addresses need to be unique only on the local access link. A popular analogy that explains local addressing is that there can be only a single street address of 2000 Pennsylvania Avenue in Washington, DC, but there can be a 2000 Pennsylvania Avenue in every town in the United States. Likewise, DLCIs must be unique on each access link, but the same DLCI numbers can be used on every access link in your network. For example, in Figure 13-7, notice that DLCI 40 is used on two access links to describe two different PVCs. No conflict exists, because DLCI 40 is used on two different access links.

Figure 13-7   *Frame Relay Addressing with Router A Sending to Routers B and C*

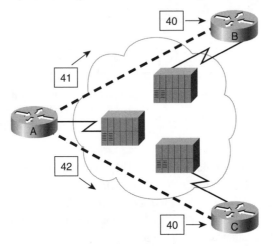

Local addressing, which is the common term for the fact that DLCIs are locally significant, is a fact. It is how Frame Relay works. Simply put, a single access link cannot use the same DLCI to represent multiple VCs on the same access link. Otherwise, the Frame Relay switch would not know how to forward frames correctly. For instance, in Figure 13-7, Router A must use different DLCI values for the PVCs on its local access link (41 and 42 in this instance).

Frame Relay Global Addressing

Most people get confused about DLCIs the first time they think about the local significance of DLCIs and the existence of only a single DLCI field in the Frame Relay header. Global addressing solves this problem by making DLCI addressing look like LAN addressing in concept. Global addressing is simply a way of choosing DLCI numbers when planning a Frame Relay network so that working with DLCIs is much easier. Because local addressing is a fact, global addressing does not change these rules. Global addressing just makes DLCI assignment more obvious—as soon as you get used to it.

Here's how global addressing works: The service provider hands out a planning spreadsheet and a diagram. Figure 13-8 is an example of such a diagram, with the global DLCIs shown.

Figure 13-8 *Frame Relay Global DLCIs*

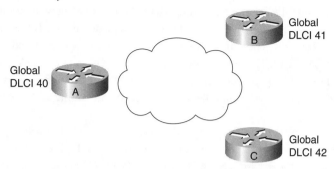

Global addressing is planned as shown in Figure 13-8, with the DLCIs placed in Frame Relay frames as shown in Figure 13-9. For example, Router A uses DLCI 41 when sending a frame to Router B, because Router B's global DLCI is 41. Likewise, Router A uses DLCI 42 when sending frames over the VC to Router C. The nice thing is that global addressing is much more logical to most people, because it works like a LAN, with a single MAC address for each device. On a LAN, if the MAC addresses are MAC-A, MAC-B, and MAC-C for the three routers, Router A uses destination address MAC-B when sending frames to Router B and uses MAC-C as the destination to reach Router C. Likewise, with global DLCIs 40, 41, and 42 used for Routers A, B, and C, respectively, the same concept applies. Because DLCIs address VCs, the logic is something like this when Router A sends a frame to Router B: "Hey, local switch! When you get this frame, send it over the VC that we agreed to number with DLCI 41." Figure 13-9 outlines this example.

Figure 13-9 *Frame Relay Global Addressing from the Sender's Perspective*

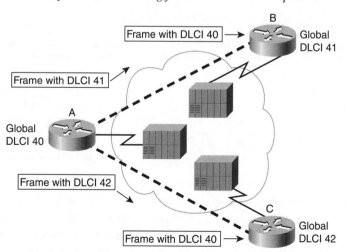

Router A sends frames with DLCI 41, and they reach the local switch. The local switch sees the DLCI field and forwards the frame through the Frame Relay network until it reaches the switch connected to Router B. Then Router B's local switch forwards the frame out the access link to Router B. The same process happens between Router A and Router C when Router A uses DLCI 42. The beauty of global addressing is that you think of each router as having an address, like LAN addressing. If you want to send a frame to someone, you put his or her DLCI in the header, and the network delivers the frame to the correct DTE.

The final key to global addressing is that the Frame Relay switches actually change the DLCI value before delivering the frame. Did you notice that Figure 13-9 shows a different DLCI value as the frames are received by Routers B and C? For example, Router A sends a frame to Router B, and Router A puts DLCI 41 in the frame. The last switch changes the field to DLCI 40 before forwarding it to Router B. The result is that when Routers B and C receive their frames, the DLCI value is actually the sender's DLCI. Why? Well, when Router B receives the frame, because the DLCI is 40, it knows that the frame came in on the PVC between itself and Router A. In general, the following are true:

- The sender treats the DLCI field as a destination address, using the destination's global DLCI in the header.

- The receiver thinks of the DLCI field as the source address, because it contains the global DLCI of the frame's sender.

Figure 13-9 describes what happens in a typical Frame Relay network. Service providers supply a planning spreadsheet and diagrams with global DLCIs listed. Table 13-5 gives you an organized view of what DLCIs are used in Figure 13-9.

Table 13-5 *DLCI Swapping in the Frame Relay Cloud of Figure 13-9*

The Frame Sent by Router	With DLCI Field	Is Delivered to Router	With DLCI Field
A	41	B	40
A	42	C	40
B	40	A	41
C	40	A	42

Global addressing makes DLCI addressing more intuitive for most people. It also makes router configuration more straightforward and lets you add new sites more conveniently. For instance, examine Figure 13-10, which adds Routers D and E to the network shown in Figure 13-9. The service provider simply states that global DLCIs 43 and 44 are used for these two routers. If these two routers also have only one PVC to Router A, all the DLCI planning is complete. You know that Router D and Router E use DLCI 40 to reach Router A and that Router A uses DLCI 43 to reach Router D and DLCI 44 to reach Router E.

Figure 13-10 *Adding Frame Relay Sites: Global Addressing*

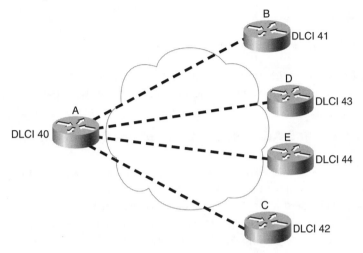

The remaining examples in this chapter use global addressing in any planning diagrams unless otherwise stated. One practical way to determine whether the diagram lists the local DLCIs or the global DLCI convention is this: If two VCs terminate at the same DTE, and a single DLCI is shown, it probably represents the global DLCI convention. If one DLCI is shown per VC, local DLCI addressing is depicted.

Now that you have a better understanding of how Frame Relay uses DLCIs to address each VC, causing the correct delivery of frames over a Frame Relay cloud, the next section moves up to Layer 3, examining the IP addressing conventions that can be used over Frame Relay.

Network Layer Concerns with Frame Relay

Frame Relay networks have both similarities and differences as compared to LAN and point-to-point WAN links. These differences introduce some additional considerations for passing Layer 3 packets across a Frame Relay network. You need to concern yourself with a couple of key issues relating to Layer 3 flows over Frame Relay:

■   Choices for Layer 3 addresses on Frame Relay interfaces

■   Broadcast handling

In particular, the Frame Relay implementation in Cisco defines three different options for assigning subnets and IP addresses on Frame Relay interfaces:

■   One subnet containing all Frame Relay DTEs

■   One subnet per VC

■   A hybrid of the first two options

This section examines the three main options for IP addressing over Frame Relay, as well as broadcast handling, which impacts how routing protocols work over Frame Relay.

Frame Relay Layer 3 Addressing: One Subnet Containing All Frame Relay DTEs

Figure 13-11 shows the first alternative, which is to use a single subnet for the Frame Relay network. This figure shows a fully meshed Frame Relay network because the single-subnet option is typically used when a full mesh of VCs exists. In a full mesh, each router has a VC to every other router, meaning that each router can send frames directly to every other router. This more closely resembles how a LAN works. So, a single subnet can be used for all the routers' Frame Relay interfaces, as configured on the routers' serial interfaces. Table 13-6 summarizes the addresses used in Figure 13-11.

Figure 13-11   *Full Mesh with IP Addresses*

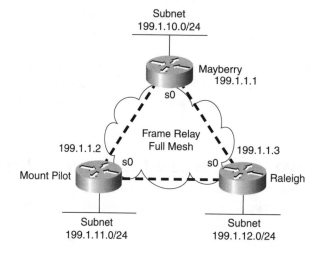

Table 13-6 *IP Addresses with No Subinterfaces*

Router	IP Address of Frame Relay Interface
Mayberry	199.1.1.1
Mount Pilot	199.1.1.2
Raleigh	199.1.1.3

The single-subnet alternative is straightforward, and it conserves your IP address space. It also looks like what you are used to with LANs, which makes it easier to conceptualize. Unfortunately, most companies build partial-mesh Frame Relay networks, and the single-subnet option has some deficiencies when the network is a partial mesh.

Frame Relay Layer 3 Addressing: One Subnet Per VC

The second IP addressing alternative, having a single subnet for each VC, works better with a partially meshed Frame Relay network, as shown in Figure 13-12. Boston cannot forward frames directly to Charlotte, because no VC is defined between the two. This is a more typical Frame Relay network, because most organizations with many sites tend to group applications on servers at a few centralized locations, and most of the traffic is between each remote site and those servers.

Figure 13-12 *Partial Mesh with IP Addresses*

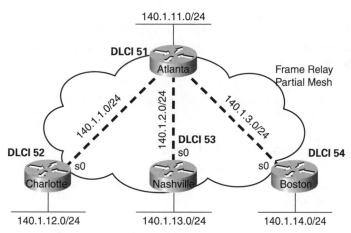

The single-subnet-per-VC alternative matches the logic behind a set of point-to-point links. Using multiple subnets instead of one larger subnet wastes some IP addresses, but it overcomes some issues with distance vector routing protocols.

Table 13-7 shows the IP addresses for the partially meshed Frame Relay network shown in Figure 13-12.

Table 13-7   *IP Addresses with Point-to-Point Subinterfaces*

Router	Subnet	IP Address
Atlanta	140.1.1.0	140.1.1.1
Charlotte	140.1.1.0	140.1.1.2
Atlanta	140.1.2.0	140.1.2.1
Nashville	140.1.2.0	140.1.2.3
Atlanta	140.1.3.0	140.1.3.1
Boston	140.1.3.0	140.1.3.4

Cisco IOS Software has a configuration feature called *subinterfaces* that creates a logical subdivision of a physical interface. Subinterfaces allow the Atlanta router to have three IP addresses associated with its Serial0 physical interface by configuring three separate subinterfaces. A router can treat each subinterface, and the VC associated with it, as if it were a point-to-point serial link. Each of the three subinterfaces of Serial0 on Atlanta would be assigned a different IP address from Table 13-7 (Chapter 14 shows several sample configurations).

NOTE   The example uses IP address prefixes of /24 to keep the math simple. In production networks, point-to-point subinterfaces typically use a prefix of /30 (mask 255.255.255.252), because that allows for only two valid IP addresses—the exact number needed on a point-to-point subinterface. Of course, using different masks in the same network means your routing protocol must also support VLSM.

Frame Relay Layer 3 Addressing: Hybrid Approach

The third alternative for Layer 3 addressing is a hybrid of the first two alternatives. Consider Figure 13-13, which shows a trio of routers with VCs between each of them, as well as two other VCs to remote sites.

Two options exist for Layer 3 addressing in this case. The first is to treat each VC as a separate Layer 3 group. In this case, five subnets are needed for the Frame Relay network. However, Routers A, B, and C create a smaller full mesh between each other. This allows Routers A, B, and C to use one subnet. The other two VCs—one between Routers A and D and one between Routers A and E—are treated as two separate Layer 3 groups. The result is a total of three subnets.

Figure 13-13 *Hybrid of Full and Partial Mesh*

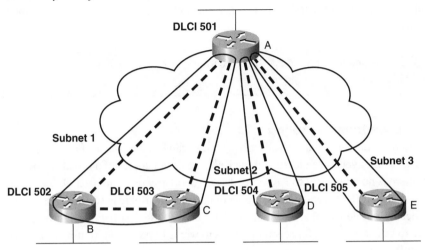

To accomplish either style of Layer 3 addressing in this third and final case, subinterfaces are used. Point-to-point subinterfaces are used when a single VC is considered to be all that is in the group—for instance, between Routers A and D and between Routers A and E. Multipoint subinterfaces are used when more than two routers are considered to be in the same group—for instance, with Routers A, B, and C.

Multipoint subinterfaces logically terminate more than one VC. In fact, the name "multipoint" implies the function, because more than one remote site can be reached via a VC associated with a multipoint subinterface.

Table 13-8 summarizes the addresses and subinterfaces that are used in Figure 13-13.

Table 13-8 *IP Addresses with Point-to-Point and Multipoint Subinterfaces*

Router	Subnet	IP Address	Subinterface Type
A	140.1.1.0/24	140.1.1.1	Multipoint
B	140.1.1.0/24	140.1.1.2	Multipoint
C	140.1.1.0/24	140.1.1.3	Multipoint
A	140.1.2.0/24	140.1.2.1	Point-to-point
D	140.1.2.0/24	140.1.2.4	Point-to-point
A	140.1.3.0/24	140.1.3.1	Point-to-point
E	140.1.3.0/24	140.1.3.5	Point-to-point

What will you see in a real network? Most of the time, point-to-point subinterfaces are used, with a single subnet per PVC. However, you should understand all options for the CCNA exams.

NOTE   Chapter 14 provides full configurations for all three cases illustrated in Figures 13-11, 13-12, and 13-13.

Layer 3 Broadcast Handling

After contending with Layer 3 addressing over Frame Relay, the next consideration is how to deal with Layer 3 broadcasts. Frame Relay can send copies of a broadcast over all VCs, but there is no equivalent to LAN broadcasts. In other words, no capability exists for a Frame Relay DTE to send a single frame into the Frame Relay network and have that frame replicated and delivered across multiple VCs to multiple destinations. However, routers need to send broadcasts for several features to work. In particular, routing protocol updates are either broadcasts or multicasts.

The solution to the Frame Relay broadcast dilemma has two parts. First, Cisco IOS software sends copies of the broadcasts across each VC, assuming that you have configured the router to forward these necessary broadcasts. If there are only a few VCs, this is not a big problem. However, if hundreds of VCs terminate in one router, for each broadcast, hundreds of copies could be sent.

As the second part of the solution, the router tries to minimize the impact of the first part of the solution. The router places the copies of the broadcasts in a different output queue than the one for user traffic so that the user does not experience a large spike in delay each time a broadcast is replicated and sent over every VC. Cisco IOS software can also be configured to limit the amount of bandwidth that is used for these replicated broadcasts.

Although such scalability issues are more likely to appear on the CCNP Routing exam, a short example shows the significance of broadcast overhead. If a router knows 1000 routes, uses RIP, and has 50 VCs, 1.072 MB of RIP updates is sent every 30 seconds. That averages out to 285 kbps. (The math is as follows: 536-byte RIP packets, with 25 routes in each packet, for 40 packets per update, with copies sent over 50 VCs. 536 * 40 * 50 = 1.072 MB per update interval. 1.072 * 8 / 30 seconds = 285 kbps.) That's a lot of overhead!

Knowing how to tell the router to forward these broadcasts to each VC is covered in the section "Frame Relay Configuration and Verification" in Chapter 14. The issues that relate to dealing with the volume of these updates are more likely a topic for the CCNP and CCIE exams.

Controlling Speed and Discards in the Frame Relay Cloud

This chapter has already examined the most important topics in Frame Relay relative to how Frame Relay delivers frames over the network. This final short section examines a few strategies you can use to fine-tune the operation of a Frame Relay network.

The Frame Relay header includes three single-bit flags that Frame Relay can use to help control what occurs inside the Frame Relay cloud. These bits can be particularly useful when one or more sites use an access rate—the clock rate of the access link—that far exceeds the CIR of a VC. For example, if a router has a T1 Frame Relay access link, but only a 128-kbps committed information rate (CIR) on a VC that goes over that link, the router can send a lot more data into the Frame Relay network than the business contract with the Frame Relay provider allows. This section examines 3 bits that impact how the switches might help control the network when the network gets congested because of these speed mismatches—namely, the Forward Explicit Congestion Notification (FECN), Backward Explicit Congestion Notification (BECN), and Discard Eligibility (DE) bits.

FECN and BECN

To deal with instances in which a router can send more data than the VC allows, IOS includes a feature called *Traffic Shaping*, which enables a router to send some packets, wait, send more, wait again, and so on. Traffic Shaping allows the router to decrease the overall rate of sending bits to a speed slower than the access rate, and maybe even as low as the CIR of a VC. For instance, with a T1 access link and a 128-kbps CIR, Traffic Shaping could be defined to send an average of only 256 kbps over that VC. The idea is that the Frame Relay provider will probably discard a lot of traffic if the router averages sending data over that VC at close to T1 speed, which is 12 times the CIR in this case. However, the Frame Relay provider may not discard traffic if the average rate is only 256 kbps—twice the CIR in this case.

You can set Traffic Shaping to use a single speed, or to adapt to range between two speed settings. When it's configured to adapt between two speeds, if the network is not congested, the higher speed is used; when the network is congested, the router adapts so that it shapes using the lower rate.

To adapt the shaping rates, the routers need a way to know whether congestion is occurring—and that's where FECN and BECN are used. Figure 13-14 shows the basic use of the FECN and BECN bits.

Figure 13-14   *Basic Operation of FECN and BECN*

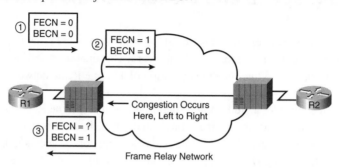

FECN and BECN are bits in the Frame Relay header. At any point—either in a router or inside the Frame Relay cloud—a device can set the FECN bit, meaning that this frame itself has experienced congestion. In other words, congestion exists in the forward direction of that frame. In Figure 13-14, in Step 1, the router sends a frame, with FECN=0. The Frame Relay switch notices congestion and sets FECN=1 in Step 2.

The goal of the whole process, however, is to get the sending router—R1 in this figure—to slow down. So, knowing that it set FECN in a frame in Step 2 in the figure, the Frame Relay switch *can* set the BECN bit in the next frame going back to R1 on that VC, shown as Step 3 in the figure. The BECN tells R1 that congestion occurred in the direction opposite, or backward, of the direction of the frame. In other words, it says that congestion occurred for the frame sent by R1 to R2. R1 can then choose to slow down (or not), depending on how Traffic Shaping is configured.

The Discard Eligibility (DE) Bit

When the provider's network becomes congested, it seems reasonable for the provider to try to discard the frames sent by customers that are causing the congestion. The providers typically build their networks to handle traffic loads far in excess of the collective CIRs for all VCs. However, if one or more customers abuse the right to send data at speeds far in advance of their contracted CIR speeds, the provider rightfully could discard only traffic sent by those customers.

Frame Relay protocols define a means to lessen the blow when the customer sends more than CIR bits per second over a VC, causing the provider to discard some frames. The customer can set the DE bit in some frames. If the provider's switches need to discard frames because of congestion, the switches can discard the frames with the DE bit set. If the customer sets the DE bit in the right frames, such as for less important traffic, the customer can ensure that the important traffic gets through the Frame Relay network, even when the provider has to discard traffic. When the provider's network is not so congested, the customer can send lots of extra data through the Frame Relay network without its being discarded.

Exam Preparation Tasks

Review All the Key Topics

Review the most important topics from this chapter, noted with the key topics icon. Table 13-9 lists these key topics and where each is discussed.

Key
Topic

Table 13-9 *Key Topics for Chapter 13*

Key Topic Element	Description	Page Number
Figure 13-1	Figure listing several terms related to a Frame Relay topology	462
Table 13-2	Table listing key Frame Relay terms and definitions	463
List	Two important functions of the Frame Relay LMI	467
Table 13-4	Frame Relay LMI types and LMI type configuration keywords	468
Figure 13-6	Figure showing headers and positions for the Cisco and IETF additional Frame Relay headers	469
Figure 13-9	Figure showing the concept of Frame Relay global addressing	471
List	Three options of subnets used on a Frame Relay network	474
Figure 13-14	Operation and use of the FECN and BECN bits	480

Complete the Tables and Lists from Memory

Print a copy of Appendix J, "Memory Tables" (found on the CD), or at least the section for this chapter, and complete the tables and lists from memory. Appendix K, "Memory Tables Answer Key," also on the CD, includes completed tables and lists for you to check your work.

Definitions of Key Terms

Define the following key terms from this chapter, and check your answers in the glossary:

> Access link, access rate, Committed Information Rate (CIR), data-link connection identifier (DLCI), Frame Relay DCE, Frame Relay DTE, Frame Relay mapping, Inverse ARP, Local Management Interface (LMI), nonbroadcast multiaccess (NBMA), permanent virtual circuit (PVC), virtual circuit (VC)

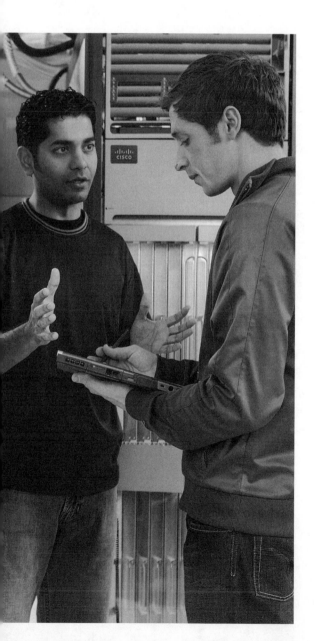

This chapter covers the following subjects:

Frame Relay Configuration and Verification:
This section shows you how to configure the
required and optional Frame Relay features, with
basic verification of each feature.

Frame Relay Troubleshooting: This section
examines a process by which an engineer can find
the root cause of why one Frame Relay router
cannot ping another Frame Relay router.

CHAPTER 14

Frame Relay Configuration and Troubleshooting

Chapter 13, "Frame Relay Concepts," introduced and explained the main concepts behind Frame Relay. This chapter shows you how to configure the features on Cisco routers, how to verify that each feature works, and how to troubleshoot problems with forwarding packets over a Frame Relay network.

"Do I Know This Already?" Quiz

The "Do I Know This Already?" quiz allows you to assess whether you should read the entire chapter. If you miss no more than one of these eight self-assessment questions, you might want to move ahead to the "Exam Preparation Tasks" section. Table 14-1 lists the major headings in this chapter and the "Do I Know This Already?" quiz questions covering the material in those sections. This helps you assess your knowledge of these specific areas. The answers to the "Do I Know This Already?" quiz appear in Appendix A.

Table 14-1 *"Do I Know This Already?" Foundation Topics Section-to-Question Mapping*

Foundation Topics Section	Questions
Frame Relay Configuration and Verification	1–5
Frame Relay Troubleshooting	6–8

1. Imagine two Cisco routers, R1 and R2, using a Frame Relay service. R1 connects to a switch that uses LMI type ANSI T1.617, and R2 connects to a switch that uses ITU Q.933a. What keywords could be used in the R1 and R2 configuration so that the LMIs work correctly?

   a. **ansi** and **itu**

   b. **T1617** and **q933a**

   c. **ansi** and **q933a**

   d. **T1617** and **itu**

   e. This won't work with two different types.

2. BettyCo has five sites, with routers connected to the same Frame Relay network. VCs have been defined between each pair of routers. Betty, the company president, will fire anyone who configures anything that could just as easily be left as a default. Which of the following configuration commands, configured for the Frame Relay network, would get the engineer fired?

    a. **ip address**

    b. **encapsulation**

    c. **lmi-type**

    d. **frame-relay map**

    e. **frame-relay inverse-arp**

3. WilmaCo has some routers connected to a Frame Relay network. R1 is a router at a remote site, with a single VC back to WilmaCo's headquarters. The R1 configuration currently looks like this:

```
interface serial 0/0
  ip address 10.1.1.1 255.255.255.0
  encapsulation frame-relay
```

Wilma, the company president, has heard that point-to-point subinterfaces are cool, and she wants you to change the configuration to use a point-to-point subinterface. Which of the following commands do you need to use to migrate the configuration?

    a. **no ip address**

    b. **interface-dlci**

    c. **no encapsulation**

    d. **encapsulation frame-relay**

    e. **frame-relay interface-dlci**

4. WilmaCo has another network, with a main site router that has ten VCs connecting to the ten remote sites. Wilma now thinks that multipoint subinterfaces are even cooler than point-to-point. The current main site router's configuration looks like this:

```
interface serial 0/0
  ip address 172.16.1.1 255.255.255.0
  encapsulation frame-relay
```

Wilma wants you to change the configuration to use a multipoint subinterface. Which of the following do you need to use to migrate the configuration? (Note: DLCIs 101 through 110 areused for the ten VCs.)

a. **interface-dlci 101 110**

b. **interface dlci 101-110**

c. Ten different **interface-dlci** commands

d. **frame-relay interface-dlci 101 110**

e. **frame-relay interface dlci 101-110**

f. Ten different **frame-relay interface-dlci** commands

5. Which of the following commands lists the information learned by Inverse ARP?

a. **show ip arp**

b. **show arp**

c. **show inverse arp**

d. **show frame-relay inverse-arp**

e. **show map**

f. **show frame-relay map**

6. Which of the following are Frame Relay PVC status codes for which a router sends frames for the associated PVC?

a. Up

b. Down

c. Active

d. Inactive

e. Static

f. Deleted

7. Central site router RC has a VC connecting to ten remote routers (R1 through R10), with RC's local DLCIs being 101 through 110, respectively. RC has grouped DLCIs 107, 108, and 109 into a single multipoint subinterface S0/0.789, whose current status is "up and up." Which of the following must be true?

a. Serial 0/0 could be in an up/down state.

b. The PVC with DLCI 108 could be in an inactive state.

c. The **show frame-relay map** command lists mapping information for all three VCs.

d. At least one of the three PVCs is in an active or static state.

8. Frame Relay router R1 uses interface S0/0 to connect to a Frame Relay access link. The physical interface is in an up/down state. Which of the following could cause this problem?

   a. The access link has a physical problem and cannot pass bits between the router and switch.

   b. The switch and router are using different LMI types.

   c. The router configuration is missing the **encapsulation frame-relay** command on interface S0/0.

   d. The router received a valid LMI status message that listed some of the DLCIs as inactive.

Foundation Topics

This chapter has two main sections. The first section examines Frame Relay configuration, along with explanations of several **show** commands. The second section discusses how to approach and troubleshoot Frame Relay problems.

Frame Relay Configuration and Verification

Frame Relay configuration can be very basic or somewhat detailed, depending on how many default settings can be used. By default, Cisco IOS automatically senses the LMI type and automatically discovers the mapping between DLCI and next-hop IP addresses (using Inverse ARP). If you use all Cisco routers, the default to use Cisco encapsulation works without any additional configuration. If you also design the Frame Relay network to use a single subnet, you can configure the routers to use their physical interfaces without any subinterfaces—making the configuration shorter still. In fact, using as many default settings as possible, the only new configuration command for Frame Relay, as compared to point-to-point WANs, is the **encapsulation frame-relay** command.

The CCNA exams' Frame Relay questions can be difficult for a couple of reasons. First, Frame Relay includes a variety of optional settings that can be configured. Second, for network engineers who already have some experience with Frame Relay, that experience may be with one of the three main options for Frame Relay configuration (physical, multipoint, or point-to-point), but the exams cover all options. So, it is important for the exams that you take the time to look at samples of all the options, which are covered here.

Planning a Frame Relay Configuration

Engineers must do a fair amount of planning before knowing where to start with the configuration. Although most modern Enterprises already have some Frame Relay connections, when planning for new sites, you must consider the following items and communicate them to the Frame Relay provider, which in turn has some impact on the routers' Frame Relay configurations:

- Define which physical sites need a Frame Relay access link installed, and define the clock rate (access rate) used on each link

- Define each VC by identifying the endpoints and setting the CIR

- Agree to an LMI type (usually dictated by the provider)

Additionally, the engineer must choose the particular style of configuration based on the following. For these items, the enterprise engineer does not need to consult the Frame Relay provider:

■ Choose the IP subnetting scheme: one subnet for all VCs, one subnet for each VC, or a subnet for each fully meshed subset.

■ Pick whether to assign the IP addresses to physical, multipoint, or point-to-point subinterfaces.

■ Choose which VCs need to use IETF encapsulation instead of the default value of "cisco." IETF encapsulation is typically used when one router is not a Cisco router.

After the planning has been completed, the configuration steps flow directly from the choices made when planning the network. The following list summarizes the configuration steps, mainly as a tool to help remind you of all the steps when you're doing your final exam preparation. Feel free to refer to this list as the upcoming examples show you how to configure the various options. (There is no need to memorize the steps; the list is just a tool to help organize your thinking about the configuration.)

Step 1   Configure the physical interface to use Frame Relay encapsulation (**encapsulation frame-relay** interface subcommand).

Step 2   Configure an IP address on the interface or subinterface (**ip address** subcommand).

Step 3   (Optional) Manually set the LMI type on each physical serial interface (**frame-relay lmi-type** interface subcommand).

Step 4   (Optional) Change from the default encapsulation of **cisco** to **ietf** by doing the following:

   a. For all VCs on the interface, add the **ietf** keyword to the **encapsulation frame-relay** interface subcommand.

   b. For a single VC, add the **ietf** keyword to the **frame-relay interface-dlci** interface subcommand (point-to-point subinterfaces only) or to the **frame-relay map** command.

Step 5   (Optional) If you aren't using the (default) Inverse ARP to map the DLCI to the next-hop router's IP address, define static mapping using the **frame-relay map ip** *ip-address dlci* **broadcast** subinterface subcommand.

Step 6 On subinterfaces, associate one (point-to-point) or more (multipoint) DLCIs with the subinterface in one of two ways:

   a. Using the **frame-relay interface-dlci** *dlci* subinterface subcommand

   b. As a side effect of static mapping using the **frame-relay map ip** *ip-address dlci* **broadcast** subinterface subcommand

The rest of this section shows examples of all these configuration steps, along with some discussion about how to verify that the Frame Relay network is working correctly.

A Fully Meshed Network with One IP Subnet

The first example shows the briefest possible Frame Relay configuration, one that uses just the first two steps of the configuration checklist in this chapter. The design for the first example includes the following choices:

■ Install an access link into three routers.

■ Create a full mesh of PVCs.

■ Use a single subnet (Class C network 199.1.1.0) in the Frame Relay network.

■ Configure the routers using their physical interfaces.

Take the default settings for LMI, Inverse ARP, and encapsulation. Examples 14-1, 14-2, and 14-3 show the configuration for the network shown in Figure 14-1.

Figure 14-1 *Full Mesh with IP Addresses*

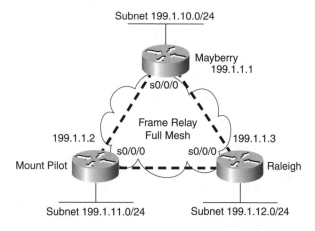

Example 14-1 *Mayberry Configuration*

```
interface serial0/0/0
 encapsulation frame-relay
 ip address  199.1.1.1  255.255.255.0
!
interface fastethernet 0/0
 ip address  199.1.10.1  255.255.255.0
!
router eigrp 1
 network 199.1.1.0
 network 199.1.10.0
```

Example 14-2 *Mount Pilot Configuration*

```
interface serial0/0/0
 encapsulation frame-relay
 ip address  199.1.1.2  255.255.255.0
!
interface fastethernet 0/0
 ip address  199.1.11.2   255.255.255.0
!
router eigrp 1
 network 199.1.1.0
 network 199.1.11.0
```

Example 14-3 *Raleigh Configuration*

```
interface serial0/0/0
 encapsulation frame-relay
 ip address  199.1.1.3  255.255.255.0
!
interface fastethernet 0/0
 ip address  199.1.12.3   255.255.255.0
!
router eigrp 1
 network 199.1.1.0
 network 199.1.12.0
```

The configuration is simple in comparison with the protocol concepts. The **encapsulation frame-relay** command tells the routers to use Frame Relay data-link protocols instead of the default, which is HDLC. Note that the IP addresses on the three routers' serial interfaces are all in the same Class C network. Also, this simple configuration takes advantage of the following IOS default settings:

- The LMI type is automatically sensed.

- The (default) encapsulation is Cisco instead of IETF.

- PVC DLCIs are learned via LMI status messages.

- Inverse ARP is enabled (by default) and is triggered when the status message declaring that the VCs are up is received.

Configuring the Encapsulation and LMI

In some cases, the default values are inappropriate. For example, you must use IETF encapsulation if one router is not a Cisco router. For the purpose of showing an alternative configuration, suppose that the following requirements were added:

- The Raleigh router requires IETF encapsulation on both VCs.

- Mayberry's LMI type should be ANSI, and LMI autosense should not be used.

To change these defaults, the steps outlined as optional configuration Steps 3 and 4 in the configuration checklist should be used. Examples 14-4 and 14-5 show the changes that would be made to Mayberry and Raleigh.

Example 14-4 *Mayberry Configuration with New Requirements*

```
interface serial0/0/0
 encapsulation frame-relay
 frame-relay lmi-type ansi
 frame-relay map ip 199.1.1.3 53 ietf
 ip address 199.1.1.1  255.255.255.0
! rest of configuration unchanged from Example 14-1.
```

Example 14-5 *Raleigh Configuration with New Requirements*

```
interface serial0/0/0
 encapsulation frame-relay ietf
 ip address  199.1.1.3  255.255.255.0

! rest of configuration unchanged from Example 14-3.
```

These configurations differ from the previous ones (in Examples 14-1 and 14-3) in two ways. First, Raleigh changed its encapsulation for both its PVCs with the **ietf** keyword on the **encapsulation** command. This keyword applies to all VCs on the interface. However, Mayberry cannot change its encapsulation in the same way, because only one of the two VCs terminating in Mayberry needs to use IETF encapsulation, and the other needs to use Cisco encapsulation. So Mayberry is forced to code the **frame-relay map** command, referencing the DLCI for the VC to Raleigh, with the **ietf** keyword. With that command, you can change the encapsulation setting per VC, as opposed to the configuration on Raleigh, which changes the encapsulation for all VCs.

The second major change is the LMI configuration. The LMI configuration in Mayberry would be fine without any changes, because the default use of LMI autosense would recognize ANSI as the LMI type. However, by coding the **frame-relay lmi-type ansi** interface subcommand, Mayberry must use ANSI, because this command not only sets the LMI type, it also disables autonegotiation of the LMI type.

> **NOTE**   The LMI setting is a per-physical-interface setting, even if subinterfaces are used, so the **frame-relay lmi-type** command is always a subcommand under the physical interface.

Mount Pilot needs to configure a **frame-relay map** command with the **ietf** keyword for its VC to Raleigh, just like Mayberry. This change is not shown in the examples.

Frame Relay Address Mapping

Figure 14-1 does not even bother listing the DLCIs used for the VCs. The configurations work as stated, and frankly, if you never knew the DLCIs, this network would work! However, for the exams, and for real networking jobs, you need to understand an important concept related to Frame Relay—Frame Relay address mapping. Figure 14-2 shows the same network, this time with global DLCI values shown.

Figure 14-2 *Full Mesh with Global DLCIs Shown*

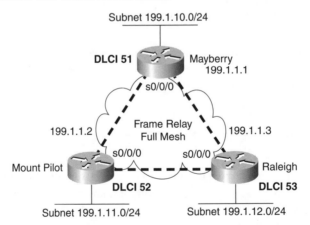

Frame Relay "mapping" creates a correlation between a Layer 3 address and its corresponding Layer 2 address. The concept is similar to the ARP cache for LAN interfaces. For example, the IP Address Resolution Protocol (ARP) cache used on LANs is an example of Layer 3-to-Layer 2 address mapping. With IP ARP, you know the IP address of another device on the same LAN, but not the MAC address; when the ARP completes, you know another device's LAN (Layer 2) address. Similarly, routers that use Frame Relay need a mapping between a router's Layer 3 address and the DLCI used to reach that other router.

This section discusses the basics of why mapping is needed for LAN connections and Frame Relay, with a focus on Frame Relay. Here's a more general definition of mapping:

> The information that correlates to the next-hop router's Layer 3 address, and the Layer 2 address used to reach it, is called mapping. Mapping is needed on multiaccess networks.

Thinking about routing helps make the need for mapping more apparent. Imagine that a host on the Mayberry Ethernet sends an IP packet to a host on the Mount Pilot Ethernet. The packet arrives at the Mayberry router over the LAN, and Mayberry discards the Ethernet header and trailer. Mayberry looks at the routing table, which lists a route to 199.1.11.0, outgoing interface Serial 0/0/0, and next-hop router 199.1.1.2, which is Mount Pilot's Frame Relay IP address.

The next decision that the router must make to complete the process points out the need for mapping: What DLCI should Mayberry put in the Frame Relay header? We configured no DLCIs. However, it would work as configured! To see the answer, consider Example 14-6, which shows some important commands that can be used to see how Mayberry makes the right choice for the DLCI.

Example 14-6 **show** *Commands on Mayberry, Showing the Need for Mapping*

```
Mayberry#show ip route
Codes: C - connected, S - static, I - IGRP, R - RIP, M - mobile, B - BGP
       D - EIGRP, EX - EIGRP external, O - OSPF, IA - OSPF inter area
       N1 - OSPF NSSA external type 1, N2 - OSPF NSSA external type 2
       E1 - OSPF external type 1, E2 - OSPF external type 2, E - EGP
       i - IS-IS, L1 - IS-IS level-1, L2 - IS-IS level-2, ia - IS-IS inter area
       * - candidate default, U - per-user static route, o - ODR
       P - periodic downloaded static route

Gateway of last resort is not set

D    199.1.11.0/24 [90/2195456] via 199.1.1.2, 00:00:26, Serial0/0/0
C    199.1.10.0/24 is directly connected, Fastethernet0/0
D    199.1.12.0/24 [90/2185984] via 199.1.1.3, 00:01:04, Serial0/0/0
C    199.1.1.0/24 is directly connected, Serial0/0/0
C    192.68.1.0/24 is directly connected, Fastethernet0/0
C    192.168.1.0/24 is directly connected, Fastethernet0/0

Mayberry#show frame-relay pvc
```

continues

Example 14-6 **show** *Commands on Mayberry, Showing the Need for Mapping (Continued)*

```
PVC Statistics for interface Serial0/0/0 (Frame Relay DTE)


                Active     Inactive     Deleted      Static
   Local          2           0            0            0
   Switched       0           0            0            0
   Unused         0           0            0            0


DLCI = 52, DLCI USAGE = LOCAL, PVC STATUS = ACTIVE, INTERFACE = Serial0/0/0

   input pkts 46           output pkts 22          in bytes 2946
   out bytes 1794          dropped pkts 0          in FECN pkts 0
   in BECN pkts 0          out FECN pkts 0         out BECN pkts 0
   in DE pkts 0            out DE pkts 0
   out bcast pkts 21       out bcast bytes 1730
   pvc create time 00:23:07, last time pvc status changed 00:21:38


DLCI = 53, DLCI USAGE = LOCAL, PVC STATUS = ACTIVE, INTERFACE = Serial0/0/0

   input pkts 39           output pkts 18          in bytes 2564
   out bytes 1584          dropped pkts 0          in FECN pkts 0
   in BECN pkts 0          out FECN pkts 0         out BECN pkts 0
   in DE pkts 0            out DE pkts 0
   out bcast pkts 18       out bcast bytes 1584
   pvc create time 00:23:08, last time pvc status changed 00:21:20


Mayberry#show frame-relay map
Serial0/0/0 (up): ip 199.1.1.2 dlci 52(0x34,0xC40), dynamic,
              broadcast,, status defined, active
Serial0/0/0 (up): ip 199.1.1.3 dlci 53(0x35,0xC50), dynamic,
              broadcast,, status defined, active
```

The example highlights all the related information on Mayberry for sending packets to network 199.1.11.0/24 off Mount Pilot. Mayberry's route to 199.1.11.0 refers to outgoing interface Serial 0/0/0 and to 199.1.1.2 as the next-hop address. The **show frame-relay pvc** command lists two DLCIs, 52 and 53, and both are active. How does Mayberry know the DLCIs? Well, the LMI status messages tell Mayberry about the VCs, the associated DLCIs, and the status (active).

Which DLCI should Mayberry use to forward the packet? The **show frame-relay map** command output holds the answer. Notice the highlighted phrase "ip 199.1.1.2 dlci 52" in the output. Somehow, Mayberry has mapped 199.1.1.2, which is the next-hop address in the route, to the correct DLCI, which is 52. So, Mayberry knows to use DLCI 52 to reach next-hop IP address 199.1.1.2.

Mayberry can use two methods to build the mapping shown in Example 14-6. One uses a statically configured mapping, and the other uses a dynamic process called *Inverse ARP*. The next two small sections explain the details of each of these options.

Inverse ARP

Inverse ARP dynamically creates a mapping between the Layer 3 address (for example, the IP address) and the Layer 2 address (the DLCI). The end result of Inverse ARP is the same as IP ARP on a LAN: The router builds a mapping between a neighboring Layer 3 address and the corresponding Layer 2 address. However, the process used by Inverse ARP differs for ARP on a LAN. After the VC is up, each router announces its network layer address by sending an Inverse ARP message over that VC. This works as shown in Figure 14-3.

Figure 14-3 *Inverse ARP Process*

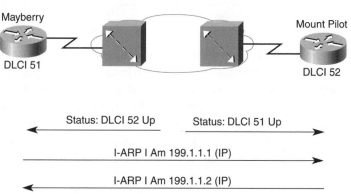

As shown in Figure 14-3, Inverse ARP announces its Layer 3 addresses as soon as the LMI signals that the PVCs are up. Inverse ARP starts by learning the DLCI data link layer address (via LMI messages), and then it announces its own Layer 3 addresses that use that VC. Inverse ARP is enabled by default.

In Example 14-6, Mayberry shows two different entries in the **show frame-relay map** command output. Mayberry uses Inverse ARP to learn that DLCI 52 is mapped to next-hop IP address 199.1.1.2 and that DLCI 53 is mapped to next-hop IP address 199.1.1.3. Interestingly, Mayberry learns this information by receiving an Inverse ARP from Mount Pilot and Raleigh, respectively.

Table 14-2 summarizes what occurs with Inverse ARP in the network shown in Figure 14-2.

Table 14-2 *Inverse ARP Messages for Figure 14-2*

Sending Router	DLCI When the Frame Is Sent	Receiving Router	DLCI When the Frame Is Received	Information in the Inverse ARP Message
Mayberry	52	Mount Pilot	51	I am 199.1.1.1.
Mayberry	53	Raleigh	51	I am 199.1.1.1.
Mount Pilot	51	Mayberry	52	I am 199.1.1.2.
Mount Pilot	53	Raleigh	52	I am 199.1.1.2.
Raleigh	51	Mayberry	53	I am 199.1.1.3.
Raleigh	52	Mount Pilot	53	I am 199.1.1.3.

To understand Inverse ARP, focus on the last two columns of Table 14-2. Each router receives some Inverse ARP "announcements." The Inverse ARP message contains the sender's Layer 3 address, and the Frame Relay header, of course, has a DLCI in it. These two values are placed in the Inverse ARP cache on the receiving router. For example, in the third row, Mayberry receives an Inverse ARP. The DLCI is 52 when the frame arrives at Mayberry, and the IP address is 199.1.1.2. This is added to the Frame Relay map table in Mayberry, which is shown in the highlighted part of the **show frame-relay map** command in Example 14-6.

Static Frame Relay Mapping

You can statically configure the same mapping information instead of using Inverse ARP. In a production network, you probably would just go ahead and use Inverse ARP. For the exams, you need to know how to configure the static map command statements. Example 14-7 lists the static Frame Relay map for the three routers shown in Figure 14-2, along with the configuration used to disable Inverse ARP.

Example 14-7   frame-relay map *Commands*

```
Mayberry
interface serial 0/0/0
 no frame-relay inverse-arp
 frame-relay map ip 199.1.1.2 52 broadcast
 frame-relay map ip 199.1.1.3 53 broadcast
Mount Pilot
interface serial 0/0/0
 no frame-relay inverse-arp
 frame-relay map ip 199.1.1.1 51 broadcast
 frame-relay map ip 199.1.1.3 53 broadcast
```

Example 14-7   **frame-relay map** *Commands (Continued)*

```
Raleigh
interface serial 0/0/0
 no frame-relay inverse-arp
 frame-relay map ip 199.1.1.1 51 broadcast
 frame-relay map ip 199.1.1.2 52 broadcast
```

The **frame-relay map** command entry for Mayberry, referencing 199.1.1.2, is used for packets in Mayberry going to Mount Pilot. When Mayberry creates a Frame Relay header, expecting it to be delivered to Mount Pilot, Mayberry must use DLCI 52. Mayberry's **frame-relay map** statement correlates Mount Pilot's IP address, 199.1.1.2, to the DLCI used to reach Mount Pilot—namely, DLCI 52. Likewise, a packet sent back from Mount Pilot to Mayberry causes Mount Pilot to use its **map** statement to refer to Mayberry's IP address of 199.1.1.1. Mapping is needed for each next-hop Layer 3 address for each Layer 3 protocol being routed. Even with a network this small, the configuration process can be laborious.

> **NOTE**   The **broadcast** keyword is required when the router needs to send broadcasts or multicasts to the neighboring router—for example, to support routing protocol messages such as Hellos.

A Partially Meshed Network with One IP Subnet Per VC

The second sample network, based on the environment shown in Figure 14-4, uses point-to-point subinterfaces. Examples 14-8 through 14-11 show the configuration for this network. The command prompts are included in the first example because they change when you configure subinterfaces.

Figure 14-4   *Partial Mesh with IP Addresses*

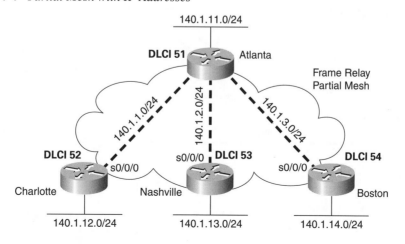

Example 14-8 *Atlanta Configuration*

```
Atlanta(config)#interface serial0/0/0
Atlanta(config-if)#encapsulation frame-relay

Atlanta(config-if)#interface serial 0/0/0.1 point-to-point
Atlanta(config-subif)#ip address 140.1.1.1  255.255.255.0
Atlanta(config-subif)#frame-relay interface-dlci 52

Atlanta(config-fr-dlci)#interface serial 0/0/0.2 point-to-point
Atlanta(config-subif)#ip address 140.1.2.1 255.255.255.0
Atlanta(config-subif)#frame-relay interface-dlci 53

Atlanta(config-fr-dlci)#interface serial 0/0/0.3 point-to-point
Atlanta(config-subif)#ip address 140.1.3.1 255.255.255.0
Atlanta(config-subif)#frame-relay interface-dlci 54

Atlanta(config-fr-dlci)#interface fastethernet 0/0
Atlanta(config-if)#ip address 140.1.11.1 255.255.255.0
```

Example 14-9 *Charlotte Configuration*

```
interface serial0/0/0
 encapsulation frame-relay
!
interface serial 0/0/0.1 point-to-point
 ip address 140.1.1.2  255.255.255.0
 frame-relay interface-dlci 51
!
interface fastethernet 0/0
 ip address 140.1.12.2 255.255.255.0
```

Example 14-10 *Nashville Configuration*

```
interface serial0/0/0
 encapsulation frame-relay
!
interface serial 0/0/0.2 point-to-point
 ip address 140.1.2.3 255.255.255.0
 frame-relay interface-dlci 51
!
interface fastethernet 0/0
 ip address 140.1.13.3 255.255.255.0
```

Example 14-11 *Boston Configuration*

```
interface serial0/0/0
 encapsulation frame-relay
!
interface serial 0/0/0.3 point-to-point
 ip address 140.1.3.4 255.255.255.0
 frame-relay interface-dlci 51
!
interface fastethernet 0/0
 ip address 140.1.14.4  255.255.255.0
```

Again, defaults abound in this configuration, but some defaults are different than when you're configuring on the physical interface. The LMI type is autosensed, and Cisco encapsulation is used, which is just like the fully meshed examples. Inverse ARP is not really needed on point-to-point subinterfaces, but it is enabled by default in case the router on the other end of the VC needs to use Inverse ARP, as explained later in this section.

Two new commands create the configuration required with point-to-point subinterfaces. First, the **interface serial 0/0/0.1 point-to-point** command creates logical subinterface number 1 under physical interface Serial 0/0/0. The **frame-relay interface-dlci** subinterface subcommand then tells the router which single DLCI is associated with that subinterface.

An example of how the **frame-relay interface-dlci** command works can help. Consider router Atlanta in Figure 14-4. Atlanta receives LMI messages on Serial0/0/0 stating that three PVCs, with DLCIs 52, 53, and 54, are up. Which PVC goes with which subinterface? Cisco IOS software needs to associate the correct PVC with the correct subinterface. This is accomplished with the **frame-relay interface-dlci** command.

The subinterface numbers do not have to match on the router on the other end of the PVC, nor does the DLCI number. In this example, I just numbered the subinterfaces to be easier to remember. In real life, it is useful to encode some information about your network numbering scheme into the subinterface number. For example, a company might encode part of the carrier's circuit ID in the subinterface number so that the operations staff could find the correct information to tell the telco when troubleshooting the link. Many sites use the DLCI as the subinterface number. Of course, useful troubleshooting information, such as the DLCI, the name of the router on the other end of the VC, and so on, could be configured as text with the **description** command as well. In any case, there are no requirements for matching subinterface numbers. This example just matches the subinterface number to the third octet of the IP address.

Assigning a DLCI to a Particular Subinterface

As mentioned in the configuration checklist at the beginning of the "Frame Relay Configuration and Verification" section, when configuring subinterfaces, the DLCIs must be associated with each subinterface in one of two ways. Examples 14-8 through 14-11 showed how to associate the DLCIs using the **frame-relay interface-dlci** subinterface subcommand. The alternative configuration would be to use the **frame-relay map** command as a subinterface subcommand on multipoint subinterfaces or as a physical interface subcommand. This command would both associate a DLCI with the subinterface and statically configure a mapping of Layer 3 next-hop IP address to that DLCI.

The router disables Inverse ARP on a subinterface when the **frame-relay map** command is configured. So, when using static maps on the router on one end of the VC, keep in mind that the router on the other end of the VC will not receive any Inverse ARP messages and may also then need to be configured with the **frame-relay map** command.

Comments About Global and Local Addressing

When you take the Cisco CCNA exams, if a figure for a question shows three or more routers, you should be able to easily decide whether the figure implies local or global DLCI values. For instance, Figure 14-4 shows a main site with three PVCs, one to each remote site. However, only one DLCI is shown beside the main site router, implying the use of global addressing. If local DLCIs were used, the figure would need to show a DLCI for each PVC beside the main site router.

In cases where a figure for a question shows only two routers, the figure might not imply whether local or global DLCI addressing is used. In those cases, look for clues in the question, answers, and any configuration. The best clues relate to the following fact:

> On any given router, only local DLCI values are in the configuration or **show** commands.

Again, consider Figure 14-4 along with Examples 14-8 through 14-11. The figure shows global DLCIs, with DLCI 51 beside the Atlanta router. However, the **frame-relay interface-dlci** commands on the Atlanta router (Example 14-8) and the Atlanta **show** commands in upcoming Example 14-12 list DLCIs 52, 53, and 54. Although Figure 14-4 makes it obvious that global addressing is used, even if only two routers had been shown, the **show** commands and configuration commands could have helped identify the correct DLCIs to use.

Frame Relay Verification

Example 14-12 shows the output from the most popular Cisco IOS software Frame Relay EXEC commands for monitoring Frame Relay, as issued on router Atlanta.

Example 14-12 *Output from EXEC Commands on Atlanta*

```
Atlanta#show frame-relay pvc

PVC Statistics for interface Serial0/0/0 (Frame Relay DTE)

              Active      Inactive      Deleted       Static
   Local        3            0             0             0
   Switched     0            0             0             0
   Unused       0            0             0             0
DLCI = 52, DLCI USAGE = LOCAL, PVC STATUS = ACTIVE, INTERFACE = Serial0/0/0.1

   input pkts 843           output pkts 876           in bytes 122723
   out bytes 134431         dropped pkts 0            in FECN pkts 0
   in BECN pkts 0           out FECN pkts 0           out BECN pkts 0
   in DE pkts 0             out DE pkts 0
   out bcast pkts 876        out bcast bytes 134431
   pvc create time 05:20:10, last time pvc status changed 05:19:31
 --More--
DLCI = 53, DLCI USAGE = LOCAL, PVC STATUS = ACTIVE, INTERFACE = Serial0/0/0.2

   input pkts 0             output pkts 875           in bytes 0
   out bytes 142417         dropped pkts 0            in FECN pkts 0
   in BECN pkts 0           out FECN pkts 0           out BECN pkts 0
   in DE pkts 0             out DE pkts 0
   out bcast pkts 875        out bcast bytes 142417
   pvc create time 05:19:51, last time pvc status changed 04:55:41
 --More--
DLCI = 54, DLCI USAGE = LOCAL, PVC STATUS = ACTIVE, INTERFACE = Serial0/0/0.3

   input pkts 10            output pkts 877           in bytes 1274
   out bytes 142069         dropped pkts 0            in FECN pkts 0
   in BECN pkts 0           out FECN pkts 0           out BECN pkts 0
   in DE pkts 0             out DE pkts 0
   out bcast pkts 877        out bcast bytes 142069
   pvc create time 05:19:52, last time pvc status changed 05:17:42

Atlanta#show frame-relay map
Serial0/0/0.3 (up): point-to-point dlci, dlci 54(0x36,0xC60), broadcast
          status defined, active
Serial0/0/0.2 (up): point-to-point dlci, dlci 53(0x35,0xC50), broadcast
          status defined, active
Serial0/0/0.1 (up): point-to-point dlci, dlci 52(0x34,0xC40), broadcast
          status defined, active
```

continues

Example 14-12   *Output from EXEC Commands on Atlanta (Continued)*

```
Atlanta#debug frame-relay lmi
Frame Relay LMI debugging is on
Displaying all Frame Relay LMI data

Serial0/0/0(out): StEnq, myseq 163, yourseen 161, DTE up
datagramstart = 0x45AED8, datagramsize = 13
FR encap = 0xFCF10309
00 75 01 01 01 03 02 A3 A1

Serial0/0/0(in): Status, myseq 163
RT IE 1, length 1, type 1
KA IE 3, length 2, yourseq 162, myseq 163
```

The **show frame-relay pvc** command lists useful management information. For instance, the packet counters for each VC, plus the counters for FECN and BECN, can be particularly useful. Likewise, comparing the packets/bytes sent on one router versus the counters of what is received on the router on the other end of the VC is also quite useful. This reflects the number of packets/bytes lost inside the Frame Relay cloud. Also, the PVC status is a great place to start when troubleshooting.

The **show frame-relay map** command lists mapping information. With the earlier example of a fully meshed network, in which the configuration did not use any subinterfaces, a Layer 3 address was listed with each DLCI. In this example, a DLCI is listed in each entry, but no mention of corresponding Layer 3 addresses is made. The whole point of mapping is to correlate a Layer 3 address to a Layer 2 address, but there is no Layer 3 address in the **show frame-relay map** command output! The reason is that the information is stored somewhere else. Subinterfaces require the use of the **frame-relay interface-dlci** configuration command. Because these subinterfaces are point-to-point, when a route points out a single subinterface, the DLCI to use to send frames is implied by the configuration. Mapping via Inverse ARP or static **frame-relay map** statements is needed only when more than two VCs terminate on the interface or subinterface, because those are the only instances in which confusion about which DLCI to use might occur.

The **debug frame-relay lmi** output lists information for the sending and receiving LMI inquiries. The switch sends the status message, and the DTE (router) sends the status inquiry. The default setting with Cisco IOS software is to send, and to expect to receive, these status messages. The Cisco IOS software **no keepalive** command is used to disable the use of LMI status messages. Unlike other interfaces, Cisco keepalive messages do not flow from router to router over Frame Relay. Instead, they are simply used to detect whether the router has connectivity to its local Frame Relay switch.

A Partially Meshed Network with Some Fully Meshed Parts

You can also choose to use multipoint subinterfaces for a Frame Relay configuration. This last sample network, based on the network shown in Figure 14-5, uses both multipoint and point-to-point subinterfaces. Examples 14-13 through 14-17 show the configuration for this network. Table 14-3 summarizes the addresses and subinterfaces used.

Figure 14-5 *Hybrid of Full and Partial Mesh*

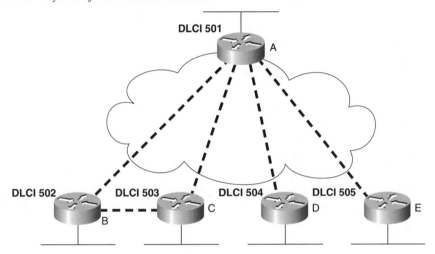

Example 14-13 *Router A Configuration*

```
interface serial0/0/0
 encapsulation frame-relay
!
interface serial 0/0/0.1 multipoint
 ip address 140.1.1.1  255.255.255.0
 frame-relay interface-dlci 502
 frame-relay interface-dlci 503
!
interface serial 0/0/0.2 point-to-point
 ip address 140.1.2.1 255.255.255.0
 frame-relay interface-dlci 504
!
interface serial 0/0/0.3 point-to-point
 ip address 140.1.3.1 255.255.255.0
 frame-relay interface-dlci 505
```

Example 14-14 *Router B Configuration*

```
interface serial0/0/0
 encapsulation frame-relay
!
interface serial 0/0/0.1 multipoint
 ip address 140.1.1.2  255.255.255.0
 frame-relay interface-dlci 501
 frame-relay interface-dlci 503
```

Example 14-15 *Router C Configuration*

```
interface serial0/0/0
 encapsulation frame-relay
!
interface serial 0/0/0.1 multipoint
 ip address 140.1.1.3  255.255.255.0
 frame-relay interface-dlci 501
 frame-relay interface-dlci 502
```

Example 14-16 *Router D Configuration*

```
interface serial0/0/0
encapsulation frame-relay
!
interface serial 0/0/0.1 point-to-point
 ip address 140.1.2.4  255.255.255.0
 frame-relay interface-dlci 501
```

Example 14-17 *Router E Configuration*

```
interface serial0/0/0
 encapsulation frame-relay
!
interface serial 0/0/0.1 point-to-point
 ip address 140.1.3.5 255.255.255.0
 frame-relay interface-dlci 501
```

Table 14-3 *IP Addresses with Point-to-Point and Multipoint Subinterfaces*

Router	Subnet	IP Address	Subinterface Type
A	140.1.1.0/24	140.1.1.1	Multipoint
B	140.1.1.0/24	140.1.1.2	Multipoint
C	140.1.1.0/24	140.1.1.3	Multipoint
A	140.1.2.0/24	140.1.2.1	Point-to-point

Table 14-3 *IP Addresses with Point-to-Point and Multipoint Subinterfaces (Continued)*

Router	Subnet	IP Address	Subinterface Type
D	140.1.2.0/24	140.1.2.4	Point-to-point
A	140.1.3.0/24	140.1.3.1	Point-to-point
E	140.1.3.0/24	140.1.3.5	Point-to-point

Multipoint subinterfaces work best when you have a full mesh between a set of routers. On Routers A, B, and C, a multipoint subinterface is used for the configuration referencing the other two routers, because you can think of these three routers as forming a fully meshed subset of the network.

The term multipoint simply means that there is more than one VC, so you can send and receive to and from more than one VC on the subinterface. Like point-to-point subinterfaces, multipoint subinterfaces use the **frame-relay interface-dlci** command. Notice that there are two commands for each multipoint subinterface in this case, because each of the two PVCs associated with this subinterface must be identified as being used with that subinterface.

Router A is the only router using both multipoint and point-to-point subinterfaces. On Router A's multipoint Serial0/0/0.1 interface, DLCIs for Router B and Router C are listed. On Router A's other two subinterfaces, which are point-to-point, only a single DLCI needs to be listed. In fact, only one **frame-relay interface-dlci** command is allowed on a point-to-point subinterface, because only one VC is allowed. Otherwise, the configurations between the two types are similar.

No mapping statements are required for the configurations shown in Examples 14-13 through 14-17, because Inverse ARP is enabled on the multipoint subinterfaces by default. No mapping is ever needed for the point-to-point subinterface, because the only DLCI associated with the interface is statically configured with the **frame-relay interface-dlci** command.

Example 14-18 lists another **show frame-relay map** command, showing the mapping information learned by Inverse ARP for the multipoint subinterface. Notice that the output now includes the Layer 3 addresses, whereas the same command when using point-to-point subinterfaces (in Example 14-12) did not. The reason is that the routes might refer to a next-hop IP address reachable out a multipoint interface, but because more than one DLCI is

associated with the interface, the router needs mapping information to match the next-hop
IP address to the correct DLCI.

Example 14-18 *Frame Relay Maps and Inverse ARP on Router C*

```
RouterC#show frame-relay map
Serial0/0/0.1 (up): ip 140.1.1.1 dlci 501(0x1F5,0x7C50), dynamic,
              broadcast,, status defined, active
Serial0/0/0.1 (up): ip 140.1.1.2 dlci 502(0x1F6,0x7C60), dynamic,
              broadcast,, status defined, active


RouterC#debug frame-relay events
Frame Relay events debugging is on

RouterC#configure terminal
Enter configuration commands, one per line.  End with Ctrl-Z.
RouterC(config)#interface serial 0/0/0.1
RouterC(config-subif)#shutdown
RouterC(config-subif)#no shutdown
RouterC(config-subif)#^Z
RouterC#

Serial0/0/0.1: FR ARP input
Serial0/0/0.1: FR ARP input
Serial0/0/0.1: FR ARP input
datagramstart = 0xE42E58, datagramsize = 30
FR encap = 0x7C510300
80 00 00 00 08 06 00 0F 08 00 02 04 00 09 00 00
8C 01 01 01 7C 51 8C 01 01 03

datagramstart = 0xE420E8, datagramsize = 30
FR encap = 0x7C610300
80 00 00 00 08 06 00 0F 08 00 02 04 00 09 00 00
8C 01 01 02 7C 61 8C 01 01 03
```

The messages about Inverse ARP in the **debug frame-relay events** output are not so
obvious. One easy exercise is to search for the hex version of the IP addresses in the output.
These addresses are highlighted in Example 14-18. For example, the first 4 bytes of
140.1.1.1 are 8C 01 01 01in hexadecimal. This field starts on the left side of the output, so
it is easy to recognize.

Frame Relay Troubleshooting

Frame Relay has many features and options that can be configured. For both real life and the exams, troubleshooting Frame Relay problems often means that you need to look at all the routers' configurations and make sure that the configurations meet the requirements. The LMI types must match or be autosensed, the Layer 3 mapping information has been learned or statically mapped, the right DLCI values have been associated with each subinterface, and so on. So, to be well prepared for the CCNA exams, you should review and memorize the many Frame Relay configuration options and what each option means.

However, the exams may have Frame Relay questions that require you to determine a problem without looking at the configuration. This second major section of this chapter examines Frame Relay troubleshooting, with emphasis on how to use **show** commands, along with the symptoms of a problem, to isolate the root cause of the problem.

A Suggested Frame Relay Troubleshooting Process

To isolate a Frame Relay problem, the process should start with some pings. Optimally, pings from an end-user host on a LAN, to another host on a remote LAN, can quickly determine if the network currently can meet the true end goal of delivering packets between computers. If that ping fails, a ping from one router to the other router's Frame Relay IP address is the next step. If that ping works, but the end user's ping failed, the problem probably has something to do with Layer 3 issues, and troubleshooting those issues was well covered in Chapters 7 and 11. However, if a ping from one router to another router's Frame Relay IP address fails, the problem is most likely related to the Frame Relay network.

This section focuses on troubleshooting problems when a Frame Relay router cannot ping another router's Frame Relay IP address. At that point, the engineer should ping the Frame Relay IP addresses of all the other routers on the other end of each VC to determine the following:

> Do the pings fail for all remote routers' Frame Relay IP addresses, or do some pings fail and some pings work?

For example, Figure 14-6 shows a sample Frame Relay network that will be used with the remaining examples in this chapter. If R1 tried to **ping** R2's Frame Relay IP address (10.1.2.2 in this case) and failed, the next question is whether R1's pings to R3 (10.1.34.3) and R4 (10.1.34.4) work.

Figure 14-6 *Sample Frame Relay Network for the Troubleshooting Examples*

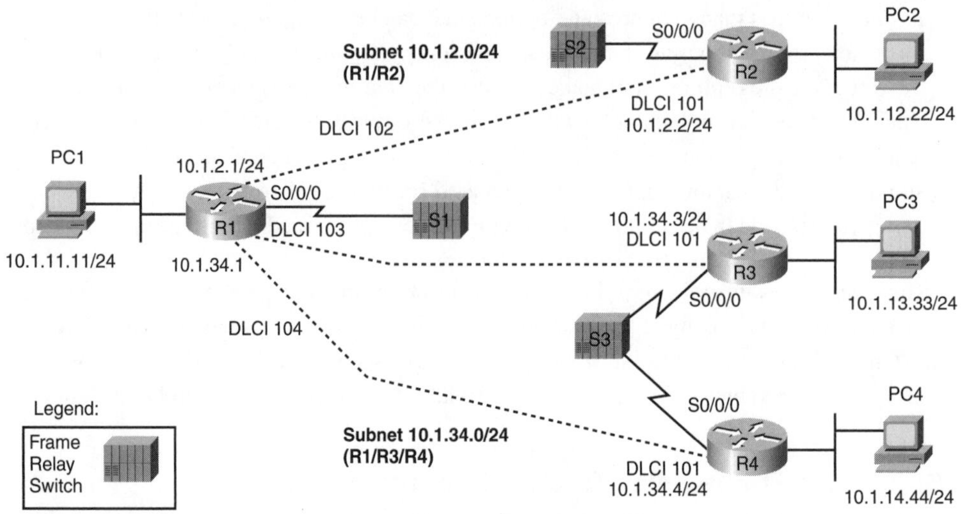

This chapter organizes its explanations of how to troubleshoot Frame Relay based on this first problem isolation step. The following list summarizes the major actions, with each step in the following list being examined in order following the list.

**Key
Topic**

If a Frame Relay router's pings fail for all remote routers whose VCs share a single access link, do the following:

Step 1   Check for Layer 1 problems on the access link between the router and the local Frame Relay switch (all routers).

Step 2   Check for Layer 2 problems on the access link, particularly encapsulation and LMI.

After resolving any problems in the first two steps, or if the original ping tests showed that the Frame Relay router can ping some, but not all, of the other Frame Relay routers whose VCs share a single access link, follow these steps:

Step 3   Check for PVC problems based on the PVC status and subinterface status.

Step 4   Check for Layer 2/3 problems with both static and dynamic (Inverse ARP) mapping.

Step 5   Check for Layer 2/3 problems related to a mismatch of end-to-end encapsulation (cisco or ietf).

Step 6   Check for other Layer 3 issues, including mismatched subnets.

The rest of this chapter explains some of the details of each step of this suggested troubleshooting process.

Layer 1 Issues on the Access Link (Step 1)

If a router's physical interface used for the Frame Relay access link is not in an "up and up" state, the router cannot send any frames over the link. If the interface has a line status (the first interface status code) of down, the interface most likely has a Layer 1 issue.

From a Layer 1 perspective, a Frame Relay access link is merely a leased line between a router and a Frame Relay switch. As such, the exact same Layer 1 issues exist for this link as for a point-to-point leased line. Because the possible root causes and suggested troubleshooting steps mirror what should be done on a leased line, refer to the section "Troubleshooting Layer 1 Problems" in Chapter 12, "Point-to-Point WANs," for more information about this step.

Layer 2 Issues on the Access Link (Step 2)

If a router's physical interface line status is up, but the line protocol status (second status code) is down, the link typically has a Layer 2 problem between the router and the local Frame Relay switch. With Frame Relay interfaces, the problem is typically related to either the **encapsulation** command or the Frame Relay LMI.

The potential problem related to the **encapsulation** command is very simple to check. If a router's serial interface configuration omits the **encapsulation frame-relay** interface subcommand, but the physical access link is working, the physical interface settles into an up/down state. If the configuration is unavailable, the **show interfaces** command can be used to see the configured encapsulation type, which is listed in the first few lines of command output.

The other potential problem relates to the LMI. LMI status messages flow in both directions between a router (DTE) and Frame Relay switch (DCE) for two main purposes:

- For the DCE to inform the DTE about each VC's DLCI and its status

- To provide a keepalive function so that the DTE and DCE can easily tell when the access link can no longer pass traffic

A router places the physical link in an up/down state when the link physically works but the router ceases to hear LMI messages from the switch. With the interface not in an up/up state, the router does not attempt to send any IP packets out the interface, so all pings should fail at this point.

A router might cease to receive LMI messages from the switch because of both legitimate reasons and mistakes. The normal legitimate purpose for the LMI keepalive function is that if the link really is having problems, and cannot pass any data, the router can notice the loss of keepalive messages and bring the link down. This allows the router to use an alternative route, assuming that an alternative route exists. However, a router might cease to receive LMI messages and bring down the interface because of the following mistakes:

- Disabling LMI on the router (with the **no keepalive** physical interface subcommand), but leaving it enabled on the switch—or vice versa

- Configuring different LMI types on the router (with the **frame-relay lmi-type** *type* physical interface subcommand) and the switch

You can easily check for both encapsulation and LMI using the **show frame-relay lmi** command. This command lists only output for interfaces that have the **encapsulation frame-relay** command configured, so you can quickly confirm whether the **encapsulation frame-relay** command is configured on the correct serial interfaces. This command also lists the LMI type used by the router, and it shows counters for the number of LMI messages sent and received. Example 14-19 shows an example from router R1 in Figure 14-6.

Example 14-19   **show frame-relay lmi** *Command on R1*

```
R1#show frame-relay lmi

LMI Statistics for interface Serial0/0/0 (Frame Relay DTE) LMI TYPE = ANSI
   Invalid Unnumbered info 0            Invalid Prot Disc 0
   Invalid dummy Call Ref 0            Invalid Msg Type 0
   Invalid Status Message 0            Invalid Lock Shift 0
   Invalid Information ID 0            Invalid Report IE Len 0
   Invalid Report Request 0            Invalid Keep IE Len 0
   Num Status Enq. Sent 122            Num Status msgs Rcvd 34
   Num Update Status Rcvd 0            Num Status Timeouts 88
   Last Full Status Req 00:00:04       Last Full Status Rcvd 00:13:24
```

For this example, router R1 was statically configured with the **frame-relay lmi-type ansi** interface subcommand, with switch S1 still using LMI type cisco. When the LMI configuration was changed, the router and switch had exchanged 34 LMI messages (of type cisco). After that change, R1's counter of the number of status enquiry messages sent kept rising (122 when the **show frame-relay lmi** command output was captured), but the counter of the number of LMI status messages received from the switch remained at 34. Just below that counter is the number of timeouts, which counts the number of times the router expected to receive a periodic LMI message from the switch but did not. In this case, the router was actually still receiving LMI messages, but they were not ANSI LMI messages so the router did not understand or recognize them.

If repeated use of the **show frame-relay lmi** command shows that the number of status messages received remains the same, the likely cause, other than a truly nonworking link, is that the LMI types do not match. The best solution is to allow for LMI autosense by configuring the **no frame-relay lmi-type** *type* physical interface subcommand, or alternatively, configuring the same LMI type that is used by the switch.

If you troubleshoot and fix any problems found in Steps 1 and 2, on all Frame Relay connected routers, all the routers' access link physical interfaces should be in an up/up state. The last four steps examine issues that apply to individual PVCs and neighbors.

PVC Problems and Status (Step 3)

The goal at this step in the troubleshooting process is to discover the DLCI of the PVC used to reach a particular neighbor and then find out if the PVC is working. To determine the correct PVC, particularly if little or no configuration or documentation is available, you have to start with the failed **ping** command. The **ping** command identifies the IP address of the neighboring router. Based on the neighbor's IP address, a few **show** commands can link the neighbor's IP address with the associated connected subnet, the connected subnet with the local router's interface, and the local router's interface with the possible DLCIs. Also, the Frame Relay mapping information can identify the specific PVC. Although this book has covered all the commands used to find these pieces of information, the following list summarizes the steps that take you from the neighbor's IP address to the correct local DLCI used to send frames to that neighbor:

Step 3a   Discover the IP address and mask of each Frame Relay interface/ subinterface (**show interfaces**, **show ip interface brief**), and calculate the connected subnets.

Step 3b   Compare the IP address in the failed **ping** command, and pick the interface/subinterface whose connected subnet is the same subnet.

Step 3c   Discover the PVC(s) assigned to that interface or subinterface (**show frame-relay pvc**).

Step 3d   If more than one PVC is assigned to the interface or subinterface, determine which PVC is used to reach a particular neighbor (**show frame-relay map**).

NOTE   As a reminder, lists like this one are meant for convenient reference when you read the chapter. It's easy to find the list when you study and want to remember a particular part of how to attack a given problem. You do not need to memorize the list, or practice it until you internalize the information.

Steps 3a, 3b, 3c, and 3d discover the correct PVC to examine. After it is discovered, Step 3 in the suggested troubleshooting process interprets the status of that PVC, and the associated interface or subinterface, to determine the cause of any problems.

This section takes a closer look at an example in which R1 cannot ping R2's 10.1.2.2 Frame Relay IP address. Before focusing on the process to determine which VC is used, it is helpful to see the final answer, so Figure 14-7 lists some of the details. For this example, R1's **ping 10.1.2.2** command fails in this case.

Figure 14-7 *Configuration Facts Related to R1's Failed **ping 10.1.2.2** Command*

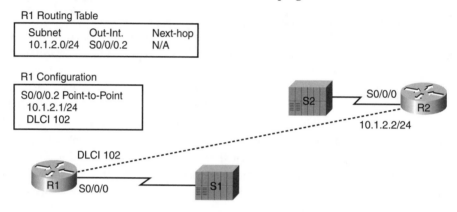

Find the Connected Subnet and Outgoing Interface (Steps 3a and 3b)

The first two substeps to find R1's PVC (DLCI) connecting to R2 (Substeps 3a and 3b) should be relatively easy assuming that you have already finished Parts II and III of this book. Any time you ping the Frame Relay IP address of a neighboring router, that IP address should be in one of the subnets also connected to the local router. To find the interface used on a local router when forwarding packets to the remote router, you just have to find that common connected subnet.

In this example, with R1 pinging 10.1.2.2, Example 14-20 shows a few commands that confirm that R1's S0/0/0.2 subinterface is connected to subnet 10.1.2.0/24, which includes R2's 10.1.2.2 IP address.

Example 14-20 *Finding Subnet 10.1.2.0/24 and Subinterface S0/0/0.2*

```
R1>show ip interface brief
Interface          IP-Address      OK? Method Status                Protocol
FastEthernet0/0    10.1.11.1       YES NVRAM  up                    up
FastEthernet0/1    unassigned      YES NVRAM  administratively down  down
Serial0/0/0        unassigned      YES NVRAM  up                    up
Serial0/0/0.2      10.1.2.1        YES NVRAM  down                  down
```

Example 14-20   *Finding Subnet 10.1.2.0/24 and Subinterface S0/0/0.2 (Continued)*

```
Serial0/0/0.5          10.1.5.1         YES manual down                  down
Serial0/0/0.34         10.1.34.1        YES NVRAM  up                    up
R1#show interfaces s 0/0/0.2
Serial0/0/0.2 is down, line protocol is down
  Hardware is GT96K Serial
  Internet address is 10.1.2.1/24
  MTU 1500 bytes, BW 1544 Kbit, DLY 20000 usec,
     reliability 255/255, txload 1/255, rxload 1/255
  Encapsulation FRAME-RELAY
  Last clearing of "show interface" counters never
```

Find the PVCs Assigned to That Interface (Step 3c)

The **show frame-relay pvc** command directly answers the question of which PVCs have
been assigned to which interfaces and subinterfaces. If the command is issued with no
parameters, the command lists about ten lines of output for each VC, with the end of the
first line listing the associated interface or subinterface. Example 14-21 lists the beginning
of the command output.

Example 14-21   *Correlating Subinterface S0/0/0.2 to the PVC with DLCI 102*

```
R1>show frame-relay pvc

PVC Statistics for interface Serial0/0/0 (Frame Relay DTE)

              Active     Inactive     Deleted       Static
  Local         1           2            0             0
  Switched      0           0            0             0
  Unused        0           0            0             0

DLCI = 102, DLCI USAGE = LOCAL, PVC STATUS = INACTIVE, INTERFACE = Serial0/0/0.2

  input pkts 33            output pkts 338        in bytes 1952
  out bytes 29018          dropped pkts 0         in pkts dropped 0
  out pkts dropped 0             out bytes dropped 0
  in FECN pkts 0           in BECN pkts 0         out FECN pkts 0
  out BECN pkts 0          in DE pkts 0           out DE pkts 0
  out bcast pkts 332       out bcast bytes 28614
  5 minute input rate 0 bits/sec, 0 packets/sec
  5 minute output rate 0 bits/sec, 0 packets/sec
  pvc create time 00:30:05, last time pvc status changed 00:04:14

DLCI = 103, DLCI USAGE = LOCAL, PVC STATUS = INACTIVE, INTERFACE = Serial0/0/0.34

  input pkts 17            output pkts 24         in bytes 1106
  out bytes 2086           dropped pkts 0         in pkts dropped 0
  out pkts dropped 0             out bytes dropped 0
```

continues

Example 14-21 *Correlating Subinterface S0/0/0.2 to the PVC with DLCI 102 (Continued)*

```
  in FECN pkts 0         in BECN pkts 0         out FECN pkts 0
  out BECN pkts 0        in DE pkts 0           out DE pkts 0
  out bcast pkts 11      out bcast bytes 674
  5 minute input rate 0 bits/sec, 0 packets/sec
  5 minute output rate 0 bits/sec, 0 packets/sec
  pvc create time 00:30:07, last time pvc status changed 00:02:57

DLCI = 104, DLCI USAGE = LOCAL, PVC STATUS = ACTIVE, INTERFACE = Serial0/0/0.34

  input pkts 41          output pkts 42         in bytes 2466
  out bytes 3017         dropped pkts 0         in pkts dropped 0
  out pkts dropped 0           out bytes dropped 0
  in FECN pkts 0         in BECN pkts 0         out FECN pkts 0
  out BECN pkts 0        in DE pkts 0           out DE pkts 0
  out bcast pkts 30      out bcast bytes 1929
  5 minute input rate 0 bits/sec, 0 packets/sec
  5 minute output rate 0 bits/sec, 0 packets/sec
  pvc create time 00:30:07, last time pvc status changed 00:26:17
```

To find all the PVCs associated with an interface or subinterface, just scan the highlighted parts of the output in Example 14-21. In this case, S0/0/0.2 is listed with only one PVC, the one with DLCI 102, so only one PVC is associated with S0/0/0.2 in this case.

Determine Which PVC Is Used to Reach a Particular Neighbor (Step 3d)

If the router's configuration associates more than one PVC with one interface or subinterface, the next step is to figure out which of the PVCs is used to send traffic to a particular neighbor. For instance, Example 14-21 shows R1 uses a multipoint subinterface S0/0/0.34 with DLCIs 103 and 104, with DLCI 103 used for the PVC to R3, and DLCI 104 for the PVC connecting to R4. So, if you were troubleshooting a problem in which the **ping 10.1.34.3** command failed on R1, the next step would be to determine which of the two DLCIs (103 or 104) identifies the VC connecting R1 to R3.

Unfortunately, you cannot always find the answer without looking at other documentation. The only **show** command that can help is **show frame-relay map**, which can correlate the next-hop IP address and DLCI. Unfortunately, if the local router relies on Inverse ARP, the local router cannot learn the mapping information right now either, so the mapping table may not have any useful information in it. However, if static mapping is used, the correct PVC/DLCI can be identified.

In the example of R1 failing when pinging 10.1.2.2 (R2), because only one PVC is associated with the correct interface (S0/0/0.2), the PVC has already been identified, so you can ignore this step for now.

PVC Status

At this point in major troubleshooting Step 3, the correct outgoing interface/subinterface and correct PVC/DLCI have been identified. Finally, the PVC status can be examined to see if it means that the PVC has a problem.

Routers use four different PVC status codes. A router learns about two of the possible status values, *active* and *inactive*, via LMI messages from the Frame Relay switch. The switch's LMI message lists all DLCIs for all configured PVCs on the access link, and whether the PVC is currently usable (active) or not (inactive).

The first of the two PVC states that is not learned using LMI is called the *static* state. If the LMI is disabled, the router does not learn any information from the switch about PVC status. So, the router lists all its configured DLCIs in the *static* state, meaning statically configured. The router does not know if the PVCs will work, but it can at least send frames using those DLCIs and hope that the Frame Relay network can deliver them.

The other PVC state, *deleted*, is used when LMI is working but the switch's LMI message does not mention anything about a particular DLCI value. If the router has configuration for a DLCI (for example, in a **frame-relay interface-dlci** command), but the switch's LMI message does not list that DLCI, the router lists that DLCI in a deleted state. This state means that the router has configured the DLCI, but the switch has not. In real life, the deleted state may mean that the router or switch has been misconfigured, or that the Frame Relay switch has not yet been configured with the correct DLCI. Table 14-4 summarizes the four Frame Relay PVC status codes.

Table 14-4 *PVC Status Values*

Key Topic

Status	Active	Inactive	Deleted	Static
The PVC is defined to the Frame Relay network	Yes	Yes	No	Unknown
The router will attempt to send frames on a VC in this state	Yes	No	No	Yes

As noted in the last row of the table, routers only send data over PVCs in an active or static state. Also, even if the PVC is in a static state, there is no guarantee that the Frame Relay network can actually send frames over that PVC, because the static state implies that LMI is turned off, and the router has not learned any status information.

The next step in the troubleshooting process is to find the status of the PVC used to reach a particular neighbor. Continuing with the problem of R1 failing when pinging R2 (10.1.2.2), Example 14-22 shows the status of the PVC with DLCI 102, as identified earlier.

Example 14-22   show frame-relay pvc *Command on R1*

```
R1>show frame-relay pvc 102

PVC Statistics for interface Serial0/0/0 (Frame Relay DTE)

DLCI = 102, DLCI USAGE = LOCAL, PVC STATUS = INACTIVE, INTERFACE = Serial0/0/0.2

  input pkts 22          output pkts 193        in bytes 1256
  out bytes 16436        dropped pkts 0         in pkts dropped 0
  out pkts dropped 0           out bytes dropped 0
  in FECN pkts 0         in BECN pkts 0         out FECN pkts 0
  out BECN pkts 0        in DE pkts 0           out DE pkts 0
  out bcast pkts 187     out bcast bytes 16032
  5 minute input rate 0 bits/sec, 0 packets/sec
  5 minute output rate 0 bits/sec, 0 packets/sec
  pvc create time 01:12:56, last time pvc status changed 00:22:45
```

In this case, R1 cannot ping R2 because the PVC with DLCI 102 is in an inactive state.

To further isolate the problem and find the root cause, you need to look deeper into the reasons why a PVC can be in an inactive state. First, as always, repeat the same troubleshooting steps on the other router—in this case, R2. If no problems are found on R2, other than an inactive PVC, the problem may be a genuine problem in the Frame Relay provider's network, so a call to the provider may be the next step. However, you may find some other problem on the remote router. For example, to create the failure and **show** commands in this section, R2's access link was shut down, so a quick examination of troubleshooting Step 1 on router R2 would have identified the problem. However, if further troubleshooting shows that both routers list their ends of the PVC in an inactive state, the root cause lies within the Frame Relay provider's network.

Finding the root cause of a problem related to a PVC in a deleted state is relatively easy. The deleted status means that the Frame Relay switch's configuration and the router's configuration do not match, with the router configuring a DLCI that is not also configured on the switch. Either the provider said it would configure a PVC with a particular DLCI, and did not, or the router engineer configured the wrong DLCI value.

Subinterface Status

Subinterfaces have a line status and protocol status code, just like physical interfaces. However, because subinterfaces are virtual, the status codes and their meanings differ a bit from physical interfaces. This section briefly examines how Frame Relay subinterfaces work and how IOS decides if a Frame Relay subinterface should be in an up/up state or a down/down state.

Frame Relay configuration associates one or more DLCIs with a subinterface using two commands: **frame-relay interface-dlci** and **frame-relay map**. Of all the DLCIs associated with a subinterface, IOS uses the following rules to determine the status of a subinterface:

- **down/down:** All the DLCIs associated with the subinterface are inactive or deleted, or the underlying physical interface is not in an up/up state.

- **up/up:** At least one of the DLCIs associated with the subinterface is active or static.

For example, to cause the problems shown in Example 14-22, R2 and R3 simply shut down their Frame Relay access links. Figure 14-8 shows the next LMI status message that switch S1 sends to R1.

Figure 14-8 *Results of Shutting Down R2 and R3 Access Links*

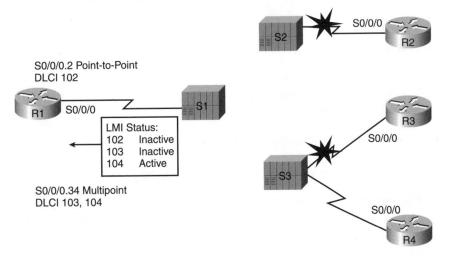

As shown in the figure, R1 uses a point-to-point subinterface (S0/0/0.2) for the VC connecting to R2, and a multipoint subinterface (S0/0/0.34) associated with the VCs to R3 and R4 (103 and 104, respectively). The beginning of Example 14-20 shows that S0/0/0.2 is in a down/down state, which is because the only DLCI associated with the subinterface (102) is inactive. However, S0/0/0.34 has two DLCIs, one of which is active, so IOS leaves S0/0/0.34 in an up/up state.

It is useful to look at subinterface status when troubleshooting, but keep in mind that just because a subinterface is up, if it is a multipoint subinterface, the up/up state does not necessarily mean that all DLCIs associated with the subinterface are working.

Frame Relay Mapping Issues (Step 4)

If you follow the first three steps of the troubleshooting process suggested in this chapter and resolve the problems at each step, at this point each router's access link interfaces should be in an up/up state, and the PVC between the two routers should be in an active (or static) state. If the routers still cannot ping each other's Frame Relay IP addresses, the next thing to check is the Frame Relay address mapping information, which maps DLCIs to next-hop IP addresses.

This section does not repeat the detailed coverage of address mapping that appears in both Chapter 13 and this chapter. However, for perspective, the following list points out some tips and hints as reminders when you perform this troubleshooting step:

On point-to-point subinterfaces:

■ These subinterfaces do not need Inverse ARP or static mapping, because IOS simply thinks that the subnet defined on the subinterface is reachable via the only DLCI on the subinterface.

■ The **show frame-relay map** command output still lists these subinterfaces, but with no next-hop IP address.

On physical interfaces and multipoint subinterfaces:

■ They need to use either Inverse ARP or static mapping.

■ The **show frame-relay map** command should list the remote router's Frame Relay IP address and the local router's local DLCI for each PVC associated with the interface or subinterface.

■ If you're using static mapping, the **broadcast** keyword is needed to support a routing protocol.

For completeness, Example 14-23 shows the output of the **show frame-relay map** command on router R1 from Figure 14-6, with no problems with the mapping. (The earlier problems that were introduced have been fixed.) In this case, interface S0/0/0.2 is a point-to-point subinterface, and S0/0/0.34 is a multipoint, with one Inverse ARP-learned mapping and one statically configured mapping.

Example 14-23 show frame-relay map *Command on R1*

```
R1#show frame-relay map
Serial0/0/0.34 (up): ip 10.1.34.4 dlci 104(0x68,0x1880), static,
               broadcast,
               CISCO, status defined, active
Serial0/0/0.34 (up): ip 10.1.34.3 dlci 103(0x67,0x1870), dynamic,
               broadcast,, status defined, active
Serial0/0/0.2 (up): point-to-point dlci, dlci 102(0x66,0x1860), broadcast
          status defined, active
```

End-to-End Encapsulation (Step 5)

The end-to-end encapsulation on a PVC refers to the headers that follow the Frame Relay header, with two options: the Cisco-proprietary header and an IETF standard header. The configuration details were covered earlier in this chapter, in the section "Configuring the Encapsulation and LMI."

As it turns out, a mismatched encapsulation setting on the routers on opposite ends of the link might cause a problem in one particular case. If one router is a Cisco router, using Cisco encapsulation, and the other router is a non-Cisco router, using IETF encapsulation, pings may fail because of the encapsulation mismatch. However, two Cisco routers can understand both types of encapsulation, so it should not be an issue in networks with only Cisco routers.

Mismatched Subnet Numbers (Step 6)

At this point, if the problems found in the first five of the six troubleshooting steps have been resolved, all the Frame Relay problems should be resolved. However, if the two routers on either end of the PVC have mistakenly configured IP addresses in different subnets, the routers will not be able to ping one another, and the routing protocols will not become adjacent. So, as a last step, you should confirm the IP addresses on each router, and the masks, and ensure that they connect to the same subnet. To do so, just use the **show ip interface brief** and **show interfaces** commands on the two routers.

Exam Preparation Tasks

Review All the Key Topics

Review the most important topics from this chapter, noted with the key topics icon. Table 14-5 lists these key topics and where each is discussed.

Table 14-5   *Key Topics for Chapter 14*

Key Topic Element	Description	Page Number
List	Frame Relay configuration checklist	488
List	Default Frame Relay settings in IOS	490
Definition	Frame Relay address mapping concept and definition	493
Figure 14-3	Frame Relay Inverse ARP process	495
List	Six-step Frame Relay troubleshooting checklist	508
List	Summary of the two main functions of LMI	509
Table 14-4	List of PVC status values and their meanings	515
List	Reasons for subinterfaces to be up/up or down/down	517
List	Summary of mapping information seen on point-to-point subinterfaces	518
List	Summary of mapping information seen on multipoint subinterfaces	518

Complete the Tables and Lists from Memory

Print a copy of Appendix J, "Memory Tables" (found on the CD), or at least the section for this chapter, and complete the tables and lists from memory. Appendix K, "Memory Tables Answer Key," also on the CD, includes completed tables and lists for you to check your work.

Read the Appendix F Scenarios

Appendix F, "Additional Scenarios," contains five detailed scenarios. They give you a chance to analyze different designs, problems, and command output and show you how concepts from several different chapters interrelate. Scenario 4 examines a variety of options and issues related to implementing Frame Relay.

Command Reference to Check Your Memory

Although you should not necessarily memorize the information in the tables in this section, this section does include a reference for the configuration and EXEC commands covered in this chapter. Practically speaking, you should memorize the commands as a side effect of reading the chapter and doing all the activities in this exam preparation section. To see how well you have memorized the commands as a side effect of your other studies, cover the left side of the table, read the descriptions on the right side, and see if you remember the command.

Table 14-6 *Chapter 14 Configuration Command Reference*

Command	Description
encapsulation frame-relay [ietf]	Interface configuration mode command that defines the Frame Relay encapsulation that is used rather than HDLC, PPP, and so on.
**frame-relay lmi-type {ansi	q933a	cisco}**	Interface configuration mode command that defines the type of LMI messages sent to the switch.
bandwidth *num*	Interface subcommand that sets the router's perceived interface speed.
frame-relay map {*protocol protocol-address dlci*} **[broadcast] [ietf	cisco]**	Interface configuration mode command that statically defines a mapping between a network layer address and a DLCI.
keepalive *sec*	Interface configuration mode command that defines whether and how often LMI status inquiry messages are sent and expected.
interface serial *number.sub* **[point-to-point	multipoint]**	Global configuration mode command that creates a subinterface or references a previously created subinterface.
frame-relay interface-dlci *dlci* **[ietf	cisco]**	Subinterface configuration mode command that links or correlates a DLCI to the subinterface.

Table 14-7 *Chapter 14 EXEC Command Reference*

Command	Description
show interfaces [*type number*]	Shows the physical interface status.
show frame-relay pvc [**interface** *interface*][*dlci*]	Lists information about the PVC status.
show frame-relay lmi [*type number*]	Lists LMI status information.
debug frame-relay lmi	Displays the contents of LMI messages.
debug frame-relay events	Lists messages about certain Frame Relay events, including Inverse ARP messages.

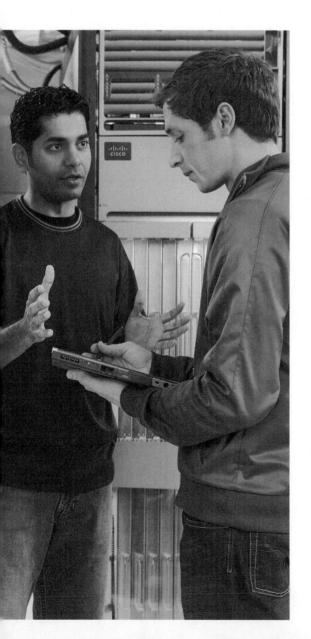

This chapter covers the following subjects:

VPN Fundamentals: This section describes the main goals and benefits of VPNs.

IPsec VPNs: This section explains how the IP Security (IPsec) protocol architecture provides the main features needed in both site-to-site and access VPNs.

SSL VPNs: This final section examines the use of the Secure Socket Layer (SSL) protocol that is included in common web browsers today.

CHAPTER **15**

Virtual Private Networks

A company with one main site and ten remote sites could buy ten T1 lines, one each from the central site to each remote office. A more cost-effective solution would be to use Frame Relay. However, especially because the remote sites often need access to the Internet, it is even more cost effective to simply connect each office to the Internet, and send traffic between sites over the Internet, using the Internet as a WAN.

Unfortunately, the Internet is not nearly as secure as leased lines and Frame Relay. For example, for an attacker to steal a copy of data frames passing over a leased line, the attacker would have to physically tap into the cable, oftentimes inside a secure building, under the street, or at the telco central office (CO); all of these actions can result in a jail sentence. With the Internet, an attacker can find less intrusive ways to get copies of packets, without even having to leave his home computer, and with a much smaller risk of getting carted off to jail.

Virtual private networks (VPN) solve the security problems associated with using the Internet as a WAN service. This chapter explains the concepts and terminology related to VPNs.

"Do I Know This Already?" Quiz

The "Do I Know This Already?" quiz allows you to assess whether you should read the entire chapter. If you miss no more than one of these six self-assessment questions, you might want to move ahead to the section "Exam Preparation Tasks." Table 15-1 lists the major headings in this chapter and the "Do I Know This Already?" quiz questions covering the material in those headings so that you can assess your knowledge of these specific areas. The answers to the "Do I Know This Already?" quiz appear in Appendix A.

Table 15-1 *"Do I Know This Already?" Foundation Topics Section-to-Question Mapping*

Foundation Topics Section	Questions
VPN Fundamentals	1–2
IPsec VPNs	3–5
SSL VPNs	6

1. Which of the following terms refers to a VPN that uses the Internet to connect the sites of a single company, rather than using leased lines or Frame Relay?

   a. Intranet VPN

   b. Extranet VPN

   c. Access VPN

   d. Enterprise VPN

2. Which of the following are not considered to be desirable security goals for a site-to-site VPN?

   a. Message integrity checks

   b. Privacy (encryption)

   c. Antivirus

   d. Authentication

3. Which of the following functions could be performed by the IPsec IP Authentication Header?

   a. Authentication

   b. Encryption

   c. Message integrity checks

   d. Anti-replay

4. Which of the following is considered to be the best encryption protocol for providing privacy in an IPsec VPN as compared to the other answers?

   a. AES

   b. HMAC-MD5

   c. HMAC-SHA-1

   d. DES

   e. 3DES

5. Which three of the following options would be the most commonly used options for newly purchased and installed VPN components today?

   a. ASA

   b. PIX firewall

   c. VPN concentrator

   d. Cisco router

   e. Cisco VPN client

6. When using the Cisco Web VPN solution, with the client using a normal web browser without any special client software, which of the following are true?

   a. The user creates a TCP connection to a Web VPN server using SSL.

   b. If the user connects to a normal web server inside the enterprise, and that server only supports HTTP and not SSL, those packets pass over the Internet unencrypted.

   c. The Web VPN server connects to internal web servers on behalf of the Web VPN client, translating between HTTP and SSL as need be.

   d. The web VPN client cannot connect without at least thin-client SSL software installed on the client.

Foundation Topics

This chapter has three main sections. The first section introduces the basic concept of a VPN. The second (and largest) section examines some of the details of building VPNs using the rules defined in the IP Security (IPsec) RFCs. The last section explains the basics of an alternative VPN technology called SSL.

VPN Fundamentals

Leased lines have some wonderful security features. The router on one ends knows with confidence the identity of the device on the other end of the link. The receiving router also has good reason to believe that no attackers saw the data in transit, or even changed the data to cause some harm.

Virtual private networks (VPN) try to provide these same secure features as a leased line. In particular, they provide the following:

- **Privacy:** Preventing anyone in the middle of the Internet (man in the middle) who copies the packet in the Internet from being able to read the data

- **Authentication:** Verifying that the sender of the VPN packet is a legitimate device and not a device used by an attacker

- **Data integrity:** Verifying that the packet was not changed as the packet transited the Internet

- **Antireplay:** Preventing a man in the middle from copying packets sent by a legitimate user, and then later resending the packets to appear to be a legitimate user

To accomplish these goals, two devices near the edge of the Internet create a VPN, sometimes called a *VPN tunnel*. These devices add headers to the original packet, with these headers including fields that allow the VPN devices to perform all the functions. The VPN devices also encrypt the original IP packet, meaning that the original packet's contents are undecipherable to anyone who happens to see a copy of the packet as it traverses the Internet.

Figure 15-1 shows the general idea of what typically occurs with a VPN tunnel. The figure shows a VPN created between a branch office router and a Cisco Adaptive Security Appliance (ASA). In this case, the VPN is called a site-to-site VPN, because it connects two sites of a company, in particular. This VPN is also called site-to-site *intranet* VPN, because it connects sites that belong inside a single company.

Figure 15-1 *VPN Tunnel Concepts for a Site-to-Site Intranet VPN*

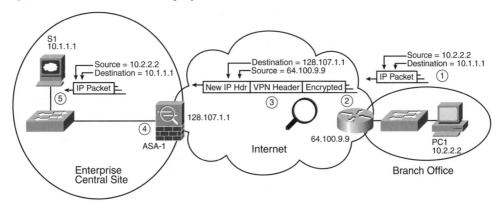

The figure shows the following steps, which explain the overall flow in the figure:

1. Host PC1 (10.2.2.2) on the right sends a packet to the web server (10.1.1.1), just as it would without a VPN.

2. The router encrypts the packet, adds some VPN headers, adds another IP header (with public IP addresses), and forwards the packet.

3. A man in the middle copies the packet but cannot change the packet without being noticed, and cannot read the contents of the packet.

4. ASA-1 receives the packet, confirms the authenticity of the sender, confirms that the packet has not been changed, and then decrypts the original packet.

5. Server S1 receives the unencrypted packet.

The benefits of using an Internet-based VPN as shown in Figure 15-1 are many. The cost of a high-speed Internet connection is typically much less than that of either a leased line or a Frame Relay WAN. The Internet is seemingly everywhere, making this kind of solution available worldwide. And by using VPN technology and protocols, the communications are secure.

> **NOTE** The term *tunnel* generically refers to any protocol's packet that is sent by encapsulating the packet inside another packet. The term *VPN tunnel* implies that the encapsulated packet has been encrypted, whereas the term *tunnel* does not imply whether the packet has been encrypted.

VPNs can be built with a variety of devices and for a variety of purposes. Figure 15-2 shows an example of three of the primary reasons for building an Internet VPN today.

Figure 15-2 *Intranet, Extranet, and Access VPNs*

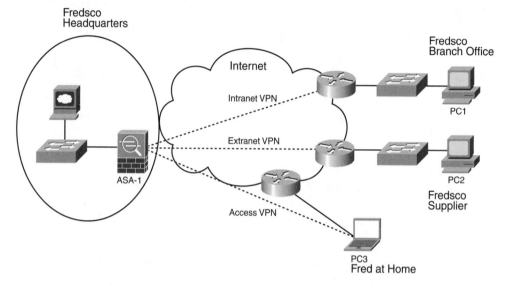

In the top part of the figure, the central site and a remote branch office of a fictitious company (Fredsco) are connected with an intranet VPN. The middle of the figure shows Fredsco connecting to another company that supplies parts to Fredsco, making that VPN an extranet VPN. Finally, when Fred brings his laptop home at the end of the day and connects to the Internet, the secure VPN connection from the laptop back into the Fredsco network is called a remote access VPN, or simply an access VPN. In this case, the laptop itself is the end of the VPN tunnel, rather than the Internet access router. Table 15-2 summarizes the key points about these three types of VPNs.

Key
Topic

Table 15-2 *Types of VPNs*

Type	Typical Purpose
Intranet	Connects all the computers at two sites of the same organization, typically using one VPN device at each site
Extranet	Connects all the computers at two sites of different but partnering organizations, typically using one VPN device at each site
Access	Connects individual Internet users to the enterprise network

To build a VPN, one device at each site needs to have hardware and/or software that understand a chosen set of VPN security standards and protocols. The devices include the following:

- **Routers:** In addition to packet forwarding, the router can provide VPN functions as well. The router can have specialized add-on cards that help the router perform the encryption more quickly.

- **Adaptive Security Appliances (ASA):** The Cisco leading security appliance that can be configured for many security functions, including VPNs.

- **PIX firewalls:** The older product line of Cisco firewall products that can perform VPN functions in addition to working as a firewall. New installations today would instead use an ASA.

- **VPN concentrators:** An older product line from Cisco, these devices provide a hardware platform to specifically act as the endpoint of a VPN tunnel. New installations today would instead use an ASA.

- **VPN client:** For access VPNs, the PC might need to do the VPN functions; the laptop needs software to do those functions, with that software being called a *VPN client.*

Next, the text examines the use of a set of protocols called IPsec to create VPNs.

IPsec VPNs

IPsec is an architecture or framework for security services for IP networks. The name itself is not an acronym, but rather a shortened version of the title of the RFC that defines it (RFC 4301, *Security Architecture for the Internet Protocol*), more generally called IP Security, or IPsec.

IPsec defines a set of functions, for example, authentication and encryption, and some rules regarding each of those functions. However, like the TCP/IP protocol architecture defines many protocols, some of which are alternatives to each other, IPsec allows the use of several different protocol options for each VPN feature. One of IPsec's strengths is that its role as an architecture allows it to be added to and changed over time as improvements to security protocols are made.

The following sections examine the components of IPsec, beginning with encryption, followed by key exchange, message integrity, and authentication.

IPsec Encryption

If you ignore the math—and thankfully, you can—IPsec encryption is not too difficult to understand. IPsec encryption uses a pair of encryption algorithms, which are essentially math formulas, that meet a couple of requirements. First, the two math formulas are a matched set:

■ One to hide (encrypt) the data

■ Another to re-create (decrypt) the original data from the encrypted data

Besides those somewhat obvious functions, the two math formulas were chosen so that if you intercept the encrypted text, but do not have the secret password (called an encryption key), decrypting that one packet would be difficult. Additionally, the formulas are also chosen so that if an attacker did happen to decrypt one packet, that information would not give the attacker any advantages in decrypting the other packets.

The process for encrypting data for an IPsec VPN works generally as shown in Figure 15-3. Note that the encryption key is also known as the session key, shared key, or shared session key.

Figure 15-3 *Basic IPsec Encryption Process*

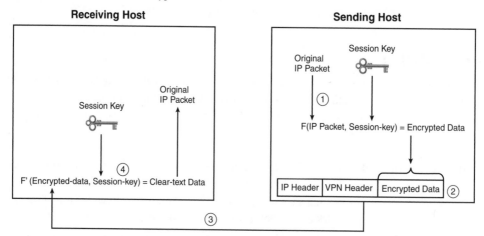

The four steps highlighted in the figure are as follows:

1. The sending VPN device (like the remote office router in Figure 15-1) feeds the original packet and the session key into the encryption formula, calculating the encrypted data.

2. The sending device encapsulates the encrypted data into a packet, which includes the new IP header and VPN header.

3. The sending device sends this new packet to the destination VPN device (ASA-1 back in Figure 15-1).

4. The receiving VPN device runs the corresponding decryption formula, using the encrypted data and session key—the same value as was used on the sending VPN device—to decrypt the data.

IPsec supports several variations on the encryption algorithms, some of which are simply more recently developed and better, while some have other trade-offs. In particular, the length of the keys has some impact on both the difficulty for attackers to decrypt the data, with longer keys making it more difficult, but with the negative result of generally requiring more processing power. Table 15-3 summarizes several of these options and the lengths of the keys.

Table 15-3 *Comparing VPN Encryption Algorithms*

Key Topic

Encryption Algorithm	Key Length (Bits)	Comments
Data Encryption Standard (DES)	56	Older and less secure than the other options listed here
Triple DES (3DES)	56 x 3	Applies three different 56-bit DES keys in succession, improving the encryption strength versus DES
Advanced Encryption Standard (AES)	128 and 256	Considered the current best practice, with strong encryption and less computation than 3DES

IPsec Key Exchange

The use of a shared common key value (also called symmetric keys) for encryption causes a bit of chicken-and-egg problem: If both devices need to know the same key value before they can encrypt/decrypt the data, how can the two devices send the key values to each over the network without having to send the keys as clear text, open to being stolen by an attacker?

The problem related to *key distribution* has existed since the idea of encryption was first created. One simple but problematic option is to use Pre-Shared Keys (PSK), a fancy term for the idea that you manually configure the values on both devices. With PSKs, you might just exchange keys by calling the engineer at the remote site, or sending a letter, or (don't do this at home) sending an unsecure e-mail with the key value.

The problem with PSKs is that even if no one steals the shared encryption key, it is only human nature that the PSKs will almost never change. It's like changing your password on a website that never requires you to change your password: You might never think about it, no one makes you change it, and you do not want to have to remember a new password. However, for better security, the keys need to be changed occasionally because even though the encryption algorithms make it difficult to decrypt the data, it is technically possible for an attacker to break a key, and then be able to decrypt the packet. Dynamic key exchange protocols allow frequent changes to encryption keys, significantly reducing the amount of lost data if an attacker compromises an encryption key.

IPsec, as a security architecture, calls for the use of *dynamic key exchange* through a process defined by RFC 4306 and called Internet Key Exchange (IKE). IKE (RFC 4306) calls for the use of a specific process called Diffie-Hellman (DH) key exchange, named after the inventors of the process. DH key exchange overcomes the chicken-and-egg problem with an algorithm that allows the devices to make up and exchange keys securely, preventing anyone who can see the messages from deriving the key value.

The primary configuration option for DH key exchange is the length of the keys used by the DH key exchange process to encrypt the key exchange messages. The longer the encryption key that needs to be exchanged, the longer the DH key needs to be. Table 15-4 summarizes the main three options.

Table 15-4   *DH Options*

Option	Key Length
DH-1	768-bit
DH-2	1024-bit
DH-5	1536-bit

IPsec Authentication and Message Integrity

IPsec has several options for the authentication and message integrity process as well. Authentication generally refers to the process by which a receiving VPN device can confirm that a received packet was really sent by a trusted VPN peer. Message integrity, sometimes referred to as message authentication, allows the receiver to confirm that the message was not changed in transit.

IPsec authentication and message integrity checks use some of the same general concepts as does the encryption and key exchange process, so this text does not go into a lot of detail. However, it is useful to understand the basics.

Message integrity checks can be performed by the IPsec Authentication Header (AH) protocol using a shared (symmetric) key concept, like the encryption process, but using a hash function rather than an encryption function. The hash works similarly to the frame check sequence (FCS) concept in the trailer of most data-link protocols, but in a much more secure manner. The hash (a type of math function), with the formal name of Hashed-based Message Authentication Code (HMAC), results in a small number that can then be stored in one of the VPN headers. The sender calculates the hash and sends the results in the VPN header. The receiver recomputes the hash, using a shared key (same key value on both ends), and compares the computed value with the value listed in the VPN header. If the two values match, it means that the data fed into the formula by the sender matches what was fed into the formula by the receiver, so the receiver knows that the message did not change in transit.

These integrity check functions with HMAC typically use a secret key that needs to be at least twice as long as the encryption key that encrypts the message. As a result, several HMAC options have been created over the years. For example, the long-supported message digest algorithm 5 (MD5) standard uses a 128-bit key, allowing it to support VPNs that use the 56-bit DES encryption key length.

> **NOTE**   If the VPN uses ESP to encrypt the packets, the HMAC message integrity function is not needed, because the attacker would have had to break the encryption key before she could have possibly altered the contents of the message.

The authentication process uses a public/private key concept similar to DH key exchange, relying on the idea that a value encrypted with the sender's private key can be decrypted with the sender's public key. Like the message integrity check, the sender calculates a value and puts it in the VPN header, but this time using the sender's private key. The receiver uses the sender's public key to decrypt the transmitted value, comparing it to the value listed in the header. If the values match, the receiver knows that the sender is authentic.

Table 15-5 summarizes a few of the specific protocols and tools available for IPsec authentication and message integrity.

Table 15-5   *IPsec Authentication and Message Integrity Options*

Function	Method	Description
Message integrity	HMAC-MD5	HMAC-MD5 uses a 128-bit shared key, generating a 128-bit hash value.
Message integrity	HMAC-SHA	HMAC–Secure Hash Algorithm defines different key sizes (for example, SHA-1 [160], SHA-256 [256], and SHA-512 [512]) to support different encryption key sizes. Considered better than MD5 but with more compute time required.
Authentication	Pre-Shared Keys	Both VPN devices must be preconfigured with the same secret key.
Authentication	Digital signatures	Also called Rivest, Shamir, and Adelman (RSA) signatures. The sender encrypts a value with its private key; the receiver decrypts with the sender's public key and compares with the value listed by the sender in the header.

The ESP and AH Security Protocols

To perform the VPN functions described in this chapter, IPsec defines two security protocols, with each protocol defining a header. These headers are shown in generic form back in Figure 15-1 as the VPN header. These headers simply provide a place to store information that is needed for the various VPN functions. For example, the message integrity process requires that the sender place the results of the hash function into a header and transmit the header (as part of the entire message) to the receiving VPN device, which then uses the value stored in that header to complete the message integrity check.

Two of the protocols defined by IPsec are the Encapsulating Security Payload (ESP) and the IP Authentication Header (AH). ESP defines rules for performing the main four functions for VPNs, as mentioned throughout this chapter and as summarized in Table 15-6. AH supports two features, namely, authentication and message integrity. A particular IPsec VPN might only use one of the two headers, or both. For example, AH could provide authentication and message integrity, with ESP providing data privacy (encryption).

Table 15-6 *Summary of Functions Supported by ESP and AH*

Key
Topic

Feature	Supported by ESP?	Supported by AH?
Authentication	Yes (weak)	Yes (strong)
Message integrity	Yes	Yes
Encryption	Yes	No
Antireplay	Yes	No

IPsec Implementation Considerations

IPsec VPNs provide a secure connection through the unsecure Internet so that hosts can behave as if they are connected directly to the corporate network. For site-to-site VPNs, the end-user hosts have no idea that a VPN even exists, just as would be the case with a leased line or Frame Relay WAN. The user can use any application, just as if he were connected to the LAN at the main office.

IPsec remote access VPN users enjoy the same functions as do site-to-site VPN users, providing the user access to any and all allowed applications. However, remote access VPNs do require some additional effort in that each host needs to use the Cisco VPN client software. This software implements the IPsec standards on the PC, rather than requiring VPN support on a separate device. The installation is not difficult, but it is an additional bit of work for each host, whereas compared to a site-to-site VPN implemented with an already installed Cisco router, the only requirement might be an upgrade of the Cisco IOS.

To ease the installation and configuration of VPNs, Cisco provides a framework and a set of functions called *Easy VPN*. The problem solved by Easy VPN can be easily understood by considering the following example. A company has 200 remote sites with which it wants to create an intranet VPN using the Internet. Additionally, this company wants extranet site-to-site VPN connections to a dozen partners. Finally, 2000 employees own laptops, and they all at least occasionally bring home their laptops and connect to the enterprise network through the Internet. And, IPsec has many options for each function, requiring configuration at each site.

Easy VPN helps solve the administration headaches in such an environment by allowing a Cisco Easy VPN server, typically the central site VPN device (for example, an ASA), to dynamically inform the remote site devices as to their IPsec VPN configurations. The remote devices—routers, ASAs, laptops with Cisco VPN client software, and so on—act as Easy VPN clients, connecting to the Easy VPN server and downloading the configuration settings.

Next, the final section of this chapter briefly examines an alternative VPN technology called SSL.

SSL VPNs

Today's commonly used web browsers all support a protocol called *Secure Socket Layer (SSL)*. These same browsers also typically support a follow-on but less-well-known standard called *Transport Layer Security (TLS)*. This section explains how SSL can be used to create access VPNs.

> **NOTE**   Rather than refer to both SSL and TLS throughout this section, the text uses the more popular SSL term alone. SSL and TLS are not truly equivalent protocols, but they perform the same functions, and they are equal to the level of depth described in this chapter.

Web browsers use HTTP to connect to web servers. However, when the communications with the web server need to be secure, the browser switches to use SSL. SSL uses well-known port 443, encrypting data sent between the browser and the server, and authenticating the user. Then, the HTTP messages flow over the SSL connection.

Most people have used SSL, oftentimes without knowing it. If you have ever used a website on the Internet, and needed to supply some credit card information or other personal information, the browser probably switched to using SSL. Most browsers show an icon that looks like a padlock, with the padlock open when not using SSL and the padlock closed (locked) when using SSL.

Web servers can choose when and how to implement SSL. Because SSL requires more work, many web servers just use HTTP for supplying general information, switching to use SSL only when the user needs to supply sensitive information, such as login credentials and financial information. However, when an enterprise's internal web servers need to send data to a home user on the other side of the Internet, rather than a user on the enterprise's local LAN, the server might need to secure all communications to the client to prevent the loss of data.

Cisco solves some of the problems associated with internal web access for Internet-based users with a feature called Web VPN. Unlike IPsec VPNs, Web VPN typically only allows web traffic, as opposed to all traffic. However, a large majority of enterprise applications today happen to be web-enabled. For example, most end users need access to internal applications, which run from internal web servers and possibly to an e-mail server. If a user can check her e-mail from a web browser, most if not all the functions needed by that user can be performed from a web browser, and Web VPN can provide a reasonable solution.

Web VPN secures an enterprise home user's connection to the enterprise network by using SSL between the end user and a special Web VPN server. Figure 15-4 shows the general idea.

Figure 15-4   *Web VPN Using SSL*

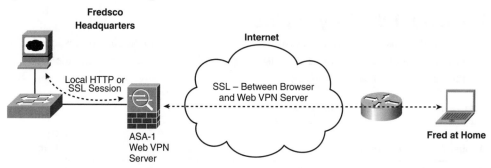

To use Web VPN, the Internet-based user opens any web browser and connects to a Cisco Web VPN server. The Web VPN server can be implemented by many devices, including an ASA. This connection uses SSL for all communications, using the built-in SSL capabilities in the web browser, so that all communications between the client and the Web VPN server are secure.

The Web VPN server acts as a web server, presenting a web page back to the client. The web page lists the enterprise applications available to the client. For example, it might list all the typical enterprise web-based applications, the e-mail server's web-based server, and other web-based services. When the user selects an option, the Web VPN server connects to that service, using either HTTP or SSL, as required by the server. The Web VPN server then passes the HTTP/SSL traffic to and from the real server over the SSL-only connection back to the Internet-based client. As a result, all communications over the Internet are secured with SSL.

The strength of this Web VPN solution is that it requires no software or special effort from the client. Employees can even use their home computer, someone else's computer, or any Internet-connected computer, and connect to the host name of the Web VPN server.

The negative with Web VPN is that it only allows the use of a web browser. If you need to use an application that cannot be accessed using a browser, you have a couple of options. First, you could implement IPsec VPNs, as already discussed. Alternately, you could use a variation on Web VPN in which the client computer loads an SSL-based thin client, much in concept like the IPsec-based Cisco VPN client used with IPsec VPNs. The client computer could then connect to the Web VPN server using the thin client, and the Web VPN server would simply pass the traffic from the PC through to the local LAN, allowing access as if the client were connected to the main enterprise network.

Exam Preparation Tasks

Review All the Key Topics

Review the most important topics from this chapter, noted with the Key Topics icon in the outer margin of the page. Table 15-7 lists a reference of these key topics and the page numbers on which each is found.

Table 15-7 *Key Topics for Chapter 15*

Key Topic Element	Description	Page Number
List	Desired security features for VPNs	528
Table 15-2	Three types of VPNs and their typical purpose	530
Figure 15-3	Significant parts of the VPN encryption process	532
Table 15-3	Facts about the three IPsec VPN encryption algorithms for encrypting the entire packet	533
Table 15-4	Three DH key exchange options and key lengths	534
Table 15-6	Summary of functions supported by the IPsec ESP and AH protocols	537

Complete the Tables and Lists from Memory

Print a copy of Appendix J, "Memory Tables," (found on the CD) or at least the section for this chapter, and complete the tables and lists from memory. Appendix K, "Memory Tables Answer Key," also on the CD, includes completed tables and lists to check your work.

Definitions of Key Terms

Define the following key terms from this chapter, and check your answers in the glossary:

Diffie-Hellman key exchange, IPsec, shared key, SSL, VPN, VPN client, Web VPN

Cisco Published ICND2 Exam Topics*
Covered in This Part

Implement an IP addressing scheme and IP Services to meet network requirements in a medium-size Enterprise branch office network

- Describe the technological requirements for running IPv6 (including: protocols, dual stack, tunneling, etc)

- Describe IPv6 addresses

Implement, verify, and troubleshoot NAT and ACLs in a medium-size Enterprise branch office network.

- Explain the basic operation of NAT

- Configure Network Address Translation for given network requirements using CLI

- Troubleshoot NAT implementation issues

* Always recheck http://www.cisco.com for the latest posted exam topics.

Part V: Scaling the IP Address Space

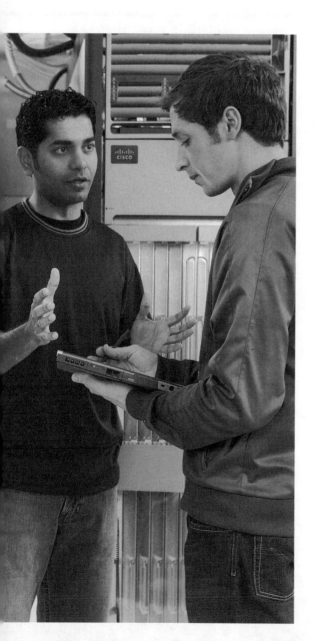

This chapter covers the following subjects:

Perspectives on IPv4 Address Scalability: This section explains the most significant need that drove the requirement for NAT back in the 1990s.

Network Address Translation Concepts: This section explains how several different variations of NAT work.

NAT Configuration and Troubleshooting: This section describes how to configure NAT, as well as how to use **show** and **debug** commands to troubleshoot NAT problems.

CHAPTER 16

Network Address Translation

This chapter begins Part V, "Scaling the IP Address Space." The two chapters in this part of the book relate to each other in that they explain the two most important solutions to what was a huge obstacle for the growth of the Internet. The problem was that the IPv4 address space would have been completely consumed by the mid-1990s without some significant solutions. One of the most significant short-term solutions was Network Address Translation (NAT), which is the focus of this chapter. The most significant long-term solution is IPv6, which attacks the problem by making the address space very large. IPv6 is covered in the next chapter.

This chapter begins with brief coverage of Classless Interdomain Routing (CIDR), which helps Internet service providers (ISP) manage the IP address space, and private IP addressing. The remaining majority of the chapter explains the concepts and configurations related to NAT.

"Do I Know This Already?" Quiz

The "Do I Know This Already?" quiz allows you to assess whether you should read the entire chapter. If you miss no more than one of these nine self-assessment questions, you might want to move ahead to the section "Exam Preparation Tasks." Table 16-1 lists the major headings in this chapter and the "Do I Know This Already?" quiz questions covering the material in those headings so that you can assess your knowledge of these specific areas. The answers to the "Do I Know This Already?" quiz appear in Appendix A.

Table 16-1 *"Do I Know This Already?" Foundation Topics Section-to-Question Mapping*

Foundation Topics Section	Questions
Perspectives on IPv4 Address Scalability	1–3
Network Address Translation Concepts	4–5
NAT Configuration and Troubleshooting	6–9

1. What does CIDR stand for?

   a. Classful IP Default Routing

   b. Classful IP D-class Routing

   c. Classful Interdomain Routing

   d. Classless IP Default Routing

   e. Classless IP D-class Routing

   f. Classless Interdomain Routing

2. Which of the following summarized subnets represent routes that could have been created for CIDR's goal to reduce the size of Internet routing tables?

   a. 10.0.0.0 255.255.255.0

   b. 10.1.0.0 255.255.0.0

   c. 200.1.1.0 255.255.255.0

   d. 200.1.0.0 255.255.0.0

3. Which of the following are not private addresses according to RFC 1918?

   a. 172.31.1.1

   b. 172.33.1.1

   c. 10.255.1.1

   d. 10.1.255.1

   e. 191.168.1.1

4. With static NAT, performing translation for inside addresses only, what causes NAT table entries to be created?

   a. The first packet from the inside network to the outside network

   b. The first packet from the outside network to the inside network

   c. Configuration using the **ip nat inside source** command

   d. Configuration using the **ip nat outside source** command

5. With dynamic NAT, performing translation for inside addresses only, what causes NAT table entries to be created?

   a. The first packet from the inside network to the outside network

   b. The first packet from the outside network to the inside network

   c. Configuration using the **ip nat inside source** command

   d. Configuration using the **ip nat outside source** command

6. NAT has been configured to translate source addresses of packets received from the inside part of the network, but only for some hosts as identified by an Access Control List. Which of the following commands identifies the hosts?

    a. **ip nat inside source list 1 pool barney**

    b. **ip nat pool barney 200.1.1.1 200.1.1.254 netmask 255.255.255.0**

    c. **ip nat inside**

    d. **ip nat inside 200.1.1.1 200.1.1.2**

    e. None of the other answers are correct.

7. NAT has been configured to translate source addresses of packets received from the inside part of the network, but only for some hosts. Which of the following commands identifies the outside local IP addresses that are translated?

    a. **ip nat inside source list 1 pool barney**

    b. **ip nat pool barney 200.1.1.1 200.1.1.254 netmask 255.255.255.0**

    c. **ip nat inside**

    d. **ip nat inside 200.1.1.1 200.1.1.2**

    e. None of the other answers are correct

8. Examine the following configuration commands:

    ```
    interface Ethernet0/0
     ip address 10.1.1.1 255.255.255.0
     ip nat inside
    interface Serial0/0
     ip address 200.1.1.249 255.255.255.252
    ip nat inside source list 1 interface Serial0/0
    access-list 1 permit 10.1.1.0 0.0.0.255
    ```

    If the configuration is intended to enable source NAT overload, which of the following commands could be useful to complete the configuration?

    a. The **ip nat outside** command

    b. The **ip nat pat** command

    c. The **overload** keyword

    d. The **ip nat pool** command

9. Examine the following **show** command output on a router configured for dynamic NAT:

```
-- Inside Source
access-list 1 pool fred refcount 2288
 pool fred: netmask 255.255.255.240
    start 200.1.1.1 end 200.1.1.7
    type generic, total addresses 7, allocated 7 (100%), misses 965
```

Users are complaining about not being able to reach the Internet. Which of the following is the most likely cause?

a. The problem is not related to NAT, based on the information in the command output.

b. The NAT pool does not have enough entries to satisfy all requests.

c. Standard ACL 1 cannot be used; an extended ACL must be used.

d. The command output does not supply enough information to identify the problem.

Foundation Topics

This chapter covers the details of NAT using three major sections. The first section explains the challenges to the IPv4 address space caused by the Internet revolution of the 1990s. The second section explains the basic concept behind NAT, how several variations of NAT work, and how the Port Address Translation (PAT) option conserves the IPv4 address space. The final section shows how to configure NAT from the Cisco IOS Software command-line interface (CLI), and how to troubleshoot NAT.

For those of you following the optional reading plan for which you move back and forth between this book and *CCENT/CCNA ICND1 Official Exam Certification Guide*, note that Chapter 17 of that book also covers NAT and PAT, with the configuration performed from the Security Device Manager (SDM). This chapter necessarily covers some of the same underlying concepts, but with a much fuller description of the concepts and configuration.

Perspectives on IPv4 Address Scalability

The original design for the Internet required every organization to ask for, and receive, one or more registered classful IP network numbers. The people administering the program ensured that none of the IP networks were reused. As long as every organization used only IP addresses inside its own registered network numbers, IP addresses would never be duplicated, and IP routing could work well.

Connecting to the Internet using only a registered network number, or several registered network numbers, worked well for a while. In the early to mid-1990s, it became apparent that the Internet was growing so fast that all IP network numbers would be assigned by the mid-1990s! Concern arose that the available networks would be completely assigned, and some organizations would not be able to connect to the Internet.

The main long-term solution to the IP address scalability problem was to increase the size of the IP address. This one fact was the most compelling reason for the advent of IP version 6 (IPv6). (Version 5 was defined much earlier, but was never deployed, so the next attempt was labeled as version 6.) IPv6 uses a 128-bit address, instead of the 32-bit address in IPv4. With the same or improved process of assigning unique address ranges to every organization connected to the Internet, IPv6 can easily support every organization and individual on the planet, with the number of IPv6 addresses theoretically reaching above 10^{38}.

Many short-term solutions to the addressing problem were suggested, but three standards worked together to solve the problem. Two of the standards work closely together: Network Address Translation (NAT) and private addressing. These features together allow organizations to use unregistered IP network numbers internally and still communicate well with the Internet. The third standard, Classless Interdomain Routing (CIDR), allows ISPs to reduce the wasting of IP addresses by assigning a company a subset of a network number rather than the entire network. CIDR also can allow ISPs to summarize routes such that multiple Class A, B, or C networks match a single route, which helps reduce the size of Internet routing tables.

CIDR

CIDR is a global address assignment convention, defining how the Internet Assigned Numbers Authority (IANA), its member agencies, and ISPs should assign the globally unique IPv4 address space to individual organizations. CIDR, defined in RFC 4632 (http://www.ietf.org/rfc/rfc4632.txt), has two main goals. First, its policies dictate that address assignment choices should aid the process of aggregating (summarizing) multiple network numbers into a single routing entity, reducing the size of Internet routers' routing tables. The second goal is to allow ISPs to assign address ranges to their customers of sizes other than an entire Class A, B, or C network, reducing waste, and putting off the date at which no more IPv4 addresses are available to assign to new organizations and people wanting to connect to the Internet. The following sections explain a little more detail about each of CIDR's two main goals.

Route Aggregation for Shorter Routing Tables

One of the main goals of CIDR is to allow easier route aggregation in the Internet. Imagine a router in the Internet with a route to every Class A, B, and C network on the planet! More than 2 million Class C networks exist! If Internet routers had to list every classful network in their routing tables, the routers would have to have a lot of memory, and routing table searches would require a lot of processing power. By aggregating the routes, fewer routes would need to exist in the routing table.

Figure 16-1 shows a typical case of how CIDR might be used to consolidate routes to multiple Class C networks into a single route. In the figure, imagine that ISP 1 owns Class C networks 198.0.0.0 through 198.255.255.0 (these might look funny, but they are valid Class C network numbers). Without CIDR, all other ISPs' routing tables would have a separate route to each of the 2^{16} Class C networks that begin with 198. With CIDR, as shown in the figure, the other ISPs' routers have a single route to 198.0.0.0/8—in other words, a route to all hosts whose IP address begins with 198. More than 2 million Class C networks alone exist, but CIDR has helped Internet routers reduce their routing tables to a more manageable size—in the range of a little over 200,000 routes by early 2007.

Figure 16-1 *Typical Use of CIDR*

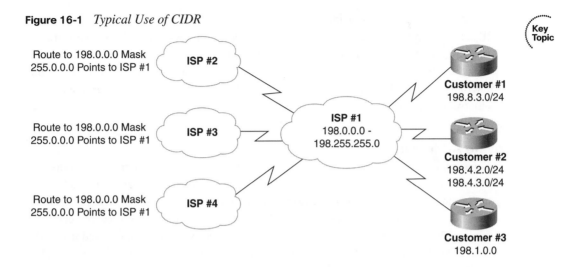

By using a routing protocol that exchanges the mask as well as the subnet/network number, a *classless* view of the number can be attained. In other words, treat the grouping as a math problem, ignoring the Class A, B, and C rules. For example, 198.0.0.0/8 (198.0.0.0, mask 255.0.0.0) defines a set of addresses whose first 8 bits are equal to decimal 198. ISP 1 advertises this route to the other ISPs, which need a route only to 198.0.0.0/8. In its routers, ISP 1 knows which Class C networks are at which customer sites. This is how CIDR gives Internet routers a much more scalable routing table—by reducing the number of entries in the tables.

For CIDR to work as shown in Figure 16-1, ISPs need to be in control of consecutive network numbers. Today, IP networks are allocated by administrative authorities for various regions of the world. The regions in turn allocate consecutive ranges of network numbers to particular ISPs in those regions. This allows summarization of multiple networks into a single route, as shown in Figure 16-1.

IPv4 Address Conservation

CIDR also helps reduce the chance of our running out of IPv4 addresses for new companies connecting to the Internet. Furthermore, CIDR allows an ISP to allocate a subset of a Class A, B, or C network to a single customer. For example, imagine that ISP 1's customer 1 needs only ten IP addresses and that customer 3 needs 25 IP addresses. ISP 1 does something like this: It assigns IP subnet 198.8.3.16/28, with assignable addresses 198.8.3.17 to 198.8.3.30, to customer 1. For customer 3, ISP 1 suggests 198.8.3.32/27, with 30 assignable addresses (198.8.3.33 to 198.8.3.62). The ISP has met the customers' needs and still not used all of Class C network 198.8.3.0.

CIDR helps prevent the wasting of IP addresses, thereby reducing the need for registered IP network numbers. Instead of two customers consuming two entire Class C networks, each consumes a small portion of a single Class C network. At the same time, CIDR, along with the intelligent administration of consecutive network numbers to each ISP, allows the Internet routing table to support a much smaller routing table in Internet routers than would otherwise be required.

Private Addressing

Some computers might never be connected to the Internet. These computers' IP addresses could be duplicates of registered IP addresses in the Internet. When designing the IP addressing convention for such a network, an organization could pick and use any network number(s) it wanted, and all would be well. For example, you can buy a few routers, connect them in your office, and configure IP addresses in network 1.0.0.0, and it would work. The IP addresses you use might be duplicates of real IP addresses in the Internet, but if all you want to do is learn on the lab in your office, everything will be fine.

When building a private network that will have no Internet connectivity, you can use IP network numbers called *private internets*, as defined in RFC 1918, *Address Allocation for Private Internets* (http://www.ietf.org/rfc/rfc1918.txt). This RFC defines a set of networks that will never be assigned to any organization as a registered network number. Instead of using someone else's registered network numbers, you can use numbers in a range that are not used by anyone else in the public Internet. Table 16-2 shows the private address space defined by RFC 1918.

Key Topic

Table 16-2 *RFC 1918 Private Address Space*

Range of IP Addresses	Class of Networks	Number of Networks
10.0.0.0 to 10.255.255.255	A	1
172.16.0.0 to 172.31.255.255	B	16
192.168.0.0 to 192.168.255.255	C	256

In other words, any organization can use these network numbers. However, no organization is allowed to advertise these networks using a routing protocol on the Internet.

You might be wondering why you would bother to reserve special private network numbers when it doesn't matter whether the addresses are duplicates. Well, as it turns out, you can use private addressing in an internetwork, and connect to the Internet at the same time, as long as you use Network Address Translation (NAT). The rest of the chapter examines and explains NAT.

Network Address Translation Concepts

NAT, defined in RFC 3022, allows a host that does not have a valid, registered, globally unique IP address to communicate with other hosts through the Internet. The hosts might be using private addresses or addresses assigned to another organization. In either case, NAT allows these addresses that are not Internet-ready to continue to be used and still allows communication with hosts across the Internet.

NAT achieves its goal by using a valid registered IP address to represent the private address to the rest of the Internet. The NAT function changes the private IP addresses to publicly registered IP addresses inside each IP packet, as shown in Figure 16-2.

Figure 16-2 *NAT IP Address Swapping: Private Addressing*

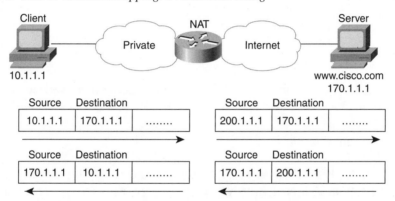

Notice that the router, performing NAT, changes the packet's source IP address when the packet leaves the private organization. The router performing NAT also changes the destination address in each packet that is forwarded back into the private network. (Network 200.1.1.0 is a registered network in Figure 16-2.) The NAT feature, configured in the router labeled NAT, performs the translation.

Cisco IOS Software supports several variations of NAT. The next few pages cover the concepts behind several of these variations. The section after that covers the configuration related to each option.

Static NAT

Static NAT works just like the example shown in Figure 16-2, but with the IP addresses statically mapped to each other. To help you understand the implications of static NAT, and to explain several key terms, Figure 16-3 shows a similar example with more information.

Figure 16-3 *Static NAT Showing Inside Local and Global Addresses*

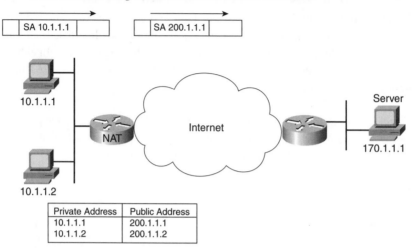

First, the concepts: The company's ISP has assigned it registered network 200.1.1.0. Therefore, the NAT router must make the private IP addresses look like they are in network 200.1.1.0. To do so, the NAT router changes the source IP addresses in the packets going from left to right in the figure.

In this example, the NAT router changes the source address ("SA" in the figure) of 10.1.1.1 to 200.1.1.1. With static NAT, the NAT router simply configures a one-to-one mapping between the private address and the registered address that is used on its behalf. The NAT router has statically configured a mapping between private address 10.1.1.1 and public, registered address 200.1.1.1.

Supporting two IP hosts in the private network requires a second static one-to-one mapping using a second IP address in the public address range. For example, to support 10.1.1.2, the router statically maps 10.1.1.2 to 200.1.1.2. Because the enterprise has a single registered Class C network, it can support at most 254 private IP addresses with NAT, with the usual two reserved numbers (the network number and network broadcast address).

The terminology used with NAT, particularly with configuration, can be a little confusing. Notice in Figure 16-3 that the NAT table lists the private IP addresses as "private" and the public, registered addresses from network 200.1.1.0 as "public." Cisco uses the term *inside local* for the private IP addresses in this example and *inside global* for the public IP addresses.

In Cisco terminology, the enterprise network that uses private addresses, and therefore needs NAT, is the "inside" part of the network. The Internet side of the NAT function is the "outside" part of the network. A host that needs NAT (such as 10.1.1.1 in the example) has the IP address it uses inside the network, and it needs an IP address to represent it in the outside network. So, because the host essentially needs two different addresses to represent it, you need two terms. Cisco calls the private IP address used in the inside network the *inside local* address and the address used to represent the host to the rest of the Internet the *inside global* address. Figure 16-4 repeats the same example, with some of the terminology shown.

Figure 16-4   *Static NAT Terminology*

Key Topic

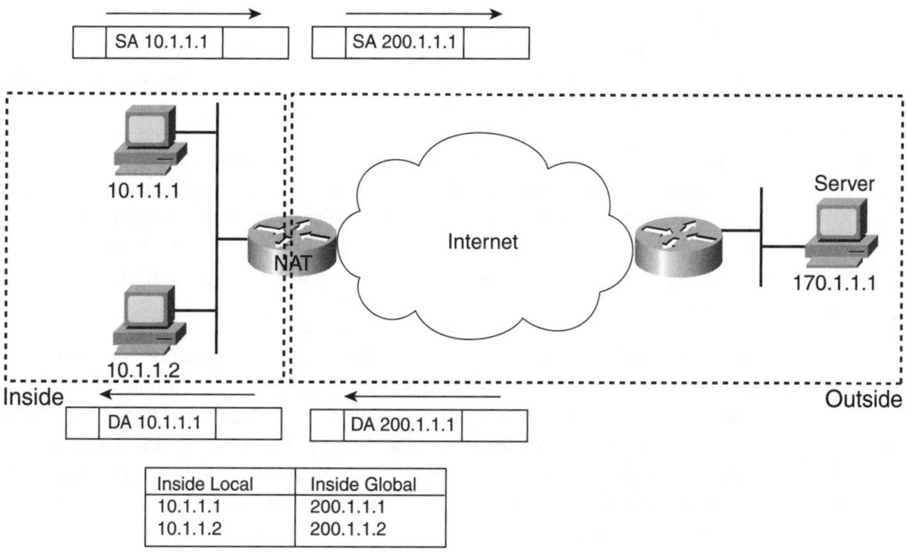

| SA 10.1.1.1 | | SA 200.1.1.1 |

10.1.1.1

Internet

Server

NAT

170.1.1.1

10.1.1.2

Inside   Outside

| DA 10.1.1.1 | | DA 200.1.1.1 |

Inside Local	Inside Global
10.1.1.1	200.1.1.1
10.1.1.2	200.1.1.2

Most typical NAT configurations change only the IP address of inside hosts. Therefore, the current NAT table shown in Figure 16-4 shows the inside local and corresponding inside global registered addresses. However, the outside host IP address can also be changed with NAT. When that occurs, the terms *outside local* and *outside global* denote the IP address used to represent that host in the inside network and the outside network, respectively. Table 16-3 summarizes the terminology and meanings.

Key
Topic

Table 16-3 *NAT Addressing Terms*

Term	Meaning
Inside local	In a typical NAT design, the term *inside* refers to an address used for a host inside an enterprise. An inside local is the actual IP address assigned to a host in the private enterprise network. A more descriptive term might be *inside private*.
Inside global	In a typical NAT design, the term *inside* refers to an address used for a host inside an enterprise. NAT uses an inside global address to represent the inside host as the packet is sent through the outside network, typically the Internet. A NAT router changes the source IP address of a packet sent by an inside host from an inside local address to an inside global address as the packet goes from the inside to the outside network. A more descriptive term might be *inside public*, because when using RFC 1918 addresses in an enterprise, the inside global address represents the inside host with a public IP address that can be used for routing in the public Internet.
Outside global	In a typical NAT design, the term *outside* refers to an address used for a host outside an enterprise—in other words, in the Internet. An outside global address is the actual IP address assigned to a host that resides in the outside network, typically the Internet. A more descriptive term might be *outside public*, because the outside global address represents the outside host with a public IP address that can be used for routing in the public Internet.
Outside local	NAT can translate the outside IP address—the IP address that represents the host outside the enterprise network—although this is not a popular option. When a NAT router forwards a packet from the inside network to the outside, when using NAT to change the outside address, the IP address that represents the outside host as the destination IP address in the packet header is called the outside local IP address. A more descriptive term might be *outside private*, because when using RFC 1918 addresses in an enterprise, the outside local address represents the outside host with a private IP address from RFC 1918.

Dynamic NAT

Dynamic NAT has some similarities and differences compared to static NAT. Like static NAT, the NAT router creates a one-to-one mapping between an inside local and inside global address and changes the IP addresses in packets as they exit and enter the inside network. However, the mapping of an inside local address to an inside global address happens dynamically.

Dynamic NAT sets up a pool of possible inside global addresses and defines matching criteria to determine which inside local IP addresses should be translated with NAT. For example, in Figure 16-5, a pool of five inside global IP addresses has been established: 200.1.1.1 through 200.1.1.5. NAT has also been configured to translate any inside local addresses that start with 10.1.1.

Figure 16-5 *Dynamic NAT*

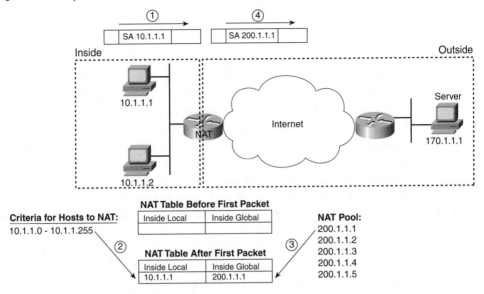

The numbers 1, 2, 3, and 4 in the figure refer to the following sequence of events:

1. Host 10.1.1.1 sends its first packet to the server at 170.1.1.1.

2. As the packet enters the NAT router, the router applies some matching logic to decide whether the packet should have NAT applied. Because the logic has been configured to match source IP addresses that begin with 10.1.1, the router adds an entry in the NAT table for 10.1.1.1 as an inside local address.

3. The NAT router needs to allocate an IP address from the pool of valid inside global addresses. It picks the first one available (200.1.1.1, in this case) and adds it to the NAT table to complete the entry.

4. The NAT router translates the source IP address and forwards the packet.

The dynamic entry stays in the table as long as traffic flows occasionally. You can configure a timeout value that defines how long the router should wait, having not translated any packets with that address, before removing the dynamic entry. You can also manually clear the dynamic entries from the table using the **clear ip nat translation** * command.

NAT can be configured with more IP addresses in the inside local address list than in the inside global address pool. The router allocates addresses from the pool until all are allocated. If a new packet arrives from yet another inside host, and it needs a NAT entry, but all the pooled IP addresses are in use, the router simply discards the packet. The user must try again until a NAT entry times out, at which point the NAT function works for the next host that sends a packet. Essentially, the inside global pool of addresses needs to be as large as the maximum number of concurrent hosts that need to use the Internet at the same time—unless you use PAT, as is explained in the next section.

Overloading NAT with Port Address Translation (PAT)

Some networks need to have most, if not all, IP hosts reach the Internet. If that network uses private IP addresses, the NAT router needs a very large set of registered IP addresses. With static NAT, for each private IP host that needs Internet access, you need a publicly registered IP address, completely defeating the goal of reducing the number of public IPv4 addresses needed for that organization. Dynamic NAT lessens the problem to some degree, because every single host in an internetwork should seldom need to communicate with the Internet at the same time. However, if a large percentage of the IP hosts in a network will need Internet access throughout that company's normal business hours, NAT still requires a large number of registered IP addresses, again failing to reduce IPv4 address consumption.

The NAT Overload feature, also called Port Address Translation (PAT), solves this problem. Overloading allows NAT to scale to support many clients with only a few public IP addresses. The key to understanding how overloading works is to recall how hosts use TCP and User Datagram Protocol (UDP) ports. Figure 16-6 details an example that helps make the logic behind overloading more obvious.

The top part of the figure shows a network with three different hosts connecting to a web server using TCP. The bottom half of the figure shows the same network later in the day, with three TCP connections from the same client. All six connections connect to the server IP address (170.1.1.1) and port (80, the well-known port for web services). In each case, the server differentiates between the various connections because their combined IP address and port numbers are unique.

NAT takes advantage of the fact that the server doesn't care whether it has one connection each to three different hosts or three connections to a single host IP address. So, to support lots of inside local IP addresses with only a few inside global, publicly registered IP addresses, NAT overload (PAT) translates both the address and possibly the port numbers as well. Figure 16-7 outlines the logic.

Figure 16-6 *Three TCP Connections: From Three Different Hosts and from One Host*

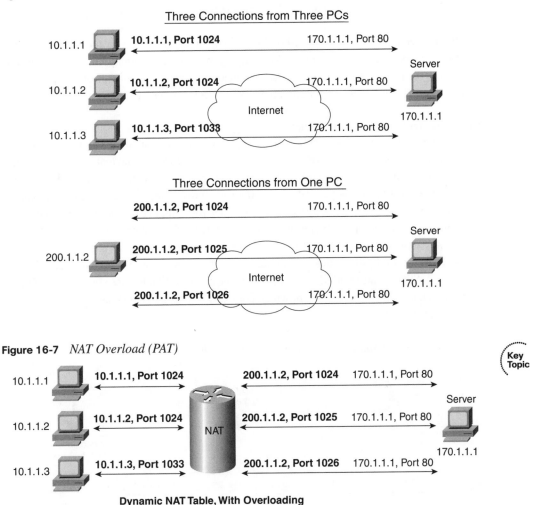

Figure 16-7 *NAT Overload (PAT)*

Key
Topic

When PAT creates the dynamic mapping, it selects not only an inside global IP address but also a unique port number to use with that address. The NAT router keeps a NAT table entry for every unique combination of inside local IP address and port, with translation to the inside global address and a unique port number associated with the inside global address. And because the port number field has 16 bits, NAT overload can use more than 65,000 port numbers, allowing it to scale well without needing many registered IP addresses—in many cases, needing only one outside global IP address.

Of the three types of NAT covered in this chapter so far, PAT is by far the most popular option. Static NAT and Dynamic NAT both require a one-to-one mapping from the inside local to the inside global address. PAT significantly reduces the number of required registered IP addresses compared to these other NAT alternatives.

Translating Overlapping Addresses

The first three NAT options explained in the previous sections are the most likely to be used in most networks. However, yet another variation of NAT exists, one that allows translation of both the source and destination IP address. This option is particularly helpful when two internetworks use overlapping IP address ranges, for example, when one organization is not using private addressing but instead is using a network number registered to another company. If one company inappropriately uses a network number that is registered appropriately to a different company, and they both connect to the Internet, NAT can be used to allow both companies to communicate to hosts in the Internet and to each other. To do so, NAT translates both the source and the destination IP addresses in this case. For example, consider Figure 16-8, in which company A uses a network that is registered to Cisco (170.1.0.0).

Figure 16-8 *NAT IP Address Swapping: Unregistered Networks*

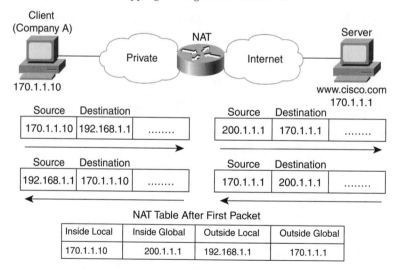

With an overlapping address space, a client in company A cannot send a packet to the legitimate IP host 170.1.1.1—or, if it did, the packet would never get to the real 170.1.1.1. Why? The routing tables inside the company (on the left) probably have a route matching 170.1.1.1 in its routing table. For host 170.1.1.10 in the figure, it is in the subnet in which the "private" 170.1.1.1 would reside, so host 170.1.1.10 would not even try to forward packets destined for 170.1.1.1 to a router. Instead, it would forward them directly to host 170.1.1.1, assuming that it was on the same LAN! NAT can solve this problem, but both the source and the destination addresses must be changed as the packet passes through the NAT router. In Figure 16-8, notice that the original packet sent by the client has a destination address of 192.168.1.1. That address, called the *outside local* address, represents the server outside the company. *Outside* means that the address represents the host that physically sits in the "outside" part of the network. *Local* means that this address represents the host on the private side of the network.

As the packet passes through the NAT router (from left to right), the source address is changed, just like in the previous examples. However, the destination address is also changed, in this case, to 170.1.1.1. The destination address is also called the *outside global* address at this point, because it represents a host that is always physically on the outside network, and the address is the global, publicly registered IP address that can be routed through the Internet.

The NAT configuration includes a static mapping between the real IP address (outside global), 170.1.1.1, and the private IP address (outside local) used to represent it inside the private network—192.168.1.1.

Because the client initiates a connection to the server on the right, the NAT router not only must translate addresses, but it also must modify Domain Name System (DNS) responses. The client, for example, performs a DNS request for www.cisco.com. When the DNS reply comes back (from right to left) past the NAT router, NAT changes the DNS reply so that the client in the company thinks that www.cisco.com's IP address is 192.168.1.1.

Today, given a choice, companies tend to simply use private addressing to avoid the need to translate both IP addresses in each packet. Also, the NAT router needs a static entry for every server in the overlapped network number—a potentially painstaking task. By using private addresses, you can use NAT to connect the network to the Internet and reduce the number of registered IP addresses needed, and have to perform only the NAT function for the private address in each packet.

Table 16-4 summarizes the use of NAT terminology in Figure 16-8.

Table 16-4   *NAT Addressing Terms as Used in Figure 16-8*

Term	Value in Figure 16-8
Inside local	170.1.1.10
Inside global	200.1.1.1
Outside global	170.1.1.1
Outside local	192.168.1.1

NAT Configuration and Troubleshooting

In the following sections, you read about how to configure the three most common variations of NAT: static NAT, dynamic NAT, and PAT, along with the **show** and **debug** commands used to troubleshoot NAT.

Static NAT Configuration

Static NAT configuration, as compared to the other variations of NAT, requires the fewest configuration steps. Each static mapping between a local (private) address and a global (public) address must be configured. Additionally, the router must be told on which interfaces it should use NAT, because NAT does not have to be enabled on every interface. In particular, the router needs to know each interface and whether the interface is an inside or outside interface. The specific steps are as follows:

Step 1   Configure interfaces to be in the inside part of the NAT design using the **ip nat inside** interface subcommand.

Step 2   Configure interfaces to be in the outside part of the NAT design using the **ip nat outside** interface subcommand.

Step 3   Configure the static mappings with the **ip nat inside source static** *inside-local inside-global* global configuration command.

Figure 16-9 shows the familiar network used in the description of static NAT earlier in this chapter, which is also used for the first several configuration examples. In Figure 16-9, you can see that FredsCo has obtained Class C network 200.1.1.0 as a registered network number. That entire network, with mask 255.255.255.0, is configured on the serial link between FredsCo and the Internet. With a point-to-point serial link, only two of the 254 valid IP addresses in that network are consumed, leaving 252 addresses.

Figure 16-9 *NAT IP Address Swapping: Private Networks*

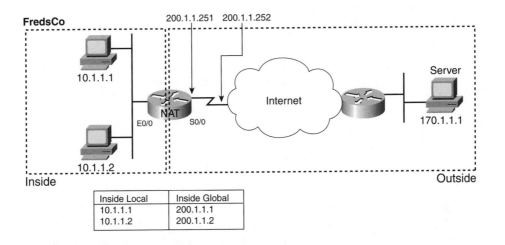

When planning a NAT configuration, you must find some IP addresses to use as inside global IP addresses. Because these addresses must be part of some registered IP address range, it is common to use the extra addresses in the subnet connecting the enterprise to the Internet—for example, the extra 252 IP addresses in network 200.1.1.0 in this case. The router can also be configured with a loopback interface and assigned an IP address that is part of a globally unique range of registered IP addresses.

Example 16-1 lists the NAT configuration, using 200.1.1.1 and 200.1.1.2 for the two static NAT mappings.

Example 16-1 *Static NAT Configuration*

```
NAT# show running-config
!
! Lines omitted for brevity
!
interface Ethernet0/0
 ip address 10.1.1.3 255.255.255.0
 ip nat inside
!
interface Serial0/0
 ip address 200.1.1.251 255.255.255.0
 ip nat outside
!
ip nat inside source static 10.1.1.2 200.1.1.2
ip nat inside source static 10.1.1.1 200.1.1.1
```

continues

Example 16-1 *Static NAT Configuration (Continued)*

```
NAT# show ip nat translations
Pro Inside global      Inside local      Outside local    Outside global
--- 200.1.1.1          10.1.1.1          ---              ---
--- 200.1.1.2          10.1.1.2          ---              ---

NAT# show ip nat statistics
Total active translations: 2 (2 static, 0 dynamic; 0 extended)
Outside interfaces:
  Serial0/0
Inside interfaces:
  Ethernet0/0
Hits: 100  Misses: 0
Expired translations: 0
Dynamic mappings:
```

The static mappings are created using the **ip nat inside source static** command. The **inside** keyword means that NAT translates addresses for hosts on the inside part of the network. The **source** keyword means that NAT translates the source IP address of packets coming into its inside interfaces. The **static** keyword means that the parameters define a static entry, which should never be removed from the NAT table because of timeout. Because the design calls for two hosts, 10.1.1.1 and 10.1.1.2, to have Internet access, two **ip nat inside** commands are needed.

After creating the static NAT entries, the router needs to know which interfaces are "inside" and which are "outside." The **ip nat inside** and **ip nat outside** interface subcommands identify each interface appropriately.

A couple of **show** commands list the most important information about NAT. The **show ip nat translations** command lists the two static NAT entries created in the configuration. The **show ip nat statistics** command lists statistics, listing things such as the number of currently active translation table entries. The statistics also include the number of hits, which increments for every packet for which NAT must translate addresses.

Dynamic NAT Configuration

As you might imagine, dynamic NAT configuration differs in some ways from static NAT, but it has some similarities as well. Dynamic NAT still requires that each interface be identified as either an inside or outside interface, and of course static mapping is no longer required. Dynamic NAT uses an access control list (ACL) to identify which inside local (private) IP addresses need to have their addresses translated, and it defines a pool of registered public IP addresses to allocate. The specific steps are as follows:

Step 1   As with static NAT, configure interfaces to be in the inside part of the NAT design using the **ip nat inside** interface subcommand.

Step 2   As with static NAT, configure interfaces to be in the outside part of the NAT design using the **ip nat outside** interface subcommand.

Step 3   Configure an ACL that matches the packets coming in inside interfaces for which NAT should be performed.

Step 4   Configure the pool of public registered IP addresses using the **ip nat pool** *name first-address last-address* **netmask** *subnet-mask* global configuration command.

Step 5   Enable dynamic NAT by referencing the ACL (Step 3) and pool (Step 4) with the **ip nat inside source list** *acl-number* **pool** *pool-name* global configuration command.

The next example uses the same network topology as the previous example (see Figure 16-9). In this case, the same two inside local addresses, 10.1.1.1 and 10.1.1.2, need translation. The same inside global addresses used in the static mappings in the previous example, 200.1.1.1 and 200.1.1.2, are instead placed in a pool of dynamically assignable inside global addresses. Example 16-2 shows the configuration as well as some **show** commands.

Example 16-2   *Dynamic NAT Configuration*

```
NAT# show running-config
!
! Lines omitted for brevity
!
interface Ethernet0/0
 ip address 10.1.1.3 255.255.255.0
 ip nat inside
!
interface Serial0/0
 ip address 200.1.1.251 255.255.255.0
 ip nat outside
!
ip nat pool fred 200.1.1.1 200.1.1.2 netmask 255.255.255.252
ip nat inside source list 1 pool fred
!
access-list 1 permit 10.1.1.2
access-list 1 permit 10.1.1.1
! The next command lists one empty line because no entries have been dynamically
! created yet.
NAT# show ip nat translations
```

continues

Example 16-2 *Dynamic NAT Configuration (Continued)*

```
NAT# show ip nat statistics
Total active translations: 0 (0 static, 0 dynamic; 0 extended)
Outside interfaces:
  Serial0/0
Inside interfaces:
  Ethernet0/0
Hits: 0  Misses: 0
Expired translations: 0
Dynamic mappings:
-- Inside Source
access-list 1 pool fred refcount 0
 pool fred: netmask 255.255.255.252
    start 200.1.1.1 end 200.1.1.2
    type generic, total addresses 2, allocated 0 (0%), misses 0
```

The configuration for dynamic NAT includes a pool of inside global addresses as well as an IP access list to define the inside local addresses for which NAT is performed. The **ip nat pool** command lists the first and last numbers in a range of inside global addresses. For example, if the pool needed ten addresses, the command might have listed 200.1.1.1 and 200.1.1.10. The required **netmask** parameter performs a kind of verification check on the range of addresses. If the address range would not be in the same subnet assuming the configured **netmask** was used, then IOS will reject the **ip nat pool** command. In this case, subnet 200.1.1.0, mask 255.255.255.252 (the configured **netmask**) would include 200.1.1.1 and 200.1.1.2 in the range of valid addresses, so IOS accepts this command.

Like static NAT, dynamic NAT uses the **ip nat inside source** command. Unlike static NAT, the dynamic NAT version of this command refers to the name of the NAT pool it wants to use for inside global addresses—in this case, fred. It also refers to an IP ACL, which defines the matching logic for inside local IP addresses. The **ip nat inside source list 1 pool fred** command maps between hosts matched by ACL 1 and the pool called fred, which was created by the **ip nat pool fred** command.

Example 16-2 ends with a couple of **show** commands that confirm that the router does not yet have any NAT translation table entries. At first, the **show ip nat translations** and **show ip nat statistics** commands display either nothing or minimal configuration information. At this point, neither host 10.1.1.1 nor 10.1.1.2 has sent any packets, and NAT has not created any dynamic entries in the NAT table or translated addresses in any packets.

The **show ip nat statistics** command at the end of the example lists some particularly interesting troubleshooting information with two different counters labeled "misses," as highlighted in the example. The first occurrence of this counter counts the number of times a new packet comes along, needing a NAT entry, and not finding one. At that point, dynamic NAT reacts and builds an entry. The second misses counter at the end of the command output lists the number of misses in the pool. This counter only increments when dynamic NAT tries to allocate a new NAT table entry and finds no available addresses, so the packet cannot be translated—probably resulting in an end user not getting to the application.

To see the misses counter and several other interesting facts, Example 16-3 continues the example started in Example 16-2. This example shows the results when hosts 10.1.1.1 and 10.1.1.2 start creating TCP connections, in this case with Telnet. This example picks up where Example 16-2 left off.

Example 16-3 *Verifying Normal Dynamic NAT Operation*

```
! A Telnet from 10.1.1.1 to 170.1.1.1 happened next; not shown
!
NAT# show ip nat statistics
Total active translations: 1 (0 static, 1 dynamic; 0 extended)
Outside interfaces:
  Serial0/0
Inside interfaces:
  Ethernet0/0
Hits: 69  Misses: 1
Expired translations: 0
Dynamic mappings:
-- Inside Source
access-list 1 pool fred refcount 1
 pool fred: netmask 255.255.255.252
    start 200.1.1.1 end 200.1.1.2
    type generic, total addresses 2, allocated 1 (50%), misses 0
NAT# show ip nat translations
Pro Inside global     Inside local      Outside local      Outside global
--- 200.1.1.1         10.1.1.1          ---                ---
NAT# clear ip nat translation *

!
! telnet from 10.1.1.2 to 170.1.1.1 happened next; not shown
!
NAT# show ip nat translations
Pro Inside global     Inside local     Outside local      Outside global
--- 200.1.1.1         10.1.1.2         ---                ---
!
! Telnet from 10.1.1.1 to 170.1.1.1 happened next; not shown
!
NAT# debug ip nat
IP NAT debugging is on

01:25:44: NAT: s=10.1.1.1->200.1.1.2, d=170.1.1.1 [45119]
01:25:44: NAT: s=170.1.1.1, d=200.1.1.2->10.1.1.1 [8228]
01:25:56: NAT: s=10.1.1.1->200.1.1.2, d=170.1.1.1 [45120]
01:25:56: NAT: s=170.1.1.1, d=200.1.1.2->10.1.1.1 [0]
```

The example begins with host 10.1.1.1 telnetting to 170.1.1.1 (not shown), with the NAT router creating a NAT entry. The NAT table shows a single entry, mapping 10.1.1.1 to 200.1.1.1. Note that the first misses counter in the **show ip nat statistics** command lists 1 miss, meaning that the first packet in host 10.1.1.1's TCP connection to 170.1.1.1 occurred and caused the router to not find a NAT table entry, incrementing the counter. The misses counter at the end of the output did not increment, because the router was able to allocate a pool member and add a NAT table entry. Also note that the last line lists statistics on the number of pool members allocated (1) and the percentage of the pool currently in use (50%).

The NAT table entry times out after a period of inactivity. However, to force the entry out of the table, the **clear ip nat translation *** command can be used. As shown in Table 16-7 at the end of the chapter, this command has several variations. Example 16-3 uses the brute force option—**clear ip nat translation ***—which removes all dynamic NAT table entries. The command can also delete individual entries by referencing the IP addresses.

After clearing the NAT entry, host 10.1.1.2 telnets to 170.1.1.1. The **show ip nat translations** command now shows a mapping between 10.1.1.2 and 200.1.1.1. Because 200.1.1.1 is no longer allocated in the NAT table, the NAT router can allocate it for the next NAT request. (Cisco IOS tends to pick the lowest available IP address when choosing the next IP address from the pool.)

Finally, at the end of Example 16-3, you see that host 10.1.1.1 has telnetted to another host in the Internet, plus the output from the **debug ip nat** command. This **debug** command causes the router to issue a message every time a packet has its address translated for NAT. You generate the output results by entering a few lines from the Telnet connection from 10.1.1.1 to 170.1.1.1. Notice that the output implies a translation from 10.1.1.1 to 200.1.1.2, but it does not imply any translation of the outside address.

NAT Overload (PAT) Configuration

NAT overload, as mentioned earlier, allows NAT to support many inside local IP addresses with only one or a few inside global IP addresses. By essentially translating the private IP address and port number to a single inside global address, but with a unique port number, NAT can support many (over 65,000) private hosts with only a single public, global address.

Two variations of PAT configuration exist in IOS. If PAT uses a pool of inside global addresses, the configuration looks exactly like dynamic NAT, except the **ip nat inside source list** global command has an **overload** keyword added to the end. If PAT just needs to use one inside global IP address, PAT can use one of its interface IP addresses. Because NAT can support over 65,000 concurrent flows with a single inside global address, a single public IP address can support an entire organization's NAT needs.

The following checklist details the configuration when using a NAT pool:

Use the same steps for configuring dynamic NAT, as outlined in the previous section, but include the **overload** keyword at the end of the **ip nat inside source list** global command.

The following checklist details the configuration when using an interface IP address as the sole inside global IP address:

Step 1   As with dynamic and static NAT, configure inside interfaces with the **ip nat inside** interface subcommand.

Step 2   As with dynamic and static NAT, configure outside interfaces with the **ip nat outside** interface subcommand.

Step 3   As with dynamic NAT, configure an ACL that matches the packets coming in inside interfaces.

Step 4   Configure the **ip nat source list** *acl-number* **interface** *interface name/ number* **overload** global configuration command, referring to the ACL created in Step 3 and to the interface whose IP address will be used for translations.

Example 16-2 shows a dynamic NAT configuration. To convert it to a PAT configuration, the **ip nat inside source list 1 pool fred overload** command would be used instead, simply adding the **overload** keyword.

The next example shows PAT configuration using a single interface IP address. Figure 16-10 shows the same familiar network, with a few changes. In this case, the ISP has given FredsCo a subset of network 200.1.1.0: CIDR subnet 200.1.1.248/30. In other words, this subnet has two usable addresses: 200.1.1.249 and 200.1.1.250. These addresses are used on either end of the serial link between FredsCo and its ISP. The NAT feature on FredsCo's router translates all NAT addresses to its serial IP address, 200.1.1.249.

In Example 16-4, which shows the NAT overload configuration, NAT translates using inside global address 200.1.1.249 only, so the NAT pool is not required. In the example, as implied in Figure 16-10, host 10.1.1.1 creates two Telnet connections, and host 10.1.1.2 creates one Telnet connection, causing three dynamic NAT entries, each using inside global address 200.1.1.249, but each with a unique port number.

Figure 16-10 *NAT Overload and PAT*

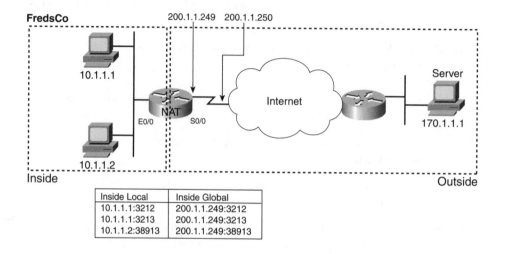

Registered Subnet: 200.1.1.248, Mask 255.255.255.252

Inside Local	Inside Global
10.1.1.1:3212	200.1.1.249:3212
10.1.1.1:3213	200.1.1.249:3213
10.1.1.2:38913	200.1.1.249:38913

Example 16-4 *NAT Overload Configuration*

```
NAT# show running-config
!
! Lines Omitted for Brevity
!
interface Ethernet0/0
 ip address 10.1.1.3 255.255.255.0
 ip nat inside
!
interface Serial0/0
 ip address 200.1.1.249 255.255.255.252
 ip nat outside
!
ip nat inside source list 1 interface Serial0/0 overload
!
access-list 1 permit 10.1.1.2
access-list 1 permit 10.1.1.1
!

NAT# show ip nat translations
Pro Inside global      Inside local      Outside local      Outside global
tcp 200.1.1.249:3212   10.1.1.1:3212     170.1.1.1:23       170.1.1.1:23
tcp 200.1.1.249:3213   10.1.1.1:3213     170.1.1.1:23       170.1.1.1:23
tcp 200.1.1.249:38913  10.1.1.2:38913    170.1.1.1:23       170.1.1.1:23
NAT# show ip nat statistics
```

Example 16-4 *NAT Overload Configuration (Continued)*

```
Total active translations: 3 (0 static, 3 dynamic; 3 extended)
Outside interfaces:
  Serial0/0
Inside interfaces:
  Ethernet0/0
Hits: 103  Misses: 3
Expired translations: 0
Dynamic mappings:
-- Inside Source
access-list 1 interface Serial0/0 refcount 3
```

The **ip nat inside source list 1 interface serial 0/0 overload** command has several parameters, but if you understand the dynamic NAT configuration, the new parameters shouldn't be too hard to grasp. The **list 1** parameter means the same thing as it does for dynamic NAT: Inside local IP addresses matching ACL 1 have their addresses translated. The **interface serial 0/0** parameter means that the only inside global IP address available is the IP address of the NAT router's interface serial 0/0. Finally, the **overload** parameter means that overload is enabled. Without this parameter, the router does not perform overload, just dynamic NAT.

As you can see in the output of the **show ip nat translations** command, three translations have been added to the NAT table. Before this command, host 10.1.1.1 creates two Telnet connections to 170.1.1.1, and host 10.1.1.2 creates a single Telnet connection. Three entries are created, one for each unique combination of inside local IP address and port.

NAT Troubleshooting

The first three major parts of this book devote an entire chapter to troubleshooting. In each of those parts, the chapters cover a wide variety of topics that are related in regard to the technical topics covered in each chapter. The troubleshooting chapters (3, 7, and 11) explain the details of troubleshooting each technology area, but they also help pull some of the related concepts together.

The majority of NAT troubleshooting issues relate to getting the configuration correct. The following list summarizes some hints and tips about how to find the most common NAT configuration problems. Following the list, the text explains one common routing problem that can prevent NAT from working, which relates mainly to ensuring that the configuration is correct.

- Ensure that the configuration includes the **ip nat inside** or **ip nat outside** interface subcommand. These commands enable NAT on the interfaces, and the inside/outside designation is important.

- For static NAT, ensure that the **ip nat source static** command lists the inside local address first and the inside global IP address second.

- For dynamic NAT, ensure that the ACL configured to match packets sent by the inside host match that host's packets, before any NAT translation has occurred. For example, if an inside local address of 10.1.1.1 should be translated to 200.1.1.1, ensure that the ACL matches source address 10.1.1.1, not 200.1.1.1.

- For dynamic NAT without PAT, ensure that the pool has enough IP addresses. Symptoms of not having enough addresses include a growing value in the second misses counter in the **show ip nat statistics** command output, as well as seeing all the addresses in the range defined in the NAT pool in the list of dynamic translations.

- For PAT, it is easy to forget to add the **overload** option on the **ip nat inside source list** command. Without it, NAT works, but PAT does not, often resulting in users' packets not being translated and hosts not being able to get to the Internet.

- Perhaps NAT has been configured correctly, but an ACL exists on one of the interfaces, discarding the packets. Note that IOS processes ACLs before NAT for packets entering an interface, and after translating the addresses for packets exiting an interface.

Finally, the NAT function on one router can be impacted by a routing problem that occurs on another router. The routers in the outside part of the network, oftentimes the Internet, need to be able to route packets to the inside global IP addresses configured on the NAT router. For example, Figure 16-4, earlier in this chapter, shows the flow of packets from inside to outside, and outside to inside. Focusing on the outside-to-inside flow, the routers in the Internet needed to know how to route packets to public registered IP address 200.1.1.1. Typically, this address range would be advertised by a dynamic routing protocol. So, if a review of the NAT configuration shows that the configuration looks correct, look at the routes in both the NAT router and other routers to ensure that the routers can forward the packets, based on the addresses used on both sides of the router performing the NAT function.

Exam Preparation Tasks

Review All the Key Topics

Review the most important topics from this chapter, noted with the Key Topics icon in the outer margin of the page. Table 16-5 lists a reference of these key topics and the page numbers on which each is found. Also, note that any configuration checklists should be reviewed and studied for the content, but you don't need to memorize the step numbers or order—they are just convenient tools for remembering all the steps.

Table 16-5 *Key Topics for Chapter 16*

Key Topic Element	Description	Page Number
Figure 16-1	CIDR global IPv4 address assignment and route aggregation concept	551
Table 16-2	List of private IP network numbers	552
Figure 16-2	Main concept of NAT translating private IP addresses into publicly unique global addresses	553
Figure 16-4	Typical NAT network diagram with key NAT terms listed	555
Table 16-3	List of four key NAT terms and their meanings	556
Figure 16-7	Concepts behind address conservation achieved by NAT Overload (PAT)	559
List	Configuration checklist for static NAT	562
List	Configuration checklist for dynamic NAT	565
List	Summary of differences between dynamic NAT configuration and PAT using a pool	569
List	Configuration checklist for PAT configuration using an interface IP address	569
List	The most common NAT errors	571-572

Complete the Tables and Lists from Memory

Print a copy of Appendix J, "Memory Tables," (found on the CD) or at least the section for this chapter, and complete the tables and lists from memory. Appendix K, "Memory Tables Answer Key," also on the CD, includes completed tables and lists to check your work.

Definitions of Key Terms

Define the following key terms from this chapter, and check your answers in the glossary:

CIDR, inside global, inside local, NAT overload, outside global, outside local, PAT, private IP network

Command Reference to Check Your Memory

While you should not necessarily memorize the information in the tables in this section, this section does include a reference for the configuration and EXEC commands covered in this chapter. Practically speaking, you should memorize the commands as a side effect of reading the chapter and doing all the activities in this exam preparation section. To check to see how well you have memorized the commands as a side effect of your other studies, cover the left side of the table with a piece of paper, read the descriptions on the right side, and see whether you remember the command.

Table 16-6   *Chapter 16 Configuration Command Reference*

Command	Description
ip nat {**inside** | **outside**}	Interface subcommand to enable NAT and identify whether the interface is in the inside or outside of the network
ip nat inside source {**list** {*access-list-number* | *access-list-name*}} {**interface** *type number* | **pool** *pool-name*} [**overload**]	Global command that enables NAT globally, referencing the ACL that defines which source addresses to NAT, and the interface or pool from which to find global addresses
ip nat pool *name start-ip end-ip* {**netmask** *netmask* | **prefix-length** *prefix-length*}	Global command to define a pool of NAT addresses

Table 16-7 *Chapter 16 EXEC Command Reference*

Command	Description
show ip nat statistics	Lists counters for packets and NAT table entries, as well as basic configuration information
show ip nat translations [**verbose**]	Displays the NAT table
clear ip nat translation { *	[**inside** *global-ip local-ip*] [**outside** *local-ip global-ip*]}	Clears all or some of the dynamic entries in the NAT table, depending on which parameters are used
clear ip nat translation *protocol* **inside** *global-ip global-port local-ip local-port* [**outside** *local-ip global-ip*]	Clears some of the dynamic entries in the NAT table, depending on which parameters are used
debug ip nat	Issues a log message describing each packet whose IP address is translated with NAT

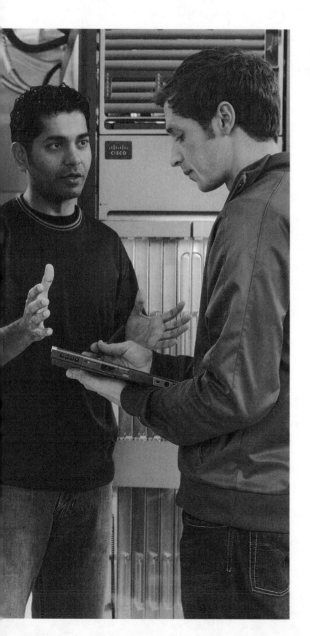

This chapter covers the following subjects:

Global Unicast Addressing, Routing, and Subnetting: This section introduces the concepts behind unicast IPv6 addresses, IPv6 routing, and subnetting using IPv6, all in comparison to IPv4.

IPv6 Protocols and Addressing: This section examines the most common protocols used in conjunction with IPv6.

Configuring IPv6 Routing and Routing Protocols: This section shows how to configure IPv6 routing and routing protocols on Cisco routers.

IPv6 Transition Options: This section explains some of the options for migrating from IPv4 to IPv6.

CHAPTER 17

IP Version 6

IP version 6 (IPv6), the replacement protocol for IPv4, is well known for a couple of reasons. IPv6 provides the ultimate solution for the problem of running out of IPv4 addresses in the global Internet by using a 128-bit address—approximately 10^{38} total addresses, versus the mere (approximate) $4*10^9$ total addresses in IPv4. However, IPv6 has been the ultimate long-term solution for over ten years, in part because the interim solutions, including Network Address Translation/Port Address Translation (NAT/PAT), have thankfully delayed the day in which we truly run out of public unicast IP addresses.

This chapter focuses on IPv6 addressing and routing, in part because the primary motivation for the eventual migration to IPv6 is to relieve the address constraints of IPv4. This chapter also briefly introduces some of the other features of IPv6, as well as explains some of the reasons for the need for IPv6.

"Do I Know This Already?" Quiz

The "Do I Know This Already?" quiz allows you to assess whether you should read the entire chapter. If you miss no more than one of these nine self-assessment questions, you might want to move ahead to the section "Exam Preparation Tasks." Table 17-1 lists the major headings in this chapter and the "Do I Know This Already?" quiz questions covering the material in those headings so that you can assess your knowledge of these specific areas. The answers to the "Do I Know This Already?" quiz appear in Appendix A.

Table 17-1 *"Do I Know This Already?" Foundation Topics Section-to-Question Mapping*

Foundation Topics Section	Questions
Global Unicast Addressing, Routing, and Subnetting	1, 2
IPv6 Protocols and Addressing	3–5
Configuring IPv6 Routing and Routing Protocols	6–8
IPv6 Transition Options	9

1.   Which of the following is the most likely organization from which an enterprise could obtain an administrative assignment of a block of IPv6 global unicast IP addresses?

    a.   An ISP

    b.   ICANN

    c.   An RIR

    d.   Global unicast addresses are not administratively assigned by an outside organization.

2.   Which of the following is the shortest valid abbreviation for FE80:0000:0000:0100:0000:0000:0000:0123?

    a.   FE80::100::123

    b.   FE8::1::123

    c.   FE80::100:0:0:0:123:4567

    d.   FE80:0:0:100::123

3.   Which of the following answers lists a multicast IPv6 address?

    a.   2000::1:1234:5678:9ABC

    b.   FD80::1:1234:5678:9ABC

    c.   FE80::1:1234:5678:9ABC

    d.   FF80::1:1234:5678:9ABC

4.   Which of the following answers list either a protocol or function that can be used by a host to dynamically learn its own IPv6 address?

    a.   Stateful DHCP

    b.   Stateless DHCP

    c.   Stateless autoconfiguration

    d.   Neighbor Discovery Protocol

5.   Which of the following help allow an IPv6 host to learn the IP address of a default gateway on its subnet?

    a.   Stateful DHCP

    b.   Stateless RS

    c.   Stateless autoconfiguration

    d.   NDP

6. Which of the following are routing protocols that support IPv6?

   a. RIPng

   b. RIP-2

   c. OSPFv2

   d. OSPFv3

   e. OSPFv4

7. In the following configuration, this router's Fa0/0 interface has a MAC address of 4444.4444.4444. Which of the following IPv6 addresses will the interface use?

```
ipv6 unicast-routing
ipv6 router rip tag1
interface FastEthernet0/0
 ipv6 address 3456::1/64
```

   a. 3456::C444:44FF:FE44:4444

   b. 3456::4444:44FF:FE44:4444

   c. 3456::1

   d. FE80::1

   e. FE80::4644:44FF:FE44:4444

   f. FE80::4444:4444:4444

8. In the configuration text in the previous question, RIP was not working on interface Fa0/0. Which of the following configuration commands would enable RIP on Fa0/0?

   a. **network 3456::/64**

   b. **network 3456::/16**

   c. **network 3456::1/128**

   d. **ipv6 rip enable**

   e. **ipv6 rip tag1 enable**

9. Which of the following IPv4-to-IPv6 transition methods allows an IPv4-only host to communicate with an IPv6-only host?

   a. Dual-stack

   b. 6to4 tunneling

   c. ISATAP tunneling

   d. NAT-PT

Foundation Topics

The world has changed tremendously over the last 10–20 years as a result of the growth and maturation of the Internet and networking technologies in general. Twenty years ago, no global network existed to which the general populace could easily connect. Ten years ago, the public Internet had grown to the point where people in most parts of the world could connect to the Internet, but with most Internet users being the more computer-savvy people. Today, practically everyone seems to have access, through their PCs, handheld devices, phones, or even the refrigerator.

The eventual migration to IPv6 will likely be driven by the need for more addresses. Practically every mobile phone supports Internet traffic, requiring the use of an IP address. Most new cars have the ability to acquire and use an IP address, along with wireless communications, allowing the car dealer to contact the customer when the car's diagnostics detect a problem with the car. Some manufacturers have embraced the idea that all their appliances need to be IP enabled.

Besides the sheer growth in the need for IPv4 addresses, edicts from governmental agencies could drive demand for IPv6. As of this writing, the U.S. government had set a date in 2008 by which all government agencies should be running IPv6 in their core IP networks. Such initiatives can help drive adoption of IPv6.

While the two biggest reasons why networks might migrate to IPv6 are the need for more addresses and mandates from government organizations, at least IPv6 includes some attractive features and migration tools. Some of those advantages are as follows:

- **Address assignment features:** IPv6 address assignment allows easier renumbering, dynamic allocation, and recovery of addresses, with nice features for mobile devices to move around and keep their IP address (thereby avoiding having to close and reopen an application).

- **Aggregation:** IPv6's huge address space makes for much easier aggregation of blocks of addresses in the Internet.

- **No need for NAT/PAT:** Using publicly registered unique addresses on all devices removes the need for NAT/PAT, which also avoids some of the application layer and VPN-tunneling issues caused by NAT.

- **IPsec:** IPsec works with both IPv4 and IPv6, but it is required on IPv6 hosts, so you can rely on support for IPsec as needed for VPN tunneling.

- **Header improvements:** While it might seem like a small issue, the IPv6 header improves several things compared to IPv4. In particular, routers do not need to recalculate a header checksum for every packet, reducing per-packet overhead. Additionally, the header includes a flow label that allows easy identification of packets sent over the same single TCP or User Datagram Protocol (UDP) connection.

- **Transition tools:** As is covered in the last major section of this chapter, IPv6 has many tools to help with the transition from IPv4 to IPv6.

The worldwide migration from IPv4 to IPv6 will not be an event, or even a year on the calendar. Rather, it will be a long process, a process that has already begun. Network engineers have a growing need to learn more about IPv6. This chapter covers the basics of IPv6, ending with some discussions about the issues of living in a world in which both IPv4 and IPv6 will likely coexist for quite a long time.

> **NOTE** *Information Week* (http://www.informationweek.com) published an interesting article about the need to migrate to IPv6, around the time this book was being completed. To see the article, search the website for the article "The Impending Internet Address Shortage."

Global Unicast Addressing, Routing, and Subnetting

One of the original design goals for the Internet was that all organizations would register and be assigned one or more public IP networks (Class A, B, or C). By registering to use a particular public network number, the company or organization using that network was assured by the numbering authorities that no other company or organization in the world would be using the addresses in that network. As a result, all hosts in the world would have globally unique IP addresses.

From the perspective of the Internet infrastructure, in particular the goal of keeping Internet routers' routing tables from getting too large, assigning an entire network to each organization helped to some degree. The Internet routers could ignore all subnets, instead having a route for each classful network. For example, if a company registered and was assigned Class B network 128.107.0.0/16, the Internet routers just needed one route for that entire network.

Over time, the Internet grew tremendously. It became clear by the early 1990s that something had to be done, or the growth of the Internet would grind to a halt when all the public IP networks were assigned, and no more existed. Additionally, the IP routing tables in Internet routers were becoming too large for the router technology of that day. So, the Internet community worked together to come up with both some short-term and long-term solutions to two problems: the shortage of public addresses and the size of the routing tables.

The short-term solutions included a much smarter public address assignment policy, where public addresses were not assigned as only Class A, B, and C networks, but as smaller subdivisions (prefixes), reducing waste. Additionally, the growth of the Internet routing tables was reduced by smarter assignment of the address ranges. For example, assigning the Class C networks that begin with 198 to only a particular Internet service provider (ISP) in a particular part of the world allowed other ISPs to use one route for 198.0.0.0/8—in other words, all addresses that begin with 198—rather than a route for each of the 65,536 different Class C networks that begin with 198. Finally, NAT/PAT achieved amazing results by allowing a typical home or small office to consume only one public IPv4 address, greatly reducing the need for public IPv4 addresses.

The ultimate solution to both problems is IPv6. The sheer number of IPv6 addresses takes care of the issue of running out of addresses. The address assignment policies already used with IPv4 have been refined and applied to IPv6, with good results for keeping the size of IPv6 routing tables smaller in Internet routers. The following sections provide a general discussion of both issues, in particular how global unicast addresses, along with good administrative choices for how to assign IPv6 address prefixes, aid in routing in the global Internet. These sections conclude with a discussion of subnetting in IPv6.

Global Route Aggregation for Efficient Routing

By the time IPv6 was being defined in the early 1990s, it was clear that thoughtful choices about how to assign the public IPv4 address space could help with the efficiency of Internet routers by keeping their routing tables much smaller. By following those same well-earned lessons, IPv6 public IP address assignment can make for even more efficient routing as the Internet migrates to IPv6.

The address assignment strategy for IPv6 is elegant, but simple, and can be roughly summarized as follows:

- Public IPv6 addresses are grouped (numerically) by major geographic region.

- Inside each region, the address space is further subdivided by ISP inside that region.

- Inside each ISP in a region, the address space is further subdivided for each customer.

The same organizations handle this address assignment for IPv6 as for IPv4. The Internet Corporation for Assigned Network Numbers (ICANN, http://www.icann.org) owns the process. ICANN assigns one or more IPv6 address ranges to each Regional Internet Registry (RIR), of which five exist at the time of publication, roughly covering North America, Central/South America, Europe, Asia/Pacific, and Africa. These RIRs then subdivide their assigned address space into smaller portions, assigning prefixes to different

ISPs and other smaller registries, with the ISPs then assigning even smaller ranges of
addresses to their customers.

NOTE   The Internet Assigned Numbers Authority (IANA) formerly owned the address
assignment process, but it was transitioned to ICANN.

The IPv6 global address assignment plan results in more efficient routing, as shown in
Figure 17-1. The figure shows a fictitious company (Company1) that has been assigned an
IPv6 prefix by a fictitious ISP, NA-ISP1 (standing for North American ISP number 1). The
figure lists the American Registry for Internet Numbers (ARIN), which is the RIR for North
America.

Figure 17-1   *Conceptual View of IPv6 Global Routes*

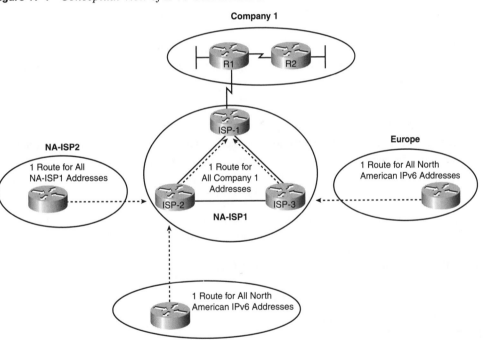

As shown in the figure, the routers installed by ISPs in other major geographies of the world
can have a single route that matches all IPv6 addresses in North America. While hundreds
of ISPs might be operating in north America, and hundreds of thousands of enterprise
customers of those ISPs, and tens of millions of individual customers of those ISPs, all the
public IPv6 addresses can be from one (or a few) very large address blocks—requiring only
one (or a few) routes on the Internet routers in other parts of the world. Similarly, routers

inside other ISPs in North America (for example, NA-ISP2, indicating North American ISP number 2 in the figure) can have one route that matches all address ranges assigned to NA-ISP1. And the routers inside NA-ISP1 just need to have one route that matches the entire address range assigned to Company1, rather than needing to know about all the subnets inside Company1.

Besides keeping the routers' routing table much smaller, this process also results in fewer changes to Internet routing tables. For example, if NA-ISP1 signed a service contract with another enterprise customer, NA-ISP1 could assign another prefix inside the range of addresses already assigned to NA-ISP1 by ARIN. The routers outside NA-ISP1's network—the majority of the Internet—do not need to know any new routes, because their existing routes already match the address range assigned to the new customer. The NA-ISP2 routers (another ISP) already have a route that matches the entire address range assigned to NA-ISP1, so they do not need any more routes. Likewise, the routers in ISPs in Europe and South America already have a route that works as well.

While the general concept might not be too difficult, a specific example can help. Before seeing a specific example, however, it helps to know a bit about how IPv6 addresses and prefixes are written.

Conventions for Representing IPv6 Addresses

IPv6 conventions use 32 hexadecimal numbers, organized into 8 quartets of 4 hex digits separated by a colon, to represent a 128-bit IPv6 address. For example:

2340:1111:AAAA:0001:1234:5678:9ABC:1234

Each hex digit represents 4 bits, so if you want to examine the address in binary, the conversion is relatively easy if you memorize the values shown in Table 17-2.

Table 17-2 *Hexadecimal/Binary Conversion Chart*

Hex	Binary	Hex	Binary
0	0000	8	1000
1	0001	9	1001
2	0010	A	1010
3	0011	B	1011
4	0100	C	1100
5	0101	D	1101
6	0110	E	1110
7	0111	F	1111

Writing or typing 32 hexadecimal digits, while more convenient than doing the same with 128 binary digits, can still be a pain. To make things a little easier, two conventions allow you to shorten what must be typed for an IPv6 address:

- Omit the leading 0s in any given quartet.

- Represent 1 or more consecutive quartets of all hex 0s with a double colon (::), but only for one such occurrence in a given address.

> **NOTE** For IPv6, a quartet is one set of 4 hex digits in an IPv6 address. Eight quartets are in each IPv6 address.

For example, consider the following address. The bold digits represent digits in which the address could be abbreviated.

FE00:**0000:0000:000**1:**0000:0000:0000:00**56

This address has two different locations in which one or more quartets have 4 hex 0s, so two main options exist for abbreviating this address, using the :: abbreviation in one or the other location. The following two options show the two briefest valid abbreviations:

- FE00::1:0:0:0:56

- FE00:0:0:1::56

In particular, note that the :: abbreviation, meaning "one or more quartets of all 0s," cannot be used twice, because that would be ambiguous. So, the abbreviation FE00::1::56 would not be valid.

Conventions for Writing IPv6 Prefixes

IPv6 prefixes represent a range or block of consecutive IPv6 addresses. The number that represents the range of addresses, called a *prefix*, is usually seen in IP routing tables, just like you see IP subnet numbers in IPv4 routing tables.

Before examining IPv6 prefixes in more detail, it is helpful to review a few terms used with IPv4. IPv4 addresses can be analyzed and understood using either *classful addressing* rules or *classless addressing* rules. (This book and *CCENT/CCNA ICND1 Official Exam Certification Guide* both use classful terminology for the most part.) Classful addressing means that the analysis of an IP address or subnet includes the idea of a classful network number, with a separate network part of the address. The top part of Figure 17-2 reviews these concepts.

Figure 17-2 *IPv4 Classless and Classful Addressing, and IPv6 Addressing*

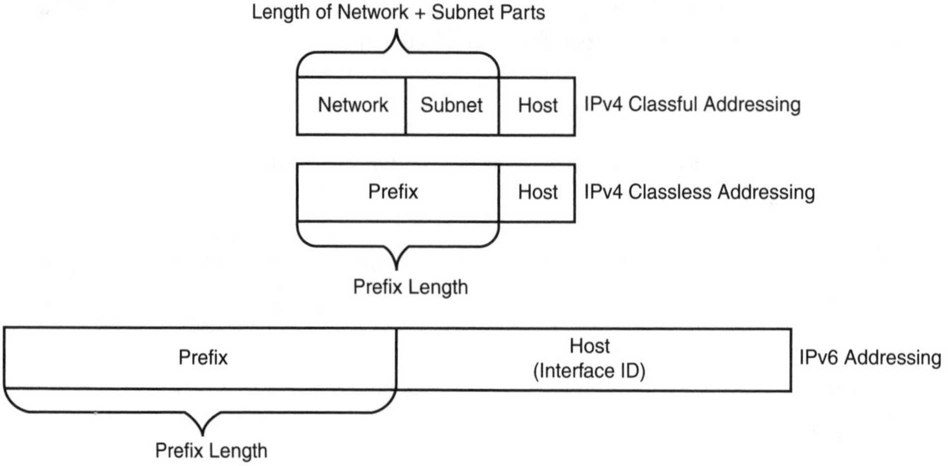

Length of Network + Subnet Parts

| Network | Subnet | Host | IPv4 Classful Addressing |

| Prefix | Host | IPv4 Classless Addressing |

Prefix Length

| Prefix | Host (Interface ID) | IPv6 Addressing |

Prefix Length

Thinking about IPv4 addressing as classful addresses helps to fully understand some issues in networking. With classful addressing, for example, the written value 128.107.3.0/24 means 16 network bits (because the address is in a Class B network) and 8 host bits (because the mask has 8 binary 0s), leaving 8 subnet bits. The same value, interpreted with classless rules, means prefix 128.107.3.0, prefix length 24. Same subnet/prefix, same meaning, same router operation, same configuration—it's just two different ways to think about the meaning of the numbers.

IPv6 uses a classless view of addressing, with no concept of classful addressing. Like IPv4, IPv6 prefixes list some value, a slash, and then a numeric prefix length. Like IPv4 prefixes, the last part of the number, beyond the length of the prefix, is represented by binary 0s. And finally, IPv6 prefix numbers can be abbreviated with the same rules as IPv4 addresses. For example, consider the following IPv6 address that is assigned to a host on a LAN:

2000:1234:5678:9ABC:1234:5678:9ABC:1111/64

This value represents the full 128-bit IP address; in fact, you have no opportunities to abbreviate this address. However, the /64 means that the prefix (subnet) in which this address resides is the subnet that includes all addresses that begin with the same first 64 bits as the address. Conceptually, it is the same logic as an IPv4 address. For example, address 128.107.3.1/24 is in the prefix (subnet) whose first 24 bits are the same values as address 128.107.3.1.

Like with IPv4, when writing or typing a prefix, the bits past the end of the prefix length are all binary 0s. In the IPv6 address shown previously, the prefix in which the address resides would be as follows:

2000:1234:5678:9ABC:**0000:0000:0000:0000**/64

When abbreviated, this would be:

2000:1234:5678:9ABC::/64

Next, one last fact about the rules for writing prefixes before seeing some examples and moving on. If the prefix length is not a multiple of 16, the boundary between the prefix and the host part of the address is inside a quartet. In such cases, the prefix value should list all the values in the last octet in the prefix part of the value. For example, if the address just shown with a /64 prefix length instead had a /56 prefix length, the prefix would include all the first 3 quartets (a total of 48 bits), plus the first 8 bits of the fourth octet. The last 8 bits (last 2 hex digits) of the fourth octet should now be binary 0s. So, by convention, the rest of the fourth octet should be written, after being set to binary 0s, as follows:

2000:1234:5678:9A**00**::/56

The following list summarizes some key points about how to write IPv6 prefixes:

■ The prefix has the same value as the IP addresses in the group for the first number of bits, as defined by the prefix length.

Key Topic

■ Any bits after the prefix-length number of bits are binary 0s.

■ The prefix can be abbreviated with the same rules as IPv6 addresses.

■ If the prefix length is not on a quartet boundary, write down the value for the entire quartet.

Examples can certainly help a lot in this case. Table 17-3 shows several sample prefixes, their format, and a brief explanation.

Table 17-3 *Example IPv6 Prefixes and Their Meanings*

Prefix	Explanation	Incorrect Alternative
2000::/3	All addresses whose first 3 bits are equal to the first 3 bits of hex number 2000 (bits are 001)	2000/3 (omits ::) 2::/3 (omits the rest of the first quartet)
2340:1140::/26	All addresses whose first 26 bits match the listed hex number	2340:114::/26 (omits the last digit in the second quartet)
2340:1111::/32	All addresses whose first 32 bits match the listed hex number	2340:1111/32 (omits ::)

Almost as important to this convention is to note which options are not allowed. For example, 2::/3 is not allowed instead of 2000::/3, because it omits the rest of the octet, and a device could not tell whether 2::/3 means "hex 0002" or "hex 2000." Only leading 0s in a quartet, and not trailing 0s, can be omitted when abbreviating an IPv6 address or prefix.

Now that you understand a few of the conventions about how to represent IPv6 addresses and prefixes, a specific example can show how ICANN's IPv6 global unicast IP address assignment strategy can allow the easy and efficient routing shown back in Figure 17-1.

Global Unicast Prefix Assignment Example

IPv6 standards reserve the 2000::/3 prefix—which, when interpreted more fully, means all addresses that begin with binary 001 or either a hex 2 or 3—as global unicast addresses. Global unicast addresses are addresses that have been assigned as public and globally unique IPv6 addresses, allowing hosts using those addresses to communicate through the Internet without the need for NAT. In other words, these addresses fit the purest design for how to implement IPv6 for the global Internet.

Figure 17-3 shows an example set of prefixes that could result in a company (Company1) being assigned a prefix of 2340:1111:AAAA::/48.

Figure 17-3   *Example IPv6 Prefix Assignment in the Internet*

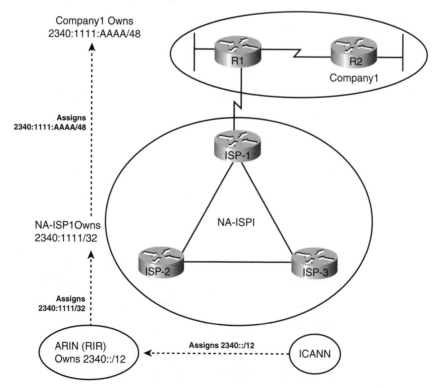

The process starts with ICANN, which owns the entire IPv6 address space, and assigns the rights to *registry prefix* 2340::/12 to one of the RIRs, ARIN in this case (North America). This means that ARIN has the rights to assign any IPv6 addresses that begin with the first 12 bits of hex 2340 (binary value 0010 0011 0100). For perspective, that's a large group of addresses—2^{116} to be exact.

Next, NA-ISP1 asks ARIN for a prefix assignment. After ARIN ensures that NA-ISP1 meets some requirements, ARIN might assign *ISP prefix* 2340:1111::/32 to NA-ISP1. This too is a large group—2^{96} addresses to be exact. For perspective, this one address block might well be enough public IPv6 addresses for even the largest ISP, without that ISP ever needing another IPv6 prefix.

Finally, Company1 asks its ISP, NA-ISP1, for the assignment of an IPv6 prefix. NA-ISP1 assigns Company1 the site prefix 2340:1111:AAAA::/48, which is again a large range of addresses—2^{80} in this case. In the next paragraph, the text shows what Company1 could do with that prefix, but first, examine Figure 17-4, which presents the same concepts as shown in Figure 17-1, but now with the prefixes shown.

Figure 17-4 *IPv6 Global Routing Concepts*

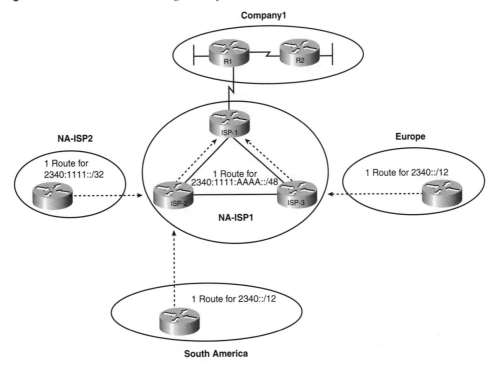

The figure shows the perspectives of routers outside North America, routers from another ISP in North America, and other routers in the same ISP. Routers outside North America can use a route for prefix 2340::/12, knowing that ICANN assigned this prefix to be used only by ARIN. This one route could match all IPv6 addresses assigned in North America. Routers in NA-ISP2, an example alternative ISP in North America, need one route for 2340:1111::/32, the prefix assigned to NA-ISP1. This one route could match all packets destined for all customers of NA-ISP1. Inside NA-ISP1, its routers need to know to which NA-ISP1 router to forward packets to for that particular customer (the router named ISP-1 in this case), so the routes inside NA-ISP1's routers lists a prefix of 2340:1111:AAAA/48.

Subnetting Global Unicast IPv6 Addresses Inside an Enterprise

The original IPv4 Internet design called for each organization to be assigned a classful network number, with the enterprise subdividing the network into smaller address ranges by subnetting the classful network. This same concept of subnetting carries over from IPv4 to IPv6, with the enterprise subnetting the prefix assigned by its ISP into smaller prefixes. When thinking about the IPv6 subnetting concept, you could make the following general analogies with classful IPv4 subnetting to help understand the process:

- The prefix assigned to the enterprise by the ISP, which must be the same for all IPv6 addresses in one enterprise, is like the IPv4 network part of an address.

- The enterprise engineer extends the length of the prefix, borrowing host bits, to create a subnet part of the address.

- The last/third major part is the host part of the address, called the *interface ID* in IPv6, and is meant to uniquely identify a host inside a subnet.

For example, Figure 17-5 shows a more detailed view of the Company1 enterprise network shown in several of the earlier figures in this chapter. The design concepts behind how many subnets are needed with IPv6 are identical to those for IPv4: A subnet is needed for each VLAN and for each serial link, with the same options for subnets with Frame Relay. In this case, two LANs and two serial links exist, so Company1 needs four subnets.

The figure also shows how the enterprise engineer extended the length of the prefix as assigned by the ISP (/48) to /64, thereby creating a 16-bit subnet part of the address structure. The /48 prefix is generally called the *site prefix*, and the longer prefix used on each link is called a *subnet prefix*. To create this extra 16-bit subnet field, the engineer uses the same concept as with IPv4 when choosing a subnet mask by borrowing bits from the host field of an IPv4 address. In this case, think of the host field as having 80 bits (because the prefix assigned by the ISP is 48 bits long, leaving 80 bits), and the design in Figure 17-5 borrows 16 bits for the subnet field, leaving a measly 64 bits for the host field.

Figure 17-5 *Company1 Needs Four Subnets*

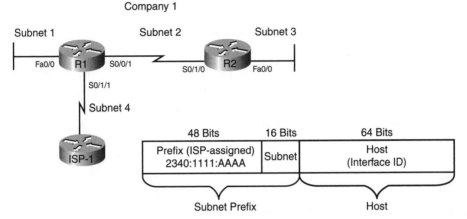

A bit of math about the design choices can help provide some perspective on the scale of IPv6. The 16-bit subnet field allows 2^{16}, or 65,536, subnets—overkill for all but the very largest organizations or companies. (There are also no worries about a zero or broadcast subnet in IPv6!) The host field is seemingly even more overkill: 2^{64} hosts per subnet, which is more than 1,000,000,000,000,000,000 addresses per subnet. However, a good reason exists for this large host or interface ID part of the address, because it allows one of the automatic IPv6 address assignment features to work well, as is covered in the section "IPv6 Host Address Assignment," later in this chapter.

Figure 17-6 takes the concept to the final conclusion, assigning the specific four subnets to be used inside Company1. Note that the figure shows the subnet fields and prefix lengths (64 in this case) in bold.

Figure 17-6 *Company1 with Four Subnets Assigned*

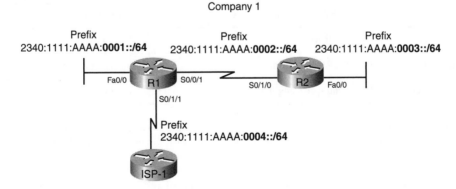

NOTE   The subnet numbers in the figure could be abbreviated slightly, removing the three leading 0s from the last shown quartets.

Figure 17-6 just shows one option for subnetting the prefix assigned to Company1. However, any number of subnet bits could be chosen, as long as the host field retained enough bits to number all hosts in a subnet. For example, a /112 prefix length could be used, extending the /48 prefix by 64 bits (4 hex quartets). Then, for the design in Figure 17-6, you could choose the following four subnets:

- 2340:1111:AAAA::0001:0000/112

- 2340:1111:AAAA::0002:0000/112

- 2340:1111:AAAA::0003:0000/112

- 2340:1111:AAAA::0004:0000/112

By using global unicast IPv6 addresses, Internet routing can be very efficient and enterprises can have plenty of IP addresses and plenty of subnets, with no requirement for NAT functions to conserve the address space.

Prefix Terminology

Before wrapping up this topic, a few new terms need to be introduced. The process of global unicast IPv6 address assignment examines many different prefixes, with many different prefix lengths. The text scatters a couple of more specific terms, but for easier study, Table 17-4 summarizes the four key terms, with some reminders of what each means.

Table 17-4   *Example IPv6 Prefixes and Their Meanings*

Term	Assignment	Example from Chapter 17
Registry prefix	By ICANN to an RIR	2340::/12
ISP prefix	By an RIR to an ISP[1]	2340:1111/32
Site prefix	By an ISP to a customer (site)	2340:1111:AAAA/48
Subnet prefix	By an enterprise engineer for each individual link	2340:1111:AAAA:0001/64

[1]While an RIR can assign a prefix to an ISP, an RIR can also assign a prefix to other Internet registries, which can subdivide and assign additional prefixes, until eventually an ISP and then its customers are assigned some unique prefix.

The next sections of this chapter broaden the discussion of IPv6 to include additional types of IPv6 addresses, along with the protocols that control and manage several common functions for IPv6.

IPv6 Protocols and Addressing

IPv4 hosts need to know several basic facts before they can succeed in simple tasks like opening a web browser to view a web page. IPv4 hosts typically need to know the IP address of one or more Domain Name System (DNS) servers so that they can use DNS protocol messages to ask a DNS server to resolve that name into an IPv4 address. They need to know an IP address of a router to use as a default gateway (default router), with the host sending packets destined to a host in a different subnet to that default router. The host, of course, needs to know its unicast IPv4 IP address and mask—or, as stated with classless terminology, its IPv4 address and prefix length—from which the host can calculate the prefix (subnet) on that link.

IPv6 hosts need the same information—DNS IP addresses, default router IP address, and their own address/prefix length—for the same reasons. IPv6 hosts still use host names, and they need to have the host name resolved into an IPv6 address. IPv6 hosts still send packets directly to hosts on the same subnet, but they send packets to the default router for off-subnet destinations.

While IPv6 hosts need to know the same information, IPv6 changes the mechanisms for learning some of these facts compared to IPv4. The following sections examine the options and protocols through which a host can learn these key pieces of information. At the same time, these sections introduce several other types of IPv6 addresses that are used by the new IPv6 protocols. The end of these sections summarizes the details and terminology for the various types of IPv6 addresses.

DHCP for IPv6

IPv6 hosts can use Dynamic Host Configuration Protocol (DHCP) to learn and lease an IP address and corresponding prefix length (mask), the IP address of the default router, and the DNS IP address(es). The concept works basically like DHCP for IPv4: The host sends a (multicast) IPv6 packet searching for the DHCP server. When a server replies, the DHCP client sends a message asking for a lease of an IP address, and the server replies, listing an IPv6 address, prefix length, default router, and DNS IP addresses. The names and formats of the actual DHCP messages have changed quite a bit from IPv4 to IPv6, so DHCPv4 and DHCPv6 differ in detail, but the basic process remains the same. (DHCPv4 refers to the version of DHCP used for IPv4, and DHCPv6 refers to the version of DHCP used for IPv6.)

DHCPv4 servers retain information about each client, like the IP address leased to that client and the length of time for which the lease is valid. This type of information is called *state information*, because it tracks the state or status of each client. DHCPv6 servers happen to have two operational modes: stateful, in which the server tracks state information, and stateless, in which the server does not track state information. Stateful DHCPv6 servers fill the same role as the older DHCPv4 servers, while stateless DHCPv6 servers fill one role in an IPv6 alternative to stateful DHCP. (Stateless DHCP, and its purpose, is covered in the upcoming section "Learning the IP Address(es) of DNS Servers.")

One difference between DHCPv4 and stateful DHCPv6 is that IPv4 hosts send IP broadcasts to find DHCP servers, while IPv6 hosts send IPv6 multicasts. IPv6 multicast addresses have a prefix of FF00::/8, meaning that the first 8 bits of an address are binary 11111111, or FF in hex. The multicast address FF02::1:2 (longhand FF02:0000:0000:0000:0000:0000:0001:0002) has been reserved in IPv6 to be used by hosts to send packets to an unknown DHCP server, with the routers working to forward these packets to the appropriate DHCP server.

IPv6 Host Address Assignment

When using IPv4 in enterprise networks, engineers typically configure static IPv4 addresses on each router interface with the **ip address** interface subcommand. At the same time, most end-user hosts use DHCP to dynamically learn their IP address and mask. For Internet access, the router can use DHCP to learn its own public IPv4 address from the ISP.

IPv6 follows the same general model, but with routers using one of two options for static IPv6 address assignment, and with end-user hosts using one of two options for dynamic IPv6 address assignment. The following sections examine all four options. But first, to appreciate the configuration options, you need a little more information about the low-order 64 bits of the IPv6 address format: the interface ID.

The IPv6 Interface ID and EUI-64 Format

Earlier in this chapter, Figure 17-5 shows the format of an IPv6 global unicast address, with the second half of the address called the host or interface ID. The value of the interface ID portion of a global unicast address can be set to any value, as long as no other host in the same subnet attempts to use the same value. (IPv6 includes a dynamic method for hosts to find out whether a duplicate address exists on the subnet before starting to use the address.) However, the size of the interface ID was purposefully chosen to allow easy autoconfiguration of IP addresses by plugging the MAC address of a network card into the interface ID field in an IPv6 address.

MAC addresses are 6 bytes (48 bits) in length, so for a host to automatically decide on a value to use in the 8-byte (64-bit) interface ID field, IPv6 cannot simply copy just the MAC address. To complete the 64-bit interface ID, IPv6 fills in 2 more bytes. Interestingly, to do so, IPv6 separates the MAC address into two 3-byte halves, and inserts hex FFFE in between the halves, to form the interface ID field, as well as setting 1 special bit to binary 1. This format, called the EUI-64 format, is shown in Figure 17-7.

Figure 17-7 *IPv6 Address Format with Interface ID and EUI-64*

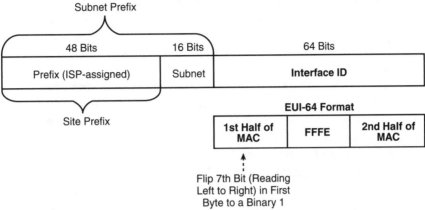

Although it might seem a bit convoluted, it works. Also, with a little practice, you can look at an IPv6 address and quickly notice the FFFE late in the address, and then easily find the two halves of the corresponding interface's MAC address.

To be complete, the figure points out one other small detail regarding the EUI-64 interface ID value. Splitting the MAC address into two halves, and injecting FFFE, is easy. However, the EUI-64 format requires setting the seventh bit in the first byte of the value to binary 1. The underlying reason is that Ethernet MAC addresses are listed with the low-order bits of each byte on the left, and the high-order bits on the right. So, the eighth bit in a byte (reading from left to right) is the highest-order bit in the address, and the seventh bit (reading from left to right) is the second highest-order bit. This second highest-order bit in the first byte— the seventh bit reading from left to right—is called the universal/local (U/L) bit. Set to binary 0, it means that the MAC address is a burned-in MAC address. Set to 1, it means that the MAC address has been configured locally. EUI-64 says that the U/L bit should be set to 1, meaning local.

For example, the following two lines list a host's MAC address and corresponding EUI-64 format interface ID, assuming the use of an address configuration option that uses the EUI-64 format:

■ 0034:5678:9ABC

■ 0234:56FF:FE78:9ABC

NOTE   To change the seventh bit (reading left-to-right) in the example, convert hex 00 to binary 00000000, change the seventh bit to 1 (00000010), and then convert back to hex, for hex 02 as the first two digits.

Static IPv6 Address Configuration

Two options for static IPv6 address configuration are covered in this book, and both are available on both routers and hosts: static configuration of the entire address, and static configuration of a /64 prefix with the host calculating its EUI-64 interface ID to complete the IP address. This section shows the concept using routers.

To configure an IPv6 address on an interface, the router needs an **ipv6 address** *address/ prefix-length* [**eui-64**] interface subcommand on each interface. If the **eui-64** keyword is not included, the address must represent the entire 128-bit address. If the **eui-64** keyword is included, the address should represent the 64-bit prefix, with the router creating the interface ID using the EUI-64 format. The *prefix-length* parameter should be the length of the subnet prefix. For example, Example 17-1 lists the commands on Router R1 from Figure 17-6 earlier in this chapter, which is one of Company1's enterprise routers. It uses the site prefix length of /64. The example shows both versions of the command (with and without the **eui-64** keyword.)

Example 17-1   *Configuring Static IPv6 Addresses*

```
! The first interface is in subnet 1, and will use EUI-64 as the Interface ID
!
interface FastEthernet0/0
 ipv6 address 2340:1111:AAAA:1::/64 eui-64
! The next interface spells out the whole 128 bits, abbreviated. The longer
! version is 2340:1111:AAAA:0002:0000:0000:0000:0001/64. It is in subnet 2.
!
interface Serial0/0/1
 ipv6 address 2340:1111:AAAA:2::1/64
! The third interface is in subnet 4, with EUI-64 format Interface ID again.
!
interface Serial0/1/1
 ipv6 address 2340:1111:AAAA:4::/64 eui-64
!
R1#show ipv6 interface fa0/0
FastEthernet0/0 is up, line protocol is up
  IPv6 is enabled, link-local address is FE80::213:19FF:FE7B:5004
  Global unicast address(es):
    2340:1111:AAAA:1:213:19FF:FE7B:5004, subnet is 2340:1111:AAAA:1::/64 [EUI]
! Lines omitted for brevity
R1#show ipv6 interface S0/0/1
Serial0/0/1 is up, line protocol is up
  IPv6 is enabled, link-local address is FE80::213:19FF:FE7B:5004
  Global unicast address(es):
    2340:1111:AAAA:2::1, subnet is 2340:1111:AAAA:2::/64
! Lines omitted for brevity
R1#show ipv6 interface s0/1/1
Serial0/1/1 is up, line protocol is up
```

Example 17-1 *Configuring Static IPv6 Addresses (Continued)*

```
IPv6 is enabled, link-local address is FE80::213:19FF:FE7B:5004
Global unicast address(es):
  2340:1111:AAAA:4:213:19FF:FE7B:5004, subnet is 2340:1111:AAAA:4::/64 [EUI]
! Lines omitted for brevity
```

The end of the example lists the full global unicast IPv6 address as part of the **show ipv6 interface** command. When using the EUI-64 option, this command is particularly useful, because the configuration command does not list the entire IPv6 address. Note that if the EUI format is used, the **show ipv6 interface** command notes that fact (see interfaces Fa0/0 and S0/1/1, versus S0/0/1). Also, routers do not have MAC addresses associated with some interfaces, including serial interfaces, so to form the EUI-64–formatted interface ID on those interfaces, routers use the MAC address of a LAN interface. In this case, S0/1/1's interface ID is based on Fa0/0's MAC address.

Stateless Autoconfiguration and Router Advertisements

IPv6 supports two methods of dynamic configuration of IPv6 addresses. One uses a stateful DHCPv6 server, which as mentioned earlier, works the same as DHCP in IPv4 in concept, although many details in the messages differ between DHCPv4 and DHCPv6. IPv6 also supplies an alternative called *stateless autoconfiguration* (not to be confused with stateless DHCP). With stateless autoconfiguration, a host dynamically learns the /64 prefix used on the subnet, and then calculates the rest of its address by using an EUI-64 interface ID based on its network interface card (NIC) MAC address.

The stateless autoconfiguration process uses one of many features of the IPv6 Neighbor Discovery Protocol (NDP) to discover the prefix used on the LAN. NDP performs many functions for IPv6, all related to something that occurs between two hosts in the same subnet. For example, one part of NDP replaces the IPv4 ARP protocol. IPv4 ARP allows devices on the same subnet—neighbors—to learn each other's MAC address. Because this and many other activities occur only inside the local subnet between neighbors on the same link, IPv6 collected these basic functions into one protocol suite, called NDP.

Stateless autoconfiguration uses two NDP messages, namely router solicitation (RS) and router advertisement (RA) messages, to discover the IPv6 prefix used on a LAN. The host sends the RS message as an IPv6 multicast message, asking all routers to respond to the questions "What IPv6 prefix(es) is used on this subnet?" and "What is the IPv6 address(es) of any default routers on this subnet?" Figure 17-8 shows the general idea, on subnet 1 from Figure 17-6, with PC1 sending an RS, and router R1 replying with the IPv6 prefix used on the LAN and R1's own IPv6 address as a potential default router.

Figure 17-8   *Example NDP RS/RA Process to Find the Default Routers*

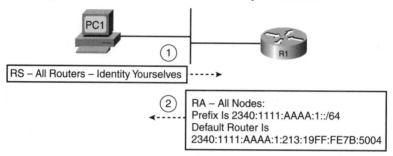

> **NOTE**   IPv6 allows multiple prefixes and multiple default routers to be listed in the RA message; the figure just shows one of each for simplicity's sake.

IPv6 does not use broadcasts. In fact, there is no such thing as a subnet broadcast address, a network-wide broadcast address, or an equivalent of the all-hosts 255.255.255.255 broadcast IPv4 address. Instead, IPv6 uses multicast addresses. By using a different multicast IPv6 address for different functions, a computer that has no need to participate in a particular function can simply ignore those particular multicasts, reducing the impact to the host. For example, the RS message only needs to be received and processed by routers, so the RS message's destination IP address is FF02::2, which is the address reserved in IPv6 to be used only by IPv6 routers. RA messages are sent to a multicast address intended for use by all IPv6 hosts on the link (FF02::1), so not only will the host that sent the RS learn the information, but all other hosts on the link will also learn the details.

Table 17-5 summarizes some of the key details about the RS/RA messages.

Table 17-5   *Details of the RS/RA Process*

Message	RS	RA
Multicast destination	FF02::2	FF02::1
Meaning of multicast address	All routers on this link	All IPv6 nodes on this link

IPv6 Address Configuration Summary

This chapter covers four methods for assigning IPv6 addresses to hosts or router interfaces. Two variations use static configuration, while two dynamically learn the address. However, with both static and dynamic configuration, two alternatives exist—one that supplies the entire IPv6 address and one that allows the host to calculate the EUI-64 interface ID. Table 17-6 summarizes the configuration methods.

Table 17-6 *IPv6 Address Configuration Options*

Static or Dynamic	Option	Portion Configured or Learned
Static	Do not use EUI-64	Entire 128-bit address
Static	Use EUI-64	Just the /64 prefix
Dynamic	Stateful DHCPv6	Entire 128-bit address
Dynamic	Stateless autoconfiguration	Just the /64 prefix

Discovering the Default Router with NDP

In IPv4, hosts discover their default router (default gateway) either through static configuration on the host or, more typically, with DHCP. IPv6 can use both of these same options as well, plus the NDP RS/RA messages as explained in the previous section. The NDP router discovery process occurs by default on IPv6 hosts and routers, so while the stateful DHCPv6 server can supply the IP address(es) of the possible default routers, it is perfectly reasonable in IPv6 to simply not bother to configure these details in a stateful DHCP server, allowing the built-in NDP RS/RA messages to be used instead.

The default router discovery process is relatively simple. Routers automatically send RA messages on a periodic basis. These messages list not only the sending router's IPv6 address but also all the known routers on that subnet. A host can wait for the next periodic RA message or request that all local routers send an RA immediately by soliciting the routers using the RS message.

Learning the IP Address(es) of DNS Servers

Like IPv4 hosts, IPv6 hosts typically need to know the IP address of one or more DNS servers to resolve names into the corresponding IP address. Oftentimes, the host also needs to learn the DNS domain name to use. And like IPv4 hosts, IPv6 hosts can be told these IP addresses using (stateful) DHCP. When a host (or router for that matter) learns its IPv6 address using stateful DHCP, the host can also learn the DNS server IP addresses and the domain name, taking care of this particular detail.

Stateless DHCP, which is most useful in conjunction with stateless autoconfiguration, is an alternative method for finding the DNS server IP addresses and the domain name. A host that uses stateless autoconfiguration can learn its IPv6 address and prefix automatically, as well as learn its default router IP address, in both cases using NDP RS/RA messages. However, the stateless autoconfiguration process does not help a host learn the DNS IP addresses and domain name. So, stateless DHCP supplies that information using the same messages as stateful DHCP. However, to supply this information, the server does not need to track any state information about each client, so a stateless DHCP server can be used.

Table 17-7 summarizes some of the key features of stateful and stateless DHCPv6.

Table 17-7 *Comparison of Stateless and Stateful DHCPv6 Services*

Feature	Stateful DHCP	Stateless DHCP
Remembers IPv6 address (state information) of clients that make requests	Yes	No
Assigns IPv6 address to client	Yes	No
Supplies useful information, like DNS server IP addresses	Yes	Yes
Is most useful in conjunction with stateless autoconfiguration	No	Yes

IPv6 Addresses

This chapter has already introduced the concepts behind the general format of IPv6 addresses, the ideas behind global unicast IPv6 addresses, and some details about multicast IPv6 addresses. The following sections round out the coverage of addressing, specifically the three categories of IPv6 address:

■ **Unicast:** IP addresses assigned to a single interface for the purpose of allowing that one host to send and receive data.

■ **Multicast:** IP addresses that represent a dynamic group of hosts for the purpose of sending packets to all current members of the group. Some multicast addresses are used for special purposes, like with NDP messages, while most support end-user applications.

■ **Anycast:** A design choice by which servers that support the same function can use the same unicast IP address, with packets sent by clients being forwarded to the nearest server, allowing load balancing across different servers.

Unicast IPv6 Addresses

IPv6 supports three main classes of unicast addresses. One of these classes, global unicast IP addresses, closely matches the purpose of IPv4 public IP addresses. Global unicast addresses are assigned by ICANN and the RIRs for the purpose of allowing globally unique IPv6 addresses for all hosts. These addresses come from inside the 2000::/3 prefix, which includes all addresses that begin with 2 or 3 (hex).

The next class of IPv6 unicast addresses covered here, *unique local* unicast addresses, have the same function as IPv4 RFC 1918 private addresses. In IPv4, most every enterprise, and most every Internet-connected small or home office, uses IPv4 private networks. *Unique local* unicast addresses begin with hex FD (FD00::/8), with the format shown in Figure 17-9.

NOTE   The original IPv6 RFCs defined a private address class called *site local*, meaning local within a site (organization). The original site local address class has been deprecated and replaced with unique local unicast addresses.

Figure 17-9 *Unique Local Address Format*

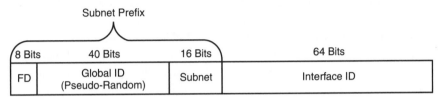

To use these addresses, an enterprise engineer would choose a 40-bit global ID in a pseudorandom manner, with the goal that hopefully the addresses will be unique in the universe. In reality, pseudorandom is probably a number made up by the engineer. The 16-bit subnet field and 64-bit interface ID work just like with global unicast addresses, numbering different subnets and hosts and allowing EUI-64 assignment of the interface ID. As usual, the engineer could avoid using EUI-64, using easier-to-remember values like 0000:0000:0000:0001 as the interface ID.

Link local addresses are the third class of unicast IPv6 addresses covered here. IPv4 has no concepts like the link local IP address. IPv6 uses these addresses when sending packets over the local subnet; routers never forward packets destined for link local addresses to other subnets.

Link local addresses can be useful for functions that do not need to leave the subnet, in particular because a host can automatically derive its own link local IP address without sending packets over the subnet. So, before sending the first packets, the host can calculate its own link local address so that the host has an IPv6 address to use when doing its first overhead messages. For example, before a host sends an NDP RS (router solicitation) message, the host will have already calculated its link local address. The host uses its link local address as the source IP address in the RS message.

Link local addresses come from the FE80::/10 range. No specific configuration is required, because a host forms these addresses by using the first 10 bits of hex FE80 (binary 1111111010), 54 more binary 0s, and the last 64 bits being the host's EUI-64 format interface ID. Figure 17-10 shows the format.

Figure 17-10 *Link Local Address Format*

10 Bits	54 Bits	64 Bits
FE80/10 1111111010	All 0s	Interface ID

Routers also use link local addresses on each interface enabled to support IPv6. Like hosts, routers automatically calculate their link local IP addresses. In fact, Example 17-1 earlier in this chapter listed the (R1) router's link local IP addresses in the output of the **show ipv6 interface** command output. Interestingly, routers normally use link local addresses as the next-hop IP address in IPv6 routes, rather than the neighboring router's global unicast or unique local unicast address.

Multicast and Other Special IPv6 Addresses

Multicast addresses can be used to communicate to dynamic groupings of hosts, with the sender sending a single packet and with the network replicating that packet as needed so that all hosts listening for packets sent to that multicast address receive a copy of the packet. IPv6 can limit the scope of where routers forward multicasts based on the value in the first quartet of the address. This book only examines multicasts that should stay on a local link; these addresses all begin with FF02::/16, so they are easily recognized.

For reference, Table 17-8 lists some of the more commonly seen IPv6 multicast addresses. Of particular interest are the addresses chosen for use by Routing Information Protocol (RIP), Open Shortest Path First (OSPF), and Enhanced IGRP (EIGRP), which somewhat mirror the multicast addresses each protocol uses for IPv4.

Table 17-8 *Common Link Local Multicast Addresses*

Purpose	IPv6 Address	IPv4 Equivalent
All IP nodes on the link	FF02::1	Subnet broadcast address
All routers on the link	FF02::2	N/A
OSPF messages	FF02::5, FF02::6	224.0.0.5, 224.0.0.6
RIP-2 messages	FF02::9	224.0.0.9
EIGRP messages	FF02::A	224.0.0.10
DHCP relay agents (routers that forward to the DHCP server)	FF02::1:2	N/A

Before completing the discussion of IPv6 addressing, you should know about a couple of special IPv6 addresses. First, IPv6 supports the concept of a loopback IP address, as follows:

::1 (127 binary 0s and a 1)

Just like the IPv4 127.0.0.1 loopback address, this address can be used to test a host's software. A packet sent by a host to this address goes down the protocol stack, and then right back up the stack, with no communication with the underlying network card. This allows testing of the software on a host, particularly when testing new applications.

The other special address is the :: address (all binary 0s). This address represents the unknown address, which hosts can use when sending packets in an effort to discover their IP addresses.

Summary of IP Protocols and Addressing

This chapter has covered a lot of concepts and details about IPv6 addresses, many of which require some work to remember or memorize. This short section pulls several concepts from throughout this major section on IPv6 protocols and addresses together before moving on to some details about routing protocols and router configuration.

When an IPv6 host first boots, it needs to do several tasks before it can send packets through a router to another host. When using one of the two methods of dynamically learning an IPv6 address that can be used to send packets past the local routers to the rest of a network, the first few initialization steps are the same, with some differences in the later steps. The following list summarizes the steps a host takes when first booting, at least for the functions covered in this chapter:

Step 1 The host calculates its IPv6 link local address (begins with FE80::/10).

Step 2 The host sends an NDP router solicitation (RS) message, with its link local address as the source address and the all-routers FF02::2 multicast destination address, to ask routers to supply a list of default routers and the prefix/length used on the LAN.

Step 3 The router(s) replies with an RA message, sourced from the router's link local address, sent to the all-IPv6-hosts-on-the-link multicast address (FF02::1), supplying the default router and prefix information.

Step 4 If the type of dynamic address assignment is stateless autoconfiguration, the following occur:

    a. The host builds the unicast IP address it can use to send packets through the router by using the prefix learned in the RA message and calculating an EUI-64 interface ID based on the NIC MAC address.

    b. The host uses DHCP messages to ask a stateless DHCP server for the DNS server IP addresses and domain name.

Step 4   If the type of dynamic address assignment is stateful DHCP, the host uses DHCP messages to ask a stateful DHCP server for a lease of an IP address/prefix length, as well as default router addresses, the DNS server IP addresses, and domain name.

> **NOTE**   Other tasks occur when a host initializes as well, but they are beyond the scope of this book.

IPv6 includes many different types of addresses, including unicast and multicast. By way of summary, Table 17-9 lists the types of IPv6 addresses mentioned by this chapter, with a few details, for easier reference when studying.

Table 17-9   *Common Link Local Multicast Addresses*

Type of Address	Purpose	Prefix	Easily Seen Hex Prefix(es)
Global unicast	Unicast packets sent through the public Internet	2000::/3	2 or 3
Unique local	Unicast packets inside one organization	FD00::/8	FD
Link Local	Packets sent in the local subnet	FE80::/10	FE8, FE9, FEA, FEB
Multicast (link local scope)	Multicasts that stay on the local subnet	FF02::/16	FF02

Configuring IPv6 Routing and Routing Protocols

To support IPv6, all the IPv4 routing protocols had to go through varying degrees of changes, with the most obvious being that each had to be changed to support longer addresses and prefixes. The following sections first examine a few details about routing protocols and then show how to configure IPv6 routing and routing protocols on Cisco routers.

IPv6 Routing Protocols

As with IPv4, most IPv6 routing protocols are interior gateway protocols (IGP), with Border Gateway Protocol (BGP) still being the only exterior gateway protocol (EGP) of note. All these current IGPs and BGP have been updated to support IPv6. Table 17-10 lists the routing protocols and their new RFCs (as appropriate).

Table 17-10 *Updates to Routing Protocols for IPv6*

Routing Protocol	Full Name	RFC
RIPng	RIP Next Generation	2080
OSPFv3	OSPF version 3	2740
MP-BGP4	Multiprotocol BGP-4	2545/4760
EIGRP for IPv6	EIGRP for IPv6	Proprietary

Each of these routing protocols has to make several changes to support IPv6. The actual messages used to send and receive routing information have changed, using IPv6 headers instead of IPv4 headers and using IPv6 addresses in those headers. For example, RIPng sends routing updates to the IPv6 destination address FF02::9, instead of the old RIP-2 IPv4 224.0.0.9 address. Also, the routing protocols typically advertise their link local IP address as the next hop in a route, as will be shown in the upcoming Example 17-2.

The routing protocols still retain many of the same internal features. For example, RIPng, being based on RIP-2, is still a distance vector protocol, with hop count as the metric and 15 hops as the longest valid route (16 is infinity). OSPFv3, created specifically to support IPv6, is still a link-state protocol, with cost as the metric but with many of the internals, including link-state advertisement (LSA) types, changed. As a result, OSPFv2, as covered in Chapter 9, "OSPF," is not compatible with OSPFv3. However, the core operational concepts remain the same.

IPv6 Configuration

Cisco router IOS enables the routing (forwarding) of IPv4 packets by default, with IPv4 being enabled on an interface when the interface has an IPv4 address configured. For IPv4 routing protocols, the routing protocol must be configured, with the **network** command indirectly enabling the routing protocol on an interface.

IPv6 configuration follows some of these same guidelines, with the largest difference being how to enable a routing protocol on an interface. Cisco router IOS does not enable IPv6 routing by default, so a global command is required to enable IPv6 routing. The unicast IP addresses need to be configured on the interfaces, similar to IPv4. The routing protocol needs to be globally configured, similar to IPv4. Finally, the routing protocol has to be configured on each interface as needed, but with IPv6, the process does not use the **network** router subcommand.

This section shows an example configuration, again showing Router R1 from the Company1 enterprise network shown in earlier figures in this chapter. The example uses

RIPng as the routing protocol. The following list outlines the four main steps to configure IPv6:

Key Topic

Step 1   Enable IPv6 routing with the **ipv6 unicast-routing** global command.

Step 2   Enable the chosen routing protocol. For example, for RIPng, use the **ipv6 router rip** *name* global configuration command.

Step 3   Configure an IPv6 unicast address on each interface using the **ipv6 address** *address/prefix-length* [**eui-64**] interface command.

Step 4   Enable the routing protocol on the interface, for example, with the **ipv6 rip** *name* **enable** interface subcommand (where the name matches the **ipv6 router rip** *name* global configuration command).

Example 17-2 shows the configuration, plus a few **show** commands. Note that the IP address configuration matches the earlier Example 17-1. Because Example 17-1 showed the address configuration, this example shows gray highlights on the new configuration commands only.

Example 17-2   *Configuring IPv6 Routing and Routing Protocols on R1*

```
R1#show running-config
! output is edited to remove lines not pertinent to this example
ipv6 unicast-routing
!
interface FastEthernet0/0
 ipv6 address 2340:1111:AAAA:1::/64 eui-64
 ipv6 rip atag enable
!
interface Serial0/0/1
 ipv6 address 2340:1111:AAAA:2::1/64
 ipv6 rip atag enable
!
interface Serial0/1/1
 ipv6 address 2340:1111:AAAA:4::/64 eui-64
 ipv6 rip atag enable
!
ipv6 router rip atag
!
R1#show ipv6 route
IPv6 Routing Table - 10 entries
Codes: C - Connected, L - Local, S - Static, R - RIP, B - BGP
       U - Per-user Static route
       I1 - ISIS L1, I2 - ISIS L2, IA - ISIS interarea, IS - ISIS summary
       O - OSPF intra, OI - OSPF inter, OE1 - OSPF ext 1, OE2 - OSPF ext 2
       ON1 - OSPF NSSA ext 1, ON2 - OSPF NSSA ext 2
R   ::/0 [120/2]
```

Example 17-2 *Configuring IPv6 Routing and Routing Protocols on R1 (Continued)*

```
        via FE80::213:19FF:FE7B:2F58, Serial0/1/1
C   2340:1111:AAAA:1::/64 [0/0]
        via ::, FastEthernet0/0
L   2340:1111:AAAA:1:213:19FF:FE7B:5004/128 [0/0]
        via ::, FastEthernet0/0
C   2340:1111:AAAA:2::/64 [0/0]
        via ::, Serial0/0/1
L   2340:1111:AAAA:2::1/128 [0/0]
        via ::, Serial0/0/1
R   2340:1111:AAAA:3::/64 [120/2]
        via FE80::213:19FF:FE7B:5026, Serial0/0/1
C   2340:1111:AAAA:4::/64 [0/0]
        via ::, Serial0/1/1
L   2340:1111:AAAA:4:213:19FF:FE7B:5004/128 [0/0]
        via ::, Serial0/1/1
L   FE80::/10 [0/0]
        via ::, Null0
L   FF00::/8 [0/0]
        via ::, Null0
R1#show ipv6 interface brief
FastEthernet0/0             [up/up]
    FE80::213:19FF:FE7B:5004
    2340:1111:AAAA:1:213:19FF:FE7B:5004
FastEthernet0/1            [up/up]
    unassigned
Serial0/0/0                [administratively down/down]
    unassigned
Serial0/0/1                [up/up]
    FE80::213:19FF:FE7B:5004
    2340:1111:AAAA:2::1
Serial0/1/0                [administratively down/down]
    unassigned
Serial0/1/1                [up/up]
    FE80::213:19FF:FE7B:5004
    2340:1111:AAAA:4:213:19FF:FE7B:5004
```

The configuration itself does not require a lot of work beyond the IPv6 address configuration shown previously in Example 17-1. The **ipv6 router rip** *name* command requires a name (formally called a tag) that is just a text name for the routing process. Example 17-2 shows the configuration, using a RIP tag named "atag". This tag does not have to match between the various routers. Otherwise, the configuration itself is straightforward.

The **show ipv6 route** command lists all the IPv6 routes, listing some important differences as highlighted in the command output. First, note the first few lines of highlighted output in that command, and the new routing code "L". For each interface with a unicast address, the router adds the usual connected route for the prefix connected to that interface. For example, the first highlighted line inside this command lists 2340:1111:AAAA:1::/64, which is the subnet connected to R1's Fa0/0 interface. The output also lists a host route— a /128 prefix length route—as a local route. Each of these local routes, as noted with the code "L," lists the specific address on each interface, respectively.

The next highlighted lines in that same **show ipv6 route** command list some interesting next-hop information in a RIP-learned route. The example highlights the route to subnet 3, listing outgoing interface S0/0/1, but the next-hop address is R2's link local IP address of FE80::213:19FF:FE7B:5026. IPv6 routing protocols typically advertise the link local addresses as next-hop addresses.

Finally, the last part of the example shows the output of the **show ipv6 interface brief** command, which lists the unicast IP addresses on each interface. The highlighted lines first show the link local address (each starts with FE8), and then the global unicast address, on R1's Fa0/0 interface. Each of the three interfaces used in this example has both the link local address, which is automatically generated, and the global unicast addresses configured, as shown in the first part of Example 17-2.

Configuring host names and DNS servers on routers for IPv4 can be a small convenience, but for IPv6, it might well be a necessity. Because of the length of IPv6 addresses, even a simple **ping** command requires a fair amount of typing and referring to other command output or documentation. So, just as with IPv4, you might want to configure static host names on routers, or refer to a DNS server, with the following two commands. Note that the commands and syntax are the same as the commands for IPv4, just with IPv6 addresses used as parameters.

- **ip host** *name ipv6-address* [*second-address* [*third-address* [*fourth-address*]]]

- **ip name-server** *server-address1* [*server-address2...server-address6*]

The first command configures a host name only known to the local routers, while the second refers to a DNS server. Note that the router attempts to act as a DNS client by default, based on the default **ip domain-lookup** global configuration command. However, if the **no ip domain-lookup** command has been configured, change the command back to **ip domain-lookup** to begin using DNS services.

While the configuration and **show** commands in Example 17-2 can be useful for learning the basics, much more is required before an internetwork can be ready for an IPv6 deployment. (*Deploying IPv6 Networks*, by Ciprian Popoviciu et al., published by Cisco Press, is a great resource if you want to read more.) The next section takes a brief look at one of the larger deployment issues, namely, how to support users during a worldwide migration from IPv4 to IPv6, which might take decades.

IPv6 Transition Options

While IPv6 solves a lot of problems, an overnight migration from IPv4 to IPv6 is ridiculous. The number of devices on Earth that use IPv4 number is well into the billions, and in some cases, even if you wanted to migrate to IPv6, the devices or their software might not even have IPv6 support, or at least well-tested IPv6 support. The migration from IPv4 to IPv6 will at least take years, if not decades.

Thankfully, much time and effort have been spent thinking about the migration process and developing standards for how to approach the migration or transition issue. The following sections introduce the main options and explain the basics. In particular, these sections examine the idea of using dual stacks, tunneling, and translation between the two versions of IP. Note that no one solution is typically enough to solve all problems; in all likelihood, a combination of these tools will need to be used in most every network.

IPv4/IPv6 Dual Stacks

The term *dual stacks* means that the host or router uses both IPv4 and IPv6 at the same time. For hosts, this means that the host has both an IPv4 and IPv6 address associated with each NIC, that the host can send IPv4 packets to other IPv4 hosts, and that the host can send IPv6 packets to other IPv6 hosts. For routers, it means that in addition to the usual IPv4 IP addresses and routing protocols covered in many of the other chapters of this book, the routers would also have IPv6 addresses and routing protocols configured, as shown in this chapter. To support both IPv4 and IPv6 hosts, the router could then receive and forward both IPv4 packets and IPv6 packets.

The dual stack approach can be a reasonable plan of attack to migrate an enterprise to IPv6 for communications inside the enterprise. The routers could be easily migrated to use dual stacks, and most desktop operating systems (OS) support IPv6 today. In some cases, the upgrade may require new software or hardware, but this approach allows a slower migration, which is not necessarily a bad thing, because the support staff needs time to learn how IPv6 works.

Tunneling

Another tool to support the IPv4-to-IPv6 transition is tunneling. Many types of tunneling exist, but in this case, the tunnel function typically takes an IPv6 packet sent by a host and encapsulates it inside an IPv4 packet. The IPv4 packet can then be forwarded over an existing IPv4 internetwork, with another device removing the IPv4 header, revealing the original IPv6 packet. The concept is very much like a VPN tunnel, as explained in Chapter 15, "Virtual Private Networks."

Figure 17-11 shows a typical example with a type of tunnel generically called an IPv6-to-IPv4 tunnel, meaning IPv6 inside IPv4. The figure shows a sample enterprise internetwork in which hosts on some of the LANs have migrated to IPv6, but the core of the network still runs IPv4. This might be the case during an initial testing phase inside an enterprise, or it could be commonly done with an IPv4-based ISP that has customers wanting to migrate to IPv6.

Figure 17-11   *Example IPv6-to-IPv4 Tunnel, Physical and Logical View*

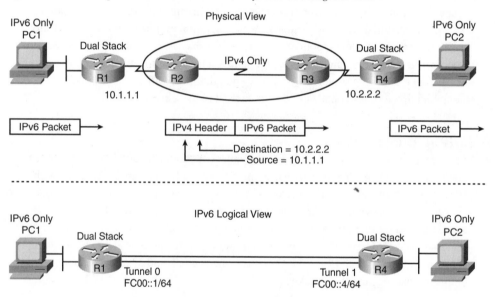

In the figure, the IPv6-based PC1 sends an IPv6 packet. Router R1 then encapsulates or tunnels the IPv6 packet into a new IPv4 header, with a destination IPv4 address of an address on Router R4. Routers R2 and R3 happily forward the packet, because it has a normal IPv4 header, while R4 de-encapsulates the original IPv6 packet, forwarding it to IPv6-based PC2. It's called a tunnel in part because the IPv6 packets inside the tunnel can't be seen while traversing the tunnel; the routers in the middle of the network, R2 and R3 in this case, perceive the packets as IPv4 packets.

Several types of IPv6-to-IPv4 tunnels exist. To perform the tunneling shown by the routers in Figure 17-11, the first three of the following types of tunnels could be used, with the fourth type (Teredo tunnels) being used by hosts:

- **Manually configured tunnels (MCT):** A simple configuration in which tunnel interfaces, a type of virtual router interface, are created, with the configuration referencing the IPv4 addresses used in the IPv4 header that encapsulates the IPv6 packet.

- **Dynamic 6to4 tunnels**: This term refers to a specific type of dynamically created tunnel, typically done on the IPv4 Internet, in which the IPv4 addresses of the tunnel endpoints can be dynamically found based on the destination IPv6 address.

- **Intra-site Automatic Tunnel Addressing Protocol (ISATAP):** Another dynamic tunneling method, typically used inside an enterprise. Unlike 6to4 tunnels, ISATAP tunnels do not work if IPv4 NAT is used between the tunnel endpoints.

- **Teredo tunneling:** This method allows dual-stack hosts to create a tunnel to another host, with the host itself both creating the IPv6 packet and encapsulating the packet inside an IPv4 header.

Figure 17-12 shows the basic idea behind the Teredo tunnel.

Figure 17-12   *Example Encapsulation for a Teredo Host-Host Tunnel*

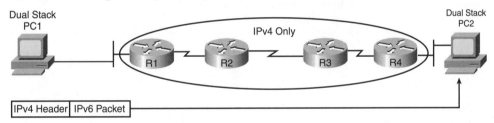

Translating Between IPv4 and IPv6 with NAT-PT

Both classes of IPv6 transition features mentioned so far in this chapter, dual stack and tunnels, rely on the end hosts to at least support IPv6, if not both IPv4 and IPv6. However, in some cases, an IPv4-only host needs to communicate with an IPv6-only host. A third class of transition features needs to be used in this case: a tool that translates the headers of an IPv6 packet to look like an IPv4 packet, and vice versa.

In Cisco routers, Network Address Translation–Protocol Translation (NAT-PT), defined in RFC 2766, can be used to perform the translation. To do its work, a router configured with NAT-PT must know what IPv6 address to translate to which IPv4 address and vice versa, the same kind of information held in the traditional NAT translation table. And like traditional NAT, NAT-PT allows static definition, dynamic NAT, and dynamic PAT, which can be used to conserve IPv4 addresses.

Transition Summary

Table 17-11 summarizes the transition options for IPv6 for easier reference and study.

Key
Topic

Table 17-11   *Summary of IPv6 Transition Options*

Name	Particular Type	Description
Dual stack	—	Supports both protocols, and sends IPv4 to IPv4 hosts and IPv6 to IPv6 hosts
Tunnel	MCT	Tunnel is manually configured; sends IPv6 through IPv4 network, typically between routers
Tunnel	6to4	Tunnel endpoints are dynamically discovered; sends IPv6 through IPv4 network, typically between routers
Tunnel	ISATAP	Tunnel endpoints are dynamically discovered; sends IPv6 through IPv4 network between routers; does not support IPv4 NAT
Tunnel	Teredo	Typically used by hosts; host creates IPv6 packet and encapsulates in IPv4
NAT-PT	—	Router translates between IPv4 and IPv6; allows IPv4 hosts to communicate with IPv6 hosts

Exam Preparation Tasks

Review All the Key Topics

Review the most important topics from this chapter, noted with the Key Topics icon in the outer margin of the page. Table 17-12 lists a reference of these key topics and the page numbers on which each is found.

Key
Topic

Table 17-12 *Key Topics for Chapter 17*

Key Topic Element	Description	Page Number
Figure 17-1	Route aggregation concepts in the global IPv6 Internet	583
List	Rules for abbreviating IPv6 addresses	585
List	Rules for writing IPv6 prefixes	587
Figure 17-3	Example prefix assignment process	588
List	Major steps in subdividing a prefix into a subnet prefix in an enterprise	590
Figure 17-5	Example and structure of IPv6 subnets	591
Figure 17-7	Structure of IPv6 addresses and EUI-64 formatted interface ID	595
Table 17-6	List of four main options to IPv6 address configuration	599
Table 17-7	Comparisons of IPv6 stateful and stateless DHCP services	600
List	Different types and purposes of IPv6 addresses	600
Figure 17-10	Format and structure of link local addresses	602
List	Summary of the steps a host takes to learn its address, prefix length, DNS, and default router	603
Table 17-9	Summary of prefixes and purpose of most common types of IPv6 addresses	604
List	Configuration checklist for IPv6 configuration	606
Table 17-11	List of IPv6 transition options	612

Complete the Tables and Lists from Memory

Print a copy of Appendix J, "Memory Tables," (found on the CD) or at least the section for this chapter, and complete the tables and lists from memory. Appendix K, "Memory Tables Answer Key," also on the CD, includes completed tables and lists to check your work.

Definitions of Key Terms

Define the following key terms from this chapter, and check your answers in the glossary:

> Dual stacks, global unicast address, ISP prefix, link local address, NAT-PT, Neighbor Discovery Protocol (NDP), Regional Internet Registry (RIR), registry prefix, site prefix, stateful DHCP, stateless autoconfiguration, stateless DHCP, subnet prefix, unique local address

Command Reference to Check Your Memory

While you should not necessarily memorize the information in the tables in this section, this section does include a reference for the configuration and EXEC commands covered in this chapter. Practically speaking, you should memorize the commands as a side effect of reading the chapter and doing all the activities in this exam preparation section. To check to see how well you have memorized the commands as a side effect of your other studies, cover the left side of the table with a piece of paper, read the descriptions on the right side, and see whether you remember the command.

Table 17-13   *Chapter 17 Configuration Command Reference*

Command	Description
ipv6 unicast-routing	Global command that enables IPv6 routing on the router
ipv6 router rip *tag*	Global command that enables RIPng
ipv6 rip *name* **enable**	Interface subcommand that enables RIPng on the interface
ipv6 address {*ipv6-address/prefix-length*	*prefix-name sub-bits/prefix-length*} **eui-64**	Interface subcommand that manually configures either the entire interface IP address, or a /64 prefix with the router building the EUI-64 format interface ID automatically
ipv6 host *name ipv6-address1* [*ipv6-address2...ipv6-address4*]	Global command to create a static host name definition
ip name-server *server-address1* [*server-address2...server-address6*]	Global command to point to one or more name servers, to resolve a name into either an IPv4 or IPv6 address
[**no**] **ip domain-lookup**	Global command that enables the router as a DNS client, or with the **no** option, disables the router as a DNS client

Table 17-14 *Chapter 17 EXEC Command Reference*

Command	Description
show ipv6 route	Lists IPv6 routes
show ipv6 route *ip-address*	Lists the route(s) this router would match for packets sent to the listed address
show ipv6 route [*prefix/prefix-length*]	Lists the route for the specifically listed prefix/length
show ipv6 interface [*type number*]	Lists IPv6 settings on an interface, including link local and other unicast IP addresses
show ipv6 interface brief	Lists interface status and IPv6 addresses for each interface

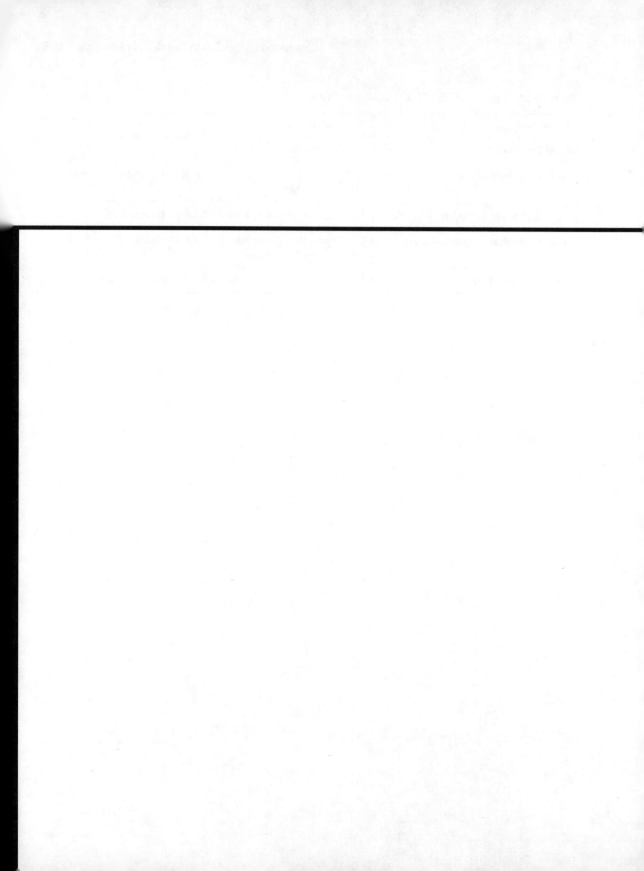

Part VI: Final Preparation

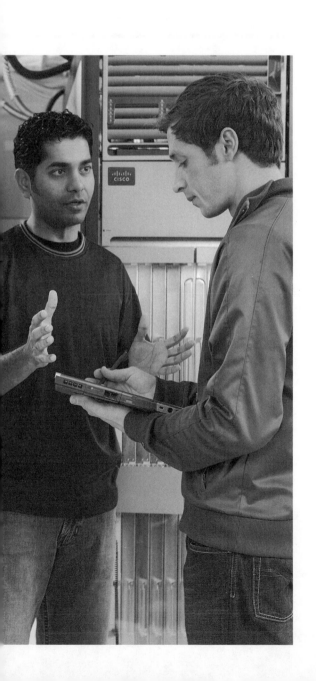

Final Preparation

The first 17 chapters of this book cover the technologies, protocols, commands, and features you need to understand to pass the ICND2 exam. Although these chapters supply the detailed information, most people need more preparation than simply reading the first 17 chapters. This chapter details a set of tools and a study plan to help you complete your preparation for the exams.

If you're preparing for the CCNA exam by reading both this book and the *CCENT/CCNA ICND1 Official Exam Certification Guide*, you know that both books have a final preparation chapter. However, you can refer to just this chapter to read about the suggested study plan, because this chapter refers to the tools in both this book and the ICND1 book. Just look for the text highlighted in gray, like this sentence, for suggestions that apply to CCNA (640-802) exam preparation, but not to ICND2 (640-816) exam preparation.

This short chapter has two main sections. The first section lists the exam preparation tools that can be useful at this point in your study process. The second section lists a suggested study plan now that you have completed all the earlier chapters.

NOTE This chapter references many of the book's chapters and appendixes, as well as tools available on the CD. Some of the appendixes, beginning with Appendix D, are included only on the CD that comes with this book. To access those, just insert the CD and make the appropriate selection from the opening interface.

Tools for Final Preparation

This section lists some information about the available tools and how to access them.

Exam Engine and Questions on the CD

The CD includes an exam engine—software that displays and then grades a set of exam-realistic questions. These include simulation (sim) questions, drag-and-drop, and many scenario-based questions that require the same level of analysis as the questions on the ICND2 and CCNA exams. Using the exam engine, you can either practice using the questions in Study Mode or take a simulated (timed) ICND2 or CCNA exam.

The installation process has two major steps. The CD includes a recent copy of the exam engine software, supplied by Boson Software (http://www.boson.com). The practice exam—the database of ICND2 exam questions—is not on the CD. Instead, the practice exam resides on the http://www.boson.com web server, so the second major step is to activate and download the practice exam.

> **NOTE**   The cardboard CD case in the back of this book includes the CD and a piece of paper. The paper lists the activation key for the practice exam associated with this book. *DO NOT LOSE THE ACTIVATION KEY.*

Install the Software from the CD

The software installation process is pretty routine compared with other software installation processes. The following steps outline the process:

Step 1   Insert the CD into your PC.

Step 2   The software that automatically runs is the Cisco Press software to access and use all CD-based features, including the exam engine, viewing a PDF of this book, and viewing the CD-only appendices. From the main menu, click the option to **Install the Exam Engine**.

Step 3   Respond to prompt windows, as you would with any typical software installation process.

The installation process might give you the option to register the software. This process requires that you establish a login at the http://www.boson.com website. You will need this login to activate the exam, so feel free to register when prompted. If you already have a login at the http://www.boson.com site, you don't need to register again. Just use your existing login.

Activate and Download the Practice Exam

After the exam engine is installed, you should activate the exam associated with this book:

Step 1   Start the Boson Exam Environment (BEE) software from the Start menu. It should be installed in a Cisco Press folder on your computer.

Step 2   The first time you start the software, it should ask you to either log in, or register an account. If you do not already have an account with Boson, select the option to register a new account. (You must register to download and use the exam.)

Step 3   After you are registered, the software might prompt you to download the latest version of the software, which you should do. Note that this process updates the exam engine software (formally called the Boson Exam Environment). It does not activate the practice exam.

Step 4   To activate and download the exam associated with this book, from the exam engine main window, click the **Exam Wizard** button.

Step 5   From the Exam Wizard pop-up window, select **Activate a purchased exam** and click the **Next** button. (Although you did not purchase the exam directly, you purchased it indirectly when you purchased this book.)

Step 6   On the next screen, enter the Activation Key from the paper inside the cardboard CD holder in the back of the book, and click the **Next** button.

Step 7   The activation process downloads the practice exam. When this is done, the main exam engine menu should list a new exam, with a name such as "ExSim for Cisco Press ICND2 ECG." If you do not see the exam, be sure you have selected the My Exams tab on the menu. You may need to click the plus sign icon (+) to expand the menu to see the exam.

At this point, the software and practice exam are ready to use.

Activating Other Exams

You need to go through the exam software installation process and the registration process only once. After that, for each new exam, only a few steps are required. For example, if you bought both this book and the *CCENT/CCNA ICND1 Official Exam Certification Guide*, you could follow the steps listed here to install the software and activate the exam associated with this book. Then, for the practice exam associated with the ICND1 book, which has about 150 exam-realistic ICND1 questions, you need to follow only a few more steps. All you have to do is start the exam engine (if it is not still up and running) and follow Steps 4 through 6 from the preceding list. In fact, if you purchase other Cisco Press books, or purchase a practice exam from Boson, you just need to activate each new exam as described in Steps 4 through 6.

You can also purchase additional practice exams from Boson directly from its website. When you purchase an exam, you receive an activation key, and then you can activate and download the exam—again without requiring any additional software installation.

The Cisco CCNA Prep Center

Cisco provides a wide variety of CCNA preparation tools at a Cisco Systems website called the CCNA Prep Center. The CCNA Prep Center includes demonstrations of the exam's user interface, sample questions, informational videos, discussion forums, and other tools.

To use the CCNA Prep Center, you need a registered login at http://www.cisco.com. To register, simply go to http://www.cisco.com, click **Register** at the top of the page, and supply some information. (You do not need to work for Cisco or one of its partners to get a login.)

After you have registered, proceed to http://www.cisco.com/go/prepcenter, and look for the link to the CCNA Prep Center. There, you can log in and explore the many features.

Subnetting Videos, Reference Pages, and Practice Problems

Being able to analyze the IP addressing and subnetting used in any IPv4 network may be the single most important skill for all the CCNA exams. The *CCENT/CCNA ICND1 Official Exam Certification Guide*'s Chapter 12, "IP Addressing and Subnetting," covers most of those details, with this book's Chapter 5, "VLSM and Route Summarization," adding to the puzzle by explaining VLSM. (In case you do not have the ICND1 book, ICND1's Chapter 12 is included with this book as CD-only Appendix H, "ICND1 Chapter 12: IP Addressing and Subnetting.")

This book includes several tools to help you practice and refine your subnetting skills:

■ **Subnetting Reference Pages:** CD-only Appendix E, "Subnetting Reference Pages," summarizes the binary and decimal shortcut processes explained in both ICND1's Chapter 12 and this book's Chapter 5. Each reference page lists a single process related to subnetting, along with reference information useful for that process. These summarized processes may be a more convenient tool when you're practicing subnetting, as compared to flipping pages in the subnetting chapters, looking for the correct process.

■ **Subnetting Videos:** The DVD included with this book has a series of subnetting videos. These videos show you how to use the shortcut processes to find the answers to popular subnetting questions. You can select and play the videos from a simple menu that starts when you insert the DVD into a DVD drive.

■ **Subnetting Practice:** CD-only Appendix D, "Subnetting Practice," contains a variety of subnetting practice problems, including 25 problems for which you need to find the subnet number, subnet broadcast address, and range of valid IP addresses. This appendix shows you how to use both binary and shortcut processes to find the answers.

Scenarios

As mentioned in the introduction to this book, some of the exam questions require you to use the same skills commonly used to troubleshoot problems in real networks. The troubleshooting sections and chapters of both the ICND1 and ICND2 books help prepare you for those kinds of questions.

Another way to prepare for troubleshooting questions on the exams is to think through many different network scenarios, predicting what should occur, and investigating whether the network is performing as it should. Appendix F, "Additional Scenarios," in both this book and the ICND1 book, includes several scenarios that include some tasks you should attempt before reading the suggested solution listed later in the appendix. By reading these scenarios and doing the exercises, you can practice some of the skills required when analyzing and troubleshooting networks.

Study Plan

You could simply study using all the available tools, as mentioned earlier in this chapter. However, this section suggests a particular study plan, with a sequence of tasks that may work better than just using the tools randomly. However, feel free to use the tools in any way and at any time that helps you fully prepare for the exam.

If you are only preparing for the ICND2 exam, you can ignore the gray highlighted portions of this study plan. If you are studying for the CCNA exam by using the ICND1 book as well, include the tasks highlighted in gray.

The suggested study plan separates the tasks into four categories:

- **Recall the Facts:** Activities that help you remember all the details from the first 17 chapters of this book.

- **Practice Subnetting:** You must master subnetting to succeed on the ICND1, ICND2, and CCNA exams. This category lists the items you can use to practice subnetting skills.

- **Build Troubleshooting Skills Using Scenarios:** To answer some exam questions that present a scenario, you may need to recall facts, do subnetting math quickly and accurately, and use a hands-on simulator—all to answer a single question. This plan section suggests activities that help you pull together these different skills.

- **Use the Exam Engine to Practice Realistic Questions:** You can use the exam engine on the CD to study using a bank of unique exam-realistic questions available only with this book.

Recall the Facts

As with most exams, you must recall many facts, concepts, and definitions to do well on the test. This section suggests a couple of tasks that should help you remember all the details:

Step 1 **Review and repeat, as needed, the activities in the "Exam Preparation Tasks" section at the end of each chapter.** Most of these activities help you refine your knowledge of a topic while also helping you memorize the facts. For CCNA exam preparation, do this for Chapters 2 through 17 in the ICND1 book, as well as Chapters 1 through 17 in this book.

Step 2 **Review all the "Do I Know This Already?" quiz questions at the beginning of the chapters.** Although the questions might be familiar, reading through them again will help improve your recall of the topics covered in the questions. Also, the DIKTA questions tend to cover the most important topics from the chapter, and it never hurts to drill on those topics.

Practice Subnetting

Without question, absolutely the most important skill you need to succeed in passing the ICND1, ICND2, and CCNA exams is to be able to accurately, confidently, and quickly answer subnetting questions. The CCNA exams all have some element of time pressure; the most stressful questions are the sim, simlet, and subnetting questions. So, you should practice subnetting math and processes until you can consistently find the correct answer in a reasonable amount of time.

Before I suggest how you should prepare for subnetting questions, please note that there are many alternative methods for finding the answers to subnetting questions. For example, you can use binary math for all 32 bits of the addresses and subnet numbers. Alternatively, you could recognize that 3 of the 4 octets in most subnetting problems are easily predicted without binary math, and then use binary math in the final interesting octet. Another option would be to use decimal shortcuts. (This topic is covered in ICND1's Chapter 12 and this book's Appendix H.) Shortcuts require no binary math, but they do require you to practice a process until you've memorized it. You can even use variations on these processes as taught in other books or classes.

Whichever process you prefer, you should practice it until you can use it accurately, confidently, and quickly.

The following list of suggested activities includes practice activities that you can use regardless of the process you choose. In some cases, this list includes items that help you learn the shortcuts included with this book:

Step 1   **View or Print Appendix E, "Subnetting Reference Pages."** This short CD-only appendix includes a series of single-page summaries of the subnetting processes found in ICND1's Chapter 12 (and this book's Appendix H, which is a copy of ICND1's Chapter 12.) Appendix E includes reference pages that summarize both the binary and decimal shortcut subnetting processes.

Step 2   **Watch the subnetting videos found on the CCNA video DVD found in the back of this book.** These videos show examples of how to use some of the more detailed shortcut processes to help ensure that you know how to use the processes. CCNA exam candidates: The subnetting videos are on DVDs included with both books. They are identical, so you can watch the videos from either DVD.

Step 3   **View or print Appendix D, "Subnetting Practice."** This CD-only appendix includes enough subnetting practice problems so that, through repetition, you can significantly improve your speed and internalize the shortcut processes. Plan on working on these problems until you can consistently get the right answer, quickly, and you no longer have to sit back and think about the process for finding the answer. The goal is to make the process for finding the answers to such problems automatic. CCNA exam candidates: the ICND2 Appendix D contains all the problems from ICND1's Appendix D, plus a few others, so use ICND2's Appendix D.

Step 4   **Practice Subnetting with Cisco's Subnetting Game.** Cisco has a subnetting game, available at the Cisco CCNA Prep Center. It prompts you with various subnetting scenarios, and makes practicing subnetting fun. Just go to the CCNA Prep Center (http://www.cisco.com/go/prepcenter), log in with your Cisco.com User ID, select the **Additional Information** tab, and look for the link to download the game. (If you do not have a login, you can establish one from this web page.)

Step 5   **Develop your own practice problems using a subnet calculator.** You can download many free subnet calculators from the Internet, including one available from Cisco as part of the CCNA Prep Center. You can make up your own subnetting problems like those in Appendix D, do the problems, and then test your answers by using the subnet calculator.

Build Troubleshooting Skills Using Scenarios

Just as a real problem in a real network may be caused by a variety of issues—a routing protocol, a bad cable, Spanning Tree, an incorrect ACL, or even errors in your documentation about the internetwork—the exam makes you apply a wide range of knowledge to answer individual questions. The one activity for this section is as follows:

- **Review the scenarios included in Appendix F of this book.** These scenarios make you think about issues covered in multiple chapters of the book. They also require more abstract thought to solve the problem. CCNA exam candidates should review the scenarios in Appendix F of both books.

Use the Exam Engine

The exam engine includes two basic modes:

- **Study mode** is most useful when you want to use the questions to learn and practice. In study mode, you can select options such as whether you want to randomize the order of the questions, randomize the order of the answers, automatically see the answers, refer to specific sections of the text that reside on the CD, and many other options.

- **Simulation mode** presents questions in a timed environment, providing you with a more exam realistic experience. However, it restricts your ability to see your score as you progress through the exam, view the answers as you are taking the exam, and refer to sections of the text. These timed exams not only allow you to study for the actual ICND2 and CCNA exams, they also help you simulate the time pressure of the actual exam.

Choosing Study or Simulation Mode

Both study mode and simulation mode are useful for preparing for the exams. It's easy to choose one of the modes from the exam engine's user interface. The following steps show you how to move to the screen where you select study or simulation mode:

Step 1 Click the **Choose Exam** button. The exam should be listed under the title **ExSim for Cisco Press ICND2 ECG**.

Step 2 Click the exam's name once, to highlight it.

Step 3 Click the **Load Exam** button.

The engine should display a window. Here you can choose **Simulation Mode** or **Study Mode** using the radio buttons on the right side of the window.

Choosing the Right Exam Option

The exam engine has many options. You need to choose from one of the three listed exams on the left side of the window, and select either simulation or study mode. Additionally, depending on these two choices, you can potentially modify many other small settings. Although this is a useful tool, it can be difficult to figure out which options to choose to perform the following four primary tasks:

- Study for the ICND2 exam

- Study for the CCNA exam

- Simulate the ICND2 exam

- Simulate the CCNA exam

To support the ability to study for and simulate both the ICND2 and CCNA exams, the practice test includes two separate hidden question banks. The first bank includes about 150 unique questions written specifically for the ICND2 exam. The second bank includes a subset of the ICND1 question bank written for the *CCENT/CCNA ICND1 Official Exam Certification Guide*.

When studying for or simulating the CCNA exam, you must choose an option that includes both the ICND2 and ICND1 questions. To study for or simulate the ICND2 exam, you must choose an exam option that includes only ICND2 questions. The following list outlines the three options from the menu, and the questions served by the exam engine for each choice:

- **Cisco ICND2 Exam:** ICND2 questions only

- **Custom Exam:** ICND2 questions only

- **Full CCNA Exam:** Both ICND1 and ICND2 questions

You might want to experiment with some of the options. After you have chosen to either study using these questions or simulate an exam, Table 18-1 lists the four main options, along with how to pick the right options from the user interface.

Table 18-1   *Directions for What to Choose from the Menu to Study or Simulate the Exam*

If you want to...	choose this exam...	...and this mode...	...and modify these additional settings:
Study for ICND2	Cisco ICND2 Book Exam	Study	No specific settings required
Simulate ICND2	Custom Exam	—	Select the timed exam option, 55 questions, 75 minutes. Deselect **Show current score during exam** and select **Never** under **Show answers and explanations**.
Study for CCNA	Full CCNA Exam	Study	No specific settings are required
Simulate CCNA	Full CCNA Exam	Simulation	No specific settings are required

In addition to these main four study options, the custom exam option has a particularly useful feature for exam study. With this option, by clicking the **Modify Settings** button, you can select the questions to study by chapter. So, if you want to use the question bank for study, and you are studying by chapter or groups of chapters, you can select the questions associated with those chapters.

Summary

The tools and suggestions listed in this chapter were designed with one goal in mind: to help you develop the skills required to pass the ICND2 and CCNA exams. This book, and its companion ICND1 book, were developed not just to tell you the facts, but to help you learn how to apply the facts. No matter what your experience level when you take the exams, it is our hope that the broad range of preparation tools, and even the structure of the books and the focus on troubleshooting, will help you pass the exams with ease. I wish you well on the exams.

Part VII: Appendixes

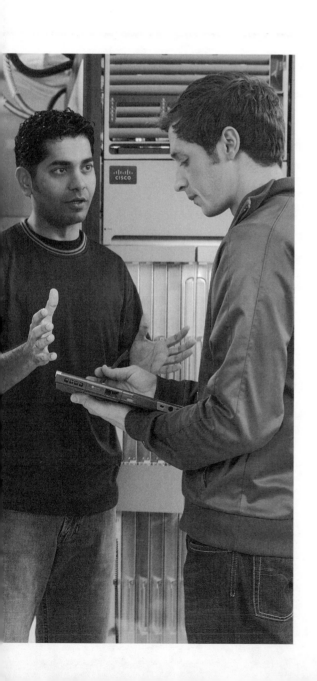

Answers to the "Do I Know This Already?" Quizzes

Chapter 1

1. B

2. D. While a subnet and a VLAN are not equivalent concepts, the devices in one VLAN are typically in the same subnet, and vice versa.

3. B

4. C

5. B and C

6. A and C. The **auto** setting means that the switch can negotiate trunking, but it can only respond to negotiation messages, and it cannot initiate the negotiation process. So, the other switch must be configured to trunk or to initiate the negotiation process (based on being configured with the **dynamic desirable** option.)

7. A. The default VTP setting of VTP server mode means that the switch can configure VLANs, so the VLAN is configured. However, being in server mode, the configuration commands only show up in the show vlan brief command output, and are not listed as part of the running-config file.

8. B and C

9. C. VTP does not require a password, although if a password is used, the password must match. VTP sends VTP updates immediately after a VLAN database change. However, VTP only sends VTP messages over trunks, and 2960s default to using a trunking administrative mode of **auto**, which does not initiate the trunking negotiation process. So, none of the switches automatically form a trunk, and no VTP messages are sent.

10. C and D. The domain name and password must be equal, and the switches must connect using a trunk before VTP will work. It is normal to have some switches as servers and some as clients. A mismatched pruning configuration setting does not prevent the synchronization of VLAN databases.

Chapter 2

1. A and B. Listening and Learning are transitory port states, used only when moving from the Blocking to the Forwarding State. Discarding is not an 802.1d STP port state.

2. C and D. Listening and Learning are transitory port states, used only when moving from the Blocking to the Forwarding state. Discarding is not an 802.1d STP port state. Forwarding and Blocking are stable states.

3. C. The smallest numeric bridge ID wins the election.

4. B. Nonroot switches forward Hellos received from the root; the root sends these Hellos based on the root's configured Hello timer.

5. E

6. B and D. The IEEE 802.1w standard, called Rapid STP, provides much faster STP convergence.

7. B and D. RSTP uses port states of Forwarding, Learning, and Discarding, with Forwarding and Learning States performing the same basic functions as the STP port states with the same name.

8. B and C

9. B. Cisco switches use the extended system ID format for bridge IDs by default, in which the priority field is broken down into a base priority value (32,768 in this case) plus the VLAN ID. The priority of this switch allows it to be capable of being the root switch, but the command output does not supply enough information to know whether this switch is currently root.

10. B. The two interfaces default to a port cost of 19 (Fa0/13) and 4 (Gi0/1), making SW3's cost to reach the root 10 + 19 = 29 out Fa0/13, and 20 + 4 = 24 over Gi0/1. SW3 therefore chooses Gi0/1 as its root port. SW3 could then advertise a cost of 24 (cost to reach the root) Hello out Fa0/13, but it would be inferior to the Hello already being received on Fa0/13 (cost 10), so SW3 would not choose Fa0/13 as a designated port.

Chapter 4

1. D. The host might need to use Dynamic Host Configuration Protocol (DHCP) to acquire an IP address, and it would likely use Domain Name System (DNS) to resolve www.ciscopress.com into an IP address. It would also use Address Resolution Protocol (ARP) to find the default gateway's MAC address, because the ARP cache would have been cleared as part of the boot process.

2. B. The **ping 2.1.1.2** command does not use a host name, so no DNS server is required. A DHCP client does not need to know the DHCP server's IP address to use DHCP. There's no such thing as an ARP server. However, to send the packet to another subnet, the PC needs to know the IP address of its default gateway.

3. A and F

4. C. With the **no ip subnet-zero** command configured, the router will not allow any interfaces to be configured with an IP address in the zero subnet. Of the listed answers, subnet 10.0.0.0 255.254.0.0 is a zero subnet, with a range of addresses from 10.0.0.1 to 10.1.255.254. The **ip address 10.1.2.2 255.254.0.0** command would be rejected.

5. A, C, E. The **ip route** command must define the static route; the "s" in the output means "static". However, the interface referenced or implied by the route must also be up/up, and IP must be enabled on the outgoing interface as well, typically with the configuration of the **ip address** command.

6. A. The correct syntax lists a subnet number, then a subnet mask in dotted decimal form, and then either an outgoing interface or a next-hop IP address.

7. A

8. B. With classless routing enabled, the router uses the default route if no other routes are matched. The line beginning "Gateway of last resort . . ." lists the IP address of the next-hop router, 168.13.1.101, which will be used as the default route.

Chapter 5

1. B, C, and D

2. A. Note that sometimes VLSM stands for variable-length subnet masking, which refers to the process of using different masks in the same classful network, whereas variable-length subnet mask refers to the subnet masks themselves.

3. C and D. Subnet 10.5.0.0 255.255.240.0 implies range 10.5.0.0–10.5.15.255, which does not overlap. 10.4.0.0 255.254.0.0 implies range 10.4.0.0–10.5.255.255, which does overlap. 10.5.32.0 255.255.224.0 implies range 10.5.32.0–10.5.63.255, which does overlap. 10.5.0.0 255.255.128.0 implies range 10.5.0.0– 10.5.127.255, which does overlap.

4. C. All the listed answers include the range of all three subnets, except for 10.3.64.0 255.255.224.0, which implies an address range of 10.3.64.0–10.3.95.255. Of the other three answers, 10.3.64.0 255.255.192.0 is the smallest range (10.3.64.0–10.3.127.255). It also happens to be the smallest single summary route that includes all three subnets listed in the question.

5. C and D. 10.0.0.0 255.0.0.0 implies a range of all addresses that begin with 10, and 10.1.0.0 255.255.0.0 implies a range of all addresses that begin with 10.1, so both these answers include all the address ranges listed in the question. 10.1.32.0 255.255.224.0 implies a range of 10.1.32.0–10.1.63.255, which includes all addresses listed in the question. 10.1.55.0 255.255.255.0 implies a range of only 10.1.55.0–10.1.55.255, which does not include all addresses. 10.1.48.0 255.255.248.0 implies a range of 10.1.48.0–10.1.55.255, which omits two of the subnets listed in the question.

6. B, C, and D

7. A, B, and C

8. A. Discontiguous networks are allowed as long as autosummarization is disabled. OSPF does not even support autosummarization, so using OSPF would solve the problem. RIP-1 cannot disable autosummarization. EIGRP can disable autosummarization, but it is on by default.

Chapter 6

1. A and C. Standard ACLs check the source IP address. The address range 10.1.1.1– 10.1.1.4 can be matched by an ACL, but it requires multiple **access-list** commands. Matching all hosts in Barney's subnet can be accomplished with the **access-list 1 permit 10.1.1.0 0.0.0.255** command.

2. D. 0.0.0.255 matches all packets that have the same first 3 octets. This is useful when you want to match a subnet in which the subnet part comprises the first 3 octets, as in this case.

3. E. 0.0.15.255 matches all packets with the same first 20 bits. This is useful when you want to match a subnet in which the subnet part comprises the first 20 bits, as in this case.

4. E and F. Extended ACLs can look at the Layer 3 (IP) and Layer 4 (TCP, UDP) headers, and a few others, but not any application layer information. Named extended ACLs can look for the same fields as a numbered extended ACL.

5. A and E. The correct range of ACL numbers for extended IP access lists is 100 to 199 and 2000 to 2699. The answers that list the **eq www** parameter after 10.1.1.1 match the source port number, and the packets are going toward the web server, not away from it.

6. E. Because the packet is going toward any web client, you need to check for the web server's port number as a source port. The client IP address range is not specified in the question, but the servers are, so the source address beginning with 172.16.5 is the correct answer.

7. E. Named extended IP ACLs can match the exact same set of fields as can numbered extended IP ACLs.

8. A and C. Before IOS 12.3, numbered ACLs must be removed and then reconfigured to remove a line from the ACL. As of IOS 12.3, you can also use ACL configuration mode and sequence numbers to delete one ACL line at a time.

9. C. The authorized Cisco curriculum makes the suggestion in answer C for extended IP ACLs, suggesting that standard ACLs be placed as close to the destination as possible.

10. C. Dynamic ACLs require the user to telnet to the router and authenticate using a username and password, which then causes the router to permit packets sent by the host.

Chapter 8

1. A and B

2. D and F

3. C and D

4. B, C, D, and E

5. B. Distance vector protocols rely on periodic full routing updates from their neighbors to confirm that the neighbor is still working.

6. D. Split horizon causes a router to not advertise routes out an interface if the route would cause packets to be sent out that same interface.

7. D. Route poisoning means advertising the failed route with an "infinite" metric, as opposed to simply ceasing to advertise the route. Poison reverse is route poisoning by advertising a route that previously was not advertised because of split horizon.

8. D. The router should not immediately send a full update. Instead, distance vector protocols immediately send a partial routing update, listing just the poisoned route.

9. B. Link-state protocols reflood each LSA on a periodic but longer timer. With RIP, the update timer is 30 seconds, and with OSPF, the timer is 30 minutes.

10. B. Link-state protocols collect information about the internetwork in the form of LSAs, which sit in memory in the link-state database. The router then runs the SPF algorithm to calculate that router's best metric route to reach each subnet.

Chapter 9

1. A. OSPF calculates metrics based on the cost associated with each interface. OSPF, by default, calculates interface cost based on the bandwidth setting.

2. A and D. OSPF uses the SPF algorithm, conceived by a mathematician named Dijkstra.

3. A and D. Routers must use the same authentication type and, if so, the same authentication key. Additionally, the subnet number and range of addresses, as calculated from the interfaces' IP addresses and masks, must be the same subnet.

4. B. Neighboring OSPF routers that complete the database exchange are considered fully adjacent and rest in a Full neighbor state.

5. D and E. The DR is elected based on the highest OSPF priority. If there is a tie, it is based on the highest OSPF RID. However, after the DR is elected, the DR role cannot be taken over by a better router until the DR and BDR have lost connectivity to the subnet. The DR attempts to be fully adjacent to all other routers on the subnet as part of the optimized database exchange process.

6. B. The **network 10.0.0.0 0.255.255.255 area 0** command works, because it matches all interfaces whose first octet is 10. The **network 10.0.0.1 0.255.255.0 area 0** command uses matching logic that matches all interfaces whose first octet is 10 and last octet is 1, which matches all three interface IP addresses. However, the wildcard mask used in OSPF **network** commands can have only one string of consecutive binary 1s, with all other digits as binary 0s, and this wildcard mask breaks that rule.

7. A. The **network 0.0.0.0 255.255.255.255 area 0** command matches all IP addresses as a result of the 255.255.255.255 wildcard mask, so this command enables OSPF in Area 0 on all interfaces. The answer with wildcard mask 0.255.255.0 is illegal, because it represents more than one string of binary 0s separated by binary 1s. The answer with x's is syntactically incorrect. The answer with wildcard mask 255.0.0.0 means "Match all addresses whose last 3 octets are 0.0.0," so none of the three interfaces are matched.

8. A, B, and E

9. B and D. For R2's neighbor state for R3 to be Full, R2 and R3 must have passed the authentication process as required by R2's configuration. The only way to configure a matching authentication key is with the **ip ospf message-digest-key** command, so answer B is correct. However, R3 may enable MD5 authentication in two ways: one using the command listed in answer A and also by configuring the OSPF subcommand **area x authentication message-digest**, which changes the default for all interfaces in that area. So Answer A is not correct, because that command is not required. R1's failure could be for many reasons, making D correct and C incorrect.

10. D. The OSPF **maximum-paths** *number* router subcommand sets the number of equal-cost routes added to the routing table. This command defaults to a setting of 4.

Chapter 10

1. A and B

2. D

3. B. The Feasible Distance (FD) is, for all known routes to reach a subnet, the metric for the best of those routes. The best route is called the successor route, and it is added to the IP routing table.

4. C. A route's reported distance (RD) is the metric used by the neighbor that advertised the route. A router uses it to determine which routes meet the feasibility condition for whether the route can be a feasible successor route.

5. A and C. The EIGRP **network** command supports a parameter of a classful network, enabling EIGRP on all interfaces in that classful network, or an address and wildcard mask. In the latter case, interface IP addresses that match the configured address, when applying ACL-like logic with the wildcard mask, match the command.

6. C and D. The EIGRP **network 10.0.0.2 0.0.0.0** command exactly matches the interface with address 10.0.0.2 because of the wildcard mask, enabling EIGRP on that interface. The EIGRP ASN value must match on both routers. The **network 10** command is syntactically incorrect; the entire classful network must be configured.

7. C. The first number in parentheses is the computed metric for a route, and the second number is the reported distance (RD) for the route. The route through 10.1.6.3 is the successor route, so it is not a feasible successor route. For the other two routes, only the third route's RD is less than or equal to the feasible distance (the metric of the successor route).

8. B and D. The MD5 key must be configured. It is not configured with an interface subcommand, but rather as part of a key chain. The useful lifetime of a key may be configured, but it is not required.

9. F

Chapter 12

1. C. Of the possible answers, only PAP and CHAP are PPP authentication protocols. PAP sends the password as clear text between the two devices.

2. C. The PPP Link Control Protocol (LCP) controls functions that apply to the link regardless of the Layer 3 protocol, including looped link detection, link quality monitoring, and authentication.

3. A and D. Both routers need an **encapsulation ppp** command, and both also will need IP addresses, before the ping will work. R1 does not need a **clock rate** command, because R2 is connected to the DCE cable.

4. D. The **username** command on one router should refer to the case-sensitive hostname of the other router.

5. B and D. The output lists encapsulation PPP, meaning that it is configured to use PPP. The line and protocol status are both up, LCP is open, and both CDPCP and IPCP are open, meaning that IP and CDP packets can be sent over the link.

6. C and D. Physical layer problems typically result in a line status (first status code) value of "down." A remote router IP address in a different subnet would not prevent a PPP-configured interface from reaching a protocol status (second line status) of "up." If the other end of the link was misconfigured to use HDLC, or if it was configured for PPP but CHAP authentication failed, the interface could be in an "up and down" state, as shown.

7. B. With PPP, two routers can use IP addresses in different subnets on opposite ends of the links, and a ping to the other router's serial IP address works. However, this subnet mismatch causes routing protocols to fail when forming neighbor relationships to exchange routes, so neither router learns EIGRP routes from the other.

Chapter 13

1. C. The LMI manages the link between the DTE and the switch, including noticing when a virtual circuit (VC) comes up or goes down.

2. A and D. The DTE typically sits at the customer site, and the DCE sits at the service provider site. Frame Relay switches send LMI messages to DTEs (typically routers) to signal VC status. A Frame Relay frame does not have a source and destination DLCI, but a single DLCI field.

3. A

4. C. The DLCI addresses a VC, not a router. The DLCI value in the frame as it crosses the local link represents that VC on that link. Because the question refers to a frame crossing the access link connected to R1, 222 is the local DLCI on R1 that identifies that VC.

5. B and C. The global DLCIs represent the DLCI the other routers use when sending frames over their local access links. So, when R1 sends a frame to R2, when the frame crosses R2's access link, the network has changed the DLCI to R1's global DLCI, 101. Similarly, when R3 sends a frame to R1, as the frame crosses R3's access link, the frame has R1's global DLCI in it, 101.

6. A. A single subnet can be used in any Frame Relay topology, but with a full mesh, a single subnet can be used with no tricky issues related to routing protocols.

7. D. BarneyCo has a total of ten VCs. With all of them configured on point-to-point subinterfaces, you need ten subnets, because you need one subnet per VC.

8. A. The frame that experienced the congestion was going from R1 to R2, so the frame with the Backward (opposite direction) Explicit Congestion Notification (BECN) bit set would go in the opposite direction, from R2 back to R1.

Chapter 14

1. C. The correct keywords are **ansi** and **q933**. However, the routers autodetect the LMI type by default, so not configuring the LMI also works.

2. C, D, and E. The LMI type is autosensed by default. Inverse ARP is on by default as well, meaning that it does not need to be enabled with the **frame-relay inverse-arp** command, nor do any static mapping statements need to be added.

3. A and E. The IP address moves to the subinterface, so it needs to be removed from the serial interface first (with the **no ip address** command). The encapsulation stays on the physical interface. The **frame-relay interface-dlci** command must be used on the subinterface so that the router knows which DLCI goes with which subinterface—even if only one DLCI exists.

4. F. You can code only one DLCI on a **frame-relay interface-dlci** command, and you need one for each VC under the multipoint interface.

5. F

6. C and E. Up and down are not PVC status codes. Inactive means that the switch thinks a defined PVC is not working, and deleted means that the DLCI is not defined at the switch.

7. D. For a Frame Relay subinterface to be in an up/up state, the underlying physical interface must be in an up/up state, and at least one of the PVCs associated with the subinterface must be in one of the two working PVC states (active or static).

8. B and C. For a Frame Relay physical interface to have a line status of "up," the same physical layer features as used on leased lines must be working. To also have a protocol status of "down," either the router is missing the **encapsulation frame-relay** command, or the router and switch disagree about the LMI type.

Chapter 15

1. A. Extranet VPNs connect sites in different but cooperating companies. Access VPNs provide access to individual users, typically from home or while traveling. The term "enterprise VPN" is not generally used to describe a type of VPN.

2. C. Antivirus software is an important security function, but it is not a function provided by the VPN itself.

3. A and C. Encapsulating Security Payload (ESP) headers support all four of the functions listed in the answers, whereas the Authentication Header (AH) only supports authentication and message integrity.

4. A. Of these answers, only Data Encryption Standard (DES), Triple DES (3DES), and Advanced Encryption Standard (AES) are encryption tools for encrypting the entire packet. AES provides better encryption and less computation time among the three options.

5. A, D, and E. All the devices and software listed in the answers can be used to terminate a VPN tunnel. However, ASAs have replaced PIX firewalls and VPN concentrators in the Cisco product line.

6. A and C. The client always uses Secure Socket Layer (SSL) to connect to the Web VPN server, so all Internet communications are encrypted. One major advantage of Web VPN is that the client does not need to have any client software, just using the built-in SSL capabilities of typical web browsers.

Chapter 16

1. F

2. D. CIDR's original intent was to allow the summarization of multiple Class A, B, and C networks to reduce the size of Internet routing tables. Of the answers, only 200.1.0.0 255.255.0.0 summarizes multiple networks.

3. B and E. RFC 1918 identifies private network numbers. It includes Class A network 10.0.0.0, Class B networks 172.16.0.0 through 172.31.0.0, and Class C networks 192.168.0.0 through 192.168.255.0.

4. C. With static NAT, the entries are statically configured. Because the question mentions translation for inside addresses, the **inside** keyword is needed in the command.

5. A. With dynamic NAT, the entries are created as a result of the first packet flow from the inside network.

6. A. The **list 1** parameter references an IP ACL, which matches packets, identifying the inside local addresses.

7. E. When translating inside addresses, the outside address is not translated, so the outside local address does not need to be identified in the configuration.

8. A and C. The configuration is missing the **overload** keyword in the **ip nat inside source** command and in the **ip nat outside** interface subcommand on the serial interface.

9. B. The last line mentions that the pool has seven addresses, with all seven allocated, with the misses counter close to 1000—meaning that close to 1000 new flows were rejected because of insufficient space in the NAT pool.

Chapter 17

1. A. One method for IPv6 global unicast address assignment is that ICANN allocates large address blocks to RIRs, RIRs assign smaller address blocks to ISPs, and ISPs assign even smaller address blocks to their customers.

2. D. Inside a quartet, any leading 0s can be omitted, and one sequence of 1 or more quartets of all 0s can be replaced with double colons (::). The correct answer replaces the longer 3-quartet sequence of 0s with ::.

3. D. Global unicast addresses begin with 2000::/3, meaning that the first 3 bits match the value in hex 2000. Similarly, unique local addresses match FD00::/8, and link local addresses match FE80::/10 (values that begin with FE8, FE9, FEA, and FEB hex). Multicast IPv6 addresses begin with FF00::/8, meaning that the first 2 hex digits are F.

4. A and C. IPv6 supports stateful DHCP, which works similarly to IPv4's DHCP protocol to dynamically assign the entire IP address. Stateless autoconfiguration also allows the assignment by finding the prefix from some nearby router and calculating the interface ID using the EUI-64 format.

5. A and D. Stateless autoconfiguration only helps a host learn and form its own IP address, but it does not help the host learn a default gateway. Stateless RS is not a valid term or feature. Neighbor Discovery Protocol (NDP) is used for several purposes, including the same purpose as ARP in IPv4, and for learning configuration parameters like a default gateway IP address.

6. A and D. OSPFv3, RIPng, EIGRP for IPv6, and MP-BGP4 all support IPv6.

7. C and E. The configuration explicitly assigns the 3456::1 IP address. The interface also forms the EUI-64 interface ID (4644:44FF:FE44:4444), adding it to FE80::/64, to form the link local IP address.

8. E. RIPng configuration does not use a **network** command; instead, the **ipv6 rip** command is configured on the interface, listing the same tag as on the **ipv6 router rip** command, and the **enable** keyword.

9. D. Network Address Translation–Protocol Translation (NAT-PT) translates between IPv4 and IPv6, and vice versa. The two tunneling methods allow IPv6 hosts to communicate with other IPv6 hosts, sending the packets through an IPv4 network. Dual-stack allows a host or router to concurrently support both protocols.

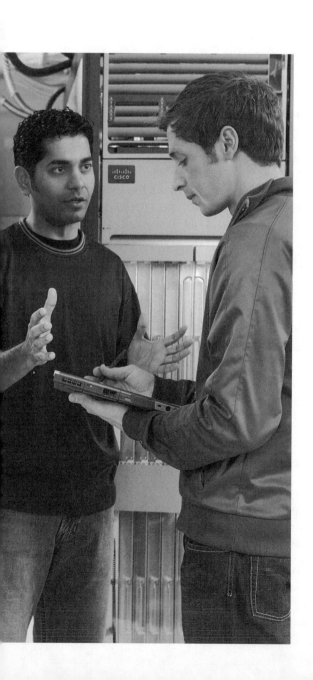

Decimal to Binary Conversion Table

This appendix provides a handy reference for converting between decimal and binary formats for the decimal numbers 0 through 255. Feel free to refer to this table when practicing any of the subnetting problems found in this book and on the CD-ROM.

Although this appendix is useful as a reference tool, note that if you plan to convert values between decimal and binary when doing the various types of subnetting problems on the exams, instead of using the shortcut processes that mostly avoid binary math, you will likely want to practice converting between the two formats before the exam. For practice, just pick any decimal value between 0 and 255, convert it to 8-bit binary, and then use this table to find out if you got the right answer. Also, pick any 8-bit binary number, convert it to decimal, and again use this table to check your work.

Decimal Value	Binary Value	Decimal Value	Binary Value	Decimal Value	Binary Value	Decimal Value	Binary Value
0	00000000	32	00100000	64	01000000	96	01100000
1	00000001	33	00100001	65	01000001	97	01100001
2	00000010	34	00100010	66	01000010	98	01100010
3	00000011	35	00100011	67	01000011	99	01100011
4	00000100	36	00100100	68	01000100	100	01100100
5	00000101	37	00100101	69	01000101	101	01100101
6	00000110	38	00100110	70	01000110	102	01100110
7	00000111	39	00100111	71	01000111	103	01100111
8	00001000	40	00101000	72	01001000	104	01101000
9	00001001	41	00101001	73	01001001	105	01101001
10	00001010	42	00101010	74	01001010	106	01101010
11	00001011	43	00101011	75	01001011	107	01101011
12	00001100	44	00101100	76	01001100	108	01101100
13	00001101	45	00101101	77	01001101	109	01101101
14	00001110	46	00101110	78	01001110	110	01101110
15	00001111	47	00101111	79	01001111	111	01101111
16	00010000	48	00110000	80	01010000	112	01110000
17	00010001	49	00110001	81	01010001	113	01110001
18	00010010	50	00110010	82	01010010	114	01110010
19	00010011	51	00110011	83	01010011	115	01110011
20	00010100	52	00110100	84	01010100	116	01110100
21	00010101	53	00110101	85	01010101	117	01110101
22	00010110	54	00110110	86	01010110	118	01110110
23	00010111	55	00110111	87	01010111	119	01110111
24	00011000	56	00111000	88	01011000	120	01111000
25	00011001	57	00111001	89	01011001	121	01111001
26	00011010	58	00111010	90	01011010	122	01111010
27	00011011	59	00111011	91	01011011	123	01111011
28	00011100	60	00111100	92	01011100	124	01111100
29	00011101	61	00111101	93	01011101	125	01111101
30	00011110	62	00111110	94	01011110	126	01111110
31	00011111	63	00111111	95	01011111	127	01111111

Decimal Value	Binary Value	Decimal Value	Binary Value	Decimal Value	Binary Value	Decimal Value	Binary Value
128	10000000	160	10100000	192	11000000	224	11100000
129	10000001	161	10100001	193	11000001	225	11100001
130	10000010	162	10100010	194	11000010	226	11100010
131	10000011	163	10100011	195	11000011	227	11100011
132	10000100	164	10100100	196	11000100	228	11100100
133	10000101	165	10100101	197	11000101	229	11100101
134	10000110	166	10100110	198	11000110	230	11100110
135	10000111	167	10100111	199	11000111	231	11100111
136	10001000	168	10101000	200	11001000	232	11101000
137	10001001	169	10101001	201	11001001	233	11101001
138	10001010	170	10101010	202	11001010	234	11101010
139	10001011	171	10101011	203	11001011	235	11101011
140	10001100	172	10101100	204	11001100	236	11101100
141	10001101	173	10101101	205	11001101	237	11101101
142	10001110	174	10101110	206	11001110	238	11101110
143	10001111	175	10101111	207	11001111	239	11101111
144	10010000	176	10110000	208	11010000	240	11110000
145	10010001	177	10110001	209	11010001	241	11110001
146	10010010	178	10110010	210	11010010	242	11110010
147	10010011	179	10110011	211	11010011	243	11110011
148	10010100	180	10110100	212	11010100	244	11110100
149	10010101	181	10110101	213	11010101	245	11110101
150	10010110	182	10110110	214	11010110	246	11110110
151	10010111	183	10110111	215	11010111	247	11110111
152	10011000	184	10111000	216	11011000	248	11111000
153	10011001	185	10111001	217	11011001	249	11111001
154	10011010	186	10111010	218	11011010	250	11111010
155	10011011	187	10111011	219	11011011	251	11111011
156	10011100	188	10111100	220	11011100	252	11111100
157	10011101	189	10111101	221	11011101	253	11111101
158	10011110	190	10111110	222	11011110	254	11111110
159	10011111	191	10111111	223	11011111	255	11111111

ICND2 Exam Updates: Version 1.0

Over time, reader feedback allows Cisco Press to gauge which topics give our readers the most problems when taking the exams. Additionally, Cisco may make small changes in the breadth of exam topics or in emphasis of certain topics. To assist readers with those topics, the author creates new materials clarifying and expanding upon those troublesome exam topics. As mentioned in the introduction, the additional content about the exam is contained in a PDF document on this book's companion website at http://www.ciscopress.com/title/158720181x. The document you are viewing is Version 1.0 of this appendix.

This appendix presents all the latest update information available at the time of this book's printing. To make sure you have the latest version of this document, you should be sure to visit the companion website to see if any more recent versions have been posted since this book went to press.

This appendix attempts to fill the void that occurs with any print book. In particular, this appendix does the following:

- Mentions technical items that might not have been mentioned elsewhere in the book

- Covers new topics when Cisco adds topics to the ICND2 or CCNA exam blueprints

- Provides a way to get up-to-the-minute current information about content for the exam

Always Get the Latest at the Companion Website

You are reading the version of this appendix that was available when your book was printed. However, given that the main purpose of this appendix is to be a living, changing document, it is very important that you look for the latest version online at the book's companion website. To do so:

1. Browse to http://www.ciscopress.com/title/158720181x.

2. Select the **Downloads** option under the **More Information** box.

3. Download the latest "ICND2 Appendix C" document.

> **NOTE**   Note that the downloaded document has a version number. If the version of the PDF on the website is the same version as this appendix in your book, your book has the latest version, and there is no need to download or use the online version.

Technical Content

The current version of this appendix does not contain any additional technical coverage. This appendix is here simply to provide the instructions to check online for a later version of this appendix.

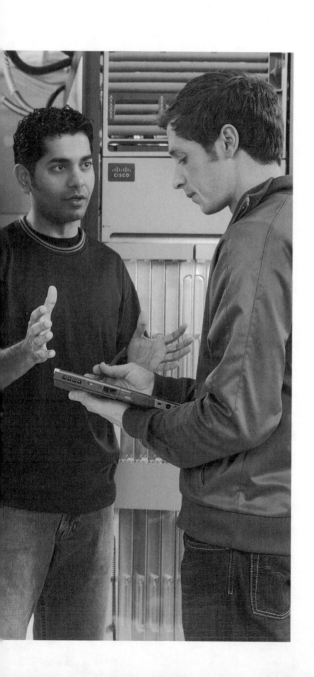

GLOSSARY

ABR Area Border Router. A router using OSPF in which the router has interfaces in multiple OSPF areas.

access link In Frame Relay, the physical serial link that connects a Frame Relay DTE, usually a router, to a Frame Relay switch. The access link uses the same physical layer standards as do point-to-point leased lines.

access rate See AR.

ACL Access control list. A list configured on a router to control packet flow through the router, such as to prevent packets with a certain IP address from leaving a particular interface on the router.

administrative distance In Cisco routers, a means for one router to choose between multiple routes to reach the same subnet when those routes are learned by different routing protocols. The lower the administrative distance, the more preferred the source of the routing information.

administrative mode See trunking administrative mode.

alternate port In RSTP 802.1w, a port role used to denote an interface that is currently receiving an inferior Hello BPDU, making it a possible replacement for the root port. Also used in the Cisco 802.1d STP implementation.

AR Access Rate. In Frame Relay, the speed at which bits are sent over an access link.

Area Border Router See ABR.

ARP Address Resolution Protocol. An Internet protocol used to map an IP address to a MAC address. Defined in RFC 826.

ASBR Autonomous System Border Router. A router using OSPF in which the router learns routes via another source, typically another routing protocol, exchanging routes that are external to OSPF with the OSPF domain.

asynchronous   Describes a convention for sending data with digital signals. The sender and receiver operate at the same speeds, but no attempt is made to dynamically cause the sender and receiver to adjust their speeds based on the other device's speed.

Autonomous System Border Router   See ASBR.

autosummarization   A routing protocol feature in which a router that connects to more than one classful network advertises summarized routes for each entire classful network when sending updates out interfaces connected to other classful networks.

B

backup designated router   An OSPF router connected to a multiaccess network that monitors the work of the designated router (DR) and takes over the work of the DR if the DR fails.

backup port   In RSTP 802.1w, a port role used when multiple interfaces on one switch connect to a single collision domain. This makes one interface the designated port (DP), and one or more others become available to replace the DP (backup role).

balanced hybrid   Refers to one of three general types of routing protocol algorithms. The other two are distance vector and link-state. EIGRP is the only routing protocol that Cisco classifies as using a balanced hybrid algorithm.

Bc   Committed burst. A Frame Relay term referring to the number of bits that can be sent during a defined time interval. This helps measure if/when the DTE has, on average, sent more data over a VC than the speed defined in the traffic contract.

BECN   Backward explicit congestion notification. The bit in the Frame Relay header that implies that congestion is occurring in the opposite (backward) direction from the frame. Switches and DTEs can react by slowing the rate at which data is sent in that direction.

Blocking State   In 802.1d STP, a port state in which no received frames are processed, and the switch forwards no frames out the interface, with the exception of STP messages.

Boolean AND   A math operation performed on a pair of one-digit binary numbers. The result is another one-digit binary number. 1 AND 1 yields 1; all other combinations yield 0.

BPDU   Bridge protocol data unit. The generic name for Spanning Tree Protocol messages.

BPDU Guard   A Cisco switch feature that listens for incoming STP BPDU messages, disabling the interface if any are received. The goal is to prevent loops when a switch connects to a port expected to only have a host connected to it.

BRI   Basic Rate Interface. An ISDN interface composed of two bearer channels and one data (D) channel for circuit-switched communication of voice, video, and data.

bridge ID (BID)   An 8-byte identifier for bridges and switches used by STP and RSTP. It is composed of a 2-byte priority field followed by a 6-byte System ID field that is usually filled with a MAC address.

bridge protocol data unit   See BPDU.

broadcast address   See subnet broadcast address.

broadcast domain   A set of all devices that receive broadcast frames originating from any device in the set. Devices in the same VLAN are in the same broadcast domain.

broadcast subnet   When subnetting a Class A, B, or C network, the one subnet in each classful network for which all subnet bits have a value of binary 1. The subnet broadcast address in this subnet has the same numeric value as the classful network's network-wide broadcast address.

C

CHAP   Challenge Handshake Authentication Protocol. A security feature defined by PPP that allows either or both endpoints on a link to authenticate the other device as a particular authorized device.

CIDR   An RFC-standard tool for global IP address range assignment. CIDR reduces the size of Internet routers' IP routing tables, helping deal with the rapid growth of the Internet. The term classless refers to the fact that the summarized groups of networks represent a group of addresses that do not confirm to IPv4 classful (Class A, B, and C) grouping rules.

CIDR notation   See prefix notation.

CIR   Committed Information Rate. In Frame Relay and ATM, the average speed at which bits can be transferred over a virtual circuit according to the business contract between the customer and the service provider.

circuit switching   The switching system in which a dedicated physical circuit path must exist between the sender and the receiver for the duration of the "call." Used heavily in the telephone company network.

classful addressing   A concept in IPv4 addressing that defines a subnetted IP address as having three parts: network, subnet, and host.

classful network   An IPv4 Class A, B, or C network. It is called a classful network because these networks are defined by the class rules for IPv4 addressing.

classful routing   A variation of the IPv4 forwarding (routing) process that defines the particulars of how the default route is used. The default route is used only if the classful network in which the packet's destination address resides is missing from the router's routing table.

classful routing protocol   An inherent characteristic of a routing protocol. Specifically, the routing protocol does not send subnet masks in its routing updates. This requires the protocol to make assumptions about classful networks and makes it unable to support VLSM and manual route summarization.

classless addressing   A concept in IPv4 addressing that defines a subnetted IP address as having two parts: a prefix (or subnet) and a host.

classless interdomain routing (CIDR)   See CIDR.

classless routing   A variation of the IPv4 forwarding (routing) process that defines the particulars of how the default route is used. The default route is always used for packets whose destination IP address does not match any other routes.

classless routing protocol   An inherent characteristic of a routing protocol. Specifically, the routing protocol sends subnet masks in its routing updates, thereby removing any need to make assumptions about the addresses in a particular subnet or network. This allows the protocol to support VLSM and manual route summarization.

Committed Information Rate (CIR)   See CIR.

contiguous network   In IPv4, a internetwork design in which packets being forwarded between any two subnets of a single classful network only pass through the subnets of that classful network.

convergence   The time required for routing protocols to react to changes in the network, removing bad routes and adding new, better routes so that the current best routes are in all the routers' routing tables.

counting to infinity   An unfortunate side effect of distance vector routing protocols in which the routers slowly increase the metric for a failed route until the metric reaches that routing protocol's finite definition of a maximum metric (called infinity).

CSU/DSU   Channel service unit/data service unit. A device that connects a physical circuit installed by the telco to some CPE device, adapting between the voltages, current, framing, and connectors used on the circuit to the physical interface supported by the DTE.

D

Database Description   An OSPF packet type that lists brief descriptions of the LSAs in the OSPF LSDB.

data-link connection identifier (DLCI)   See DLCI.

DCE   Data communications equipment. From a physical layer perspective, the device providing the clocking on a WAN link, typically a CSU/DSU, is the DCE. From a packet-switching perspective, the service provider's switch, to which a router might connect, is considered the DCE.

DE   Discard eligible. The bit in the Frame Relay header that, if frames must be discarded, signals a switch to choose this frame to discard instead of another frame without the DE bit set.

Dead Timer   In OSPF, a timer used for each neighbor. A router considers the neighbor to have failed if no Hellos are received from that neighbor in the time defined by the timer.

deny   An action taken with an ACL that implies that the packet is discarded.

designated port   In both STP and RSTP, a port role used to determine which of multiple interfaces, each connected to the same segment or collision domain, should forward frames to the segment. The switch advertising the lowest-cost Hello BPDU onto the segment becomes the DP.

designated router   In OSPF, on a multiaccess network, the router that wins an election and is therefore responsible for managing a streamlined process for exchanging OSPF topology information between all routers attached to that network.

Diffie-Hellman Key Exchange   A key exchange protocol in which two devices can exchange information over a public network. Combined with some preexisting secrets, this allows them to calculate a symmetric key known only to them.

Diffusing Update Algorithm (DUAL)   See DUAL.

Dijkstra Shortest Path First (SPF) algorithm   The name of the algorithm used by link-state routing protocols to analyze the LSDB and find the least-cost routes from that router to each subnet.

directed broadcast address   The same as a subnet broadcast address.

disabled port   In STP, a port role for nonworking interfaces—in other words, interfaces that are not in a connect or up/up interface state.

Discarding State   An RSTP interface state in which no received frames are processed, and the switch forwards no frames out the interface, with the exception of RSTP messages.

discontiguous network   In IPv4, a internetwork design in which packets being forwarded between two subnets of a single classful network must pass through the subnets of another classful network.

distance vector   The logic behind the behavior of some interior routing protocols, such as RIP and IGRP. Distance vector routing algorithms call for each router to send its entire routing table in each update, but only to its neighbors. Distance vector routing algorithms can be prone to routing loops but are computationally simpler than link-state routing algorithms. Also called Bellman-Ford routing algorithm.

DLCI   Data-Link Connection Identifier. The Frame Relay address that identifies a VC on a particular access link.

DTE   Data terminal equipment. From a Layer 1 perspective, the DTE synchronizes its clock based on the clock sent by the DCE. From a packet-switching perspective, the DTE is the device outside the service provider's network, typically a router.

DUAL   Diffusing Update Algorithm. A convergence algorithm used in EIGRP when a route fails and a router does not have a feasible successor route. DUAL causes the routers to send EIGRP Query and Reply messages to discover alternate loop-free routes.

dual stacks   In IPv6, a mode of operation in which a host or router runs both IPv4 and IPv6.

dynamic ACL   A type of ACL that goes beyond traditional IP ACLs to dynamically permit traffic from a host if the host's user first connects to the router via Telnet and passes an authentication process.

E

EIGRP   Enhanced Interior Gateway Routing Protocol. An advanced version of IGRP developed by Cisco. Provides superior convergence properties and operating efficiency and combines the advantages of link-state protocols with those of distance vector protocols.

encoding   The conventions for how a device varies the electrical or optical signals sent over a cable to imply a particular binary code. For instance, a modem might encode a binary 1 or 0 by using one frequency to mean 1 and another to mean 0.

EtherChannel   A Cisco-proprietary feature in which up to eight parallel Ethernet segments between the same two devices, each using the same speed, can be combined to act as a single link for forwarding and Spanning Tree Protocol logic.

extended access list   A list of IOS **access-list** global configuration commands that can match multiple parts of an IP packet, including the source and destination IP address and TCP/UDP ports, for the purpose of deciding which packets to discard and which to allow through the router.

extended ping   An IOS command in which the **ping** command accepts many other options besides just the destination IP address.

exterior gateway protocol (EGP)   A routing protocol that was designed to exchange routing information between different autonomous systems.

F

feasibility condition   In EIGRP, when a router has learned of multiple routes to reach one subnet, if the best route's metric is X, the feasibility condition is another route whose reported distance is <= X.

feasible distance   In EIGRP, the metric of the best route to reach a subnet.

feasible successor   In EIGRP, a route that is not the best route (successor route) but that can be used immediately if the best route fails, without causing a loop. Such a route meets the feasibility condition.

FECN   Forward explicit congestion notification. The bit in the Frame Relay header that signals to anything receiving the frame (switches and DTEs) that congestion is occurring in the same direction as the frame.

FTP   File Transfer Protocol. An application protocol, part of the TCP/IP protocol stack, used to transfer files between network nodes. FTP is defined in RFC 959.

filter   Generally, a process or a device that screens network traffic for certain characteristics, such as source address, destination address, or protocol. This process determines whether to forward or discard that traffic based on the established criteria.

forward   To send a frame toward its ultimate destination by way of an internetworking device.

forward delay   An STP timer, defaulting to 15 seconds, used to dictate how long an interface stays in both the Listening state and Learning state. Also called the forward delay timer.

Forwarding State   An STP and RSTP port state in which an interface operates unrestricted by STP.

forward route   From one host's perspective, the route over which a packet travels from that host to some other host.

Frame Relay   An international standard data-link protocol that defines the capabilities to create a frame-switched (packet-switched) service, allowing DTE devices (typically routers) to send data to many other devices using a single physical connection to the Frame Relay service.

Frame Relay DCE   The Frame Relay switch.

Frame Relay DTE   The customer device connected to a Frame Relay access link, typically a router.

Frame Relay mapping   The information that correlates, or maps, a Frame Relay DLCI to the Layer 3 address of the DTE on the other end of the VC identified by the local DLCI.

framing   The conventions for how Layer 2 interprets the bits sent according to OSI Layer 1. For example, after an electrical signal has been received and converted to binary, framing identifies the information fields inside the data.

full duplex   Generically, any communication in which two communicating devices can concurrently send and receive data. Specifically for Ethernet LANs, the ability of both devices to send and receive at the same time. This is allowed when there are only two stations in a collision domain. Full duplex is enabled by turning off the CSMA/CD collision detection logic.

Full State   In OSPF, a neighbor state that implies that the two routers have exchanged the complete (full) contents of their respective LSDBs.

full update   With IP routing protocols, the general concept that a routing protocol update lists all known routes. See also partial update.

fully adjacent   In OSPF, a characterization of the state of a neighbor in which the two neighbors have reached the Full state.

G

global unicast address   A type of unicast IPv6 address that has been allocated from a range of public globally unique IP addresses as registered through ICANN, its member agencies, and other registries or ISPs.

H

HDLC   High-Level Data-Link Control. A bit-oriented synchronous data link layer protocol developed by the International Organization for Standardization (ISO). Derived from synchronous data-link control (SDLC), HDLC specifies a data encapsulation method on synchronous serial links using frame characters and checksums.

Hello   (Multiple definitions) 1) A protocol used by OSPF routers to discover, establish, and maintain neighbor relationships. 2) A protocol used by EIGRP routers to discover, establish, and maintain neighbor relationships. 3) In STP, refers to the name of the periodic message sourced by the root bridge in a spanning tree.

Hello BPDU   The STP and RSTP message used for the majority of STP communications, listing the root's Bridge ID, the sending device's Bridge ID, and the sending device's cost with which to reach the root.

Hello interval   With OSPF and EIGRP, an interface timer that dictates how often the router should send Hello messages.

Hello timer   In STP, the time interval at which the root switch should send Hello BPDUs.

holddown   A Distance Vector protocol state assigned to a route placed so that routers neither advertise the route nor accept advertisements about it for a specific length of time (the holddown timer). Holddown is used to flush bad information about a route from all routers in the network. A route typically is placed in holddown when a link in that route fails.

I

IEEE 802.11   The IEEE base standard for wireless LANs.

IEEE 802.1ad   The IEEE standard for the functional equivalent of the Cisco-proprietary EtherChannel.

IEEE 802.1d   The IEEE standard for the original Spanning Tree Protocol.

IEEE 802.1Q   The IEEE-standard VLAN trunking protocol. 802.1Q includes the concept of a native VLAN, for which no VLAN header is added, and a 4-byte VLAN header is inserted after the original frame's type/length field.

IEEE 802.1s   The IEEE standard for Multiple Instances of Spanning Tree (MIST), which allows for load balancing of traffic among different VLANs.

IEEE 802.1w   The IEEE standard for an enhanced version of STP, called Rapid STP, which speeds convergence.

IEEE 802.3   The IEEE base standard for Ethernet-like LANs.

IGRP   Interior Gateway Routing Protocol. An old, no-longer-supported Interior Gateway Protocol (IGP) developed by Cisco.

inferior Hello   When comparing two or more received Hello BPDUs, a Hello that lists a numerically larger root Bridge ID than another Hello, or a Hello that lists the same root Bridge ID but with a larger cost.

infinity   In the context of IP routing protocols, a finite metric value defined by the routing protocol that is used to represent an unusable route in a routing protocol update.

inside global   A NAT term referring to the IP address used for a host inside the trusted part of the network, but in packets as they traverse the global (untrusted) part of the network.

inside local   A NAT term referring to the IP address used for a host inside the trusted part of the network, but in packets as they traverse the local (trusted) part of the network.

interior gateway protocol (IGP)   A routing protocol designed to be used to exchange routing information inside a single autonomous system.

Inter-Switch Link (ISL)   The Cisco-proprietary VLAN trunking protocol that predated 802.1Q by many years. ISL defines a 26-byte header that encapsulates the original Ethernet frame.

Inverse ARP   A Frame Relay protocol with which a router announces its Layer 3 address over a VC, thereby informing the neighbor of useful Layer-3-to-Layer-2 mapping information.

IP Control Protocol (IPCP)   A control protocol defined as part of PPP for the purpose of initializing and controlling the sending of IPv4 packets over a PPP link.

IPsec   The term referring to the IP Security Protocols, which is an architecture for providing encryption and authentication services, typically when creating VPN services through an IP network.

ISDN   Integrated Services Digital Network. A communication protocol offered by telephone companies that permits telephone networks to carry data, voice, and video.

ISL   See Inter-Switch Link.

ISP prefix   In IPv6, the prefix that describes an address block that has been assigned to an ISP by some Internet registry.

K

keepalive   A feature of many data-link protocols in which the router sends messages periodically to let the neighboring router know that the first router is still alive and well.

L

LAPF   Link Access Procedure Frame Bearer Services. Defines the basic Frame Relay header and trailer. The header includes DLCI, FECN, BECN, and DE bits.

learn   Transparent bridges and switches learn MAC addresses by examining the source MAC addresses of frames they receive. They add each new MAC address, along with the port number of the port on which it learned of the MAC address, to an address table.

Learning State   In STP, a temporary port state in which the interface does not forward frames, but it can begin to learn MAC addresses from frames received on the interface.

leased line   A transmission line reserved by a communications carrier for a customer's private use. A leased line is a type of dedicated line.

Link Control Protocol   A control protocol defined as part of PPP for the purpose of initializing and maintaining a PPP link.

link local address   A type of unicast IPv6 address that represents an interface on a single data link. Packets sent to a link local address cross only that particular link and are never forwarded to other subnets by a router. Used for communications that do not need to leave the local link, such as neighbor discovery.

link-state   A classification of the underlying algorithm used in some routing protocols. Link-state protocols build a detailed database that lists links (subnets) and their state (up, down), from which the best routes can then be calculated.

link-state advertisement (LSA)   In OSPF, the name of the data structure that resides inside the LSDB and describes in detail the various components in a network, including routers and links (subnets).

link-state database (LSDB)   In OSPF, the data structure in RAM of a router that holds the various LSAs, with the collective LSAs representing the entire topology of the network.

link-state request   An OSPF packet used to ask a neighboring router to send a particular LSA.

link-state update   An OSPF packet used to send an LSA to a neighboring router.

Listening State   A temporary STP port state that occurs immediately when a blocking interface must be moved to a Forwarding state. The switch times out MAC table entries during this state. It also ignores frames received on the interface and doesn't forward any frames out the interface.

Local Management Interface (LMI)   A Frame Relay protocol used between a DTE (router) and DCE (Frame Relay switch). LMI acts as a keepalive mechanism. The absence of LMI messages means that the other device has failed. It also tells the DTE about the existence of each VC and DLCI, along with its status.

LSA   See link-state advertisement.

M

mask   See subnet mask.

MaxAge   In STP, a timer that states how long a switch should wait when it no longer receives Hellos from the root switch before acting to reconverge the STP topology. Also called the MaxAge Timer.

metric   A numeric measurement used by a routing protocol to determine how good a route is as compared to other alternate routes to reach the same subnet.

MLP   Multilink Point-to-Point Protocol. A method of splitting, recombining, and sequencing frames across multiple point-to-point WAN links.

MTU   Maximum transmission unit. The maximum packet size, in bytes, that a particular interface can handle.

N

named access list   An ACL that identifies the various statements in the ACL based on a name, rather than a number.

NAT   Network Address Translation. A mechanism for reducing the need for globally unique IPv4 addresses. NAT allows an organization with addresses that are not globally unique to connect to the Internet by translating those addresses into globally routable address space.

NAT overload   See Port Address Translation (PAT).

NAT-PT   An IPv6 feature in which packets are translated between IPv4 and IPv6.

NBMA   See nonbroadcast multiaccess.

neighbor   In routing protocols, another router with which a router decides to exchange routing information.

Neighbor Discovery Protocol (NDP)   A protocol that is part of the IPv6 protocol suite, used to discover and exchange information about devices on the same subnet (neighbors). In particular, it replaces the IPv4 ARP protocol.

neighbor table   For OSPF and EIGRP, a list of routers that have reached neighbor status.

nonbroadcast multiaccess (NBMA)   A characterization of a type of Layer 2 network in which more than two devices connect to the network, but the network does not allow broadcast frames to be sent to all devices on the network.

O

OSPF   Open Shortest Path First. A popular link-state IGP that uses a link-state database and the Shortest Path First (SPF) algorithm to calculate the best routes to reach each known subnet.

outside global   A NAT term referring to an IP address used for a host in the outside (untrusted) part of the network, for packets as they traverse the outside part of the network, which is usually the global Internet.

outside local   A NAT term referring to an IP address used for a host in the outside (untrusted) part of the network, for packets as they traverse the inside (trusted), or local, part of the network.

overlapping subnets   An (incorrect) IP subnet design condition in which one subnet's range of addresses includes addresses in the range of another subnet.

P

packet switching   A WAN service in which each DTE device connects to a telco using a single physical line, with the possibility of being able to forward traffic to all other sites connected to the same service. The telco switch makes the forwarding decision based on an address in the packet header.

PAP   Password Authentication Protocol. A PPP authentication protocol that allows PPP peers to authenticate one another.

partial mesh   A network topology in which more than two devices could physically communicate, but by choice, only a subset of the pairs of devices connected to the network are allowed to communicate directly.

partial update   With IP routing protocols, the general concept that a routing protocol update lists a subset of all known routes. See also full update.

PAT   See Port Address Translation.

periodic update   With routing protocols, the concept that the routing protocol advertises routes in a routing update on a regular periodic basis. This is typical of distance vector routing protocols.

permanent virtual circuit (PVC)   A preconfigured communications path between two Frame Relay DTEs, identified by a local DLCI on each Frame Relay access link, that provides the functional equivalent of a leased circuit, but without a physical leased line for each VC.

permit   An action taken with an ACL that implies that the packet is allowed to proceed through the router and be forwarded.

poisoned route   A route in a routing protocol's advertisement that lists a subnet with a special metric value, called an infinite metric, that designates the route as a failed route.

poison reverse   A distance vector poisoned route advertisement for a subnet that would not have been advertised because of split-horizon rules but is now advertised as a poison route.

port   (Multiple definitions) 1) In TCP and UDP, a number that is used to uniquely identify the application process that either sent (source port) or should receive (destination port) data. 2) In LAN switching, another term for switch interface.

Port Address Translation (PAT)   A NAT feature in which one Inside Global IP address supports more than 65,000 concurrent TCP and UDP connections.

PortFast   A switch STP feature in which a port is placed in an STP Forwarding state as soon as the interface comes up, bypassing the Listening and Learning states. This feature is meant for ports connected to end-user devices.

PPP   Point-to-Point Protocol. A data-link protocol that provides router-to-router and host-to-network connections over synchronous and asynchronous circuits.

prefix notation   A shorter way to write a subnet mask in which the number of binary 1s in the mask is simply written in decimal. For instance, /24 denotes the subnet mask with 24 binary 1 bits in the subnet mask. The number of bits of value binary 1 in the mask is considered to be the prefix.

PRI   Primary Rate Interface. An ISDN interface to primary rate access. Primary rate access consists of a single 64-kbps D channel plus 23 (T1) or 30 (E1) B channels for voice or data.

private address   Several Class A, B, and C networks that are set aside for use inside private organizations. These addresses, as defined in RFC 1918, are not routable through the Internet.

private IP network   One of several classful IPv4 network numbers that will never be assigned for use in the Internet, meant for use inside a single enterprise.

private key   A secret value used in public/private key encryption systems. Either encrypts a value that can then be decrypted using the matching public key, or decrypts a value that was previously encrypted with the matching public key.

problem isolation   The part of the troubleshooting process in which the engineer attempts to rule out possible causes of the problem, narrowing the possible causes until the root cause of the problem can be identified.

protocol type   A field in the IP header that identifies the type of header that follows the IP header, typically a Layer 4 header, such as TCP or UDP. ACLs can examine the protocol type to match packets with a particular value in this header field.

public key   A secret value used in public/private key encryption systems. Either encrypts a value that can then be decrypted using the matching private key, or decrypts a value that was previously encrypted with the matching private key.

PVC   See permanent virtual circuit.

R

Rapid Spanning Tree Protocol (RSTP)   Defined in IEEE 802.1w. Defines an improved version of STP that converges much more quickly and consistently than STP (802.1d).

reflexive ACL   A type of ACL that goes beyond traditional IP ACLs to monitor the addition of new user sessions. The router reacts to add an ACL entry that matches that session's IP addresses and TCP or UDP port numbers.

Regional Internet Registry (RIR)   The generic term for one of five current organizations that are responsible for assigning the public, globally unique IPv4 and IPv6 address space.

registry prefix   In IPv6, the prefix that describes a block of public, globally unique IPv6 addresses assigned to a Regional Internet Registry by ICANN.

reported distance   From one EIGRP router's perspective, the metric for a subnet as calculated on a neighboring router and reported in a routing update to the first router.

reverse route   From one host's perspective, for packets sent back to the host from another host, the route over which the packet travels.

RIP   Routing Information Protocol. An Interior Gateway Protocol (IGP) that uses distance vector logic and router hop count as the metric. RIP version 1 (RIP-1) has become unpopular. RIP version 2 (RIP-2) provides more features, including support for VLSM.

root bridge   See root switch.

root port   In STP, the one port on a nonroot switch in which the least-cost Hello is received. Switches put root ports in a Forwarding state.

root switch   In STP, the switch that wins the election by virtue of having the lowest Bridge ID, and, as a result, sends periodic Hello BPDUs (the default is 2 seconds).

routable protocol   See routed protocol.

routed protocol   A Layer 3 protocol that defines a packet that can be routed, such as IPv4 and IPv6.

router ID (RID)   In OSPF, a 32-bit number, written in dotted decimal, that uniquely identifies each router.

route summarization   The process of combining multiple routes into a single advertised route, for the purpose of reducing the number of entries in routers' IP routing tables.

routing protocol   A set of messages and processes with which routers can exchange information about routes to reach subnets in a particular network. Examples of routing protocols include Enhanced Interior Gateway Routing Protocol (EIGRP), Open Shortest Path First (OSPF), and Routing Information Protocol (RIP).

RSTP   See Rapid Spanning Tree Protocol.

S

secondary IP address   The second (or more) IP address configured on a router interface, using the **secondary** keyword on the **ip address** command.

Secure Sockets Layer (SSL)   A security protocol that is integrated into commonly used web browsers that provides encryption and authentication services between the browser and a website.

segment   (Multiple definitions) 1) In TCP, a term used to describe a TCP header and its encapsulated data (also called an L4PDU). 2) Also in TCP, the set of bytes formed when TCP breaks a large chunk of data given to it by the application layer into smaller pieces that fit into TCP segments. 3) In Ethernet, either a single Ethernet cable or a single collision domain (no matter how many cables are used).

shared key   A reference to a security key whose value is known by both the sender and receiver.

site prefix   In IPv6, the prefix that describes a public globally unique IPv6 address block that has been assigned to an end-user organization (for example, an Enterprise or government agency). The assignment typically is made by an ISP or Internet registry.

SLSM   Static-length subnet mask. The usage of the same subnet mask for all subnets of a single Class A, B, or C network.

Spanning Tree Protocol (STP)   A protocol defined by IEEE standard 802.1d. Allows switches and bridges to create a redundant LAN, with the protocol dynamically causing some ports to block traffic, so that the bridge/switch forwarding logic will not cause frames to loop indefinitely around the LAN.

split horizon   A distant vector routing technique in which information about routes is prevented from exiting the router interface through which that information was received. Split-horizon updates are useful in preventing routing loops.

SSL   See Secure Sockets Layer.

standard access list   A list of IOS global configuration commands that can match only a packet's source IP address for the purpose of deciding which packets to discard and which to allow through the router.

stateful DHCP   A term used in IPv6 to contrast with stateless DHCP. Stateful DHCP keeps track of which clients have been assigned which IPv6 addresses (state information).

stateless autoconfiguration   A feature of IPv6 in which a host or router can be assigned an IPv6 unicast address without the need for a stateful DHCP server.

stateless DHCP   A term used in IPv6 to contrast with stateful DHCP. Stateless DHCP servers don't lease IPv6 addresses to clients. Instead, they supply other useful information, such as DNS server IP addresses, but with no need to track information about the clients (state information).

subinterface   One of the virtual interfaces on a single physical interface.

subnet   A subdivision of a Class A, B, or C network, as configured by a network administrator. Subnets allow a single Class A, B, or C network to be used and still allow for a large number of groups of IP addresses, as is required for efficient IP routing.

subnet broadcast address   A special address in each subnet—specifically, the largest numeric address in the subnet—designed so that packets sent to this address should be delivered to all hosts in that subnet.

subnet mask   A 32-bit number that describes the format of an IP address. It represents the combined network and subnet bits in the address with mask bit values of 1 and represents the host bits in the address with mask bit values of 0.

subnet prefix   In IPv6, a term for the prefix that is assigned to each data link, acting like a subnet in IPv4.

successor   In EIGRP, the route to reach a subnet that has the best metric and should be placed in the IP routing table.

summary route   A route created via configuration commands to represent routes to one or more subnets with a single route, thereby reducing the size of the routing table.

SVC   Switched virtual circuit. A VC that is set up dynamically when needed.

switch   A network device that filters, forwards, and floods frames based on each frame's destination address. The switch operates at the data link layer of the Open System Interconnection (OSI) reference model.

synchronous   The imposition of time ordering on a bit stream. Practically, a device tries to use the same speed as another device on the other end of a serial link. However, by examining transitions between voltage states on the link, the device can notice slight variations in the speed on each end and can adjust its speed accordingly.

T

TFTP Trivial File Transfer Protocol. An application protocol that allows files to be transferred from one computer to another over a network, but with only a few features, making the software require little storage space.

topology database The structured data that describes the network topology to a routing protocol. Link-state and balanced hybrid routing protocols use topology tables, from which they build the entries in the routing table.

triggered update A routing protocol feature in which the routing protocol does not wait for the next periodic update when something changes in the network, instead immediately sending a routing update.

trunk In campus LANs, an Ethernet segment over which the devices add a VLAN header that identifies the VLAN in which the frame exists.

trunking Also called VLAN trunking. A method (using either the Cisco ISL protocol or the IEEE 802.1Q protocol) to support multiple VLANs that have members on more than one switch.

trunking administrative mode The configured trunking setting on a Cisco switch interface, as configured with the **switchport mode** command.

trunking operational mode The current behavior of a Cisco switch interface for VLAN trunking.

two-way state In OSPF, a neighbor state that implies that the router has exchanged Hellos with the neighbor, and all required parameters match.

U

unique local address A type of IPv6 unicast address meant as a replacement for IPv4 private addresses.

update timer The time interval that regulates how often a routing protocol sends its next periodic routing updates. Distance vector routing protocols send full routing updates every update interval.

V

variable-length subnet mask(ing)   See VLSM.

variance   IGRP and EIGRP compute their metrics, so the metrics for different routes to the same subnet seldom have the exact same value. The variance value is multiplied with the lower metric when multiple routes to the same subnet exist. If the product is larger than the metrics for other routes, the routes are considered to have "equal" metric, allowing multiple routes to be added to the routing table.

VC   Virtual circuit. A logical concept that represents the path that frames travel between DTEs. VCs are particularly useful when comparing Frame Relay to leased physical circuits.

virtual LAN (VLAN)   A group of devices connected to one or more switches that are grouped into a single broadcast domain through configuration. VLANs allow switch administrators to place the devices connected to the switches in separate VLANs without requiring separate physical switches. This creates design advantages of separating the traffic without the expense of buying additional hardware.

virtual private network (VPN)   A set of security protocols that, when implemented by two devices on either side of an unsecure network such as the Internet, can allow the devices to send data securely. VPNs provide privacy, device authentication, anti-replay services, and data integrity services.

VLAN   See virtual LAN.

VLAN configuration database   The name of the collective configuration of VLAN IDs and names on a Cisco switch.

vlan.dat   The default file used to store a Cisco switch's VLAN configuration database.

VLAN Trunking Protocol (VTP)   A Cisco-proprietary messaging protocol used between Cisco switches to communicate configuration information about the existence of VLANs, including the VLAN ID and VLAN name.

VLSM   Variable-length subnet mask(ing). The ability to specify a different subnet mask for the same Class A, B, or C network number on different subnets. VLSM can help optimize available address space.

VoIP   Voice over IP. The transport of voice traffic inside IP packets over an IP network.

VPN   See virtual private network.

VPN client   Software that resides on a PC, often a laptop, so that the host can implement the protocols required to be an endpoint of a VPN.

VTP   See VLAN Trunking Protocol.

VTP client mode   One of three VTP operational modes for a switch with which switches learn about VLAN numbers and names from other switches, but which does not not allow the switch to be directly configured with VLAN information.

VTP pruning   The VTP feature by which switches dynamically choose interfaces on which to prevent the flooding of frames in certain VLANs when the frames do not need to go to every switch in the network.

VTP server mode   One of three sets of operating characteristics (modes) in VTP. Switches in server mode can configure VLANs, tell other switches about the changes, and learn about VLAN changes from other switches.

VTP transparent mode   One of three sets of operating characteristics (modes) in VTP. Switches in transparent mode can configure VLANs, but they do not tell other switches about the changes, and they do not learn about VLAN changes from other switches.

W

web VPN   A tool offered by Cisco in which a user can use any common web browser to securely connect using SSL to a web VPN server, which then connects to the user's Enterprise web-based applications—applications that may or may not support SSL.

wildcard mask   The mask used in Cisco IOS ACL commands and OSPF and EIGRP **network** commands.

Z

zero subnet   For every classful IPv4 network that is subnetted, the one subnet whose subnet number has all binary 0s in the subnet part of the number. In decimal, the 0 subnet can be easily identified because it is the same number as the classful network number.

Index

VLAN 689

determining nonroot switches,
100-102
determining root switches, 99-100
determining RP, 100-102
VLSM, 297
configuring overlapping subnets,
293-295
overlapping subnets, 295-296
recognizing VLSM usage, 292
VTP, 44
best practices, 51-52
determining the problem, 44-49
switch connections, 50-51
trunking, 50-51
trunk interfaces, 28
trunking (VLAN), 11-12
802.1Q, 13-15
allowed VLAN lists, 33-36
configuring, 29-33
IP phones, 36-37
ISL, 13-15
LAN switching, troubleshooting, 132-135,
143-146
security, 37
VTP, 16
avoiding via Transparent mode, 20
client mode, 17-19
feature comparison summary, 23
pruning, 22
server mode, 17-19
storing VLAN configurations, 20-21
switch requirements, 19
troubleshooting, 50-51
versions of, 21
tunneling
IPv6, 609-611
VPN, 529
**Two-way neighbor state (OSPF neighbors),
355**

U -V

**UDP (User Datagram Protocol), matching
port numbers in extended ACL, 246-248**
unicast frames, forwarding, 151-154
unicast IPv6 addresses, 600-601
updates
ICND1 exam, 649-650

triggered updates, distance vector loops,
326
update messages (EIGRP), 381

variance command, 390, 400
VC (virtual circuits)
CIR, 463
Frame Relay, 462-466
layer 3 addressing, 475-476
*partially meshed networks with one IP
subnet per VC, 497-500*
verifying
Dynamic NAT configurations, 567-568
Frame Relay configurations, 501-502
STP default operations, 90-92
video tutorials, subnetting, 622
virtual connections. *See* VC (virtual circuits)
VLAN (Virtual Local Area Networks), 9-11
Administrative mode, 29, 33
configuration database, 20-21
Configuration mode, 25
configuring, 24
allowed VLAN lists, 33-36
full configuration, 25-27
shorter configurations, 28-29
storing configurations, 20-21
trunking configuration, 29-33
database configuration revision numbers,
17
Database mode, 25
IP routing, 178, 180
IP subnets, 16
LAN switching, troubleshooting, 132-134,
143-146
self-assessments, 5-7
STP configuration, 89
synchronization, 19
tagging, 11
trunking, 11-12
802.1Q, 13-15
allowed VLAN lists, 33-36
configuring, 29-33
IP phones, 36-37
ISL, 13-15
security, 37
verifying, 33
VLAN ID, 11
VMPS, 25

Cisco Systems

Cisco Press

3 STEPS TO LEARNING

STEP 1

First-Step

STEP 2

Fundamentals

STEP 3

Networking
Technology Guides

STEP 1 **First-Step**—Benefit from easy-to-grasp explanations.
No experience required!

STEP 2 **Fundamentals**—Understand the purpose, application,
and management of technology.

STEP 3 **Networking Technology Guides**—Gain the knowledge
to master the challenge of the network.

NETWORK BUSINESS SERIES

The Network Business series helps professionals tackle the
business issues surrounding the network. Whether you are a
seasoned IT professional or a business manager with minimal
technical expertise, this series will help you understand the
business case for technologies.

Justify Your Network Investment.

Look for Cisco Press titles at your favorite bookseller today.

Visit **www.ciscopress.com/series** for details on each of these book series.

CISCO SYSTEMS

Cisco Press

SAVE UP TO 30%

Become a member and save at **ciscopress.com**!

Complete a **user profile** at ciscopress.com today to become a member and benefit from **discounts up to 30% on every purchase** at ciscopress.com, as well as a more customized user experience. Your membership will also allow you access to the entire Informit network of sites.

Don't forget to subscribe to the monthly Cisco Press newsletter to be the first to learn about new releases and special promotions. You can also sign up to get your first **30 days FREE on Safari Bookshelf** and preview Cisco Press content. Safari Bookshelf lets you access Cisco Press books online and build your own customized, searchable electronic reference library.

Visit **www.ciscopress.com/register** to sign up and start saving today!

The profile information we collect is used in aggregate to provide us with better insight into your technology interests and to create a better user experience for you. You must be logged into ciscopress.com to receive your discount. Discount is on Cisco Press products only; shipping and handling are not included.

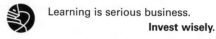

Learning is serious business.
Invest wisely.

SEARCH THOUSANDS
OF BOOKS FROM
LEADING PUBLISHERS

Safari® Bookshelf is a searchable electronic reference library for IT professionals that features more than 2,000 titles from technical publishers, including Cisco Press.

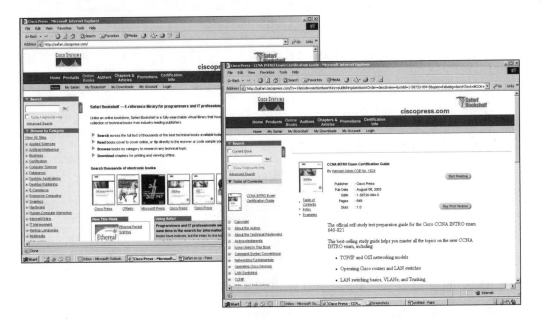

With Safari Bookshelf you can

- **Search** the full text of thousands of technical books, including more than 70 Cisco Press titles from authors such as Wendell Odom, Jeff Doyle, Bill Parkhurst, Sam Halabi, and Karl Solie.

- **Read** the books on My Bookshelf from cover to cover, or just flip to the information you need.

- **Browse** books by category to research any technical topic.

- **Download** chapters for printing and viewing offline.

With a customized library, you'll have access to your books when and where you need them—and all you need is a user name and password.

Safari
BOOKS ONLINE
ENABLED

THIS BOOK IS SAFARI ENABLED

INCLUDES FREE 45-DAY ACCESS TO THE ONLINE EDITION

The Safari® Enabled icon on the cover of your favorite technology book means the book is available through Safari Bookshelf. When you buy this book, you get free access to the online edition for 45 days.

Safari Bookshelf is an electronic reference library that lets you easily search thousands of technical books, find code samples, download chapters, and access technical information whenever and wherever you need it.

TO GAIN 45-DAY SAFARI ENABLED ACCESS TO THIS BOOK:

- Go to **http://www.ciscopress.com/safarienabled**

- Complete the brief registration form

- Enter the coupon code found in the front of this book before the "Contents at a Glance" page

If you have difficulty registering on Safari Bookshelf or accessing the online edition, please e-mail customer-service@safaribooksonline.com.